Communications
in Computer and Information Science   1114

Commenced Publication in 2007
Founding and Former Series Editors:
Phoebe Chen, Alfredo Cuzzocrea, Xiaoyong Du, Orhun Kara, Ting Liu,
Krishna M. Sivalingam, Dominik Ślęzak, Takashi Washio, Xiaokang Yang,
and Junsong Yuan

More information about this series at http://www.springer.com/series/7899

Pablo H. Ruiz · Vanessa Agredo-Delgado (Eds.)

Human-Computer Interaction

5th Iberoamerican Workshop, HCI-Collab 2019
Puebla, Mexico, June 19–21, 2019
Revised Selected Papers

 Springer

Editors
Pablo H. Ruiz 🆔
Corporación Universitaria Comfacauca -
Unicomfacauca and Universidad del Cauca
Popayán, Colombia

Vanessa Agredo-Delgado 🆔
Corporación Universitaria Comfacauca -
Unicomfacauca and Universidad del Cauca
Popayán, Colombia

ISSN 1865-0929   ISSN 1865-0937   (electronic)
Communications in Computer and Information Science
ISBN 978-3-030-37385-6   ISBN 978-3-030-37386-3   (eBook)
https://doi.org/10.1007/978-3-030-37386-3

This Springer imprint is published by the registered company Springer Nature Switzerland AG
The registered company address is: Gewerbestrasse 11, 6330 Cham, Switzerland

Preface

The Human-Computer Interaction (HCI) studies the exchange of information between people who use technological elements. Its objective is to make this exchange efficient: minimizing errors, increasing satisfaction, reducing frustration, and making the interaction between people and technological elements more productive. HCI research has evolved, proposing and improving the different paradigms for the design and evaluation of the interaction of humans with technology. This area of knowledge allows us to know the relevance of each of the three elements of the equation: the human being (user), the computer/mobile device (system), and the interaction (transmission of information in two ways).

This book conglomerates a set of works related to HCI, written by authors from different countries, such as Colombia, Argentina, Peru, Ecuador, Mexico, Spain, Chile, France, Brazil, Saudi Arabia, and the USA. The papers are presented in specialized topics such as: Emotional Interfaces, Usability, HCI and Video Games, Computational Thinking, Collaborative Systems, IoT, Software Engineering, and ICT in Education.

We present papers that describe models, design patterns, implementations, evaluations of existing applications, and systemic reviews; all of which are very important aspects within HCI. This work is the result of the HCI-Collab Network, which is a collaborative network that supports the teaching-learning processes within the HCI area. All paper submissions were reviewed by three experts. Authors removed personal details, the acknowledgments section, and any references that may disclose the authors' identity. Papers which did not meet this criteria were rejected without reviews. All contributions were written following the Springer template, and the first anonymous version was submitted in PDF format.

The 5th Ibero-American Workshop in HCI (HCI-Collab 2019) call for papers attracted 55 submissions, of which 35 were accepted and invited to send an extended version as a long article in English, of which 31 accepted the invitation and are presented in this book. Reviewing was performed by national and international reviewers. Moreover, the EasyChair system was used for the management and review of submissions.

We are grateful to all authors whose sent their articles, to the organizers, and Springer.

October 2019

Pablo H. Ruiz
Vanessa Agredo-Delgado

Organization

Program Committee Members

Julio Abascal	University of the Basque Country, Spain
Agustin Lagunes Dominguez	Universidad Veracruzana, Mexico
Alberto L. Morán	Universidad Autónoma de Baja California, Mexico
Alejandro Fernández	LIFIA - Facultad de Informática - Universidad Nacional de La Plata, Argentina
Alessandra Reyes-Flores	Universidad Veracruzana, Mexico
Alfredo Garcia	Benemérita Universidad Autonoma de Puebla, Mexico
Alfredo Mendoza	Universidad Autónoma de Zacatecas, Mexico
Andrés Solano	Universidad Autónoma de Occidente, Colombia
Andres Saul De La Serna Tuya	Benemérita Universidad Autónoma de Puebla, Mexico
Anselmo Frizera Neto	Universidade Federal do Espírito Santo, Brazil
Antonia Huertas	Universitat Oberta de Catalunya, Spain
Antonio Peñalver Benavent	Universidad Miguel Hernández de Elche, Spain
Beatriz Beltran	Benemérita Universidad Autónoma de Puebla, Mexico
Blanca Pedroza	Benemérita Universidad Autónoma de Puebla, Mexico
Blanca Nydia Perez Camacho	Benemérita Universidad Autónoma de Puebla, Mexico
Carina Gonzalez-González	Universidad de La Laguna, Spain
Carlos Arturo Torres Gastelú	Universidad Veracruzana, Mexico
Cesar A. Collazos	Universidad del Cauca, Colombia
Christian Sturm	University of Applied Sciences, Germany
Claudia Deco	Universidad Nacional de Rosario, Argentina
Claudia González Calleros	Benemérita Universidad Autónoma de Puebla, Mexico
Cristian Rusu	Pontificia Universidad Católica de Valparaiso, Chile
Cristina Manresa-Yee	University of Balearic Islands, Spain
Daminana Leyva	Benemérita Universidad Autónoma de Puebla, Mexico
Daniel Mocencahua Mora	Benemérita Universidad Autónoma de Puebla, Mexico
Daniela Quiñones	Pontificia Universidad Católica de Valparaíso, Chile
Darnes Vilariño Ayala	Benemérita Universidad Autónoma de Puebla, Mexico
David Cespedes	Benemérita Universidad Autónoma de Puebla, Mexico
Diego Torres	LIFIA - Facultad de Informática - Universidad Nacional de La Plata, Argentina
Eduardo Fernández	INCO - Universidad de la República, Uruguay
Enric Mor	Universitat Oberta de Catalunya, Spain
Erika Martínez	Benemérita Universidad Autónoma de Puebla, Mexico

Francisco Montero	Universidad de Castilla-La Mancha, Spain
Francisco Luis Gutiérrez Vela	Universidad de Granada, Spain
Gabriela Sánchez	Universidad de las Américas Puebla, Mexico
Gerardo Rocha	Instituto Tecnológico y de Estudios Superiores de Monterrey, Mexico
Giovanni Chavez	Universidad Popular Autónoma del Estado de Puebla, Mexico
Guillermina Sánchez	Benemérita Universidad Autónoma de Puebla, Mexico
Gustavo Rossi	LIFIA - Facultad de Informática - Universidad Nacional de La Plata, Argentina
Huizilopoztli Luna-García	Universidad Autónoma de Zacatecas, Mexico
Imelda García López	Instituto Tecnológico de Sonora, Mexico
Ismael Esquivel	Universidad Veracruzana, Mexico
Jaime Muñoz-Arteaga	Universidad Autónoma de Aguascalientes, Mexico
José Antonio Macías Iglesias	Universidad Autónoma de Madrid, Spain
José Antonio Pow-Sang	Pontificia Universidad Católica del Perú, Peru
José Guadalupe Arceo Olague	Universidad Autónoma de Zacatecas, Mexico
Jose Maria Celaya Padilla	CONACyT - Universidad Autónoma de Zacatecas, Mexico
José Pascual Molina Massó	Universidad de Castilla-La Mancha, Spain
Jose Rafael Rojano Caceres	Universidad Veracruzana, Mexico
Josefa Somodevilla	Benemérita Universidad Autónoma de Puebla, Mexico
Josefina Guerrero Garcia	Benemérita Universidad Autónoma de Puebla, Mexico
Juan Manuel Gonzalez Calleros	Benemérita Universidad Autónoma de Puebla, Mexico
Juan Miguel López	University of the Basque Country, Spain
Liliana Rodríguez-Vizzuett	Universidad Autónoma de Aguascalientes, Mexico
Luz Edith Herrera Diaz	Universidad Veracruzana, Mexico
Manuel Ortega Cantero	Universidad de Castilla-La Mancha, Spain
Maria Villegas	Universidad del Quindío, Colombia
Maria Dolores Lozano	Universidad de Castilla-La Mancha, Spain
Maria J. Somodevilla	Benemérita Universidad Autónoma de Puebla, Mexico
Maria Luisa Velasco Ramirez	Benemérita Universidad Autónoma de Puebla, Mexico
Mario Rossainz	Benemérita Universidad Autónoma de Puebla, Mexico
Marta Rosecler Bez	Universidade Feevale, Brazil
Martin Larrea	Universidad Nacional del Sur, Argentina
Martín-Santiago Domínguez-González	Benemérita Universidad Autónoma de Puebla, Mexico
Mayela Coto	Universidad Nacional, Costa Rica
Mayra Nayeli Márquez Specia	Benemérita Universidad Autónoma de Puebla, Mexico
Miguel Redondo	Universidad de Castilla-La Mancha, Spain
Milagros Cruz	Benemérita Universidad Autónoma de Puebla, Mexico

Pablo Ruiz	Corporación Universitaria Comfacauca – Unicomfacauca, Colombia
Pascual Gonzalez	Universidad Castilla-La Mancha, Spain
Patricia Paderewski	Universidad de Granada, Spain
Paula Escudeiro	Instituto Superior de Estudios Psicológicos, Spain
Philippe Palanque	University of Toulouse, France
Ricardo Mendoza-Gonzalez	Instituto Tecnológico de Aguascalientes, Mexico
Roberto Garcia	Universidad de Lleida, Spain
Roberto Solis Robles	Universidad Autónoma de Zacatecas, Mexico
Rosa Sandoval	Benemérita Universidad Autónoma de Puebla, Mexico
Rosa Maria Gil	Universidad de Lleida, Spain
Rubén-Edel Navarro	Universidad Veracruzana, Mexico
Sandra-Cano	Universidad San Buenaventura, Colombia
Sergio-Zepeda	Universidad Autónoma Metropolitana Unidad Cuajimalpa, Mexico
Silvia T. Acuña	Universidad Autónoma de Madrid, Spain
Soraia Silva Prietch	Universidade Federal de Mato Grosso, Brazil
Toni Granollers	Universidad de Lleida, Spain
Vanessa Agredo-Delgado	Corporación Universitaria Comfacauca – Unicomfacauca, Colombia
Victor Morales	Benemérita Universidad Autónoma de Puebla, Mexico
Victor Peñeñory	Universidad de San Buenaventura, Colombia
Víctor López-Jaquero	Universidad de Castilla-La Mancha, Spain
Victor M. Gonzalez	Instituto Tecnológico Autónomo de México, Mexico
Victor M. R. Penichet	Universidad de Castilla-La Mancha, Spain
Virginica Rusu	Universidad de Playa Ancha, Chile
Yadira Navarro	Benemérita Universidad Autónoma de Puebla, Mexico
Yenny Mendez	Universidad Nacional Abierta y a Distancia, Mexico
Yesenia Nohemi Gonzalez	Instituto Tecnológico de Apizaco, Mexico

Academic Committee President

Juan Manuel González Calleros	Benemérita Universidad Autónoma de Puebla, México

Program Committee President

César Alberto Collazos	Universidad del Cauca, Colombia

Editorial Committee

Pablo H. Ruiz	Corporación Universitaria Comfacauca - Unicomfacauca and Universidad del Cauca, Colombia
Vanessa Agredo-Delgado	Corporación Universitaria Comfacauca - Unicomfacauca and Universidad del Cauca, Colombia

Contents

A Groupware Usability-Oriented Evaluation Methodology Based on a Fuzzy Linguistic Approach

Luz A. Sánchez-Gálvez[1,2](✉) , Juan Manuel Fernández-Luna[2] ,
and Mario Anzures-García[1]

[1] Facultad de Ciencias de la Computación, Benemérita Universidad Autónoma
de Puebla, Puebla, Mexico
{sanchez.galvez,mario.anzures}@correo.buap.mx
[2] Departamento de Ciencias de la Computación e Inteligencia Artificial, E.T.S.I.
Informática y de Telecomunicación, Universidad de Granada, Granada, Spain
jmluna@decsai.ugr.es

Abstract. Nowadays, many organizations or groups of persons must carry out group work effectively. Groupware typically provides a shared workspace, which is displayed through shared user interfaces by group members, with appropriate resources to accomplish a common task. Consequently, an adequate design and development of groupware requires that the shared user interfaces offer a high level of usability for the users' interaction and the utilization of the shared resources. In this paper, a groupware usability evaluation methodology, specifically for the shared user interfaces, is proposed. This methodology provides an evaluation instrument that collects the users' perceptions through four dimensions—effectiveness, efficiency, learnability and satisfaction—In addition, the gap theory of quality service, and a fuzzy linguistic approach using aggregation operators—which operate directly with words—are applied. Accordingly, the methodology shows to be a significant, innovative contribution to the research area on groupware usability evaluation. A case study to validate methodology, is presented.

Keywords: Usability evaluation methodology · Groupware · Fuzzy linguistic approach · Aggregation operators · SERVQUAL

1 Introduction

Currently, many organizations or groups of persons whose members are geographically distributed, must carry out their work in an effective way. Groupware is a computer-based system that supports groups of people who are engaged in a common task (or goal), and it provides an interface to a shared environment [1]. This definition implies that the groupware development must be focused to manage and control a user's group by supplying a shared workspace, which provides communication, collaboration and coordination among these users. Nevertheless, many people get frustrated with this kind of software as they argue it does not adequately support them, i.e. it does not match the users' tasks and needs. This occurs, since shared workspace interface design

© Springer Nature Switzerland AG 2019
P. H. Ruiz and V. Agredo-Delgado (Eds.): HCI-COLLAB 2019, CCIS 1114, pp. 1–16, 2019.
https://doi.org/10.1007/978-3-030-37386-3_1

often relies too much on trial-and-error techniques, which need to be improved in order to systematically develop better groupware systems. Accordingly, the groupware evaluation is necessary in several situations, although, it is frequently done in an ad-hoc manner or not at all. Therefore, it represents a challenging effort for developers and researchers, since existing methods have significant limitations.

The high cost of evaluation is one of the reasons why groupware systems are not frequently evaluated. On the one hand, the evaluation process could require the use of resources—time, users, experts, labs—hard to find or inaccessible. This applies especially, but not exclusively, to controlled laboratory experiments, depending on how complete or accurate the diagnosis should be. On the other hand, several evaluation methods are either descriptive or prescriptive and therefore provide little support for comparing design options and predicting usability results.

Usability is a discipline of applying sound scientific observation, measurement, and design principles to the creation and maintenance of systems in order to bring about the greatest ease of use [2]. The concept of usability focuses mainly on the use of an interface and how people use it to carry out their tasks. If an interface is not able to satisfy its users, then it will not be able to succeed in the long term. Therefore, the aim is to design both usable and useful groupware. In such a way, it is important to base the design on the work that must be done by the users' interaction.

In recent decades, usability studies have received significant attention in the groupware field. Therefore, its design and development has been reinforced with the various approaches to usability evaluation, which have somehow served as guidelines in the groupware evaluation research. Thus, these have greatly helped to propose new approaches to usability evaluation, as well as to diagnose problems and hence improve the design of groupware interfaces.

Accordingly, the users play an important role in acquiring knowledge about their work as well as for usability testing. As a consequence, a groupware usability evaluation methodology, specifically for shared user interface, and a case study of groupware usability evaluation, are presented in this paper. The methodology proposes an low cost and subjective evaluation instrument, which collects the users' perceptions by four dimensions—effectiveness, efficiency, satisfaction and learnability—In addition, the gap theory of service quality and a fuzzy linguistic model using aggregation operators of linguistic information—which operate directly with words—are used. So, the methodology proves to be a significant and innovative contribution to the area of groupware usability evaluation research.

The paper is organized as follows: Sect. 2 presents the background of the proposed groupware usability methodology. Section 3 details a fuzzy-based groupware usability evaluation methodology. Section 4 describes the application and validation of the methodology. Finally, conclusions and future works are depicted in Sect. 5.

2 Background

This section presents the background for the proposed groupware usability evaluation methodology in this paper. It starts with the description of the discipline groupware and the usability in the context of groupware. Then, it continues with a review and analysis of groupware usability evaluation methods, which provides an important context. Finally, the gap theory of quality service, and linguistic approach are defined.

2.1 Groupware

Groupware provides the shared workspace, where users will perform group work; allowing [3]: *Communication*, it enables the interaction among persons, which is characterized by the users, the information that is shared, and the means or artefacts used; *Collaboration*, it denotes a higher degree of users participation for achieving a certain goal, through their express participation in group activities; and *Coordination*, it manages dependencies among activities carried out into a group to accomplish an objective; providing concurrency mechanisms to reduce racing conditions and guarantee mutually exclusive resource usage.

The session is a term to denote a shared workspace established by polices that define the group organizational structure to support interaction of a group of individuals, geographically distributed, perform collective tasks. The users' interaction is coordinated by the concurrency mechanism to avoid conflicts, due to the cooperative and competitive activities among users, by supplying dynamically generated, temporary permissions to collaborating users. The permissions granted to users depend on the roles that they can play and specify which user can send, receive, or manipulate shared data at a given moment. Furthermore, to cooperate, users must be aware of the presence of other members during the session and of the actions that each one has carried out and is carrying out (group awareness). In such way, a common context be established, and activities coordinated, thereby avoiding surprises and reducing the probability of conflicts in the group. This is achieved by using a mechanism notification, which to ensure the consistency of shared information; indicating to each participant happens it in this shared workspace. As well, in groupware a group memory should be proven, as it is important to count with a historical about use of the shared resources.

2.2 Usability in the Context of Groupware

In the literature, there are several definitions of the concept of usability, which provide different and complementary points of view in each research area. In Human–Computer Interaction (HCI), the most widely accepted definition of usability is the provided for ISO standard 9241-11 [4]: "the extent to which a product can be used by specified users to achieve specific goals with *effectiveness*, *efficiency* and *satisfaction* in a specified context of use". So, usability implies the interaction of users with the software product and can be seen as the product's capability to meet customer expectations.

Nielsen, defines: "usability is a quality attribute that assesses how easy user interfaces are to use" and further breaks down the concept into the following five quality components [5]: *Learnability*: How easy is it for users to accomplish basic tasks the first time they encounter the design? *Efficiency*: Once users have learned the design, how quickly can they perform tasks? *Memorability*: When users return to the design after a period of not using it, how easily can they reestablish proficiency? *Errors*: How many errors do users make, how severe are these errors, and how easily can they recover from the errors? *Satisfaction*: How pleasant is it to use the design?

These definitions of usability directly impact how it is evaluated, since each method or technique employed in these evaluations may focus on distinct aspects of the term usability (e.g., effectiveness of user task, learnability of user interfaces). A usability evaluation is a systematic process composed of a set of well-defined activities for collecting usage data related to end-user interaction with a software product and/or how the specific properties of this software product contribute to achieve a certain degree of usability [6, 7].

Furthermore, a metric is a way to measure or evaluate a software product, whose characteristics or attributes can receive a numerical or nominal value to explain or conjecture about its validity and adequacy. Consequently, for usability, metrics are an essential element allowing the validity and adequacy of interactive products to be studied and, thus, to evaluate their usability; as well as, to help to compare, infer and draw specific conclusions. Four types of metrics are considered to measure usability: direct, indirect, objective, and subjective, which implies the intervention of human judgment. In this manner, it is possible to quantify the experience that the user is acquiring when using the software product, the way in which interacts, behaves and acts with that product. So, usability metrics contribute to the development of software products according to the needs and wishes of users considering their limitations and usage contexts.

For these reasons, to establish the groupware usability evaluation methodology, in this paper, the groupware usability is defined as: *"The degree to which a groupware supports the interaction among group users, as well as between the users and the shared workspace"*. This definition assumes that a groupware system is already usable by examining whether the group interaction grants: *Effectiveness, Efficiency, Learnability*, and *Satisfaction*. In addition, this methodology uses observable, quantifiable and subjective metrics to make timely decisions at key moments and improve the interface appearance.

2.3   State of Art About Groupware Usability Evaluation Methods

In summary, existing methods for groupware usability evaluation can be classified into two main groups: evaluation methods based on expert evaluators, and evaluation methods based on users' perception.

2.3.1   Expert Evaluators-Based Evaluation Methods
In these methods, the evaluation is based on expert evaluators:

– **Groupware Heuristic Evaluation** [8] is an adaptation of the Nielsen's heuristic evaluation methodology [5, 9–11] to groupware. A set of eight usability heuristics that evaluators can use to inspect shared workspace and see how users support teamwork. Evaluators identify usability problems recording the violated heuristic, a severity rating and optionally, a solution to the problematic. The problems are then filtered, classified and consolidated into a list, which is used to improve the application.
– **Groupware walkthrough** [12] is a usability inspection technique based on cognitive walkthrough [13], for single-user software that incorporates user descriptions

and tasks. It involves three types of contextual information: a description of the users and the knowledge they possess; descriptions of the tasks the users will perform with the system; and a list of the correct actions that a user must perform to accomplish the tasks with a prototype. It has two components: a group task model for identifying and analyzing real-world collaborative tasks that captures the variability and multiple courses of action in group work; and a walkthrough process for assessing a system's support for those tasks that guides evaluators as they step through tasks and evaluate the groupware interface. Once scenario specifications and task analyses have been compiled. Evaluators step through the tasks and determine how well the interface supports group members in working toward and achieving the intended outcome.

- **Human-Performance Models** [14] such as the Keystroke-Level Model [15] are based on a cognitive architecture that approximates single-user interaction at a low level of detail (e.g. perceptual, motor, and cognitive processors), which is adapted to groupware: the conventional information flows are considerably changed to reflect collaborative actions, mutual awareness, and interdependence; and the focus and granularity should not remain on the interactions between the user and the physical interface but should significantly change to reflect the interactions among users, mediated by the physical interface. Evaluators define physical interface that may be decomposed into several shared workspaces, and critical scenarios focused on the collaborative actions for shared workspaces. Finally, they compare group performance in the critical scenarios to predict execution times.

- **"Quick-and-dirty" Ethnography** [16]. Ethnography refers to the qualitative description of human social phenomena to produce detailed descriptions of the work activities of actors within specific domains. The intention is to see activities as social actions embedded within a socially organized domain and accomplished in and through the day to day activities of participants. Evaluators carry out brief studies of the group work to provide it and suggest to designers the deficiencies of a system, thus allowing existing and future systems to be improved. "Quick and dirty" provides a broad understanding, which is capable of sensitizing designers particularly to issues which have a bearing on the acceptability and usability of an envisaged system rather than on the specifics of design.

- **Scenario-Based Evaluation** [17]. A scenario is "a concrete description of an activity that the user engages in when performing a specific task, a description sufficiently detailed so the design implications can be inferred and reasoned about". In addition, a complete scenario includes an actor, which may be a specified individual but can be represented as a prototypical role; a setting describing the context in which the scenario occurs; task goals describing the motivation behind performing a scenario; and claims, which are statements about the effects or consequences of using the system [18]. Scenarios and claims provide a tangible, traceable basis for both general and concrete analyses, which are based on actual use of the system. This technique suggests evaluative claims about features of the system, and contextual information about the organization. It is useful for identifying failures to system use that need enhancement.

- **Knowledge Management Approach** [19]. This method is based on knowledge and knowledge flow. It measures whether the tool helps users to detect knowledge flows, to disseminate them, to store previous experience and to reuse it. The knowledge flow process is comprised of six phases (knowledge creation, accumulation, sharing, utilization, internalization), which are also the areas to be evaluated by this approach. To perform evaluation, each area has a list of associated questions, which may be used as a checklist by evaluators.

This first group of methods can be applied to shared workspaces but have a descriptive or prescriptive nature that depends on inspections performed by multiple usability experts. These quantitative lab-based methods although evaluates the usability, they do not make use of information about users and their work contexts.

2.3.2   Users Perception-Based Evaluation Methods

In these methods, the evaluation is based on users' perception:

- **Groupware Task Analysis** [8, 20] combines high-level hierarchical task analysis and field observations for addressing all stages of groupware design. It is based on a conceptual framework including agents, group work, and situation, similar to the work models defined by the Contextual Design approach [21].
- **Collaboration Usability Analysis** [22] is a task analysis technique designed to represent collaboration of a group task in a shared workspace. It is based hierarchical task analysis, which provides flexibility in the ways that tasks are composed and executed. The task hierarchy includes scenarios to describe the high-level context of the collaborative situation, tasks to indicate specific goals within the scenario, and task instantiations to represent individual and collaborative ways of carrying out the task.
- **Mechanics of Collaboration** [23] is a conceptual framework for developing discount usability evaluation techniques that can be applied to shared-workspace groupware. The framework bases on to support mechanics of collaboration: the low level actions and interactions that must be carried out to complete a task in a shared manner. These include communication, coordination, planning, monitoring, assistance, and protection. The framework also includes gross measures of these mechanics: effectiveness, efficiency, and satisfaction.
- **Perceived Value** [24]. The approach is centered on a variable–Perceived Value–measuring several external product attributes of meetingware that can be negotiated between developers and users. This evaluation concerns measuring the Perceived Value attributed by the users to the technology. Perceived Value can provide a metric about the alignment of the developers' and users' expectations. This metric can then be used to make preliminary decisions about the feasibility of a meetingware project, and intermediate assessments of the development process.
- **E-MAGINE** [25]. The aim is to support groups to efficiently assess the groupware applications that fit them best. The method focuses on knowledge sharing groups and follows a modular structure. It is based on the Contingency Perspective in order to structurally characterize groups in their context, and the new ISO-norm for Information Communications Technology tools, Quality in Use. It comprises two phases. The initial phase leads to a first level profile and provides an indication of possible mismatches between group and application. The formulation of this profile

has the benefit of providing a clear guide for further decisions on what instruments should be applied in the final phase of the evaluation process.

This second group of methods is targeted at allows for high-level task analysis or predicting performance in coordinated work scenarios where users react to predefined events not even requiring group awareness. These proposals evaluate groupware by using the shared workspace context through task analysis, mechanics of collaboration, group setting, and perceived value. However, they do not consider the complete interaction in shared space, quality of service, questionnaires to capture users' perception, nor the information evaluation in a qualitative way. Therefore, this paper provides a groupware usability evaluation methodology of low cost (it does not require the use of labs and experts), and qualitative (it captures users' perceived value by Fuzzy Linguistic Approach) to suggest a number of commendations for improving groupware systems (using gap theory of quality service, SERVQUAL). This methodology focus on the user's interaction in the shared workspace and resources.

2.4 SERVQUAL

SERVQUAL [26] evaluation methodology is based on the theory of service quality—assessment applied in the environment of enterprises and organizations. The key element is the customer satisfaction. Service quality is related to diminishing the distance between the customers' expectations and his final perception. Consequently, customers will evaluate, positively or negatively, the quality of a service where their prior perceptions were either higher or lower than expected. In SERVQUAL to evaluating the service quality, Minimum required level of service; Expected level of service; and the level perceived by the use, are considered. Based on the users' feedback, it is possible to define two variables for detecting the strengths and weaknesses i.e. Adequacy of Service (the difference between the perceived value and the minimum value) indicating the areas where the service is below the level expected by the user, and Service Excellence (the difference between the perceived value and the expected value) that identifies areas where it provides a better service than that expected by the user.

2.5 Linguistic Approach

The information cannot always be evaluated in a quantitative manner, sometimes it is necessary to do it qualitatively. The existence of qualitative variables inherent to human behavior, or external environment elements which are difficult to quantify objectively lead individuals to express their opinions better, by using linguistic terms instead of precise numerical values. A linguistic variable differs from a numerical one in that its values are not numbers but words or sentences in a natural or artificial language [27].

When a linguistic model is used, the existence of a suitable set of terms or labels according to the problem domain is assumed, then, the individuals can express their perceptions. The ordinal fuzzy linguistic model [28] is very useful as it simplifies the computing by eliminating the complexity of having to define a grammar.

An ordinal fuzzy linguistic modeling [29] is used in this paper to represent the users' perceptions with words, based on the linguistic aggregation operators LOWA and LWA [28], in order to evaluate groupware usability.

The Linguistic Ordered Weighted Averaging (LOWA) is an operator used to aggregate non-weighted ordinal linguistic information, i.e., linguistic information values with equal importance. The Linguistic Weighted Averaging (LWA) is an operator used to aggregate weighted linguistic information, i.e., linguistic information values have different importance. In order to calculate both operators, this paper follows the definitions established on [27].

3   A Fuzzy-Based Groupware Usability Evaluation Methodology

In this work, a groupware usability evaluation methodology, specifically for the shared user interface has been developed. Therefore, this methodology takes an approach that requires the establishment of dimensions to measure usability, based on standards: ISO 9241-11 [4] and Nielsen's definition [9]. Consequently, it considers four dimensions: effectiveness, efficiency, satisfaction, and learnability. These in 20 items—which capture the users' perceptions to assess the usability degree of groupware—have been represented. Furthermore, the methodology uses a fuzzy linguistic model by aggregation operators with linguistic information, which handle words directly. They are important to allow sorting and classifying all data from an aggregation process—without any loss of linguistic information—This methodology, also, draws on SERVQUAL that is based on the gap theory of service quality and focused on assessing private sector institutions; by measuring the overall service quality.

Deficiencies on groupware usability could be identified through SERVQUAL. Therefore, the proposed methodology of usability evaluation in this paper, could offer commendations for prioritizing improvements and guaranteeing a proper interface design for groupware, based on users' preferences.

4   Application and Validation of the Proposed Methodology

The groupware usability evaluation methodology is based on the development, evaluation and reliability of the questionnaire, as well as the results' analysis, from where a series of recommendations to improve the groupware usability can be provided. For implementing this methodology the following stages are performed:

1. The establishing of dimensions of the usability.
2. The proposal of the questionnaire.
3. The applying of the groupware usability evaluation.
4. The results obtained of the groupware usability evaluation.
5. The commendations suggested.

4.1 The Establishing of Dimensions of the Usability

The usability is a multidimensional concept. In this paper, four dimensions of usability —effectiveness, efficiency, satisfaction and learnability—are proposed to assess groupware usability (see Table 1).

Table 1. Dimensions of methodology.

Dimension	Sub criteria	Definition
Effectiveness		It refers to successful completion of collaborative tasks, where a user group achieve common goals at each stage
Efficiency		It refers to the resources (such as time or effort) required to carry out a successfully collaborative task by the group interaction
Learnability		The groupware should be easy to learn and to understand; it should be easy for the group to achieve a collaborative task by using the shared workspace
Satisfaction	Easiness of use	It refers to the group perception of the use of the shared workspace
	Information organization	It is to assess whether the structure, design, and organization of the system reach the group' goals
	Clear labeling	It refers to the clear labeling of the groupware from the user group point of view, and whether the terminology used is easy to understand
	Visual aspect	It evaluates the groupware design concerning its visual appealing, as well as the group awareness and group memory provision
	Error recovery	It has to do with the easiness for recovering from errors made in each task by the group
	Navigability	It refers to the easiness that group may have to access from one shared interface to another

4.2 The Proposal of the Questionnaire

An important part of the usability research has been the designing of a questionnaire. The items for measuring the groupware usability, were based on the literature on usability evaluation studies. First, it was necessary to establish the dimensions. Consequently, the measurement items were generated and modified to reflect the unique features of the groupware. Thus, twenty items establish the questionnaire (see Table 2) to capture the users' perceptions on the rate of groupware usability, based on the proposed dimensions of usability. Users must answer the questions about their personal experience when interacting with the groupware.

Table 2. Questionnaire.

Dimension	Item
Effectiveness	Can you usually complete a shared task by using the groupware?
	Can you successfully interact through the groupware system?
	Do the shared resources of the groupware system satisfy your needs of group awareness, and memory?
	In general, is the groupware system useful to help you achieve the common goal?
Efficiency	Can you complete a collaborative task quickly by using the groupware?
	Do you obtain results quickly by using the groupware system?
	Does the user interface gives you expeditious access to groupware system shared resources?
	Is the access to information resources quick and easy to use?
Learnability	Was learning to use the groupware system easy?
	Are the terms used on groupware easily understandable?
	Is the groupware system help well organized?
	Are new users able to utilize the shared resources without considerable effort?
Satisfaction	What is your main fulfillment when using groupware system?
	What is the rate of access of groupware system?
	Is the organization and distribution of information on the groupware system clear?
	Is the language used by tags on the groupware system appropriate, organized and clearly enough?
	Is the groupware system visually appealing?
	Does the groupware system allow an easy error recovery?
	Are the resources offered by groupware satisfactory?
Global usability	What is the general usability of the groupware system?

4.3 The Applying of the Groupware Usability Evaluation

The evaluation instrument has been applied to the groupware implemented by a semantic methodological approach [30, 31]. This includes two roles: (1) The professor, who can register himself and enter to this shared workspace, create groups, upload and download files both his and those of the students, publish messages and respond to those made by others; and (2). The students, who can register themselves and enter in the shared space and access courses, load and unload files (homework and course materials that have been uploaded by the professor), make publications and to reply to them. Therefore, loading files and publishing message are two essentials collaborative interactions, which make use both the shared workspace and the group awareness.

In the case study, the participants were asked to fill out a pre-questionnaire concerning demographic data—level of education, age, and gender, use frequency of the groupware and level of computer skills. A total of 43 users participated in the groupware usability evaluation—including students and professors of undergraduate.

The usability evaluation questionnaire was examined bearing in mind the following steps:

1. The users expressed their judgment by completing the questionnaires (see Table 1). The scale for this model is S = {VL = Very Low, L = Low, M = Medium, H = High, VH = Very High}.

   As a result for each one of the users u_j (u_1, u_2,...u_n) and for each questionnaire item i_k (i_1, i_2,...i_m), m is the total number of questions; there is a tuple (mv_{jk}, pv_{jk}, ev_{jk}) of the minimum value—mv—, perceived value—pv—and the expected value—ev—, for each user u_j and for each question i_k.

2. To compute the global users' opinion concerning each item i_k of the tuple (mv_{jk}, pv_{jk}, ev_{jk}), the following aggregation operators are used:

   2.1. LOWA [27] is used if all users are considered to bear the same importance.

   $$mv_k = \Phi_Q(mv_{1k}...,mv_{nk})$$
   $$pv_k = \Phi_Q(pv_{1k}...,pv_{nk})$$
   $$ev_k = \Phi_Q(ev_{1k}...,ev_{nk})$$

   2.2. LWA [27] is used when each user is considered to bear a different level of importance.

   $$mv_k = \Phi_Q((UI(u_1, i_k), mv_{1k}),..., (UI(u_n, i_k),mv_{nk}))$$
   $$pv_k = \Phi_Q((UI(u_1, i_k), pv_{1k}),..., (UI(u_n, i_k), pv_{nk}))$$
   $$ev_k = \Phi_Q((UI(u_1, i_k), ev_{1k}),..., (UI(u_n, i_k), ev_{nk}))$$

   Where $UI(u_j, i_k)$ S is the level of relative linguistic importance assigned to a user u_j for the item i_k.

3. The overall review of all questions of the tuple (mv, pv, ev) is calculated similarly to the previous step, by using aggregation operators:

   LOWA [27] is used when all the items are considered to bear the same importance.

   $$mv_k = \Phi_Q(mv_1, ..., mv_m)$$
   $$pv_k = \Phi_Q(pv_1, ..., pv_m)$$
   $$ev_k = \Phi_Q(ev_1, ..., ev_m)$$

   LWA [27] is used when each item is considered to carry a different level of importance.

   $$mv = \Phi_Q((II(i_1), mv_1), ..., (II(i_m),mv_m))$$
   $$pv = \Phi_Q((II(i_1), pv_1), ..., (UI(i_m), pv_m))$$
   $$ev = \Phi_Q((II(i_1), ev_1), ..., (UI(i_m), ev_m))$$

   Where $II(i_k)$ S is the level of relative linguistic importance assigned to item i_k.

4. The gap theory of service quality is applied to each item. The tolerance zone is located between the minimum and the expected values. The difference between the perceived and the minimum values, is called Service Adequacy—SA—and the Service Superiority—SS—is the difference between the expected values and the perceived ones. Therefore, for each item i_k, SA_k and SS_k are computed as follows [27]:

$$SA_k = D(pv_k, mv_k)$$
$$SS_k = D(ev_k, ev_k)$$

In the other hand, it is important to verify the reliability of the evaluation instrument, when questionnaires for evaluating the groupware usability are applied, therefore, it is advisable to use the Cronbach's alpha [32]. Cronbach's alpha allows to quantify the level of reliability of an evaluation scale, built from k variables observed. Assuming that the variables are related to the qualitative interest data; the k variables should achieve stable, consistent measurements with a high level of correlation among themselves. A questionnaire is considered reliable when Cronbach's alpha is greater than 0.80. The formula for Cronbach's alpha is:

$$\propto = \left[\frac{k}{k-1} \right] \left[1 - \frac{\sum_{i=1}^{k} S_i^2}{S_t^2} \right]$$

S_i^2 is the item variance i;
S_t^2 is the item variance of all observed values;
K in the item number of the questionnaire;

4.4 The Results Obtained of the Groupware Usability Evaluation

Both a quantitative and a qualitative analysis are accomplished in the groupware usability evaluation. The qualitative analysis focuses on calculating the aggregation operators LOWA and LWA; it is based on proposed linguistic labels on the scale.

The LOWA operator requires to obtain the combination of the users' perception for each item. Thus, Table 3 summarizes the result of the combined aggregation of the users' perception for the three assessed values: minimum, perceived, and expected values, regarding the groupware as well as their corresponding gap. On the other hand, the Fig. 1 shows a radial chart that summarizes the user responses to the questionnaire items on the minimum, perceived and expected levels. This type of chart was used, as SERVQUAL encourages its use to display the results obtained with the LOWA operator. As shown there in, the usability of the minimum value is perceived with a medium value by most users, unlike the perceived and the expected values which show a tendency towards a higher level of groupware usability.

The LWA operator allows perceiving the opinion of all users on items with a different level of importance; which is suitable to evaluate the usability on this work, because it contemplates four dimensions: efficiency, effectiveness, learnability, and satisfaction. So, the level of importance will vary according to the dimension that is being assessed. In case of measuring effectiveness, items 1, 2, 3, and 4 would have a VH (Very High) level of importance, while the remaining items present a VL (Very Low) level of importance as shown in Table 4.

On the other hand, concerning the quantitative analysis, item 20 has been planted to measure the satisfaction of the user's overall groupware usability. Figure 2 displays that 19 out of the 43 respondents have a high (H) overall satisfaction when evaluating

Table 3. Results of the LOWA operator.

Item	Minimum	Perceived	Expected	Usability adequacy	Usability excellence
1	M	H	H	L	VL
2	L	H	H	L	VL
3	L	H	H	L	VL
4	M	H	VL	L	VL
5	M	H	H	L	VL
6	M	H	VL	L	VL
7	L	H	H	L	VL
8	H	H	VL	L	VL
9	L	H	H	L	VL
10	L	H	H	M	VL
11	H	H	VL	M	VL
12	L	H	M	M	L+
13	H	H	M	M	L+
14	VL	VL	VL	M	L+
15	M	H	VL	B	VL
16	M	H	H	B	VL
17	M	VL	VL	M	VL
18	M	VL	VL	M	VL
19	M	H	H	L	VL
20	L	H	H	L	VL

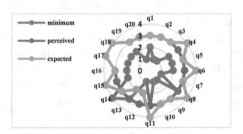

Fig. 1. Radial chart of the LOWA operator.

Table 4. LWA operator for the effectiveness dimension.

LWA: effectiveness		
Minimum	Perceived	Expected
M	H	H

groupware usability; while 7 of them show a Very High (VH) level; 13 show a Medium (M) value, and the other 4 present a Low (L) value. As mentioned above, the evaluation questionnaire reliability, was calculated using Cronbach's alpha, obtaining a value equal to 0.89 for the minimum value; 0.91 for perceived value; and 0.93 for the expected value, which means such a reliability is fairly acceptable.

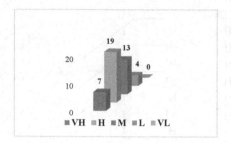

Fig. 2. Chart of the 20 item.

4.5   The Commendations Suggested

Overall, the groupware usability evaluation results have been satisfactory. However, the adequacy gap indicates that the improvement should focus primarily on two-dimensions; learnability and satisfaction. In the former, the adjustments should be directed to improve and simplify the access control, both the shared resources and application itself. So, it is advisable to specify users, tasks, and resources involved in shared workspace in a clear, simply way. While in the latter, the changes should be oriented to improve the navigability in collaborative workspace, group awareness and memory. So, including widgets, menu, messages or icons, that allow to indicate users connected, resources used or changed, state of each user or resource, historical of each resource modified; which clearly inform and orient about the shared workspace situation. As for the interface, three commendations are made: To modify its organization to simplify and improve its navigability; to focus on the resources offered by the groupware, eliminating or reducing those that are strange to it, and using a clear terminology that would improve the appearance of the groupware. These interface adjustments help to simplify the interaction among users, and these with the system.

5   Conclusions and Future Work

A low-cost groupware usability evaluation methodology that can identify shared workspace specific usability problems and can be considerable potential for using it to improve groupware systems usability, has been developed. In the methodology, the basic principles of usability have been combined with models of service quality (the gap theory of service quality has set the pace to suggest a number of commendations for improving groupware systems) and fuzzy logic models as the use of aggregation operators of linguistic information with a measurement scale was raised five linguistic labels specifically applied to groupware usability evaluation. In this research, a measuring instrument that collects users' perceptions based on the four dimensions to evaluate the groupware usability is proposed. Cronbach's alpha for verifying the reliability of the measurement instrument was used. A qualitative study was also carried out using descriptive statistics to compare the results with those obtained by the aggregation operators, which showed that their use for the methodology, is appropriate. Future work will focus on applying diverse linguistic quantifiers to calculate the weights of aggregation operators, which allow us improving this methodology.

References

1. Ellis, C.A., Gibs, S.J., Rein, G.L.: Groupware: some issues and experiences. Commun. ACM **34–1**, 39–58 (1991). https://doi.org/10.1145/99977.99987
2. Pearrow, M.: Web Site Usability Handbook. Charles River Media, Rockland (2000)
3. Anzures-García, M., Sánchez-Gálvez, L.A., Hornos, M., Paderewski, P.: Facilitating the development of collaborative applications with the MVC architectural pattern. In: Chapter 15, Software Engineering: Methods, Modeling, and Teaching, vol. 4, pp. 268–290 (2017)
4. International Organization for Standardization, Technical Committee of Ergonomics. 1998. Ergonomic requirements for office work with visual display terminals (VDTs): Part 11: Guidance on usability (ISO No. 9241–11)
5. Nielsen, J.: Usability Engineering. Academic Press, Cambridge, Mass (1993)
6. Fernandez, A., Insfran, E., Abrahão, S.: Usability evaluation methods for the web: a systematic mapping study. Inf. Softw. Technol. **53**, 789–817 (2011). https://doi.org/10.1016/j.infsof.2011.02.007
7. Sánchez-Gálvez, L.A., Fernández-Luna, J.M.: A usability evaluation methodology of digital library. In: The Seventh International Conference on Information, Process, and Knowledge Management (eKNOW 2015), Lisbon, Portugal, pp. 22–27 (2015)
8. Baker, K., Greenberg, S., Gutwin, C.: Empirical development of a heuristic evaluation methodology for shared workspace groupware. In: CSCW 2002, pp. 96–105 (2002). https://doi.org/10.1145/587078.587093
9. Nielsen, J., Robert, L.M.: Usability Inspection Methods. Wiley, New York (1994). https://doi.org/10.1145/259963.260531
10. Nielsen, J., Molich, R.: Heuristic evaluation user interfaces. In: CHI, pp. 249–256. ACM (1990). https://doi.org/10.1145/97243.97281
11. Nielsen, J.: Finding usability problems through heuristic evaluation. In: CHI 1992, pp. 372–380. ACM (1992). https://doi.org/10.1145/142750.142834
12. Pinelle, D., Gutwin, C.: Groupware walkthrough: adding context to groupware usability evaluation. In: CHI 2002, pp. 455–462. ACM Press (2002). https://doi.org/10.1145/503376.503458
13. Polson, P., Lewis, C., Rieman, J., Wharton, C.: Cognitive walkthroughs: a method for theory-based evaluation of user interfaces. Int. J. Man-Mach. Stud. **36**, 741–773 (1992). https://doi.org/10.1016/0020-7373(92)90039-N
14. Antunes, P., Ferreira, A., Pino, J.A.: Analyzing shared workspaces design with human-performance models. In: Dimitriadis, Y.A., Zigurs, I., Gómez-Sánchez, E. (eds.) CRIWG 2006. LNCS, vol. 4154, pp. 62–77. Springer, Heidelberg (2006). https://doi.org/10.1007/11853862_6
15. Card, S.K., Moran, T.P., Newell, A.: The keystroke-level model for user performance time with interactive systems. Comm. ACM **23–7**, 396–410 (1980). https://doi.org/10.1145/358886.358895

16. Hughes, J., King, V., Rodden, T., Andersen, H.: Moving out from the control room: ethnography in system design. In: CSCW 1994, pp. 429–439. ACM Press (1994). https://doi.org/10.1145/192844.193065

17. Haynes, S., Purao, S., Skattebo, A.: Situating evaluation in scenarios of use. In: CSCW 2004, pp. 92–101. ACM Press (2004). https://doi.org/10.1145/1031607.1031624

18. Carroll, J.M.: Scenario-Based Design: Envisioning Work and Technology in System Development. Wiley, New York (1995). https://doi.org/10.1109/tpc.1996.544582

19. Vizcaíno, A., Martinez, M., Aranda, G., Piattini, M.: Evaluating collaborative applications from a knowledge management approach. In: WETICE 2005, pp. 221–225. IEEE (2005). https://doi.org/10.1109/wetice.2005.36

20. Van der Veer, G., van Welie, M.: Task based groupware design: putting theory into practice. In: DIS20000: Proceedings of the conference on Designing interactive systems, New York City, New York, USA, pp. 326–337 (2000). https://doi.org/10.1145/347642.347781

21. Beyer, H., Holtzblatt, K.: Contextual Design: Defining Customer-Centered Systems. Morgan Kaufmann Publishers, San Francisco (1998)

22. Pinelle, D., Gutwin, C., Greenberg, S.: Task analysis for groupware usability evaluation: modeling shared-workspace tasks with the mechanics of collaboration. ACM Trans. Comput.-Hum. Interact. **10–4**, 281–311 (2003). https://doi.org/10.1145/966930.966932

23. Gutwin, C., Greenberg, S.: The mechanics of collaboration: developing low cost usability evaluation methods for shared workspaces. In: WETICE 2000, pp. 98–103. IEEE (2000). https://doi.org/10.1109/enabl.2000.883711

24. Antunes, P., Costa, C.J.: Perceived value: a low-cost approach to evaluate meetingware. In: Favela, J., Decouchant, D. (eds.) CRIWG 2003. LNCS, vol. 2806, pp. 109–125. Springer, Heidelberg (2003). https://doi.org/10.1007/978-3-540-39850-9_10

25. Huis in't Veld, M., Andriessen, J., Verburg, R.: E-magine: the development of an evaluation method to assess groupware applications. In: WETICE 2003, pp. 153–164 (2003)

26. Parasuraman, A., Zeithaml, V.A., Berry, L.L.: SERVQUAL: a multiple-item scale for measuring customer perceptions of service quality. J. Retail. **64**, 12–40 (1988)

27. Herrera, F., Herrera-Viedma, E., Verdegay, J.L.: Direct approach processes in group decision making using linguistic OWA operators. Fuzzy Sets Syst. **79**, 175–190 (1996). https://doi.org/10.1016/0165-0114(95)00162-X

28. Heradio, R., Cabrerizo, F.J., Fernández-Amorós, D., Herrera, M., Herrera-Viedma, E.: A fuzzy linguistic model to evaluate the quality of library 2.0 functionalities. Int. J. Inform. Manag. **33**, 642–654 (2013). https://doi.org/10.1016/j.ijinfomgt.2013.04.001

29. Zadeh, L.A.: The concept of a linguistic variable and its applications to approximate reasoning. Part III. Inf. Sciences **9–1**, 43–80 (1975). https://doi.org/10.1016/0020-0255(75)90036-5

30. Anzures-García, M., Sánchez-Gálvez, L.A., Hornos, M.J., Paderewski, P.: A workflow ontology to support knowledge management in a group's organizational structure. Int. J. Comp. Sci. Appl. **22–1**, 163–178 (2018). https://doi.org/10.13053/CyS-22-1-2781

31. Anzures-García, M., Sánchez-Gálvez, L.A., Hornos, M.J., Paderewski, P.: Tutorial function groupware based on a workflow ontology and a directed acyclic graph. IEEE Latin Am. Trans. **16–1**, 294–300 (2018). https://doi.org/10.1109/TLA.2018.8291487

32. Bojórquez, A., López, L., Hernández, M.E., Jiménez, E.: Utilización del alfa de Cronbach para validar la confiabilidad de un instrumento de medición de satisfacción del estudiante en el uso del software Minitab. In: Innovation in Engineering, Technological and Ed. for Competitiveness and Prosperity, pp. 14–16 (2013)

A Reformation Proposal of the Process Phase in the Computer-Supported Collaborative Learning

Vanessa Agredo-Delgado[1,2]([⊠]) [iD], Pablo H. Ruiz[1,2] [iD],
Cesar A. Collazos[2] [iD], and Habib M. Fardoun[3,4] [iD]

[1] Corporación Universitaria Comfacauca – Unicomfacauca,
Street 4 Number 8–30, Popayan, Colombia
{vagredo, pruiz}@unicomfacauca.edu.co
[2] Department of Computing, University of Cauca,
Street 5 Number. 4 – 70, Popayan, Colombia
ccollazo@unicauca.edu.co
[3] Infomation Systems, Faculty of Computing and Information Technology,
King Abdulaziz University, Jeddah, Saudi Arabia
hfardoun@kau.edu.sa
[4] Computer Science Department, College of Arts and Science,
Applied Science University, Al Eker, Bahrain

Abstract. One of the important needs of the companies is form interdisciplinary expert groups on specific topics that contribute to a decision-making process and the solution of complex problems, more efficiently, which has led to seeking the challenge of achieving an adequate collaboration and better productivity, allowing common objectives to be achieved through interaction with the rest of the group. The education has not been foreign to this need, since it is intended to support students to be more prepared in their collaborative skills and to form collaborative citizens who, together, can solve key problems of society. This is where the definition of computer-supported collaborative learning (CSCL) appears, which focuses mainly on the study of how people can learn together with the help of computers. The CSCL is divided into three phases according to its temporal execution: Pre-Process, Process and Post-Process. The Process phase is carried out mainly by the students, where the interactions of the learning process and collaboration are materialized. In this paper, we propose an elements refinement of the Process stage, in addition to its validation through the usefulness, applicability, and ease of use. Obtaining as a result that, our proposal is useful and applicable, but despite this, due to the amount of information necessary for its ap-plication it does not ease of use. Thus, we have contributed to the enrichment of the learning process elements in the Process stage which can be used in the execution of the collaborative activities.

Keywords: Education · Computer supported collaborative learning · Collaborative elements · Collaborative learning process phases

© Springer Nature Switzerland AG 2019
P. H. Ruiz and V. Agredo-Delgado (Eds.): HCI-COLLAB 2019, CCIS 1114, pp. 17–29, 2019.
https://doi.org/10.1007/978-3-030-37386-3_2

1 Introduction

Thanks to various studies, it has been proven that the computer-supported collaborative learning [1] (CSCL) it favors individual learning and fosters social skills, it has also been proven that students who work collaboratively develop better attitudes towards the learning process, dedicate more time to the task of learning, are more tolerant, listen more to the opinions of others and have better negotiation skills. In addition, from the teacher's viewpoint, the use of computers as a learning tool allows for a more detailed follow-up of the process, since the different tools and applications can incorporate a record of the activities. In this way, the teacher can review the process that each student has followed in their learning, guide the process and observe the mistakes made [2]. On the other hand, the analysis of the collaboration allows measuring the interactive process that takes place during a collaborative activity [3]. From this viewpoint, it is important to be able to detect what degree of collaboration is having or has taken place during the group learning process [4]. To guide the learning process, according to [5], is divided into three phases: Pre-Process, Process and Post-Process. The first phase Pre-Process begins with the activity design and specification, in addition, the activity content, the main tasks and the objectives to be achieved by participating groups are designed. In the Process phase, the collaboration activity is executed to achieve the objectives, where each member develops collaborative skills such as explanation, argumentation, regulation, negotiation, communication among others. At the end of the activity, in the Post-Process phase, the activity coordinator performs an individual and collective review to verify the achievement of the proposed objective. Currently, there are proposals that include some of the elements or techniques that constitute the collaborative learning ambit [6–8], which does not cover all the design needs of collaborative activities and much less monitoring and evaluation mechanisms. Consequently, the need arises to create a proposal that, with technological accompaniment, guides the collaborative learning activities execution, to improve the collaboration outcomes of the students involved process [9]. For this reason, in this paper, we propose a refinement to the Process stage through of its elements (activities, roles, inputs, outputs and, monitoring and evaluation mechanisms), also, we validate this refinement through its usefulness, applicability, and ease of use. According to the validation, it can be considered that our proposal is useful and applicable, but despite this, it was found that due to the amount of information necessary for its application it does not ease of use.

This paper is structured, section two: related work, the section three: redefinition of the Process phase elements, which shows the evolution of each element, section four show the application of this phase through a case study and finally the section five the conclusions and future work section.

2 Related Work

Ramirez et al. [10] presented a guide for the computer-supported collaborative learning activities design called CSCoLAD, which used a web tool that provided a mechanism to support all collaborative learning process. The guide design was based on theoretical references, such as those proposed by Johnson et al. [11] regarding the phases that are incorporated in the collaborative learning process and the definition that it proposes about collaborative activity and its characteristics, adding activities given by the expert's experience. This work helped as a basis for the redefinition of the Process phase elements show in this paper and for the addition of monitoring and evaluation elements, thus allowing increased collaboration among the activity members, concepts that were not considered in this first version presented in CSCoLAD.

On the other hand, the method presented by Chacón [12], enable the collaborative activities structuring and thus stimulate the technology incorporation more efficiently in teaching and learning processes, taking advantage of Web 2.0 tools to design and develop collaborative activities. Lund [13] proposed a model for designing teaching-learning activities, in collaborative and geographically distributed environments, in an experimental format. This model, called CODILA+A, was oriented to universities that dictate computer science careers, this model has a template that guides the teacher in the activities design, its exposed guidelines or characteristics and revision for each collaborative activity carried out. A script called Strategic Guide for Problem Solving proposed by King [14] was designed to foment student interactions when solving complex problems, which was based on a strategic question sequence that guides the participants in the problem-solving activity, controlling the content of their interactions while solving the activity together. Fischer et al. [15] proposed a study on the convenience of using scripts in the collaborative activities design and development. In this study a series of experiments with different groups was done, obtaining that some of these development activities with the scripts support and others without such help. Gallardo et al. [16] designed a computational environment to support one of the most commonly used techniques in collaborative learning environments such as JIGSAW [4]. This type of tool was linked to the collaborative learning technique and has not been structured in a generic way so that it can adapt to any other technique. Hernández et al. [17] presented a high-level tool for the collaborative activities design based on patterns, called COLLAGE, created with the purpose of helping teachers in the process of creating their collaborative designs through the reuse and patterns customization, in order to that they are effective and adapted to the needs of a learning situation.

3   Redefining the Process Phase Elements

As shown, Ramírez et al. [10], presented the first version of the activities for each process phase set forth in [5], which generated a guide for the collaborative learning activities design assisted by computer. The steps of creating the guide followed by Ramirez et al. [10] was: the first step was the study of the process for the collaborative activities design proposed by Johnson et al. [18], after, they analyze the classification of these activities in the Pre-Process phases, Process and Post-Process. With the support of the authors such as Dillenbourg [1], Johnson et al. [11], Lund [13], and Collazos et al. [5], a proposal is carried out, obtaining a CSCoLAD guide first version. This proposal is repeatedly evaluated by experts in the collaborative learning area, who propose improvements and new recommendations that will be adapted to the guide, in order to obtain a CSCoLAD guide final version. Once this final version is available, it is described in the format of patterns, how to execute each one activity exposed in the guide, in order to facilitate the interpretation, within a collaborative learning environment.

Starting from the guide defined in CSCoLAD project and the deficiencies related to maintaining collaboration during the activity execution according by Collazos [9], it was observed the need to monitor and evaluate the collaborative learning process, through by incorporation of new elements at process for increasing the collaboration between the participants, it is for this reason that a redefinition of the Process phase elements and of the CSCoLAD guide was carried out. For the definition of our proposal of refinement, we define some stages, the launch stage: where approval was given and the proposal to be made communicated, after, the definition stage: the characteristics at the group level were defined, activities, and technology. Evaluation mechanisms for the activities in each phase were defined for CSCoLAD and templates were created for data collection. A formulation stage: conceptual models were developed of how the collaborative processes were executed with its activities, groups, tools where the process possible improvements were identifying. A metrics stage: a set of indicators and collaboration metrics were described. It was defined which factors that must be considered for the creation of the groups, the activities design, and the tools. A mechanisms stage: mechanisms that allow the evaluation and monitoring of the collaborative process were created which were presented in [19]. According to the previous stages, we obtained the first refinement, then, it was evaluated by experts in the collaborative learning area, who proposed some improvements and recommendations that were incorporated. In this first refinement was implemented a software tool that supported each process phase. An improvement stage: it was defined an improved conceptual model of the collaborative learning process that allowed us solving the shortcomings found in activities, roles, and tools that were part of collaborative learning, in addition to having a formal specification of the activities of Process phase presented in [20], a test stage: within order to evaluate and validate the proposed conceptual infrastructure field tests were elaborated in various classrooms, using like supporting the defined tool in [21]. Finally, we obtained recommendations and results that allowed us to improve our proposal.

According to the stages that were shown previously, as one of the results, some deficiencies and improvement opportunities in CSCoLAD were identified (See Table 1):

Table 1. Improvement opportunities

Deficiency	Opportunities
Lack of steps to develop collaborative activity by the teacher	Manual for management of collaborative activity preparation
The teacher does not have a record of the objectives, which are seen by the participants	PDF generator to describe the collaborative activity
The teacher cannot form groups automatically to manage them	Tool for creating groups
The teacher needs to design roles and assign them to the student with their tasks	Tool for role assignment
There is no automatic control of the start and end of activities	Report on delivery dates and control of these
The teacher has no knowledge of how to make chats, forums, wikis to incentive collaboration	Collaboration incentive mechanisms: Chat, forums, wikis, emails
There is no monitoring of tasks	Monitoring of activities carried out
There is no way where the teacher can test whether the success criteria are being met	Success criteria evaluation
The teacher cannot keep track of the activities and give feedback	Mechanisms for teacher feedback of activities carried out for students
The teacher does not have a manual to know the best practices and the guidelines to follow in a collaborative activity	Manual of general recommendations to carry out the collaborative learning process
It is necessary to have records of all activities to know actions by students	Handling of records for the activities carried out

To support the improvement opportunities identified in the previous table, each activity of the process phase was assigned mechanism to execution, an application strategy, responsible, inputs, outputs, evaluation mechanisms and monitoring mechanisms. Table 2 shows a summary of the most important items assigned to each activity.

In order to verify that the proposed elements were adequate, seven experts in the area were asked to do an evaluation where they were requested that each activity, each monitoring and evaluation mechanisms are given a score: 1–5 considering the relevance that each one of them (1 is little relevant and 5 highly relevant). With the results obtained by the experts, the arithmetic calculation of these values is applied, those activities that have an inferior value to those defined in the limits, they were discarded in the final proposal of this work (In Table 3 shows the value obtained by the experts in each activity):

Table 2. Monitoring and evaluation mechanisms for the Process phase

Number of the activity	Activity	Evaluation mechanisms	Monitoring mechanisms
1	Briefly describe learning activity	Checklist of the collaborative activity compliance, a survey with students or experts on the subject	Record of the information delivery by the teacher of each task to be performed
2	Groups formation	List of formed groups and characteristics	Forums according to the corresponding group, group chats
3	Roles assign	List of roles assigned, activities and responsibilities to be fulfilled	The teacher monitor activities compliance. Have a chat seeing the role and their actions
4	Materials distribution	Checklist of the materials used assigned, materials history used	Fulfillment monitoring the activity that has been assigned and the material use
5	Activity start	Actions and situations record that goes beyond what is stipulated, the messages and activities sent with the student's schedule and name	Have a history of the time that the students spend in the corresponding activities and their participation in the group activities
6	Keep the collaboration moment	Record of messages sent, and activities carried out, actions list with which the teacher should react during the activity	Contact with students. The teacher sends to the students who don't collaborate, messages and change the groups
7	Test the success criteria	Student checklists of activity completion, collaboration checklist among team members	Look the student's activities and the activities fulfillment required
8	Conduct a formative evaluation	Surveys experts on the subject, keep track of past activities	Evaluations record made to the students according to the activities theme
9	Feedback	Past activities record, delivery of solutions to activities	Record of support provided for feedback, a mistakes compendium made by the groups
10	Present the activity closing	Socialization record among the students of the activities carried out and the results obtained	Chat to socialize the results by group, it can use forums, wikis, among others
11	The groups compare their results with each other	Concepts record evaluated by the groups according to the results obtained	Chat to socialize the results by group, it can use forums, wikis, among others

The criterion of Statistical Fashion (Mo) was used to find the value that has the highest absolute frequency in the distribution of data, and thus define the threshold with which it is statistically determined which elements of the refinement are included and which will not be included according to expert validation. The threshold value was Mo = 3.72, the activities that have a value lower than this will not be included in the refinement. For this reason, it can be determined that all activities defined are relevant to the Process phase, considering that recommendations were given for some activities which allowed to enrich the phase elements. Finally, for each activity was specified, subtasks, steps, roles, inputs, outputs, monitoring, and evaluation mechanisms. In Fig. 1. is shown each activity with its subtasks associated:

Table 3. Arithmetic calculation of the experts

Activity	X
1	4,3
2	4,2
3	4,3
4	4,3
5	4,4
6	4,5
7	4,1
8	4,2
9	4,4
10	4,1
11	3,9

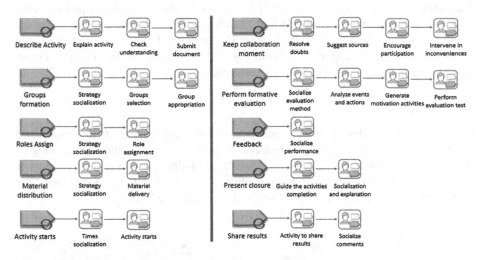

Fig. 1. Activities with its subtasks associated

As an example, below is shown only the information specification of activity "*Describe activity*", the same was done with each of the other activities proposed, in addition to each task the steps that comprise it was defined, and for each step were defined a monitoring mechanism, an evaluation mechanism, and its description (See Table 4).

Table 4. Describe activity information

Name	Describe activity
Description	To explain and describe the activity with the goals, success criteria, tasks, duration, roles, evaluation, and expectations towards students and with this description a teacher can determine if the activity fits their course or not
Inputs	A document, where chose the activity to be carried out, goal list, success criteria list, activity duration list, task list with time and role assignment
Outputs	Activity explanation and the tasks to be performed, document containing the explanation, the activity limits, what it wants to achieve and how it is going to do it
Role	Teacher

4   Case Study

According to refinement that was shown above, a case study was developed in which MEPAC [22], was used as a support tool, which allowed to support the teacher in the collaborative learning process in each phase (Pre-process, Process, Post-process), and we are focusing the support of monitoring and evaluation in the Process Phase, applying each element redefined in this research.

4.1   Context

This case study was developed in an academic context, applying the refinement in two university courses of a systems engineering program, specifically in the Object-Oriented Programming (See Fig. 2), and Data Base Modeling (See Fig. 3) courses. The first course was constituted by 16 undergraduate students of first and second year. The second course was constituted by 10 students of second and third year.

Fig. 2. Course object-oriented programming

Fig. 3. Course data base modeling

4.2 Objective

The objective was to validate the elements refinement (activities, roles, inputs, outputs, monitoring and evaluation mechanisms) of the collaborative learning process in the Process stage. Therefore, the question for this case study is: Does the refinement of the collaborative learning elements of the Process phase is useful, applicable and easy to use, in the undergraduate academic environment?

4.3 Selection of the Case Study

The unit of analysis is the academic environment within a collaborative learning process in an academic environment, the primary source of information is the teacher and the participating groups, who are responsible for the Process phase, his selection responded to availability criteria [23] of a subject with interest in applying collaborative activities to his course. According to Benbasat et al. [23], the case study is Holistic, the collaborative activity selected was because it is a real case in teaching (it is a sufficiently complete case to evaluate the applicability of the proposal).

4.4 Metrics and Indicators of the Case Study

The indicators detailed description and its metrics are the following:

Utility: The utility is defined as the property by which the refinement of the Process phase achieves the proposed improvement objectives for the collaborative learning process. The metrics that have been established to calculate the utility are:

- The range of students who approve the activity must be between 80% and 100%.
- The range of students who consider that the refinement of the elements is a positive support for the course should be between 80% and 100%.
- The percentage of the number of questions that have a positive impact obtained from the perception of the teacher between level four and five (five being the highest degree of utility) must be greater than or equal to 80%.

Applicability: Applicability is defined as the property by which refinement can be easily employed to obtain favorable improvement results for the collaborative learning process. The metrics that have been established to determine the applicability are:

- The answers average about applicability obtained from the teacher perception must be greater than or equal to 80%. With values between four and five, where five is the highest degree of applicability.
- The effort to apply the refinement must be on average of a collaborative activity (average duration of 3 to 4 h).

Ease of use: Ease of use is defined as the degree of ease with which a person can understand and apply the Process phase refinement. The metrics that have been established to determine the ease of use are:

- The average from the teacher perception of ease of use obtained that is between 1 and 5 (5 being the highest degree of ease of use) must be greater than or equal to 80%.
- The number of explanation questions for using that the teacher and the students made to the formulator of the refinement to apply the elements, should be below 3 questions per hour.

4.5   Case Study Execution

The case study application began with the Pre-process phase, in which the teacher used MEPAC tool and with a form performed the collaborative activity design. In the following session, the teacher performed the second form related to the Process phase, considering some activities already defined in the Pre-process, and taking the help given to execute this phase. The form presented in the tool for this phase contains the following elements:

Describe the activity:
Clear explanation of the activity to be carried out:
Define the activity limits (to be achieved with the activity):
Steps sequence to be followed in the activity:
Groups formation:
Group formation (participant's names in each group created):
To assign roles:
Students names with the assignment of each role created in the groups:
Description for each role and work justification performed by each student:
Materials distribution:
Groups name with the material definition delivered to each of them:
Activity start:
Activity start time and date:
Estimated time and date of activity completion:
Description of each task with the estimated duration:
Maintain the collaboration moment:
Define means to answer doubts, queries, and problems:
Resources suggestion and information sources regarding the activity designed:
Strategies to increase collaboration among students, during the activity execution:
Test the success criteria:
Describe activity success criteria:
Conduct a formative evaluation:
Define the evaluation about the activity theme carried out:
Field to locate the evaluation to be carried out:
Feedback:
Mechanisms to be handled to provide feedback on the activities carried out:
Present the activity closing:
Mechanisms to be used for the teacher to guide the activities completion carried out:
Strategy within each group to complete the activities carried out (for example: sharing within each group in pairs what was learned within the class):

To do the groups compare their results with each other:
Strategy for groups to share the results:

After the teacher filled out each field of the Process phase, the software tool MEPAC generates a PDF of this second phase, and with this guide the teacher executes the activity designed on the course students. In order to carry out this Process phase, the monitoring and evaluation mechanisms of the activities carried out that allowed the teacher's intervention at appropriate times were applied to achieve the proposed objective.

After executing the activity with the students, the teacher makes the form for the Post-process. For all these processes the times were measured, and the observations were recorded according to the protocols and templates established at each process phase. At the session end, a survey was given to the investigated subject to measure the satisfaction degree, utility, and ease of use of the application of the refined elements.

4.6 Results

As a result of the execute case study we obtain the following values for the indicators defined:

Utility

- The percentage of the students who approved the activity before the refinement was 70.8%, while after the application of the refinement this percentage was 88.2%. Bearing in mind, that the activity carried out before the refinement and afterward was the same, to compare the obtained grades.
- The survey conducted to students allows determining that the refinement is positive support for the course development, with an average of 86% of the students that classify the refinement at a high level of utility.
- 80% of the questions answered by the teacher determine that the refinement is at a high level of positive impact on the course.

Applicability

- The teacher perception regarding the applicability of the refinement of the elements is 85%.
- The effort involved in the application was on average 4 h per person.

Ease of Use

- The teacher perception of ease of use was in 20%.
- The number of explanation questions by the teacher per hour was 5, and by the student was 4.

Discussion
In summary, the results show that the application of the Process phase redefined elements is simple; the terminology used is very close to the teaching environment, considering the perception of both the teacher and the student. The students perceived that the tools provided to them support the development of their activities. This was

evident through students' communication, via the MEPAC software tool, as they had to listen to each other's viewpoints and to work as an effective team. Furthermore, from the teacher's perspective, it is possible to classify the phase elements as useful taking into consideration the positive impact that was generated on the activity performed, and the positive impact that generates the forms use to guide collaborative activity definition and execution. Regarding the level of ease of use, the results specify that refinement is not classified as easily use because it requires a lot of information to follow each of the activities and their specifications, but it does provide mechanisms for its application in this context. Likewise, from the perspective of the teacher, it can be observed that in order to comply with all the stages a great effort is needed in terms of time per person.

5 Conclusions and Future Work

The refinement is useful to achieve the goals proposed according to the perception of the teacher, the students and when obtaining satisfactory results in the execution of the activity. In addition to being applicable to the collaborative learning processes area. Although the teacher requires a considerable time amount the first time it is applied, due to the lack of knowledge and inexperience of the needs to define a collaborative activity. The teacher needs an explanation of the use of some elements defined in the refinement that was not clear enough and some additional information about the description.

To achieve the success of the refinement application, MEPAC tool was essential to support this process and to allows the monitoring of each one activity, providing the necessary mechanisms to achieve the collaboration among the participants.

As future work, it is necessary to execute more case studies in order to refine the improvement of the collaborative learning process, considering the teacher and student roles in any of the phases of the process (Pre-Process, Process, Post-Process), with the support of MEPAC.

References

1. Dillenbourg, P.: What do you mean by collaborative learning? In: Collaborative Learning: Cognitive and Computational Approaches, pp. 1–19. Elsevier, Oxford (1999)
2. Hämäläinen, R.: Designing and investigating pedagogical scripts to facilitate computer-supported collaborative learning. Koulutuksen tutkimuslaitos (2008)
3. Jacobs, G.M., Siowck Lee, G., Ball, J.: Learning cooperative learning via cooperative learning: a sourcebook of lesson plans for teacher education on cooperative learning. Kagan Cooperative Learning (1995)
4. Collazos, C.A., Guerrero, L.A., Pino, J.A., Ochoa, S.F.: Collaborative scenarios to promote positive interdependence among group members. In: Favela, J., Decouchant, D. (eds.) CRIWG 2003. LNCS, vol. 2806, pp. 356–370. Springer, Heidelberg (2003). https://doi.org/10.1007/978-3-540-39850-9_30
5. Collazos, C.A., et al.: Evaluating collaborative learning processes using system-based measurement. Educ. Technol. Soc. 10(3), 257–274 (2007)

6. Lasker, R.D., Weiss, E.S., Miller, R.: Partnership synergy: a practical framework for studying and strengthening the collaborative advantage. Milbank Quarter. **79**(2), 179–205 (2001)
7. Muñoz González, J.M., Rubio García, S., Cruz Pichardo, I.M.: Strategies of collaborative work in the classroom through the design of video games. Digit. Educ. Rev. **27**, 69–84 (2015)
8. Castro, Y.P.C., Molina, R.: Collaborative learning in superior education with learning virtual objects LVO. Adv. Educ. Technol. 141–146 (2014)
9. Collazos, C.A.: Diseño de actividades de aprendizaje colaborativo asistido por computador. Rev. Educ. Ingeniería **9**(17), 143–149 (2014)
10. Ramirez, D., Bolaños, J., Collazos, C.A.: Guía para el diseño de actividades de aprendizaje colaborativo asistida por computador (CSCoLAD). Monografía de Trabajo de Grado, Universidad del Cauca, Popayan (2013)
11. Johnson, D.W., Johnson, R.T., Holubec, E.J.: The New Circles of Learning: Cooperation in the Classroom and School. ASCD, Alexandria (1994)
12. Chacón, J.: Modelo para el diseño de actividades colaborativas mediante la utilización de herramientas web 2.0. Learn. Rev. (2012)
13. Lund, M.: Modelo de apoyo para la preparación de actividades experimentales destinadas a la enseñanza de Ingeniería de Software en ambientes colaborativos y distribuidos geográficamente. Maestría en informática, Escuela de Postgrado Universidad Nacional de la Matanza (2012)
14. King, A.: Effects of training in strategic questioning on children's problem-solving performance. J. Educ. Psychol. **83**(3), 307–315 (1991)
15. Fischer, F., Kollar, I., Mandl, H., Haake, J.M.: Scripting Computer-Supported Collaborative Learning: Cognitive, Computational and Educational Perspective. Springer, Heidelberg (2007). https://doi.org/10.1007/978-0-387-36949-5
16. Gallardo, T., Guerrero, L.A., Collazos, C., Pino, J.A., Ochoa, S.: Supporting JIGSAW-type collaborative learning. In: 36th Annual Hawaii International Conference on System Sciences (2003)
17. Hernández-Leo, D., et al.: COLLAGE: a collaborative learning design editor based on patterns. JSTOR **9**(1) (2006)
18. Johnson, D.W., Johnson, R.T.: Making cooperative learning work. Theory Pract. **38**(2), 67–73 (1999)
19. Agredo Delgado, V., Collazos, C.A., Paderewski, P.: Definición de mecanismos para evaluar, monitorear y mejorar el proceso de aprendizaje colaborativo. Tecnol. Educ. Rev. CONAIC **3**(3), 18–28 (2016)
20. Agredo Delgado, V., Collazos, C.A., Paderewski, P.: Aplicación del procedimiento formal definido para evaluar, monitorear y mejorar el proceso de aprendizaje colaborativo en su etapa de Proceso mediante la creación de mecanismos. I+T+C Investigación, Tecnología y Ciencia, pp. 57–68 (2016)
21. Agredo Delgado, V., Ruiz, P.H., Collazos, C.A., Hurtado Alegria, J.A.: Aplicando agile SPI–process para la construcción de mecanismos de monitoreo, evaluación y mejora del proceso de aprendizaje colaborativo. Gerencia Tecnol. Inform.-GTI J. **15**(43) (2017)
22. Agredo Delgado, V., Ruiz, P.H., Collazos, C.A., Fardoun, H.M., Noaman, A.Y.: Software tool to support the improvement of the collaborative learning process. In: Solano, A., Ordoñez, H. (eds.) CCC 2017. CCIS, vol. 735, pp. 442–454. Springer, Cham (2017). https://doi.org/10.1007/978-3-319-66562-7_32
23. Benbasat, I., Goldstein, D.K., Mead, M.: The case research strategy in studies of information systems. MIS Q. **11**(3), 369–386 (1987)

A Serious Game Proposal to Reinforce Reading Comprehension in Scholars

Luis Alejandro Hernández Rentería[1] , Alberto Ramírez Lujano[2] ,
Madeleine Contreras Davito[3] , David Bonilla Carranza[4] ,
and Adriana Peña Pérez Negrón[4(✉)]

[1] Universidad de Guadalajara CIEP, Escuela Militar de Aviación No. 16,
Col. Ladrón de Guevara, 44600 Guadalajara, Jalisco, Mexico
luis.hernandez@administrativos.udg.mx
[2] Instituto de Estudios Universitarios, Calle Montemorelos Nº 3503,
Col. Rinconada de la Calma, 45070 Zapopan, Jalisco, Mexico
arramirez@amerike.edu.mx
[3] Universidad de Guadalajara, Sistema de Universidad Virtual, Av. Enrique Díaz
de León No. 782, Col. Moderna, 44190 Guadalajara, Jalisco, Mexico
mgabriela@suv.udg.mx
[4] Universidad de Guadalajara CUCEI, Blvd. Marcelino García Barragán #1421,
44430 Guadalajara, Jalisco, Mexico
jose.bcarranza@academicos.udg.mx,
adriana.pena@cucei.udg.mx

Abstract. Reading comprehension is a cognitive activity, which development promotes complex and fundamental processes helpful to access learning; it is connected to the world understanding in a participatory way. Consequently, it is essential to acquire this ability at an early age. Particularly for children, the videogames motivational aspect makes them an attractive resource in reading comprehension. In this paper is presented the development process of a serious game as a support for the reading comprehension process. The videogame is oriented to strategies related to syntax through fill-in-the-blank exercises. The game tutorial is illustrative for the children to understand the game mechanics, the avatar movements and the interaction with the game elements; an exploratory study was conducted to observe its effectiveness.

Keywords: Serious games · Reading fostering · Game design · Tutorial design

1 Introduction

Decoding text is the baseline for reading. However, a single-by-single word reading is not enough to comprehend what is written. Comprehensive reading involves word decoding along with language understanding [1]. Although decoding and comprehension are highly related, a person with decoding word ability does not necessarily have also comprehensive reading skills.

Reading comprehension relays on several factors, both text and reader related. Text related are for example, the type of text or the amount of new information, and reader

P. H. Ruiz and V. Agredo-Delgado (Eds.): HCI-COLLAB 2019, CCIS 1114, pp. 30–41, 2019.
https://doi.org/10.1007/978-3-030-37386-3_3

related are the reader's prior knowledge or decoding skills, which includes even affective factors such as motivation or self-perception [2].

The development of comprehensive reading is crucial for another cognitive process such as the development of thought [3]. And therefore, it is important to acquire this ability at an early stage, for the child to go successfully through the first years of the scholar stage.

People who lack the ability of reading comprehension requires to experience diverse literate practices, preferable with different strategies to build the tools to interpret and organize texts on their mind [4]. As Dubbels [4] pointed out, comprehension is transmedia, this means that it does not depend only on formal printed material. Also, other key processes for comprehending printed material are helpful in different communications and media. Dubbels [4] also stated that games represent a medium to build comprehension, because they provide interaction, feedback and demand mastery, with the incentive to reengage in the development of different skills.

Nowadays, children are digital natives. They interact with technology on an everyday basis. New trends in pedagogic reinforce the use of ICT to motivate active learning [5] because as has been established, motivation is a fundamental factor in learning. Serious games are one of these trends, these are video and computer games with other than just entertaining purposes, mainly with training or educational aims [6]. Therefore the use of videogames that comprises technology media and games represent an adequate platform to reinforce reading comprehension.

1.1 Related Work

In [3] a study was conducted with 228 children in 5th grade, with the aim to evaluate four designed strategies for reading comprehension: (1) activating prior knowledge, (2) clarifying difficult words, (3) making schematic representations, and (4) formulating the main idea of the text. Results showed that children were able to apply the comprehension strategies in different contexts. Authors summarized that by immersing children in a learning environment, based on highly interactive instructional techniques, they fostered the adoption of helpful comprehension strategies.

Regarding serious games, in [7] was presented a game prototype designed under the frame of the TERENCE European project [8], aimed to improve reading comprehension skills in primary school poor comprehends. The learning task consisted of reading a story, then play with smart games for the stimulation of inference making about the stories, and then playing with relaxing games to motivate the learner. The paper presents the design and development of the playing material.

A serious game to improve reading comprehension skills in 3rd graders was developed by [9]. They applied a User Centered Design, particularly the child-centered interaction proposed in [10]. They followed three stages for the design: (1) the design of the menus, characters, scenarios, textures, scripts, among other items, (2) the development of the actions and functionalities to interact with the game, and (3) the application of a functionality test. This serious game follows a storyline approach. A study was conducted to measure usability and acceptance with good results.

In our case, as a request from the program to promote reading "*Letras para Volar*" (Letters to Fly) from the Universidad de Guadalajara, a serious game was proposed to encourage reading comprehension in children in the range of 7 to 9 years old. Our approach consists on completing a task in order to get a reward, that in this case are missing words of a sentence that they have to locate in the correct place. Fill-in-the-blank is a well-known technique frequently used in exercises for reading comprehension. This involves word decoding, syntaxes knowledge, and reading comprehension in order to situate the recovered words in their correct place, according to the text of the story.

In the next Sect. 2 the game design is presented, and in Sect. 3 is presented an exploratory test focused on the game tutorial effectiveness, finally, in Sect. 4 conclusions and future work are discussed.

2 Serious Game Design

BrinCuentos is the name of the proposed videogame; its name derives from the mix of two words in Spanish, jump and stories, since its principal game mechanics is jumping.

BrinCuentos is categorized as a serious game because its primary purpose is not pure entertainment, and therefore its development process is not necessarily identical to the one for entertainment games.

Mildner and Floyd Mueller [11] pointed out the design of serious games presents two particular different challenges, when compared with regular game design. First, serious games have to be both attractive and effective, requiring a balance of task difficulty and skill level; and second, they require involving domain experts. Serious games design has to be conducted holistically avoiding just inserting to the serious content in a game or vice versa. The game design takes care of the relevant aspects of the internal structure and external structure, while the game production takes care of content production and game programming.

As Abeele et al. [12] recommended on their framework for design and development of serious games, BrinCuentos followed their four pillars: (1) a player-centered design, (2) an iterative development, (3) an interdisciplinary teamwork, and (4) the integration of play and learning. Their interactive development approach consists of three main phases: *concept design, game design* and *games development*. In the concept phase stage the understanding of the players and the involved domain is acquire. In the design phase the concept is transformed into a detailed game that serves as input for the final phase. In the final phase, game development and user tests are specified, and also the risks that could represent delays or problems.

Figure 1 depicts the development process of BrinCuentos. Defining the design challenge and a review of the state of the art were part of the concept design. Then for the game design were used the next techniques: an executive script, action verbs identification, brainstorming, and paper prototyping. Finally, for the game development the digital prototyping development, test and the release version were accomplished, by following an iterative and incremental approach. These steps are next briefly described, while they are linked to BrinCuentos examples.

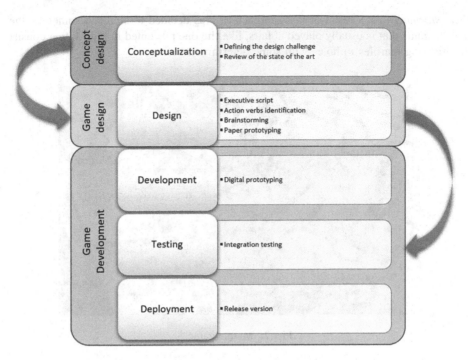

Fig. 1. Iterative cycle of the serious game development

Defining the Design Challenge. In this step, the main objective, the audience, and the platform were decided. For example, *the video game promotes reading for children in the range of 7 to 9 ages. It has to be compatible with Android-based mobile platforms.* Here was determined that BrinCuentos intended to have simple rules and to be somehow easy to master, so the player does not require investing major time to learn how to play it.

State of the Art Review. Similar products on the market, directly or indirectly tackling the design challenges were reviewed trying to identify achievements and deficiencies on each one of them. That is to say, written material, games, videogames or apps aimed to promote reading with the same target audience as BrinCuentos were reviewed.

Executive Script. This is an approach that provides a narrative context for the game mechanics design. For example, "*A monster that devours words from books arrives at the Earth. People can no longer read. Your mission will be to defeat those monsters and return the missing words to the books".*

Action Verbs Identification. Action verbs were selected from the executive script as key for the game mechanics. Taken for the previous example of the executive script: *devour* and *return.* Returning words to their place on the text, which represents a fill-in-the-blank exercise. From this step arose the question: How can we make fill-in-the-blank exercises fun?

Brainstorming. As a result of this approach, it was decided to simulate somehow the marble game that is usually played at fairs, like the one presented in Fig. 2, that consist on throwing marbles to holes with some determined value.

Fig. 2. Marble game

Then a paper prototype was designed and tested within our target audience, at the popular First Literary Festival organized by the *"Letras para Volar"* program of the Universidad de Guadalajara, which took place at the center of Guadalajara city. Figure 3 shows the paper prototype being tested at the festival.

Digital Prototype. In this stage the elements of the game's execution environment that were validated in the paper prototype were implemented. Here, the Unity™ game engine was used.

Integration Testing. The assembly between the different components as a unite was verified. Also an exploratory test presented on this paper in Sect. 3 was conducted.

Release Version. Brincuentos was decided to be distributed through the Google Play Store™.

The conceptual design took around 8 months, while the production took around fourteen months.

2.1   Videogame Mechanics

After downloading the game, a tutorial is presented. This tutorial is detailed in the next Sect. 3. The proper game starts with the user selecting a female or male avatar. A series of three sequential stories are available; the first one is *"Dany el ensuciador"* (Dany the dirty one) written by Andres López, and the second one is *"Las reglas de la manada"*

(The rules of the pack) written by María Furquet. These two short stories are property of AMCO International Education Services, LLC. The last story is Tassie, written by Alberto Ramírez Lujano. The stories were broken down in small parts with sequential sentences of the general story; they are called "pages" in the game.

Fig. 3. The paper prototype tested with the target audience at the Literary Festival

The player has to climb by jumping on small different type of platforms (see the left image of Fig. 4); the mobile device gyroscope is used to articulate the avatar's jumping direction. On his/her way up, the player can stomp monsters and defeat them to recover the words represented by spheres (or marbles). When the player arrives at the top there is a book, as can be seen in the right image of Fig. 4.

Afterward, again using the mobile device gyroscope, the player can place the missing words on its place, avoiding obstacles like monsters, black holes or mines. If the word is misplaced, the monster eats it; otherwise, the monster is defeated by the sphere. When all the words are correctly placed, the player gets a new page of the story. The accumulated pages can be read when a new page is earned.

Fig. 4. Climbing stage to recover missing words

Fig. 5. Placing the words stage

On its way, the player earns points, represented by diamonds. The number of accumulated diamonds is placed at the right top corner of the game (see Figs. 4 and 5). With these diamonds, the player "pays" to unblock the next story.

3 Exploratory Test for the Game Tutorial

As mentioned, BrinCuentos design was driven by managing simple rules easy to understand and master. The game mechanics are explained in a game based tutorial, that is, instead of only written instructions, images and the user interaction conducts the tutorial.

The tutorial start with the image shown in Fig. 6, on it can be observed on the right bottom corner a mobile device figure with arrows, the mobile device figure moves to show how the device has to be manipulated to start the game. The sphere with the word "*Jugar*" (play) has to be moved, when the sphere touches the diamonds they disappear, and when it touches the monster it disappear and the sphere takes its place, then you have to touch the play sphere to continue.

Fig. 6. Starting game screen

Then the story regarding the monsters that are eating words goes on seven sequential screens, and then the game for the tutorial starts. In the first page two sentences with missing words replaced by monsters can be seen, and the word "*Jugar*" (play) in a bottom that when is touched triggers the tutorial game. Then the player has to select a male or female lion, his/her avatar. In the next screen, similar to the one shown in Fig. 7, it also appears the white figure of the mobile device figure, this time with only two arrows that show how to move it in order to jump through the platforms. The only way to get to the top is by jumping on the one placed monster, this shows the words the player wins by defeating it, on the left bottom corner.

Fig. 7. Tutorial screen with a figure for instructions

Then the two earned words have to be placed in their right place to continue. Here the sentences have the instructions to place the spheres, see Fig. 8; the first sentence translation is "Hit the monster with the right word", the word "the" is represented by a monster, and the second one translation is "The monsters eat the wrong words", the word "eat" is also represented by a monster.

Fig. 8. Tutorial screen with instructions like game

3.1 Methods and Materials

An exploratory test was conducted with the aim to understand to what extent the tutorial helps the kids to understand the mechanics of the game. The talk aloud usability test adaptation from Doker and Reitsman [13] was selected because this test uncovers more problems than when children answer specific questions. It consists of asking the children what they are doing while they perform the application; though, children have to be encouraged to keep talking.

Five children voluntarily played the game with their parents' consent. Two male, one is 8 years old and one is 10 years old, and three female, two are 7 years old and one is 8 years old, as shown in Table 1.

Table 1. Participants data.

ID	Age	Gender
P1	8	F
P2	7	F
P3	7	F
P4	8	M
P5	10	M

The 10 years old child was included to asked him to play without performing the tutorial. The other four kids "played" the tutorial and started to play the game with the "Dany the dirty one" story for only a few minutes, however, one girl (P1) played until she got the first page.

The game was played at an Acer™ Tablet Model Iconia One7 with Android system, 7" screen, 8 GB ROM and 1 GB RAM.

Each child was taken by an adult to a room with doors open trying to avoid distractions. The children were told that they were going to be sound taped. They were instructed as follows: "*Hello, we need your help to find out if a videogame is well done and if it is fun*", then they were asked their data: name, age, and gender. Then they answered two questions: (1) "Have you ever played videogames in a cellular phone?, and (2) Have you ever played videogames in a tablet? Then they were instructed "*While you are playing comment to us about what you are doing*" when they staid quite for a while they were encouraged to comment on what they were doing. At the end they answered two more questions: (1) Did you like the game? And (2) Do you remember what was the story about?

3.2 Results

All the participants had experience playing videogames in tablets, and P1 and P3 did not have experience in smartphones, these results are shown in the second and third column of Table 2. The time to complete the tutorial varied in the range to 3:04 to 8:08 min, as shown in the fourth column of Table 2. The participant with the ID P5 is the 10-year-old child that was asked to play the game without following the tutorial, he could not found out how to manage the avatar jumping by himself, so the game was restarted for him with the tutorial.

Table 2. Participants' time to complete the tutorial.

ID	Smart phone	Tablet	Time to complete the tutorial
P1	✗	✓	3:04
P2	✓	✓	8:08
P3	✗	✓	3:18
P4	✓	✓	5:29
P5	✓	✓	5:20

As was observed during the test, the moving figure with the mobile device and the arrows, was a helpful tool to show the children how to manipulate the table to direct their avatars' jumps. They understood at the very moment what they had to do.

Regarding the instructions for the spheres, only two children (P1 and P3) explained out loud how they had to choose what sphere was on what place. The other three children seem to solve the task by a trial and error approach, however, this was not confirmed by a direct question.

Only P3 asked questions, like "how do I play this?", "what do I have to do?", or "how do I move this?", the questions were answered with questions to guide her to found out by herself how to play. The other participants just commented on what they were doing.

The five children expressed that they like the game, and they remembered the introduction story of the tutorial game. They also expressed that they only need more practice to master the game.

This exploratory test helped us to understand the extent to which the children comprehend the tutorial instructions. We believe, that even if they do not read the instructions for the spheres in the tutorial, during the game they will figure out the convenience of understanding where the spheres should go on the first place, instead of using a trial and error approach, however, this has to be tested.

P1 was the only that finished the first page of the game. It took her around half an hour to complete it. This can be seen as a drawback in the game, but we consider that as any game, with practice the player get better scores, and the difficulties him/her to stay interested in it. Although, this requires more inquiry, especially regarding the support for reading comprehension main target of the game.

4 Conclusions and Future Work

Because of the motivational nature of videogames, particularly in children from this technology era, a serious game was designed with the aim to support reading comprehension in children of the ages of 7 to 9 years old. The steps for its design are here described. Game design elements such as rewards and narrative are part of this serious game proposal.

An important factor of the design was to keep the game fun for the users while improving their comprehension reading abilities and avoiding the sense of being in a traditional learning scenario.

An exploratory test on the tutorial as a game was conducted. Results showed that the game as tutorial was helpful for the children to understand some mechanics of the game, although, it seems that others could be reinforced.

For future work, we will compare this serious game results regarding reading comprehension on a long-term approach.

The game is available at Google Play Store™ and to this day it has around 500 downloads.

Acknowledgment. We would like to thank the *"Letras para Volar"* program, and the Coordinación de Innovación Educativa y Pregrado of the Universidad de Guadalajara. Also, we are grateful to John Moreno for his support. And finally, we want to acknowledge the work of the game programmer Manuel Iván Herrera Maciel, and the game artist Nidia Angélica Bautista Cosío.

References

1. Gough, P.B., Tunmer, W.E.: Decoding, reading, and reading disability. Remed. Spec. Educ. **7**, 6–10 (1986). https://doi.org/10.1177/074193258600700104
2. De Corte, E., Verschaffel, L., Van De Ven, A.: Improving text comprehension strategies in upper primary school children: a design experiment. Br. J. Educ. Psychol. **71**(4), 531–559 (2001). https://doi.org/10.1348/000709901158668
3. Bravo Valdivieso, L.: El aprendizaje del lenguaje escrito y las ciencias de la lectura. Un límite entre la psicología cognitiva, las neurociencias y la educación. Límite **11**(36), 50–59 (2016)
4. Dubbles, B.: Video games, reading, and transmedial comprehension. In: Handbook of Research on Effective Electronic Gaming in Education, pp. 251–276. IGI Global (2009). https://doi.org/10.4018/978-1-59904-808-6.ch015
5. Kiryakova, G., Angelova, N., Yordanova, L.: Gamification in education. In: Proceedings of 9th International Balkan Education and Science Conference (2014)
6. He, L., Hu, X., Wei, D.: The case analysis of Serious Game in community vocational education. In: Proceedings of 2011 International Conference on Computer Science and Network Technology, vol. 3, pp. 1863–1866. IEEE (2011). https://doi.org/10.1109/iccsnt.2011.6182333
7. De la Prieta, F., Di Mascio, T., Gennari, R., Marenzi, I., Vittorini, P.: Playing for improving the reading comprehension skills of primary school poor comprehenders. In: Proceedings of the PDSG 2012 Workshop. CEUR-WS (2012)
8. TERENCEProjectWebSite. http://www.terenceproject.eu/. Accessed 20 Feb 2019
9. Gaytán-Lugo, L.S., Santana-Mancilla, P.C., Santarrosa-García, A., Medina-Anguiano, A., Gallardo, S.C.H., García-Ruíz, M.Á.: Developing a serious game to improve reading comprehension skills in third graders. Res. Comput. Sci. **89**, 71–79 (2015)
10. Tan, J., Goh, D., Ang, R., Huan, V.: Child-centered interaction in the design of a game for social skills intervention. ACM Comput. Entertain. **9**, 2 (2011). https://doi.org/10.1145/1953005.1953007
11. Mildner, P., Floyd Mueller, F.: Design of serious games. In: Dörner, R., Göbel, S., Effelsberg, W., Wiemeyer, J. (eds.) Serious Games, pp. 57–82. Springer, Cham (2016). https://doi.org/10.1007/978-3-319-40612-1_3
12. Vanden Abeele, V., et al.: P-III: a player-centered, iterative, interdisciplinary and integrated framework for serious game design and development. In: De Wannemacker, S., Vandercruysse, S., Clarebout, G. (eds.) ITEC/CIP/T 2011. CCIS, vol. 280, pp. 82–86. Springer, Heidelberg (2012). https://doi.org/10.1007/978-3-642-33814-4_14
13. Donker, A., Reitsma, P.: Usability testing with young children. In: Proceedings of the 2004 Conference on Interaction Design and Children: Building a Community, pp. 43–48. ACM, June 2004. https://doi.org/10.1145/1017833.1017839

A Study for the Identification of a Full-Body Gesture Language for Enabling Natural User Interaction

David Céspedes-Hernández[(⊠)] [iD]
and Juan Manuel González-Calleros [iD]

Facultad de Ciencias de la Computación,
Benemérita Universidad Autónoma de Puebla, Puebla, Mexico
dcespedesh@gmail.com, jumagoca78@gmail.com

Abstract. Most proposals addressing gesture recognition consider two main stages: gesture identification in a source and association between gestures and meanings. About the semantic meaning of gestures, it is important to consider that due to their cultural and linguistic specificity each of them may be mapped to many concepts and vice versa, making them ambiguous and incompletely defined. From the HCI perspective, there is work in the literature presenting elicitation studies on which researchers find gestures sets to allow user interaction with tailored applications under determined contexts. In this paper, we present a full-body language for enabling gesture-based interaction in different contexts. For this purpose, 70 users were asked to provide the gestures they would use as commands within different existing applications, keeping awareness of the relationship between the tasks they were asked to do on the applications and abstract tasks, resulting on 980 gestures which were compared for generating a reduced set of 68 gestures consisting on their graphic representation, a textual description, an anthropometric characterizations for each of them, and generic labels. Interpretation and insights obtained during the experiment are also reported.

Keywords: Gesture-based interaction · Natural User Interfaces · User-defined gesture set

1 Introduction

Gestures are (static or dynamic) expressive, meaningful body motions involving physical movements of the fingers, hands, arms, legs, head or face. Through gestures, it is possible to communicate in a nonverbal way and enrich verbal communication as well [1]. In the Computer Science field, Natural User Interfaces, and specifically Gesture Recognition (GR) is currently being applied to several domains such as children-computer interaction; forensic identification and detection; rehabilitation and medical monitoring; navigation and manipulation in virtual environments; distance learning assistance; security; athlete training; and entertainment applications [2–5]. Besides, hardware and software are constantly being developed supporting such interaction modality.

© Springer Nature Switzerland AG 2019
P. H. Ruiz and V. Agredo-Delgado (Eds.): HCI-COLLAB 2019, CCIS 1114, pp. 42–56, 2019.
https://doi.org/10.1007/978-3-030-37386-3_4

GR is a challenging problem for which proposed solutions typically involve at least two stages: gesture identification, and gesture-meaning matching. Gesture identification is achieved through wearable devices, by using vision-based techniques, or through the processing of wireless signals. Interaction through wearables typically requires users to carry uncomfortable devices [6], while vision-based techniques, in turn, content with other problems related to occlusion [7], and processing of wireless signals has not been thoroughly explored and regularly involves the use of devices like radars and routers [8]. Each data gathering device varies along several dimensions, including accuracy, resolution, latency, the range of motion, user comfort, and cost [1].

Gestures are often specific to a determined language and culture, hence, giving them standard meaning is not possible. Also, since the semantic meaning of the gestures that a person does depends on his/her mental model, there are many-to-one mappings from concepts to gestures and vice versa. Thus, gestures are ambiguous and incompletely specified [9]. Taking this into consideration, the objective of this paper is on reporting the realization of elicitation experiments for proposing a full- body language for enabling natural user interaction in different contexts through the use of reified versions of abstract tasks.

The rest of the paper is structured into sections. The second section is dedicated to describing the state of the art, including the definition of capability models that were used for identification of the body parts to be considered as well as their movements, and the description of related works on the proposition of user-defined gestures sets. In section three, the followed method and the performed experiments are described, so in the fourth section, the results and its discussion are addressed. Finally, the fifth section is aimed at presenting the conclusions of the project and the future work to be done.

2 State of the Art

When designing interactive applications, it is important to consider the context in which the to be implemented system is going to be used. The analysis of the context of use has been addressed in several works, most of them from an HCI perspective, agreeing on that it can be separated into three dimensions: user, platform, and environment [10]. For the purposes of this paper, and aligned to the defined problem, this section is focused on describing a method for modeling users and for identifying their capabilities, as well as on presenting related works about the creation of user- defined gestures sets.

Originally proposed as part of a framework for modeling virtual users for automatic simulated accessibility and ergonomic testing of applications, in [11] a Generic Virtual User Model (GVUM) and a full-body capability model are described. Considering the GVUM representation it is possible to notice that the human body consists of six main components: neck, spinal column, left upper limb, right upper limb, left lower limb, and right lower limb. In a more detailed level, upper limbs include shoulders, elbows, forearms, wrists, and hands containing fingers, while lower limbs include in turn hip, thighs, knees, ankles, and foot toes.

Using the GVUM as previously described, it is possible to anatomically model users, but not to represent their interaction with user interfaces. This objective was achieved by defining a capability model, consisting of 108 classes corresponding to systems, body parts, features, and motions. A summary of the body parts that are listed as part of the GVUM related to their motions according to the capability model is presented in Table 1.

Being able to identify all of the possible movements that users can perform in order to interact with user interfaces through full-body gestures, allows to drive experiments focused on the definition of interaction gestures sets and to characterize such gestures. In this order of ideas, in the literature, it is possible to find works from authors addressing the definition of gesture sets for interacting through different means. Some of those works were analyzed prior design and planning of the present project and are described in the following lines.

Typically, gesture elicitation studies, based on the procedure of guessability studies [19], are conducted with the purpose of identifying those gestures corresponding to specific tasks according to the mental model of a group of users. This approach, which has become a standard in HCI, seeks that after obtaining gesture vocabularies considering the information provided by users, these vocabularies are used as commands within an application to positively impact usability and UX evaluations.

However, although the proposals based on elicitation studies report encouraging results in terms of overall satisfaction and motivation with respect to the use of gestural interfaces [20], it is important to note that most studies in the area are not statistically representative, limiting their conclusions to specific groups of users with similar contexts, and leading to the conclusion that if an application should be available for different populations, multiple elicitation studies should be carried out, making projects more expensive and reducing their viability.

In the context of surface computing, in [12] Wobbrock et al. stated that gestures that are defined by system designers are appropriate only for early prototype testing, while for a production environment it is desirable to have gestures that are reflective of the users' mental model. That work is only focused on the analysis of gestures of 1 or 2 hands for performing 27 commands, due to the restrictions of the platform of interest. The results were shown as graphic representations along with the level of agreement that was reached for every single command. In that work, it is asserted that the participants preferred 1-hand gestures for 25 of the 27 defined commands, participants employed reversible gestures for dichotomous actions, multiple participants provided gestures using areas out of the screen edges and above it, leading to think that the surface device must have the ability to track gestures using other mechanisms rather than only the touchscreen.

With regards to applying GR in augmented reality applications, in [13] Piumsomboon et al. addressed the definition of a user-defined gesture set for allowing designers to achieve natural interaction in such type of systems. In their experiments, 20 participants were asked to provide gestures for 40 tasks, resulting in 800 gestures that were compared for obtaining levels of agreement.

The results of the experiment were reported as graphical representations of the consensus set of gestures along with textual explanations of them and labels for their identification. Also, in this proposal, it is affirmed that the definition of the gesture set

Table 1. Body parts from the GVUM related to movements from the capability model [11].

Body part	Associated motion from the capability model
Neck	Flexion, extension, right lateral flexion, right lateral rotation, left lateral flexion and left lateral rotation
Spinal column	Flexion, extension, right lateral flexion, right lateral rotation, left lateral flexion and left lateral rotation
Shoulders	External rotation, extension, flexion, internal rotation, abduction, and adduction
Elbows	Extension, Hyperextension, and flexion
Forearms	Supination, pronation
Wrists	Extension, flexion, radial deviation, and ulnar deviation
Hand	Supination and pronation
Finger	Adduction, extension, abduction, flexion, and hyperextension
Hip	Adduction, abduction, internal rotation, flexion, external rotation, and extension
Thighs	Flexion and extension
Knees	Flexion and extension
Ankles	Dorsiflexion, plantar flexion, eversion, and inversion
Foot toes	Extension and flexion

was affected by causes such as the mental model of users and their experience on the use of determined platforms. Even though gesture detection was achieved using a depth sensor making it possible to examine full-body gestures, the proposal was only focused on hands and fingers gestures.

In the literature, it is also possible to find works addressing the definition of full-body gesture vocabularies and applied to navigation and control domains. Such is the case of [14] in which users were asked to perform full-body gestures for controlling a humanoid robot. In that study, Obaid et al. proposed navigational commands and analyzed gestures provided by users, reporting agreement scores, time performances, and graphical representations of the consensus set. Along with the obtention of the gestures set, significant insights were discussed like the need of the definition of points of view when trying to recognize gestures for navigation, i.e. if users' motion is being tracked using cameras in front of them, it is possible to misunderstand the direction of the gestures.

From this state of the art and by executing a more exhaustive revision of the literature, it is possible to see that related works follow methodologies consisting on: the definition of the body parts to be analyzed; the selection of participants and description of their characteristics; the implementation of GR software; the obtention of data from users; and the explanation of the gathered results in terms of agreement, time performance, graphical representations of the gestures, gestures labeling, and additional observations. Next section is dedicated to the description of the method that was followed in this specific project and the description of the performed experiment.

3   A Study for the Identification of a Full-Body Gesture Language for Enabling Natural User Interaction

In accordance with the expressed objective and considering the capability model which was summarized in Table 1, this work is focused on the recognition of full-body gestures, specifically on movements of the neck tracked through the position of the head, upper limbs observed as arms and hands, and lower limbs to be analyzed considering legs and feet.

During preliminary studies, it was noticed that all of the gestures performed by specific users were significantly different from those performed by others for the same tasks. After thoroughly reviewing possible causes for this issue and exploring alternatives, we identified research addressing the influence of creativity on the use and development of technology [15]. Then, we searched on creativity tests and found the Aulive test which is available online and allows to measure users' creativity delivering an average result and considering eight dimensions: abstraction, connection, perspective, curiosity, boldness, paradox, complexity, and persistence. We then asked users to get their creativity tested and found some of the users getting creativity levels high above or under the average, were the same as those performing gestures that were not consistent with the others.

As a total, 70 subjects without experience on the use of gesture-based interaction applications were selected for participation and separated into 5 groups with 14 users each. The first group, dedicated to neck gestures, consisted of 9 females and 5 males between 19 and 79 years old. The second group which was created for arm gestures observation consisted of 7 female and 8 males aged between 17 and 67 years.

The third group, for hand gestures, was composed of an equal number of female and male users between 20 and 63 years. The fourth group, for legs gestures, involved 7 females and 7 males aged between 13 and 53 years. Finally, the fifth group in which feet gestures were observed, was composed of 7 females and 7 males between 12 and 52 years. Users were selected and equally distributed in such way according to the punctuation they received as average on the Aulive creativity test. Users who received scores wide above, or wide below the average were discarded.

Once the participants were selected and the groups were defined, it was time to drive experiments for finding interaction vocabularies for each of the above-mentioned body parts. This kind of elicitation studies is carried out by implementing applications. Nonetheless, the implementation of systems based on gesture interaction represents a challenge itself, and as our objective is on identifying gestures for general purposes, and not on assessing the interaction of a specific application nor defining commands, the development is out of the scope of this specific work, and it was decided to consider a different approach.

The Wizard of Oz technique has been used throughout the history of the development of interactive systems [16], and in particular, in the field of natural interfaces development as it is a way to collect data for mixed reality environments or movement commands for interaction with kids [17] among other application domains. Following this technique, the designed experiment consisted on asking users to use their own body gestures to interact with different applications using only specified body parts and giving them the feeling that those commands actually worked on the application, but actually providing the input to the programs through keyboard commands.

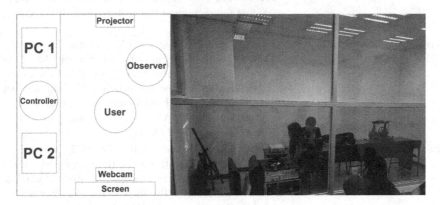

Fig. 1. Experiment setup following the Wizard of Oz technique [16] and its disposition in a Gesell chamber.

The setup of the experiment, as shown in Fig. 1, took place in a Gesell room and included two computers (PC1 and PC2), the first one for retrieving users' movement information from a webcam and allowing to document the experiment; while the second one was connected to a projector for providing the user with feedback and simulating users' interaction with the system. An observer of the experiment was designated and located next to the user in order to provide support in case any doubt arises. The experiment controller managed the devices to document the experiment and to explain how each user performed the activity.

During the experiment, users were asked to provide the gestures they would use to perform 14 commands within different applications and contexts. The 70 tasks that were defined are presented in Table 2. When users carried out gestures for each of the requested commands, data was gathered including response time, a video record of the corresponding gesture, and a score given by the same user with respect to how natural they thought the gesture was for the task. As a total, 980 records were acquired and then processed through manual labeling, manual comparison, to finally be assigned with an agreement score. The results of the performed experiment and the proposed gestures set are discussed in the next section.

Table 2. Tasks to be observed during the experiment.

Body part (application/context)	Tasks
Head (Instagram)	Find profiles (N1), Add image (N2), Pick image (N3), Take photo (N4), Record video (N5), View notifications (N6), View profile (N7), Like post (N8), Post story (N9), Add emoji (N10), Add hashtag (N11) Accept follow request (N12), Tag friend (N13), Edit profile (N14)
Arms (Smart home)	Open gate (A1), Close gate (A2), Turn lights on (A3), Turn lights off (A4), Turn air conditioner on (A5), Turn air conditioner off (A6), Turn TV on (A7) Turn TV off (A8), Turn TV volume up (A9), Turn TV volume down (A10), Change TV channel (next) (A11), Change TV channel (previous) (A12), Turn water pump on (A13), Turn water pump off (A14)
Hands (Facebook)	View posts (H1), View notifications (H2), View messages (H3), Create a group (H4), Like post (H5), Love post (H6), Write a message (H7) Add friend (H8), Upload photo (H9), Tag friend (H10), Block user (H11), Create an event (H12), Start video call (H13), Start call (H14)
Legs (Crash Bandicoot game)	Move down in the main menu (L1), Move up in the main menu (L2), Select option in the main menu (L3), Move forward in 3D (L4), Move left in 3D (L5), Hit a box in 3D (L6), Jump an obstacle in 3D (L7), Smash a box in 3D (L8), Move forward in 2 ½D (L9), Jump an obstacle in 2 ½D (L10), Hit a box in 2 ½D (L11), Smash a box in 2 ½D (L12), Duck in 3D (L13), Exit minigame in 2 ½D (L14)
Feet (Android phone control, media player, Web browser)	Answer phone call (F1), Hang up a phone call (F2), Go to the home screen (F3), Start voice search (F4)
	Play/Pause (F5), Quit player (F6), Go to previous track (F7), Shuffle play (F8), Turn volume up (F9), Turn volume down (F10)
	Move cursor to the left (F11), Move cursor to the right (F12), Zoom in (F13), Zoom out (F14)

4   Results and Discussion

Those gestures with the higher agreement rates for each task were characterized according to the capability model which was presented in the state of the art, described in natural language, depicted in a graphical representation, generically relabeled for their quick identification, and taken as part of a new gestures set which is described in Table 3 and depicted in Fig. 3. In case of having ties on the times in which two or more gestures were performed for a task, the situation would be solved using the grade users gave them and the response time in which they were done.

Table 3. Labels, agreement scores, descriptions, and characterization of the user-defined gesture set.

Label (Agreement score)	Textual description	Characterization according to capability model
G001 (5/14)	Tilt the head to the right	Right lateral flexion of the neck
G002 (3/14)	Turn the head to the right	Right lateral rotation of the neck
G003 (3/14)	Tilt the head to the left	Left lateral flexion of the neck
G004 (5/14)	Lift both shoulders	Flexion of both shoulders
G005 (2/14)	Lift both shoulders twice	Flexion of both shoulders twice
G006 (3/14)	Tilt the head to the right twice	Right lateral flexion of the neck twice
G007 (3/14)	Look down	Flexion of the neck
G008 (4/14)	Nod twice	Flexion and extension of the neck twice
G009 (4/14)	Look up	Extension of the neck
G010 (3/14)	Turn the head to the left	Left lateral rotation of the neck
G011 (2/14)	Lift the left shoulder	Flexion of the left shoulder
G012 (2/14)	Move both shoulders forward	Adduction of both shoulders
G013 (2/14)	Lift the left shoulder twice	Flexion of left shoulder twice
G014 (2/14)	Lift the left shoulder and tilt the head to the left	Flexion of the left shoulder and left lateral flexion of the neck
G015 (6/14)	Move the left arm to the left and the right arm to the right	Extension of both shoulders, extension of both elbows
G016 (6/14)	Starting with both arms extended, bring them to the body	Starting with the extension of both shoulders and elbows, flex both shoulders
G017 (6/14)	Lift the right arm	Abduction of the right shoulder, extension of the right elbow
G018 (4/14)	Lower the right arm	Adduction of the right shoulder, extension of the right elbow
G019 (1/14)	Move the right wrist to the right	Flexion of the right elbow, and internal rotation of the right shoulder
G020 (1/14)	Starting with the arm extended, move the right wrist forward	Starting with the right elbow extended, flex the right elbow
G021 (4/14)	Move the left wrist to the left	Flexion of the left elbow, and internal rotation of the left shoulder
G022 (4/14)	Starting with the right arm flexed, move right wrist forward	Starting with the right elbow flexed, rotate the right shoulder
G023 (6/14)	Lift the left arm	Abduction of the left shoulder, extension of the left elbow
G024 (6/14)	Lower the left arm	Adduction of the right shoulder, extension of the right elbow
G025 (4/14)	Move the left wrist to the left	Starting with the left elbow flexed, rotate the left shoulder

(*continued*)

Table 3. (*continued*)

Label (Agreement score)	Textual description	Characterization according to capability model
G026 (4/14)	Move the left wrist to the right	Starting with the right elbow flexed, rotate the right shoulder
G027 (4/14)	Starting with the arm flexed and the wrist pointing up, lower the elbow	Starting with the elbow flexed, adduct the shoulder
G028 (4/14)	Starting with the arm flexed and the wrist pointing up, move the wrist to point down	Starting with the elbow flexed, flex the shoulder
G029 (5/14)	Using only the forefinger, point forward	Flexion of all fingers but the second one
G030 (2/14)	Turn the right wrist from right to left with the forefinger and the middle finger extended	Flexion of all fingers but the second and third ones along with the wrist flexion
G031 (1/14)	Pointing up with the forefinger only, flex the fingertip twice	Starting with all fingers flexed but the second one, flex the second finger twice
G032 (2/14)	Using both hands, reach with the forefinger each other thumb creating a 'frame' form	Extension of the first and the second fingers of both hands, reaching the second finger of the left hand with the first finger of the right one, and the second finger of the right hand with the first finger of the left one
G033 (13/14)	Use only one thumb to point up	Flex all fingers and extend the first one
G034 (8/14)	Join each finger of one hand to those on the other creating a heart-like shape	Flex all fingers and reach each one of the fingers of one hand with the same finger of the other
G035 (3/14)	Use both hands for 'typing' in the air	Starting with all fingers extended, quickly flex and extend all of them
G036 (4/14)	Using the forefingers of both hands, make a 'plus sign'	Extending only the second finger of each hand, use one of them to point up and put the other one perpendicularly in order to make a 'plus sign'
G037 (2/14)	With thumb and forefinger extended, move the forefinger down to reach the thumb without touching it	Starting with only the first and the second fingers extended, lightly flex the second finger towards the first one without reaching it
G038 (2/14)	With the palm forward, touch the thumb with the little finger	Starting with all fingers extended, hyperflex the first and the fifth fingers so they touch each other
G039 (7/14)	Using the forefingers of both hands, make an 'x sign'	Extending only the second finger of each hand, use one of them to point up and put the other one perpendicularly in order to make an 'x sign'

(*continued*)

Table 3. (*continued*)

Label (Agreement score)	Textual description	Characterization according to capability model
G040 (1/14)	Using only the forefinger, make a triangle in the air	Extending only the second finger, draw a triangle in the air either rotating the elbow or the shoulder
G041 (2/14)	Using only the forefinger, make a circle in the air	Extending only the second finger, draw a circle in the air either rotating the elbow or the shoulder
G042 (9/14)	Flex all fingers but the little finger and the thumb	Flex all fingers and extend only the first and the fifth one
G043 (3/14)	Slide the left foot backward	Extend the hip above of the left leg
G044 (6/14)	Slide the right foot forward	Flex the hip above of the right leg
G045 (5/14)	Stomp	Flex a knee, then, quickly extend it
G046 (4/14)	Step forward	Flex the hip, extend a knee, extend the hip
G047 (3/14)	Slide the left foot to the left	Abduction of the hip above the left leg.
G048 (5/14)	Kick	Flex the hip, flex a knee, then extend it
G049 (5/14)	Jump using both legs	Flex the hips, flex the knees, flex the ankles, then extend the ankles and the knees pushing the body up
G050 (3/14)	Lift a leg and then stomp	Flex the hip, flex a knee, then, quickly extend the hip and the knee
G051 (3/14)	Walk forward	Repeat with each lower limb: Flex the hip, extend the knee, extend the hip
G052 (7/14)	Rotate the left ankle	Plantar flexion, adduction, dorsiflexion, abduction of an ankle
G053 (5/14)	Jump using both legs twice	Flex the hips, flex the knees, flex the ankles, then extend the ankles and the knees pushing the body up twice
G054 (5/14)	Duck	Flexion of the hips, flexion of the knees, plantar flexion of the ankles
G055 (3/14)	Slide the left foot to the left	Adduction of the hip above the left leg
G056 (4/14)	Slide the left foot to the right	Adduction of the hip above the right leg
G057 (6/14)	Get on tiptoes	Plantar flexion
G058 (4/14)	Get on tiptoes and move forward	Plantar flexion, extend the hip
G059 (3/14)	Get on tiptoes/raise foot	Plantar flexion, flex the knee/extend the knee
G060 (6/14)	Rotate the left foot up	Eversion of the left foot
G061 (4/14)	Make an 'x sign' with a foot	Plantar flexion, draw an 'x sign' using the toe tip
G062 (4/14)	Rotate both feet in	Eversion of both feet

(*continued*)

Table 3. (*continued*)

Label (Agreement score)	Textual description	Characterization according to capability model
G063 (5/14)	Separate both feet	Adduction of both ankles
G064 (7/14)	Rotate the left foot out	Inversion of the left foot
G065 (5/14)	Move the left foot forward	Extend the left knee
G066 (8/14)	Rotate the left foot to the left	Eversion, dorsiflexion, inversion, plantar flexion
G067 (7/14)	Rotate the left foot to the right	Inversion, dorsiflexion, eversion, plantar flexion
G068 (5/14)	Split the toes	Abduction of all toes

It was interesting to see that even though users were asked to use only movements from a determined part of the body and that it would be correct to use same gestures for different commands, they mostly felt more comfortable using different gestures for each command, and particularly in the case of head and feet motion groups, they commented that the use of the single part of the body was not enough to express what they thought, extending motions to shoulders and ankles respectively. Therefore, the final gestures set contains such type of movements as well.

If well the gesture set was created using specific tasks on existing applications, it is possible to see that they may be applicable to other similar contexts as most of them describe abstract activities such as turn on, turn off, open, close, move up, and move down. An interesting insight is on that agreement scores for the consensus gestures from the head (avg. 0.22, stddev. 0.08), legs (avg. 0.32, stddev. 0.09) and feet (avg. 0.36, stddev. 0.11) were not significantly lower when compared to gestures from hands (avg. 0.31, stddev. 0.26) and arms (avg. 0.31, stddev. 0.12) as we expected considering that HCI is usually achieved using upper limbs.

From the observation during the experiment, this was caused by two reasons, the first one regarding the mental model that users have and the second one concerning that if well it is not common to interact with applications using only head, legs, and feet movements, the degrees of freedom they allow reduce the number of gestures that users feel comfortable doing reducing the options they have and raising the probabilities of having similar movements. Moreover, the standard deviation calculated over the agreement scores showed the highest value for the hands' gestures. In regard to this, we noticed that gestures which were constantly repeated by users for a specific task, such as G033 for H5, are already being in use in real human-to-human interaction with similar meaning or may have similar representation on widely used platforms and adopted as de-facto standards. This is coherent with the observations in [18] regarding technology and culture influence on gestural interaction.

On the other hand, other tasks that do not have a standard gestural representation such as H2, H3, and H4, got lower agreement scores. We observed that the main cause for this, is on that hands have more degrees of freedom and therefore it is possible to have more gestures from them. Expressiveness allowed by upper limbs significantly

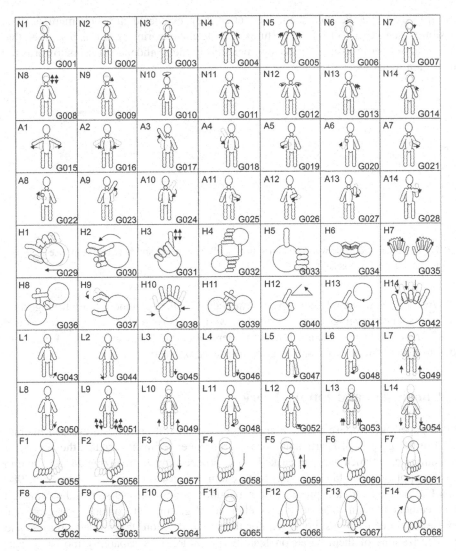

Fig. 2. Graphic representation of the obtained user-defined gesture set including the identifiers of tasks and their associated gestures.

affected agreement, consider that there were only 4 tasks for which users provided completely different gestures and that such tasks belong to the arms (A5 and A6) and hands groups (H3 and H12). Furthermore, it is also possible to see that gestures G048 and G049 got the highest agreement score (5/14) for two tasks each, hence resulting on the reduction of the vocabulary of gestures from 70 expected gestures to 68.

As previously mentioned, response times were also recorded, and users were asked to evaluate the gestures they provided. It was interesting to notice that younger users responded, on average, faster than the older ones did, and that the faster users provided gestures for a specific command, the better they evaluated the movement as it is possible to see in Fig. 3 for head gestures. During the experiment, it was perceived that both of these metrics were affected significantly by the confidence of users towards the interaction modality.

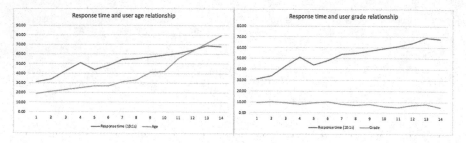

Fig. 3. The relationship between response time and users' age, and between response time and gestures grade for head gestures.

We expected to see relationships existing between the agreement score for a gesture and its associated average response time, as well as between the agreement scores and users' grades for each gesture, however, there does not seem to be any. Final considerations and future work are described in the next section.

5   Conclusion and Future Work

In this paper, we propose a user-defined language for full-body gesture-based interaction. For this purpose, 70 participants took part in an experiment based on the Wizard of Oz technique, in which they were asked to provide gestures for realizing 14 tasks within specific applications which are aligned to canonical tasks. From the experiment, 980 records were obtained, and processed for manual labeling, comparison, and calculation of agreement rate, in order to finally elicit a 68-gesture set containing a graphical representation of each gesture, labels for their identification, textual descriptions, and characterizations of them based on features presented in a capability model. It was noticed that users' characteristics such as experience, confidence, age, and mental model, as well as additional facets like comfort, expressiveness and the degree of freedom of body parts, affect the gestures, response time, and evaluation of gestures.

Additionally, it was observed during the performance of the elicitation experiments that isolating users from the influence of digital and technological products is a complex challenge. It is common to observe in the results of these studies the influence and presence of digital metaphors for the execution of specific commands. In this sense, researchers in the area have proposed the use of different strategies to be applied in elicitation experiments. Such is the case of Morris et al. [21] who proposed carrying out these experiments by adding physical activities and requesting the production of multiple gestures per task to reduce the likelihood that they will be affected by previous experiences and external influences.

The impact of additional factors such as creativity and the influence of the use of technology were superficially considered in this work, but it will be necessary to drive additional experiments in order to precisely determine the dimensions of such aspects that affect gestural elicitation.

As the tasks from the experiment correspond to abstract tasks, our gesture vocabulary will allow the implementation of full-body gesture-based applications for general purposes, keeping in mind that additional gestures may be necessary for extension and tailoring. As future work, it will be necessary to develop a tool for GR and automatic labeling, as well as means to allow usability and user experience testing on gesture-based applications working with user-defined commands.

References

1. Mitra, S., Acharya, T.: Gesture recognition: a survey. IEEE Trans. Syst. Man Cybern. C Appl. Rev. **37**(3), 311–324 (2007). https://doi.org/10.1109/tsmcc.2007.893280
2. Schlömer, T., Poppinga, B., Henze, N., Boll, S.: Gesture recognition with a Wii controller. In: Proceedings of the 2nd International Conference on Tangible and Embedded Interaction, Bonn, Germany, 18–20 February, pp. 11–14. ACM, New York (2008). https://doi.org/10.1145/1347390.1347395
3. Liang, R.H., Ouhyoung, M.: A real-time continuous gesture recognition system for sign language. In: Proceedings of the Third IEEE International Conference on Automatic Face and Gesture Recognition, Nara, Japan, 14–16 April, pp. 558–567. IEEE (1998). https://doi.org/10.1109/afgr.1998.671007
4. Daniloff, J.K., Noll, J.D., Fristoe, M., Lloyd, L.L.: Gesture recognition in patients with aphasia. J. Speech Hear. Disord. **47**(1), 43–49 (1982). https://doi.org/10.1044/JSHD.4701.43
5. Jia, P., Hu, H.H., Lu, T., Yuan, K.: Head gesture recognition for hands-free control of an intelligent wheelchair. Ind. Robot **34**(1), 60–68 (2007). https://doi.org/10.1108/01439910710718469
6. Norman, D.A.: Natural user interfaces are not natural. Interactions **17**(3), 6–10 (2010). https://doi.org/10.1145/1744161.1744163
7. Malima, A.K., Özgür, E., Çetin, M.: A fast algorithm for vision-based hand gesture recognition for robot control. In: 14th Signal Processing and Communications Applications, Antalya, Turkey, 17–19 April. IEEE (2006). https://doi.org/10.1109/siu.2006.1659822
8. Wan, Q., et al.: Gesture recognition for smart home applications using portable radar sensors. In: 2014 36th Annual International Conference of the IEEE Engineering in Medicine and Biology Society (EMBC). IEEE (2014). https://doi.org/10.1109/embc.2014.6945096
9. Chandler, J., Schwarz, N.: How extending your middle finger affects your perception of others: learned movements influence concept accessibility. J. Exp. Soc. Psychol. **45**(1), 123–128 (2009). https://doi.org/10.1016/J.JESP.2008.06.012
10. Calvary, G., Coutaz, J., Thevenin, D., Limbourg, Q., Bouillon, L., Vanderdonckt, J.: A unifying reference framework for multi-target user interfaces. Interact. Comput. **15**(3), 289–308 (2003). https://doi.org/10.1016/S0953-5438(03)00010-9
11. Kaklanis, N., Moschonas, P., Moustakas, K., Tzovaras, D.: Virtual user models for the elderly and disabled for automatic simulated accessibility and ergonomy evaluation of designs. Univ. Access Inf. Soc. **12**(4), 403–425 (2013). https://doi.org/10.1007/s10209-012-0281-0

12. Wobbrock, J.O., Morris, M.R., Wilson, A.D.: User-defined gestures for surface computing. In: Proceedings of the SIGCHI Conference on Human Factors in Computing Systems, Boston, USA, 04–09 April, pp. 1083–1092. ACM, New York (2009). https://doi.org/10.1145/1518701.1518866

13. Piumsomboon, T., Clark, A., Billinghurst, M., Cockburn, A.: User-defined gestures for augmented reality. In: Kotzé, P., Marsden, G., Lindgaard, G., Wesson, J., Winckler, M. (eds.) INTERACT 2013. LNCS, vol. 8118, pp. 282–299. Springer, Heidelberg (2013). https://doi.org/10.1007/978-3-642-40480-1_18

14. Obaid, M., Häring, M., Kistler, F., Bühling, R., André, E.: User-defined body gestures for navigational control of a humanoid robot. In: Ge, S.S., Khatib, O., Cabibihan, J.-J., Simmons, R., Williams, M.-A. (eds.) ICSR 2012. LNCS (LNAI), vol. 7621, pp. 367–377. Springer, Heidelberg (2012). https://doi.org/10.1007/978-3-642-34103-8_37

15. Motaghi, H.: Creativity and technology in the context of creative industries, dissertation. Université du Québec à Montréal (2015)

16. Dow, S., Lee, J., Oezbek, C., MacIntyre, B., Bolter, J.D., Gandy, M.: Wizard of Oz interfaces for mixed reality applications. In: CHI 2005 Extended Abstracts on Human Factors in Computing Systems, Portland, USA, 2–7 April, pp. 1339–1342. ACM, New York (2005). https://doi.org/10.1145/1056808.1056911

17. Höysniemi, J., Hämäläinen, P., Turkki, L.: Wizard of Oz prototyping of computer vision-based action games for children. In: Proceedings of the 2004 Conference on Interaction Design and Children: Building a Community, Maryland, USA, 01–03 June, pp. 27–34. ACM, New York (2004). https://doi.org/10.1145/1017833.1017837

18. Hoff, L., Hornecker, E., Bertel, S.: Modifying gesture elicitation: do kinaesthetic priming and increased production reduce legacy bias? In: Proceedings of the TEI 2016: Tenth International Conference on Tangible, Embedded, and Embodied Interaction. ACM (2016). https://doi.org/10.1145/2839462.2839472

19. Connell, S., Kuo, P.Y., Liu, L., Piper, A.M.: A Wizard-of-Oz elicitation study examining child-defined gestures with a whole-body interface. In: Proceedings of the 12th International Conference on Interaction Design and Children, pp. 277–280. ACM, June 2013. https://doi.org/10.1145/2485760.2485823

20. Liu, J., Zhong, L., Wickramasuriya, J., Vasudevan, V.: uWave: accelerometer-based personalized gesture recognition and its applications. Pervasive Mob. Comput. 5(6), 657–675 (2009). https://doi.org/10.1016/J.PMCJ.2009.07.007

21. Morris, M.R., Danielescu, A., Drucker, S., Fisher, D., Lee, B., Wobbrock, J.O.: Reducing legacy bias in gesture elicitation studies. Interactions 21(3), 40–45 (2014)

A Visual Analytics Framework Case Study: Understanding Colombia's National Administrative Department of Statistics Datasets

Pierre Raimbaud[1,2]([⊠]) [iD], Jaime Camilo Espitia Castillo[1] [iD],
and John A. Guerra-Gomez[3] [iD]

[1] Systems and Computing Engineering, Imagine Group,
Universidad de los Andes, Bogota, D.C., Colombia
p.raimbaud@uniandes.edu.co, camilospn@gmail.com
[2] LiSPEN, Arts et Métiers, Institut Image, Chalon-sur-Saone, France
pierre.raimbaud@ensam.eu
[3] Northeastern University, San Jose, California, USA
john.guerra@gmail.com

Abstract. In a world filled with data, it is expected for a nation to take decisions informed by data. However, countries need to first collect and publish such data in a way meaningful for both citizens and policy makers. A good thematic classification could be instrumental in helping users to navigate and find the right resources on a rich data repository, such as the one collected by the DANE (*Departamento Administrativo Nacional de Estadística*, i.e. the Colombia's National Administrative Department of Statistics). The Visual Analytics Framework is a methodology for conducting visual analysis developed by T. Munzner et al.1 that could help with this task. This paper presents a case study applying such framework conducted to help the DANE to better visualize their data repository, and also to understand it better by using another classification extracted from its metadata. It describes the three main analysis tasks identified and the proposed solutions. Usability testing results during the process helped to correct the visualizations and make them adapted to decision-making. Finally, we explained the collection of insights generated from them.

Keywords: Visual analytics · Data repositories · Open data

1 Introduction

The DANE (Departamento Administrativo Nacional de Estadística, i.e. the Colombia's National Administrative Department of Statistics) is the Colombian public organization responsible for collecting, analyzing and distributing the country's national statistics. The total amount of data that this institution owns is one of the largest in the country (among public institutions), since it periodically gathers information about all the major topics, from population statistics, to public access to services, among many others. Because of this, one of DANE's main goals is that public policies in Colombia become

© Springer Nature Switzerland AG 2019
P. H. Ruiz and V. Agredo-Delgado (Eds.): HCI-COLLAB 2019, CCIS 1114, pp. 57–72, 2019.
https://doi.org/10.1007/978-3-030-37386-3_5

more data-driven [1]. However, this is rarely the case, as public institutions suffer data availability and/or classification issues. Aware of these issues, the DANE wants to improve its data management, by applying visual analytics methods, resulting in building and delivering better tools to the public policy-making structures.

Concretely, the DANE owns data coming from both administrative records (called administrative registers (AR) afterwards) and the derived statistical analyses conducted on them i.e. statistical operations (called statistical operations (SO) afterwards) and f. This paper addresses these two main types of data. Note that here we will not consider the final data collected by the DANE when they apply the questions or requests contained in an administrative register or a statistical operation, but we will consider the characteristics of the administrative registers and the statistical operations themselves, meaning their attributes and characteristics, in other terms all their metadata. So, our original data will be the DANE inventories of statistical operations and administrative registers. Figure 1 illustrates this main distinction.

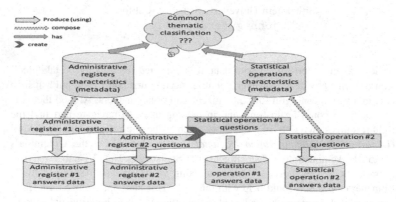

Fig. 1. DANE's data distribution and explanation of the problematic: does a new thematic classification coming from the metadata of the administrative registers and statistic operation exist?

Based on these considerations, the main objective of this project is to build a tool to understand and visualize the DANE data, particularly by organizing it through the topics and keywords present among the metadata of different groups of statistical operations and administrative registers, ultimately allowing decision-makers to have right overviews of topics and to find which statistical operations and administrative registers are related to one in particular, thanks to this classification (see Fig. 1).

2   Related Work

2.1   Tamara Munzner's Framework

For this project, we used Munzner's visualization framework [2] to abstract and understand the data, the users' tasks and to choose the best idioms that allow the users to complete these tasks. It has three dimensions: the WHAT, the WHY and the HOW.

WHAT: It refers to the available data for the visualization. The basic abstractions of the dataset arrangements are tables, networks, fields and geometry. In a dataset, we can find items, or nodes and links, and its attributes. Data can be static, or dynamic (e.g. a data stream) and the items/nodes attributes can be ordered or categorical.

WHY: It refers to the tasks abstraction that must feature mainly one action (a verb) and one target (a noun). Task abstraction aims to clarify what is the main purpose of a visualization, and its potential secondary purposes. It can vary from high to low level (meaning depending on how precise you want to define it), and range from presenting trends (at high level, it would be to consume data) to identifying outliers.

HOW: It refers to the design choices to visualize the data and to interact for performing the tasks. The two objectives here are to decide which visual channels like size, color, etc. will represent the data, and to choose the right marks, or the visual representations for the data (geometric primitives like lines, points, areas) for the visualization. At this stage, the idea is to choose the visual encoding and the idiom (or representation) that best suits the WHAT and WHY, to develop the visualization accordingly. This "HOW" part relies on two principles: expressiveness and effectiveness. The first one means that the chosen visual encoding should express all (and only) the information contained in the dataset, and that the visualization should show the information as it was in the dataset, in terms of data characteristics and its links with the chosen idioms. The effectiveness means that the chosen channels should always be the highest ranked ones, according to the nature of the attributes that they represent (these links between attributes and channels are referenced in the literature).

To illustrate this concept, we want to present some examples of visualizations like the ones we used further in this work. First, a bar chart (HOW) allows to summarize distribution (WHY), and to show extremes (WHY) if it also uses order (ascending or descending). Indeed, Elzer et al. [3] showed its efficiency for this kind of tasks, but note that another possible idiom for these tasks is the stacked bar chart, as Indramoto et al. [4] explained it. However, in the stack bar chart, the focus is more on combining both single-attribute and overall-attribute comparisons rather than making only single-attribute comparisons for one or more dataset (this is our case, see Sect. 3). Furthermore, notice that here we derived the original dataset, a table, to a network dataset. In this case, following Munzner's framework, this kind of dataset is composed by nodes and links (whereas tables are composed by items) - it can be relevant to show these links or not, depending on the task. About our project data, remember that one of our aims is also to discover a new thematic classification. As Ochs et al. [5] showed it, ontologies manipulations and representations are crucial nowadays, but required much work, so they presented a software framework for doing the following tasks: derivation, clustering and visualization as a network. So, based on their study, we can note that another visualization for ontologies is the treemap [6]. In our case, we used this last representation, and also the radial force representation (see Sect. 3); note that in both cases, one of the most critical point is the usage of forces to separate the nodes, depending on one attribute or relationship. Hilbert et al. explained the usefulness and importance of the them in a network visualization; indeed, forces allow to separate and form groups, also called clusters [7]. This approach is useful for our work because we

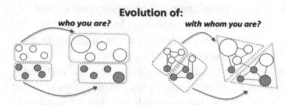

want to permit the public policy-makers to make decisions based on visualizations that show a new classification, so in this case it could be shown thanks to the use of clustering (see Fig. 2).

Fig. 2. Network visualization with forces for clustering by Hilbert et al.

2.2 Projects with Similar Issues

Here, we will present some related work that faced the same issues that we did, either from the policymakers' point of view or the visual analytics tools designers' one.

First, about public policy and data-driven policy making, Brazil had useful data about some activities in their cities, but the authorities were not using them for prioritizing the different public policies. Thus, Petrini et al. [8] applied an analytic hierarchy process (AHP) on their data and then they build some visualizations that show them adequately. As the policymakers were evaluating various priorities at the same time (environmental, economic, social), the stack bar chart was the good idiom (Fig. 3).

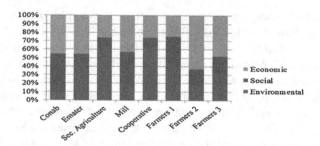

Fig. 3. Classification of thematic by priorities (multiple values for the priorities) by Petrini et al.

But first, clean data and metadata is necessary: it is a common but complex issue to deal with uncleaned data. So, Liu et al. [9] proposed a framework for cleansing (Fig. 4).

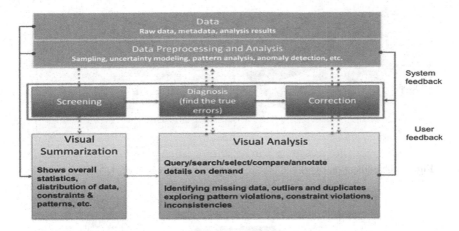

Fig. 4. Visual analytics framework for steering data quality by Liu et al.

We can note that their process could be a complementary approach to Munzner's one, because they gave more importance to the steps of creation and evaluation of the visualization, whereas Munzner's framework focuses on abstraction (what, why, how).

Moreover, even when the ontologies have been created especially for the final users, there are real needs of availability and accuracy, meaning that these ontologies would be useless otherwise. About this issue, Kamdar et al. made a study about the usage/the access by the users of the ontologies in the biomedical field [10], about which queries the specialists made, and how they combined results. In this paper, we can see the importance of creating ontologies, that they must be user or task/issue-designed, and that they can also be viewed from a "macro" point of view, where ontologies can be combined between themselves. In the Fig. 5, we can see how ontologies can be built.

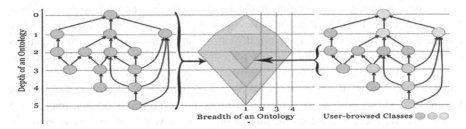

Fig. 5. Analysis of the composition of ontologies and their depth by Kamdar et al.

To sum up, in this section we have described some common issues with our project: ontologies or classifications are truly required for policy making, sometimes with an additional classification (priorities: "meta-classification", Petrini et al.). Then we have noted that other frameworks for creating visualizations than the Munzner's one exist,

Fig. 6. Classification by global/macro topic (in Spanish, source: DANE website)

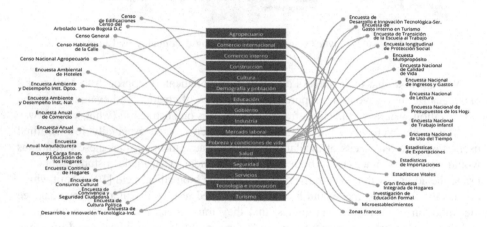

Fig. 7. Classification by sub-themes, linked to the surveys (in Spanish, source: DANE website)

with other focuses than abstraction, such as cleansing (Liu et al.). We have also seen that these classifications must be accessible and accurate (Kamdar et al.). That leads us to our case study: the classification of the DANE metadata and its usage in visualizations. Currently, the DANE public policy-making tools don't satisfy their final users, because the classification used does not fit with policy making, and the visualizations are not appropriate to the tasks that the policymakers want to perform. Particularly, they need to be able to discover (identify) easily which statistical operation or administrative register is the most useful for a specific policy. Figures 6 and 7 show examples of the current classification and visualizations. The classification may be too generic/inappropriate, and the visualizations don't show where the information is.

3   Applying the Visual Analytics Framework

Here we will present how we applied the framework for our three main tasks. But, before that, we should explain how we built a new classification from the metadata, resulting in a new dataset, derived from the others, so we can build task 2 (T2) and task

3 (T3) visualizations. The creation of this dataset can be considered as task 0 **(T0)**, called a derivation task. To do it, we used natural language processing on the original datasets, an acceptable way since the datasets were about 500 lines and 20 columns maximum, after cleansing. To use a commercial natural language processing tool was a valid option, but we created our own to process the words and build the new dataset in the same tool. First, it read all the lines of the file, build a dictionary of keywords that are repeated more than X times (using an exclusion list: determinants or repetitive and useless words such as register), and build the nodes and the links of the new dataset, based on the keywords occurrences in the metadata for each item. Here we explain the three abstractions, and our prototypes, obtained by applied the framework. You will find a summary for each task (details in the next sections):

T1: How many statistical operations and administrative registers are there for each topic (in the original classification)?
T2: How many statistical operations and administrative registers are there for each new topic, considering a new classification coming from the metadata?
T3: Which administrative registers and statistical operations are more related to a specific topic (new classification)?

Task 1 (T1)

What: the original datasets – three tables, two of administrative registers and one of statistical operations (items), with, among others, the following attributes: name (categorical attribute), kind of data (categorical) and thematic area (categorical)
Why: **summarize the distribution (considering the old classification)**
How: idiom: bar chart; mark: lines; channel: depending on the visualizations, vertical or horizontal position, and color hue, one for the registers, one for the operations
Prototype: see Figs. 8 and 9.
Principal insight (see more in Sect. 4): large difference between the numbers of administrative registers and statistical operations on the macro-category "Economics".

Task 2 (T2)

What: a new dataset derived from the previous tables – a network where the nodes (items) are the administrative registers, or the statistical operations, or the keywords of a new classification, and the links represent when an administrative register or a statistical operation matches with a keyword, one or more time; some attributes: name (categorical attribute) and new keyword groups (categorical attribute).
Why: **summarize the distribution (considering the new classification)**
How: idiom: treemap; mark: point; channel: color hue, spatial region
Prototype: see Figs. 10 and also 11 (auxiliary visualization - details on demand)
Principal insight (see more in Sect. 4): "Labor market" was the penultimate sub-theme in the old classification vs. "Companies" is the 4th with our new classification.

Task 3 (T3)
What: a new dataset derived from the original ones (the same as in task 2)
Why: **identify features/extremes** (which nodes are **more related** to a theme, **with the new classification)**
How: idiom: radial force; mark: points; channel: radial position and color hue
Prototype: see Fig. 12
Principal insight (more in Sect. 4): with the keyword "Health", "Individual register of health service delivery– RIPS", is the most important administrative register.

As explained in previous sections, the main objective here is to use and understand better the DANE data to allow decision-making, resulting into two main aims: first, to determine new topics (useful for decision making on public policies) that can emerge from the metadata, and to evaluate which different statistical operations and administrative registers are more linked to a topic, and secondly, once found this information, to provide some appropriate visualizations to the policymakers. Therefore, we developed for this case study a visual analytics tool, by applying the Munzner's framework. As there were three main different tasks, it is composed of three main components: for the task T1, several context visualizations to analyze the current state of the information held by the DANE (Sect. 3.1), then for the task T2, a treemap visualization to understand the results of the natural language processing used to find more relevant major topics (a new thematic classification for decision making) around the DANE's datasets (Sect. 3.2), and finally for the task T3, a radial force visualization to navigate between and into the identified topics and to provide a final tool for policymakers that shows which are the most relevant sources of information according to a topic (Sect. 3.3).

3.1 Task 1: General and Contextualization Task, on the Original Dataset

The first set of visualizations aims to represent the current inventory. The main task T1 is to *summarize* the *distributions* (WHY) of both datasets to answer the questions:

- How many statistical operations and administrative registers exist here?
- What is the proportion of statistical operations and administrative registers in the three major topics (economics, social and environmental)?
- What is the proportion of statistical operations and administrative registers in each of the 30+ specific topics (for example, health, education, etc.)?

The datasets that we used were two inventories of administrative registers and one inventory of statistical operations (WHAT) (three tables in total).

Based on the analysis made using the Munzner's framework, the best visual encoding (HOW) to provide this kind of overview is to use bar charts where the statistical operations and administrative registers are differentiated by colors. The horizontal position indicates that there are several categories (administrative registers VS statistical operations, economics VS social...), whereas vertically the size of the bars shows items quantities differences. Fig. 13 shows the first three general and context visualizations developed. Figure 9 shows two other visualizations developed to present the distribution of the attribute "sub-theme", allowing to know the global distribution of these sub-themes for all these administrative registers and statistical operations. We used the same encoding since it is still the best one for *summarizing the distributions,* and to *identify extremes* (secondary task), we used the technique "separate order and align" for that purpose). About this last point, if considering only administrative registers (on the left in Fig. 9.), the most present sub-theme is "currency – bank and finance" whereas looking only at statistical operations (on the right), it is "agriculture".

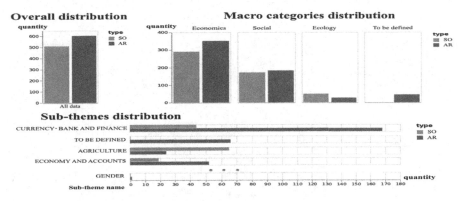

Fig. 8. Bar chart visualizations based on sub-themes from the original data.

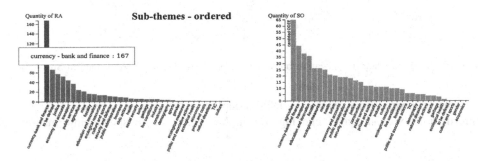

Fig. 9. Bar chart visualizations about original sub-themes, with "separate order and align".

3.2   Task 2: New Dataset, New Classification, but Which Distribution?

Here we present the T2 task visualization: *summarize the distribution with the new classification* (WHY). We used a treemap and a bar chart (HOW). It uses the derived dataset, that contains nodes and links (WHAT), each node being a statistical operation or an administrative register, and each link being a relationship between nodes, particularly between a "register/operation" node and a "keyword" node. We used clustering for grouping them by (new) themes. For separating the clusters, we used the force-in-a-box algorithm (https://github.com/john-guerra/forceInABox), by J. Guerra. Thus, this visualization allows to have a global vision (*summarize distribution*) of the new different themes: transport (*transporte*), research (*investigación*) etc. It also allows to detect that services (*servicio*) and credits (*crédito*) are the themes that most appear (*identify extremes*). Both in the tree map (by nature) and in the bar chart (common technique), we applied the technique "separate order and align" for completing this secondary task. In Fig. 12, administrative registers and statistical operations are considered, whereas in Fig. 12, they are separated. However, we notice that the top themes are globally the same, considering them separately (Fig. 12: services (*servicio*), planning (*planeación*)) or in total (Fig. 10: top3:services, credits, planning).

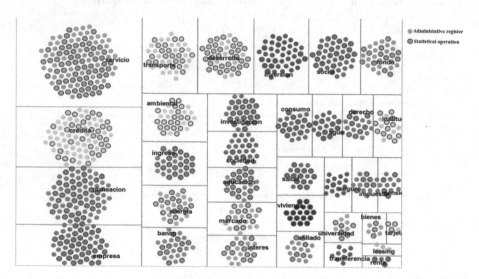

Fig. 10. Tree map chart visualization on new themes (derived data – DANE data in Spanish).

The following visualization is a table, coupled to the previous treemap that give information about an item by clicking on it in the treemap, to get specific information.

Table for detailed information

Name:
ESTADISTICAS DE SERVICIOS AEROPORTUARIOS
Type: OOEE
Statistical operations related to:
Operations:
Consolidar informacion estadistica de los servicios de escala en a eropuerto (Handling)

Fig. 11. Auxiliary view, a table, of the treemap visualization (DANE data in Spanish)

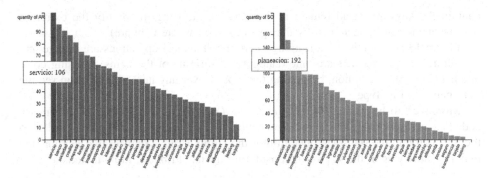

Fig. 12. Bar chart visualization on new themes, in blue the administrative registers, in orange the statistical operations (derived data – DANE data in Spanish).

3.3 Task 3: Given a Keyword, Which Are the Items More Linked to It?

To navigate between the new topics and the nodes associated to it, we created a visualization where the user can type a word, and then explore the statistical operations and administrative registers that feature this keyword in their metadata, in top-down order. As a result, the main task T3 of the visualization is to *identify features* (WHY).

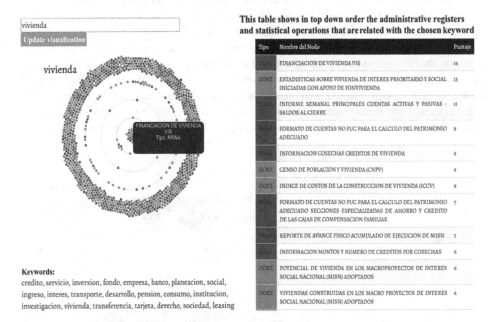

Fig. 13. Radial force visualization and its auxiliary view on the right (DANE data in Spanish)

In this visualization, we used the radial force idiom (HOW), using forces to order the items depending on how much they fit with the written keyword (separate and order). It means that, after choosing the keyword, the user can see that the statistical operations and administrative registers that contain the keyword are more or less attracted to the center depending on the number of occurrences (the ones that do not contain the keyword at all remain in the border), allowing to identify the extremes (similar items can be identified by the spatial region where they are).

Figure 13 shows this visualization, where the statistical operations are orange and the administrative registers are blue (categorical attribute of the items, so using color hue is effective). In addition, by putting the mouse over any item, the user can see the item name and its type.

Moreover, to help *identifying the extremes* (WHY), right to the visualization, we added an auxiliary view, a table, where the elements are ordered in descendant order, so the user can find the statistical operation or the administrative register that features the major occurrences of the keyword, considering all its attributes, in its metadata.

4 Experiment and Results

4.1 Experiment

To validate our work, we organized an experiment where the experts from the DANE were invited to try our tool with all the visualizations created according to the tasks explained before, and according to our application of the visual analytics framework. In total, there were 8 participants, 6 females and 2 males. 5 of them were working in the R&D department (in other words, "our clients", the people who asked for the tool) and 3 were working in the department responsible for the planning based on statistics (in other words, the final users of our future tool, apart from the policymakers). All the participants had to follow these instructions: "first, try to get new themes about registers and operations (with the treemap now, but actually, during the experiment, with a network visualization, see Sect. 4.2); then get some information about one item (with the coupled table); after that, write a word about one theme of your interest and discover which are the registers and operations more related with this keyword (with the radial visualization); finally, read the name of the most important register/operation in the coupled table".

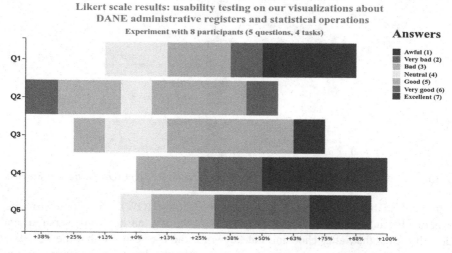

Fig. 14. Results of the experiment with the users (Likert scale graph).

4.2   Results

First, note that in this experience, the users were using and evaluating a previous version of our visual analytics tool that the one in this paper. Thanks to these results, we have been able to correct our visualizations. So, these results show how our work has evolved. It also shows that to apply the visual analytics framework may often require iterations, with several users experiments (and that some tasks may require more iterations than others). The following results come from a post-experiment questionnaire, where the users evaluated the quality of our visualizations (usability and completion of the tasks). Using Likert scale, we asked closed questions, one for each visualization and task. The idea of this usability testing questionnaire was to determine if the visualizations were answering or not to the previously defined issues of the DANE (with the Visual Analytics Framework, visualizations must be built according to the tasks defined using abstraction, from the original tasks described by users). Moreover, we asked open questions to get some feedback, for making corrections. Finally, according to the results, that would be discussed in the next section, we created the final visualizations that are presented in the paper in Sect. 3. So notice that in this experience, the tool had only two parts not three (the context visualizations part, for the task T1, were missing), composed of four visualizations: a network visualization (where the forces were not separating the clusters of nodes as good as in the treemap, which is the "evolution" of this visualization after the experience) and its coupled table, for the task T2, and the radial force visualization and its coupled table, for the task T3.

- Q1 - What is your general impression with this tool?
- Q2 - Have you been able to explore a new classification of the items?
- Q3 - Have you been able to obtain the detail for one of these items?
- Q4 - Have you been able to discover the items in relation with a theme?
- Q5 - Have you been able to identify the item more related with a theme?

5   Discussion

According to the results, both the quality results shown on the Likert scale graph (see Fig. 14), and the feedback given by the experts indicate that the task they performed with more difficulty (almost 50% of the participants grade it between 1 and 4 included) was the one asked in Q2: explore the new classification in the network visualization (T2). On the contrary, the easiest task for them (100% of them grade it between 4 and 7 included) was the one asked in Q4: discover the items in relation with one theme in the radial force visualization (T3). As a result, we did more corrections on the visualization used in Q2, so it is the only visualization where we had to completely modify the idiom (visual encoding) used, transforming the visualization from a network visualization at that moment (clusters might not be appearing so clearly, but the relationships/links between elements do appear better) to a treemap now (on the contrary, the focus is clearly on clustering) – to sum up, both idioms use nodes and forces, but, in our case, the clustering was clearer with the treemap visualization.

Additionally, we noticed, both in the comments and the qualitative results (apart from Q2 results), thanks to Q1 results, with 25% of neutral grade (4), that something might be missing, apart from the current visualizations and their corrections, something that shows better the purpose of our tool and why did we create it. In other terms: to understand where we are going, we should know what were the original data? Were there some insights in the original data? The next visualizations are showing different data? What is the difference with the new thematic classification? What are the new insights? All these questions can be considered as a first task for the users (T1). So, that is why we finally added the context visualizations part and organized the tool into three parts and not two: context - T1 (original data), treemap - T2 (derived data) and radial force visualization - T3 (derived data).

6 Insights

The new (corrected) visualizations (presented in the Sect. 3) allow to discover some insights about the statistical data and their classification in new themes.

First, thanks to the context visualizations based on the initial data, we discovered than globally more information could be generated because there are more registers than operations (remember that the administrative registers create the statistical operations). We noticed this particularly for the macro category "Economics". By looking also at the visualization by sub-themes, it is confirmed, with more details: the sub-themes "Currency, banks and finance" and "Accounts and economics" appear as some of the ones where there is much difference between the number of registers and the number of operations, and both are belonging to the macro category "Economics".

Then, thanks to the new derived data and the treemap visualization, we can discover other insights. First, by looking to the terms that appear, on one hand this visualization confirms that the macro category and sub-theme currently used are quite coherent with the metadata. For example, we can find as new keywords "research" (*investigación*), "credits" (*crédito*), "market" (*mercado*), whereas that, in the current sub-theme, there were "education and innovation", "business", "economy and accounts" etc. But, in the other hand, this visualization also suggests that the categories and sub-themes used currently may not be so accurate in term of distribution, because in the current classification, "labor market" is the penultimate sub-theme whereas "company" (*empresa*) is the fourth one with our new thematic classification. Another insight is that this visualization gives us more details about a previous insight from the first visualizations: in the current category "Economics", the focus for generating new operations from registers should be done more precisely on the ones that contains in their metadata the words "leasing" or "transactions", since we observe in this visualization that there are no statistical operations about these subjects, only registers.

Finally, some other insights have been revealed thanks to the radial force visualization. As our final tool in this study for decision making on public policies, we can notice that, thanks to it, people, without being an expert about data manipulation, can identify easily which registers and operations are more related to a specific theme: for example about "Housing" (the chosen keyword), the most important administrative register is "Housing financing VIS", or for "Health it is "Individual register of health service delivery – RIPS". To conclude, this last visualization, by grouping in the center the elements with more relevance but separating them into two categories, for being administrative registers or statistical operations by using two different colors, allows at a glance to notice for one thematic if the relevant elements are mostly of one kind of information (because visually it will be mostly of one color), and as a result, it can confirm that more statistical operations should be generated in this thematic or not (so we could make some "priorities" about statistical operation generations). So, for example, following with the theme "Economics", we can notice for the keyword "credits" that more statistical operations could be generated (there are much more administrative registers).

7 Conclusion

Finally, by applying our approach, we obtained useful visualizations that confirmed that the DANE owns highly relevant information for the country and that they should continue developing more data analysis tools, to provide them to public policymakers to maximize the usage of their data. The visual analytics tools permit both policymakers and citizens to locate where the relevant information is, and allows its understanding, ultimately enhancing policies and fostering data-driven businesses. So, we might think that our contribution helped the DANE to understand that their data are very valuable, and that with such approaches, these data can be classified and presented in a way that allow the policymakers to use it for public policies making. As written in the previous section, thanks to this study and its visualizations, the DANE learned, among other insights, that, even if they held a large amount of data about economics, they could explore and use it better: more statistical operations could be generated, especially about topics such as leasing or transactions. This insight might be the most relevant because parts of it appeared in most of the different visualizations.

About future work, it could be interesting to explore other possibilities about our natural language processing tool (the one for getting the keywords that appear in the metadata), and also to think about how could we grade differently the administrative registers or statistical operations that belong to a theme (currently it is based on the number of occurrences of the keywords in the metadata – the DANE has already confirmed it interest for this avenue). Finally, another possibility of future work could be to study which visualization would be appropriate for showing the relationships between the administrative registers and the statistic operations that are linked (because this register produces this operation) while the visualization shows the clusters of nodes by thematic.

References

1. OECD: OECD Digital Government Studies Digital Government Review of Colombia Towards a Citizen-Driven Public Sector. OECD Publishing, France (2018). https://doi.org/10.1787/9789264291867-en
2. Munzner, T.: Visualization Analysis and Design, 1st edn. A K Peters Visualization Series/CRC Press, Natick, Massachusetts (2014). ISBN 10: 9781466508910, ISBN 13: 978-1466508910

3. Elzer, S., Carberry, S., Zukerman, I.: The automated understanding of simple bar charts. Artif. Intell. **175**(2), 526–555 (2011). https://doi.org/10.1016/j.artint.2010.10.003
4. Indratmo, Howorko, L., Boedianto, J., Daniel, B.: The efficacy of stacked bar charts in supporting single-attribute and overall-attribute comparisons. Vis. Inform. **2**(3), 155–165 (2018). https://doi.org/10.1016/j.visinf.2018.09.002
5. Ochs, C., Geller, J., Perl, Y., Musen, M.A.: A unified software framework for deriving, visualizing, and exploring abstraction networks for ontologies. J. Biomed. Inform. **62**, 90–105 (2016). https://doi.org/10.1016/j.jbi.2016.06.008
6. Shneiderman, B.: Tree visualization with tree-maps: 2-D space-filling approach. ACM Trans. Graph. **11**(1), 92–99 (1992). https://doi.org/10.1145/102377.115768
7. Hilbert, M., Oh, P., Monge, P.: Evolution of what? A network approach for the detection of evolutionary forces. Soc. Netw. **47**, 38–46 (2016). https://doi.org/10.1016/j.socnet.2016.04.003
8. Petrini, M.A., Rocha, J., Brown, J.C., Bispo, R.: Using an analytic hierarchy process approach to prioritize public policies addressing family farming in Brazil. Land Use Policy **51**, 85–94 (2016). https://doi.org/10.1016/j.landusepol.2015.10.029
9. Liu, S., et al.: Steering data quality with visual analytics: the complexity challenge. Vis. Inform. **2**(4), 191–197 (2018). https://doi.org/10.1016/j.visinf.2018.12.001
10. Kamdar, M.R., Walk, S., Tudorache, T., Musen, M.A.: Analyzing user interactions with biomedical ontologies: a visual perspective. J. Web Semant. **49**, 16–30 (2018). https://doi.org/10.1016/j.websem.2017.12.002

Alcohol Detection in a Car's Cab Using MQ3 and First Approaches to Sensing: Laboratory Tests

Jonathan Samuel Romero-González[1]([⊠]) [iD],
Huizilopoztli Luna-García[1] [iD], José M. Celaya-Padilla[2] [iD],
Hamurabi Gamboa-Rosales[1] [iD], Jorge I. Galván-Tejada[1] [iD],
Carlos E. Galván-Tejada[1] [iD], José G. Arceo-Olague[1] [iD],
and Roberto Solís-Robles[1] [iD]

[1] Centro de Investigación e Innovación Automotriz de México (CIIAM),
Universidad Autónoma de Zacatecas, Jardín Juárez 147, Centro,
98000 Zacatecas, Zac, Mexico
jona95rg@gmail.com, {hlugar,hamurabigr,gatejo,
ericgalvan,arceojg,rsolis}@uaz.edu.mx
[2] CONACYT, Centro de Investigación e Innovación Automotriz de México
(CIIAM), Universidad Autónoma de Zacatecas, Jardín Juárez 147, Centro,
98000 Zacatecas, Zac, Mexico
jose.celaya@uaz.edu.mx

Abstract. It is a matter of interest to the automotive industry and the authorities to prevent alcohol consumption in drivers, crashes and run-over deaths caused by drunk drivers are the leading cause of death among Mexican youth, according to the Deputy General Directorate of Youth Integration (DGAIJ) in Mexico. Likewise, the Pan American Health Organization (PAHO) in terms of roads, notes that Mexico ranks seventh worldwide in deaths from crashes and run-ins due to alcohol consumption while driving. On the other hand, in recent years, technology has been incorporated into automobiles which aims to help in safety material for both the driver and passengers; however, efforts are needed to increase the safety of pedestrians. Derived from the above, and with the purpose of addressing the identified problem, this work shows the design of a prototype to detect alcohol in the cabin of a vehicle using MQ3 alcohol sensors installed in the ventilation ducts of a car. Laboratory tests were performed and the results were satisfactory since different levels were detected in alcohol intensity. Finally, the result of the evaluation allowed us to improve the initial design of the prototype.

Keywords: Alcohol detection · Automotive industry · Raspberry Pi · MQ3 sensor

1 Introduction

Over the years, methods and systems have been developed to prevent alcohol consumption in motorists, including fines, prevention information and implementation of road safety seals who use an electronic "breathalyser" device to determine the level of

© Springer Nature Switzerland AG 2019
P. H. Ruiz and V. Agredo-Delgado (Eds.): HCI-COLLAB 2019, CCIS 1114, pp. 73–84, 2019.
https://doi.org/10.1007/978-3-030-37386-3_6

alcohol present in the drivers' breath, however, this method has not been a viable solution, since it is easy to evade them and even comments from certain authorities recognize that they cannot always implement this type of action since they are exceeded by the great demand that this represents. With the purpose of helping to solve this problem, various technological systems have been developed that seeks to prevent drunk driving. For example, the proposal developed by Sakairi et al. [1], which consists of a coupling of an alcohol and a breathing sensors installed behind the steering wheel (see Fig. 1), where it is necessary for the driver to blow on the sensors every time he wants to start the car in order to detect breath alcohol and in a positive case, inhibit the ignition of the car.

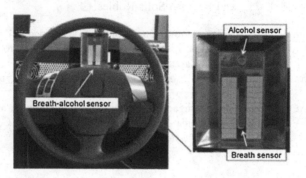

Fig. 1. Breathing and alcohol sensor, available in [1].

This method is efficient and meets the main objective of detecting alcohol in the driver's breath, however, the ergonomics of the system is a problem since it is very uncomfortable in the long term to be blowing to be able to start the vehicle.

A solution to this ergonomics problem is the proposal generated by Kulkarni and Thakur [2], which consists of attaching an alcohol sensor and capturing images of the eyes in real time by means of a camera. These images are then processed by a Raspberry, which compares them to images of closed and open eyes in a database. With these comparisons, it determines when a driver has his eyes closed beyond the threshold value, assuming the user has drowsiness, and in case of detecting levels high alcohol inside the car or drowsiness, the system sends a warning signal.

Although this proposal solves the problem of ergonomics, another inconvenience arises since the eyes closed or a slow frequency in the blinking of the eyes occurs at a late stage or what translates as high levels of alcohol in the blood, so that a state of drunkenness cannot be determined at an early stage (objective of this study) since according to the US National Library of Medicine the symptoms of euphoria and motor impairment occur at an early stage [3]. These symptoms are the cause of accidents and driving crashes while intoxicated.

Kumari et al. [4], develop a system that uses physiological behaviors as a way of preventing alcohol-induced accidents and drowsiness. Alcohol consumption causes certain changes in physiological behavior, for example, heart rhythm, involuntary movements of the head or frequency in the blinking of the eyes, which can be tracked using glasses that include sensors such as camera and accelerometer, see Fig. 2.

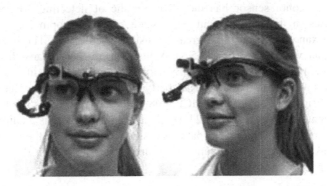

Fig. 2. Lens for detecting drowsiness and drunk people, available in [4].

The accuracy of this method is satisfactory since heart rhythm, eye blinking and head movement are involved as variables to predict or classify drowsiness and drunkenness, however, ergonomics and system comfort is all. On the contrary, since it is uncomfortable for the user to wear the lenses each time the car is desired, that is, it is an intrusive solution, additionally, in addition, it is possible to present certain situations, for example, the wear of the lenses (scratches), fogging caused by perspiration or moisture of the body which could result in an inconvenience for user visibility and data processing.

Another alternative to this problem was developed by Takahashi, Hiramatsu, and Tetsuishi [5], which consists of the detection of alcohol by means of a camera, in order to avoid drunk driving. The method detects whether a driver has drunk alcohol or not, using images of the skin color on either the face or parts that the camera captures. According to the author, the body temperature rises when you are under the influence of alcohol, and this is easily identifiable with the color of the skin. To classify the parts that are useful in the detection of alcohol, a 3-layer neural network is used, obtaining as a result that the best parts of the body to predict are the cheeks, neck and hands, however, it is important to mention that the detection by means of images is not the best option since the variables of illumination, distance and contrast, are unstable variables, therefore, it is difficult to classify a user in a drunken state.

2 Materials and Methods

This project aims to detect alcohol inside the car through the use of alcohol sensors (MQ3), which will be installed in the ventilation slots of the car, likewise, a Raspberry Pi and free software were used for the processing of the information (Python), and in this way identify and classify the alcohol levels inside the car cabin. It is important to mention that to obtain the optimum performance of the sensors it is necessary to consider the following conditions: closed windows and air conditioning on, so that the sensor values are stable and remain without fluctuations that may affect the classification.

The MQ-3 alcohol sensor has the characteristic of detecting concentrations of flammable gases in the environment on a scale of 25–500 ppm [6], for example, benzene and hexane, however, it has greater sensitivity to alcohol. The sensor output is an analog signal which can vary 0–5 V (Volts), where 0 V means the absence of alcohol and 5 V an alcohol concentration. Before the signal processing, it is necessary to transform it into digital, since the Raspberry Pi does not have the characteristic of reading analog signals. For this, the MCP3008 10-bit converter was used, obtaining a digital signal that varies from 0 to 1024, see Fig. 3. Finally, there is a hardware device (Raspberry Pi) responsible of the signal processing, depending on the level of alcohol detected, it makes decisions, for example, to turn on an alarm or in that case it could prevent the car from starting.

Fig. 3. Prototype for alcohol detection (Laboratory Tests).

Although this method considers certain conditions for optimal operation, it is necessary to mention that this project is part of an integral system that includes several sensors not only for the detection of alcohol, but also for detection of infants, recognition of distracted driver, among others. The system is in the process of development implementing technology related to the Internet of Things and artificial intelligence for the analysis and processing of massive data.

For the design and development of this method, the User Centered Design (UCD) process was used to generate feedback capable of persuading a person and preventing them from driving in a Drunk state. This process is defined as the design or development of products and services based on the needs of the users, see Fig. 4.

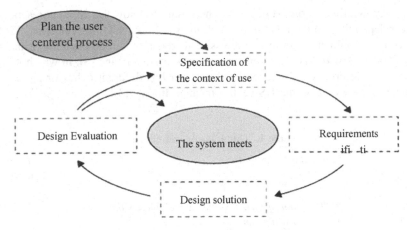

Fig. 4. ISO Standard 9241-210: 2010 [7].

The selection of the DCU method is due to the intention of creating an intuitive and functional feedback that can persuade people not to drive while intoxicated, placing the user at the center of the design and development of such feedback.

3   DCU Process Implementation

Each of the phases of the DCU process shown in the Fig. 4 are described below:

Usage context specification, refers to the environment surrounding the user, in this case, the interior of the car. Taking into account the Fig. 5, we can say that the alcohol sensors will be installed in the parts indicated by the label of "Alcohol sensors" and the feedback will be displayed in the area indicated by the "Warning icon" label.

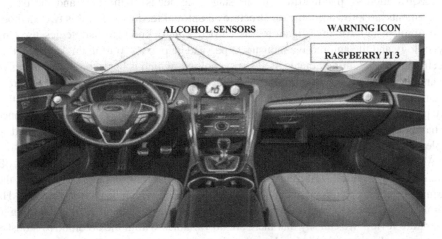

Fig. 5. Environment surrounding the driver.

Similarly, within the context of use it is necessary to know the different reactions of the driver depending on the level of alcohol ingested, for which the reference Table 1 generated by "Movimet", a group of professionals related to urban planning, is taken as a basis, planning, road, transportation and urban tourism signage [8], in which 7 levels of alcohol are described and at each level the user has different behavior and effects. These effects are based on the US central medical library [3].

Table 1. Drunk levels and effects.

Level of difficulty driving	Effects on the person	Types of users
Without difficulty	*Full domain of their faculties, which means that they have not ingested alcohol*	*Type 1*
Moderate	*Decrease the ability to respond to danger, slower decisions or become confusing*	*Type 2*
Moderate	*Vision problems not focusing properly and lack of attention to their surroundings*	*Type 3*
Severe	*The movements of the body are delayed and a feeling of euphoria and confidence appears, which makes you drive aggressively and without fear of danger*	*Type 4*
Critical	*Slow and inaccurate reflexes accompanied by lack of visual concentration*	*Type 5*
Critical	*Unpredictable behavior and it is impossible to make decisions with certainty*	*Type 6*
Critical	*Gradually lose consciousness as a prelude to alcohol-induced coma*	*Type 7*

Requirements Specification, at this stage, the needs of the user and the design requirements are known in order to structure an optimal feedback. For this two methods were applied, (1) An investigation was carried out to know the strategies used by psychology and the automotive industry to persuade a person. Within this investigation a technique was identified that is used in psychology, which is based on punishments or rewards [9]. For example, within the automotive industry the seat belt is used, where it is punished with the sound of an alarm to disturb the user's environment and in that way persuade him to put on his seat belt or reward him by deactivating the alarm once he has put it on. Derived from the above, the following elements were identified to implement the technique.

Alarm: the alarm will have to have the following characteristic, less than 90 dB (Intensity of the sound) with the aim of not causing hearing damage, to generate the alarm an electronic component called "buzzer" was used which has 85 dB and 2.4 kHz so it is within the established standards to not cause hearing damage [10]. According to a literature review we can say that there are no variables within the automotive industry to determine the type of sound and the duration of the alarm, since this is determined by each of the car brands, but it is intended that for each increase in the level of alcohol the alarm intensity automatically will increase and thereby create more cognitive alertness in the user and remain active or in the best case persuade him not to drive while intoxicated.

Warning icon: the colors used in the icon, selected according to the signaling rules which indicate red for danger or prohibition, yellow in case of warning or attention and green indicating safety or stability [11]. Regarding the symbology, the signage of a bottle and a glass was incorporated as it is associated with alcohol consumption, in addition the standards were used in the figures of road displays, circle for prohibition and triangle for danger or attention [11, 12]. In accordance with the standards set out above, it is proposed to use a circle with red colors indicating danger, yellow for attention or warning and green for stability, see Fig. 6.

Fig. 6. Proposed icon for identification of drunkenness (Color figure online)

Finally, so that the symbol was as intuitive as possible, a survey was carried out, and this was developed with the results of it.

Music blocking: this punishment is established due to the characteristic of euphoria and trust that is presented in users when they are under the influence of alcohol, according to the AAP (American Academy of Pediatrics, for its acronym in English) the propitious music the appearance of this characteristic or amplifies it, making it more difficult to persuade the user [13].

Ignition lock: it is established when the user does not have the ability to handle or is evident his lack of sanity regarding his decisions or movements. It should be noted that the last two punishments proposed are part of the integral system, and are not integrated into the prototype presented.

A simple survey was conducted in order to know the opinion of people (drivers) about the development of the prototype. This survey was applied to 30 people, the questions were: (1) Have you ever driven while drunk? the result was 61.1% have not driven under the influence of alcohol while 38.9% have driven while intoxicated. (2) Do you think it is convenient to install an alcohol detection system? (3) Do you think it is convenient for the system to intervene in the car? The results obtained were 5.6% rejection and 94.4% approval since users considered the system as a method of safety and accident prevention, they had more acceptance by people from senior citizens, considering an effective method to provide security for their children and family members. Finally, an open question was applied (4) How would you like the system to alert you when alcohol has been detected in the car? The question was very important since, derived from it, the visual and auditory feedback was developed to the end user, that is, the driver. The results of the survey are presented in Fig. 7.

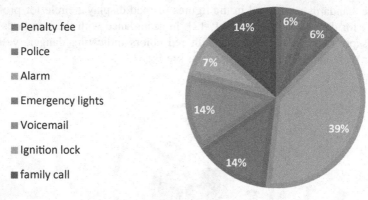

Fig. 7. Survey Results.

Production of design solutions, this phase uses the information obtained from the 2 previous stages to generate a prototype and the respective feedback, in this case, for each of the 7 levels of alcohol; which can represent the level of alcohol in the car cabin or the level of drunkenness of a person, Table 2 shows the user classification (alcohol level), and the visual and auditory feedback provided by the system.

Design Evaluation, this stage is of the utmost importance since the design is approved or rejected according to the opinion of the users. For this, a sample of the population was taken and an evaluation of 5 questions was applied on a Likert scale. The questions were: (1) On a scale from 1 to 5 how intense is the lighting of the icon?, (1 means low lighting and 5 very bright), the result: 60% in 3, 20% in 4, 20% in 5, it is concluded that the intensity is adequate since the lighting is visible to the user; (2) Is the lighting of the icon annoying? Result: 80% does not bother and 20% if, it is concluded that the color and illumination of the icon is adequate, since it is visible and does not irritate the view of users; (3) Is the alarm intensity annoying? Result: 60% yes and 40% no, it is concluded that the intensity is above the accepted limit; (4) Do you consider the alarm frequency correct? Result: 60% yes and 40% no, it is concluded that the intensity and frequency of the alarm must be modified; (5) What would you change about the feedback? Result: some would modify the design, however, most accepted it.

Table 2. Feedback for each of the users.

Types of users	Icon color	Feedback
Type 1		*Off*
Type 2		*Alarm every second for 10 seconds*
Type 3		*Alarm every 600 milliseconds for a continuous time*
Type 4		*Alarm every 400 milliseconds for a continuous time* *Music lock*
Type 5		*Alarm every 200 milliseconds for a continuous time* *Music lock* *Ignition lock*
Type 6		*Alarm every 200 milliseconds for a continuous time* *Music lock* *Ignition lock*

Type 7

Text message to a family member or acquaintance to let you know the status of the user

Music lock

Ignition lock

Alarm every 400 milliseconds for a continuous time

4   Results and Discussion

Given the results obtained in the last stage of the DCU process, where users evaluated the prototype and recommendations were issued, the system feedback was redesigned, see Table 3.

Table 3. Modified feedback

Types of users	Modified feedback	Observations
Type 1	*Off*	*None*
Type 2	*Alarm every 4 min for a continuous time*	*This change is due to the fact that it does not make sense to sound the alarm only once since the user would lose the cognitive alert*
Type 3	*Alarm every 3 min and 30 s for a continuous time*	*The time interval for the alarm sound was very short because it was very chaotic for the user, so the time interval was extended*
Type 4	*Alarm every 3 min for a continuous time* *Music lock*	*In the same way that in the previous stage the time interval is extended*
Type 5	*Music lock* *Ignition lock*	*When the ignition lock occurs, there is no need to sound the alarm, as this may bother the user or cause discomfort or stress*
Type 6	*Music lock* *Ignition lock*	*In the same way that in the stage the alarm sound is removed*
Type 7	*Text message to a family member or acquaintance to let you know the status of the user* *Music lock* *Ignition lock*	*In the same way that in the stage the alarm sound is removed*

Regarding the alarm sound, as mentioned above, the intensity was annoying, so the level in decibels (dB) was reduced, in this way a softer and less stressful sound was obtained. Finally, the code responsible for the processing of the information contained in the Raspberry Pi was redesigned and optimized, since delays were identified that slowed the transitions from one feedback to another, giving the user a perspective of discomfort improving the sensitivity and speed to the system.

5 Conclusion

Drunk driving incidents are events that happen very frequently and the problem of not being able to prevent these incidents has led to the death of many people, so various prevention methods have been developed, however, new ones are necessary contributions to solve the problem that they consider adequate visual and auditory feedback. This document shows the development of a device that provides feedback for the driver by identifying alcohol in a car cabin. The development of the prototype is based on the process of User Centered Design with the purpose of including the driver (end user) in each stage of the system development. Some results show, for example, the different design perspectives that users have, as well as 94.4% approval in an alcohol detection system.

However, it is important to mention that this is the first approach in the development of a comprehensive system that will allow the presence of alcohol in the car cabin to be validated in different ways that the driver is drunk. For this, it is planned to implement artificial intelligence techniques for the processing of data from various sources.

Acknowledgments. The authors thank the academic and student community for the Master of Science in Information Processing (MCPI) and Industrial Electronics Engineering (IEI) programs of the Autonomous University of Zacatecas - Mexico, as well as the Zacatecas Council of Science, Technology and Innovation (COZCyT) for the support received.

References

1. Sakairi, M.: Water-cluster-detecting breath sensor and applications in cars for detecting drunk or drowsy driving. IEEE Sens. J. **12**(5), 1078–1083 (2012). https://doi.org/10.1109/jsen.2011.2163816
2. Kulkarni, S.S., Harale, A.D., Thakur, A.V.: Image processing for driver's safety and vehicle control using raspberry Pi and webcam. In: 2017 IEEE International Conference on Power, Control, Signals and Instrumentation Engineering (ICPCSI) (2017). https://doi.org/10.1109/icpcsi.2017.8391917
3. Consumo y nivel seguro del alcohol: MedlinePlus enciclopedia médica. https://medlineplus.gov/spanish/ency/article/001944.htm. Accessed 27 May 2019
4. Kumari, B.M.K., Sethi, S., Kumar P.R., Kumar, N., Shankar, A.: Detection of driver drowsiness using eye blink sensor. Int. J. Eng. Technol. **7**(3.12), 498 (2018). https://doi.org/10.14419/ijet.v7i3.12.16167

5. Takahashi, K., Hiramatasu, K., Tetsuishi, M.: Experiments on detection of drinking from face images using neural networks. In: 2015 Second International Conference on Soft Computing and Machine Intelligence (ISCMI) (2015). https://doi.org/10.1109/iscmi.2015.12
6. Alcohol gas sensor (Model: MQ-3). https://cdn.sparkfun.com/datasheets/Sensors/Biometric/MQ-3%20ver1.3%20-%20Manual.pdf. Accessed 02 Feb 2019
7. ISO - International Organization for Standardization. https://www.iso.org/standard/52075.html. Accessed 02 Feb 2019
8. Alcohol: Efectos, niveles, riesgos y consecuencias. http://www.movimet.com/2013/12/alcohol-efectos-niveles-riesgos-y-consecuencias/. Accessed 10 Dec 2019
9. Técnicas de persuasión – GestioPolis. https://www.gestiopolis.com/tecnicas-de-persuasion/. Accessed 19 Dec 2018
10. Productos de audio—DigiKey. Recuperado. https://www.digikey.com/product-detail/es/cui-inc/CEM-1206S/102-1155-ND/412414/. Accessed 20 Dec 2018
11. Seven. http://www.seven.com.ve/empnorma.php/. Accessed 20 Dec 2018
12. Secretaria de Comunicaciones y Transportes: Señalamiento. http://www.sct.gob.mx/carreteras/direccion-general-de-conservacion-de-carreteras/publicaciones/senalamiento/. Accessed 27 May 2019
13. La música y el estado de ánimo, American Academy of Pediatrics. https://www.healthychildren.org/Spanish/healthy-living/emotional-wellness/Paginas/Music-and-Mood.aspx. Accessed 19 Dec 2018

An Architecture of Reactive Interfaces Proposal

Laura Sanely Gaytán-Lugo$^{(\boxtimes)}$ ⓘ,
Pablo Armando Alcaraz-Valencia ⓘ,
Mayra G. Terrones ⓘ, and Esteban Hernández ⓘ

School of Mechanical and Electrical Engineering, Universidad de Colima,
Colima, Mexico
{laura, pablo_alcaraz, mterrones, ehernandez10}@ucol.mx

Abstract. This paper presents a proposal for the development of reactive user communication interfaces, popularly known as widgets. This proposal aims to dispense with the Application Development Kits (ADKs), promoting the integration of an open and cross-platform reference framework specialized in the development of applications. Likewise, the 3D interfaces are designed as a mechanism for user interaction as optical illusions. The transit route to follow is to resort to the forms of programming proposed in the traditional programming paradigms: (a) imperative programming; (b) procedural programming; and, (c) object-oriented programming. Later it is exposed the integration of a specialized frame of reference in the systematization of an encoding process that leads to the development of 3D interfaces is exposed. The initial design process consists of the identification of three subsystems that establish a verifiable framework for work, control and communication, from which an architectural design based on components and modules is established. As future work it is visualized to work in the way in which the interfaces will be evaluated in terms of effectiveness and efficiency, as well as finding a meaningful way to apply this proposal particularly in the educational area.

Keywords: Reactive interfaces · Widgets · User graphic interfaces

1 Introduction

In terms of interaction and usability, the Graphical User Interfaces (GUI) take advantage of people's predisposition to remember visual information, by interacting in events through circumstantial actions [1]. The latter in contrast to the possibility of managing information through texts (See Fig. 1).

A user's communication Reactive Interface or widget corresponds to an assertive way of conceptualizing the programming paradigm present in an IGU. For this, the objective of a reactive interface is focused on providing the user with graphic scenarios, from which it is possible to interact through specific functionalities. Likewise, a reactive interface produces an output of information whose purpose may vary based on (1) who requires as a destination, or (2) the result of information management performed through this software entity [2]. For this work, a reactive interface is defined as

© Springer Nature Switzerland AG 2019
P. H. Ruiz and V. Agredo-Delgado (Eds.): HCI-COLLAB 2019, CCIS 1114, pp. 85–96, 2019.
https://doi.org/10.1007/978-3-030-37386-3_7

Fig. 1. GUI can be used to reflect a set of points to interact with in order to discover meaningful information about specific topics.

a symbol whose representation in a graphical user interface is given through objects: buttons, text boxes, images, among others.

Nowadays, the development of reactive interfaces is carried out through Application Development Kits (ADK). These work environments provide code editors dedicated to the design of objects inside user interfaces in order to manipulate and process data [3]. An important detail is that the scope of the reactive interfaces varies based on the management information to be made between (a) person & electronic device, (b) person & an electronic device & a process, or (c) a person & an electronic device & a person.

Likewise, to implement ADKs in the development of reactive interfaces implies to the programmer the use of an Application Programming Interface (API) which unifies the operability of the software into several work environments (phones, tablets, computers and internet). This last is expensive in terms of money because of the prices related to use libraries that allow the functionality of the reactive interface into different operating systems [4]. In other words, the use of ADKs compromise the coding work of developers to the use of tools dedicated to get money in order to operate. Considerations such as maintaining the reactive interface, its portability and the reusability is tied costly to the licensing business software development.

2   Solution Proposal

Given the need to develop reactive interfaces for communication with the user by dispending the use of popular KDAs, and in order to promote the integration of an open and cross-platform framework, specialized in the development of applications to interact with holographic interfaces in 3D as an optical illusions, the route to follow consists on resorting the way of programming proposed in the traditional programming paradigms: (a) imperative programming, based on instructions; (b) procedural programming, which consists on summing imperative programming plus method implementation; and (c) object-oriented programming, which merges procedural programming through the definition of objects.

As the first step of our work proposal in the systematization of coding to develop reactive (3D) interfaces based on widgets, the initial process consisted in the identification of three subsystems that establish an architectural design based on modules and components. This last resulted as a consequence of an analysis of user's requirements which was taken as a case study. The idea was to development an interactive and virtual environment to produce immersion in order to understand information from auditory texts inputs (see Fig. 1).

In this sense, it is important to note this case of study is designed to explore meaning that emerges from the relationships built from the analysis, through cultural baggage, inferences and assumptions [5].

3 Requirements Analysis

3.1 User Requirements

The goal of this project is to integrate an open and cross-platform reference framework specialized in the development of applications based on interaction with holograms as optical illusions. Therefore, it is necessary to define in parallel what the role of the virtual environment will result from such integration.

In this sense and based on the defined problem approach, is required an implicit exploration of the context through the culmination of purposes, which in the best case will result in the user's comprehension about specific topics.

For this purpose, we will use the listening comprehension process when learning English as a second language. In this order, as a vehicle of transit, in the process of listening when there is a purpose, it is involved the generation of small tasks to interact visually and aurally by relating them to previous experiences, and consequently to get access to specific information contained in audio-texts [5]. The idea of this approach is to prevent a person (the user of an interactive tool based on holographic widgets as optical illusions) from translating each linguistic element perceived through the ear. The above, given the need to store each part of the newly acquired information, and later to incorporate it into the understanding process that occurs in real time (see Fig. 1).

For this last, the way of the interaction happens between the user, the practice and the holographic tool based on widgets (Holotank), does not require to generate oral responses that verify the communication comprehension from the interlocutor. The validation of this process of communication is given based on the interaction that the user undertakes towards the virtual environment, and through the selection of options as a response.

Thus, the development of such interaction mechanism proposed is based on the practice of interaction in Table 1 where immersion occurs from three approaches dedicated to show how to address information perceived auditorily: (1) correlational (2) transgressive and (3) potential. Also, the immersion development is segmented and proposed as stages, where the definition of the requirements to be satisfied in terms of system development was feasible.

In this order, the first user requirement in the system to be analyzed corresponds to the correlational level, where the user's objective in this first stage corresponds to recognize a subject by analyzing content in the audio-text through the cultural

Table 1. Objectives in the analysis of information in audio texts through interaction with widgets based on 3D holograms.

CS level	Textual analysis	Self reflective dimension	Objectives in the skills	Objectives in practice
Correlation	How can we recognize the subject analyzed?	How do we recognize ourselves in the subject analyzed?	Stimulate cultural baggage to position the user on the subject	Provide a graphic and auditory environment that allows contextualizing the user through the selection of options
Transgression	Where do we find the finished text?	Where are we regarding the subject analyzed?	Stimulate the ability to infer or assume in a logical-relational way, based on the rethinking of new ideas from contextualization	The graphic and auditory environment is turned into a system that evaluates relational connections through the selection of options
Potentiality	How can we rethink the subject analyzed?	How can we rethink ourselves the subject analyzed?	Provide feedback regarding the meaning of the auditory text produced that the user has generated	The graphic environment links the conceptual nodes to show an approximation of the meaning of the auditory text

background. For this, the interaction between the user and the HoloTank tool corresponds to discarding the options opposed to the theme that transits in an audio-text. The above happens when the user clicks with the index finger on the three-dimensional images that are not related to the subject, or with respect to the analysis of the information that is happening in an auditory way (Table 2).

For the requirement of the level of transgression, it is based on the previous contextualization (in which the user was positioned within a theme) that the HoloTank tool presents a series of selectable graphic options. These options are grouped into four menus. The idea is that through the auditory text a three-dimensional object is selected, by clicking with the index finger on one of these options. Consequently, a menu of four more options is activated, consistent with the selected alternative. The value of this type of interaction lies in the construction of a story congruent with the audio-text that is being analyzed, and the selection of one of the four graphic options whose purpose is to materialize and represent, only what is understood (Table 3).

Table 2. The user requirement representative of the correlational level in the user's positioning within the subject to be analyzed.

Interaction	Representation	Description
Theoretical	Textual	Recognize the analyzed issue of sde out
	Self-reflective	Position yourself within the subject to finalized
	Conceptual	A story, an historical theme or a cultural representation
	Objective of the correlation	Stimulate the cultural background of a person to place him on the subject to be analyzed
Practical	Objective of the tool	Provide a graphic and auditory environment that allows the user to contextualize, through interaction with three-dimensional objects and the selection of options

Table 3. The user requirement representative of the transgressive level in recognition for the construction of the subject to be analysed.

Interaction	Representation	Description
Theoretical	Textual	Where do you recognize the subject analyzed?
	Self-reflective	Where do we find ourselves regarding the subject analyzed?
	Conceptual	Through texts, time and space, modalities, cultures and languages
	Objective of the correlation	Stimulate the ability to infer or suppose in a logical-relational way, the time and space where the subject takes place
Practical	Objective of the tool	The graphic and auditory environment turns into a system that evaluates the relational connections that make up the context of the subject in question, through the selection of options

Thus, the user requirement at the level of potentiality is the result of having positioned the user within the subject analyzed (at the correlational level), and the consequent construction of a story through the graphic and auditory context that is presented (during the transgressive level). The objective of this last stage of interaction is the contemplation of the set of events that constructed the outcome presented, and the proximity of said resolution to the expected objective (Table 4).

Table 4. The user requirement representative of the level of potential in the construction of a conclusion.

Interaction	Representation	Description
Theoretical	Textual	How does the user rethink the analyzed topic?
	Self-reflective	How does the user rethink the subject analyzed?
	Conceptual	Based on: (a) a cultural and historical position, in relation to (b) a social reality, (c) political, (d) economic or (e) a power structure
	Objective of the correlation	Provide feedback on the meaning of the auditory text and what the user of the tool concluded
Practical	Objective of the tool	The graphic environment links the conceptual nodes to show an approximation of the meaning of the auditory text

4 Systems Requirements

Once the user requirements have been determined with respect to the development of a computer system, it is necessary a bridge that allows the system's programmer to understand what the end user needs through the practice [6]. In this sense, the author recommends the implementation of a methodology called "use cases", which allows to organize in a graphic way the textual requirements provided by the user and clarify the newly collected requests.

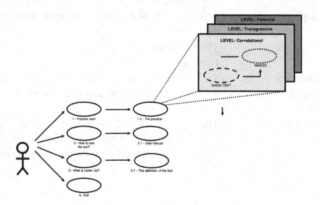

Fig. 2. Use case: correlation, transgression and potential in audiovisual interaction with auditory texts.

The purpose of a use case is to establish in order the sequences of interaction between the user and the services provided by the HoloTank tool under construction. For this, the use cases must contain all the significant activities of the user with respect to the system, as well as the way in which these activities are related.

Thus, the result of obtaining the textual user requirements, and the transformation of these into a use case, derives in the specifications that, in terms of procedures, the software developer requires, to start programming the HoloTank tool [7].

Then in Fig. 3 occurs the transformation of user requirements into system requirements for each node. That is, the node from which the user starts the proposed practice for immersion in the context. The idea of such transformation benefits both the project manager and the programmer. This last happens because of the format works as a checklist's template through which it is possible to verify if there is synchrony between the events that the user triggers when interacting with the HoloTank tool, since these are activated from the objects in the communication interface provided to the user.

Table 5. System requirements at the start of practice.

Function	Start up the contextualization system
Description	Provide a starting point for the tactile interaction system, whose objective is to provide holographic and auditory interfaces in the work of contextualization with respect to a subject subject to analysis
Inputs	The selection of a holographic option through a touch interface
Source	Option one of the holographic menus presented when starting the HoloTank tool
Outputs	Holographic interface of tactile interaction whose objective is to place the user within a graphic and auditory context, such that it requires analysis to advance within it
Destination	Menu of four selectable holographic options, consistent with the initialization of the practice at the correlation level
Requirements	Initialization of the HoloTank tool through the command instructions executed in the Ubuntu 14.04 operating system terminal
Precondition	Start the virtual environment from the command console where the necessary settings for the use of the video camera are located, as a mechanism for interaction with holographic images as optical illusions
Postcondition	Access to the interaction interfaces whose purpose is to provide the user with graphic and auditory interaction interfaces in the context analysis
Collateral effects	The data collection system begins which, based on the interaction with holographic images, recreates a history susceptible to multiple outcomes

Likewise, these types of tables provide a description about the flow of information that takes place in the system, as well as the influence of this on other nodes. Such is the case of Table 5, in which in the "Precondition" section is established, where the said node depends on a previous one, which once it is finished with its work leads the user to restart the practice (Table 6).

After obtaining the system requirements from the nodes present in the case of use provided in Fig. 2, it is possible to generate a sequence diagram defining the process of interaction between the user and the three levels of immersion in the context through 3D holograms and audio-text (see Fig. 3).

Table 6. Requirements system for practice.

Function	Place the user in the context analysis
Description	Provide a holographic and auditory environment that allows the user to access the context of the subject analyzed through the selection of options that react to touch
Inputs	The selection of a holographic option through a touch interface.
Source	A menu of four holographic options
Outputs	Holographic and auditory feedback
Destination	Menu of four selectable holographic options, consistent with the newly selected option
Requirements	Menus of chained holographic and auditory options that always lead to the conclusion of a topic. The above based on the selection of previous options
Precondition	Select the system option that starts the practice at the level of correlation, transgression and potentiality
Postcondition	At the conclusion of the analysis of the information presented at the levels of correlation, transgression and potentiality, the user is driven to restart the system
Collateral effects	The approach of the conclusion is established (at the level of correlation), the knot of the story is developed (at the level of transgression), and the end of the immersion is reached in the graphic and auditory context (at the level of potentiality)

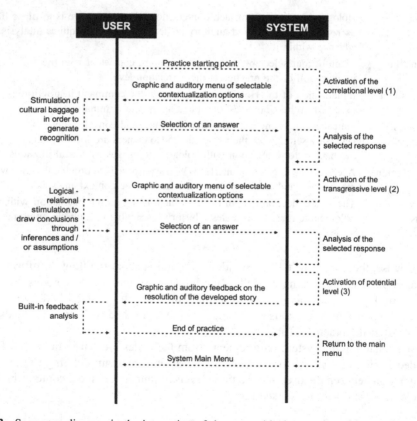

Fig. 3. Sequence diagram in the interaction of the user with the practice of immersion in the context, through the level of correlation, transgression and potentiality

In this way, the sequence diagram provides a visualization mechanism that sets in motion the requirements of the HoloTank tool in order to verify congruence between the activation of events through interaction with system objects (the user and the software) contained in it.

5   Content System Design of the Tool

Different types of graphics were made for the design of the system that allowed to recreate a general panorama about the structure of the system in general and its operation. Below to this section it is showed the architectural diagrams dedicated to identifying the subsystems that make the tool work. Also, it is shown the components and modules in which these subsystems are divided.

5.1   Architectural Design

In the following Figure, an architectural block diagram is shown in which a general overview of the structure of the developed system is shown. In said diagram each table represents a subsystem and the arrows indicate the flow of the data that transits from one side to another. The boxes within the tables indicate that the subsystem has been broken down into parts (into modules).

Regarding the interaction with 3D holograms, the components in which the architecture of the general system is divided are described below. The objective of this section is to describe the process in which an authentic frame of reference was created for the design of holographic interfaces through optical illusions.

The processing subsystem is responsible for generating the interaction that the user requires to communicate with the HoloTank tool. This subsystem provides a communication interface to response how and when to interact through the pointer defined in the subsystem (Fig. 4).

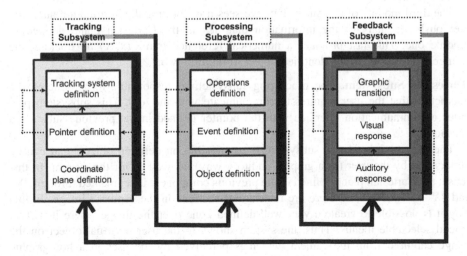

Fig. 4. Proposal architectural design.

The feedback subsystem provides the most perceptible software layer to the user, since their goal is to provide a virtual communication mechanism with the developed system, in order to achieve user immersion with an environment (graphic and auditory) dedicated to contextualizing specific themes.

5.2 Design of Modules and Components

Once the general architecture of the system to be developed is defined, and all the subsystems that give functional meaning to the possibilities of interaction between the user and the software tool are identify, the next stage of the software design consists of in decomposing subsystems into modules [8].

Tracking Subsystem. The tracking subsystem is responsible for storing zeros and ones dynamically to find combinations of data susceptible to analysis. The above means to perform an exploration of information in images that varies from thirty-two to sixty-four per second.

In this sense, there are three tasks to be performed on each of the images analyzed in said unit of time, that is, (1) the definition, (2) the search and (3) the location of an object. The first module of this component is responsible for defining an information search space through a Cartesian coordinate plane, which is accessed when the camera is activated. This allows the system to establish a starting point in the search of information, so it can be detected a pointer in movement captured in the image.

The second module of this first component or subsystem searches for a single moving element within the Cartesian space defined in the previous module. The goal of this module is to discriminate the information that is not necessary in an image. This last in order to only process the information that is significant to the system (the pointer captured in the image). Therefore, it was established that the pointer would be a circular element in the image, colored in fluorescent green. The color chosen for the object to be identified in the moving image is convenient since fluorescent green is rare to find in the environment.

The third module of this subsystem oversees transforming the information analyzed previously. It analyzes the information that lies in the Cartesian plane defined in module one. This last provides a numerical reference frame (x, y) by tracking the change of position of the identified object in module two.

Processing Subsystem. The processing subsystem is responsible for producing the interaction that the user requires to communicate with the tool. This subsystem provides a communication interface with the pointer defined in the previous subsystem component.

The first module of this subsystem is responsible on defining objects that can be understood by the user (in a graphic-auditory way), as well as for the system. In this sense, the Cartesian plane defined in the previous component is segmented through "X" and "Y" coordinates, so there are rectangular sections in the captured image. In this way it is possible to create a very well-defined zone over the image where it will be placed selectable menus. Thus, the system shows to the user a virtual object on the image captured from the camera, which is perceived by the user in a holographic illusion way, so that it becomes a selectable option that can be chosen by using the fluorescent green pointer.

The second module consists in the definition of the events in which the object defined in the previous module will be susceptible of interaction. That is, for this system an event begins when it is detected the green pointer within a certain zone of the Cartesian plane figured over the image captured by the camera. This space may or may not be a selectable menu, but the idea is that in this component could be possible to discern such an event.

Once the objects are defined in the communication interfaces with the user, the third module takes place by taking charge of connecting such objects with the events of the previous module through a action - reaction process. If the pointer controlled by the user is within certain zone of the image captured by the camera, and object exists in it, then an event will be triggered, that is, the event may correspond to "click" on a selectable menu.

Feedback Subsystem. The feedback subsystem provides the most perceptible software layer to the user, since the main goal consists on providing a virtual communication mechanism by enhancing the context of an audio text. This means to make possible that the user gets immerse into a virtual environment (graphic and auditory) dedicated to contextualize ideas about specific topics.

The first module is responsible for providing the sound feedback according to the selected object and the triggered event. This module displays the sound effects that correspond to: clicking on the selectable menus, letting the user know if the chosen options are correct, and especially to present an auditory atmosphere congruent with the theme presented both graphically and textually.

The second module of this component (or subsystem) provides a graphical, virtual and interactive communication interface, projected on the plane that the camera focuses on. This functions as a starting point for the selection of options based on the textual history that will be developed by been activated when they are selected with the pointer. This offers different types of feedback from the events unleashed in the practice presented to through the tool.

To finish with this component, the third transition module refers to the organization of the distribution of the graphic elements presented to the user, given the selected objects, the events that are triggered, the text of the practice to be developed, the recycling of graphics, and auditory elements.

6 Discussion

Regarding ADKs, it results that they are not expendable for the development of 3D GUI's, especially when it comes to build usable prototypes and experiment with them quickly. Nevertheless, in relation of effectiveness when using 3D interfaces located in the same physical space of the user, attention must be paid on how to address the interaction goals and how to reach them.

In this sense, the 3D Graphic Interfaces as optical illusions should verify their efficiency based on two axes: (1) when validating whether the interaction of the user with the interface produces incremental usability given the frequency of use, and (2) when quantifying the efficiency (or quality) present in the interaction experience.

7 Future Work

As future work it is planned to find a suitable way to evaluate the proposed GUI based 3D holograms as optical illusions. For this, it is intended to start with a literature review regarding on how to evaluate these kind of user interfaces in terms of efficiency and effectiveness. From this, it will be determined if it is possible to use an existing instrument, or if it must be designed and validated.

Although, our proposal is intended to influence different areas related to GUI and the internet of things, an important aspect of your work is to apply it in the major of education. Therefore, the importance of consolidating and instrument that quantifies the effectiveness of our proposal in terms of usability.

References

1. Galitz, W.: The Essential Guide to User Interface Design: An Introduction to GUI Design Principles and Techniques. Wiley Publishing, Indianapolis (2007)
2. Android Developers.: Build an App Widget. https://developer.android.com/guide/topics/appwidgets/overview. Accessed 11 Dec 2018
3. Android Developers: Accessory Development Kit. https://stuff.mit.edu/afs/sipb/project/android/docs/tools/adk/index.html. Accessed 23 Dec 2018
4. University of Birmingham: How much does it cost to build a mobile app? https://intranet.birmingham.ac.uk/collaboration/mobile-apps/faqs/budget.aspx
5. Alcaraz-Valencia, P., Gaytán-Lugo, L., Hernández-Gallardo, S., Maciel, R.: The role of technology in audio texts' comprehension for English as a second language. In: Andujar, A. (ed.) Recent Tools for Computer-and Mobile-Assisted Foreign Language Learning. IGI-Global, USA (2019)
6. Cockburn, A.: Writing Effective Use Cases. The Crystal Collection for Software Professionals. Addison-Wesley Professional, Reading (2000)
7. Inayat, I., Salim, S.S., Marczak, S., Daneva, M., Shamshirband, S.: A systematic literature review on agile requirements engineering practices and challenges. Comput. Hum. Behav. **51**, 915–929 (2015). https://doi.org/10.1016/j.chb.2014.10.046
8. Mantle, M., Lichty, R.: Managing the Unmanageable: Rules, Tools, and Insights for Managing Software People and Teams. Addison-Wesley, Boston (2012)

An Augmented Reality-Based Application Relying on the Use of Tangible User Interfaces for English Teaching to Children Between 10 and 12 Years

Liliana Rodríguez-Vizzuett[1]([✉]) [iD], Josefina Guerrero-García[2] [iD],
and Ivan Olmos-Pineda[2] [iD]

[1] Facultad de Ciencias de la Electrónica,
Benemérita Universidad Autónoma de Puebla, Puebla, Mexico
lliliana.rodriguezvizzuett@viep.com.mx
[2] Facultad de Ciencias de la Computación,
Benemérita Universidad Autónoma de Puebla, Puebla, Mexico
joseguga01@gmail.com, ivanoprkl@gmail.com

Abstract. One of the main challenges associated to the foreign language teaching-learning process is lack of motivation from students. In the literature it is reported that it is possible to promote motivation towards such process through the realization of educational activities on familiar environments created by using animations and digital sounds. In this paper, the process that was followed for the implementation of an Augmented Reality-based application to support the development of the listening comprehension skill in children between 10- and 12-years learning English as foreign language is presented, considering educational content provided by certification institutions and technological elements. A preliminary assessment of interface prototypes by driving an experiment using the Wizard of Oz technique was also addressed.

Keywords: Augmented Reality · Tangible user interfaces · English language learning

1 Introduction

According to information from the Mexican organization *Instituto Mexicano para la Competitividad* [1], only 5% of Mexican population can understand English language. Moreover, *Mexicanos Primero* (http://www.mexicanosprimero.org/) reports that 14.7% of the 50,000 English language teachers in public institutions do not understand such language, and that 23.8% of them reach the A1 level from the Common European Framework of Reference for Languages (CEFR) [2] which is the expected level for students enrolled in the fourth degree of the elementary school.

English language teaching (ELT) was not considered a mandatory subject in the Mexican educational model for 2016 [3], however, it is in the 2017 version implemented since 2018, leading to think that new strategies and tools are required as means to support teaching tasks. The Mexican national program for ELT in elementary education has determined that the abilities to be developed during the fifth and the sixth

© Springer Nature Switzerland AG 2019
P. H. Ruiz and V. Agredo-Delgado (Eds.): HCI-COLLAB 2019, CCIS 1114, pp. 97–112, 2019.
https://doi.org/10.1007/978-3-030-37386-3_8

grades of elementary school are equivalent to the level A2 of the CEFR [2]. For the purposes of this research work, only abilities related to the listening comprehension skill presented in Table 1 are considered.

Table 1. Listening comprehension ability for the A2 CEFR level.

Listening comprehension ability
Can understand phrases and expressions related to areas of most immediate priority (e.g. very basic personal and family information, shopping, local geography, employment) provided speech is clearly and slowly articulated
Can understand enough to be able to meet needs of a concrete type provided speech is clearly and slowly articulated

Considering the above-mentioned problematic, and for providing a tool to aid to solve it, in the literature it is possible to find works reporting the advantages of using Augmented Reality (AR) to promote motivation and as a mean to reinforce knowledge acquisition [4, 5]. Furthermore, in [6] it is reported that the use of AR in the education domain, allows the creation of contents otherwise unviable, consents the realization of activities in in-door environments, and promotes collaboration and interactivity. AR is an interaction paradigm, which is result of the combination of the processing capabilities of computers, and elements from the real environment [7]. In recent years, several prototypes and applications relying on AR had been created in areas such as computer graphics, Human Computer Interaction (HCI), and collaborative work including the following sectors: architecture, engineering, planning, games, and education [8–10].

Aligned to the exposed problematic, considering the characteristics of the Mexican context, and inspired by the positive insights regarding motivation and aiding on the diminution of negative effects like anxiety and frustration, the goal of this work is to present the design of an AR-based application for ELT to children between 10 and 12 years specifically to develop listening comprehension skills. The viability of the solution is supported by the fact of that in Mexico, the introduction of commercial smartphones made AR-based applications available to several population strata. Information provided in 2015 by the Mexican national statistics and geography institute (INEGI) shows that 55.2% of Mexicans aged 6 and above, already had access to smartphones making them potential users of such type of applications.

The remainder of this paper is structured into sections. Section 2 presents the state of the art including important concepts for the realization of this work. In Sect. 3, we present the design process of ARTUI describing user stories and the description of the functionalities of each of the modules to be developed. Section 4 is dedicated to the design of an assessment for the developed application and to describe the gathered results. And finally, in Sect. 5 conclusions and future work are provided.

2 State of the Art

In this section, a literature review on relevant concepts for understanding the proposal is presented including technology applied to the English teaching domain, AR applied to the education field, tangible user interfaces and related work.

2.1 Technology Applied to the ELT Domain

During the decades of 1970 and 1980, computer assisted language learning was developed with the support of teaching methodologies which encourage this process through predefined exercises [11]. According to [12], this type of learning may be addressed from three approaches: the behaviorist approach, based on observation, practice, reinforcements, and habits formation; the communicative approach, supported by cognitive theories which emphasized that learning is a process of discovery, expression and development; and the integrative approach, using multimedia as support to the teaching activities, and relying on the Web, emphasizing the use of the language in a real-life context [13]. Among the technological developments implemented, it is possible to identify e-books, management tools, web quests, and forums. Later, between 1990 and 2000, the terms e-learning presenting tools for remote education [14], and b-learning as a merge of in-classroom and virtual education were introduced [15]. During this decade, platforms for the development of abilities and social networks for sharing information were created. Finally, after 2010 m-learning was presented as a teaching modality which allows to create remote learning environments using mobile devices [16]. The development of mobile applications for teaching enables student interaction and motivates them using gamification elements. The massification of mobile devices has encouraged the implementation of AR-based applications for educational purposes which are addressed in the following subsection.

2.2 Augmented Reality Applied to the Education Domain

With the purpose of understanding the impact of AR when applied to the educational context, we performed a systematic literature review. The results of such review in terms of the objectives and results of the analyzed works are reported in Table 2.

Table 2. Results of the literature review on AR and the educational domain.

Works	Objectives	Results
[17–19]	To create AR-based tools to support the learning of different concepts and to perform studies for understanding the advantages of the use of AR for teaching different subjects	Improvement of the language learning process. AR-based applications enable teachers to perform better presentations. By enriching educational processes with the use of AR, students report to have fun while learning, making it easier for them
[21–28]	To create augmented books supported by 3D resources, to develop tools to support teaching processes, and to implement applications overlapping virtual resources on real objects	AR is useful as support for teaching as it allows the development of tools which use motivates students. It was observed that attention levels and general satisfaction were increased in educational environments supported by AR applications
[29]	To create tools for teaching sciences	Proposition of a development process for allowing AR use in educational domains using free Software
[30]	To compare the traditional teaching processes with AR assisted processes	Children making use of AR-based applications are more engaged as they are encouraged to create and control instead of only analyzing and describing

2.3 Tangible User Interfaces

The term Tangible User Interfaces (TUI), coined by Fitzmaurice and defined as a physical identifier for accomplishing virtual tasks were first described as comprehensive UI [31]. TUIs augment the real physical environment and add digital information to common physical objects [32]. The objective pursued with the implementation of TUIs is then, to manipulate digital information using everyday objects which are present in users' contexts. TUIs allow to realize physical representations through technology, making virtual environments more real and intuitive for users. Multiple authors refer that physical action is important during learning processes and that tangible objects may provide opportunities to think over the application of the obtained knowledge and the real world. TUIs are employed for reaching a better performance in learning tasks and may also be an alternative to GUI as they allow direct manipulation, enabling users to control applications and to navigate through data by selecting and posing physical objects and not only representations of them [33].

In the domain of education, TUIs provide benefits like reduction in the time to learn the use of the interface; diminution of the cognitive effort when learning, giving the opportunity of focusing on the content rather than on the use of the application; and a continuous representation of objects of interest by applying quick, reversible and incremental actions which are immediately visible. Finally, TUIs enable multiple users to interact with an application by sharing objects and hence, promoting collaborative work and natural interaction [33]. A specific type of TUI requires mobile computing and wireless technology like Bluetooth, RFID cards, Near Field Communication (NFC) tags, infrared beacons, WiFi, etc. In this specific proposal NFC tags are being used. NFC was developed by Philips® and Sony® in 2002 and consists on the integration of mobile phones and radio frequency technology and provides simple and safe communication between devices. NFC allows to automatically identify products, components, animals, people and everyday objects using tags [34].

2.4 Related Work

The introduction and massive availability of mobile devices make AR-based applications accessible to different population strata. Considering this fact along with the already described problematic regarding the impact of AR on the motivation towards the learning of a foreign language [5], and the intention of proposing an strategy based on the use of such applications as a means to reinforce the learning process, in (Table 3). it is possible to find a summarized comparison of related works on the use of AR and its application to the ELT domain in terms of their objectives and the obtained results.

In the next section, we address the design of ARTUI, an AR-based application relying on TUI and which content was created according to material provided by language certification entities and incorporating the use of gamification resources.

Table 3. Related works of AR applied to the ELT domain.

Works	Objectives	Results
[4, 5, 35–38]	To develop AR-based tools to incentivize reading and for teaching basic vocabulary and grammar to non-native English speakers	Motivation towards language learning was increased and educational material was created. It was concluded that the supervised use of this type of tools reports benefits
[39–41]	To implement AR-based systems in order to analyze teachers' perception towards such type of technology and for enhancing students' English level, and to create a virtual classroom with the use of AR based on learning theory	Students reported having fun when interacting with such type of technology, they feel less pressured and seem to be more interested in the class. AR-based games showed a positive impact in the educational process, specifically for progressive recognition of words and concepts
[42, 43]	To create teaching material based on the content of textbooks combining AR with ordinary resources	Learning was improved and enriched as motivation increased. Besides, researchers found that the use of AR is recommended as support to learning processes independently of the educational level

3   Application Design

As part of a spiral Software development process model, in order to gather requirements, interviews with final users (teachers and students of English language) within three educational institutions were scheduled. The interviews, following a qualitative approach were created specifically to allow understanding the main challenges that actors face during the EL educational process. In this sense, teachers were also asked about the didactic material that they currently use when teaching and about their perception towards the use of instructive Software to support their classes. From the interviews, the following requirements and clarifications were identified:

1. The application will be used by children between 10 and 12 years as they are completing elementary school and according to the official educational program, they must reach an equivalent to the A2 level of the CEFR.
2. The application to be implemented will be focused on the development of listening comprehension skills.
3. The content to be used should be based in material provided by entities for preparing language certifications.
4. The typography to be used must be understandable by children.
5. The used vocabulary should be adequate to the level A2 from the CEFR.
6. Colors to be used in the application should attract children's attention.
7. The application should not rely on the use of an Internet connection.
8. It is necessary to provide a teacher role in the application in order to allow analysis of the progress of each student individually and as part of a team.

From the above-mentioned requirements along with the characterization of students and teachers and after observation of ELT sessions, it was decided to develop an application entitled ARTUI. ARTUI was conceptualized as a mobile application enclosing two main activities. The first one is a word to 3-D model dictionary in which, supported by AR, students may be able to find words associated to the A2 level of the CEFR taking Cambridge's "Flyers" book as reference, and that are useful for interacting with the other module within the app. The second activity within of ARTUI consists on telling the student a story and evaluating if he/she was able to comprehend it by asking related questions. Students should answer using NFC tags stuck to each of the faces of a cube which works as TUI.

Table 4. Sign up and Login User Stories.

Id	User story	Description	Gamification resource
1	User sign up (teacher)	As a teacher, I want to sign up to the application entering my personal data, selecting the school to which I'm enrolled and the group to which I teach. Besides, I want to choose an avatar, so my profile can be easily identified	Avatar
2	User sign up (student)	As a student, I want to sign up to the application entering my personal information, selecting the group and school to which I belong to, and selecting an avatar to distinguish my profile	Avatar
3	Login (student)	As a registered student, I want to login to the application with my user name	NA
4	Login (teacher)	As a registered teacher, I want to login to the application with my user name	NA
5	Activity selection	As a logged student, I want to see the available activities within the application and be able to select any of them	NA
6	Team registration	As a logged student, I want to be able to choose my team mates from a list, name my team, and select an avatar so we can be distinguished from other teams	Avatar

After gathering and describing functional and non-functional requirements, self-explanatory user stories were created in order to have a more organized and precise representation of them. Such stories, presented in Tables 4, 5 6, 7 and 8, resulted on the implementation of 4 modules in the first iteration: user sign up and login, "Dictionary" activity, "Story" activity, and evaluation; as well as on additional modules to be implemented in a second iteration.

Table 5. Dictionary activity user stories.

Id	User story	Description	Gamification resource
7	"Dictionary" activity selection	As a logged student, I want to select the "Dictionary" activity from a list	NA
8	"Dictionary" activity presentation	As a logged student, I want to see a list of words in English in the screen, and that when I select one of them, either a related 3D model, video, image, or audio is displayed	NA

Table 6. Story activity user stories.

Id	User story	Description	Gamification resource
9	"Story" activity selection	As a logged student, I want to select the "Story" activity from a list	NA
10	"Story" activity selection	As a logged student, I want to be able to select the story that I want to listen to	NA
11	"Story" activity presentation	As a logged student, I want to listen to the story which I previously selected	NA

Table 7. Evaluation of the story activity user stories.

Id	User story	Description	Gamification resource
12	Select evaluation of the "Story" activity	As a logged student, I want to advance to the evaluation section of the listened story	NA
13	Show evaluation of the "Story" activity	As a logged student, I want to listen to questions about the listened story	NA
14	Answer evaluation of the "Story" activity	As a logged student, I want the system to show answer options to the asked question. I want to be able to select any of those options and receive either feedback or rewards depending on the correctness of my answer	Feedback, use of rewards

Table 8. User Stories to be implemented in the second iteration.

Id	User story	Description	Gamification resource
15	Get reports	As a logged teacher, I want to be able to see reports about activities by student and by group	NA
16	Select level of difficulty	As a logged student, I want to be able to select a level of difficulty and to see it reflected on the available stories and their related questions	NA

Next subsections are dedicated to describing the implemented modules according to the presented user stories.

3.1 Sign up and Login Module

This module is divided into two parts. The first one allows new users to sign up to the application. To this purpose, users should specify whether they are students or teachers. As it can be seen in Fig. 1, in case a student is signing in, the application asks him/her for his/her first name, last name, a user name, age, gender, the group to which they belong to, and an avatar with which the student will be represented. As shown in Fig. 1, if the user is a teacher, he/she will be asked to provide first name, last name, user name, the school of enrollment, and the groups to which he/she teaches.

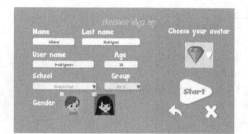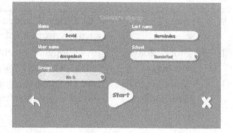

Fig. 1. Student's sign up interface.

The second part of this module consists on allowing users to log into the application using the username they provided when creating their accounts. The use of this functionality is simple, when starting the application users should input their usernames into a text box in the screen and tap on the "Login" button. The application will validate the existence of the user in the database. The implementation of this module required the design and development of a database using MySQL, the connection to the database is managed using PHP and integrated to the Unity game engine in which the project runs.

3.2 Dictionary Module

In the dictionary module, which user interface is presented in Fig. 2, a word-object dictionary supported by AR is provided. Once users are logged in and they selected the "Dictionary" activity from the menu, they may see a list of available words, as well as the camera view. For using this feature, a TUI is given to users in the form of a cube. Two of the cube faces show ARTUI's application logo. After selecting a word and pointing the camera to any of the above referred cube faces, users can listen to the correct pronunciation of the word, and to see a 3D model associated to it.

Fig. 2. Dictionary module interface with cube as TUI.

The development of this module was achieved using the Vuforia platform and its integration to the Unity game engine, as well as with the addition of free 3D models available in online libraries. The audio resources were recorded by native speakers of the language. The technical challenge, which was faced, was on associating one single marker with multiple resources depending on users' choice.

3.3 Story Presentation Module

The story presentation module, illustrated in Fig. 3, presents multiple stories to users and is intended to aid on the improvement of the listening comprehension ability. To this purpose, images and audio resources are used. The stories included in the ARTUI application are extracted from material provided by certification and educational institutions such as Cambridge's 'Fun for Flyers', McMillan education's 'I'm Ready', University of Dayton's 'Do it!', and Pearson's 'Sunshine'. The implementation of this module was completely achieved using the Unity game engine. All the audio resources within the module are recorded by native speakers of the EL taking care of the speed and diction considering the users skills.

Fig. 3. Story presentation module interface.

3.4 Evaluation Module

In the evaluation module, which user interface is presented in Fig. 4, users are provided with a series of questions related to a previously listened story along with the elapsed time for completing the activity. Such questions are presented in text and audio making it easier for students to understand them. In the same way, answer options are presented. This module considers the use of a cube with four NFC tags attached to four of its faces. Another cube was also made using AR markers. In order to use of the AR-based interaction, users have the option to choose whether they will use their NFC reader or through their camera. To interact in this last modality, it is necessary to focus the camera of the mobile device running the application on the cube taking care that only the face with the chosen option is visible, the device then detects the corresponding marker, validates the given answer, and shows the proper feedback.

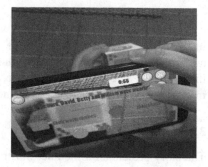

Fig. 4. Evaluation module interface and cube with NFC tags and AR Markers as TUI.

The faces of the cube containing NFC tags are identified using colors and images attached to them. Such colors are consistent with the presented options and allow users to associate each of the cube faces to the options displayed. For choosing an option, users must first take the cube and locate the NFC sensor in the mobile device, then, take the desired face of the cube close to the sensor and wait for the application to detect the tag. The application will display a message letting the user know whether the option selected was correct or wrong. Depending on the attempts that users take to provide a correct answer, they are rewarded with gold, silver, or bronze stars. As a first assessment of the developed application, we drove an experiment with EL teachers from different institutions. The design of such evaluation along with the obtained results are presented in the following section.

4   Design of Assessment and Results

As a parallel process to the development of the application and taking advantage of the model-based approach applied, we decided to evaluate the created user interfaces and workflow in an early stage in order to be able to correct any potential failures in posterior testing. For this experiment, we recruited 6 teachers from three schools. As up to this moment we only counted on user interfaces, the experiment was performed in compliance to the Wizard of Oz technique [44]. To record data from the experiment, an instrument including the list of tasks to be performed and cells for documenting the execution time and mistakes made as the one described in Table 9 was created.

Table 9. Tasks to be performed during the experiment along with the average results.

Task ID	Task	Execution time	Mistakes
1	Start application	3 s	0
2	Sign up as student	7.8 s	0.4
3	Sign up as teacher	5.4 s	0
4	Login to the application	2.4 s	0
5	Select "Dictionary" activity	3 s	0
6	Select word from the dictionary	1.8 s	0
7	Go back to main menu	2.6 s	0.2
8	Select "Story" activity	5.6 s	0
9	Play story	2.2 s	0
10	Repeat story	1.6 s	0.2
11	Go to evaluation	5 s	0
12	Select right answer	2.6 s	0
13	Select wrong answer	4.2 s	0
14	Exit application	2 s	0
15	Go to credits section	3.2	0

Once the experiment was performed and the gathered information was analyzed, it was possible to see that in average the tasks that took more time to be performed are "Sign up as student" and "Select story activity". Also, the task in which more mistakes were made (2) was "Sign up as student", leading to think that users needed some time to get used to the user interface and that this interface should be simplified for optimizing its use. After the interaction with the user interfaces, participants were asked to answer the CSUQ questionnaire [45] for measuring usability in terms of four dimensions: System usability, information quality, interface quality, and general satisfaction. The processed data reported that our application received for system usability an average score of 6.77 out of 7 (stddev = 0.24), for information quality an average score of 6.5 out of 7 (stddev = 0.27), for interface quality an average score of 6.47 out of seven (stddev = 0.6), and finally for general satisfaction an average score of 6.6 out of seven (stddev = 0.54).

Once teachers interacted with the developed application, an assessment instrument was applied to them in order to evaluate the content of the application. Such questionnaire was answered by the five teachers participating in the experiment. The instrument consists of 12 items that are measured through a Likert scale, where 1 corresponds to total disagreement and 5 to total agreement. This instrument was developed to evaluate the quality of the application content in terms of educational level, number of questions, vocabulary used, graphic resources, images and the use of tangible elements as an interaction mechanism within the application. According to the results gathered from the application of the mentioned instrument, it was observed that in general, teachers consider that the content of the application is adequate to the target level (A2). Moreover, in the second item, analyzing if the content is adequate for the educational level, an average of 4.4 out of 5 was obtained (stddev = 0.54), meaning that teachers think that the content within the application is appropriate to the A2 level. For the item referring to the number of questions in the presented activity, an average of 4.4 out of 5 (stddev = 0.54) was obtained. Despite obtaining this average score, teachers recommended adding more questions to evaluate the comprehension of the presented story. As for the vocabulary sufficiency in the application, an average of 4.8 out of 5 (stddev = 0.44) was recorded. Teachers agreed on how the vocabulary was presented to them since they commented that the fact of seeing the object in a closer way to reality would make it more attractive for the students to consult the dictionary with the vocabulary covered in the activity. Regarding the support that the application provides to solve the activities, an average of 4.2 out of 5 was obtained (stddev = 0.44). Some teachers had problems to complete specific activities since they did not understand the meaning of some buttons, but they believed that children would not have problems to carry out such tasks. When asked about if they think that the quality of the audios helps to carry out the activities, an average of 4.6 out of 5 (stddev = 0.54) was gotten, and they mentioned that the audios were very clear so that the children should not have problems for accomplishing the activities within the application. In a similar fashion, for the item on whether the images were representative of the activities, an average of 4.8 out of 5 (stddev = 0.44) was obtained and the teachers commented that they were adequate since these images were associated with the story presented to the students. About the item that refers to whether the content promotes learning, an average of 4.6 out of 5 (stddev = 0.54) was provided. Teachers agreed on that the stories presented were based on the books to which their students usually have access. For this item, the participants mentioned that it would be appropriate to group the stories according to the agenda that was followed in classroom sessions, since this would work as a guide for the teachers to evaluate the students.

Concerning the item of the use of tangible elements for learning, an average of 4.6 out of 5 (stddev = 0.89) was obtained. For most of the teachers participating, the use of tangible objects was interesting and caused curiosity to know how they would be used within the application, when the instructions to be followed were explained to them, they commented that it would be very entertaining for the children and that this would be useful for them to make their classes more dynamic and that the children would not get bored and would always be motivated to participate in the class. For the item referring to the simplicity of the content, an average of 3.8 out of 5 (stddev = 1.09) was obtained. Teachers mentioned that the content was simple to apply mainly because there were few stories to be evaluated. Finally, in the item about the amount of questions for the learning evaluation, an average of 4.8 out of 5 was obtained (stddev = 0.44). Teachers mentioned that it would be good to add levels of complexity for the stories and increase the number of questions so that they could really be evaluated in terms of comprehension.

Based on the presented results, in the next section we describe the identified conclusions and future work.

5   Conclusions and Future Work

In this paper, the design, development and partial assessment of ARTUI, an AR-based application for support to the ELT, is presented. Following a traditional Software development process, the requirement gathering stage was achieved by interviewing English teachers and through direct observation of in-classroom activities. The collected requirements were expressed as user stories making them easier to be developed and tracked. After generating the user stories, a model-based approach was followed for the implementation of user interfaces and their associated functionalities. In order to take advantage of the followed approach and considering that the application of the Wizard of Oz technique would allow to drive an experiment for understanding issues related to navigation and interaction, prior termination of the development phase, a partial assessment was done with teachers from three institutions. During the evaluation, considering that high scores were obtained in the CSUQ questionnaire, it was possible to notice that teachers appreciate the proposal and that its use results easy and intuitive, and to see that the use of ARTUI in classroom sessions is viable and may positively impact English learning. The development of ARTUI involved technical challenges such as the management of the database and its integration to the Unity engine, the use of the Vuforia platform in Unity and its configuration to work as expected, and the detection and identification of NFC tags from the Unity engine. In a first version of the ARTUI application, it had an evaluation module using a cube with NFC tags, however, due to the needs presented by teachers, the same module was implemented, but with the option of using AR instead of such tags, for enabling this, it was necessary to add markers to four of the cube faces so that they could be identified by the camera of mobile devices.

As future work, it was identified that following a spiral Software process model, a second iteration is required in order to implement functionalities like the addition of difficulty levels, the implementation of reports and the creation of additional content adequate to other skills. Also, if well the partial assessment was encouraging, content and interaction evaluation must be done with more teachers and students in order to assure quality and pertinence of the solution.

References

1. de los Piñón, N.A.G., del Sánchez, S.C.H., del Nares, Y.C.P.: Las TIC en la enseñanza del inglés en educación básica. Revista Electrónica Sobre Tecnología, Educación Y Sociedad **4** (7) (2017)
2. Consejo De Europa: Marco común europeo de referencia para las lenguas. Strasburgo: Consejo de Europa, Ministerio de Educación, Cultura y Deporte/Instituto Cervantes (2002)
3. Secretaría de Educación Pública. El Modelo Educativo 2016 (2016)
4. Lee, L.K., Chau, C.H., Chau, C.H., Ng, C.T.: Using augmented reality to teach Kindergarten students English vocabulary. In: 2017 International Symposium on Educational Technology (ISET), pp. 53–57. IEEE (2017). https://doi.org/10.1109/ISET.2017.20

5. Hsieh, M.-C.: Teachers' and students' perceptions towards augmented reality materials. In: 2016 5th IIAI International Congress on Advanced Applied Informatics (IIAI-AAI) (1), pp. 1180–1181 (2016). https://doi.org/10.1109/iiai-aai.2016.39
6. Prendes Espinosa, C.: Realidad aumentada y educación: análisis de experiencias prácticas. Píxel-Bit. Revista de Medios y Educación **46**, 187–203 (2015). https://doi.org/10.12795/pixelbit.2015.i46.12
7. Azuma, R., Baillot, Y., Behringer, R., Feiner, S., Julier, S., MacIntyre, B.: Recent advances in augmented reality. IEEE Comput. Graph. Appl. **21**(6), 34–47 (2001). https://doi.org/10.1109/38.963459
8. Dubois, E.: Chirurgie Augmentée: un Cas de Réalité Augmentée; Conception et Réalisation Centrées sur l'Utilisateur (Doctoral dissertation, Université Joseph-Fourier-Grenoble I) (2001)
9. Kaufmann, H., Schmalstieg, D.: Mathematics and geometry education with collaborative augmented reality. In: ACM SIGGRAPH 2002 Conference Abstracts and Applications, pp. 37–41. ACM (2002). https://doi.org/10.1145/1242073.1242086
10. Klopfer, E., Perry, J., Squire, K., Jan, M.F.: Collaborative learning through augmented reality role playing. In: Proceedings of the 2005 Conference on Computer Support for Collaborative Learning: Learning 2005: The Next 10 years!, pp. 311–315. International Society of the Learning Sciences (2005)
11. Gündüz, N.: Computer assisted language learning. J. Lang. Linguist. Stud. **1**(2), 193–214 (2005)
12. Warschauer, M.: Computers and language learning: an overview. Lang. Learn. **31**, 57–71 (1998). https://doi.org/10.1017/S0261444800012970
13. Beatty, K.: Teaching & Researching: Computer-Assisted Language Learning. Routledge, Abingdon (2013)
14. Cesteros, A.: Las Plataformas E-Learning Para La Enseñanza Y El Aprendizaje Universitario en Internet. Las Plataformas De Aprendizaje. Del Mito a La Realidad, pp. 45–73 (2010)
15. Chérrez, E.: El B-learning como estrategia metodológica para mejorar el proceso de enseñanza-aprendizaje de los estudiantes de inglés de la modalidad semipresencial del departamento especializado de idiomas de la Universidad Técnica de Ambato, p. 503 (2014)
16. Montoya, M.S.: Dispositivos de mobile learning para ambientes virtuales: implicaciones en el diseño y la enseñanza. Apertura, pp. 82–96 (2008)
17. Moralejo, L., Sanz, C. Pesado, P.M., Baldassarri, S.: Avances en el diseño de una herramienta de autor para la creación de actividades educativas basadas en realidad aumentada. TE & ET (2014)
18. Gupta, N., Rohil, M.K.: Exploring possible applications of augmented reality in education. In: 2017 4th International Conference on Signal Processing and Integrated Networks (SPIN), pp. 437–441. IEEE (2017). https://doi.org/10.1109/SPIN.2017.8049989
19. Kiat, L.B., Ali, M.B., Halim, N.D.A., Ibrahim, H.B.: Augmented reality, virtual learning environment and mobile learning in education: a comparison. In: 2016 IEEE Conference on e-Learning, e-Management and e-Services (IC3e), pp. 23–28. IEEE (2016). https://doi.org/10.1109/IC3e.2016.8009034
20. Lee, H.S., Lee, J.W.: Mathematical education game based on augmented reality. In: Pan, Z., Zhang, X., El Rhalibi, A., Woo, W., Li, Y. (eds.) Edutainment 2008. LNCS, vol. 5093, pp. 442–450. Springer, Heidelberg (2008). https://doi.org/10.1007/978-3-540-69736-7_48
21. Gazcón, N.F., Larregui, J.I., Castro, S.M.: La Realidad Aumentada como complemento motivacional. TE & ET (2016)
22. Eras Montaño, E.J.: Realidad aumentada como propuesta metodológica para la enseñanza en un entorno de aprendizaje escolar (Tesis de Licenciatura) (2016)

23. Freitas, R., Campos, P.: SMART: a system of augmented reality for teaching 2nd grade students. In: Proceedings of the 22nd British HCI Group Annual Conference on People and Computers: Culture, Creativity, Interaction-Volume 2, pp. 27–30. BCS Learning & Development Ltd. (2008)

24. Kirner, T.G., Reis, F.M.V., Kirner, C.: Development of an interactive book with augmented reality for teaching and learning geometric shapes. In: 2012 7th Iberian Conference on Information Systems and Technologies (CISTI), pp. 1–6. IEEE (2012)

25. Di Serio, Á., Ibáñez, M.B., Kloos, C.D.: Impact of an augmented reality system on students' motivation for a visual art course. Comput. Educ. **68**, 586–596 (2013). https://doi.org/10.1016/j.compedu.2012.03.002

26. Gutiérrez, R.C., Martínez, M.D.V.D.M., Bravo, J.A.H., Bravo, J.R.H.: Tecnologías emergentes para la enseñanza de las Ciencias Sociales. Una experiencia con el uso de Realidad Aumentada en la formación inicial de maestros. Digit. Educ. Rev. **27**, 138–153 (2015). https://doi.org/10.1344/der.2015.27.138-153

27. Peula, J.M., Zumaquero, J.A., Urdiales, C., Barbancho, A.M., Sandoval, F.: Realidad Aumentada aplicada a herramientas didácticas musicales. Grupo ISIS, Málaga (2007)

28. Delgado, R.G., Parra, N.S., Trujillo, P.M.N.: AR-Learning: libro interactivo basado en realidad aumentada con aplicación a la enseñanza. Tejuelo: Didáctica de la Lengua y la Literatura. Educación **8**, 74–88 (2013)

29. Sánchez, S.Á., Martín, L.D., González, M.Á.G., García, T.M., Menéndez, F.A., Méndez, C.R.: El Arenero Educativo: La Realidad Aumentada un nuevo recurso para la enseñanza. EDMETIC **6**(1), 105–123 (2016). https://doi.org/10.21071/edmetic.v6i1.5810

30. Kerawalla, L., Luckin, R., Seljeflot, S., Woolard, A.: "Making it real": exploring the potential of augmented reality for teaching primary school science. Virtual Reality **10**(3–4), 163–174 (2006). https://doi.org/10.1007/s10055-006-0036-4

31. Fitzmaurice, G.W., Buxton, W.: Graspable user interfaces. University of Toronto (1997)

32. Ishii, H., Ullmer, B.: Tangible bits: towards seamless interfaces between people, bits and atoms. In: Proceedings of the ACM SIGCHI Conference on Human Factors in Computing Systems, pp. 234–241. ACM (1997)

33. Xu, D.: Tangible user interface for children-an overview. In: Proceedings of the UCLAN Department of Computing Conference (2005)

34. Tapia, D.I., Cueli, J.R., García, Ó., Corchado, J.M., Bajo, J., Saavedra, A.: Identificacion por radiofrecuencia: fundamentos y aplicaciones. In: Proceedings de las primeras Jornadas Científicas sobre RFID, Ciudad Real, Spain, pp. 1–5 (2007)

35. Dalim, C.S.C., Dey, A., Piumsomboon, T., Billinghurst, M., Sunar, S.: TeachAR: an interactive augmented reality tool for teaching basic English to non-native children. In: Proceedings of IEEE International Symposium on Mixed and Augmented Reality Adjunct, pp. 344–345 (2016). https://doi.org/10.1109/ISMAR-Adjunct.2016.0046

36. Amaia, A.M., Iñigo, A.L., Jorge, R.L.B., Enara, A.G.: Leihoa: a window to augmented reality in early childhood education. In: 2016 International Symposium on Computers in Education, SIIE 2016: Learning Analytics Technologies (2016). https://doi.org/10.1109/siie.2016.7751836

37. Barreira, J., Bessa, M., Pereira, L.C., Adão, T., Peres, E., Magalhães, L.: MOW: augmented reality game to learn words in different languages: case study: learning English names of animals in elementary school. In: 2012 7th Iberian Conference on Information Systems and Technologies (CISTI), pp. 1–6. IEEE (2012)

38. Martínez, A.A., Benito, J.R.L., González, E.A., Ajuria, E.B.: An experience of the application of augmented reality to learn English in Infant education. In: 2017 International Symposium on Computers in Education (SIIE), pp. 1–6. IEEE (2017). https://doi.org/10.1109/SIIE.2017.8259645

39. Liu, T.Y., Tan, T.H., Chu, Y.L.: 2D barcode and augmented reality supported English learning system. In: Proceedings - 6th IEEE/ACIS International Conference on Computer and Information Science, ICIS 2007; 1st IEEE/ACIS International Workshop on E-Activity, IWEA 2007, (ICIS), pp. 5–10 (2007). https://doi.org/10.1109/ICIS.2007.1

40. Zhou, L., Zhang, S.: Design research and practice of augmented reality textbook. In: 2014 International Conference of Educational Innovation through Technology, pp. 16–20 (2014). https://doi.org/10.1109/EITT.2014.11

41. Yang, M.T., Liao, W.C., Shih, Y.C.: VECAR: virtual English classroom with markerless augmented reality and intuitive gesture interaction. In: Proceedings - 2013 IEEE 13th International Conference on Advanced Learning Technologies, ICALT 2013, pp. 439–440. (2013). https://doi.org/10.1109/ICALT.2013.134

42. Hsieh, M.-C., Koong Lin, H.-C.: A conceptual study for augmented reality e-learning system based on usability evaluation. Commun. Inf. Sci. Manag. Eng. 1(8), 5–7 (2011)

43. Vate-U-Lan, P.: The seed shooting game: an augmented reality 3D pop-up book. In: 2013 2nd International Conference on E-Learning and E-Technologies in Education, ICEEE 2013, pp. 171–175. (2013). https://doi.org/10.1109/ICeLeTE.2013.6644368

44. Llisterri, J.: Las tecnologías del habla: Entre la ingeniería y la lingüística. In: Actas del Congreso Internacional "La Ciencia ante el Público. Cultura humanística y desarrollo científico y tecnológico", Universidad de Salamanca, Instituto Universitario de Estudios de la Ciencia y Tecnología, pp. 44–67 (2003)

45. Lewis, J.R.: IBM computer usability satisfaction questionnaires: psychometric evaluation and instructions for use. Int. J. Hum.-Comput. Interact. 7(1), 57–78 (1995). https://doi.org/10.1080/10447319509526110

Artificial Neural Networks for the Study of Cosmic Rays

Enrique Varela[1,2]([✉]) [iD], Irving Gabriel[2] [iD], Alejandro Quiroz[2] [iD],
Luis Angel Báez[2] [iD], Humberto Salazar[1,2] [iD], and Luis Villaseñor[3] [iD]

[1] Facultad de Ciencias Físico Matemáticas BUAP, Avenida San Claudio
y 18 sur, Colonia San Manuel, Puebla, Mexico
{enrique.varela,humberto.salazar}@correo.buap.mx
[2] Laboratorio Nacional de Supercómputo del Sureste de México (LNS),
Boulevard Valsequillo y Av. Las torres, 72570 Puebla, Mexico
{irving.gabriel,alejandro.quirozf}@correo.buap.mx,
baez@inaoep.mx
[3] Universidad de Morelia, Fray Antonio de Lisboa y Av. Tata Vasco,
Morelia, Mexico
lvillasen@gmail.com

Abstract. In this paper, we use artificial neural networks (ANNs) techniques to reconstruct the mass composition of high energy cosmic rays. We train artificial neural networks using a high-performance computing cluster with 12 Nvidia Tesla V100 GPUs from the Laboratorio Nacional de Supercómputo del Sureste de México (LNS), and a database of approximately *4.8 million* Monte Carlo (MC) simulations of extensive air showers (EAS) using the hadronic interaction model Sibyll 2.3 with two primaries: Protons and Irons, between the energy ranges of 10^{17} to 10^{19} eV. The longitudinal development profile of EAS produced by ultra-high energy cosmic rays carries physical information related to the interaction properties of the primary particles with atmospheric nuclei. We extract from the MC values of the longitudinal profile of air showers trough atmospheric depth on different energy ranges, the variable called Xmax (depth of EAS maximum development), which is strongly correlated with the composition of the primary cosmic ray, in order to predict Xmax values for very high-energy cosmic rays by using ANNs. These methods can be used to train a neural network with real EAS events and predict outcomes where statistical limitations with normal means cannot say much.

Keywords: Artificial neural networks · Cosmic rays · NVIDIA V100

1 Introduction

The study of ultra-high energy cosmic rays (above 10^{17} eV) is performed by large ground-level observatories, such as Pierre Auger Observatory (PAO) located in Mendoza Argentina. The measurements made by their detectors allow the reconstruction of cosmic rays that induce extensive air showers (EAS) when they interact with the nuclei of the atmosphere. The parameters that are analyzed are the arrival

© Springer Nature Switzerland AG 2019
P. H. Ruiz and V. Agredo-Delgado (Eds.): HCI-COLLAB 2019, CCIS 1114, pp. 113–123, 2019.
https://doi.org/10.1007/978-3-030-37386-3_9

direction, its energy, the atmospheric depth where the maximum of the shower was developed and other observables.

Many of the cosmic-ray reconstruction methods are based on Monte Carlo simulations [1] to make more tractable the complex mathematics required. These Monte Carlo methods are used, for example, in the study of the cosmic ray spectrum [2]. Monte Carlo simulations, together with different hadronic interaction models, are also used to determine the mass composition of the primary particle of the cosmic rays [3].

The study of the composition of very high energy cosmic rays is an important to elucidating the not yet well-understood origin of these particles. The atmospheric depth where the longitudinal development of the EAS generated by a primary cosmic ray reaches its maximum generation of secondary particles is called X_{max}. This parameter is an observable sensitive to the mass, i.e., different nuclei/masses have different distributions of X_{max} [4]. In this work, we study, for example, the development of X_{max} as a function of energy.

Astroparticle physics has benefited recently with the emerging computational sciences, such as data science techniques using *machine* and *deep learning* through artificial neural network algorithms (ANNs). Scientists who are experts in the detection and reconstruction of cosmic rays using large observatories placed at ground level are comparing the standard methods to perform the reconstruction of extensive air showers with the new tools from deep learning [5]. In addition, the estimation of the content of muons in the air showers has also benefited from machine and deep learning methods [6]. ANNs are also employed in techniques for the detection of cosmic rays in neutron monitors [7].

2   Input Data for the Artificial Neural Network

2.1   Mass Composition X_{max}

The present work consists of the analysis of simulated events of extensive air showers, EAS, induced by cosmic rays using a back-propagation neural network. We use these novel techniques as a predictive model to determine the X_{max} parameter as a function of energy, the errors involved in the predictions do not depend strongly on the energy of the primaries. In a later work we will use these methods to train a neural network with real data from the PAO observatory to overcome some statistical limitations that appear with the use of normal methods.

In the present work we focus on the study of X_{max}, since, as mentioned, this parameter is sensitive to the composition of the primary cosmic ray so that different primary nuclei have different distributions of X_{max} [4].

2.2   Production of Simulated Events

The first step is the generation of data to be used to train the *ANN;* for this we used two datasets of Monte Carlo simulations (*MC*) of extensive air showers. These MC simulations were created with the CONEX v4r37 code [8, 9], using *Sibyll 2.3* as the particle interaction model [10].

In total we simulated 3×10^5 showers per primary (protons and iron nuclei) for each energy interval separated intervals Log [Energy/eV] = 0.25 covering the range of $10^{17}-10^{19}$ eV.

These MC simulations require a lot of CPU-time and consume many computing resources since each event is simulated on a different computing core, and, the simulation time depends on the energy of the primary; e.g., a MC event of an Iron primary of 10^{17} eV with a thousand showers takes about 2 days to be calculated on an average desktop PC, while a 10^{18} eV event can take a week. So, a high-performance computer with a robust processing capacity is needed to execute the computing jobs in parallel. The MC simulations used for this work were created previously for another research on the CPUs cluster *"Cuetlaxcoapan"* of the *Laboratorio Nacional de Supercómputo del Sureste de México (LNS)* [11], i.e., we use these existing data as input for the present work.

3 Hardware

The computer equipment used to perform the training is the high-performance equipment provided by the LNS. This supercomputer consists of CPUs of the latest generation described below:

IBM Power System AC922, each one with
    2 x POWER9 20-core Processor, 2.4 GHz (3.0 GHz turbo)
    160 threads: x4 per core
    1 TB RAM Memory:
        16 x 64GiB RDIMM DDR4 2666 MHz
    4 x 16 GB SXM2 NVIDIA Tesla V100 GPUs with NVLink Air-Cooled

Each GPU NVIDIA Tesla V100 features:
    GPU Architecture: NVIDIA Volta
    NVIDIA Tensor Cores: 640
    NVIDIA CUDA® Cores: 5,120
    Double-Precision Performance: 7.8 TFLOPS
    Single-Precision Performance: 15.7 TFLOPS
    Tensor Performance: 125 TFLOPS
    GPU Memory: 16GB HBM2
    Memory Bandwidth: 900GB/sec
    Interconnect Bandwidth: 300GB/sec

The LNS has three IBM Power System AC922 servers with 4 *NVIDIA Tesla V100 GPU* each, which can be used to train deep neural networks in parallel with up to 12 GPUs; for this phase of the project we used only one GPU.

Neural network training was performed on both the *POWER9 CPUs* and the *NVIDIA Tesla V100 GPU* using CUDA Cores.

We used previous work [5, 6] as a reference to determine the parameters suitable for the model of our *ANN* and the appropriate hardware for training it. The cited papers were done using an *NVIDIA GeForce GTX 1080 GPU* card, which has 2560 CUDA Cores, 8 GB of memory, and a bandwidth of 320 GB/sec, resulting in a performance of ~ 0.2773 TFLOPS in double precision operations. In comparison, the hardware characteristics and performance of the *Tesla V100 GPUs* greatly exceed in all respects the GTX 1080 cards, with a performance ~ 28 times greater. Based on these comparisons we anticipated to reduce ANN training times considerably below ~ 100 s.

4   Data Preparation

The database used during the analysis is a sample of approximately *4.8 million* data registers described in Sect. 2.2. From this dataset, we extracted only the energy in (Log [Energy/eV]) and the atmospheric depth corresponding to the maximum development of the simulated cosmic rays X_{max} [gr/cm^2].

For the ANN to represent the data accurately, the database was partitioned into secondary sets for training and the subsequent evaluation of the model generated by the ANN. This partition included *samples* that represent the entire behavior, so before splitting the data, all registers from the database were previously randomized [12].

Next, we defined the percentage of data used for network training and validation testing. For the models of networks generated in this work, we used 70% of the total data for the training phase and 30% for the validation phase.

Data normalization is a common practice in the preparation of the information to be processed when an ANN algorithm has more than two variables (columns) with different numerical ranges since the downward gradient converges faster to a local minimum or global minimum, thus avoiding possible oscillations in the loss function during training. This effect can also be noticed in the method called *support vector classification* (SVC), where data need to be scaled for further analysis [13].

We used the Z-score method for standardization which is one of the best methods to compare data from different samples. Using this technique not only provides the ability to rescale the data as typical normalization would, but also groups the data. Z-score standardization is obtained with:

$$z = (x - \mu)/\sigma \tag{1}$$

Where:

x: Data to analyze.
μ: Average.
σ: Standard deviation.

Another benefit of implementing the standardization is the possibility of estimating the distance of the data from the average; this standardization was also applied to the primary energies (LogE).

5   ANN Architecture

We programmed the ANN model in *Python* language, using the *TensorFlow* library and the *Keras* framework, both designed for the creation of machine learning algorithms. This keeps the development environment simple and robust for the modeling of neural networks.

Using mean squared error (MSE) as the loss function, we generated a polynomial regression with an artificial neural network, which underwent multiple design changes throughout the development of the research in order to determine the appropriate number of neurons. We followed this procedure because there is currently no general methodology that, given a problem, establishes a defined neural network architecture [14].

As stated, the loss function is described by the following expression:

$$MSE = \frac{1}{n}\sum\nolimits_{i=1}^{n} (y_i - \tilde{y}_i)^2 \tag{1}$$

n: Number of values.

y: Real value.

ỹ: Predicted value.

The model obtained consists of an input layer with the energy level (LogE) and X_{max} as input data, followed by multiple dense hidden layers (fully connected) with 256, 512 and 1024 perceptrons, which were distributed symmetrically through the network. The output layer is composed of a single perceptron (see Fig. 1).

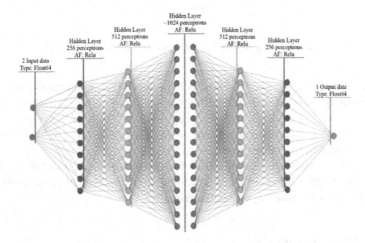

Fig. 1. Schematic of our ANN model including distribution, number of layers and perceptrons corresponding.

For our implementation of the regression *ANN*, we used a single independent variable. We tested designs of *2048, 1024, 832, 512, 256, 128, 100* and up *32* neurons for the hidden layers, distributed between *1* and *6* hidden layers, to define the best model to develop. After testing these different combinations we found no noticeable differences between error and error validation during the training of these models, and due to the great increase in time required to do so, i.e., proportional to the total number of neurons in the network, we decided to use the described architecture.

It was essential to determine the optimal number of perceptrons and layers in the network to prevent the ANN from *"memorizing"* the data with a reduction in its predicting ability (overfitting) in one extreme, or to render the model uncapable of representing the behavior of the data (underfitting) in the other extreme. We indeed found that a smaller number of perceptrons produced larger errors (underfitting), and, on the other hand, a larger number gave rise to increasing training times (overfitting) (see Fig. 2).

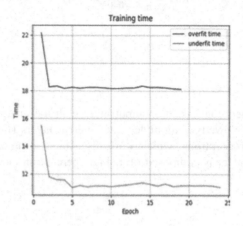

Fig. 2. Training time in seconds per epoch for each model.

Between each perceptron layer of the network, an activation function is used, which adds non-linearity to the model, and in this way, it is possible to learn more complex patterns. This function applies to both the entry layer and the hidden layers. As already mentioned, a linear regression algorithm is implemented, then a linear activation function is applied to the output layer.

The activation function used was *ReLU* (rectified linear unit), which is widely used nowadays and exhibits good results by avoiding the *vanishing gradient* problem that causes a slow learning rate on regression networks.

6 Training Parameters

The *epochs* are the number of times the regression is performed and define the proportion with which the network learns with each iteration of the weight adjustment of the perceptrons: few epochs tend to lead to the problem of *underfitting*, and too many, to *overfitting*.

A variable quantity of *epochs* was used when establishing a training stop function, which was activated when there was no decrease in the training error (loss) or the validation loss during 10 epochs. After training the model, it was determined that 21 epochs were appropriate to reach a minimum in the validation error.

The batch size is an option that can be modified at the training phase in order to determine the number of samples that will be propagated through the network for its training at the same time. We used an adequate batch size to optimize the use of RAM memory on the supercomputer that we used for the training process. Taking into account the large RAM memory of the hardware used, as well as the complexity of the ANN, given that the training process was performed with 1,674,418 samples, we experimented with batch sizes in values from 32 samples up to 10,000 samples. We decided to use the latter value for training.

Since a higher number of samples can deteriorate the quality of the model and its ability to generalize [15], an increase in the number of epochs was required to validate the errors compared to the errors obtained with much smaller batch sizes. This effect was compensated by decreasing the training time per epoch; i.e., the number of epochs that would take the network to be trained with a batch size of 512 increased by a factor of up to 1.3 times, but the training time per epoch was ~ 2.8 times faster.

7 Tests with Similar Databases

Once the network architecture was established and after having settled the parameters for training, we tested with datasets generated randomly through a program in Python language with the Numpy library. The first dataset had one million points with a range of 0 to 7 for the x-axis, and a range of -20 to 20 for the y-axis. A sinusoidal function was introduced for the generation of the data, thus preventing the data from being created with a linear distribution. The second database had two million points. For the x-axis, there is a value range of 0 to 2.3 and for the y-axis a range of 512 to 524. Again, a sinusoidal function was introduced for the data generator.

Figure 3 illustrates the results of network training for each dataset. Notice that the network identified the data following a non-linear behavior. In addition, it successfully learned the overall distribution of the data because, although the database had random values, its distribution was uniform in the established range. Additionally, we confirmed that the network did not present overfitting since it was able to predict the direction of values outside the range of the training data.

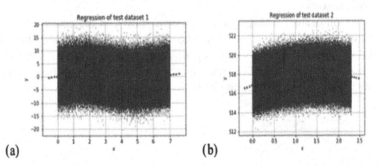

Fig. 3. Polynomial regression and data prediction, (a) first database with the wide sine function, (b) second database with a short sine function.

The number of epochs used for the network to learn the behavior of each dataset was 34 and 52 epochs respectively.

8   Results

Figure 4 shows the scheme of procedures performed during the different phases of our work.

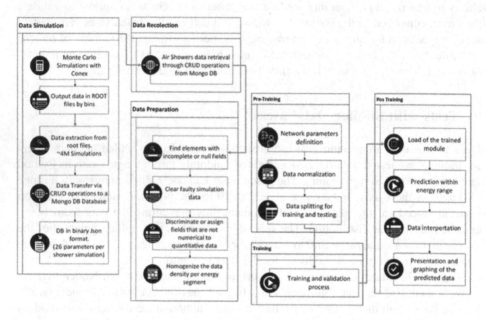

Fig. 4. Scheme of the procedures performed through the present research project.

Using the proposed ANN architecture and with the described training parameters, the network was trained to generate, at first instance, the polynomial regression of extensive air showers.

The evolution of the network training process shows, in the case of this database, that overfitting occurs. Figure 5 displays the training error (loss) and the validation error (val_loss) against the number of epochs. This error, in turn, is the difference between the estimated value and the real value. Overfitting occurs when the validation error is much higher than the training error.

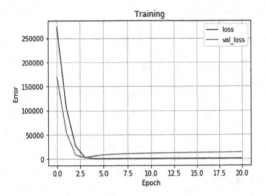

Fig. 5. Training evolution, it can be shown if there is overfitting.

Figures 6 and 7 exhibit the difference between MC's X_{max} and the X_{max} predicted by the ANN, for MC events simulated using Sibyll 2.3 as the hadronic model for both primary protons and iron nuclei, respectively.

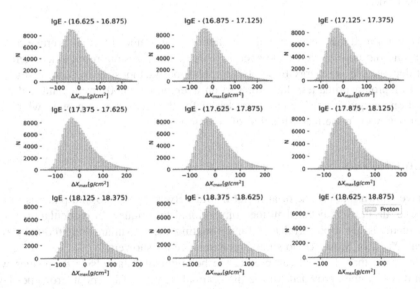

Fig. 6. Difference between *input X_{max}* and *predicted X_{max}*, by energy intervals for extensive air showers generated by a primary cosmic ray of *Proton*, simulated with the hadronic model Sibyll.

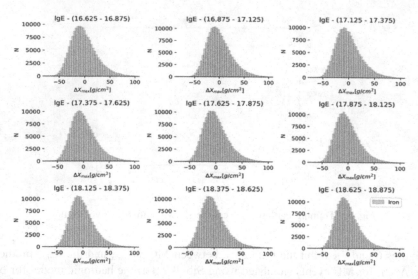

Fig. 7. Difference between *input X_{max}* minus *predicted X_{max}*, by energy intervals for extensive air showers generated by iron nuclei as primary cosmic rays, simulated with Sibyll as the hadronic model.

We confirmed that the error in the prediction of iron nuclei had an average of 9.00 gr/cm² and did not depend on the energy. This is an interesting result since there is a direct dependence on energy by applying traditional methods. In the case of the prediction of proton primaries, the error had an average of 23.00 gr/cm² and it did not depend on energy either. The error was larger for the prediction of proton, which is a known behavior in the reconstruction of cosmic rays.

9   Conclusions

We have shown that the use of artificial neural networks helps to find patterns in MC extensive air showers better than the conventional techniques. In particular, we have ANN methods are a powerful tool for estimating the maximum longitudinal development, X_{max}, of Monte Carlo simulated extensive air showers.

We found that an ANN can predict the behavior of data outside the values with which it was trained provided we use the optimal number of layers, neurons per layer and epochs. For instance, if the number of neurons is not large enough, the ANN cannot be adjusted to the data; likewise if the number of epochs is rather large but the data provided are small the ANN could overfit the known data but it would be unable to make predictions based on new data.

Even though this work uses a rather simple ANN with few input parameters, our method describes the patterns present in the simulated data and it can be adapted and applied to a broad spectrum of primary nuclei and energies of the MC simulated primary cosmic rays. In subsequent work we will use more complex ANNs and will test them with real data.

This approach will be most useful to extract X_{max} for the real cosmic ray events of the highest energies where the number of events is small. Therefore, our final conclusion is that Artificial Neural Networks and Deep Learning methods are promising tools to study the mysteries of ultra-high energy cosmic rays.

Acknowledgments. *The authors thankfully acknowledge computer resources, technical advice and support provided by Laboratorio Nacional de Supercómputo del Sureste de México (LNS), a member of the CONACYT national laboratories.*

References

1. Dunn, W.L., Shultis, J.K.: The basis of Monte Carlo. Explor. Monte Carlo Methods 21–46 (2012). https://doi.org/10.1016/b978-0-444-51575-9.00002-6
2. Abu-Zayyad, T., et al.: The cosmic-ray energy spectrum observed with the surface detector of the telescope array experiment. Astrophys. J. Lett. **768**(1), L1 (2013). https://doi.org/10.1088/2041-8205/768/1/l1
3. Carvalho Jr., W.R., Alvarez-Muñiz, J.: Determination of cosmic-ray primary mass on an event-by-event basis using radio detection. Astropart. Phys. **109**, 41–49 (2019). https://doi.org/10.1016/j.astropartphys.2019.02.005
4. Gaisser, T.K., Hillas, A.M.: Reliability of the method of constant intensity cuts for reconstructing the average development of vertical showers. In: Proceedings 15th International Cosmic Ray Conference, vol. 8, pp. 353–357 (1977)
5. Erdmann, M., Glombitza, J., Walz, D.: A deep learning-based reconstruction of cosmic ray-induced air showers. Astropart. Phys. **97**, 46–53 (2018). https://doi.org/10.1016/j.astropartphys.2017.10.006
6. Guillén, A., et al.: Deep learning techniques applied to the physics of extensive air showers. Astropart. Phys. **111**, 12–22 (2019). https://doi.org/10.1016/j.astropartphys.2019.03.001
7. Paschalis, P., Sarlanis, C., Mavromichalaki, H.: Artificial neural network approach of cosmic ray primary data processing. Solar Phys. **282**(1), 303–318 (2012). https://doi.org/10.1007/s11207-012-0125-3
8. Bergmann, T., et al.: One-dimensional hybrid approach to extensive air shower simulation. Astroparticle Phys. **26**(6), 420–432 (2007). https://doi.org/10.1016/j.astropartphys.2006.08.005
9. Pierog, T., et al.: First results of fast one-dimensional hybrid simulation of EAS using conex. Nuclear Phys. B – Proc. Suppl. **151**(1), 159–162 (2006). https://doi.org/10.1016/j.nuclphysbps.2005.07.029
10. Ahn, E., Engel, R., Gaisser, T.K., Lipari, P., Stanev, T.: Cosmic ray interaction event generator SIBYLL 2.1. Phys. Rev. D **80**(9), 094003 (2009). https://doi.org/10.1103/physrevd.80.094003
11. Laboratorio Nacional de Supercómputo del Sureste de México - LNS. Benemérita Universidad Autónoma de Puebla (n.d.). http://www.lns.org.mx/
12. Brownlee, J.: Deep Learning with Python: Develop Deep Learning Models on Theano and TensorFlow Using Keras. Machine Learning Mastery (2016)
13. Hsu, C.W., Chang, C.C., Lin, C.J.: A practical guide to support vector classification (2003). http://ntur.lib.ntu.edu.tw/bitstream/246246/2006092712291477314/1/guide.pdf
14. Stathakis, D.: How many hidden layers and nodes? Int. J. Remote Sens. **30**(8), 2133–2147 (2009). https://doi.org/10.1080/01431160802549278
15. Keskar, N.S., Mudigere, D., Nocedal, J., Smelyanskiy, M., Tang, P.T.: On large-batch training for deep learning: generalization gap and sharp minima (2016). https://arxiv.org/abs/1609.04836

Automation of Usability Inspections for Websites

Gabriel Elías Chanchí Golondrino[1]([✉]) [iD], Daniela Pérez Oliveros[2] [iD],
and Wilmar Yesid Campo Muñoz[3] [iD]

[1] Universidad de Cartagena, Cartagena, Bolívar, Colombia
gchanchig@unicartagena.edu.co
[2] Institución Universitaria Colegio Mayor del Cauca, Popayán, Cauca, Colombia
danielaperez@unimayor.edu.co
[3] Universidad del Quindío, Armenia, Quindío, Colombia
wycampo@uniquindio.edu.co

Abstract. To allow website portals to be designed according to the functional needs of users, the concept of usability has gained great importance in recent years. In this sense, according to ISO 9241-11, usability focuses on fulfilling a user's objectives with effectiveness, efficiency, and satisfaction. At usability level in websites, a set of usability inspection heuristic tests exists, such as Torres-Burriel, which, based on a set of usability criteria and heuristics, allows identifying typical usability problems. In spite of the above, execution of these types of usability tests does not only involve the inspection and evaluation of the criteria, but also the processing and analysis of the data, given that the templates for these tests are usually found in text documents. In this paper, we propose as a contribution, a software system to inspect the usability of websites, which allows evaluating the criteria associated with the heuristics and the graphic analysis of the heuristics evaluated. This software system seeks to support developers and experts to carry out usability inspections on websites.

Keywords: Inspection · Software system · Usability · Usability test · Web applications

1 Introduction

Website portals are currently the simplest and most widespread way people and companies have to publicize information about a product or service. In relation to the aforementioned, it is necessary for these sites to comply and agree with what users expect to find in them, in such a way that it manages to capture their attention without ignoring the main idea for which the website was created [1]. Due to this, the concept of usability has gained strength with the objective of users being able to fulfill their expectations of use adequately in applications in different application contexts. According to the ISO 9241-11 standard, usability is understood as the degree in which a product can be used by specific users to achieve specific objectives with effectiveness, efficiency, and satisfaction within a given context of use [2].

© Springer Nature Switzerland AG 2019
P. H. Ruiz and V. Agredo-Delgado (Eds.): HCI-COLLAB 2019, CCIS 1114, pp. 124–137, 2019.
https://doi.org/10.1007/978-3-030-37386-3_10

Various methods of web usability inspection exist among which we can highlight the heuristic test by Sirius [3] and the Torres-Burriel test [4], which, from the definition of heuristics and usability criteria, permit identifying common usability problems in different types of websites. The heuristics defined for websites in both evaluation tests mentioned, start from the general-purpose heuristics by Nielsen and are specified to the context of the websites [5]. These two types of tests define a different evaluation scale for each of the evaluation criteria considered, permitting to obtain statistics by using documents or spreadsheets, making it necessary for the evaluator to draw graphics manually on the compliance of heuristics in websites. The importance of executing these evaluation methods lies in obtaining recommendations on the website portal evaluated, permitting to provide feedback to the quality of the product software [6]. Although both website usability tests are similar regarding the heuristics and criteria proposed, the website usability test by Torres-Burriel can be considered more complete by bearing in mind a set of accessibility criteria, a currently fundamental element, to guarantee that a greater number of people can access a website independent of the context of use [7]. Thus, in this paper the heuristics of Torres-Burriel are considered, taking into account that they address the main elements of a website, including aspects related to accessibility.

This article proposes a software system for usability inspection for web applications, considering the usability test by Torres-Burriel [4]. This system permits evaluating the compliance of a set of criteria associated with the eleven heuristics of the test (general aspects, identification and information, language and drafting, labeling, navigation structure, page layout, search, multimedia elements, help, accessibility, and control and feedback), obtaining a graphic report on the percentage of compliance and the evaluation average obtained for each heuristic. The software system seeks to become a support to conduct usability inspections on website portals, to identify different elements to improve of usability of a website portal. The rest of the article is organized in the following manner: Sect. 2 presents the different phases of the methodology used for this research; Sect. 3 presents a set of concepts considered to develop this work; Sect. 4 describes the functional structure of the usability inspection software system; Sect. 5 presents a case study conducted through the software system on the website portal of the Government of Cauca; finally, Sect. 6 presents the conclusions and future work derived from this research.

2 Methodology

To develop and validate the software system for the usability inspection of websites, the following phases were considered, namely, exploration of the usability test by Torres-Burriel, design of the inspection software system, implementation of the inspection software system, and case study (see Fig. 1).

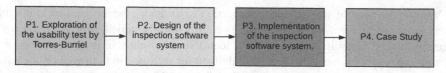

Fig. 1. Proposed methodology

Phase 1 - Exploration of the Usability Test by Torres-Burriel: this phase conducted a detailed study of each of the guidelines and criteria present in the usability test by Torres-Burriel. This was done to identify the different heuristics and criteria, as well as the format of the template used to conduct the test.

Phases 2 and 3 - Design and Development of the Software System: starting from the criteria obtained in the Torres-Burriel test and revising its structure in the document in which it is proposed, a software system was designed and developed using a system of tabs, each of which is associated with a Torres-Burriel heuristic.

Phase 4: Case study: once the software system was generated to evaluate the usability of websites, the portal of the Government of Cauca was chosen, given that by being a government-type portal, it must guarantee usability and accessibility conditions necessary considering the amount of visitors.

3   Conceptual Framework

This section includes a set of relevant concepts considered to carry out this work. These are: usability, usability test, usability test by Torres-Burriel.

3.1   Usability

Usability is understood according to ISO 9241-11 as the measure in which a system, product, or service can be used by specific users to achieve specific objectives with effectiveness, efficiency, and satisfaction within a specific context of use [1]. Likewise, it may be defined as the discipline that studies the way of designing websites for users to interact with them more easily, comfortably, and intuitively [8]. A usability test comprises a series of practices and tests performed on an application or a website to test the comfort, ease or complexity with which it is managed. Expert users or conventional users who explore in detailed manner the functionalities of the interactive system can carry out these tests. The results of the interaction of the users are consigned in a test that accounts for the usability of the software system evaluated [9]. In this work an application for the execution of usability evaluations based on the inspection of Torres-Burriel heuristics is proposed.

3.2   Heuristic Test of Torres-Burriel

Torres-Burriel propose a set of heuristics to evaluate websites, which contain the most relevant aspects to keep in mind at usability level, where for each heuristic presented a set of criteria to evaluate is provided within a range from 1 to 5 [4]. These are posed in terms of questions. Said heuristics retake some of the elements proposed in the principles by Nielsen, so that they are distributed in 11 heuristics, as shown in Table 1 [10].

Table 1. Torres-Burriel heuristics

Heuristic	Description
H1: General aspects	Aspects related with the objectives of the website, correct and easy remembrance of the external and internal URLs, adequate organization and structure of the contents in addition to using clear language, concise and familiar to the user
H2: Identification and information	Evaluates aspects related with site identity, as well as the mechanisms to contact the company, protection of personal data and authorship of contents
H3: Language and drafting	Refers to whether the website speaks the same language as the user
H4: Labeling	Expresses elements related with the meaning, adequate use and familiarity of content labels
H5: Structure and navigation	Elements referring to adequate organization, disposition, and structure of information, besides the navigation of the site
H6: Page layout	Aspects related with the distribution and appearance of the navigation elements and contents in the interface
H7: Search	Evaluates aspects referring to the search system implemented in the website related to ease of access, as well as elements related with the effectiveness of searches
H8: Multimedia elements	Aspects related with the adjustment level of the website portal's multimedia contents
H9: Help	Aspects related with the help available to users during their navigation on the site
H10: Accessibility	Aspects related with any user's ease of use of web pages, which evaluate elements with respect to font size, type, and color, weight of page, compatibility with different browsers and elements that permit navigating comfortably
H11: Control and feedback	Aspects related with the user's freedom to undo or redo actions in the navigation, as well as timely and clear information provided to them in their interaction with the website portal

In keeping with the aforementioned, Table 2 introduces the amount of criteria associated to each of the heuristics presented in Table 1. As mentioned, said criteria are presented to the evaluator in terms of questions.

Table 2. Criteria per heuristic of the test by Torres-Burriel

Heuristic	Number of criteria
H1: General aspects	9
H2: Identity and information	7
H3: Language and drafting	4
H4: Labeling	5
H5: Structures and navigation	11
H6: Page layout	7
H7: Search	6
H8: Multimedia elements	4
H9: Help	4
H10: Accessibility	8
H11: Control and feedback	6

4 Proposed Software System

The software system introduced in this work stemmed from a set of usability criteria associated with each of the 11 heuristics proposed by Torres-Burriel (Table 2). These criteria are presented in terms of questions and can be evaluated in a range from 0 to 5, with 0 being the absence of the criterion in the website portal and 5 being maximum compliance of the criterion within the portal. At design level, the software system is based on tabs, each of which comprises a heuristic and its associated criteria.

According to the aforementioned, the software system proposed is constituted by 15 tabs organized in the following manner: the first tab consigns the general data of the usability evaluation; tabs 2 to 12 include each of the usability heuristics and their associated criteria; tab 13 presents a table with the average obtained in each of the heuristics evaluated and the general average of the heuristics; tab 14 includes a graphic with the averages of each principle; finally, tab 15 presents a graphic with the percentage of compliance of each of the heuristics by Torres-Burriel.

A flow diagram illustrating the functioning of the software system is presented in Fig. 2. As observed in Fig. 2, the software system allows reviewers to evaluate one-to-one the different criteria associated with the standard's accessibility principles to, subsequently, generate statistics of the mean value per accessibility principle and of the percentage of compliance of each principle of the application to inspect. In summary, according to Fig. 2, the functionality of the tabs is grouped into three: the first instance is related with filling out the test data (first tab); the second instance includes the evaluation of the criteria of the eleven heuristics (tabs 2 to 12); and the third instance contains that related with the analysis of the statistical results and graphics of the evaluation conducted. The results obtained seek to guide evaluators on those heuristics that the website portal evaluated is not complying fully.

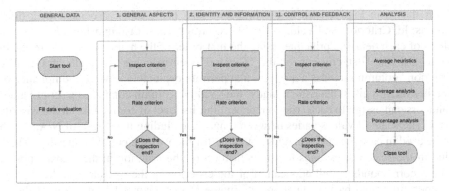

Fig. 2. Functional diagram of the software system

To comply with the idea presented in Fig. 2, a software system was constructed in Java language through tabs and with different tables per tab, using JTabbedPane (Swing class) and JTable components (see Fig. 3). Regarding the generation of the analysis graphics, the software system uses the JFreeChart library [11], which in this case permits obtaining bar graphs on the average of the evaluations per principle and their percentage of compliance.

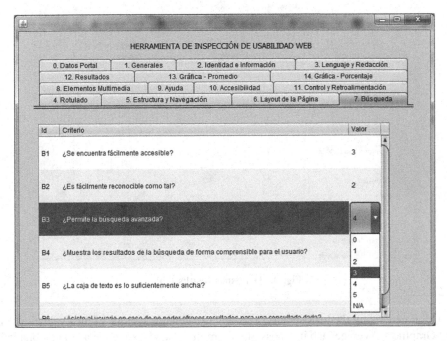

Fig. 3. Heuristics evaluation tabs

As shown in Fig. 3, each of the first four tabs has a table associated with three columns: Id, Criterion, and Value. The "Id" column permits distinguishing the different criteria of each heuristic principle, using the first letter of the heuristic and a number. In that regard, the first criterion of the "General" heuristic has the code of G1. The "Criterion" column includes a question that permits evaluators to verify compliance of the criterion of a given heuristic. Finally, the "Value" column comprises a set of values evaluators can assign to each criterion, depending its level of compliance in the website portal. The scale of values varies between 0 and 5, including the option of N/A, which can be used in case the criterion does not apply for the website portal in question. The 0 value in the scale corresponds to no application of the criterion in the website portal, while 5 corresponds to full application of the criterion in the website portal.

Upon filling out basic evaluation data (name of evaluator, URL of site to evaluate, and evaluation description) and ending the inspection by the different heuristics and usability criteria proposed by Torres-Burriel, it is possible to see in the "Results" tab the average obtained in each of the heuristics and general average obtained in the usability inspection (see Fig. 4). The average obtained within each of the heuristics permits evaluators to identify aspects of the web application that do not comply adequately with the usability criteria.

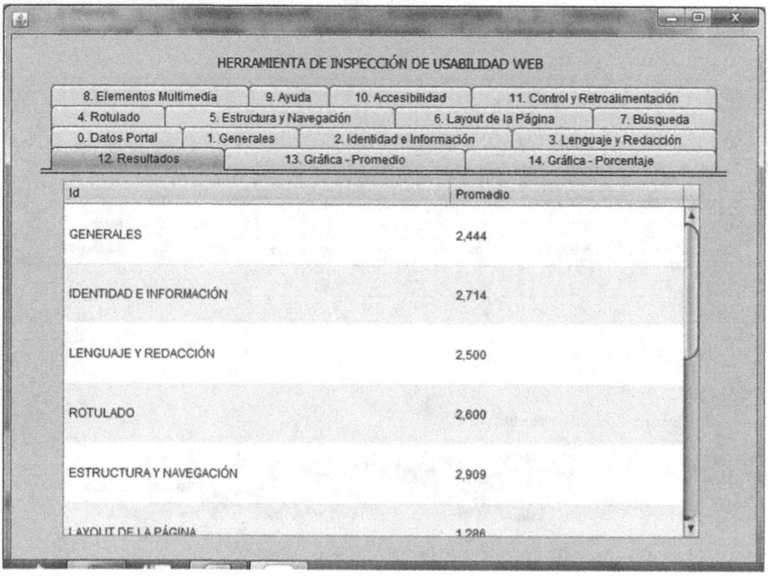

Fig. 4. Heuristics results tab

Upon generating the heuristic averages and the general average of the evaluation, in the "Graphic – Average" tab it is possible to graphically visualize the average obtained by each of the usability heuristics for websites proposed by Torres-Burriel (see Fig. 5).

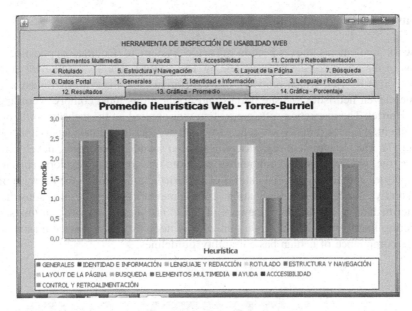

Fig. 5. "Graphic – Average" tab

Likewise, in the "Graphic – Percentage" tab, it is possible to visualize the graphic with the percentage of compliance of each of the usability heuristics for websites proposed by Torres-Burriel (see Fig. 6).

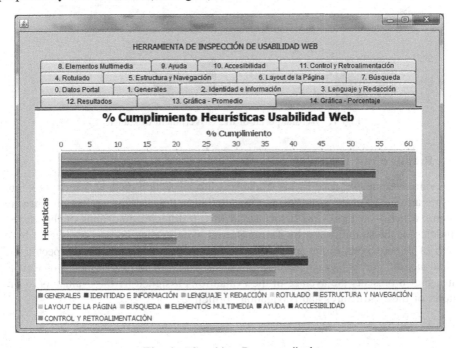

Fig. 6. "Graphic - Percentage" tab

5   Case Study

This work implements the inspection software system to facilitate application and analysis of the results of the heuristic test by Torres-Burriel and validate the heuristic test by Torres-Burriel, which proposes in its different tabs a set of criteria associated with the eleven heuristics website portals and applications must comply according to Torres-Burriel. The inspection software system was applied on the website portal of the Government of Cauca (http://www.cauca.gov.co/) in order to evaluate the usability of it (see Fig. 7). The Government of Cauca aims to plan social and economic development, promote the welfare of the community, promote the integral development of its municipalities and other territorial entities of its jurisdiction, through the exercise of its administrative functions of coordination, complementarity, concurrence, subsidiarity and intermediation, within the framework of the Constitution and laws. In this sense, considering the diversity of the target public, it is necessary to guarantee inasmuch as possible compliance of certain basic usability guidelines.

Fig. 7. Website portal of the Government of Cauca

5.1   Results of the Inspection

The evaluation method used in this article was the inspection method, which took into consideration each of the usability criteria included in the usability evaluation software system, which – in turn – are associated with the different guidelines of the eleven heuristics of the usability test by Torres-Burriel. The evaluation was conducted by a group of three experts in the area of human computer interaction, who inspected the compliance of Torres-Burriel's heuristics on the portal of the Government of Cauca. Thus, Fig. 8 presents the average of the evaluations assigned by the evaluators to the criteria of the " Structures and Navigation" principle.

Upon finishing the inspection of the Government of Cauca web page and considering the different criteria by Torres-Burriel, Fig. 9 presents one of the graphic results obtained by the usability inspection software system for web pages, which shows the average of the evaluations obtained for each of the eleven heuristics evaluated.

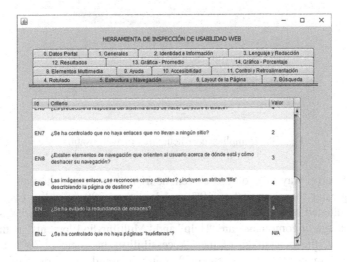

Fig. 8. Evaluation by experts

It may be noted that the portal is poorly usable, considering the inspection results, given that only one of its principles (General) reaches an average slightly above 4 (4.11) in a scale from 1 to 5, remaining <4 in the rest of the heuristics evaluated, which in mathematical terms means that only one of the heuristics achieves more than 80 percent compliance. Likewise, it is possible to analyze that six of the eleven heuristics evaluated have a compliance percentage greater than or equal to 70% and less than

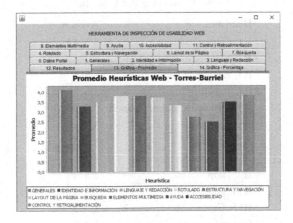

Fig. 9. Average graphic of the heuristics

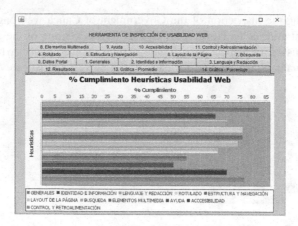

Fig. 10. Compliance of heuristics of web usability

80%. In the same way two of the eleven heuristics evaluated have a compliance percentage greater than or equal to 60% and less than 70%. Finally, two of the 11 heuristics evaluated have a compliance rate of less than 60%. The heuristics with the lowest percentage of compliance are "Help" and "Multimedia Elements" with less than 56%. Similarly, the percentage of the "Accessibility" heuristic is 70%, considered acceptable and in need of improvement, bearing in mind the variety of the public accessing the government portal evaluated (see Fig. 10).

Finally, the general usability average for the website portal is 3.466, corresponding to 69.32% compliance (see Table 3). It is convenient to consider different usability criteria for the portal to have a value >80%, which can be deemed acceptable. Thus, the inspection of the portal of the Government of Cauca helps to generate a set of recommendations keeping in mind the averages per heuristics (see Table 3), which seek to be of help to generate possible improvements, considering the number and diversity of users accessing these types of government portals.

Table 3. Average per heuristic

Heuristics	Average
H1: General aspects	4.111
H2: Identity e information	3.286
H3: Language and drafting	3.5
H4: Labeling	3.8
H5: Structures and navigation	3.8
H6: Page layout	3.714
H7: Search	3.333
H8: Multimedia elements	2.75
H9: Help	2.5
H10: Accessibility	3.5
H11: Control and feedback	3.833
General average	**3.466**

5.2 Recommendations

Pursuant to the inspection conducted of the portal of the Government of Cauca, this section presents a set of recommendations (obtained by the test coordinator) for the eleven heuristics evaluated and considering the criteria obtaining the lowest value through the assessment of the evaluators (see Table 4).

Table 4. Recommendations of usability generated

Heuristic	Recommendation
H2: Identity and Information	• It is suggested to include an additional mechanism to the PQRS, so that the citizen can contact the government of Cauca • It is suggested to present information on data protection on the portal • It is suggested to include the information of the date and the author of the different articles and news presented in the web portal
H4: Labeling	• It is suggested to include a title in all sub-pages of the web portal
H5: Structure and Navigation	• It is suggested to correct the broken links in the different portal options. Example: "Citizen Participation" • It is suggested to include the breadcrumb functionality in the different views of the portal
H6: Page Layout	• It is suggested to present the text information of the different sub-pages more concisely • It is suggested to improve the distribution of images in the articles and news of the web portal
H7: Search	• It is recommended that the search bar be more recognizable and/or distinguishable to the user • It is recommended to improve the width of the search bar in the web portal
H8: Multimedia elements	• It is recommended to improve the control by the user of the cyclic animation of the portal (forward, backward, stop) • It is recommended to present more relevant and updated information in the cyclical animation, given its visual hierarchy
H9: Help	• It is suggested to increase the number of frequently asked questions, so that they include the different procedures of the web portal • It is suggested to include frequently asked questions in a more visible section of the web portal • It is suggested to include contextual help within the forms of the web portal
H10: Accessibility	• It is suggested to improve the distribution of the elements of the page when printing it • It is suggested to use the alt attribute in the images of the different sub-pages • It is suggested to improve the font size and contrast in the different sub-pages of the portal

6   Conclusions and Future Work

The principal contribution of this research is to propose a software system for the usability inspection of web applications, keeping in mind the usability test by Torres-Burriel. This software system seeks to support developers, designers, and programmers in evaluating websites to construct more inclusive and usable websites.

The principal contribution of the software system proposed is the possibility of evaluating each of the criteria associated with the heuristics by Torres-Burriel, as well as automatically generating the graphic of averages and the graphic of percentage of compliance of the heuristics by Torres-Burriel. The above indicators are intended to be helpful in terms of improving the overall design of the evaluated portal and the increase in its number of potential users.

It is worth highlighting that portals, like that of the Government of Cauca, when aimed at a broad and diverse public, must pay great attention to heuristic criteria such as accessibility and help to enable inclusion and access to different users, independent of the context of use.

The Java language proved adequate to implement an inspection software system, bearing in mind the tab management component (JTabbedPane), the table management component (JTable), and the API to generate JFreeChart statistical graphics.

In reflection, it is important to highlight that given that many governmental website portals have been created by using content managers, the websites constructed through these bring along diverse usability problems that do not necessarily depend on the webpage designer, given that these managers were mostly conceived without considering usability criteria.

For future work derived from this research, the software system should include the possibility of generating automatic recommendations arising from the statistic results and graphics obtained in the test.

References

1. Jiménez, K., Pérez, D., Rengifo, S.: Propuesta de una evaluación heurística de accesibilidad para sitios web basada NTC 5854. Obras Colectivas en Ciencias de la Computación, Cali, Colombia, pp. 53–68 (2018)
2. Sánchez, W.: La usabilidad en Ingeniería de Software: definición y características. Rev. Ingeniería Innov. Fac. Ingeniería – Univ. Don Bosco 1(2), 7–21 (2011)
3. Suarez, M.C.: Sistema de evaluación de la usabilidad web orientado al usuario y basado en la determinación de tareas críticas. Editorial Universidad de Oviedo, Oviedo-España (2011)
4. Torres-Burriel Estudio: Test heurístico de Torres-Burriel. http://www.torresburriel.com/weblog/2008/11/28/plantilla-para-hacer-analisis-heuristicos-de-usabilidad/
5. Sánchez, J., Zapata, C., Jiménez, J.: Evaluación heurística de usabilidad de software para facilitar el uso del computador a personas en situación de discapacidad motriz. Revista EIA 14(27), 63–72 (2017). https://doi.org/10.24050/reia.v14i27.785
6. Covella, G.: Medición y evaluación de calidad en uso de aplicaciones web. Editorial Universidad Nacional de la Plata, La Plata-Argentina (2005). https://doi.org/10.35537/10915/4082

7. Idrobo, C., Vidal, M., Chanchí, G.E.: Guía de accesibilidad para el diseño e implementación de sitios web teniendo en cuenta la norma NTC 5854. In: Solano, A., Ordoñez, H. (eds.) Advances in Computing, pp. 572–585 (2017). https://doi.org/10.1007/978-3-319-66562-7_41

8. Yusef, H.: Introducción a la Usabilidad. Revista No Solo Usabilidad 1 (2002)

9. Gómez, M.: Test de usabilidad en entornos de Realidad Virtual. Revista No Solo Usabilidad 17 (2018)

10. Hurtado S., Pimentel, J., Chanchí, G.E.: Estudio comparativo de métodos de evaluación de usabilidad para sitios web. Desarrollo e Innovación en Ingeniería, Medellín, Colombia, pp. 129–136 (2018). https://doi.org/10.5281/zenodo.2613975

11. Librería JFreeChart. http://www.jfree.org/jfreechart/

Children Detection on Passenger Seat Using UCD and IDP: An Initial Prototype

William Castañeda Almaraz[1]([⊠]) [iD], Huizilopoztli Luna-García[1] [iD],
José M. Celaya-Padilla[2] [iD], Hamurabi Gamboa-Rosales[1] [iD],
Ricardo Mendoza-González[3] [iD], Jorge I. Galván-Tejada[1] [iD],
Carlos E. Galván-Tejada[1] [iD], Joyce S. A. Lozano-Aguilar[1] [iD],
and Roberto Solís-Robles[1] [iD]

[1] Centro de Investigación e Innovación Automotriz de México (CIIAM),
Universidad Autónoma de Zacatecas, Jardín Juárez 147, Centro,
98000 Zacatecas, Zac, Mexico
{williamcasta58, hlugar, hamurabigr, gatejo, ericgalvan,
joyce_lozag, rsolis}@uaz.edu.mx
[2] CONACYT, Centro de Investigación e Innovación Automotriz de México
(CIIAM), Universidad Autónoma de Zacatecas, Jardín Juárez 147, Centro,
98000 Zacatecas, Zac, Mexico
jose.celaya@uaz.edu.mx
[3] Tecnológico Nacional de México, Instituto Tecnológico de Aguascalientes,
Av. Adolfo López Mateos # 1801 Ote. Fracc. Bona Gens,
20256 Aguascalientes, Ags, Mexico
mendozagric@mail.ita.mx

Abstract. The negligence of drivers when carrying children on passenger vehicle occupants is a latent problem and it causes a lot of human losses. Due to the restraining children in rear seats instead of front seats reduces fatal injury risk by three-quarters for children up to age 3. The present research describes the development of an initial prototype using the User-Centered Design (UCD) development methodology and Digital Image Processing (DIP) to low level to identify people by detecting facial features. The aim of this prototype is to reduce the number of minor and lethal injuries that a child could have at the time of a vehicular accident. This initial prototype was evaluated by 30 drivers of which 14 were accompanied by a child. The results obtained from prototype specifications are composing of a visual-hearing alert which is activated when a child is detected on the passenger-seat and this indicates to change the child un a safe place.

Keywords: Prototype · Visual alert · Hearing alert · User Centered Design (UCD) · Image Digital Processing (IDP)

1 Introduction

Today the negligence of citizens in driving is not a recent problem, this has been happening since 1900 when the first car accidents occurred, this is because companies started to produce vehicles in assembly chains, lowering prices and popularizing and

© Springer Nature Switzerland AG 2019
P. H. Ruiz and V. Agredo-Delgado (Eds.): HCI-COLLAB 2019, CCIS 1114, pp. 138–149, 2019.
https://doi.org/10.1007/978-3-030-37386-3_11

boosting cars use [1]. However, it does not mean that no accidents have occurred before, the first car accident with fatal consequences was in 1896, as a result the first speeding ticket was imposed [2]. The negligence of drivers who do not take children to a correct place or do not have the necessary and appropriate equipment for the safety of minors, road traffic accidents have been the leading cause of death among children, human losses and serious injury to those involved, prematurely lost years, have been generated for decades, emotional damage, among others. Data from the National Council for Accident Prevention (CNPA) in Mexico informed car accidents are the leading cause of death among children aged 4 to 12, and points out that 50% of car deaths could be avoided if the child had been fitted with safety equipment suitable for his age and weight [3]. A study conducted by the World Health Organization (WHO) and UNICEF reported that more of 2000 children die each day from unintended injuries, and millions of injured children are disabled every year [4]. For the above, this article aims to develop a prototype to detect children on passenger seat and this persuades drivers about the child is in danger, in this way, we can reduce the amount of injuries an infant could suffer from a vehicular accident. We use the technique of Image Digital Processing to Low Level to detect children on passenger seat locating biometric points of interest, through which they were extracted information.

2   Related Works

Nowadays, there are several systems focused on the children detection as passenger seat, below we describe the three most relevant works. (A) A system integrated by sensors that automatically detects the presence of a child in the passenger seat, and it classifies people according to their physiology (weight, size) [5]; (B) The Bosch company created a control module integrated called "iBolt" which communicates through a bus system with the central electronic control of the airbag, due to the exact measurement of four points, this receives more information than just weight classification. The "iBolt" system evaluates the four measurement values and can identify the position of the seat and its modifications. With additional information, the activation of the airbag can be adapted with two or more levels gas generators to the position of the copilot's body [6]; (C) Finally, the Bebop company, who creates more secure seats by integrating fabric sensors onto an intelligent Open Computer and Software Inventory Next Generation (OCS) system. The key to this intelligence is in the characteristics of the fabric: waterproof, it consists of integrated circuits, with a thickness of approximately 1 mm. This sensor provides a higher level of detail that distinguishes the size, weight and real time movements of each occupier. Based on the static elements, the system can determine whether it is a baby seat or a person [7].

The previous information allows us to know the technology panorama that has been developed to solve the present problem. It should be noted these technologies are installed in high-end cars. For this reason, this article proposes a solution based on free software and low cost hardware, which can be implemented in cars of medium and low range.

3   Materials and Methods

The prototype design was implemented through the "User Centered Design (UCD)" methodology shown on Fig. 1.

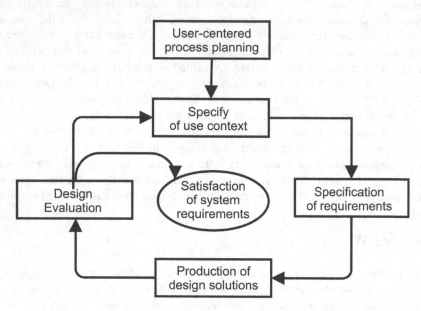

Fig. 1. User Centered Design methodology, ISO 9241-210:2010 [8].

In this section, we describe briefly each stage of the UCD methodology:

Specification of Use Context: Identification of the people who will use the product, what they will use it for, and under what conditions they will use it, that is, in what context and where they will use it.

Specification of Requirements: Identification of user needs and objectives, as well as requirements the organizational and product use.

Production of Design Solutions: From the information collected in the previous stages, prototypes are designed. Depending on each case, this activity can be broken down into different sub-stages.

Design Evaluation: This is one of the most important stages of the process, as the designs made are evaluated by the users who will use the system, as well as the requirements and the context of use. If the evaluation satisfies the requirements, the process ends, otherwise the UCD process is restarted, with the aim of refining the results obtained in each of the implemented eta-pas [8].

4   Implementation of the User Centered Design Process

To carry out the implementation of the prototype the phases of the UCD methodology were used, which are described below.

(A) Specification of Use Context. In order to determine the system use-context, we used an interview as a data collection technique, which allowed setting targets for different user profiles.

(B) Specification of the Requirements. At this stage, several questions was applied to drivers with children aboard the car, in order to gather information and make conjectures about the importance of having knowledge in safety measures with regard to children.

The surveys were applied to a sample of 30 drivers between 18 and 39 years old in the downtown of Zacatecas, Mexico. The aim of these surveys was to collect descriptive information by users (drivers) as well as the requirements required for the development of the initial prototype.

As a result of the interviews conducted, it was obtained that 100% of the respondents are aware of the damage they could cause to a child in an accident, 25% of the drivers without children admit to having put children on the passenger seat, and in turn, 90% of drivers agree that children generate a great distraction when driving. 100% of the respondents agree that there is a need for a system in automobiles that alerts children to the danger they face in a visual and additive way.

From the information acquired, the characteristics that the prototype should meet were determined:

1. Hearing Alert;
2. Visual Alert;
3. Color: Red;
4. Size: 2–3 cm;
5. Figure: Triangle.
6. Time: Undefined.

(C) Produce Design Solutions. Once the requirements have been established, it was proposed to develop the first prototype, a device when detects a child, it is activated and sends an audible alert to users indicating danger.

The first prototype implemented consists of a visual alert, it is a triangle object with size of 3×2 cm and it has an icon in the shape of a baby, has 5 perforations for led's of 5 mm. The prototype design was developed with the 3D modeling software "Solidedge" (owned by Siemens) that is a program to create 3D mechanical design with parametric methods that includes a mode-solids, creation of assemblies and trimmed drawings [9]. Figures 2 and 3 show the 3D design of the visual alert of the first prototype proposed for the visual-auditory system.

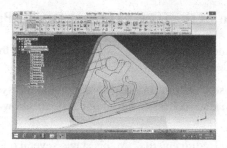

Fig. 2. Front of the visual-alert (own design).

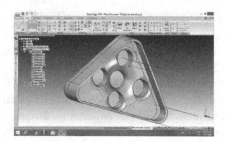

Fig. 3. Back of the visual-alert (own design).

(1) Physical-Alert Development

A 3D printer was used, which is a machine capable of printing figures with volume (width, length and height), from a computer design [10]. This process was segmented into two phases: in the first phase, the software called cure is used with which the printing characteristics are established (see Fig. 4): thickness of each layer 0.1 mm, 30% filler percentage and brackets used to prevent deformation of the part.

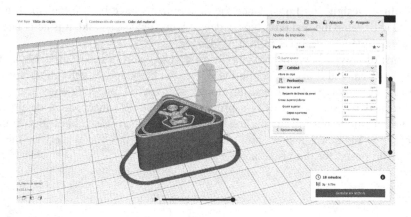

Fig. 4. Print specifications.

The second phase consisted in the execution of the printing, for it, selected colors filaments are color red and white, were selected by the respondents, as representative for alerts. In Fig. 5, the image on the left side shows the printing process and on the right side, the final result of the prototype printing is observed.

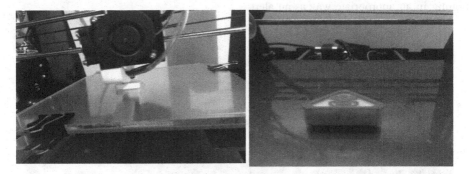

Fig. 5. Printing prototype.

(2) Hearing-Alert Development

For the development of the hearing alert, an electrical device called "Buzzer" was selected, which is capable of transforming electricity into sound. This device works at 5 v and can work with different frequencies. In the development of the hearing alert, different factors were taken into account such as: frequency, time and delay. As can be seen from the graph in Fig. 6, the audible frequencies that the human ear can respond are in the approximate range of 20 Hz–20 kHz [11]. With a frequency range of 3000 Hz at 6000 Hz it allows users to perceive more sounds or alerts. In the duration or delay of the alerts no rules were found that could help the development, so that the delay time was selected a time 1000 ms (milliseconds).

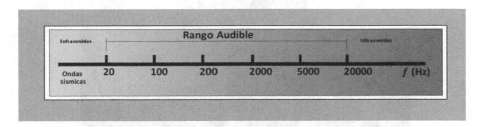

Fig. 6. Graphic of Human hearing frequencies [12].

Once the sound specifications and the creation of a physical-visual prototype were defined, the development of the functional prototype was finally carried out, which consists of a "Arduino Nano" plate, "Button" and a "Buzzer", as can be seen in Fig. 7. Arduino, is a free hardware platform, based on a board with a microcontroller and a development environment, designed to facilitate the use of electronics in multidisciplinary projects [13] with which the two alerts are encompassed. The visual alert is intended to give users better feedback on the children detection on the passenger seat and that is forbidden to take them there. It is complemented by an audible alert at a frequency of "3500 Hz" which is an appropriate frequency for different users, functioning in an appropriate way as an alert.

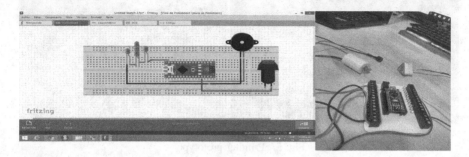

Fig. 7. Diagram of granting and prototype.

With all components integrated into a single device, the prototype was implemented in a Nissan March Model 2017 vehicle, in which the three main components of the system were placed: camera, visual-alert and hearing-alert, as shown in Fig. 8. The camera aims to simulate the image processing technique for the children detection on passenger seat.

Fig. 8. Prototype Implementation.

(D) Evaluation

The prototype was evaluated in the downtown of Zacatecas, Mexico by 30 drivers of different ages. By means of the technique "Wizard of Oz" (see Figs. 9 and 10), useful to test the prototypes of an interaction that simulates the interactive behavior and functionality of the machine through the use of a human operator [14]. The test consisted in simulating of the children detection on the passenger seat, and after pressing a button manually activate the visual-hearing alert. In such a way that users could interact with the simulated system, that is, the actual functioning of each of the visual and auditory components, and evaluate the prototype with all the characteristics established by the users.

Fig. 9. Prototype evaluation.

Fig. 10. Prototype evaluation by Wizard of Oz Technique

At the end of the simulation of the implementation of the prototype in a real environment, the participants responded to a questionnaire, where they evaluated the interaction with the device.

As a result of this evaluation, it was obtained that 100% of the surveys, according to the sound produced by the alarm, in terms of the delay of the sound 13.33% of the users suggested that it was more frequent, 93.33% of users agree that the alarm should remain until the child is moved to the appropriate seat. In the visual-alert, 100% of users agreed with the color of the alert, 86.66% of users agreed with the size of the device, and in turn suggested increasing the size of the icon by 1.0 cm, 100% of respondents agreed with the light being emitted. Finally, 100% of users agreed with the proposal of the system, because they determined that is viable and useful for motorists when correcting their actions.

In the following section are described the first approximations are in the implementation of the Low Level Digital Image Processing technique, using the process shown in Fig. 11.

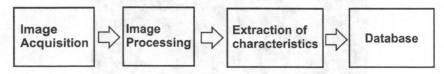

Fig. 11. Diagram of image processing.

5   Image Digital Processing Development

(1) Image Acquisition

The acquisition of images was carried out in a controlled environment, the capture of the images was carried out by a cellular (iPhone 5 ©) with a resolution 1200×1600 pixels at a distance of 70 cm, the test was made to three people (Fig. 12).

Fig. 12. Images to process.

(2) **Image Processing**

The image processing was done in the program called MATLAB, which is a Programming platform Designed specifically for Engineers and scientists, a matrix based language allowing the most natural expression of Computational Mathematics [15]. In the development of the processing, the first thing to do is a filter to the image to soften the contours, then it is done changed from RGB color space (red/green/blue) to HSV space (nuance/saturation/value) which was created by Alvy Ray Smith in 1978. HSV is also known as the color model of the hexagonal cone with the components: nuance, saturation and value [16], using channel H (nuance) was performed the extraction of characteristics of regions as area and centroids. These characteristics serve to discriminate areas that do not correspond to points of interest such as eyes and mouth (Fig. 13).

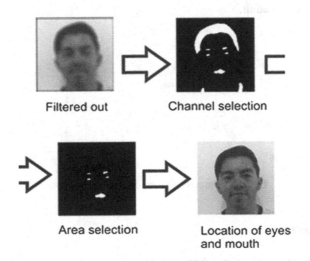

Filtered out   Channel selection

Area selection   Location of eyes
                        and mouth

Fig. 13. Image processing.

With the biometric points of interest already identified in the image the following is the extraction of characteristics, such extraction is based on the distance between eyes, distance from eyes to mouth as shown in Fig. 15 and the area of the triangle is formed by such points, such distances were extracted based on the Euclidean distance. The Euclidean distance between two points in either the plane or 3-dimensional space measures the length of a segment connecting the two points [17] in the Fig. 14 shown the formula.

$$ds(p1.p2) = \sqrt{(x1 - x2)^2 + (y1 - y2)^2}$$

Fig. 14. The distance formula.

Fig. 15. Images processed.

The characteristics are stored in a database where they are assigned the condition and assigned their respective distances as shown in Fig. 16 and which in turn will serve to generate classification models where the class of the class is finished evaluated whether a child or an adult.

	A	B	C	D	E
1	ojos	ojos-boca	Area	condi	
2	7	7.5	26.25	1	
3	7.5	9	33.75	1	
4	7.5	9	33.75	1	
5					
6					

Fig. 16. Dataset of facial-features measures.

6 Conclusions

The present investigation shows how the User Centered Design process allows to develop high fidelity prototypes, in this case, the implementation of DCU focused on the automotive sector resulted in a prototype that contributes to improving the safety of children aboard the car. It is also important to stress that the prototype it ongoing assessments, directly by interested users, allow the developer to obtain a more accurate feedback on the proposed solution of the problem being sought to solve.

For the above, the final prototype generated includes the needs of drivers: a vehicle warning system useful for drivers, of high fidelity, with a design acceptable to the users.

The future work for this project is the implementation of computational vision for the children detection, through the use of a video camera (Go pro) and the application of high level Digital Image Processing techniques (PDI), implementation of Deep learning techniques to analyze and classify infants and implement a solution of a Human Machine Interface (HMI, Human Machine Interface), which allows a better interaction of the prototype and the user in a real environment.

Acknowledgments. The authors thank the academic and student community for the programs Maestría en Ciencias del Procesamiento de la Información (MCPI) e Ingeniería en Electrónica Industrial (IEI) de la Universidad Autónoma de Zacatecas - México, also, to the Consejo Zacatecano de Ciencia, Tecnología e Innovación (COZCyT) for the support received.

References

1. Vaiustore. https://vaiu.es/accidentes-de-trafico-en-1900/. Accessed 24 Oct 2018
2. Turbo. http://www.revistaturbo.com/noticias/asi-fue-el-primer-accidente-automovilistico-de-la-historia-887. Accessed 01 Oct 2018
3. GOBIERNO DE MÉXICO. https://www.gob.mx/policiafederal/articulos/guia-para-prevenir-accidentes-de-transito-en-jovenes?idiom=es. Accessed 15 Oct 2018
4. Organización Mundial de la Salud. https://www.who.int/mediacentre/news/releases/2008/pr46/es/. Accessed 02 Nov 2018
5. Aficionados a la Mecánica. http://www.aficionadosalamecanica.net/sensores8.htm. Accessed 16 Oct 2018
6. Kasten, K., Stratmann, A., Munz, M., Dirscherl, K., Lamers, S.: iBolt technology—a weight sensing system for advanced passenger safety. In: Valldorf, J., Gessner, W. (eds.) Advanced Microsystems for Automotive Applications 2006. VDI-Buch, pp. 171–186. Springer, Heidelberg (2006). https://doi.org/10.1007/3-540-33410-6_14
7. BeBopsensors. https://bebopsensors.com/bebop-sensors-announces-automotive-seat-sensor-system/. Accessed 09 Oct 2018
8. Luna García, H.: Diseño Centrado en el Usuario. Human Machine Interface. Universidad Autónoma de Zacatecas, septiembre 2018. Accessed 01 Oct 2018
9. 3DCADportal. http://www.3dcadportal.com/solid-edge.html, Accessed 30 Nov 2018
10. Areatecnologuia. http://www.areatecnologia.com/informatica/impresoras-3d.html. Accessed 11 Oct 2018
11. Audix perfecta armonía. http://www.audix.cl/hrf_faq/que-rango-de-sonidos-son-aceptables-para-el-oido-humano/. Accessed 30 Nov 2018
12. Megafoniaysonorizacionronald. https://sites.google.com/site/megafoniaysonorizacionronald/t01-prin-bas-del-sonido/1-2-propiedades-fisicas-del-sonido/1-2-3-el-espectro-audible. Accessed 11 Nov 2018
13. Arduino. http://jamangandi2012.blogspot.com/2012/10/que-es-arduino-te-lo-mostramos-en-un.html. Accessed 06 Nov 2018
14. FJC. http://jimenezcano.blogspot.com/2013/06/mago-de-oz.html. Accessed 06 Oct 2018
15. MathWorks. https://la.mathworks.com/discovery/what-is-matlab.html. Accessed 24 Nov 2018
16. TECH-FAQ. http://www.tech-faq.com/hsv.html. Accessed 05 Oct 2018
17. ROSALIND. http://rosalind.info/glossary/euclidean-distance/. Accessed 01 Nov 2018

Collaborative Content Production Model to Reduce Digital Divide

Jaime Muñoz-Arteaga[1(✉)] 🆔, José E. Guzmán Mendoza[2] 🆔,
Héctor Cardona Reyes[3] 🆔, and Ricardo Mendoza-González[4] 🆔

[1] Universidad Autónoma de Aguascalientes, Aguascalientes, Mexico
jaime.munoz@edu.uaa.mx
[2] Universidad Politécnica de Aguascalientes, Aguascalientes, Mexico
jose.guzman@upa.edu.mx
[3] CIMAT, Zacatecas, Mexico
hector.cardona@cimat.mx
[4] Instituto Tecnológico de Aguascalientes, Aguascalientes, Mexico
mendozagric@mail.ita.mx

Abstract. Nowadays, the digital divide in underdeveloped countries is not about the provision of infrastructure and Internet connectivity, is about innovation in models and strategies for digital literacy and digital content generation. In additions, the differences in terms of access and ICT skills between different groups in society have created a problem of digital divide. To overcome this kind of problems, models and strategies are required to achieve a greater impact on the citizen and that population can develop skills that enhance inclusion in the society knowledge. This work addresses the digital divide issue as a challenge to achieve the knowledge society; it proposes a collaborative content production architectural model to generate content in order to mitigate the digital divide. This is a model-centered approach in order to have a massive content production to facilitate the integration of users with different skills. Finally, a case study describes the use of proposed architectural model in order to reduce the digital divide for large communities of librarians of in México.

Keywords: Digital divide · Content production · User interface · Architectural model

1 Introduction

Currently, several countries have adopted changes that have led to what is known as "Knowledge Society". These transformations are driven and supported on new technologies to create, transmit and disseminate information, and direct product, which is knowledge. In this sense, it is desirable to achieve a knowledge society where inclusion of individuals in the generation of knowledge can be total, so knowledge societies are sources of development for all and not for a few. However, the difference in access and use of technology has created a new form of exclusion, called "digital divide", that it can impede the economic and human development, and expand the gap between

© Springer Nature Switzerland AG 2019
P. H. Ruiz and V. Agredo-Delgado (Eds.): HCI-COLLAB 2019, CCIS 1114, pp. 150–164, 2019.
https://doi.org/10.1007/978-3-030-37386-3_12

regions and countries (international digital gap) and groups of citizens in a society (domestic digital divide) [1]. Digital divide is not limited only to a technological problem; it is a social and educational problem. The digital divide should be understood in three main concepts: access, ICT education and content [2]. On these concepts, Aguascalientes state in Mexico can be considered as one of state that has a better Internet connectivity infrastructure covering all its municipalities. However, there is still resolve the issues of ICT education -digital literacy- and content.

1.1 Digital Divide and Knowledge Society

The concept of "digital divide" appeared in conjunction with the rapid increase in Internet use in the late 1990s, and is typically defined in terms of physical access to computers. Over time the concept has been widened to include a number of issues, including the infrastructure needed to support the use of computers such as internet connections and electricity; physical barriers such as long distance to e.g. a library; economic barriers, such as being able to afford a computer; social and cultural barriers and patterns, including different social patterns in different social groups making for different uses of computers, e.g. for entertainment vs. for searching for information and taking part in politics; technical literacy, the ability to use a computer [3–5].

Sharing and creating information are a well know initiatives come from a knowledge society [6]. Ideally, the wealth generation engine in this society is knowledge, which constitutes the main factor of development and human welfare. Therefore, entering the knowledge society will allow any society access other levels of welfare and progress.

1.2 Digital Literacy and Collaborative Content Productions

In the knowledge society, a citizen has seen the need to adapt to an era of technological and social changes over the last century. This contemporary society intended to that citizens could be autonomous and own their own ideas, generators of transformations and knowledge to fostering progress in science, information technology, culture and other fields [7]. Digital literacy is a set of skills taught in order to identify and find the information needed to solve a problem [8]. In this sense, being digitally literate involves developing the knowledge and skills relating to ICT, and develop values and social attitudes and political in relation to technology [9].

One of the basic objectives pursued by the use of collaborative work is to promote proper training and proper job performance from the exchange of ideas and actions of the members involved in the management process of the organization, including the promotion of ideas, training activities and proposals for action [10].

In this work, we propose a collaborative content production model that allows collaborative content production, so that any user can collaborate and produce massively open content and use the content produced to help others users to develop basic digital skills and when these new users to appropriate these basic digital skills, they can be added to keep producing new content in order to mitigate their digital divide.

2 Collaborative Content Production Model

Today, with the wide variety of tools available on the Web 3.0 [11], allows a group of people, virtual communities, even educational institutions and companies to work collaboratively in order to create digital content on a massive scale. And once created these contents, may be available for different end users, such as older adults, Indigenous, professionals, children, etc. We believe that this collaboration can be used to produce digital content that help to reduce the digital divide.

People who join content collaboration, can work in both formal and informal environments. For example, formal collaboration can come from educational institutions, training centers, etc. Informal collaboration can occur from virtual communities and social networks. Then, it is necessary to combine these environments. For collaborative work in the production of content, this implies, using platforms that facilitate collaborative task for differentiated users. We use the term differentiated users to refer the task type that a user can performs based on the skills and competencies that provide to the content collaboration. That is, the role played by each user. A user can take the role as the coordinator who monitors and evaluates the quality of content, another user can perform the task of instructional designer, and another user can be the technical designer.

In this sense, users must develop digital skills at least at a basic level to be able to perform a variety of tasks for the collaborative production of content. In other words, users should be able to handle different interfaces, devices and technology platforms.

This situation creates another problem that relates to the need to provide training to these users, this is known as digital literacy. Digital literacy is introduced in the acquirement of some ICT technical skills. Technological skill refers to the knowledge about what the technology is, how it works, what it is for, and how it can be used to achieve specific objectives. Informational skill is the ability to recognize a need for particular information, and know how to locate, evaluate, select, summarize, and use the information effectively [12].

The collaborative learning environments allow to provide spaces which give developing individual and group skills from the discussion among users in exploring new concepts, each one responsible for their own learning [13]. Based on this premise, we propose the strategy of using the collaborative work focused on the content production with a dual purpose. The first is to provide content designed according to certain digital skills, for example, a content that allows a person to learn to use a Web browser. And the second purpose is that during the development of content, users can apply the skills acquired and consequently strengthen these skills acquired to get the social appropriation of ICTs. Thus, we determined that the collaborative work focused on digital content production promotes the acquisition of basic digital skills for users (see Fig. 1).

Servon [2] says that the problem of the digital divide can be understood as three problems: infrastructure problem, problem of digital literacy and content production problem. We're going to focus on solving the problem of content production from a collaborative approach.

However, there are few methodologies for collaborative production of content that are supported by technology platforms [14, 15]. Some systems provide collaborative platforms and are limited in relation to the tasks that users must perform, creating obstacles for collaborative work. We also want to mention that these systems require users to possess specific skills for its handling.

So, our contribution to the reduction of the digital divide is in relation to design a model based on different technological platforms that allow support the collaborative work of a group of users (with different skills) for massive content production.

There a lot open platforms available in Web 2.0 easy to use. These platforms encourage to perform the user tasks through user interfaces for collaborative work environments. To exploit these open platforms, we propose the following architecture to support the collaborative content production:

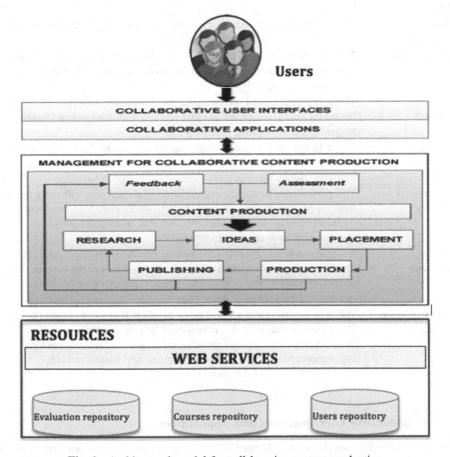

Fig. 1. Architectural model for collaborative content production

The objective of the proposed architecture is to provide support for the content production into collaborative platforms, so that users can adapt themselves depending on the environments learning. This architecture consists of four layers: (1) users,

(2) Collaborative user interfaces and applications (3) Management for collaborative content production and (4) Resources.

Next subsections present in detail every layer.

2.1 Users

In order to promote efficiency and allow people to take initiative in the content production it is important to have clearly defined roles in a multi-skilled team. In this section we propose a set of roles for collaborative content production. Table 1 shows the roles and functions or tasks that must be performed to content production.

Table 1. Roles and user task for contents production

Role	User task
Content producer	This role represents a person or a group of persons that uses various tools to produce content about a specific topic
Idea generator	This person (or group of people) identifies the big picture of the project, leads the others towards the main objective, and keeps the momentum of the project moving forward
Content reviewer	This role is in charge of reviewing the contents about a subject. Then, this person (or group) must work in close relation with the Content Organizer, proposing the appropriate modifications
Technical reviewer	This role has the function of checking all the technical aspects of the content, for example, checks the consistency of the links, revise the formulas edition, etc.
Pedagogical reviewer	This person ensures that the organization of the content will make sense from a pedagogical point of view, hence, works closely to the content organizer in order to notify missing contents, or to point out some elements that must be deeper investigated
Content organizer	It is a person able to guide the creation of a content, who has clear insights into the while providing swift feedback on all aspects of the content. This person proposes a table of contents where a collaborative production strategy will be defined in the group
Group organizer	This role is vital in order to organize the team that works in the project. The person in charge of this role should be characterized by various competencies such as project management, good social relationships, experience within the field of collaboration, and basic knowledge regarding the topic of the content

2.2 Collaborative User Interfaces and Applications

Collaborative user interfaces provide support for a group of users to perform content production tasks collaboratively. They are responsible for providing dynamism to the production process and in addition, to establish a methodology facilitating the user tasks.

The collaborative application is a layer to manage different applications to provide for the users functionalities and allowing to make different collaboration tasks through the UIs. Also, this applications support different patterns for collaboration among the users: asynchronous, synchronous, multi-synchronous, local, distributed, etc. Collaborative applications perform its tasks in terms of user interfaces for content producers according to the role the users perform.

The collaborative layer should provide user interfaces able to support a wide of tasks in collaborative environment for content production, and accessible through many possible devices. Many different applications are available to perform similar tasks and users choose those that are easier to understand and interact with and which, consequently, increase efficiency, productivity, and acceptance while reducing errors and the need for training [16].

When a user executes a task through collaborative UI, the UI sends the request to a collaborative application; this application can executes the task and returns an update to the collaborative UI so that other users can view updates (see Fig. 2).

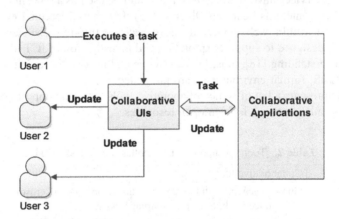

Fig. 2. Collaborative graphical user interface model

Such collaborative layer can combine different applications and user interfaces for: communication, supporting different phases of process production, searching information, managing users, assessing content, etc., this facilitates the system to be available anywhere anytime.

2.3   Management for Collaborative Content Production

The management for collaborative content production describes the workflow and user tasks for the content production using the defined collaborative UIs and applications provided by the collaborative layer.

In this layer, the collaborative production of content is handled. This administration is determined by a series of tasks that forming a collaborative process. The process includes five tasks that are oriented to the production of content: (1) research, (2) ideas, (3) placement, (4) production and (5) publishing, and two tasks that are designed to control the quality of the content: (1) feedback and (2) Assessment.

Thus, this manager allow for an easy generation/configuration of different collaborative application specific services for collaborative product/process design in international settings along the product/process development life cycle of a content, adapted to the specific needs of different users and their tasks. The platforms have to be open for different production content frameworks, i.e., they have to support different collaborative design approaches by combining different existing design tools with web services and LMS services.

2.4 Resources

Resources are on the backend which is composed of web services as a backbone for an entire architecture to operate and have the characteristics of cloud computing. Web services can provide services through Internet allowing to support formal and informal collaborative learning environments. These services include three characteristics: (a) service by demand, (b) Ubiquitous access to network and (c) configuration elasticity [17]. Also, web services have characteristic that could be used as a repository to include different kind of content as Learning Objects (LO). LOs based learning environments are mostly used within web environments, especially through distance education. The LO can be designed to support exploration and investigation of ICT ideas and help conceptual understanding [18], thus, LOs allow the end users the acquisition of digital skills. With LMS, formal environments are integrated.

Next table presents a list of some collaborative tools that can support collaborative tasks through collaborative UIs from open resources.

Table 2. Tools to support UI for collaborative tasks [21]

Collaborative UI	Collaborative tools
Research	Google, Scoop.it, Slideshare, Youtube, ZonaClic. Microsoft Academic, MyScienceWork, Scientific Journal Finder
Ideas	Mindmeister, Symbaloo, Miro, Google Calendar, Bubbl.us, IdeaBoardz
Placement	Dropbox, Google Drive, Connexions, Miro, Edocr OneDrive, pCloud, Box, Mega.
Production	Moodle, Educaplay, BookType, Connexions, Wix, Construcor, Cuadernia, Exelearning, BookStack, WordPress, Blogger
Publishing	Slideshare, Moodle, BookType, Scoop.it, Scribd, WordPress, Blogger
Feedback	Miro, MeetingBurner, Skype, Wikispaces, Moodle, Join.me, Ekiga, Google Hangouts
Assessment	Miro, Google Docs, OpenSchool ePorfolio, Watermark

With the proposed architecture, we intend to generate more flexible environments, which allow inclusion of differentiated users, with the understanding that a differentiated user can be a person or a community with different needs and characteristics. Through these flexible environments the users start as consumers of content, and after they grasp a high level of digital skills they can become content providers.

We want to emphasize that formal education is inflexible because it excludes many people who do not have the skills, qualities, requirements or resources to join formal learning environments. Older adults, indigenous communities, people with low economic resources, even very small companies are different users who need to be literate in the use of ICT to join the society of knowledge, however, no one takes care of them. Informal environments can provide possible solutions to different users.

3 Case Study

The Government Plan of Aguascalientes State 2010–2016 considers within its main activities carried Aguascalientes toward a *Knowledge Society* as a strategy for improving the quality of life of the people of Aguascalientes.

In order to illustrate our model this section presents a case study for the collaborative content production within the Fomix Project (FP) entitled *"Integral Intervention to Reduce Digital Divide in Aguascalientes State"* [19] and also poses a strategic way to develop basic digital skills through the creation of digital content collaboratively.

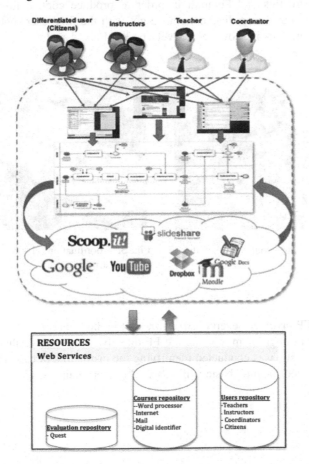

Fig. 3. Architectural model for collaborative content production for the case study

For this case study an implementation of architectural model has presented in the Fig. 3, where there are several kind of users such as: librarian, instructors, coordinator and teacher. The intermediate module are represented by an workflow specifications for management of content production as well as a series of user interfaces of web applications such as the Moodle LMS, Slideshare, Youtube, Scoop.it, Google-Doc and Drop Box. Finally, the repositories of quests, courses and user data compose the resources module.

This case study has as goal to contribute to the social appropriation of ICT in an effective and efficient to allow the entire population of Aguascalientes join the knowledge society. However, Aguascalientes is a state with very heterogeneous population, and to solve this situation we need to create different scenarios for integrating the various sectors of the population to the knowledge society.

3.1 Users

As a case study we establish a categorizing digital skills into three levels that should be acquired by instructors and librarian in order to produce content through different online resources. For this, a diagnostic have got with the final user such the librarian and the instructor. This is show respectively by the Figs. 4 and 5.

Fig. 4. Librarian filling out a digital divide questioner.

Fig. 5. Coordination of educative resources by an instructor.

Within the FP involved several *instructors* that in the future they will be the digital facilitators, and through them, operate the FP directly to the Aguascalientes librarian. But first, a diagnostic was conducted identifying the instructors of case study, they has required an updated in some basic skills as well a intermediate digital skills.

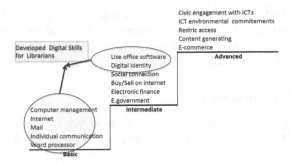

Fig. 6. Basic and intermediate digital divide levels for librarians.

Adapting the general strategy to the FP context is described as follows *"Provide instructors the ability to build additional content to reduce the digital divide attached to basic and intermediate skills established in the FP"*. So, Instructors can develop basic and intermediate digital skills (see Fig. 6) through the production of digital content collaboratively. This strategy allows one hand, creating *collaborative work scenario* and on the other, producing digital content in order to training Aguascalientes citizens. Once a librarian acquires an advanced level, as consequence he/she can become a content producer.

3.2 Collaborative User Interface

To illustrate the operation of architecture to generate scenarios that promote collaborative production of content on a massive scale, we designed the following scenario for the FP case study (Fig. 7).

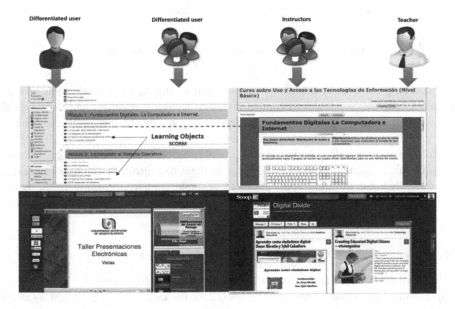

Fig. 7. Use of *Moodle, Slideshare and Scoop.it* to produce, save and use educative resources.

The scenario is developed for the Aguascalientes state in Mexico. It is based on virtual environments and distance to cover formal and informal learning, thus, different users can be integrated. Moodle and some cloud services (from Table 2) are the backbone for providing this support.

3.3   Collaborative Applications

This section presents an example of how the scenario manages and supports the processes in the next Fig. 8 on the side of the users group in relation to the role performed.

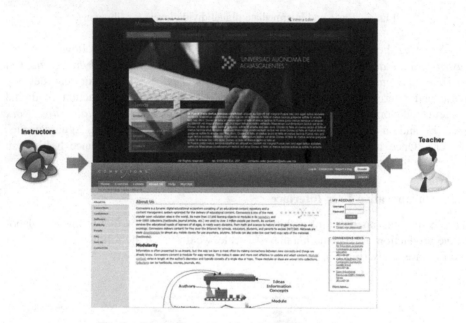

Fig. 8. Graphical user interface for content production

According the Fig. 8, the user interface help to manage the production task as fallow: A *Teacher* takes roles as content reviewer, technical reviewer and pedagogical reviewer. The teacher is responsible for periodically reviewing the production phase. Teacher valued pedagogical and technical aspects of content ensuring the quality of the content, generates a valuation report and provide feedback to the instructors. *Instructors* take role as content producer and some of them can also take the role of content reviewer. They use different applications to generate content according to the pedagogical and technical requirements. They are also based on the feedback of the teacher to make changes to the content.

3.4   Management for Collaborative Content Production

To have a better understanding of the implementation of the management for collaborative content production (described in Sect. 2.3), the tasks to be performed by users

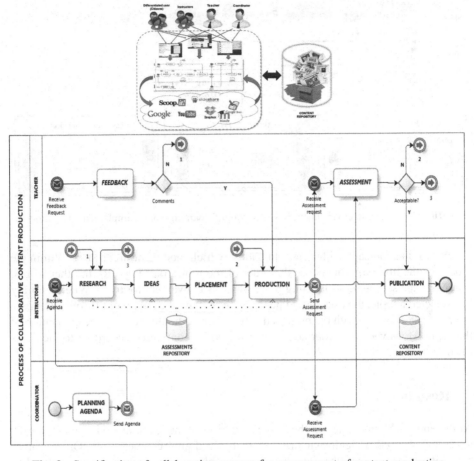

Fig. 9. Specification of collaborative process for management of content production

of case study are illustrated in Fig. 6. We decided to use BPMN [20, 21] for modeling the manager in terms of collaborative processes.

Independently that interfaces and platforms are used, Fig. 9. shows the processes that must be executed for the content production content by the users or roles. In this case, the processes are assigned to users, but, also be assigned to roles. A user can perform several roles in the process.

3.5 Resources

According to the Table 2, Moodle, Slideshare and Scoop.it are resources that integrate tools that support the task of publication for the case study. As shown in Fig. 8. Moodle, Slideshare and Scoop.it are resources; they are used as content repositories. At the same time, these resources allow all the users to have access to these content. Also, these resources can support the task of feedback and allow users to assign a score to the content.

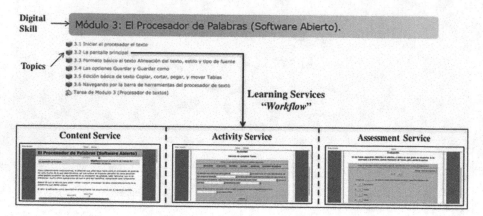

Fig. 10. Collaborative environment based-on digital learning course implemented in moodle

Within the course, the librarian can choose which module desire to start. Within the modules, the librarian can choose the order of the topics (see Fig. 10). In other words, librarians can set the better learning path, which is convenient for them. When a library has selected a topic, the user should begin by reviewing the theory of the topic, then, do the practice, continue with the proposed activities, and finally perform the evaluation of the topic. However, these four activities can also be configured according to the skills of the librarian.

4   Results

At the end of the first phase of the implementation of the learning environment, the 15 librarians showed a significant increase in basic digital competencies. On the other hand, it was noted that librarians had some problems completing activities related to intermediate digital competencies. However, all librarians were able to successfully

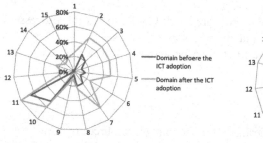

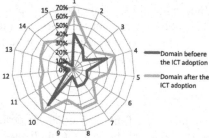

Fig. 11. Radar chart related to query: *have you ever used a composed research key content?*

Fig. 12. Radar chart related to query: *have you ever participate in academic forums?*

complete the development of the learning object. In this way, librarians have succeeded in moving from a learning community to a learning content producing community.

A user-centered evaluation has conducted asking some questions before and after the ICT adoption. The Fig. 11. shows a light evolution of librarians to use a composed research key content. Also, the Fig. 12. shows a highly evolution of librarians to participate in academic forums.

5 Conclusion

Current work presents a collaborative environment for content production as a proposal to reduce the problem of the digital divide in the state of Aguascalientes in Mexico. The proposed architectural model allows articulate collaborative strategies that allow digital content can be designed, developed and implemented within the same, and then generalized and expanded to citizenship. The case study of this work has consider as citizens the user of library, when citizens consume these contents, acquire basic digital skills Thus, it is intended that citizens are not content consumers only, in the moment they are integrating to knowledge society are able to generate new content and become content providers both individually and collectively.

Moreover, it is important to the selection of technology resources. The resources should facilitate the collaborative content production scenarios, and ensure easy access to contents. Our scenario described by the case study shows the ease in handling and performing tasks collaboratively by all roles.

As future work, we will continue working on various lines of action: (a) searching to strengthen the educational and technological features that should have digital content to be viable in other technology resources. (b) designing UI able to adapt to different learning communities; (c) integrating multicultural aspects in digital content; (d) evaluating the usability of some digital literacy services digital; (e) enhancing the UX.

References

1. Tello, E.: Information and communication technology (ICT) and the digital gap: their impact on mexican society. Univ. Knowl. Soc. J. **4**(2), 20–29 (2007). https://doi.org/10.7238/rusc.v4i2.305
2. Servon, L.: Bridging the Digital Divide: Technology, Community, and Public Policy. Malden Ma Blackwell Pub, Oxford (2002). https://doi.org/10.1002/9780470773529
3. Payne, R.K.: A Framework for Understanding Poverty, 5th edn. Aha Process Inc., Highlands (2013). ISBN 13: 978-1-938248-01-6
4. Gurstein, M.: Effective use: a community informatics strategy beyond the digital divide. First Monday **8**(12) (2003). https://doi.org/10.5210/fm.v8i12.1107
5. Grönlund, Å., Hatakka, M., Ask, A.: Inclusion in the e-service society – investigating administrative literacy requirements for using e-services. In: Wimmer, M.A., Scholl, J., Grönlund, Å. (eds.) EGOV 2007. LNCS, vol. 4656, pp. 216–227. Springer, Heidelberg (2007). https://doi.org/10.1007/978-3-540-74444-3_19
6. Olivé, L.: El libro, la lectura y las bibliotecas en la sociedad del Conocimiento. Lect. Vida **30**(3), 20–29 (2009)

7. Álvarez, E.: Cinco ventajas del aprendizaje colaborativo online. Colombia Digital (2013). Accessed 01 May 2018
8. Monge, R., Frisicaro-Pawlowski, E.: Redefining information literacy to prepare students for the 21st century workforce. Innov. High Educ. **39**, 59–73 (2013). https://doi.org/10.1007/s10755-013-9260-5
9. Pinto, M.: Información, Acción, Conocimiento y Ciudadanía. La educación escolar como espacio de interrogación y de construcción de sentido, Gedisa Barcelon (2008)
10. Carmenado, I., Figueroa, B., Gómez, F.: Methodological proposal for teamwork evaluation in the field of project management training. Proc.-Soc. Behav. Sci. **46**, 1664–1672 (2012). https://doi.org/10.1016/j.sbspro.2012.05.358
11. Hafkesbrink, J., Schroll, M.: Innovation 3.0: embedding into community knowledge - collaborative organizational learning beyond open innovation de boeck supérieur. J. Innov. Econ. Manag. (7) 55–92 (2011). https://doi.org/10.3917/jie.007.0055
12. Badilla-Quintana, M.G., Cortada-Pujol, M.: Digital literacy development of studens involved in an ICT educational project. TechEducation **73**, 632–638 (2010). https://doi.org/10.1007/978-3-642-13166-0_88
13. Lucero, M.: Entre el trabajo colaborativo y el aprendizaje colaborativo. Iberoamericana Educ. **33**, 1–21 (2003)
14. Ruiz, R.G., García, A.R., Rosell, R.M.: Media literacy education for a new prosumer citizenship. Comunicar **22**(43), 15–23 (2014). https://doi.org/10.3916/C43-2014-01
15. Atif, Y., Chou, Ch.: Digital citizenship: innovations in education, practice, and pedagogy. J. Educ. Technol. Soc. 21(1), 152–54 (2018). https://doi.org/0000-0002-7312-9089
16. Manca, M., Paternò F., Santoro C., Spano L.: Considering task pre-conditions in model-based user interface design and generation. In: Proceedings ACM SIGCHI Symposium on Engineering Interactive, pp. 149–154 (2014). https://doi.org/10.1145/2607023.2610283
17. Linthicum, D.S.: Cloud Computing and SOA Convergence in Your Enterprise: A Step-By-Step Guide. Addison-Wesley Prof., Boston (2009)
18. Baki, A., Cakroglu, U.: Learning objects in high school mathematics classrooms: implementation and evaluation. Comput. Educ. **55**, 1459–1469 (2010). https://doi.org/10.1016/j.compedu.2010.06.009
19. Muñoz-Arteaga, J.: Integral intervention to reduce digital divide in Aguascalientes State. Fomix Project in Aguascalientes (2016)
20. White, S., Miers, D., BPMN: Business Process Modeling Notation. Future Strategies Inc. (2009). https://doi.org/10.1007/978-3-642-45100-3_10
21. OMG: Business Process Model and Notation (BPMN). https://www.omg.org. Accessed 05 May 2019

Design of Home Energy Management System Using IoT Data Flow

Blanca-Nydia Pérez-Camacho[1]([⊠]) [ID],
Juan-Manuel González-Calleros[1] [ID],
and Gustavo Rodríguez-Gómez[2] [ID]

[1] Benemérita Universidad Autónoma de Puebla, Av. Sn Claudio y 14 Sur Esq.
Av. Ciudad Universitaria, 72570 Puebla, Puebla, Mexico
blancanydia.perezc@gmail.com, jumagoca78@gmail.com
[2] Instituto Nacional de Astrofísica, Óptica y Electrónica, Ciencias
Computacionales, Luis Enrique Erro 1, Sta. Ma. Tonantzintla,
72840 Puebla, Mexico
gustavo.grgrodrig@gmail.com

Abstract. A home energy management system (HEMS) is designed in order to analyze and control the way in which household appliances consumption occurs in a context. The HEMS has four objectives: to reduce consumption, to reduce costs, to reduce peak average ratio and to maximize the users' comfort. In this paper, the design of HEMS architecture is examined based on the IoT data flow architecture, and considering the constraints of the environment, user preferences and as a whole the context of use. Our architecture incudes a layer that explicity assumes the existance of an intelligent ambient (IA) which lets to denote the elements to obtain and display consumption data from the environment. Also, IA let to monitor data, which helps users for decision making related to consumption in a context where HEMS has been implemented. Also, our architecture allow the specification of users' context of use, a novel way to define the constraints of HEMS, as novel way to make things simpler and clear.

Keywords: Home Energy Management System methodology · Internet of Things · Analysis of household appliance consumption

1 Introduction

Until now, a methodology to analyze the electric consumption has not been developed from the perspective of implementation and Internet of Things (IoT) data flow architecture.

IoT has been implemented in the way to develop different application areas, like Smart Warehouse, Smart grid, Smart City, Smart meter, Smart Healthcare and Smart Home [1]. Between Smart grid and Smart home, there is a common objective to accomplish, to develop systems that make efficient electricity consumption. The systems that manage the electric consumption are called Home Energy Management System (HEMS).

The works about HEMS focused in to improve the electric consumption are about to research devices or to identify control variables [2–5], buildings consumption [3],

© Springer Nature Switzerland AG 2019
P. H. Ruiz and V. Agredo-Delgado (Eds.): HCI-COLLAB 2019, CCIS 1114, pp. 165–176, 2019.
https://doi.org/10.1007/978-3-030-37386-3_13

houses consumption [4], reduce costs [2, 6–10], sensor infrastructure [3] and control algorithms [4, 10]. Few works focus on the current challenge to develop solutions supported by IoT.

Home Energy Management System analyses how the electric energy is used and by which ones of devices are consuming range, their objectives could be one or more from these: low Peak Average Ratio (PAR), minimize costs, minimize consumption and maximizer user´s comfort [7]. To develop HEMS requires: to define objectives, variables and to identify what kind of factors needs to be considered. When HEMS works with consumption data, it needs to handle a big quantity of data [8] that could be useful to make decisions [13, 14] and it converts the problem into a multi-objective optimization problem [10]. To this kind of problem, a metaheuristic is used to find a solution to the multi-objective problem.

So, according to the characteristics of the problem, it requires to search for alternative solutions that are appropriate to the context of the problem, which consider the source of the data, the variables and the implementation of a metaheuristic to search the optimal consumption.

Rest of the paper is organized as follows, in Sect. 2 describes the literature review. A description of the layers that make up the methodology proposed to develop projects that implemented the Internet of Things is given in Sect. 3. In Sect. 4, a brief discussion is carried out. Both conclusions and future work are in Sect. 5.

2 Literature Review

A Home Energy Management System (HEMS) is a system designed to make an efficient analysis and control the context of electricity consumption. Many researchers around the world worked to make an optimal electric consumption system in different research lines like smart meter, smart grid, neural network, metaheuristic, IoT, Genetic algorithm and big data. Nadeem et al. in [11] considered to develop a HEMS to reduce consumption under a predefined level, costs and waiting time using hybrid metaheuristics schemes based on Teaching-Learning techniques. The metaheuristics used were Optimization Stopping Rule (OSR), Genetic Algorithm (GA) and Firefly Algorithm (FA). This work considered three electric devices (fridge, dishwasher, and dryer), the variables that were considered for every device: costs average per month, the cost reduction, the priority and the delay per hour per day. It is simulated by the implementation of every technique and their hybrids to each of the devices.

Yao et al. in [12] said that the energy management problem consists in to solve appliance load scheduling and grid power dispatching under a single optimization framework of a utility grid with dynamic costs, a photovoltaic module and the household appliance with three different types: interruptible, uninterruptible and time-varying; in this work was implemented a simulation of a mixed-integer linear programming framework. His future consists of two stages, first to implement a genetic algorithm, second to implement a multiobjective optimization framework.

Rahim et al. in [11] described the goal of implementing a HEMS, which is reduced to the following to reduce the costs, minimization of Peak to average ratio and maximize comfort. In this work is proposed a generic architecture for a HEMS, it models the electric consume in a house, here was considered three algorithms genetic algorithm (GA), binary particles swarm optimization (BPSO) and ant colony optimization (ACO). The GA was more efficient than BPSO and ACO in term of consumption reduction, minimizing PAR while is considered user comfort. In this work is concluded that to Minimize PAR, cost, consumption and maximize comfort is still an open problem.

Javaid et al. in [13] focused over to control electric consumption and maintenance the comfort taking into consideration the user preferences. Were implemented four algorithms: genetic algorithms (GA), teaching-learning base on optimization (TLBO), enhanced differential evolution (EDE) and enhanced differential teaching-learning algorithm (EDTL). The consumption model took two types of devices flexible and inflexible, device, consumption, and schedule of use, this model is implemented in a microgrid context.

On the other hand, Avaid et al. in [3] is presented an electric consumption model that consider houses and devices mount; the kind of devices are interruptible, not interruptible and regular application use. This model is for demand-side management to reduce peak average to ratio, costs and renewable energy that are considered tariff and time of use. The algorithms that were analyzed are bacterial foraging optimization algorithm (BFOA), genetic algorithm (GA), binary particle swarm optimization (BPSO), wind-driven optimization (WDO). In this work, a genetic binary particle swarm optimization (GBPSO) is proposed. Results showed in term of PAR reduction and execution time that GA is better than others, in term of cost reduction BPSO is better than the others, and in terms of cost and PAR GBPSO is more efficiently than the others.

Complementary work is presented by Hao and Wang where they proposed a home energy demands in [14], this system reduced cost in terms of tariff and costs, devices identified are interruptible and not interruptible. This system has implemented a game theory technique which can reduce costs and can help to increase load demand at the off-peak time. The identified peak time hours are between 8 to 24 h. Mohsin et al. developed demand-side management in [9] with the main purpose of reducing costs, PAR and time, maximize comfort in applying a harmony search algorithm (HSA). This work compared his algorithm with binary particle swarm optimization (BPSO), differential evolution (DE), genetic algorithm (GA), ant colony optimization (ACO), Hybrid Differential Evolution – Harmony Search (DE-HS), immune artificial hybrid algorithm, genetic hybrid algorithm, teaching-learning base on optimization (TLBO) and Shuffled Frog Learning (SFL). Devices types in this work are interruptible, not interruptible, flexible and inflexible. In terms of costs, PAR and consumption, HAS was better than other techniques.

In addition, Huang et al. in [15] is used as a set of models of demand systems. In the work is used a gradient (PSO) based on particle swarm optimization, the main objective was to schedule the operation of appliances to save energy and reduce cost considering user convenience. The model is simulated and compared to hybrid PSO algorithm and cooperative PSO algorithm. The proposed algorithm shows better results in a real-time application. Similarly, Matei et al. in [16] describes an IoT architecture, that consist of four layers sensors, physic, digital and meta through that the data flow. In this work were proposed to process the data in two different times, first one in the physic layer and second one in meta-layer. The first process is about to select data that reduce computational cost, and the second process is about to implement any algorithm or technique, the selection of that technique depends on implementation objectives.

Finally, Mohsin et al. concluded in [9] that a deterministic optimization is inefficient and impractical to handle a big problem. A heuristic optimization is better to implement in big data problems. Also, Silva et al. conclude in [17] that electric consumption varies according to the hour of the day, the day of the week and season.

Hoon et al. explain in [2], that IoT let to monitor, handle and control devices by WEB way. The IoT implementation let to get information from data that are generated in real-time. The great challenge for smart meters there is to develop an intelligent environment (AmI).

3   A Methodology to Design a Home Energy Management System

A Home Energy Management System analyze and control the electric area consumption. The HEMS main objectives [7] are: to reduce costs, reduce consumption, reduce PAR and maximizer user comfort. IoT could help to implement a control and monitoring a sensors infrastructure, it through the web way. So, HEMS could be developed using IoT to control the devices that are in the same red. First of all is necessary to know how IoT data flow architecture is, a proposed architecture is showed in [16]. When a comparison is made with [18], which describes cyber-physic behavior, it is observed between [16] and [18] that it is possible to identify an architecture that contemplates all the stages through which the data must pass (since its obtaining, processing, and their output). In Fig. 1, the stages are presented by which the data flow. In IoT architecture proposed the data flow through five layers called: sensor, there is a sensor architecture; physic, here is implemented an ambient intelligent (AmI), AmI extracts the context and in this stage is made a first process with sensor and user data; the data extracted pass to information module, where all the context data are gathered; behavioral awareness is processed the data and found a behavior; digital, here is created a logical object that represents the real objects; in the meta-layer all the logical objects data are processed according to particular objectives of the problem to be solved.

When is developed a HEMS and it's integrated an information layer, that occurs when IoT is implemented, the problems became a multi-objective optimization problem and this kind of problems are solved using metaheuristics [19]. To develop a HEMS requires: to identify all variables that determine the electric consumption, to know the types of devices, to identify a meta-heuristic algorithm and to propose an electric consumption model.

A Home Energy Management System (HEMS) (see Fig. 2), it consists of three modules (programming, monitor, and prediction) and a control unit [15]. In the programming module preference data is entered, which ones are sent to the control unit. The control unit performs communication between the devices, by sending and receiving the signals; and it communicates with the prediction module by sending the data that allows generating a profile of household appliances use. The logical control unit sends the consumption of each appliance to the programming module.

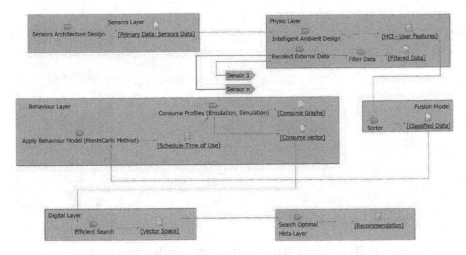

Fig. 1. DS data flow in IoT, own creation from [16] and [18].

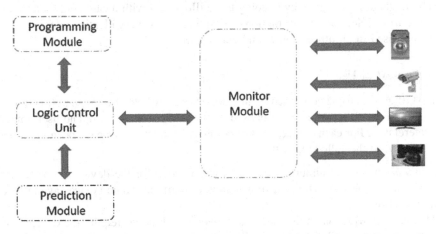

Fig. 2. Home Energy Management System architecture from [15].

After identifying the stages (Fig. 1), and the modules (Fig. 2) is possible to develop a proposition HEMS which implements IoT. The stages are placed in the module that corresponds to according to what must be generated in each of them (see Fig. 3). The proposed HEMS consists of a sensor layer, physical layer, and a prediction module. The sensor architecture and the monitor module are in the sensor layer. In the physical layer there is the intelligent environment, which is formed by a programming module, logical control unit, and information fusion module. In the prediction module, there are three layers: behavioral awareness, the digital and the goal layer. In the way to develop a HEMS based on the use of IoT, the following variables must be identified: the variables that determine the electricity consumption, the devices, the metaheuristic techniques, and a proposed model of electrical consumption.

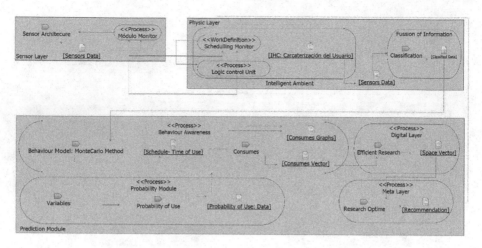

Fig. 3. Home Energy Management System with IoT, own creation.

The methodology feasibility is going to be illustrated with a case study with a real case scenario of electronic consumption corresponding to every identified device that is frequently used in an office, house, and classroom.

3.1 Context of Use

Context of use is a triple composed by the identification of electric consumption device, the environment (where the device is used, house, office, classroom), and user's needs (or preferences). For each device, a set of common characteristics have been identified. Accordingly, to the following list:

- *Minimum power*: minimum electrical power needed for the device to could function. This value was estimated from public lists of electronic devices available on their websites.
- *Maximum power*: maximum electrical power which could require the device. This value was obtained from public lists of electronic devices available on their websites.
- *Time of use*: the daily average time usage measured in hours.
- *Kind of device*: the devices are classified according to the most common appearance. For example, office supplies, video games, household appliances, electronics, lighting and security devices.
- *Type of devices*: corresponds to the category proposed in related works [6, 20, 21] that are: interruptible (I), non-interruptible (NI), flexible (F) and not-inflexible (NF). An Interruptible system refers to a system that can be turned on and off without any constraint. Interruptible devices are defined as devices that could be used in anytime, and the time of use varies according to the user needs [9, 12–14, 21]. Not-interruptible devices stop their function once they are finished, their consumption could be variable or constant [9, 11, 12, 14, 21]. Flexible devices, their functions

could be stopped and continue at another time, could be on standby too [3, 9, 12, 21] Not-flexible devices, they could not be turned off because is necessary that they have a constant function [9, 21].

3.2 Sensor Layer

Sensor Layer stores sensors raw data, also known as primary data, corresponding to the sensors' consumption readings. In a context, the set of devices may vary and the corresponding arrangement as well, we call this setup the Sensor Architecture. So, from this layer, the output is a database with the consumption readings, consumption meters, of each device that is connected to the sensor architecture of the electricity facility under a specific context.

Data acquisition nowadays could be the result of using IoT devices, or we could even build a no-invasive potentiometer using Arduino Uno and SCT-013 sensors, or any related technology. Data consumption files are obtained and stored in a DB, a sample set is listed as follows in Table 1:

Table 1. Laptop consumption.

Current (Amperes)	Power (Watts)
6.4871	1423.1668
3.9958	878.9938
4.4403	976.8803
4.7000	1059.5591
12.5839	2768.4433
9.4061	2009.3459
8.5427	1894.3894
4.9717	1059.7808
3.8485	846.6782
6.0309	1327.0713
18.2753	4020.5761
6.7826	1492.1634
6.0730	1336.0534
6.6512	1409.5651
3.1939	702.6623

The current work considers data from a specific context which every household appliance monitored by a non-invasive smart meter that represents a specific consumption that is determined by the occupants' behavior.

In our example, we implemented a database (DB) using MySQL Workbench, DB is placed in a local server. The DB contains 268 registers. Every register stores: <id_device, device_name, min_ power, max_power, freq_time, shut_down, kind_device>, some registers are showed in Table 2.

Table 2. Many registers from household appliances DB.

ID device	Device_name	Min power	Max_ power	Freq_time (use Hrs/day)	Shut_ down	Kind_ device
OF1	Cannon (three light)	6.4	400	1.5	Yes	I
OF2	Cannon (three light)	6.4	1000	1.5	Yes	I
OF3	Cannon (one light)	6.4	220	1.5	Yes	I
OF4	Cannon (one light)	6.4	236	1.5	Yes	I
OF5	CPU	14.1	250	4	Yes	F
OF6	CPU iMac 3.06 GHz	129.6	365	4	Yes	F
OF9	Digital decoder	55	55	24	Yes	I
OF10	Scanner	65	275	1	Yes	I
OF11	Fax	65	150	1	Yes	F

3.3 Physical Layer

The physical layer corresponds to the composition of the primary and user data that corresponds to a set of constraints. For this purpose, an interactive system is recommended a human-computer interface. The external data is the readings obtained from the room sensors. In a HEMS it is identified that the user data have to do with the preferences and times of use of the household appliances that are monitored through the sensor architecture; and the external data are the data obtained from the environmental conditions (temperature, humidity, presence, etc.), that is, all those data that result in a high degree of importance to be considered for the conditioning of the use of electrical devices within the area you want to control. In our case, we have built a website (see Fig. 4) where users select their devices, graphically, and coherent with the proposal of building better Legos [21].

In the website is possible to register new users and unsubscribe them (see Fig. 5). To each one of users can define their context identifying household appliances (see Fig. 6) and make reports and graphs (see Fig. 7).

In the physical layer, is founded a fusion module, too. This module works as a repository of all the data that must be considered (primary, external and user data) to solve the problem that is being studied; to later be able to group them according to the needs of the solution. The output resulting from this module is grouped data.

3.4 Prediction Module

The prediction module is formed by three layers: behavioral awareness, digital and meta layer. There is a behavioral module in the behavior layer, in which the methods or

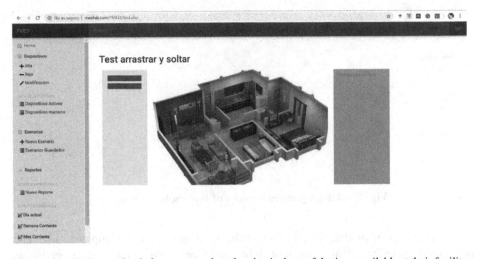

Fig. 4. A web site used to help users to select the physical set of devices available at their facility.

Fig. 5. High and low users on the web site.

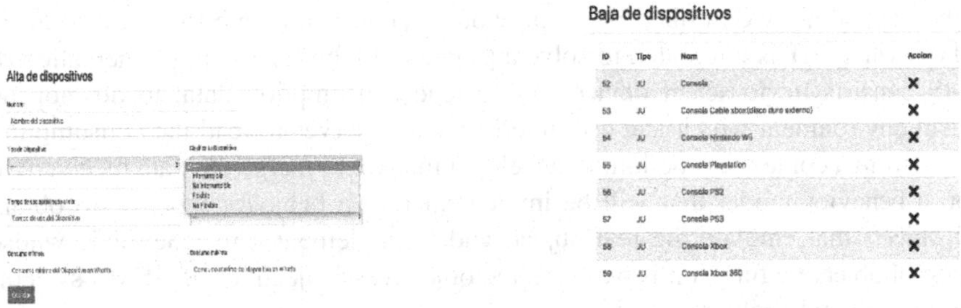

Fig. 6. High and low household appliances used to define the context.

procedures can be implemented to generate the necessary parameters according to the problem to be solved, this module includes both the user's data (which determines the restrictions to consider) as environmental data (which are the conditions for decision making).

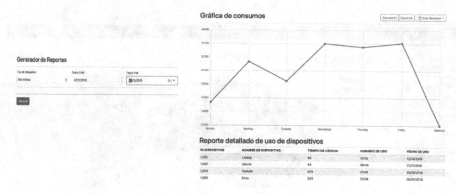

Fig. 7. Make reports and graphs of household appliances.

In the behavior module of HEMS, a behavioral model can be implemented. The behavioral model can identify the probability and time of use of the devices, giving as output the on and off schedule, and the operating time of each device; and integrate, a module capable of generating the actual consumption data that each device can have. All the resulting data pass in vector form to the next layer.

The digital layer is where the data from the previous layer arrive and space is formed with the vectors that represent the possible behavior scenarios of all the objects that are in the real world. The vector space is sent to the next layer. In a HEMS, we have a set of vectors formed from the combinations of possible consumptions that each of the devices that are being monitored may have.

In the meta-layer are implemented procedures that seek proposals for solutions to the objectives that are to be achieved according to the proposed scenario. A HEMS is a multi-objective problem and to solve it, a metaheuristic technique is implemented.

4   Discussion

From the methodology described in the previous section is possible to identify how is carried out when IoT is integrated to solve a problem. In the case of implementation of a HEMS consists in: to select devices for to read consumption data; to develop an intelligent environment which is a user interface and it serves to read the consumption data to perform a context extraction; to develop a module to merge the data received; to develop a behavior model that will be implemented in a behavior module, to obtain logical objects that emulate the real object; and to implement a metaheuristic whose definition of objective function is based on the objectives (objectives of HEMS system) to meet the original problem.

A methodology has been defined to identify the consumption variables. The methodology consists in: to identify the household appliances that are the most frequently in a house, office, and classroom; the maximum and minimum power; the frequently time of use according to the area in which HEMS is going to be implemented; and the classification to which the device belongs (I, NI, F, NF). With the devices database is possible to simulate N different scenarios with d devices each one.

The data flow in HEMS was obtained from two different ideas, one that talks about an architecture that would be considered when is implementing an IoT project, and another one when is talking about a context where is necessary to take in a count the information.

The selection of metaheuristic to be implemented is based on what has been identified in the literature, in which the constant of selecting a genetic algorithm is identified against whose results are compared to another metaheuristics implementation.

5 Conclusion and Future Work

This methodology was developed after to analyze the literature, which their focus objective was to develop a HEMS. During the literature review was observed that the development of the systems proposals only covers one or two stages of our proposed methodology. If the methodology proposed here is followed, it allows the developers to identify every requirement that needs to be met.

The proposed methodology is used as the basis to develop a HEMS, where the appliances were identified and their consumption variables too.

As future work is considered the creation of an intelligent schedule which works with the probability of use, schedules and the time of consumption of every device that is contemplated in the scenario. As well as, it is proposed the implementation of a simulator to a household appliance use where the metaheuristic technique will make an analysis and will give a user recommendation according to the user-needs and specific objectives.

References

1. Parsa, A.: Implementation of smart optimal and automatic control of electrical home appliances (IoT) (2017)
2. Kim, T.H., Ramos, C., Mohammed, S.: Smart city and IoT. Futur. Gener. Comput. Syst. **76**, 159–162 (2017). https://doi.org/10.1016/j.future.2017.03.034
3. Javaid, N., et al.: A new heuristically optimized Home Energy Management controller for smart grid. Sustain. Cities Soc. **34**, 211–227 (2017). https://doi.org/10.1016/j.scs.2017.06.009
4. Sowmya, R., Suneetha, K.R.: Data mining with big data. In: 2017 11th International Conference on Intelligent Systems and Control, pp. 246–250 (2017). https://doi.org/10.1109/ISCO.2017.7855990
5. Kakran, S., Chanana, S.: Energy scheduling of smart appliances at home under the effect of dynamic pricing schemes and small renewable energy source. Int. J. Emerg. Electr. Power Syst. **19**(2), 1–12 (2018). https://doi.org/10.1515/ijeeps-2017-0187
6. Jahn, M., Jentsch, M., Prause, C.R., Pramudianto, F., Al-Akkad, A., Reiners, R.: The energy aware smart home. In: 2010 5th International Conference on Future Information Technology (FutureTech), pp. 1–8. IEEE (2010). https://doi.org/10.1109/FUTURETECH.2010.5482712
7. Rahim, S., et al.: Exploiting heuristic algorithms to efficiently utilize energy management controllers with renewable energy sources. Energy Build. **129**, 452–470 (2016). https://doi.org/10.1016/j.enbuild.2016.08.008

8. Mocanu, D.C., Mocanu, E., Nguyen, P.H., Gibescu, M., Liotta, A.: Big IoT data mining for real-time energy disaggregation in buildings. In: 2016 IEEE International Conference on Systems, Man, and Cybernetics (SMC), pp. 3765–3769 (2017). https://doi.org/10.1109/SMC.2016.7844820
9. Mohsin, S.M., Javaid, N., Madani, S.A., Abbas, S.K.: Appliance scheduling in smart homes with harmony search algorithm for different operation time intervals, p. 1 (2018)
10. Fauvel, C., Claveau, F., Chevrel, P., Fiani, P.: A flexible design methodology to solve energy management problems. Int. J. Electr. Power Energy Syst. **97**, 220–232 (2018). https://doi.org/10.1016/j.ijepes.2017.11.005
11. Nadeem, Z., Javaid, N., Malik, A.W., Iqbal, S.: Scheduling appliances with GA, TLBO, FA, OSR and their hybrids using chance constrained optimization for smart homes. Energies **11**, 1–30 (2018). https://doi.org/10.3390/en11040888
12. Yao, L., Damiran, Z., Lim, W.H.: Energy management optimization scheme for smart home considering different types of appliances (2017)
13. Javaid, N., et al.: Demand side management in nearly zero energy buildings using heuristic optimizations. Energies **10**, 1131 (2017). https://doi.org/10.3390/en10081131
14. Hao, Y., Wang, W.: Optimal home energy management with PV system in time of use tariff environment, pp. 5–9 (2017)
15. Huang, Y., Tian, H., Wang, L.: Demand response for home energy management system. Int. J. Electr. Power Energy Syst. **73**, 448–455 (2015). https://doi.org/10.1016/j.ijepes.2015.05.032
16. Matei, O., Anton, C., Scholze, S., Cenedese, C.: Multi-layered data mining architecture in the context of Internet of Things. In: Proceedings of 2017 IEEE 15th International Conference on Industrial Informatics, INDIN 2017, pp. 1193–1198 (2017). https://doi.org/10.1109/INDIN.2017.8104943
17. Silva, B.N., Khan, M., Han, K.: Load balancing integrated least slack time-based appliance scheduling for smart home energy management. Sensors (Switzerland) **18**(3), 685 (2018). https://doi.org/10.3390/s18030685
18. Chen, S., et al.: Butler, not servant: a human-centric smart home energy management system. IEEE Commun. Mag. **55**, 27–33 (2017). https://doi.org/10.1109/MCOM.2017.1600699CM
19. Fauvel_flexible design methodology.pdf
20. Yao, L., Shen, J.Y., Lim, W.H.: Real-Time energy management optimization for smart household. In: Proceedings of 2016 IEEE International Conference on Internet Things; IEEE Green Comput. Commun. IEEE Cyber, Physical and Social Computing (IEEE Smart Data, iThings-GreenCom-CPSCom-Smart Data 2016, pp. 20–26 (2017). https://doi.org/10.1109/iThings-GreenCom-CPSCom-SmartData.2016.31
21. Jenson, S.: The future IoT: building better legos. Computer **50**, 68–71 (2017). https://doi.org/10.1109/MC.2017.48

Digital Competence in Initial Teacher Training: Construction and Pilot Test of an Evaluation Tool/Instrument

Anna Luz Acosta-Aguilera[1]([⊠]), Rubén Edel-Navarro[1],
and Yadira Navarro-Rangel[2]

[1] Universidad Veracruzana, Av. Jesús Reyes Heroles s/n Zona Universitaria,
Fracc. Costa Verde, 94294 Boca del Río, Ver, Mexico
aniluzacosta@gmail.com, redeln@gmail.com
[2] Benemérita Universidad Autónoma de Puebla, Calle 4 Sur #104, Col. Centro,
72000 Puebla de Zaragoza, Puebla, Mexico
ynavarro44@gmail.com

Abstract. The objective of the present article is to describe the process of designing and validating an implement which allows to measure the digital competence of the students from the bachelor in Secondary teaching in the area of Telesecundaria. First of all, it is set the context and evolution of the concept of digital competence in order to provide the theory to understand the structure of the tool. The design of the questionnaire was made taking as a reference some questionnaires applied by different researchers at a national and international level. 48 items were defined and these were organized into 3 dimensions based on theoretical elements from different authors. Three different types of validation were evaluated: 1. content, 2. construct and 3. consistency and reliability. The outcomes indicate high levels of reliability, also the feedback received through the opinion of experts provides valuable and trustworthy elements about the implement. The information obtained in this first procedure bring to light the need to consider technical and logistics aspects in the final application of the questionnaire as well as complement the data with another tool which is not of perception.

Keywords: Digital competence · Initial teacher training · Validation of tools

1 Introduction

Overcrowding of the Internet throughout the mid-nineties put into evidence what some authors call the *technological revolution* centered in the use of TIC, which started to reconfigure the material base of the society to a fast speed [1]. This social restructuring had a great impact in the teaching area, modifying practice and therefore the teacher's roles, since integrating this technologies requires one who is ready to innovation and conscious of the methodology implications that means proposing teaching environments in which virtuality plays an essential part in the exercise of their profession.

This form of being inside the social and school environment, which is called by some authors a digital culture or ciberculture [2] demands different ways to be and

© Springer Nature Switzerland AG 2019
P. H. Ruiz and V. Agredo-Delgado (Eds.): HCI-COLLAB 2019, CCIS 1114, pp. 177–188, 2019.
https://doi.org/10.1007/978-3-030-37386-3_14

behave that also promote different forms of communication, management and school organization, access to information and creation of data and information [3].

In this context of changes and uncertainty arise the concept of digital competence. There is a great deal of definitions, which respond to moments, contexts and specific objectives. However, in order to clarify the characteristics they have, the ones which were considered relevant for the purpose of this investigation were selected.

To Peña-López [4] digital competence is the combination of knowledge, skills and abilities, along with values and attitudes to reach objectives effectively and efficiently in context and with digital tools. It is expressed in a strategic control of five great abilities related to the different dimensions of digital competence.

He proposes 5 dimensions/aspects: (1) learning dimension, (2) informational dimension, (3) communicative dimension, (4) digital culture dimension and (5) technological dimension. He mentions that having an efficient command in the 5 aspects proposed would mean being digital competent, which would be a goal to achieve for the students and teachers.

Some of the dimensions mentioned by Peña-López [4] are closely related to what Jordi Adell exposed [5]. He indicates that digital competence is formed by five basic elements which are:

1. Informational competence: set of knowledge, skills and abilities necessary to work with information, search it, have access to it, organize it, manage it, analyze it, criticize it, evaluate it and then create new information and distribute it.
2. Technological competence: It has to do with handling the technological tools.
3. Multiple literacy: Our world is not only the society of the printing texts, since the 50's with the advent of TV, we live in an audiovisual society, the video language, photography, comics, should be part of the curriculum and not only as spectators but as authors too.
4. Generic cognitive competence, not only having access to information but being able to transform it into knowledge, requires a problem-solving ability.
5. Digital citizenship: it is the preparation to live, into the real and digital world, the preparation for a citizenship to be critic, free, integrated, able to live this society with rules and high standards of behavior in the digital world.

According to the European Commission, digital competence is the "safe and critic use of information technology for work, leisure and communication. It is sustained on the basic competence in the subject ICT: the use of computers to obtain, evaluate, store, produce, present and exchange information and communicate and participate in collaborative networks on line" [6]. This competence was included within the eight key competences established to the accomplishment of permanent learning.

In some research analyzed in relation to the work developed by Gisbert, it can be observed a clear tendency to define digital competence according to the contribution its development can have within the teaching-learning process, pointing out that the digital competence is the sum of "skills, knowledge and attitudes in technological, informational, multimedia and communicative aspects which lead to a complex multiple literacy" [7].

Therefore, it represents "a set of skills and knowledge that the individual himself must acquire and consolidate as an essential mean to move forward in his studies (at any formal stage and throughout his life)" [8].

They consider it is "a basic competence to any XXI-century citizen, from which the digital competence of a teacher derives (DCT) specific to any education professional" [8], all of this would require a teacher who had the skills, attitudes and knowledge needed to establish learning environments in context enriched by ICT.

Related to the "specific use of knowledge, skills and abilities which has to do with the development of elements and processes that allow to use efficiently, effectively and innovatively the tools and technological resources" [7].

Some other definitions which were found are more general, these are not limited only to the educational field. These defined digital competence as:

"The set of knowledge, skills, attitudes, strategies and consciousness the use of ICT and digital resources require to do tasks, solve problems, communicate, handle information, collaborate, create and share contents and also generate knowledge in an effective, efficient, adequate, critic, creative, autonomous, flexible, etic and reflexive way for work, leisure, participation, learning, socialization, consumption and empowerment" [9].

All of the above matches what it was stated by Castillejos, Torres and Lagunes [10] who say that digital competence is a key and transverse aspect which every digital citizen should develop, since they face every day the need to take advantage of technology. "Promoting them involves the critical, creative and safe use of ICT, either for work, school or every day activities".

Cabello, Cuervo, Puerta y Serrano [11] complement this definition arguing that so as to be digitally competent it is necessary to have the abilities to get, process, transmit information and transform it in knowledge. This means having the control of basic specific languages, technological and expressive resources to transmit the information, strategies to identify and solve software and hardware problems as well as logical thinking skills.

All that has been described so far allow us to identify the complexity and diversity of the concepts analyzed, which represent a foundation to the establishment of criteria according to the interest, purpose and context in which they are examined.

2 Methodology

Prior to the description of the methodological characteristics and the procedure of making the survey, the variables which support these are described. It is worth mentioning that the information presented is part of a wider research related to the pedagogical usability of TIC in initial teacher training.

2.1 Variable: Digital Competence

Digital competence of students was selected as the study variable after a thorough research on the theoretical construct developed up to date, as well as the established objectives which pretend to identify the perception students have regarding their own digital competence and at the same time, analyze the type and level of digital competence they actually possess on the basis of the assumption that this knowledge is essential for designing strategies which allow the teacher trainers provide better educational experiences related to the use of TIC to their students.

2.2 Construction of the Implement

The questionnaire at issue was elaborated after making an important search and identification of some tools that have been applied by other researchers both at national and international level, even when the exact questions were not transcribed they were considered as an important basis for the final version that it is presented.

The works from Zúñiga [12], Pech [13] and Esteve [14] were analyzed in more detail since they have developed their investigations in higher education contexts related to the educational field, that is how the three dimensions and fourteen variables of "digital competence" intended to be measured with this implement were chosen, which is shown in the Table 1.

Table 1. Dimensions of digital competence

Dimension	Indicator	Source
Learning field/area	Pedagogical value	Esteve [14], Pech [13]
	Relevance	
	Critical usage	
	Problem solving	
Information and communication field/area	Technological literacy	UNESCO [15], Zúñiga [12]
	Usage of computer systems.	
	Organisation in digital formats	
	Effective pair communication	
	Usage of social media	
	Collaboration in digital environment	
Digital culture field/area	Creation and diffusion of knowledge	Zúñiga [12], Adell [5]
	Digital citizenship	
	Social and cultural practice	
	Legal and ethical usage	

Another critical moment in the making of the implement came out when the multiple choice options in scale Likert were determined. However, after analyzing what De Villis [15] says to this matter, only four-option answers were chosen obtaining with this decision a higher reliability in the questionnaire.

Finally, a pilot implement was designed, with 48 items, which answer-options were presented in a Likert scale. These include the options "Incapable, A bit capable, Quite capable and Very capable", Table 2 distributed as follows:

Table 2. Distribution of questions per dimension

Dimension	No. of questions	Percentage
General questions	3	n/a
Dimension 1	13	29%
Dimension 2	18	40%
Dimension 3	14	31%
	TOTAL	100%

2.3 Subjects/Population

The participants were chosen randomly considering the following inclusion, exclusion and elimination criteria:

1. They have to be students of the Bachelor degree in Secondary Teaching from the area of Telesecundaria.
2. They have to be registered in the subjects of: Secondary level Teaching Basic Issues II and Educational Attention to teenagers in threatening situations.
3. They have to show interest and be willing to participate.

2.4 Pilot Test

The tool was applied at the Benemérita Escuela Normal Veracruzana (BENV) "Enrique C. Rébsamen" to a sample of 60 students from two different groups from the Bachelor in Secondary Teaching in the area of Telesecundaria in order to test the functioning of the tool and therefore to have elements to determine if the questions were clear and easy to understand by the participants.

The implementation of the tool was self-administered online through the use of LimeSurvey which is free software to elaborate and apply surveys and is simple and easy to use. The data is stored on the page www.limesurvey.org where they can be handled without difficulty.

In spite of being a self-administered questionnaire, the conducting was guided and during school time, which required to ask permission from the teachers in advance to finish their lessons 30 min before scheduled. With the support of a teacher from the research area of the BENV, it was installed a computer and a modem in which a kind of intranet was configured so that the students were able to answer in their phones or laptops without using up their download volumes.

It is important to mention that the participants were explained the purpose of the investigation and they were ensured its reliability. The implementation took place in two days at different times. There were no difficulties during the application.

3 Data Analysis

The analysis consisted in estimating descriptive statistic for each item (graphs, percentages, among others). After that it was carried out the factor analysis, the main component analysis and the reliability/internal consistence of the items analysis throughout the Cronbach's Alfa. To do so it was used the Statistical Program for Quantitative Analysis SPSS version 24.

3.1 Validity

3.1.1 Validity of Content

Validity of content refers to the need of proving that the items that form the tool represent the construct intended to be evaluated, one of the most common procedures to carry out this validation is to turn to external criteria for example, the opinion of experts [16]. This is why it was requested the assessment of three experts in digital competence, who were given a check list through which they could evaluate item by item the validity of the tool.

3.1.2 Validity of Construct

Validity of construct refers to the consistence itself has the carrying of the data in the evaluated construct [16] that means, it allows to know if it is really being measured what it is supposed to be measured, to carry out this validation it was used the Kaiser-Meyer-Olkin test (KMO) and the Bartlett's sphericity test.

3.2 Reliability Analysis

The factor analysis enables to explore the suitability and validity of the proposals made by the researcher about the acceptability of the theoretical variables which intends to build. Its objective is to reduce the number of variables for a better scientific explanation and simpler to reality. In the same way, it clusters the data produced by many empirical variables into few theoretical variable or latent variables, or factors independent among them.

4 Results

4.1 Validity of Content

Initially it was determined who would be the expert judges to whom support in the validation of the tool would be requested. It was sent to three experts whose career and knowledge in the area of digital competence and teacher training is outstanding.

They were contacted via email to ask their support. After that the tool and the corresponding check list were sent. Even when there were some comments related to the structure of the indicators in general, the judges considered appropriate and relevant the items designed for each dimension.

Verbal feedback was possible only with one of them, this was carried out through a video chat system (WebEx). He was pointing out the observations he had made, supporting each one with a reason and suggesting options to a greater understanding.

4.2   Validity of Construct

According to Castro and Galindo [16], the Table 3 Kaiser-Meyer-Olkin test (KMO) and the Barlett's sphericity test help prove if the sample is acceptable for the factoring of the variables.

Table 3. KMO and Bartlett test

Sampling adequacy measurement Kaiser-Meyer-Olkin		.765
Bartlett's sphericity test	Aprox. Chi-square	2560.611
	gl	990
	Sig.	.000

From the previous results it can be concluded that the sample is acceptable for the factoring of the variables by reaching a KMO index of 0.765 (quite close to 0.8 which is the one normally demanded). At the same time the correlation matrix turned out spherical ($p < 0.01$), and as a consequence, analyzable from the factorial point of view.

4.3   Factorial Analysis

In order to do the factorial analysis, first of all the correlation matrix is obtained with the aim of identifying if the variables share common factors which explain its variance. In the correlation matrix most of correlations resulting were highly significant ($p < 0.01$), this indicates the existence a strong correlation in most of them, this would assume the presence of common factors which explain the variance of such variables and bring together the information provided in the factors hypothetically operationalized.

4.4   Reliability Analysis

The Table 4 Cronbach's Alfa coefficient was used to do the reliability analysis, obtaining a value of 0.976 as a result the tool is considered reliable to measure what is intended to be measured.

Table 4. Cronbach's Alfa tool

Reliability statistics		
Cronbach's Alfa	Cronbach's Alfa based on standardized elements	N of elements
.976	.976	45

Subsequently a statistic fact-finding per item was made in which it could be observed in a Table 5 a standard deviation and lost values. It is worth mentioning that there were no lost values because when the questionnaire was applied all the questions were marked as mandatory and they could not be sent unless they were all answered.

Table 5. Standard deviation and lost values

		Highest value	Lowest value
		D1P12	D3P34
Valid	Number	60	60
	Lost	0	0
Deviation		0.911	0.666

Regarding to the deviation, results below .500 were found and some other above .500 without being close to 1 which tells us that there were little variation in the type of answers given. As far as statistics exploration carried out per student, the situation is very different since standard deviation is above1 in most of the cases, which reflects variation in the type of answers given.

4.5   Demographic Data

In relation to the application of the questionnaire in order to measure the digital competence of the students in Bachelor Degree in Secondary teaching with mayor in Telesecundaria, hereunder some data considered relevant for its analysis is outlined.

The questionnaire was answered by students between 18 and 22 years old. 70% were women and 30% men. This could be explained due to the fact that in Mexico, especially in elementary education, most teacher trainers are female.

In the following Table 6 it can be observed that most of the respondents (68%) is currently studying the second semester in the Bachelor Degree in Secondary teaching with mayor in Telesecundaria, with a recurring age of 19 years old (35%).

Table 6. Demographic data

		Current year of study	Gender	Age
N	Valid	60	60	60
	Lost	0	0	0
Mean		2.23	1.70	19.97
Median		2.00	2.00	20.00
Mode		2	2	19

Table 7. Statistical analysis

		Level_dim_1	Level_dim_2	Level_dim_3	Level_global
N	Valid	60	60	60	60
	Lost	0	0	0	0
Mean		2.03	2.03	2.20	2.12
Median		2.00	2.00	2.00	2.00
Mode		2	2	2	2

In the statistical analysis shown in Table 7 it can be observed the obtained results in relation to the mean, median and mode prepared taking in consideration the level of digital competence per dimension and global level.

This data allow us to infer that the median, that means the average in the values assigned, is two. This is, according to students, level 2 corresponding to an intermediate level in the development of their digital competence.

Hereafter, it is presented the analysis which was carried out by level of digital competence. It is important to mention that this was determined taking into account the grades the participants got. The results look as the following Table 8:

Table 8. Levels of digital competence

Score	Level of competence	Codification
151–180	Advanced	3
121–150	Intermediate	2
91–120	Beginner	1

The levels obtained in dimensions 1, 2 and 3 showed that the participants got an intermediate digital competence level, which means they are able to identify software to support their academic activities, make good use of TIC as an instrument that reinforce critical and reflective thought, use technology to improve quality in their products or learning evidences (homework, research, essays, writing, presentations, etc.) as well as to obtain maximum benefit from technology for their professional and personal life.

Finally, in the following Fig. 1, it is encompassed the total level of digital competence obtained in each dimension. There you can see that the prevailing level is 2 with a 55%, which corresponds to an intermediate level.

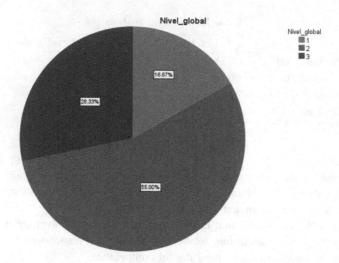

Fig. 1. Total level of digital competence obtained in each dimension

5 Discussion and Future Works

Designing a questionnaire which allows to know and analyze the digital competence a future Telesecundaria teacher has is the first step for making a proposal to the integration of TIC which promote their use through the establishment of methodologies, strategies and activities to meet the specific needs of a future Telesecundaria teacher.

While this statistical work represented a first approach to the validity analysis and reliability of the instrument, this first data allows distinguishing some changes or adjustments needed to improve the measurement scale, such as revising the structure of the dimensions to reorganize the questions in each of them.

During the implementation of the factor analysis it can be seen that in the results, the variables are not distributed in the factors or identified dimensions, the factor analysis offers a rearrangement and adjustment of the dimensions, since not all the questions were brought together in the concept dimensions proposed in the research.

The questions are focused in two out of three dimensions which were determined since the theoretical revision. (Learning area, Information and communication area and Digital culture Area)

In the same way, and derived from the implementation of the tool, some failures in the structure of the questionnaire could be identified. Some of them were pointed out by the participants (spelling and typing mistakes, an item which was double in dimension 1 and dimension 2). From the factor analysis we could identified some redundant items or the lack of differentiation among the questions, also the location of each group of questions in the dimensions which were built beforehand. These will be adjusted in the following implementations.

Apart from the conclusions expressed before, it is important to state that the results obtained during the pilot stage permitted not only knowing relevant aspects of the context of implementation but establishing a precedent to:

- Learning how to measure the digital competence of a training teacher of Telesecundaria.
- Identifying the levels of digital competence from the participants and the possible relation between this and the pedagogical usage of ICT in the initial teacher training.
- Identifying areas of opportunities which allow to strengthen the digital competence of teacher-training students at a curricular level.

As a future work, it would be convenient to develop a quantitative instrument which reinforce this perception questionnaire and evaluates the participants performance, contrasting or complementing their opinion to what they really know how to do. This is due to the fact that the results show the need to implement actions to an institutional level in order to help students get a higher standard in digital competence.

References

1. Castells, M.: La era de la información: economía, sociedad y cultura. Volumen I. La Sociedad Red. 2a ed., p. 656. Alianza Editorial, S.A. Madrid (2000)
2. Levy, P.: Cultura escrita y tecnocultura contemporánea: mediaciones cognitivas en la formación universitaria, en: Revista Nexus, No. 10, Escuela de Comunicación Social de la Universidad del Valle (2011)
3. Ramírez-Martinell, A., Casillas, M.A.(Coords.): Saberes digitales de los docentes de educación básica. Una propuesta para la discusión desde Veracruz. Veracruz: Secretaría de Educación de Veracruz. https://www.uv.mx/blogs/brechadigital/files/2017/04/Saberes-Digitales-SEV-libro-final.pdf. Accessed 23 Nov 2018
4. Peña-López, I.: La competencia digital: una propuesta. [Comentarios en una wiki en línea]. https://competenciadigital.wikispaces.com. Accessed 12 Sep 2018
5. Adell, A.: ¿Qué es la competencia digital? http://carraud.blogspot.mx/2010/10/jordi-adell-que-es-la-competencia.html. Accessed 09 Nov 2018
6. Lion, C.: Desarrollo de competencias digitales para portales de la región. Banco Interamericano de Desarrollo y Red Latinoamericana de Portales Educativos (2012). https://documentop.com/queue/desarrollo-de-competencias-digitales-para-portales-de-la-region-relpe_5a0d2f6a1723dd99282eedfb.html. Accessed 22 Aug 2018
7. Gisbert, M., Esteve, F.: Digital learners: la competencia digital de los estudiantes universitarios. La cuestión universitaria. Boletín electrónico de la Cátedra UNESCO de Gestión y Política Universitaria. No. 7 (2011). http://polired.upm.es/index.php/lacuestion universitaria/article/view/3359/3423. Accessed 30 Jan 2018
8. Silva. J., Miranda, P., Gisbert, M., Morales, J., Onetto, A.: Indicadores para evaluar la competencia digital docente en la formación inicial en el contexto chileno-Uruguayo. Revista Latinoamericana de Tecnología Educativa RELATEC **15**(3) (2016). ISSN 1695-288X
9. Punie, Y., Brecko, B.: DIGCOM: Marco Europeo de competencias digitales. European Commission (2014). http://jakintza.eus/wp-content/uploads/DIGCOMP_Donostia_ES-Rev.pdf. Accessed 17 Aug 2017
10. Castillejos, B., Torres, C., Lagunes, A.: La seguridad en las competencias digitales de los Millennials. Apertura. Revista de Innovación Educativa. Universidad de Guadalajara **8**(2) (2016). http://www.udgvirtual.udg.mx/apertura/index.php/apertura/article/view/914/586. ISSN 2007-1094. Accessed 06 Feb 2018

11. Cabello, J.L., Cuerva, J., Puerta, A., Serrano, J.: Tratamiento de la información y competencia digital en la educación. [Comentarios en una wiki en línea] https://sites.google.com/site/lascompetenciasbasicas/ticd. Accessed 03 Sep 2018
12. Zúñiga, J.: Las competencias digitales en el perfil universitario: el caso de la Facultad de Pedagogía de la Universidad Veracruzana. Universidad Veracruzana, Facultad de Pedagogía, Veracruz, México (2016)
13. Pech, S.: Competencia digital docente. Cuestionario en línea. Ciudad Real: España. https://docs.google.com/forms/d/e/1FAIpQLSeoPt3bZlU_mUIhaUCq4GjGt0AYAI5XpmcM7niSogPg3uxI1Q/viewform. Accessed 29 Mar 2018
14. Esteve, F.: La competencia digital docente Análisis de la autopercepción y evaluación del desempeño de los estudiantes universitarios de educación por medio de un entorno 3D. Departamento de Pedagogía, Universitat Rovira i Virgili. Tarragona. España (2015)
15. UNESCO Estándares de competencias en TIC para docentes. Londres: UNESCO. Recuperado el 18 de noviembre de 2014 de (2008). http://www.eduteka.org/EstandaresDocentesUnesco.php. Accessed 10 Jan 2019
16. Castro, J., Galindo, M.: Estadística Multivariable: análisis de correlaciones, Amarú: Ediciones, Salamanca: España (2000). ISBN 848196137

Exploratory Factor Analysis of a Digital Competency Questionnaire for Research

Adrián Sánchez[1](✉) ⓘ, Agustin Lagunes[2] ⓘ, Carlos A. Torres[3] ⓘ,
Juan C. Judikis[4], and Francisco López[1] ⓘ

[1] Universidad Veracruzana, 94294 Boca del Río, Veracruz, Mexico
adrianvidal2000@hotmail.com, frlopez@uv.mx
[2] Universidad Veracruzana, 94452 Ixtaczoquitlán, Veracruz, Mexico
aglagunes@uv.mx
[3] Universidad Veracruzana, 91780 Veracruz, Veracruz, Mexico
ctorres@uv.mx
[4] Universidad de Magallanes, 01855, Punta Arenas, Chile
juan.judikis@umag.cl

Abstract. Currently, citizens find themselves in a technological environment that demands a series of digital skills that must be developed to perform adequately, either in society or in any type of profession. It is of our interest that these competences allow students to perform satisfactorily in the academic field. Thus, the need to establish the level of digital skills that students require in order to carry out scientific research in a satisfactory manner. For this reason, an instrument of self-perception was adapted that gives a diagnosis of digital competences for research conducted by new university students. In order to carry out the analysis of reliability and validity of the instrument, a pilot test was implemented with a representative sample of 71 new students, belonging to a military engineering university in Veracruz, Mexico. As a result of the analysis, the instrument obtained a remarkable reliability, yielding a Cronbach's Alpha of 0.890 and its construct validity was average, obtaining a global Kaiser Meyer Olkin index of 0.718. Regarding the level of competence detected, a better perception of development was obtained in the students coming from private schools and technological baccalaureates, while the lowest levels were found in those coming from CON-ALEP, COBAEV and tele-baccalaureates. In light of the results, it is important to visualize the factors that can affect the academic development of students in order to allow them to enter universities with a better expectation of success.

Keywords: Digital competences for research · New income · Self-perception

1 Introduction

At present, the technological environment in which citizens of all types of profession are surrounded demands a series of digital competences that they must obtain in order to perform adequately in their work field and in society. For this, the European Union identifies a total of 21 digital competences grouped into 5 dimensions [1]. In the report of the European Union as part of the Project on Digital Competence (DIGCOMP), the knowledge, skills and attitudes that contribute to the Digital Competence were

© Springer Nature Switzerland AG 2019
P. H. Ruiz and V. Agredo-Delgado (Eds.): HCI-COLLAB 2019, CCIS 1114, pp. 189–210, 2019.
https://doi.org/10.1007/978-3-030-37386-3_15

determined [2]. However, there are no studies that establish the level of digital skills in Latin America, given that there are mostly researches that analyze them with perception surveys [3–12], which do not allow us to measure with certainty their level in each of the dimensions of the competition.

Table 1. Description of indicators of digital competences for research grouped by dimension. Excerpted from the DigCOMP 2.0 framework [1].

Dimension	Indicator	Description
1. Information and information literacy	1.1 Navigation, search and filtering of information and digital content	Articulate information needs, search data, information and content in digital environments, access and navigate among them. To create and update personal search strategies
	1.2 Evaluation of data, information and digital content	Analyze, compare and critically evaluate the credibility and reliability of data sources, information and digital content. Analyze, interpret and critically evaluate data, information and digital content
	1.3 Management of data, information and digital content	Organize, store and retrieve data, information and content in digital environments. Organize and process them in a structured environment
2. Communication and collaboration	2.1 Interaction through digital technologies	Interact through a variety of digital technologies and understand the appropriate digital media for a given context
	2.2 Sharing through digital technologies	To share data, information and digital content with others through appropriate digital technologies. To act as an intermediary, to know the practices of reference and attribution
	2.3 Collaboration through digital technologies	Use tools and digital technologies for collaborative processes, and for the construction and joint creation of resources and knowledge
3. Creation of digital content	3.1 Development of digital content	Create and edit digital content in different formats, to express themselves through digital media
	3.2 Integration and reworking of digital content	Modify, improve and integrate information and content in an existing body of knowledge to create new, original and relevant content and knowledge
	3.3 Copyright and licenses	Understand how copyright and licensing apply to data, information and digital content

Digital competences involve knowledge and skills in ICT management [2, 8, 13–17], as well as in digital media [14, 15] that allow managing and making proper use of information [8, 14, 15] participating in collaborative works in the network [14], which allow personal and professional development [15].

On the other hand, for some authors digital competences are defined from three stages of development [2, 18]. The first stage (Level 1) contemplates the generic digital competences that people must have in order to function in the information society. The second stage (Level 2), involves those skills that the individual is able to apply for specific purposes, so that he or she develops professionally. The third and last (Level 3), refers to those competencies that allow the individual to innovate and be creative, making a digital transformation of processes and activities, both individually and socially.

Digital competences for research are an extension of generic digital competences, since they are required to take them to a higher level when applied to a specific activity, such as research. Due to this, according to the definition of Ala-Mutka [2] and Martin and Grudziecki [18] they can be considered as digital competences of the second level. Therefore, Digital Competences for research (DCR) could be defined as the ability to search, filter, evaluate and manage data, information and digital content, which allows you to communicate and collaborate in digital media, as well as create digital content with research purposes.

In order to develop the Digital Competences for the research of university students, Lagunes Domínguez [19] recommends generating digital material focused on four main aspects: research, text processor, statistical tool and tools for qualitative and quantitative research.

While this proposed instrument is also based on the perception of students, it is worth noting that unlike those mentioned beforehand it addresses the digital skills at a higher level. This is because it is aimed at determining specifically those digital skills required by the university student to carry out scientific research throughout their academic career.

2 Methodology

2.1 Design of the Instrument

Using determined descriptors, a search was carried out in several databases (Ebsco, Dialnet, and others) of the sources (articles, theses, and others) where instruments were designed to measure digital competence, finding some questionnaires that highlight those made by Ambriz [3] and Ascencio [20]. Combining some of their items and adapting their scope, both served as the basis for the design of a self-perception questionnaire that diagnoses the level of digital competence for the research of university students.

Precisely, of the 66 items that make up the Ambriz questionnaire [3], 13 of them were taken, of which only item 13 was transcribed identically, while the others were modified. For example, 65 was taken by specifying only the type of new product to which it refers, adding the text "multimedia product". However, the remaining 11 were completely restructured in their wording, as for example item 13 that was made up of 2 main ideas (calculate and graph), which were separated and restructured. Its original wording was: "I make calculations with formulas in an electronic spreadsheet such as Excel, from a set of graphical data in a spreadsheet or data processor"; ideas that were separated into two parts. The first idea was in item 16 as follows: "I make graphics in a spreadsheet or word processor, from a set of data". While the second was: "I perform statistical calculations with formulas in an electronic spreadsheet such as Excel".

On the other hand, 30 of its 42 items were taken from the questionnaire developed by Ascencio [20]. Of these, 16 were transcribed identically, another 7 had some changes in their writing and 7 more were restructured. An example of the above could be item 7, which originally was:

"Information will be represented in graphs and tables". Its meaning was extended also contemplating the aspect of understanding. Remaining its final wording as: "I know how to present and interpret information in graphs and tables".

This questionnaire was structured from the dimensions of the digital competence for research shown in Table 1. It is composed of two parts, the first one raises 5 open response items and the second consists of 44 closed response items grouped in three dimensions, based on the self-perception of their digital competences for research.

Finally, it allows you to establish the level of your competence, classifying it as basic, intermediate and advanced, as a result of the answers in each of the actions selected in the 9 indicators that comprise it. The questionnaire is answered in an assisted way by a digital medium (computer, tablet, and others), since it was uploaded to the RIMCI network portal, when collaborating with its research projects.

2.2   Validity and Reliability

The reliability of an instrument expresses the degree of repeatability and consistency that will be obtained in the results when applied at different times. This is determined by different procedures, among which the measure of internal consistency stands out [21]. Cronbach's Alpha [22] is the coefficient most commonly used to establish the level of internal consistency of a measurement instrument. However, to establish that its consistency is sufficient to consider that it presents good reliability, the value of the alpha must be greater than 0.8, being better as it approaches the unit. Its value can also be influenced by various factors such as the length of the instrument, the variability of the sample and what level the respondent has with respect to the variable to be measured [23].

Unlike Cronbach's Alpha, the Composite Reliability Index (CR) analyzes all constructs as a whole and not one at a time. In addition, its value is not influenced by the number of items that conform to the scale, which can become a favorable point.

Its value for each factor is obtained with the formula of Fornell and Larcker [24], where it can be observed that it only depends on the factor loads and the variance of the measurement error, being this another favorable point of the composite reliability.

$$IFC_i = \frac{\left(\sum_j L_{ij}\right)^2}{\left(\sum_j L_{ij}\right)^2 + \sum_j Var\left(E_{ij}\right)} \tag{1}$$

Where:

- L_{ij} = standardized factor load of each of the j indicators.
- $Var(E_{ij})$ = variance of the error of the corresponding term.

$$Var(E_{ij}) = 1 - L_{ij}^2 \qquad (2)$$

Analyzing the formula of the composite reliability index, it can be inferred that its value tends to the unity as the variance of the measurement error decreases. On the other hand, for McDonald [25] the calculation of reliability is obtained by means of the omega coefficient (ω), which, as observed, is practically equal to the CR. The formula is:

$$\omega = \frac{\left(\sum_j \lambda\right)^2}{\left(\sum_j \lambda\right)^2 + \sum_j \left(1 - \lambda_i^2\right)} \qquad (3)$$

Where

- ω = omega coefficient.
- λ_i = i-th standardized factor load.

On the other hand, the validity of the instrument refers to how much it measures the variable or construct for which it was designed [21]. There are several types of validity, but due to the early stage in which this work is found, validity was used in pairs (prior to that of experts) and construct validity, using an exploratory factorial analysis, to determine the correlations of the elements that compose it.

The average extracted variance (AVE is obtained by the formula of Fornell and Larcker [24], from which it is deduced as the ratio between the quadratic cumulative of an i-th factor with respect to the total variance due to the measurement error of that factor.

$$AVE = \frac{\sum_j L_{ij}^2}{\sum_j L_{ij}^2 + \sum_j Var(E_{ij})} \qquad (4)$$

On the other hand, according to the Classical Test Theory (TCT) there are a series of psychometric indicators that give a measure of the quality of the instrument. These indicators are the reagent difficulty index, the reagent discrimination index, the internal reliability coefficient (Cronbach's alpha) and the bi serial point correlation coefficient [23]. The latter being the one that will be used later to analyze its quality.

Finally, the instrument was subjected to peer review, who sought to validate the content and construct, from which several enriching recommendations were obtained that led to the modification of several items before their application. The result obtained after the feedback and adaptation was applied in the pilot test.

2.3   Sample of the Pilot Test

A pilot test was conducted with new students of the August 2018–July 2019 period of a University, based in Veracruz, Mexico. To establish the number of participants that would make up the sample, a stratified probability sampling was applied, which according to what was established by Sierra [26], for a reliability level of 95.5%, its size is calculated with the formula at 2σ.

$$n = \frac{4p(100-p)N}{\sigma^2(N-1)+4p(100-p)} \quad [26]$$

(5)

Where, n is the size of the sample participants to calculate, p is the probability of their elements, N is the population, σ is the standard deviation that the sample will have over the mean, and σ^2 is the variance. Finally, a sample of 71 was obtained for the population of 247 first-year students, of whom 16 were women (22.5%) and 55 men (77.5%). The sample obtained has a reliability level of 95.5%, with a pre-established standard deviation of 10% and a probability of 50%. The total sample was randomly formed without gender distinction, fulfilling the proportion corresponding to the academic program, remaining as follows.

- Engineering in Electronics and Naval Communications (6.5%): 4 students.
- Engineering in Naval Mechanics (9.3%): 7 students.
- Naval Systems Engineering (43.7%): 31 students.
- Engineering in Hydrography (20.6%): 15 students.
- Logistics Engineering (12.1%): 9 students.
- Aeronaval Engineering (7.7%): 5 students.

3   Results

The analysis of results is presented in three parts: global frequencies, reliability analysis and instrument validity.

3.1   Global Frequencies

The data obtained through the online survey were processed with the help of IBM SPSS Statistics software, by means of a descriptive statistical analysis by frequencies. Of the sample analyzed, 55 respondents were men (77.46%) and only 16 women (22.54%), whose age range between 16 and 20 years, where the vast majority have 18, but the average age is 18.41. Because, of the 71 respondents 3 are 16 years old, 1 has 17, 38 have 18, 22 have 19 and 7 are 20 years old.

Most of the students come from private schools (35.21%), general baccalaureate (32.29%) and a technological baccalaureate such as CBTIS (19.72%) (see Fig. 1). So, it will be important to take it into consideration the light of the results.

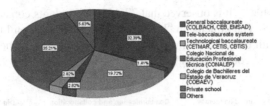

Fig. 1. Baccalaureate or high school of origin.

In the DigComp 2.1 model, Carretero et al. [27] establish various levels of competence according to the autonomy of citizens and the complexity of the tasks they are able to perform. They establish 4 ascending levels of competence, which are basic, intermediate, advanced and highly specialized level. It is important to clarify that for this instrument the items corresponding to each indicator are grouped only in basic and advanced, depending on the level of competence represented by each of the actions they perform. Therefore, in order to establish the level of competence in a similar way to the DigComp 2.1 model, only the basic, intermediate and advanced levels were used. To determine them, a decision table similar to that of Gómez, Segredo and Hernández [28] was used, based on the criteria shown in Table 2.

Table 2. Criteria to establish the level of competence of the indicator.

Level of competence	Criteria
Advanced	Achieving all basic items, and at least an advanced item
Intermediate	If it is fairly achieved at least half of the basic items and the total of advanced items are achieved correctly
	If all basic items are achieved correctly, and at least one advanced item is achieved correctly
	If at least half of the basic items are achieved correctly and achieves half of the advanced items correctly
Basic	If the above conditions are not met

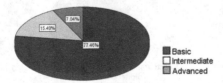

Fig. 2. Global level of digital competence for research.

The information on the level of global competence and dimension, respectively, is concentrated in circular graphs (see Figs. 2 and 3). These denote the level of basic, intermediate and advanced proficiency in percentage terms, corresponding to each of the indicators in Table 1. It is observed that 77.46% of students consider having a basic level of competence. The dimension "Information and information literacy" turned out to be the lowest with only 2.82% in advanced level, while the highest dimension was "Communication and collaboration" with 18.31% in advanced level.

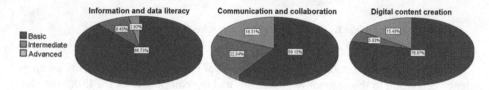

Fig. 3. Percentage of the level of digital competence for research by dimension.

In addition, the levels of competence obtained by indicator (see Fig. 4), which shows that the indicator with the worst level of domain of the respondents was 1.1, called "Navigation, search and filtering of information and digital content"; since only 1.41% reached the advanced level. While the best level of competence is 2.2, designated as "Sharing through digital technologies", given that 43.66% of respondents reached the advanced level, being this last indicator the only one where the percentage of advanced level surpasses the others.

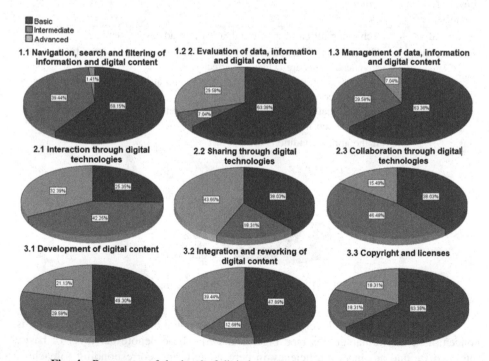

Fig. 4. Percentage of the level of digital competence for research by indicator.

Now, comparing the level of global competence that the students achieved with respect to their type of baccalaureate of origin and their sex, there was interesting information obtained. Of the students with an advanced level of digital competence for research, 4 came from private schools (80%) and only one from technological baccalaureate (20%), making a total of 5 students, of which 3 were women (60%) and 2 men (40%), whose ages were focused on 18 (80%) and 19 years (20%).

On the other hand, 11 of the respondents obtained an intermediate global level, of which 45.4% (5) coma from a general baccalaureate, and then the same proportion of technological baccalaureate, private school and other high school, with an 18.2% (2) each. As for sex, they are fairly balanced despite the fact that women are a minority, with 54.5% of men (6) and 45.5% (5) women. Most of this group was 18 years old, being specifically 45.5%, 36.4% had 19 years and the minority was 20 years old (18.2%).

It is noteworthy that most of the respondents, a total of 55, had a basic level of competence. The majority (38) of them were from three types of baccalaureates, slightly more than private school with 34.5%, followed by 18 general baccalaureate respondents who represented 32.7%. Finally, 11 were from technological baccalaureate, making up 20%; distributing the rest among graduates of CONALEP, COBAEV, tele - baccalaureate and others. It is important to highlight that 100% of the respondents of CONALEP, COBAEV and tele- baccalaureate were located in this group, considering that they have a basic level of competence. It should be mentioned that the level of basic competence is largely dominated by the male sex, representing 85.5% of this subsample.

Table 3 concentrates the distribution of levels of digital competence for research by type of baccalaureate of origin.

Table 3. Distribution of levels of digital competence for research by type of baccalaureate of origin.

Type of baccalaureate	Level		
	Basic	Intermediate	Advanced
General baccalaureate (COLBACH, CEB, EMSAD)	78.26%	21.74%	0.00%
Tele-baccalaureate system	100%	0.00%	0.00%
Technological baccalaureate (CETMAR, CETIS, CBTIS)	78.57%	14.29%	7.14%
Colegio Nacional de Educación Profesional técnica (CONALEP)	100%	0.00%	0.00%
Colegio de Bachilleres del Estado de Veracruz (COBAEV)	100%	0.00%	0.00%
Technical professional or mixed baccalaureate (CMM, BTA, MMDF, others)	0.00%	0.00%	0.00%
Without baccalaureate diploma (Open Prep, Online Prep, Single Exam or COLBACH)	0.00%	0.00%	0.00%
Private school	76.00%	8.00%	16.00%
Other	50.00%	50.00%	0.00%

3.2 Reliability Analysis of the Instrument

The self-perception instrument was subjected to a reliability analysis using the Cronbach's Alpha coefficient, in order to establish its degree of repeatability and coherence. Based on the data obtained from the pilot test, a value of 0.886 was obtained when calculating it throughout the instrument with the help of IBM SPSS Statistics® software, so it can be considered remarkably reliable. However, in order to determine if it is possible to increase the value of the coefficient, we proceeded to verify the level of correlation between the items of the instrument, based on the analysis of the element's statistics.

Table 4 shows the results of the analysis, which highlights what was obtained in item "2. Whenever I go somewhere and a WIFI network is available for free internet connection, I connect my computer and navigate", because it is the only one whose total correlation with the other items was negative, with a value of −0.020.

On the other hand, before starting the factorial analysis it is important to verify the value of the corrected total correlation of elements, since the items must be discarded or written in a different way if their value is low; that is, if they are not sufficiently correlated with each other, as to be grouped according to their latent variables or dimensions. For authors such as Cohen and Manion [29], the reference value is from 0.35, while for others such as Field [30] and Cea [31] the limit to be considered is 0.30. Thus, as one approaches the unit, the probability of grouping the items in a smaller number of factors or dimensions increases.

Table 4. Total statistics by item.

Items	Total corrected item correlation	Cronbach Alpha if item has been deleted
1. I can use different internet browsers (Google Chrome, Safari, other.)	.390	.883
2. Always I connect my computer and navigate when a WIFI network is available	−.020	.890
3. I know to search for information in several sources (virtual libraries, e-journals, online newspapers, blogs, etc.)	.515	.882
4. I use different internet search engines (Google, Bing, Yahoo, etc.) to carry out academic activities	.340	.884
5. I'm able to identify and select keywords that facilitate the most limited search of information on the Internet	.322	.884
6. I use advanced search options (site: www. url. com, filetype: pdf, etc.)	.564	.880
7. I use operators as a strategy to search for selective information (+, −, |, "X", etc.)	.525	.882

(*continued*)

Table 4. (*continued*)

Items	Total corrected item correlation	Cronbach Alpha if item has been deleted
8. I perform my academic activities with the help of ICT; I review and manage tasks and activities using technological tools such as Tablet, PC, Internet and search engines, since it's easier and enjoyable to perform	.326	.884
9. I'm able to evaluate the relevance or quality of the information located on the Internet, by means of applying criteria like authorship, reliability or other	.338	.884
10. I know that not all websites are safe to deliver my personal data, so I worry about analyzing and revise the context of this so that they are not misused	.188	.885
11. I use specialized databases for the search of reliable information (REDALYC, Google Academic, Dialnet, etc.)	.182	.886
12. I can organize the information collected from the Internet, adding the pages that interest me to bookmarks, and classifying them in subfolders under some sort criteria or tags	.423	.882
13. I can recognize and operate with different data storage media: Pen Drive, SD memory, mini SD memory, external hard drive, cloud, etc.	.337	.884
14. I connect my phone or digital camera to my computer and transfer information from one to another	.335	.884
15. When I work on some calculation template, I use the functions to perform operations	.420	.882
16. I perform graphics on a spreadsheet or word processor, from a dataset	.463	.882
17. I Make backup copies of my files and folders	.437	.882
18. I use the main functions of a word processor, a spreadsheet and an electronic presentation	.558	.880
19. I perform statistical calculations with formulas on an electronic sheet such as Excel	.421	.882
20. When I don't have in my computer of any program that I need, then I search on Internet and work with the tools online	.557	.880
21. When I participate online I do it with respect, I'm able to apply communication protocols relevant to the context and audience	.325	.884
22. When it is proposed to debate online some topic of work for the university, I do it using digital means	.261	.885

(*continued*)

Table 4. (*continued*)

Items	Total corrected item correlation	Cronbach Alpha if item has been deleted
23. I use online educational platforms	.139	.887
24. I communicate with other people for academic issues through email, chat, video conferencing, forums or social networks	.185	.886
25. When I share information, I look at the audience for which it is destined and depending on this selection the design or modality in which I will present (image, video, multimedia presentation, other.)	.248	.885
26. When I write an email, I worry about delivering clear information in order to receive a pertinent answer	.290	.884
27. I usually use Google Drive or Dropbox to share files or do work with my classmates	.318	.884
28. I collaborate in schemes of work or planning, by means of the use of a digital tool	.429	.882
29. When they propose group work in digital environment, the tasks and functions are always defined for a collaboration in harmony	.355	.883
30. I can use some digital media (Google Drive or other) to edit documents in collaboration	.457	.882
31. Whenever We work in the collaborative construction of a product I use the tool "change Control" or at least the "comments"	.374	.883
32. I know How to present and interpret information in charts and charts	.333	.884
33. When I design and elaborate a digital product I worry about sharing information of interest to the audience that follows me	.455	.882
34. I know How to design multimedia products to present information with a digital tool	.438	.882
35. I use programs to edit videos or audios	.478	.881
36. I design, create or modify blogs	.409	.883
37. I can integrate information in different formats (audio, video, text, images, etc.) in the elaboration of a work	.453	.882
38. When I build or modify a electronic presentation I notice that the protocol, colors and language is appropriate	.190	.885
39. I can transform a text content into a new multimedia product	.319	.884

(*continued*)

Table 4. (*continued*)

Items	Total corrected item correlation	Cronbach Alpha if item has been deleted
40. I recognize the legal implications for misuse of software licenses	.487	.881
41. I recognize the concept Creative Commons or Copyright when I work with information obtained from the Internet	.311	.884
42. I know How to download and install free software from the Internet	.436	.882
43. When I extract information from an internet source I incorporate it into some work done by me, I worry about quoting correctly the source of where I got it	.329	.884
44. I know when a content has similarity or plagiarism	.373	.883

Therefore, of the total correlation results shown in Table 4, it is observed that items 4, 5, 8, 9, 13, 14, 21, 27, 30, 39, 41 and 43, have a correlation between 0.3 and 0.35. While others like 2, 10, 11, 22, 23, 24, 25, 26 and 38, have less than 0.3. However, by eliminating them, the Cronbach's alpha drops to 0.871, instead of rising, in addition to the correlation between some elements falling. Now, if only item 2 of negative correlation is eliminated, the alpha increases to 0.890 and the correlation remains without considerable changes in the other items. Now, homogeneity does not increase despite calculating it by indicator, dimension, or by basic or advanced items, but in all these cases the alpha decreases.

3.3 Validity Analysis of the Instrument

When submitting the data to the Kaiser-Meyer-Olkin (KMO) test in the IBM SPSS Statistics® software, it expressed a low or negligible association obtaining an index value of 0.515, making it not recommendable to reduce the elements. As a consequence, before making the factorial analysis, it is a priority to determine which variables to remove, looking for those whose individual KMO indexes are less than 0.5 [31], placing them on the diagonal of the anti-image correlation matrix (AIC). After eliminating them, the global KMO index is recalculated to verify if factor analysis is appropriate.

Table 5. Summarized anti-image correlation matrix.

Item	2	4	9	10	21	22	23	24	25	26	30	31	34	38	39	41	43	44
2	.301																	
4		.428																
9			.403															
10				.227														
21					.406													
22						.387												
23							.418											
24								.312										
25									.366									
26										.452								
30											.453							
31												.466						
34													.439					
38														.287				
39															.450			
41																.382		
43																	.455	
44																		.386

Once AIC the matrix shown in Table 5 was analyzed, it was detected that there were many elements that presented a KMO <0.5 and that, therefore, should be eliminated, specifically items 2, 4, 9, 10, 21, 22, 23, 24, 25, 26, 30, 31, 34, 38, 39, 41, 43 and 44. After being eliminated and considering only the 26 remaining items, the CAI matrix was recalculated, where all the values of its diagonal were found to be greater than 0.5, with the lowest correlation of 0.554 corresponding to element 5 and the highest correlation of 0.807 of element 3. Thus, there was also an increase in the global KMO index reaching 0.718, considered as a mean value or normal, which allows to proceed to the factorial analysis.

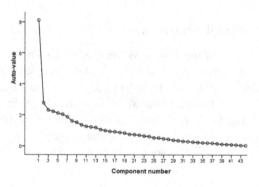

Fig. 5. Sedimentation graph.

With these new data, Bartlett's sphericity test yields an approximate Chi-square of 588,680 with 325 degrees of freedom. Its level of significance is very small (practically 0.000), which implies that the correlation matrix is not an identity matrix; validating also that there is a sufficient correlation between elements to carry out the factorial analysis.

Table 6. Rotating component matrix.

Item	Component								
	1	2	3	4	5	6	7	8	9
20	0.73	0.155							
17	0.68	-0.02							
29	0.53	0.15							
37	0.51	-0.06							
28	0.46	0.41							
15		0.831	0.049						
19		0.766	-0.02						
35		0.552	0.205						
18		0.487	0.395						
16		0.449	-0.05						
13			0.85	0.08					
42			0.737	0.07					
40			0.508	0.38					
27				0.65	0.21				
6				0.62	0.02				
7				0.61	0.09				
8				0.53	-0.11				
32					0.74	0			
33					0.73	0.07			
1						0.72	0.268		
5						0.69	-0.19		
3						0.46	-0.05		
11							0.785	0.05	
14							0.516	0	
12								0.78	0.12
36									0.77

As for the extraction test with the matrix of the total variance explained, the authors looked for the factors up to where the eigenvalues stop being greater than 1 and justify most of the variance. With this criterion a total of 9 factors were obtained, with the ninth exceeding the value of 1025, explaining 67.739% of the variance. Of these, the first factor explains 24.076% of the variance, the second one 7.921%, the third of 6.695%, the fourth 5.847% and thereafter, the other factors explain a similar percentage between 5% and 4%. The above is shown in the sedimentation graph (see Fig. 5), where it is observed that the curve begins to flatten from the fourth component, since they no longer offer a significant contribution to the variance.

Analyzing the matrix of components, the elements that are highly correlated or associated with each other are deduced. The elements of the first factor were located to the point where the correlation of the second component (second column) exceeds them (first column). Also, for the second factor, the second and third components were compared. Therefore, to locate the elements that are associated with the other factors, the same criterion was applied. Observing the rotated component matrix of Table 6, it showed that for the first factor the associated elements are 20, 17, 29, 37 and 28, in that order. While for the second the elements are 15, 19, 35, 18 and 16. This implies that 10 variables become associated to the first two factors. The associations of the other factors are clearly identified in the graph.

As a result of the factorial analysis, it showed a total of 9 factors or dimensions that make up the instrument, which coincides with the number of indicators considered in its design. However, it would require further reduction to complete the Exploratory Factor Analysis (AFE), because components eight and nine have only one associated item. The foregoing is insufficient since it is required to have at least two for each observable variable; that is, for each component or factor.

On the other hand, if the decision is made to analyze the instrument from the beginning applying the Classical Test Theory, the only items in Table 4 (second column) that do not have a bi serial point correlation coefficient higher than the minimum criteria - established (greater than 0.2) are 2, 10, 11, 23, 24 and 38. By eliminating only these items, it was necessary to recalculate the value of the bi serial point correlation coefficient on two more occasions, because new items arise with low correlation. In the second calculation, item 25 did not meet the minimum criteria established by having a 0.169 correlation, while in the third calculation it was item 26 with a correlation of 0.196. For the fourth calculation it was verified that there were no items with low correlation problems; that is, all the remaining ones met the minimum criteria. However, items 9 and 22 exceeded by far the required limit with 0.230 and 0.255, respectively.

After the TCT analysis, the assumption of normality was verified by contrasting the grades obtained by the students of the various educational programs, applying the Shapiro-Wilk test [32, 33]. Because each group of students on the test did not exceed the minimum value of 50 observations. On the contrary, if passed the Kolmogorov-Smirnov test [33] would have been used. For this, the following statistical hypotheses of normality were established:

H_0: The variable ratings in the population has a normal distribution.
H_1: The variable ratings in the population is different from a normal distribution.

The test results showed a p value (sig) in each of the groups greater than 0.05, as a consequence the theoretical or null hypothesis is accepted; that is, it is established that the data have a normal distribution as seen in Table 7, thereby fulfilling the assumption of normality (see Fig. 6).

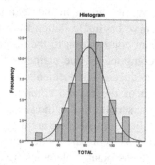

Fig. 6. Normality of grades by educational program.

When observing the graph, a slightly leptokurtic curve with negative asymmetry was obtained, having a kurtosis value of 0.245 and an asymmetry of −0.7. However, their kurtosis is considered negligible or not significant, since its absolute value is less than three times its standard error; that is, less than triple 0.563 [34]. Likewise, its asymmetry is neglected since its value is between −1 and 1, in addition to its absolute value being less than three times its standard error; that is, less than triple 0.285 [34]. Verifying again that it meets the normality assumption.

Table 7. Shapiro-Wilk Test.

Academic program	Statistical	df	Sig.
Aeronaval Engineering	0.966	5	0.850
Naval Systems Engineering	0.969	31	0.496
Engineering in Electronics and Naval Communications	0.939	4	0.647
Engineering in Hydrography	0.928	15	0.253
Logistics Engineering	0.928	9	0.464
Naval Systems Engineering	0.947	7	0.705

In proceeding with the exploratory factor analysis (AFE), an extraction method of main shaft factorization with Promax rotation was used. Estimating eight factors that explain 46.98% of the variance. Of which, items 4, 8, 29 and 31 did not meet the minimum recommended values (greater than 0.3) in their communities, obtaining values of 0.293, 0.273, 0.241 and 0.223, respectively. For its part, the standard matrix revealed that items 5, 6, 7, 9, 14, 16, 28, 29, 31, 35, 36 40, 42, 44 were not associated with any of the eight factors, so its elimination is recommended to recalculate the AFE.

When performing the AFE for the second time, again items not associated with the factors are found, specifically items 18, 30 and 37, which would cause item 13 to be eliminated as it was the only item associated with the seventh factor. It is necessary to have at least two observable variables (items) associated with each latent variable (factor). So when calculating the AFE again, a total of 16 items remain, all of them associated with one of the six factors (see Fig. 7).

The previous measurement model represents the best association and reduction of components recommended by the AFE, based on the previously mentioned method of extraction and rotation. However, inconsistencies were found in the composite reliability and in the average variance extracted, when estimating its reliability and validity with the Dr. Gaskin plugin [35], developed for the IBM SPSS Amos®. Since some factors do not meet the recommended criteria or thresholds [36], as presented in Table 8. The composite reliability (CR) must have values between 0.6 and 1, while the values of the average value extracted (AVE) must be greater than 0.5. Therefore, in order to improve these indices, it is recommended to eliminate items 12, 17, 27 and 41, which would also mean eliminating item 22, since it would be a single observable variable with its latent variable.

However, it was necessary to perform the reliability and validity calculation with the plugin twice more. Because in the second execution he encountered problems again, recommending to eliminate items 1, 3, 20, 21 and 43. While, in the third execution the minimum criteria were met in all the factors, once the items were eliminated mentioned, as presented in Table 9.

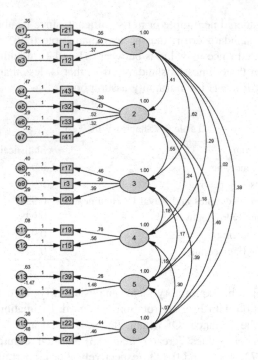

Fig. 7. Modelo de medida con seis factores.

Table 8. Validity measures of the six-factor model.

	CR	AVE	1	2	3	4	5	6
1	0.605	0.344*	0.586					
2	0.638	0.318*	0.405	0.564				
3	0.674	0.411*	0.616	0.551	0.641			
4	0.775	0.641	0.285	0.243	0.184	0.801		
5	1.367*	1.563	0.020	0.180	0.167	0.153	1.250	
6	0.484*	0.319*	0.386	0.465	0.394	0.303	−0.074	0.565

Table 9. Validity measures of the final three- factor model.

	CR	AVE	1	2	3
1	0.677	0.513	0.716		
2	0.806	0.691	0.162	0.831	
3	0.892	0.835	0.268	0.219	0.914

The final measurement model meets the established criteria, as a result of performing the Exploratory Factor Analysis (see Fig. 8). With which there is a reliability composed of dimension ranging from 0.677 to 0.892, as well as an average variance extracted between 0.513 and 0.835.

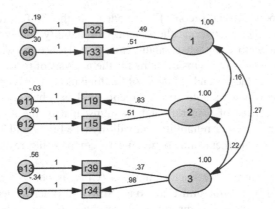

Fig. 8. Final measurement model.

4 Conclusions

It is interesting to identify some factors that influence the level of digital competence for research that students have when they arrive to university. According to the information obtained in the analysis of global frequencies, it was observed that a factor to consider is the type of baccalaureate of origin; since only a percentage of the students coming from private schools and technological baccalaureates consider they have an advanced level. While the totality of those from the CONALEP, COBAEV and tele-baccalaureate consider having a basic level. It is also worth highlighting the higher level of competence that women consider having, where it would be interesting to see if that difference is real, locating the factors to which it is due, or if it is a simple difference of perception.

Going into the analysis of the instrument, specifically in terms of its reliability, it was observed that one of the items had a negative total correlation. This could be solved by rewriting the item or deleting it; since, if it is eliminated, the value of the alpha would change from 0.886 to 0.89, being the only item that would raise it when eliminated. In addition to the above, by eliminating the items with low correlation, the value of Cronbach's alpha decreased. This allows us to infer that the poor total correlation of the items is not due to the instrument, but to the basic level that most of the respondents have, as established by Muñiz (2005) and previously mentioned in the section of validity and reliability. This is justified due to the low level of competences obtained in each of the indicators and dimensions presented in the previous point, where 77.46% of the participants demonstrated a basic level, while only 7.04% showed an advanced level.

From the first Exploratory Factorial Analysis (EFA) carried out to obtain the construct validity, the items that are loads of the latent variables (factors or components) were determined; that is, the dimensions and indicators of the proposed theoretical model were identified. Arriving at the conclusion of eliminating items 11–14, 32, 33 and 36 that were associated with indicators with little load.

In what corresponds to the second EFA made from the TCT, a reduced measurement model was reached that meets the criteria of reliability and validity, unlike the first model that failed to establish a quality measure. However, when applying the instrument, there will be two groups of items for the analysis of results. The first group is made up of the three factors and six items of the final measurement model (see Fig. 8 and Table 9), with which reliable measurements will be obtained. Meanwhile, the second group will consist of 6 factors and 16 items; that is, the same reliable items together with others of regular reliability and validity (see Fig. 7 and Table 8), in order to have a greater measurement and to be able to compare the results of the results obtained in both groups.

Currently, the Confirmatory Factor Analysis (CFA) is being carried out using a measurement model with Structural Equations (SEM), in order to determine its composite reliability, as well as its discriminant validity and convergent validity. The results obtained in the various criteria (CFI, RMSEA, AVE, etc.), as well as the process of obtaining them, will be presented in a forthcoming publication.

As a result of the results obtained, a training course is being designed to develop the level of digital skills for student research. It is planned to apply it to new students at the beginning of each school year, in order to provide them with the tools that contribute to their performance throughout their academic work. This course is being designed using the Blended Learning methodology, which is based mainly on short support videos that will be accessible at all times through the network, specifically aimed at supporting the indicators of our interest.

References

1. Vuorikari, R., Punie, Y., Carretero, S., Van Den Brande, G.: DigComp 2.0: the digital competence framework for citizens. Update Phase 1: the conceptual reference model. Publications Office of the European Union (2016). https://doi.org/10.2791/11517
2. Ala-Mutka, K.: Mapping digital competence: towards a conceptual understanding, pp. 3–12. Publications Office of the European Union (2011). http://ftp.jrc.es/EURdoc/JRC67075_TN.pdf
3. Ambriz, C.: La competencia digital de los estudiantes. Estudio de caso: alumnos de nuevo ingreso a la Escuela Superior de Ingeniería Mecánica Eléctrica Unidad Azcapotzalco (Maestría). ESIME Unidad Azcapotzalco, México (2014). https://tesis.ipn.mx/handle/123456789/14406. Accessed 27 Sep 2018
4. Aquino, S.P., Izquierdo, J., García, V., Valdés, A.A.: Percepción de estudiantes con discapacidad visual sobre sus competencias digitales en una universidad pública del sureste de México. Apertura: Revista de Innovación Educativa **8**(1), 1 (2016). http://search.ebscohost.com.ezproxy.cdigital.uv.mx:2048/login.aspx?direct=true&AuthType=ip,url,uid,cookie&db=zbh&AN=113930733&site=ehost-live
5. Carrasco, M.E., Sánchez, C., Carro, A.: Las competencias digitales en estudiantes del posgrado en educación. Revista Lasallista de Investigación **12**(2), 10–18 (2015). https://doi.org/10.22507/rli.v12n2a1
6. Castellanos, A., Sánchez, C., Calderero, J.F.: Nuevos modelos tecnopedagógicos. Competencia digital de los alumnos universitarios. Revista Electrónica de Investigación Educativa **19**(1), 1–9 (2017). https://doi.org/10.24320/redie.2017.19.1.1148

7. García, F.J.: Competencias digitales en la docencia universitaria del siglo XXI (doctoral). Universidad Complutense de Madrid. Madrid, Spain (2016). http://eprints.ucm.es/44237/1/T39101.pdf. Accessed 27 Apr 2018

8. Gisbert, M., Espuny, C., González, J.: INCOTIC. Una herramienta para la @utoevaluación diagnóstica de la competencia digital en la universidad. Profesorado 15(1), 75–90 (2011). http://www.ugr.es/local/recfpro/rev151ART5.pdf

9. Hernández, J., Reséndiz, N.M.: La construcción sociocultural de las habilidades digitales en el bachillerato: De la interacción cotidiana al estudio. Revista Multidisciplinar de Investigación Educativa 22(73), 421–444 (2017). http://www.scielo.org.mx/pdf/rmie/v22n73/1405-6666-rmie-22-73-00421.pdf. Accessed 2 May 2018

10. Hernández, E.E., Romero, S.I., Ramírez, M.S.: Evaluación de competencias digitales didácticas en cursos masivos abiertos: Contribución al movimiento latinoamericano. Comunicar XXII(44), 81–90 (2015). http://dx.doi.org/10.3916/C44-2015-09

11. Herrero, P., Lozano, J., del Toro, A., Sánchez, M.: Estudio de las competencias digitales en el espectador fan español. Palabra Clave 20(4), 917–947 (2017). https://doi.org/10.5294/pacla.2017.20.4.4

12. Murtonen, M., Olkinuora, E., Tynjälä, P., Lehtinen, E.: Do I need research skills in working life?: University students' motivation and difficulties in quantitative methods courses. Natl. Sci. Found. 1–14 (2008). https://doi.org/10.1007/s10734-008-9113-9

13. Chávez, F., Cantú, M., Rodríguez, C.: Competencias digitales y tratamiento de información desde la mirada infantil. Revista Electrónica de Investigación Educativa 18(1), 209–220 (2016)

14. Diario Oficial de la Unión Europea: Recomendación del Parlamento Europeo y del Consejo de 18 de diciembre de 2006 sobre las competencias clave para el aprendizaje permanente. Bruselas: Diario Oficial de la Unión Europea (2006). http://eur-lex.europa.eu/LexUriServ/LexUriServ.do?uri=OJ:L:2006:394:0010:0018:ES:PDF. Accessed 18 Dec 2006

15. Ferrari, A.: Digital Competence in Practice: An Analysis of Frameworks. Publications Office of the European Union, Sevilla, Spain (2012). http://ftp.jrc.es/EURdoc/JRC68116.pdf. https://doi.org/10.2791/82116

16. INTEF: Marco Común de Competencia Digital Docente (2017). http://aprende.intef.es/mccdd. Accessed Sep 2017

17. Pons, J.P.: Higher education and the knowledge society. Information and digital competencies. Revista de Universidad y Sociedad del Conocimiento 7(2) (2010). https://doi.org/10.7238/rusc.v7i2.977

18. Martin, A., Grudziecki, J.: DigEuLit: concepts and tools for digital literacy development. ITALICS: Innov. Teach. Learn. Inf. Comput. Sci. 5(4), 246–264 (2006). https://doi.org/10.11120/ital.2006.05040249

19. Lagunes Domínguez, A.: La competencia investigadora en Universitarios mediante el Blending Learning y Flipped Classroom. Estrategias de investigación socioeducativas: propuestas para la educación superior 95–112 (2016). https://www.researchgate.net/profile/Agustin_Lagunes_Dominguez/publication/316488277_La_competencia_investigadora_en_universitarios_mediante_el_Blended_Learning_y_Flipped_Classroom/links/5900c9abaca2725bd71f4a0e/La-competencia-investigadora-en-universitar

20. Ascencio, P.: Estándar de competencia digital para estudiantes de educación superior de la Universidad de Magallanes Chile (doctoral). Universidad de Barcelona., Barcelona, Spain (2017). http://hdl.handle.net/2445/119225. Accessed 10 Sep 2018

21. Hernández, R., Fernández, C., Baptista, P.: Metodología de la investigación. McGraw_Hill, México, D. F. (2014)

22. Cronbach, L.: Coefficient alpha and the internal structure of tests. Psychometrika 16, 297–334 (1951). https://doi.org/10.1007/BF02310555

23. Muñiz, J., Fidaldo, A., Garcia, E., Martinez, R., Moreno, R.: Análisis de los ítems. La Muralla, S.A. (2005)
24. Fornell, C., Larcker, D.F.: Evaluating structural equation models with unobservable variables and measurement error. J. Mark. Res. **18**(1), 39–50 (1981). https://doi.org/10.2307/3151312
25. McDonald, R.P.: Test Theory: A Unified Treatment. Lawrence Erlbaum Associates Inc., Mahwah (1999)
26. Sierra, R.: Técnicas de Investigación Social: Teoría y Ejercicios. Paraninfo Thomson-Learning, Madrid (2001)
27. Carretero, S., Vuorikari, R., Punie, Y.: The Digital Competence Framework for Citizens with Eight Proficiency Levels and Examples of Use. Publications Office of the European Union, Luxembourg (2017). https://doi.org/10.2760/38842
28. Gómez, O., Segredo, A.M., Hernández, L.: Evaluación de habilidades clínicas en estudiantes del Nuevo Programa de Formación de Médicos. Revista Cubana de Educación Médica Superior **25**(4), 486–495 (2011)
29. Cohen, L., Manion, L.: Métodos de investigación educativa. La Muralla, Madrid (2002)
30. Field, A.: Discovering Statistics Using SPSS, 3rd edn. SAGE Publications Ltd., London (2009)
31. Cea, M.: Análsis multivariable. Teoría y práctica en la investigación social. Síntesis, Madrid (2004)
32. Peat, J., Barton, B.: Medical Statistics: A Guide to Data Analysis and Critical Appraisal. Blackwell Publishing, Massachusetts (2005)
33. Oztuna, D., Elhan, A., Tuccar, E.: Investigation of four different normality tests in terms of type 1 error rate and power under different distributions. Turk. J. Med. Sci. **36**(3), 171–176 (2006)
34. Sposito, V.A., Hand, M.L., Skarpness, B.: On the efficiency of using the sample kurtosis in selecting optimal $l_p$estimators. Commun. Stat.-Simul. Comput. **12**(3), 265–272 (1983). https://doi.org/10.1080/03610918308812318
35. Gaskin, J., Lim, J.: "Master Validity Tool", AMOS Plugin. Retrieved from Gaskination's StatWiki (2016). http://statwiki.kolobkreations.com
36. Hair, J.F., Black, W.C., Babin, B.J., Anderson, R.E.: Multivariate Data Analysis, 7th edn. Prentice Hall, Upper Saddle River (2010)

Formal Protocol for the Creation of a Database of Physiological and Behavioral Signals for the Automatic Recognition of Emotions

Yesenia N. González-Meneses[1]([⊠]) (ID), Josefina Guerrero-García[1] (ID),
Carlos Alberto Reyes-García[2] (ID), Ivan Olmos-Pineda[1] (ID),
and Juan Manuel González-Calleros[1] (ID)

[1] Facultad de Ciencias de la Computación, BUAP, Av. San Claudio y 14 Sur,
Col. San Manuel Edificio CCO3, Ciudad Universitaria Puebla, Puebla,
Pue., Mexico
yeseniaglez0@gmail.com, joseguga01@gmail.com,
ivanoprkl@gmail.com, jumagoca78@gmail.com
[2] Ciencias Computacionales, INAOE, Luis Enrique Erro 1, Tonantzintla, Puebla,
Pue., Mexico
kargaxxi@inaoep.mx

Abstract. In this article the design of the experiment's protocol (elements, considerations and formalization) for to create databases of physiological and behavioral signals from college students are doing a learning activity is described. The main thing is to define a formal protocol for data capture to provide an adequate database for the study of learning-centered emotions. For the recognition of emotions in specific contexts is a fundamental task and generally is part of the data treatment stage in research that is intended to automatically identify emotions in educational environments (as interest, boredom, confusion and frustration, according to [1]).

For the execution the capture it is proposed to merge data from technologies for the acquisition of physiological and behavioral signals with the idea of integrating a vast and diverse set of data.

Keywords: Formal protocol · Database of physiological and behavioral signals · Learning-centered emotions · Automatic recognition of emotions

1 Introduction

In affective computation research, the automatic identification of emotions is a relevant problem, since it is the beginning of the study and development of human-computer interaction systems sensitive to the emotions of human beings. The human-computer interaction can be implemented from the use of physiological signal sensors for the acquisition of data. Another approach to interact has to do with the observation of human behavior through the analysis of voice, images of the face, eyes, head or body movements of people, as mentioned by [2].

The data obtained from different devices must be processed and classified based on a specific objective. For this proposal they will be captured in real educational

© Springer Nature Switzerland AG 2019
P. H. Ruiz and V. Agredo-Delgado (Eds.): HCI-COLLAB 2019, CCIS 1114, pp. 211–226, 2019.
https://doi.org/10.1007/978-3-030-37386-3_16

environments when students are performing a learning activity and subsequently used to identification learning-centered emotions. A factor that affects the performance of emotion recognizers is the difficulty to generate databases with spontaneous emotions in the wild. Therefore, the learning activity must be carried out in a real context using any education software in a computer. In this work we do not consider face-to-face classes with the intervention of a lecturer. The main objective is to build a database of physiological and behavioral signals, starting with the capture of data and ending with the selection of useful features get of database for the identification of learning-centered emotions. These data will be the basis for the implementation of a model of emotion identification with an acceptable level of accuracy, more in line with the reality within an educational context.

In the development of this article, we first do an analysis of the state of the art about databases are existing to use for the recognition of emotions. Thus, we identify a gap with respect to hybrid databases (which contain physiological and behavioral data used to recognize emotions). Nowadays, facial expression databases are what predominate in the recognition of basic emotions in general contexts. Therefore, we identify the creation of a robust database that supports the automatic classification as the first problem. To achieve this, the quality, quantity and variability in the data is essential. Therefore, the need to follow a formal protocol for data capture is a fundamental task.

So, in the last section of this article, we present the research, analysis and selection of key concepts for the design of the data capture protocol and finally, the conclusions.

2   State of the Art

A database of emotional expressions is a collection of images or video clips, speech and physiological signals related to a wide range of emotions. Its content corresponds to emotional expressions related to the context in which they were captured and then tagged, this is essential for the training, testing, and validation of algorithms for the development of emotions identification systems. The tagging of emotions can be done with a discrete or continuous scale. Most of the databases are usually based on the emotions theory of [3], which assumes the existence of six basic emotions on a discrete scale (anger, fear, disgust, surprise, joy, sadness) and neutral state, in addition to an approximate variety of 22 secondary emotions. However, in some databases the emotions are tagged in continuous arousal-valence scale [4]. Other databases include the AU (Action Units) based on FACS (Facial Action Coding System) [5]. The databases of expressions of emotions are mostly formed only by facial expressions and these are classified into posed and spontaneous. In posed expression databases, the participants are asked to display different emotional expressions, while in spontaneous expression database, the emotional expressions are natural. Spontaneous expressions differ from posed ones remarkably in terms of intensity, configuration, and duration. In most cases, the posed expressions are exaggerated, while the spontaneous ones are subtle and differ in appearance. Apart from this, synthesis of some AUs are barely achievable without undergoing the associated emotional state so it is not possible to capture physiological data since these cannot be controlled by people and therefore do not correspond to the emotion that is acted out.

In Table 1, we show a compilation of databases of facial expressions, although our interest lies in hybrid databases that contain facial images and physiological data, so far, we have only found one database of this type publicly available. The DEAP database [6] contains physiological recordings (of EEG) and facial video of an experiment where 32 volunteers watched a subset of 40 music videos. In this experiment participants are also asked to rate each video according to the emotion it caused in them. Therefore, the analysis of the databases shown in Table 1 only includes databases of facial expressions available to the public. These databases correspond to facial expressions of basic emotions, which have been captured while people perform various activities. Most of the databases are comprised of viewers watching media content (i.e. ads, movie trailers, television shows, animated gifs and online viral campaigns) and of posed facial expressions. Out of these, the most robust database for the amount for data stored is Affectiva [7].

Table 2 shows details of databases of spontaneous facial expressions. These correspond to learning-centered emotions that have been captured while students perform some learning activity in a wild setting. Some of them contain physiological data but unfortunately, they do not make them available to the public or provide information about the characteristics of these data, let alone details of the processing they do with them. Out of these, four databases are hybrids, include physiological and behavioral data. The most complete is the one mentioned in [8] in which 67 students participate and use three physiological data sensors and a video camera. In general, they have been created with data from very few participants.

From this analysis, we have identified as an area of opportunity the creation of a physiological and behavioral database supported by a formal protocol for data collection. The definition of the protocol allows us to run a controlled experiment in a natural environment and specific that can be replicated the number of times necessary to create a robust database.

3 Problem Definition

The construction of a database of physiological and behavioral signals for the automatic recognition of emotions has been an area of investigation highly active in the last years. Regardless of this, a clear solution, which is within reach of most people, is still far away. Several drawbacks have influenced the construction of an appropriate solution from a computational point of view. On one hand, a factor that affects the performance of emotion recognizers in real contexts is the difficulty to generate databases with spontaneous emotions. Generally, works are made with acted databases which provide portraits of emotions representing prototypical and intense emotions that facilitate the automatic classification.

This kind of databases are usually captured in a controlled environment, which decreases problems in the processing of information (noise, for example). In addition, it can guarantee a balanced number of samples per class. As consequence, there have not been good results when translating the knowledge extracted from these databases to real contexts [40].

Table 1. Databases facial expressions of basic emotions

Database	Facial expression	Number of subjects	Number of images/videos	Type
DEAP [6]	Analysis of continuous emotion model	32	32-channels 512 Hz EEG peripheral physiological signals and 22 face videos	Spontaneous
RAVDESS [9]	Speech: Calm, happy, sad, fearful, surprised, disgusted and neural Song: Calm, happy, sad, angry, fearful and neutral	24	7,356 video and audio files	Posed
F-M FACS 3.0 (EDU, PRO & XYZ versions) [10]	Neutral, sad, surprised, happy, fearful, angry, contemptuous and disgusted	10	4,877 videos and images sequences	Posed and spontaneous
CK ++ [11]	Neutral, sad, surprised, happy, fearful, angry and disgusted	123	593 image sequences (327 with discrete emotions labels)	Posed and spontaneous smiles
JAFFE [12]	Neutral, sad, surprised, happy, fearful, angry and disgusted	10	213 static images	Posed
MMI [13]	Disgusted, happy and surprised	43	1,280 videos and over 250 images	Posed and spontaneous
BELFAST [14]	Set 1 (disgusted, fearful, amused, frustrated, surprised)	114	570 video clips	Natural emotions
	Set 2 (disgusted, fearful, amused, frustrated, surprised, angry, sad)	82	650 videos clips	
DISFA [15]	–	27	4,845 video frames	Spontaneous
MUG [16]	Neutral, sad, surprised, happy, fearful, angry and disgusted	86	1,462 sequences	Posed
ISED [17]	Sad, surprised, happy and disgusted	50	428 videos	Spontaneous

(*continued*)

Table 1. (*continued*)

Database	Facial expression	Number of subjects	Number of images/videos	Type
RaFD [18]	Neutral, sad, contemptuous, surprised, happy, fearful, angry and disgusted	67	3 different gaze directions and 5 camera angles (8,040 images)	Posed
Oulu-CASIA NIR-VIS [19]	Surprise, happy, sad, angry, fearful and disgusted	80	3 different illumination conditions: normal, weak and dark (2,880 videos)	Posed
FERG [20]	Angry, disgusted, fearful, joyful, neutral, sad and surprised	6	55,767 images	Frontal pose
Affectnet [21]	Neutral, happy, sad, surprised, fearful, disgusted, angry and contemptuous	–	~450,000 manually annotated ~500,000 automatically annotated	Wild setting
IMPA-FACE3D [22]	Neutral frontal, joyful, sadness, surprised, angry, disgusted, fearful, opened, closed, kiss and neutral	38	534 static images	Posed
FEI [23]	Neutral and smiley	200	2,800 static images	Posed
Aff-Wild [24]	–	200	~1,250,000 manually annotated	In the wild setting
Affectiva [7]	angry, joyed, sad, surprised, fearful, disgusted and contemptuous	–	7,860,463 Faces analyzed	Spontaneous

In contrast, the databases with spontaneous records show information with emotional content that does not belong to a single class, but a mixture of them. In other cases, there are samples with a very light emotional charge, close to a neutral emotional state. In addition, databases with spontaneous emotions are usually recorded in noisy environments, such as classrooms, study rooms, entertainment areas, offices, factories or in phone conversations, which leads to the inclusion of noise. And, because of the very nature of the problem, it is not possible to ensure a balanced quantity of examples

Table 2. Databases of facial expressions that correspond to learning-centered emotions.

Database	Facial expression	Number of subjects	Number of images/videos	Type/Software tool
Own database [25]	Frustrated, confused, sad, joyful, anguished and fearful	39 students	30 to 60 min for student	Spontaneous/Intelligent Tutor System
Own database [26]	Interested, bored, frustrated, confused, surprised, pleasured, curios, happy and neutral	22 college students	Images	Spontaneous/Learning administrator system
Own database [27, 28] y [29]	Interested, bored, frustrated and excited	8 students	Video and EGG (discrete emotion labels)	Spontaneous/Intelligent Tutor System
Own database [30]	Frustrated, confused, interested and bored	29 students	Video and self-report	Spontaneous/environment to program in python
Own database [31]	Basic emotions and learning centered emotions (19 emotions and neutral state)	67 students	Video and self-report	Spontaneous/Intelligent multi-agent tutorial system for teaching the human circulatory system
Own database [32]	Frustrated, confused, interested and bored	28–30 students	Video of eyes tracking, dialogue notes with the tutor, facial expressions video, body postures, mouse and keyboard pressure sensors and voice acoustics	Spontaneous/Intelligent tutorial system for computer repair
Own database [33]	Attentive and concentrated	23, 072 instances	Video and EGG headband (Emotiv-EPOC). Extraction of Alpha and Beta waves	Spontaneous/Psychological test to induce mental states of attention and concentration
Own database [34, 35] y [36]	Pleasure, frustrated, confused, interested and bored	137 students	Video and the BROMP observation method	Spontaneous/Educational game Physics Playground
Own database [37]	Interested	22 students	Video of the Kinect and BIOPAC MP150 ECG signal acquisition system	Spontaneous/writing a summary

(*continued*)

Table 2. (*continued*)

Database	Facial expression	Number of subjects	Number of images/videos	Type/Software tool
Own database [38]	Interested	30 students	Video of Kinect V2	Spontaneous/excel course
Own database [39]	Bored, interested and neutral	44 students	Typing analysis and video	Spontaneous/writing an essay
Own database [8]	Interested, excited, confident and frustrated	2 groups of 38 and 29 high school students	Physiological sensors (video camera, mouse, chair and bracelet)	Spontaneous/Multimedia adaptive tutoring system for geometry

per class. On the other hand, a challenge to be solved is the extraction and selection of a set of characteristics that allow recognizing emotions in the data captured spontaneously. Although progress in the area has been important, there is still much to be done in realistic contexts. Therefore, it is necessary to propose and explore other approaches that allow reaching a good performance of the emotion's recognition in real world applications. An evident aspect to consider is the fact that the area of application has an important influence on the accuracy of emotion recognition, as well as the degree of intrusion of the tools used [41]. And these two aspects are crucial to consider in the creation of the database of physiological and behavioral signals in a context specific.

The problems that are usually faced in the capture of physiological and behavioral signals data in real contexts are:

1. Use of invasive technologies that cause discomfort in the capture of spontaneous expressions.
2. Synchronization precise of the different capture devices.
3. The environmental conditions where the capture takes place.
4. The correct sensing of the devices.
5. The previous emotional state of the participants.
6. The availability of the participants.
7. The physical appearance of the face (amount of hair or artifacts on the face).
8. The necessary capture time.

Due to the above mentioned, the formal design of a protocol for the capture of data (either physiological, behavioral or both) is necessary. The protocol is guide to execution of a controlled experiment with the objective of avoiding errors in the acquisition of data. This describe the technologies to be used, the capture process, the environmental conditions and the preparation of the participants. In the following sections, all the aspects to be considered in the design of a protocol for data collection are defined.

4   Designing the Protocol for the Capture of Physiological and Behavioral Data

In this section, we first describe the activities of research, analysis and selection prior to protocol design for the creation of a spontaneous database captured in real educational environments through the execution of a controlled experiment. In the second part, we propose legal, ethical and environmental (physical place) issues that should be considered in the design of a formal protocol. These activities can be seen in the diagram shown in Fig. 1, in terms of key concepts, the physiological and behavioral signals to be captured must be defined, the data acquisition technologies that will be used to capture the signals, the model of emotions on which the identification of emotions will be based and the activity in which the students will participate while their data is captured. Regarding physical aspects of the place where the experiment will be carried out, it is important to consider comfortable furniture and stable climate control. As well as the legal and ethical aspects dependent on the laws and customs of the country where the data capture will take place.

4.1   Research, Analysis and Selection of Concepts for the Design of the Data Capture Protocol

Physiological and Behavioral Signals

Physiological and behavioral responses occur during or immediately after the causal event and the signals can be quantitatively compared. There are many signals relevant to emotional responses that are physically measurable, especially by cameras, microphones, and sensors, the latter of which might be placed in physical contact with a person in a comfortable and non-invasive way.

Consider what happens when we try to recognize somebody's emotion. First, our senses detect low-level signals: motion around their mouth and eyes, perhaps a hand gesture, a pitch change in their voice and, of course, verbal cues such as the words they are using. Signals are any detectable changes that carry information or a message. Sounds, gestures, and facial expressions are signals that are observable by natural human senses, while blood pressure, hormone levels, and neurotransmitter levels require special sensing equipment. Second, patterns of signals can be combined to provide more reliable recognition. A combination of clenched hands and raised arms movements may be an angry gesture; a pattern of features extracted from an electromyogram, a skin conductivity sensor, and an acoustic pitch waveform, may indicate a state of distress. This medium-level pattern representation can often be used to decide about what emotion is present. At no point, however, do we directly observe the underlying emotional state. All that can be observed is a complex pattern of voluntary and involuntary signals, in physical (physiological signals) and behavioral forms. Deciding which signal to measure depends on the data we want to analyze and on the availability of the technologies for its capture.

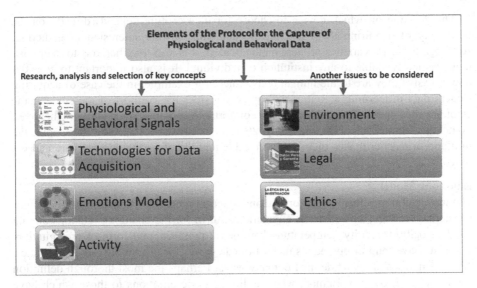

Fig. 1. Elements of the protocol for the capture of physiological and behavioral data.

Technologies for Data Acquisition

For the physiological data acquisition these technologies are electronic dispositives whose main component are sensors. These can detect events in the human body or changes in the environment and send the information to other electronics, frequently a computer processor. The sensors can measure physiological parameters related to autonomic nervous system changes. Nowadays these are already integrated into wearable human-machine interfaces that capture physiological signals that can help in the recognition of emotions, as mentioned in [42]. Brainwave diadems that send information to an electronic device in the form of an electroencephalogram (EEG) are found. Cardiovascular wristbands, which measure the heart rate and provide information in the form of an electrocardiogram (ECG). Electrothermal activity sensors, which measure the level of conductivity of the skin through sweat on the hands measured with two small electrodes of silver chloride in which an imperceptibly small voltage is applied and then the conductance between the two electrodes is measured. Thermal cameras allow to measure the temperature change of the human body associated with the different emotional states. There are also devices that measure muscle electrical activity in response to nerve stimulation of muscles, in the form of electromyography (EMG). The electromyogram signal uses small electrodes to measure a small muscle tension, which indicates contraction [43].

Regarding devices related to the identification of people's behavior -such as body postures and gestures- there are traditional video cameras, webcams or augmented reality devices that allow the recording of facial expressions and body movements, as well as eye tracking, important to the recognition of emotions. In this type of devices, there are also voice recorders, another medium used to identify emotions, as mentioned in [41].

The decision on which device to choose for data capture depends directly on the possibility of acquiring them and on the data that we are interested in gathering. Although there are varieties of them on the market, it is also true that, due to their cost, they are not available to any institution or individual. It is also important to consider how invasive they are to the human body, since, for example, in the case of acquiring student data in learning activities we should consider the comfort of the student; the emotions they show depend a lot on how comfortable and how much pleasure they feel. Something similar happens when they attend a face-to-face class at a classroom, the furniture or teacher makes them uncomfortable and therefore they do not care and get bored.

Emotions Model

The term emotion refers to relations among external incentives, thoughts, and changes in internal feelings; as weather is a remarkable term for the changing relations among wind velocity, humidity, temperature, barometric pressure, and form of precipitation. Theorists have long discussed a small set of categories for describing emotional states. "Basic emotions" may be defined in many ways. Perhaps the most thorough definition has been given by Paul Ekman, who has linked basic emotions to those which have distinctive universal facial expressions associated with them, as well as eight other properties [3]. By these criteria, Ekman identified six basic emotions or discrete emotion categories mentioned in the introduction.

Some authors have been less concerned with the existence of eight or so basic emotions and instead refer to continuous dimensions of emotion [44]. Three dimensions show up most commonly, although only the names of the first two are widely agreed on. The two most common dimensions are "arousal" (calm/excited), and "valence" (negative/positive) [4]. The other dimension is called "activation" (active/passive) [43].

In general, two dimensions cannot be used to distinguish all the basic emotions; for example, intense fear and anger lie in the same region of high arousal and negative valence. However, these two dimensions do account for the most common descriptions of mood. The lack of a definition of emotion, and the lack of agreement on whether there are basic emotions or continuous spaces of emotions are obstacles to the goals of computer-based recognition and synthesis. The question of whether to try to represent emotions with discrete categories or continuous dimensions can be considered a choice, as each representation has advantages in different applications, the best choice depends on what we are trying to explain or get [43]. For example, if colleges must answer a self-report about the emotions they are feeling when they are running a learning activity it is better to ask them with emotions categories as engagement or bored instead of continuous values for arousal, valence or activation variables.

Educational Software

Educational software incorporates multimedia content and gives users a high level of interactivity. These two features differentiate them from traditional teaching practices. Multimedia content like pictures, graphics, and sound help engage the students in their lessons. Its objective is to help fill a need for more interactive and personalized educational experiences for students. Some examples of educational software are intelligent tutorial systems, educational games and MOOCs. An essential element of this software is the student's modeling, from which it must be possible to adapt the software automatically to the requirements of each student, such as their learning style, cognitive capacity, learning curve and emotional state. The choice of educational software to be used as a virtual interactive medium depends on the characteristics of the students (age, school level, subjects of study, studies they carry out), the subject of interest and mainly learning-centered emotions that want to provoke during their interaction with it.

4.2   Issues for the Design of the Protocol

Environment

A learning environment is a "place" or a "space" where learning takes place, it is a set of physical places and the relationships that appear in it. It is a whole of objects, smells, shapes, colors, sounds, people who inhabit and relate in a physical frame [45]. The elements, components, dimensions and conditions that should be considered when planning and designing a quality learning environment are the dimensions of the space, the furniture, the lighting, temperature and ventilation, the decoration and accessories, the computer equipment that will be used and the technologies for the acquisition of data and its physical disposition.

Legal

In Mexico, the Federal Law on the Protection of Personal Data in Possession of Individuals DOF: 05/07/2010, published in the Official Gazette of the Federation on July 5th, 2010, protects the privacy of individuals with respect to the treatment we give their personal information. Its provisions are applicable to all individuals or corporations, public and private sector, both at the federal and state level, which carry out the processing of personal data in the exercise of their activities, therefore, companies such as banks, insurers, hospitals, schools, telecommunications companies, religious associations, and professionals such as lawyers, doctors, among others, are obliged to comply with what is established by this law. According to article 3 Sect. 5 of this Law, personal data is all that information that allows to identify a person.

In the capture of physiological and behavioral data we must first obtain consent for its recording, this must be done formally through the drafting of an "*informed consent letter*". In this document the participant is explained what the experiment consists of, the devices that will be used for the capture, the use that will be given to their data, the confidentiality that will be saved from them and their signature is requested with which they authorize the recording.

For any other country we must inform ourselves of the laws that protect the privacy of personal data and design our experiment being respectful of them.

Ethics

Emotions, perhaps more so than thoughts, are ultimately personal and private, providing information about the most intimate motivational factors and reactions. Any attempts to detect, recognize, not to mention manipulate, a user's emotions thus constitute the ultimate breach of ethics and will never be acceptable to computer users. Attempts to endow computers with these abilities will lead to widespread rejection of such computer systems and will help promote an attitude of distrust to computers in general.

Humans routinely detect, recognize, and respond to emotions or manipulate them in ways that most would consider highly ethical and desirable [46]. In the case of cheering up a student's mood to take better advantage of a learning activity is perfectly acceptable, more, however, although the intention is good, he should be informed of this.

4.3   Protocol, Informed Consent Letter and Emotions Test

The content of the protocol includes the description, sample population definition, data collection instruments, data acquisition technologies to use, educative software to use, experiment execution steps, data protection law and informed consent letter. In Fig. 2 we show the protocol document, informed consent letter and the emotions tests that the student will answer three times during the data capture (they serve as a self-evaluation of the emotion they are feeling from the discrete and continuous model).

Informed consent is an ethical and legal requirement for research involving human participants. It is the process where a participant is informed about all aspects of the trial. Informed consent is an inevitable requirement prior to every research involving human being as subjects for study. Obtaining consent involves informing the subject about his or her rights, the purpose of the study, procedures to be undertaken, potential risks and benefits of participation, expected duration of study, extent of confidentiality of personal identification and demographic data, so that the participation of subjects in the study is entirely voluntary [47].

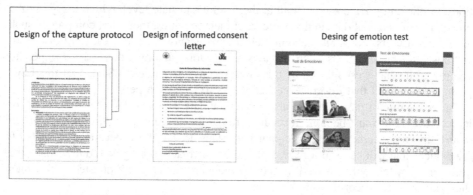

Fig. 2. Protocol, informed consent letter and emotion test.

5   Conclusions

Constructing a database with physiological and behavioral signals of humans performing activities in real environments, both controlled and uncontrolled, is a complex, laborious and time-consuming task, especially when the challenge is to integrate data from various devices to capture different signs. Due to this, the databases of expressions with emotional content that are publicly available correspond only to facial expressions and activities in which it is easier to place a video camera and record the emotional expressions. But while it is true, this is the least invasive way to capture emotional signals, it is a challenge to be able to integrate more robust databases with emotional data, both physiological and behavioral. The advantage of this proposal is to be able to relate physiological signals with the physical expression of the behavior and corroborate their correspondence, that is, for example, if the facial expression indicates happiness, what facial temperature is related to this emotion or what changes in heart rate can be associated with this emotion.

Defining the area in which the recognition is attempted and the physiological signals that are to be captured gives the pattern to the design of an experiment, formalized in a protocol for its execution. The protocol defines the details of the capture to perform a controlled experiment and is designed for a specific context. Therefore, the databases will contain data corresponding to the activity within the context defined as those mentioned in Table 2 where we show examples of databases with data captured in learning environments. The design of the capture protocol requires prior investigation about the context in which it will be executed, the kind of participants, the activity that will be carried out, the data that will be captured, the devices that will be used, the time of the capture, the emotions model, among others that may vary depending on the use that will be given to the database. Other not less important aspects that must be considered are the physical conditions of the place, furniture, legal aspects referring to the confidentiality of the captured data and ethical aspects about the treatment that will be given to the data. All these elements are described in a document that supports both the capture of data and the use that is made of them. It is important for any type of research to be backed by a document that validates the data on which the research is based and that in many occasions is a requirement to be able to publish in academic and scientific dissemination events. This work is the result of research and activities that were carried out to capture physiological and behavioral signals in a controlled learning environment with the objective of creating a database that makes better contributions to the learning-centered emotions automatic recognition. Based on the considerations mentioned in this article, the formal protocol for data capture was designed that helped us solve the problems mentioned in Sect. 3. Following the protocol, we have a control of the execution of the experiment. In this the steps to carry out the capture are listed, from the welcoming of the student, the explanation of the experiment in which they will participate and the definition of all the elements. The sample population is college engineering students, the educational software they use is a MOOC of basic algebra, exploring only the introductory module to algebra. The devices to record selected behavior signals are a Logitech Full HD Web video camera and the Kinect 360 for Windows. The devices for capturing physiological signals are an ICI 9320P thermal camera (for capturing the facial temperature), a cardiac pulse sensor implemented with Arduino and the MUSE 2 headband (both for recording the heart rate). Once we have the data, the future work to be done in this investigation is the cleaning and selection of these with the aim of structuring the database. Subsequently, a prior analysis of the data should be carried out with the idea of finding relations (manual labeling) between changes in temperature or heart rate and emotion, detected by observation of the face also considering the emotional state identified by the same student through an emotional test. The manual labeling will give us the guidelines to do it automatically. Finally, the tagged data will be the input of machine learning algorithms that once trained automatically identify emotions centered on learning, hoping to contribute both in the educational and computational area. The process of automatic identification of emotions can be integrated into the module of student modeling in educational software sensitive to students' emotions, such as intelligent tutorials, MOOCs or educational games. This with the idea of complementing the student model and consequently reinforcing the decision making of teaching strategies and assignment of activities that contribute to better levels of learning.

References

1. D'Mello, S., Graesser, A.: Dynamics of affective states during complex learning. Learn. Instr. **22**(2), 145–157 (2012). https://doi.org/10.1016/j.learninstruc.2011.10.001
2. Fuentes, C., Herskovic, V., Rodríguez, I., Gerea, C., Marques, M., Rossel, P.O.: A systematic literature review about technologies for self-reporting emotional information. J. Ambient Intell. Humaniz. Comput. 1–14 (2016). https://doi.org/10.1007/s12652-016-0430-z
3. Ekman, P.: Emotions Revealed. Recognizing Faces and Feelings to Improve Communication and Emotional Life, 1st edn. Henrry Holt and Company, New York (2003)
4. Russell, J.A.: A circumplex model of affect. J. Pers. Soc. Psychol. **39**(6), 1161–1178 (1980). https://doi.org/10.1037/h0077714
5. Ekman, P., Friesen, W., Hager, J.: Facial Action Coding System. The Manual, Salt Lake City (2002)
6. Soleymani, M., Member, S., Lee, J.: DEAP: a database for emotion analysis using physiological signals. IEEE Trans. Affect. Comput. **3**(1), 18–31 (2012)
7. el Kaliouby, R., Picard, R.W.: Affectiva Database. MIT Media Laboratory (2019). https://www.affectiva.com. Accessed 08 Apr 2019
8. Arroyo, I., Cooper, D.G., Burleson, W., Woolf, B.P., Muldner, K., Christopherson, R.: Emotion sensors go to school. Front. Artif. Intell. Appl. **200**(1), 17–24 (2009). https://doi.org/10.3233/978-1-60750-028-5-17
9. Livingstone, S.R., Russo, F.A.: The Ryerson audio-visual database of emotional speech and song (RAVDESS): a dynamic, multimodal set of facial and vocal expressions in north American English. PLoS ONE **13**(5), 14–18 (2018). https://doi.org/10.1371/journal.pone.0196391
10. Freitas-Magalhães, A.: Facial Action Coding System 3.0: Manual of Scientific Codification of the Human Face (English edition). FEELab Science Books, Porto (2018)
11. Lucey, P., Cohn, J.F., Kanade, T., Saragih, J., Ambadar, Z.: The extended Cohn-Kanade dataset (CK +): a complete facial expression dataset for action unit and emotion-specified expression. In: 2010 IEEE Computer Society Conference on in Computer Vision and Pattern Recognition Workshops (CVPRW), July 2010, pp. 94–101 (2010)
12. Lyons, M.J., Gyoba, J., Kamachi, M.: Japanese Female Facial Expressions (JAFFE), Database of Digital Images (1997)
13. Valstar, M.F., Pantic, M.: Induced disgust, happiness and surprise: an addition to the MMI facial expression database. In: Seventh International Conference on Language Resources and Evaluation (2010)
14. Sneddon, I., Mcrorie, M., Mckeown, G., Hanratty, J.: Belfast induced natural emotion database. IEE Trans. Affect. Comput. **3**(1), 32–41 (2012)
15. Mavadati, S.M., Member, S., Mahoor, M.H., Bartlett, K., Trinh, P., Cohn, J.F.: DISFA: a spontaneous facial action intensity database. IEEE Trans. Affect. Comput. **6**(1), 1–13 (2013)

16. Aifanti, N., Papachristou, C., Delopoulos, A.: The MUG facial expression database. In: 11th International Workshop on Image Analysis for Multimedia Interactive Services WIAMIS 2010, pp. 1–4 (2010). https://doi.org/10.1371/journal.pone.0009715
17. Happy, S.L., Patnaik, P., Routray, A., Guha, R.: The Indian spontaneous expression database for emotion recognition. IEEE Trans. Affect. Comput. 8(1), 131–142 (2017). https://doi.org/10.1109/TAFFC.2015.2498174
18. Langner, O., Dotsch, R., Bijlstra, G., Wigboldus, D.H.J., Hawk, S.T., van Knippenberg, A.: Presentation and validation of the Radboud Faces Database. Cogn. Emot. 24(8), 1377–1388 (2010). https://doi.org/10.1080/02699930903485076
19. Zhao: Oulu-CASIA NIR&VIS facial expression database. Center for Machine Vision and Signal Analysis. University of Oulu, Oulum, Yliopisto. http://www.cse.oulu.fi/wsgi/CMV/Downloads/Oulu-CASIA. Accessed 04 Apr 2019
20. Aneja, D., Colburn, A., Faigin, G., Shapiro, L., Mones, B.: Modeling stylized character expressions via deep learning. In: Lai, S.-H., Lepetit, V., Nishino, K., Sato, Y. (eds.) ACCV 2016. LNCS, vol. 10112, pp. 136–153. Springer, Cham (2017). https://doi.org/10.1007/978-3-319-54184-6_9
21. Mollahosseini, A., Hasani, B., Mahoor, M.H.: AffectNet: a database for facial expression, valence, and arousal computing in the wild. IEEE Trans. Affect. Comput. 10(1), 18–31 (2017). https://doi.org/10.1109/TAFFC.2017.2740923
22. Mena-Chalco, R., Marcondes, J., Velho, L.: Banco de Dados de Faces 3D: IMPA-FACE3D, Brasil (2008)
23. Thomaz, C.E.: FEI face database. Department of Electrical Engineering. Centro Universitario da FEI, São Bernardo do Campo, São Paulo, Brazil (2012). https://fei.edu.br/~cet/facedatabase.html. Accessed 04 Apr 2019
24. Zafeiriou, S., Kollias, D., Nicolaou, M.A., Papaiooannou, A., Kotsia, I.: Aff-Wild: valence and arousal 'in-the-wild' challenge. In: Computer Vision and Pattern Recognition Workshops (CVPRW), 2017, pp. 1980–1987 (2017)
25. Nye, B., et al.: Analyzing learner affect in a scenario-based intelligent tutoring system. In: André, E., Baker, R., Hu, X., Rodrigo, Ma.Mercedes T., du Boulay, B. (eds.) AIED 2017. LNCS (LNAI), vol. 10331, pp. 544–547. Springer, Cham (2017). https://doi.org/10.1007/978-3-319-61425-0_60
26. Xiao, X., Pham, P., Wang, J.: Dynamics of affective states during MOOC learning. In: André, E., Baker, R., Hu, X., Rodrigo, Ma.Mercedes T., du Boulay, B. (eds.) AIED 2017. LNCS (LNAI), vol. 10331, pp. 586–589. Springer, Cham (2017). https://doi.org/10.1007/978-3-319-61425-0_70
27. Zataraín, R., Barrón, M.L., González, F., Reyes-García, C.A.: An affective and web 3.0 based learning environment for a programming language. Telemat. Inform. (2017). https://doi.org/10.1016/j.tele.2017.03.005
28. Zatarain-Cabada, R., Barrón-Estrada, M.L., González-Hernández, F., Oramas-Bustillos, R., Alor-Hernández, G., Reyes-García, C.A.: Building a corpus and a local binary pattern recognizer for learning-centered emotions. Adv. Comput. Intell. II, 524–535 (2017)
29. Zatarain-Cabada, R., Barron-Estrada, M.L., González-Hernández, F., Rodríguez-Rangel, H.: Building a face expression recognizer and a face expression database for an intelligent tutoring system. In: Proceedings - IEEE 17th International Conference Advanced Learning Technologies ICALT 2017, no. 2161–377X/17, pp. 391–393 (2017). https://doi.org/10.1109/icalt.2017.141
30. Bosch, N., D'Mello, S.: The affective experience of novice computer programmers. Int. J. Artif. Intell. Educ. 27(1), 181–206 (2015). https://doi.org/10.1007/s40593-015-0069-5

31. Harley, J.M., Bouchet, F., Azevedo, R.: Aligning and comparing data on emotions experienced during learning with MetaTutor. In: Lane, H.C., Yacef, K., Mostow, J., Pavlik, P. (eds.) AIED 2013. LNCS (LNAI), vol. 7926, pp. 61–70. Springer, Heidelberg (2013). https://doi.org/10.1007/978-3-642-39112-5_7

32. Graesser, A.C., D'Mello, S.: Emotions during the learning of difficult material 57 (2012). https://doi.org/10.1016/b978-0-12-394293-7.00005-4

33. Arana-Llanes, J.Y., González-Serna, G., Pineda-Tapia, R., Olivares-Peregrino, V., Ricarte-Trives, J.J., Latorre-Postigo, J.M.: EEG lecture on recommended activities for the induction of attention and concentration mental states on e-learning students. J. Intell. Fuzzy Syst. 34, 3359–3371 (2017)

34. Bosch, N., et al.: Detecting student emotions in computer-enabled classrooms. In: IJCAI International Joint Conference on Artificial. Intelligence, vol. 2016-Janua, pp. 4125–4129 (2016)

35. Bosch, N., D'mello, S.K., Ocumpaugh, J., Baker, R.S., Shute, V.: Using video to automatically detect learner affect in computer-enabled classrooms. ACM Trans. Interact. Intell. Syst. 6(2), 1–26 (2016). https://doi.org/10.1145/2946837

36. Bosch, N., et al.: Automatic detection of learning-centered affective states in the wild. In: Proceedings of the 20th International Conference on Intelligent User Interfaces - IUI 2015, pp. 379–388 (2015). https://doi.org/10.1145/2678025.2701397

37. Monkaresi, H., Bosch, N., Calvo, R.A., D'Mello, S.K.: Automated detection of engagement using video-based estimation of facial expressions and heart rate. IEEE Trans. Affect. Comput. 1–14 (2016). https://doi.org/10.1109/taffc.2016.2515084

38. Almohammadi, K., Hagras, H., Yao, B., Alzahrani, A., Alghazzawi, D., Aldabbagh, G.: A type-2 fuzzy logic recommendation system for adaptive teaching. Soft. Comput. 21(4), 965–979 (2017). https://doi.org/10.1007/s00500-015-1826-y

39. Bixler, R., D'Mello, S.: Towards automated detection and regulation of affective states during academic writing. In: Lane, H.C., Yacef, K., Mostow, J., Pavlik, P. (eds.) AIED 2013. LNCS (LNAI), vol. 7926, pp. 904–907. Springer, Heidelberg (2013). https://doi.org/10.1007/978-3-642-39112-5_142

40. González-Hernández, F., Zatarain-Cabada, R., Barrón-Estrada, M.L., Rodríguez-Rangel, H.: Recognition of learning-centered emotions using a convolutional neural network. J. Intell. Fuzzy Syst. 34, 3325–3336 (2017)

41. Steidl, S.: Automatic Classification of Emotion-Related User States in Spontaneous Children's Speech. Universität Erlangen-Nürnberg, Erlangen (2009)

42. Cowie, R., et al.: Emotion recognition in human computer interaction. IEEE Signal Process. Mag. 18(1), 32–80 (2001). https://doi.org/10.1109/79.911197

43. Picard, R.W.: Affective Computing (1997). https://doi.org/10.1007/bf01238028

44. Schlosberg, H.: Three dimensions review. J. Gen. Psychol. 61(2), 81–88 (1954). https://doi.org/10.1080/00221309.1934.9917853

45. Wilson, B.G.: Constructivist Learning Environments: Case Studies in Instructional Design, p. 4. Educational Technology, New York City (1996)

46. Picard, R.W.: Affective computing: challenges. Int. J. Hum Comput Stud. 59(1–2), 55–64 (2003). https://doi.org/10.1016/S1071-5819(03)00052-1

47. Nijhawan, L., et al.: Informed consent: issues and challenges. J. Adv. Pharm. Technol. Res. 4 (3), 134–140 (2013). https://doi.org/10.4103/2231-4040.116779

Fostering Teenagers' Motivation Towards Peace Culture Workshops Using Gamification

Cristian Jurado(✉)(iD), Mónica Llano(iD), Edwin Gamboa(iD),
Yuri Bermúdez(iD), Victor Valencia(iD), and Maria Trujillo(iD)

Universidad del Valle, Cali, Colombia
{cristian.camilo.jurado,monica.llano,
edwin.gamboa,yuri.bermudez,valencia.victor,
maria.trujillo}@correounivalle.edu.co

Abstract. Multipropaz Foundation, a non-profit organization, tries to prevent violence among teenagers through formative workshops in a vulnerable zone in Cali Colombia. This foundation uses an active methodology focused on teamwork and personal growth, which helps teenagers build a life project and promote a peace culture. Teenager's sustained participation is key to achieve the expected outcomes; i.e., develop life skills, such as creative conflict resolution and leadership, and strengthen teenager's potential. However, Multipropaz has detected an intermittent participation from students resulting in a lack of adherence to the formative workshops, which may prevent students who desert or participate occasionally from achieving the expected outcomes. In this paper, we present Freiya, a user-centred gamified application developed to address the identified lack of adherence from teenagers. The motivation of a group of teenagers towards the use of Freiya as a complementary tool in a workshop was assessed using the Intrinsic Motivation Inventory (IMI). The results of the evaluation showed that most teenagers felt motivated using the application as part of the workshop. Thus, we argue that the employed approach to address teenagers' lack of motivation using gamification may be effective. Freiya is planned to be extended to generate a more interactive environment for teenagers during formative workshops.

Keywords: Teenagers · Motivation · Adherence · Peace promotion · Workshops · Freiya · Gamification · Technology enriched workshops

1 Introduction

Comuna 20 is a zone in Cali Colombia composed of 12 neighbourhoods that belong to the working class; i.e., 1 (83%), 2 (14%), 3 (3%) Colombian social strata. Only 2.2% of that population reaches higher education and the majority (42.2%) only accomplish a basic primary education level [1]. Consequently, academic and professional opportunities for them are minimal. In addition, teenagers from this zone are exposed to social conflicts such as drug addiction, thefts, gangs and violence. Multipropaz, a non-profit organisation from Cali, tries to address those issues by conducting formative workshops that foster the acquisition of conflict resolution skills. The formative workshops

© Springer Nature Switzerland AG 2019
P. H. Ruiz and V. Agredo-Delgado (Eds.): HCI-COLLAB 2019, CCIS 1114, pp. 227–237, 2019.
https://doi.org/10.1007/978-3-030-37386-3_17

include activities with an active and dynamic methodology to improve leadership and communication skills, and to foster a peace culture among teenagers. The workshops are conducted by members of the foundation (workshop facilitators) who are responsible for planning and leading the activities, in which the teenager's continuous participation is key to achieve the expected results. However, Multipropaz has detected a lack of adherence by teenagers to the workshops, which is evidenced by their intermittent participation.

Freiya is a user-centred gamified mobile application that aims to be a complementary tool to improve this lack of adherence through the generation of a more interactive environment during the training workshops. This article presents a study conducted to assess the motivation of teenagers produced by the use of this application. The results are preliminary and may serve as a basis to develop a more solid gamification strategy to address teenagers' lack of motivation in the long-term. In Sect. 2, we present works related to motivation. Then, we describe Freiya in Sect. 3. After that, we present the methods employed to validate Freiya in Sect. 4. We present and discuss the findings of the validation in Sects. 5 and 6 respectively. Finally, we conclude the paper in Sect. 7.

2 Related Work

Some studies related to human motivations towards playing or doing activities in their academic or leisure time were reviewed to understand motivation. First, a study conducted by Tischer [2] who remarks the importance of the "concept of a group leader"; whose leadership style is based on universal motivational values. Tischer [2] claims that there is a "universal structure of motivational values" [2] that explains how the students' and educators' motivations are the key of success in education processes. Educators have their own ways of teaching, conducted by methodologies or didactic ways of transmitting knowledge. In the same manner, students learn or participate in educational processes based on and determined by their own learning styles. Motivation results from educators' and students' inherent values and is the force that improve learning processes. Table 1 presents a categorization of the "universal structure of motivational values.

Regarding motivation and gamification, Roosta [3] proposes to relate the students' motivation types to elements of gamification. Accordingly, students' interests and needs should be identified; then, gamification elements that address those interests should be employed. It is proposed to categorize the students interests in front of the different elements of gamification.

Table 1. Motivational structure of human qualities [4]

Value	Description
Hedonism	It is made up of a group of values whose goal is sexual pleasure and gratification
Self-realization	Supports values based on the need for personal success by demonstrating competence, which will lead to social recognition
Social power	Seeks social status, prestige, and control over people and resources
Self-determination	Describes the values that are based on the need for independence in thought, action and choice
Conformity	It is part of the group of values that seeks control of impulses and own behaviour in accordance with social norms and expectations
Benevolence	Interest and concern for the wellbeing of close people
Security	Seeks the personal integrity of identification groups, social or personal stability
Tradition	It is expressed in the respect and acceptance of ideas and habits of society
Stimulation	The search for excitement, innovation and change
Philanthropy	It is a value directed towards the understanding and acceptance of the others, concern for the well-being of everyone

Furthermore, Table 2 [3] presents a categorization of motivation types, the mastery approach refers to students seeking the acquisition of skills. Meanwhile, mastery avoidance refers to students who do not seek comprehension of topics. Performance approach includes students who are looking for an external proof; and performance avoidance refers to students who want to avoid feeling unqualified in front of others.

Table 2. Categorisation of motivation types.

		Definition	
		Performed based	Other based
Valence	Positive (approaching success)	Mastery approach	Performance approach
	Negative (avoiding failure)	Mastery avoidance	Performance avoidance

3   Freiya

Freiya is a gamified mobile application developed using the Player Centered Design Process presented in. It is composed of two main modules, one targeted at workshop facilitators, who create and manage activities; and another at workshop participants, who use the activities to deliver answers and evidence of their work.

3.1   Workshop Facilitators Module

In this module, a workshop facilitator can create and configure three mechanics according to their needs (i.e., *RaceQr, Challenges* and *Questions*). Once a mechanic is created, a workshop facilitator obtains a code, which must be given to the workshop participants to allow them to access the created/configured activity. These mechanics are described below:

1. *RaceQr*: Consists of a question race in which facilitators can create a set of questions and the associated QR codes. In the meantime, when teenagers access a *RaceQr*, they must find and scan the codes to answer the questions. It was based on the need of workshop facilitators to assess participants' knowledge acquisition in relation to the concepts taught during the workshops. This mechanic includes the following sub-mechanics:
   a. *Leader board:* This sub-mechanic presents the order of arrival of participants during a race. It means that all participants can achieve the same score if they answer all questions correctly.
   b. *Points*: During a race, teenagers earn points when they answer a question correctly. This sub-mechanic is a numerical representation of the participants' progress. These points will be used in future versions as the core of the gamification economy strategy.
2. *Challenges*: This mechanism allows workshop facilitators to suggest challenges to teenagers, which can be solved in groups or individually. Teenagers should submit an image or audio as a solution to the challenge.
3. *Questions:* This mechanic allows workshop facilitators to choose a student (as desired or randomly) to answer a question. The smartphone of the selected participant will ring to indicate that he/she was selected.

Some of the application screens shown in Fig. 1, Image A shows the start-up and registration screen of the application. The session can be entered as a student or a workshop participant using Fb or Gmail. In the image B it is possible to visualize the screen of selection of activities, in which you can currently choose between "Race QR", "Challenges" and "Questions". Image C shows the QR race answer screen, the questions appear after scanning a QR code with the camera of the mobile device. The backgrounds and symbols of the screens and activities, are scenarios and actors of the Multipropaz Foundation, looking for an identity in the aesthetics of the application.

3.2 Workshop Participants Module

In this module, participants can access the activities programmed by a workshop facilitator using an access code. In a future phase of Freiya, participants will be able to share their badges, achievements or any progress in social networks. They will also be able to provide feedback to workshop leaders through badges and comments. Finally, they will have access to a personal profile in which they will be able to see their personal progress and reports.

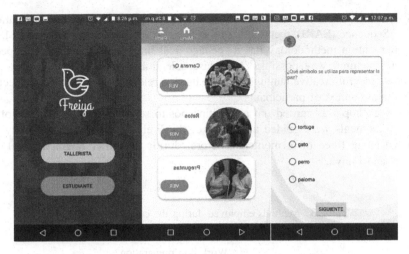

Fig. 1. Freiya screenshots (A, B and C respectively)

4   Methods

4.1   Aim of the Study

To assess Freiya's capability to motivate a group of teenagers during a peace promotion workshop using the IMI [5].

4.2   Participants

27 teenagers (12 males (44,44%) and 15 females (55,56%)) who are regular partici-pants of Multipropaz workshops participated voluntarily during the data collection. Teenagers' ages ranged from 14 to 17 years old (Mean:15,5 years, Standard Deviation: 1,29 years). 19 (70,37%) of them had a smartphone. The number of participants depended on the number of teenagers who attended the activity the day on which the study took place.

4.3   Instruments

Evaluation instruments included a group interview [6] and the Intrinsic Motivation Inventory (IMI) [5].

4.4   Procedure

An overview of the followed procedure is presented in Table 3. To validate Freiya, a workshop was conducted by two students from the Recreation Academic Program of the Universidad del Valle, who have been trained by Multipropaz foundation to be workshop facilitators. The workshop was created using the Intensive Recreational Activity Sequence (SARI) methodology [7]. According to Jonny Velasco [8], the SARI intervention methodology has a "pedagogical intention, which is developed in the most structured way possible. A precise selection of conceptual elements and techniques (playful-creative languages) to be used is relevant to address and reflect the socio-cultural context of participants".

The workshop was carried out at Multipropósito school. All the activities of the workshop moments were guided using one of the Freiya mechanics. This study was conducted along three main moments, before, during and after interaction between teenagers and Freiya.

Table 3. Methods employed during the conducted study

Moment	Employed method	Goal
Before interaction	–	Workshop preparation
During interaction	SARI [7]	Use Freiya as part of a workshop under real conditions
After interaction	IMI questionnaire [5]	Gather feedback participants' motivation (See Sect. 5)

Before interaction, the classroom was organised simulating a roundtable to break the traditional classroom scheme and promote the teenager's comfort. Furthermore, teenagers were asked to work in groups to generate a space for meeting, recognition, collaboration and affection.

During interaction, the SARI was applied and executed from using the following moments:

1. *Opening*, the goal of the session is presented, and an "icebreaker" activity is carried out to separate the teenagers into groups. this icebreaker activity consisted of a logical-mathematical game.
2. *Exploration*, a role-playing game is conducted to generate a comfortable environment between the teenagers.
3. *Negotiation*, a dramatic art technique (Fixed-Photo) was carried out using the Challenges mechanic of Freiya. The challenge consisted in creating a narrative sequence divided in 4 scenes based a topic (e.g. Colombian last peace agreement). Then, they had to draw the first 3 on a paper and capture the final scene as a collective photo.

4. *Closing*: the final stage of the SARI is a call to socialization and evaluation, which "implies a reconstruction experience, in which the individual and general process is assessed" [8] at this moment a facilitator and each group shares their narrative sequence and collective photo using Freiya. After that, a RaceQr was carried out using Freiya, with the aim of recalling the themes presented by each group. Finally, the Questions activity of Freiya is employed to gather feedback from participants regarding their impressions about he conducted workshop.

After interaction, the participants answered the IMI form to gather their impressions regarding their motivation towards the use of Freiya as part of the conducted Workshop. The IMI is a 7-point Likert scale used to evaluate the intrinsic motivation of people regarding an activity [9]. The IMI includes 7 sub-scales to assess interest/enjoyment, perceived competence, effort/importance, pressure/tension, perceived choice, value/usefulness and relatedness. When using the IMI, researchers may adapt the IMI; i.e., excluding some scale items or rephrasing of each item to match the evaluated activity. In our case, the activity is the use of Freiya as part of a workshop. Additionally, we translated all items into Spanish since participants do not have a proficient level of English. The translation was validated by an English teacher from *Universidad del Valle*. Finally, we do not include relatedness and perceived choice since the items do not meet the pursued study aim. The adapted version of the IMI is available online[1].

5   Findings

The findings suggest that most teenagers (81,48%) found interesting or enjoyed the workshop while using Freiya. As shown in Fig. 2, the mean score obtained for this sub-scale was 5.73, which reflects a positive attitude from participants regarding the use of Freiya in the workshop. Furthermore, in the Pressure/Tension sub-scale, a mean score of 2,84 was achieved, which means that most of the participants did not feel pressured or tense while using Freiya. Only 17,78% of teenagers reported to feel pressured or tense when using Freiya.

Similarly, most of the participants provided positive feedback regarding Perceived Competence and Value/Usefulness (62,95% and 67,90% respectively). The teenagers felt that the application is useful and valuable for workshop. Moreover, they felt competent while using the application during the workshop. This is shown on Fig. 2, where the mean scores for these sub-scales are 5.16 and 5.42 respectively.

Regarding the Effort/Importance sub-scale, 33.33% of the participants reported to have tried very hard to use Freiya properly during the workshop or felt that the application was not important for them. This is reflected by the obtained mean score (3,59) as shown in Fig. 2.

---

[1] Adapted IMI employed in the study (Spanish): bit.ly/2OGbJqe.

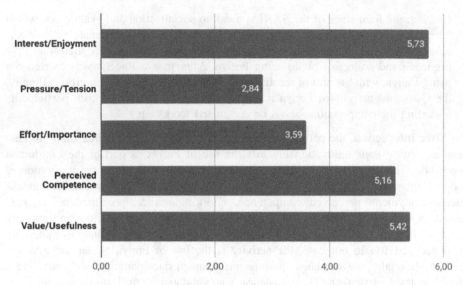

Fig. 2. Average grades on intrinsic motivations

5.1 Feedback Obtained from the Participants

During the closing activity some comments about Freiya were collected. The teenagers found funny and useful to use of a mobile application as a complementary tool in Multipropaz workshops. The RaceQr mechanic was attractive since it required participants to move around the school and working in group. They assessed this mechanic as a novel way to evaluate knowledge and get distracted from the common academic environment. Furthermore, they considered *Challenges* mechanic as a dynamic way of asking the teenagers for opinions or answers on a specific topic. Some relevant excerpts from their feedback are given below:

5. "I think using the application during the workshop was fun and makes it more dynamic.".
6. "Maybe if we could use the application individually, it would attract more our attention.".

In general, they expressed their eagerness to continue using the application during the Multipropaz workshops as an alternative to traditional methodologies employed during workshops.

Finally, they highlighted some issues of Freiya that should be addressed. For instance, during the RaceQr some of the participants had difficulties to scan the required QR codes, which represented a disadvantage for them to reach the top of the final leader board.

6 Discussion

Our findings showed that most teenagers felt motivated using Freiya during the conducted workshop. Most of the participants did not feel tense while using Freiya, which is expected since they are used to interact with mobile technologies. The most relevant reason for these results may be the use of a user-centred design approach since Freiya was developed in collaboration with Multipropaz members and considering the feedback provided by a group of teenagers. The gamification strategy was designed based on Persona models, which were developed considering socio-cultural aspects of regular Multipropaz workshop participants (teenagers). These models served as raw material for the development of the interactive, aesthetic and functional components of Freiya. As a result, we obtained a mobile application that addresses facilitators' and participants' needs. Also, the application integrates properly into current facilitators' methodologies, rather than requiring a complete change (e.g. the use of a virtual environment in a PC).

Participants' positive motivation may also be a consequence of being able to use their personal smartphones as a tool to achieve workshop goals, rather than having to put them aside as facilitators normally require them.

An unexpected outcome was related to the perceived importance. Although, the results regarding usefulness and interest were mostly positive, the participants did not consider important to use Freiya properly in the workshops. This means that the application was not totally indispensable to complete the tasks of the workshop; nevertheless, it does not mean that it was not an attractive element. Moreover, the application was used at specific moments of the workshop to fulfil specific tasks during the negotiation, exploration and closing moments (described in Sect. 4.4). In these moments, it was more a supporting tool than the main methodology of the workshop.

Furthermore, the errors that participant experienced while using *RaceQr* affected the competitive and interaction elements, which are key requirements identified in the developed Persona models. On the other hand, the *Challenges* mechanic was hindered by the unstable internet connection of the site where the workshop was held. This complicated the interaction with the application at the time of sending the photo of the challenge.

6.1 Limitations and Future Work

The most relevant limitation of our work is that the data was collected from one evaluation session of a gamified prototype. Consequently, most of the findings may be short-term responses that may change after a repeat use of the prototype. To assess teenagers' long-term motivation and adherence to Multipropaz workshops a study monitoring the use of the application for a significant period (e.g., one academic year) may be required. Also, more mechanics may be required to avoid excessive use of the mechanics included in Freiya (i.e. *RaceQr, Challenges* and *Questions*), which in turn requires a deeper knowledge of Multipropaz context to facilitate capturing particularities to develop proper and relevant content.

Regarding the obtained positive results, we argue that some of the feedback might be biased. First, only one smartphone was available per group and the whole interaction lasted 80 min. Thus, individual interaction times might be short. Additionally, the group of teenagers who tested the prototype did not have previous experiences with a similar technology; therefore, the novelty of the application may have biased their point of view. Thus, the view of older teenagers is to be validated.

Furthermore, the motivation of workshop facilitators needs to be assessed. Their point of view is also relevant since they are the ones who plan each workshop. Thus, the use of gamified application such as Freiya in a workshop depends mainly on them. Finally, the number of teenagers and facilitators who participated in the evaluation is low; thus, our results cannot be generalised.

Also, the workshop was carried out with a gamification strategy still in progress; that is to say, the application does not yet reflect everything contained in the Persona models. Thus, the mechanics of the application (*RaceQr, Challenges, Questions*), are subject to changes and their use was just for evaluation purposes. Identified errors should be corrected and more Persona models should be fully included/addressed in future versions of Freiya.

7 Conclusion

This paper presented a qualitative study to assess the capability of Freiya, a gamified mobile application, to motivate a group of teenagers during a peace promotion workshop using the IMI. Teenagers belong to a digital age that has changed communication paradigms, which results in the need of educational strategies that meet teenagers needs as digital natives. Addressing this need requires the use of user-centred approaches to understand end users' characteristics, motivations (intrinsic and extrinsic), habits and ways of understanding the world. We confirmed that using a user-centred strategy may be an effective strategy to motivate participants during a peace promotion workshop. The participants considered that Freiya may be a motivating tool to mediate and enrich workshops. Thus, Freiya may serve as a mediator in social processes targeted at improving teenagers' interest to educational processes social contexts such as Comuna 20 in Cali Colombia.

Acknowledgements. The authors would like to acknowledge the facilitators at the Multipropaz foundation and the teenagers at the Multipropósito school for their engagement and feedback provided during this study.

References

1. Municipal, C.D.A. de P., Universidad Icesi, C. de I. en E. y F., Alonso Cifuentes, J.C., Solano, J., Gallego, A.I., Arcos, M.A.: Una mirada descriptiva a las comunas de Cali (2007)
2. Tischer, I.: Heuristica Aprender La Ingenieria (2013)
3. Roosta, F., Taghiyareh, F., Mosharraf, M.: Personalization of gamification-elements in an e-learning environment based on learners' motivation (2016)
4. García del Junco, J., Medina Susanibar, E., Dutschke, G.: Una revisión exploratoria del modelo de Schwartz. Econ. gestión y Desarro **9**, 35–66 (2010)

5. Green, K.: Intrinsic motivation. J. Philos. Educ. **6**, 73–96 (1972). https://doi.org/10.1111/j. 1467-9752.1972.tb00461.x
6. Leech, B.L.: Asking questions: techniques for semistructured interviews. In: PS - Political Science and Politics (2002). https://doi.org/10.1017/S1049096502001129
7. Cobo, G.M.: Tejer Desde Adentro: La universidad Imaginada (2008)
8. Jonny Andrés, V.A.: Propuesta Metodológica de Intervencion Mediada por la Recreacion Dirigida (2014)
9. McLeod, S.: Likert Scale—Simply Psychology. https://www.simplypsychology.org/likert-scale.html. Accessed 28 May 2019

Guidelines to Evaluate the Usability and User Experience of Learning Support Platforms: A Systematic Review

Juan Salas[1]([⊠]) [iD], Alberto Chang[1] [iD], Lourdes Montalvo[1] [iD],
Almendra Núñez[1] [iD], Max Vilcapoma[1] [iD], Arturo Moquillaza[1,2] [iD],
Braulio Murillo[1] [iD], and Freddy Paz[1] [iD]

[1] Pontificia Universidad Católica del Perú, San Miguel, Lima 32, Peru
{juan.salas,montalvo.lourdes,bmurillov}@pucp.edu.pe,
{alberto.changl,almendra.nunezc,christian.vilcapomag,
amoquillaza,fpaz}@pucp.pe
[2] Universidad San Ignacio de Loyola, La Molina, Lima 12, Peru
miguel.moquillaza@usil.pe

Abstract. Nowadays, the usability and the user experience, are important aspects for the success of any software product. In the educational domain, Learning Support Platforms are not the exception, and these quality attributes become essential to guarantee an appropriate teaching process. For this reason, in this study, we present a systematic literature review whose purpose was to identify the characteristics that these types of systems must meet to obtain usable products. In the same way, the features that contribute to the assurance of a satisfying user experience have been cataloged. The purpose of this study is to establish the basis towards the elaboration of a future framework to quantify the level of usability and user experience of learning support platforms. The systematic search retrieved a total of 105 studies, from which 23 were selected as relevant. A set of 15 sub-attributes with their corresponding guidelines were identified to serve as a guide to design graphical user interfaces in a correct way in this type of software systems.

Keywords: Human-Computer Interaction · Systematic review · Usability evaluation · User experience · Guidelines and principles · Education

1 Introduction

Over the years, technology has been evolving on a large scale, which has led many organizations to take advantage of this event and make efforts to implement learning management systems (LMS), which improves the quality and scope of learning processes [1]. The Education sector is one of the most interesting sectors to analyze regarding the use of this type of LMS tools [2]. In order for the LMS to fulfill its objective efficiently, certain aspects must be considered, such as motivation, interest, commitment, focus on the task, behavior and much more [3].

Sometimes, the efficiency of the LMS is affected by the lack of usability. This is because the user could invest more effort in trying to understand the software than in

© Springer Nature Switzerland AG 2019
P. H. Ruiz and V. Agredo-Delgado (Eds.): HCI-COLLAB 2019, CCIS 1114, pp. 238–254, 2019.
https://doi.org/10.1007/978-3-030-37386-3_18

carrying out their activities. Therefore, there are two factors that must be considered for the success of the LMS: the quality of information and the way in which it is displayed to the user. According to Westfall, it was reported that 61% of people surveyed affirm that one of the inconveniences they had with LMS was learning how it works [4].

Therefore, usability is one of the key factors for the user to achieve satisfaction while using the LMS. This involves making the software easy to use and learn, with a user-friendly interface; displaying the content of a simple and orderly manner, thus preventing the user to focus on these issues [5]. Measuring usability is considered one of the great challenges, this is because there is no standard model which covers all the necessary usability attributes [6].

Heuristic evaluation is one of the most commonly used qualitative techniques to inspect software interfaces and find problems that affect usability [7]. On the other hand, quantitatively assessing the level of usability provides certain benefits, such as making objective comparisons between the software of the same type, which makes it easier for companies to make decisions to choose the best product [8]. With a numerical score, it favors the identification of the state of the level of usability of the software [9].

In this research, it is proposed to find those most important features about usability and electronic learning, as well as quantitative usability evaluations, taking into account heuristics and guidelines. To achieve this, a systematic literature review was carried out, following the Kitchenham methodology. Thus, the most important research on the subject was identified, which will serve as support to build a preliminary framework that allows quantifying the level of usability in those support tools for learning, in the near future.

2   A Systematic Literature Review

To identify those important key aspects that LMS must meet, a systematic review was conducted. The purpose of identifying those aspects was to analyze them, systematize them, and to propose in a future research, a framework to assess the usability and user experience based on the most important identified aspects.

The present systematic review was performed based on the parameters defined by Kitchenham and Charters [10]. In this case, the activities that were performed are: (1) definition of the research questions and search strategy, (2) selection of the primary studies, the extraction of the papers and (3) analysis of the results.

2.1   Research Questions

The main objective was to summarize some studies related to usability, user experience, learning management systems and usability evaluation methods. We used the PICOC table criteria in order to do this review according to the protocol established by Petticrew and Roberts [11]. In addition, we employed synonyms and related terms to find better results. These criteria are shown in Table 1.

Table 1. General concepts defined using the PICOC criteria.

Criterion	Description
Population	Web platforms that support learning
Intervention	Heuristic evaluation of usability and user experience
Comparison	Other methods of usability evaluation
Outcome	Case studies in which any method of usability evaluation is applied
Context	Academic and business context, including all types of stakeholders and empirical studies

Based on the concepts established using PICOC, we defined the following research questions oriented to identify relevant aspects in the design of graphical interfaces for learning management systems:

- **RQ1**: Which are the most relevant aspects of usability and user experience?
- **RQ2**: Which are the most important characteristics in LMS?
- **RQ3**: Which are the activities/characteristics of the usability evaluation models?
- **RQ4**: Which are the guidelines considered in other domains to evaluate usability?

2.2 Search Strategy

We defined our search strategy based on the general concepts. Some synonymous were selected to achieve a more comprehensive search. The search process was performed by using four recognized databases to search for primary studies: ACM Digital Library, IEEExplore, SCOPUS and SpringerLink. Grey literature was excluded since it is not peer reviewed.

In this phase, the search chains or queries that were used in the search engines of each database were formulated. It is important to mention that the syntax of the queries could vary according to the database that is employed. After grouping a series of concepts using the connectors AND/OR, the resulting search string was the following:

("usability" OR "user experience" OR "UX" OR "HCI") AND ("heuristic" OR "heuristic evaluation" OR "usability evaluation" OR "model evaluation usability") AND ("quantify" OR "quantitative" OR "approach quantitative" OR "comparative" OR "comparative analysis" OR "methodology to evaluate usability" OR "quantify usability" OR "measure usability" OR "method to evaluate usability") AND ("interface" OR "software" OR "web" OR "system" OR "satisfaction" OR "characteristic" OR "guideline" OR "design" OR "methodology" OR "case study") AND ("elearning" OR "e-learning" OR "learning management system" OR "LMS" OR "education" OR "higher education" OR "university" OR "e-learning system" OR "web platform to teaching" OR "web platform" OR "web system to support teaching").

2.3 Search Process and Data Extraction

In order to determine if an article must be considered as relevant, we defined the following inclusion criteria: *the study should present a methodology, framework or study case in which the usability and user experience are evaluated.* In the same way, we defined the exclusion criteria: *in the study, the specialists do not apply a usability or user experience evaluation in an intangible product as a software.* The automated search for our systematic mapping review was performed on October 20th, 2018. Table 2 shows the search results that were found. In addition, Table 3 shows the selected studies from the four databases used in this research. These studies were selected by discarding the studies that do not meet the inclusion criteria and present any of the exclusion criteria.

Table 2. Search results for RQ1, RQ2, RQ3 and RQ4.

Database name	Search results	Duplicate papers	Relevant papers
ACM Digital Library	24	–	9
IEEExplore	13	–	6
Scopus	36	4	7
SpringerLink	32	2	1
TOTAL	**105**	6	**23**

Table 3. Selected primary studies.

Study id	Author name	Year	Title
SS1 [12]	Hedegaard and Simonsen	2013	Extracting usability and user experience information from online user reviews
SS2 [13]	Al-Faries et al.	2013	Evaluating the accessibility and usability of top Saudi e-government services
SS3 [14]	Dias et al.	2014	HEUA: A heuristic evaluation with usability and accessibility requirements to assess Web systems
SS4 [6]	Hasan and Al-Sarayreh	2015	An integrated measurement model for evaluating usability attributes
SS5 [15]	Hovde	2015	Effective user experience in online technical communication courses: employing multiple methods within organizational contexts to assess usability
SS6 [16]	Choma et al.	2016	Working beyond technical aspects: an approach for driving the usability inspection adding the perspective of user experience
SS7 [17]	Quiñones et al.	2017	A methodology to develop usability/user experience heuristics
SS8 [18]	Sagar and Saha	2017	Qualitative usability feature selection with ranking: a novel approach for ranking the identified usability problematic attributes for academic websites using data mining techniques

(continued)

Table 3. (*continued*)

Study id	Author name	Year	Title
SS9 [19]	Hasan	2018	Usability problems on desktop and mobile interfaces of the Moodle Learning Management System (LMS)
SS10 [20]	AlRoobaea et al.	2013	A framework for generating a domain specific inspection evaluation method: A comparative study on social networking websites
SS11 [21]	Gordillo et al.	2014	The usefulness of usability and user experience evaluation methods on an e-Learning platform development from a developer's perspective: A case study
SS12 [22]	Iman and Rasoolzadegan	2015	Quantitative evaluation of software usability with a fuzzy expert system
SS13 [23]	Mtebe and Kissaka	2015	Heuristics for evaluating usability of Learning Management Systems in Africa
SS14 [24]	Kabir et al.	2016	An analytical and comparative study of software usability quality factors
SS15 [9]	Granollers	2016	Validación experimental de un conjunto heurístico para evaluaciones de UX de sitios web de comercio-e
SS16 [25]	Ivanović et al.	2013	Usability and privacy aspects of Moodle: Students' and teachers' perspective
SS17 [26]	Sabri et al.	2013	A quantitative approach in the usability evaluation of a courseware
SS18 [27]	Deraniyagala et al.	2015	Usability study of the EduMod eLearning Program for contouring nodal stations of the head and neck
SS19 [28]	Junus et al.	2015	Usability evaluation of the student centered e-Learning environment
SS20 [29]	Murillo et al.	2017	Usability testing as a complement of heuristic evaluation: A case study
SS21 [30]	Emang et al.	2017	Usability studies on E-Learning Platforms: Preliminary study in USM
SS22 [8]	Paz et al.	2018	Quantifying the usability through a variant of the traditional heuristic evaluation process
SS23 [31]	Aparna and Baseer	2015	SIRIUS-WUEP: A heuristic-based framework for measuring and evaluating Web usability in model-driven Web development

In addition, some secondary studies were identified applying the inclusion and exclusion criteria to the references established in the most relevant of the primary studies. These secondary papers are shown in Table 4.

Table 4. Selected secondary studies.

Study ID	Author name	Year	Title
SS24 [32]	Eason	1984	Towards the experimental study of usability
SS25 [33]	Nielsen	1993	Usability engineering
SS26 [34]	ISO 9241-11	1998	Ergonomics requirements for office work with visual display terminals (VDTs) – Part 11: Guidance on usability
SS27 [35]	ISO 9126-1	2001	Software engineering – Product quality
SS28 [36]	Reeves et al.	2002	Usability and instructional design heuristics for e-learning evaluation
SS29 [37]	Folmer et al.	2003	A framework for capturing the relationship between usability and software architecture
SS30 [38]	Abran et al.	2003	Usability meanings and interpretations in ISO standards
SS31 [39]	Rosato et al.	2004	Usability of course management systems by students
SS32 [40]	Mehlenbacher et al.	2005	Usable E-Learning: A conceptual model for evaluation and design
SS33 [41]	Dringus and Cohen	2005	An adaptable usability heuristic checklist for online courses
SS34 [42]	Ardito et al.	2005	An approach to usability evaluation of e-learning applications
SS35 [43]	Seffah et al.	2006	Usability measurement and metrics: A consolidated model
SS36 [44]	Nielsen and Loranger	2006	Prioritizing Web Usability
SS37 [45]	Bevan	2008	Classifying and selecting UX and usability measures
SS38 [46]	Ketola and Roto	2008	Exploring user experience measurement needs
SS39 [47]	Zaharias and Poylymenakou	2009	Developing a usability evaluation method for e-learning applications: Beyond functional usability
SS40 [48]	Giannakos	2009	A combinational evaluation method of computer applications
SS41 [49]	Al-Khalifa	2010	Heuristic evaluation of the usability of E-Government Websites: A case from Saudi Arabia
SS42 [50]	Al-Sarrayrih et al.	2010	Evaluation of a Moodle based learning management system applied at Berlin institute of technology based on ISO-9126
SS43 [51]	Giannakos	2010	The evaluation of an e-learning web-based platform
SS44 [52]	ISO 25010	2011	Systems and software engineering – Systems and software Quality Requirements and Evaluation (SQuaRE) – System and software quality models

(continued)

Table 4. (*continued*)

Study ID	Author name	Year	Title
SS45 [53]	Zaharias	2011	Heuristic evaluation of e-learning courses: a comparative analysis of two e-learning heuristic sets
SS46 [54]	Ghirardini	2011	E-learning methodologies. A guide for designing and developing e-learning courses
SS47 [55]	Kumar Dubey et al.	2012	Usability evaluation of object-oriented software system using fuzzy logic approach
SS48 [56]	Torrente et al.	2013	Sirius: A heuristic-based framework for measuring web usability adapted to the type of website
SS49 [57]	Şenol et al.	2014	Usability evaluation of a Moodle based learning management system
SS50 [58]	Thuseethan et al.	2014	Usability evaluation of learning management systems in Sri Lankan universities
SS51 [59]	Gupta and Ahlawat	2014	A critical analysis of a hierarchy-based usability model
SS52 [60]	Paz et al.	2015	Heuristic evaluation as a complement to usability testing: A case study in Web domain
SS53 [61]	Issa and Isaias	2015	Sustainable design: HCI, usability and environmental concerns
SS54 [62]	Rogers et al.	2015	Interaction Design - Beyond Human-Computer Interaction
SS55 [63]	Farmanesh and Samani	2015	Heuristic evaluation of the usability of LMS (Moodle) at EMU

Once these studies were obtained through the secondary review process, these were cataloged based on the relevant works. This information is shown in Table 5.

Table 5. Mapping of primary studies with secondary studies.

Primary study ID	Secondary study ID
SS1	SS25, SS26, SS29, SS35, SS37, SS38
SS2	SS41
SS3	SS25
SS4	SS25, SS26, SS30, SS35, SS37, SS44, SS47, SS51, SS54
SS5	SS32
SS6	SS24, SS36, SS53
SS7	SS26
SS8	SS25, SS47

(*continued*)

Table 5. (*continued*)

Primary study ID	Secondary study ID
SS9	*SS31, SS42, SS46, SS49, SS50*
SS10	*SS25, SS26, SS39*
SS11	*SS26, SS34, SS40, SS43*
SS12	*SS25*
SS13	*SS25, SS28, SS33, SS34, SS39, SS45*
SS14	*SS27, SS35*
SS15	–
SS16	–
SS17	–
SS18	*SS34, SS39*
SS19	*SS39*
SS20	*SS52*
SS21	*SS25, SS40, SS55*
SS22	*SS25, SS27*
SS22	*SS25, SS27*

3 Results of the Review

3.1 Relevant Aspects of Usability and User Experience

There were 18 papers that answer RQ1 (SS1, SS4, SS6, SS14, SS24, SS26, SS27, SS29, SS30, SS35, SS36, SS37, SS38, SS44, SS47, SS51, SS53, SS54). The usability/UX aspects that found in the systematic review are shown in Table 6.

Table 6. Usability and UX Aspects found by the Systematic Review Process (RQ1).

Aspect	Study id
Efficiency	*SS4, SS14, SS26, SS29, SS30, SS35, SS36, SS47, SS51, SS53, SS54*
Learnability	*SS1, SS4, SS14, SS27, SS29, SS30, SS35, SS36, SS37, SS44, SS54*
Satisfaction	*SS1, SS4, SS14, SS26, SS29, SS30, SS35, SS36, SS47, SS51, SS53*
Effectiveness	*SS4, SS14, SS26, SS30, SS35, SS37, SS47, SS51, SS53*
Accessibility	*SS4, SS35, SS37, SS44*
Memorability	*P36, SS51, SS54*
Protection	*SS35, SS37, SS54*

(*continued*)

Table 6. (*continued*)

Aspect	Study id
Universality	*SS4, SS35, SS51*
Esthetic	*SS1, SS4, SS44*
Operability	*SS4, SS14, SS27*
Errors	*SS1, SS36*
Hedonic	*SS1, SS38*
Recognizable	*SS4, SS44*
Security	*SS30, SS51*
Attractiveness	*SS14, SS27*
Reliability	*SS14, SS29*
Usability Compliance	*SS14, SS27*
Utility	*SS35, SS54*
Functionality	*SS53*
Impact	*SS38*
General Usability	*SS38*
Special Users	*SS53*
Specific Context of Use	*SS53*
Support	*SS38*
Trustfulness	*SS35*
Anticipation	*SS38*
User Difference	*SS38*
Protection against user errors	*SS44*
Aesthetics of user interface	*SS44*
Others	*SS1, SS14, SS24, SS27, SS38, SS53*

3.2 Important Characteristics in Learning Management Systems

In the same way, to answer RQ2, 14 papers were selected (SS5, SS9, SS13, SS16, SS19, SS21, SS28, SS31, SS32, SS39, SS42, SS46, SS49, SS50). According to the authors, there are relevant design aspects that contribute to satisfy the learning objectives that are frequently requested by the educational institutions when they search for learning tools. We detail some of those design aspects in Table 7.

Table 7. LMS Characteristics found by the Systematic Review Process (RQ2).

Study id	Characteristic
SS9	- *Consistency in the interface language* - *Aesthetic design of the pages* - *Appropriate content for each system page* - *Consistent information*
SS13	- *Instructional materials* - *Collaborative learning* - *Learning control* - *Feedback and evaluations* - *Accessibility* - *Motivation to learn*
SS16	- *General quality of existing teaching material* - *Tests* - *Collaborative assignments* - *Use of communication tools (forums, wikis, chats)* - *Express opinions (surveys)* - *Privacy concerns* - *Technical problems and localization (language)*
SS19	- *Content: factor consisting of the languages and terms used, support and learning materials, and other information in the system.* - *Learning and support: it is related to the characteristics of the platform for sending materials, discussions, evaluations, etc.* - *Visual design* - *Accessibility* - *Interactivity: factor related to all forms of communication in the context of learning that is facilitated by the system* - *Auto evaluation and system learning* - *Motivation to learn*

3.3 Activities and Characteristics of the Usability Evaluation Models

There were 11 papers that answer RQ3 (SS3, SS12, SS15, SS17, SS20, SS22, SS23, SS28, SS32, SS45, SS52). Some important strategies related to the process that must be followed in a usability/UX evaluation were obtained from these studies. These approaches were compared to decide how to establish the assessment framework. We show some of those strategies in Table 8.

Table 8. Characteristics/Activities of Usability Evaluations found by the Systematic Review Process (RQ3).

Study id	Characteristic
SS3	*This study proposes a questionnaire that evaluates usability and accessibility in support platforms for learning quantitatively* *- Evaluate the usability and accessibility of websites* *- It is composed of 93 requirements, which have been classified based on 10 Nielsen heuristics*
SS15	*- It is oriented to the application of electronic commerce systems* *- It is divided into 6 aspects* *- It consists of 64 guidelines that will be in charge of being evaluated for the qualification of the system* *- The objective of this is to obtain a degree of usability to determine the state of the system and - in addition - comparisons can be made between them*
SS22	*- This study presents a variation with respect to the study carried out by Granollers* *- The 'Yes' answers will have a score of 4, while the 'No' answers will be assigned the value of 0. For those questions that the evaluator feels is not met at all, you can choose a score between 1, 2, 3*
SS32	*- Group heuristics in 5 dimensions* *- They are based on activities related to teaching and learning with technology*

3.4   Guidelines to Evaluate the Usability Attribute

Finally, the RQ4 is related with the principles used in the heuristic evaluation models which allow to get the usability level - quantitatively or qualitatively - in the platforms from other domains, that can be used as well for learning support platforms. There were 18 papers that were used to answer this research question (SS2, SS3, SS7, SS8, SS10, SS11, SS18, SS23, SS25, SS28, SS32, SS33, SS34, SS40, SS41, SS43, SS48, SS55). Some the guidelines found are shown in Table 9.

Table 9. Guidelines to Evaluate Usability found in the Systematic Review Process (RQ4).

Study id	Guidelines (1/2)	Guidelines (2/2)
SS3	*- Visibility of the study of the system* *- Comparability between the framework and the real world and comparability between the designer model and the apprentice model* *- Control and freedom learners* *- Consistency and compliance with standards* *- Help and documentation*	*- Error prevention of the discard of circumferential errors related to usability* *- Recognition instead of memory* *- Flexibility and efficiency of use* *- Legitimacy and minimalism in the design* *- Identify recognition and improvement of errors*

(continued)

Table 9. (*continued*)

Study id	Guidelines (1/2)	Guidelines (2/2)
SS8	- *Organization of contents* - *Design and design evaluation.* - *Navigation* - *Search* - *Titular, titles and labels.* - *Scroll and pagination.* - *Page design* - *Home page*	- *Accessibility* - *Optimizing the user experience* - *Graphics, images and multimedia* - *Internationalization* - *Mobile* - *Security* - *Social communication media*
SS33	- *Visibility* - *Functionality* - *Esthetic* - *Feedback and help* - *Prevention of the error* - *Memorability* - *Course management*	- *Interactivity* - *Flexibility* - *Consistency* - *Efficiency* - *Reduce the redundancy* - *Accessibility*
SS34	- *Support for learning/authorship* - *Support for communication, personalization and access* - *Adaptation of the structure*	- *Facilities and technological adaptation* - *Effectiveness of teaching/authorship* - *Support efficiency*

4 Conclusions and Future Works

The usability and UX have become critical aspects to be considered in the development of software products. Nowadays, these quality attributes represent the main concerns of the software industries, since ensuring a high level of ease of use and UX in the applications, leads to establish an environment of appropriate use for the interaction with the system. The new paradigm in the software development is not only about providing the users with a tool to achieve their goals but also to ensure that the user experience is quality enough to generate satisfaction on the end user.

In this study, we performed a systematic literature review following a recognized and widely used methodology. According to this protocol, we identified 105 studies, from which 23 were selected. Furthermore, we considered 32 secondary studies, that provided more information to 4 research questions. This work allowed to identify the most relevant aspects in both usability as learning. Additionally, this review allowed to find characteristics that help to quantify the level usability and UX and some heuristics/guidelines related to domain of study.

The objective of this systematic literature review was to obtain relevant information from previous research to build a preliminary framework that allows quantifying the level of usability and UX in learning support platforms, through a checklist. Therefore, a deeper analysis should be carried out to generate the results to the objectives for the construction of the framework. Also, some of the results must be complemented and validated by interviews and expert judgment, respectively.

Acknowledgement. This study is highly supported by the Section of Informatics Engineering of the Pontifical Catholic University of Peru (PUCP) – Peru, and the "HCI, Design, User Experience, Accessibility & Innovation Technologies" Research Group (HCI-DUXAIT). HCI-DUXAIT is a research group of PUCP.

References

1. Penha, M., Correia, W., Soares, M., Campos, F., Barros, M.: Ergonomic evaluation of usability with users – application of the technique of cooperative evaluation. In: Marcus, A. (ed.) DUXU 2013. LNCS, vol. 8012, pp. 379–388. Springer, Heidelberg (2013). https://doi.org/10.1007/978-3-642-39229-0_41
2. Ilyas, M., Kadir, K.A., Adnan, Z.: Demystifying the learning management system (LMS): journey from e-learning to the strategic role. Eur. J. Bus. Manag. **9**, 12–18 (2017)
3. Cavus, N., Alhih, M.S.: Learning management systems use in science education. Procedia - Soc. Behav. Sci. **143**, 517–520 (2014). https://doi.org/10.1016/j.sbspro.2014.07.429
4. Westfall, B.: Learning Management System User Report - 2016. SoftwareAdvice.com (2016). https://www.softwareadvice.com/resources/lms-user-trends-2016/
5. Kumar, R., Hasteer, N.: Evaluating usability of a web application: a comparative analysis of open-source tools. In: Proceedings of the 2nd International Conference on Communication and Electronics Systems (ICCES 2017), Coimbatore, India, pp. 350–354 (2017). https://doi.org/10.1109/CESYS.2017.8321296
6. Hasan, L.A., Al-Sarayreh, K.T.: An integrated measurement model for evaluating usability attributes. In: Proceedings of the International Conference on Intelligent Information Processing, Security and Advanced Communication, pp. 1–6. ACM, Batna (2015). https://doi.org/10.1145/2816839.2816861
7. Granollers, T.: Usability evaluation with heuristics. new proposal from integrating two trusted sources. In: Marcus, A., Wang, W. (eds.) DUXU 2018. LNCS, vol. 10918, pp. 396–405. Springer, Cham (2018). https://doi.org/10.1007/978-3-319-91797-9_28
8. Paz, F., Paz, F.A., Sánchez, M., Moquillaza, A., Collantes, L.: Quantifying the usability through a variant of the traditional heuristic evaluation process. In: Marcus, A., Wang, W. (eds.) DUXU 2018. LNCS, vol. 10918, pp. 496–508. Springer, Cham (2018). https://doi.org/10.1007/978-3-319-91797-9_36
9. Granollers, T.: Validación experimental de un conjunto heurístico para evaluaciones de UX de sitios web de comercio-e. In: Proceedings of the 2016 IEEE 11th Colombian Computing Conference (CCC 2016), Popayan, Colombia, pp. 1–8 (2016). https://doi.org/10.1109/ColumbianCC.2016.7750783
10. Kitchenham, B., Pearl Brereton, O., Budgen, D., Turner, M., Bailey, J., Linkman, S.: Systematic literature reviews in software engineering – A systematic literature review. Inf. Softw. Technol. **51**, 7–15 (2009). https://doi.org/10.1016/j.infsof.2008.09.009
11. Petticrew, M., Roberts, H.: Systematic Reviews in the Social Sciences: A Practical Guide. Blackwell Publishing, Hoboken (2005). ISBN 978-1-405-12110-1
12. Hedegaard, S., Simonsen, J.G.: Extracting usability and user experience information from online user reviews. In: Proceedings of the SIGCHI Conference on Human Factors in Computing Systems, pp. 2089–2098. ACM, Paris (2013). https://doi.org/10.1145/2470654.2481286
13. Al-Faries, A., Al-Khalifa, H.S., Al-Razgan, M.S., Al-Duwais, M.: Evaluating the accessibility and usability of top Saudi e-government services. In: Proceedings of the 7th International Conference on Theory and Practice of Electronic Governance, pp. 60–63. ACM, Seoul (2013). https://doi.org/10.1145/2591888.2591898

14. Dias, A.L., Fortes, R.P.d.M., Masiero, P.C.: HEUA: a heuristic evaluation with usability and accessibility requirements to assess web systems. In: Proceedings of the 11th Web for All Conference, pp. 1–4. ACM, Seoul (2014). https://doi.org/10.1145/2596695.2596706

15. Hovde, M.R.: Effective user experience in online technical communication courses: employing multiple methods within organizational contexts to assess usability. In: Proceedings of the 33rd Annual International Conference on the Design of Communication, pp. 1–5. ACM, Limerick (2015). https://doi.org/10.1145/2775441.2775453

16. Choma, J., Zaina, L.A.M., Silva, T.S.d.: Working beyond technical aspects: an approach for driving the usability inspection adding the perspective of user experience. In: Proceedings of the 34th ACM International Conference on the Design of Communication, pp. 1–10. ACM, Silver Spring (2016). https://doi.org/10.1145/2987592.2987607

17. Quiñones, D., Rusu, C., Rusu, V.: A methodology to develop usability/user experience heuristics. Comput. Stand. Interfaces 59, 109–129 (2018). https://doi.org/10.1016/j.csi.2018.03.002

18. Sagar, K., Saha, A.: Qualitative usability feature selection with ranking: a novel approach for ranking the identified usability problematic attributes for academic websites using data-mining techniques. Hum.-Centric Comput. Inf. Sci. 7, 1–24 (2017). https://doi.org/10.1186/s13673-017-0111-8

19. Hasan, L.: Usability problems on desktop and mobile interfaces of the Moodle learning management system (LMS). In: Proceedings of the 2018 International Conference on E-Business and Applications, pp. 69–73. ACM, Da Nang (2018). https://doi.org/10.1145/3194188.3194192

20. AlRoobaea, R.S., Al-Badi, A.H., Mayhew, P.J.: A framework for generating a domain specific inspection evaluation method: a comparative study on social networking websites. In: Proceedings of the 2013 Science and Information Conference (SAI 2013), London, UK, pp. 757–767 (2013). ISBN 978-0-9893193-0-0

21. Gordillo, A., Barra, E., Aguirre, S., Quemada, J.: The usefulness of usability and user experience evaluation methods on an e-Learning platform development from a developer's perspective: a case study. In: Proceedings of the 2014 IEEE Frontiers in Education Conference (FIE 2014), Madrid, Spain, pp. 1–8 (2014). https://doi.org/10.1109/FIE.2014.7044340

22. Iman, M.R.H., Rasoolzadegan, A.: Quantitative evaluation of software usability with a fuzzy expert system. In: Proceedings of the 2015 5th International Conference on Computer and Knowledge Engineering (ICCKE 2015), Mashhad, Iran, pp. 325–330 (2015). https://doi.org/10.1109/ICCKE.2015.7365850

23. Mtebe, J.S., Kissaka, M.M.: Heuristics for evaluating usability of Learning Management Systems in Africa. In: Proceedings of the 2015 IST-Africa Conference, Lilongwe, Malawi, pp. 1–13 (2015). https://doi.org/10.1109/ISTAFRICA.2015.7190521

24. Kabir, M.A., Rehman, M.U., Majumdar, S.I.: An analytical and comparative study of software usability quality factors. In: Proceedings of the 2016 7th IEEE International Conference on Software Engineering and Service Science (ICSESS 2016), Beijing, China, pp. 800–803 (2016). https://doi.org/10.1109/ICSESS.2016.7883188

25. Ivanović, M., Putnik, Z., Komlenov, Ž.: Usability and privacy aspects of Moodle: students' and teachers' perspective. Informatica 37, 221–230 (2013)

26. Sabri, N.M., Mohamed, H., Soon, G.Y., Yusof, Y.m.H.: A quantitative approach in the usability evaluation of a courseware. J. Next Gener. Inf. Technol. 4, 29–38 (2013). https://doi.org/10.4156/jnit.vol4.issue2.4

27. Deraniyagala, R.L., Amdur, R.J., Boyer, A.L., Kaylor, S.: Usability study of the EduMod eLearning Program for contouring nodal stations of the head and neck. Pract. Radiat. Oncol. 5, 169–175 (2015). https://doi.org/10.1016/j.prro.2014.10.008

28. Junus, I.S., Santoso, H.B., Isal, Y.K., Utomo, A.Y.: Usability evaluation of the student centered e-Learning environment. Int. Rev. Res. Open Distance Learn. **16**, 62–82 (2015). https://doi.org/10.19173/irrodl.v16i4.2175

29. Murillo, B., Vargas, S., Moquillaza, A., Fernández, L., Paz, F.: Usability testing as a complement of heuristic evaluation: a case study. In: Marcus, A., Wang, W. (eds.) DUXU 2017. LNCS, vol. 10288, pp. 434–444. Springer, Cham (2017). https://doi.org/10.1007/978-3-319-58634-2_32

30. Emang, D.W.A.B., Lukman, R.N.I.R., Kamarulzaman, M.I.S., Zaaba, Z.F.: Usability studies on e-learning platforms: preliminary study in USM. In: Proceedings of the 2nd International Conference on Applied Science and Technology (ICAST 2017), Kedah, Malaysia, vol. 1891, pp. 1–8 (2017). https://doi.org/10.1063/1.5005373

31. Aparna, S.S., Baseer, K.K.: SIRIUS-WUEP: a heuristic-based framework for measuring and evaluating web usability in model-driven web development. In: Satapathy, S., Govardhan, A., Raju, K., Mandal, J. (eds.) Emerging ICT for Bridging the Future - Proceedings of the 49th Annual Convention of the Computer Society of India (CSI) Volume 1. Advances in Intelligent Systems and Computing, vol. 337, pp. 303–310. Springer, Cham (2015). https://doi.org/10.1007/978-3-319-13728-5_34

32. Eason, K.D.: Towards the experimental study of usability. Behav. Inf. Technol. **3**, 133–143 (1984). https://doi.org/10.1080/01449298408901744

33. Nielsen, J.: Usability Engineering. Morgan Kaufmann, Burlington (1993). ISBN 0125184050

34. ISO: Ergonomic requirements for office work with visual display terminals (VDTs) – Part 11: Guidance on usability - ISO 9241-11:1998. International Organization for Standardization (1998)

35. ISO: Software engineering – Product quality – Part 1: Quality model - ISO/IEC 9126:2001. International Organization for Standardization (2001)

36. Reeves, T.C., et al.: Usability and instructional design heuristics for E-Learning evaluation. In: Proceedings of the 2002 World Conference on Educational Multimedia, Hypermedia & Telecommunications (ED-MEDIA 2002), Denver, Colorado, USA, pp. 2–8 (2002). https://eric.ed.gov/?id=ED477084

37. Folmer, E., van Gurp, J., Bosch, J.: A framework for capturing the relationship between usability and software architecture. Softw. Process: Improv. Pract. **8**, 67–87 (2003). https://doi.org/10.1002/spip.171

38. Abran, A., Khelifi, A., Suryn, W., Seffah, A.: Usability meanings and interpretations in ISO standards. Softw. Qual. J. **11**, 325–338 (2003). https://doi.org/10.1023/A:1025869312943

39. Rosato, J., Dodds, C., Laughlin, S.: Usability of course management systems by students. Department of Computer Information Systems/Computer Science, College of Scholastica, Duluth (2006)

40. Mehlenbacher, B., et al.: Usable e-learning: a conceptual model for evaluation and design. In: 11th International Conference on Human-Computer Interaction (HCI International 2005), Las Vegas, NV, USA, pp. 1–10 (2005). http://citeseerx.ist.psu.edu/viewdoc/citations?doi=10.1.1.84.331

41. Dringus, L.P., Cohen, M.S.: An adaptable usability heuristic checklist for online courses. In: Proceedings Frontiers in Education 35th Annual Conference, Indianapolis, IN, USA (2005). https://doi.org/10.1109/FIE.2005.1611918

42. Ardito, C., et al.: An approach to usability evaluation of e-learning applications. Univ. Access Inf. Soc. **4**, 270–283 (2006). https://doi.org/10.1007/s10209-005-0008-6

43. Seffah, A., Donyaee, M., Kline, R.B., Padda, H.K.: Usability measurement and metrics: a consolidated model. Softw. Qual. J. **14**, 159–178 (2006). https://doi.org/10.1007/s11219-006-7600-8

44. Nielsen, J., Loranger, H.: Prioritizing Web Usability. New Riders Publishing, Thousand Oaks (2006). ISBN 0321350316
45. Bevan, N.: Classifying and selecting UX and usability measures. In: Proceedings of the Valid Useful User Experience Measurement (VUUM 2008), pp. 1–6. University of Iceland, Reykjavik (2008)
46. Ketola, P., Roto, V.: Exploring user experience measurement needs. In: Proceedings of the Valid Useful User Experience Measurement (VUUM 2008), pp. 23–26. University of Iceland, Reykjavik (2008). https://doi.org/10.4018/jthi.2009070104
47. Zaharias, P., Poylymenakou, A.: Developing a usability evaluation method for e-learning applications: beyond functional usability. Int. J. Hum.-Comput. Interact. **25**, 75–98 (2009). https://doi.org/10.1080/10447310802546716
48. Giannakos, M.N.: A combinational evaluation method of computer applications. J. Basic Appl. Sci. **1**, 240–242 (2009)
49. Al-Khalifa, H.S.: Heuristic evaluation of the usability of e-government websites: a case from Saudi Arabia. In: Proceedings of the 4th International Conference on Theory and Practice of Electronic Governance, pp. 238–242. ACM, Beijing (2010). http://doi.acm.org/10.1145/1930321.1930370
50. Al-sarrayrih, H.S., Knipping, L., Zorn, E.: Evaluation of a MOODLE based Learning Management System applied at Berlin Institute of Technology based on ISO-9126. In: 13th International Conference on Interactive Computer aided Learning (ICL2010), Hasselt, Belgium, pp. 1–8 (2010)
51. Giannakos, M.N.: The evaluation of an E-Learning Web-based platform. In: Proceedings of the 2nd International Conference on Computer Supported Education (CSEDU 2010), Valencia, Spain, pp. 433–438 (2010). https://doi.org/10.5220/0002799504330438
52. ISO: Systems and software engineering – Systems and software Quality Requirements and Evaluation (SQuaRE) – System and software quality models - ISO/IEC 25010:2011. International Organization for Standardization (2011)
53. Zaharias, P.: Heuristic evaluation of e-learning courses: a comparative analysis of two e-learning heuristic sets. Campus-Wide Inf. Syst. **29**, 45–60 (2012). ISSN 1065-0741
54. Ghirardini, B.: E-Learning Methodologies: A Guide for Designing and Developing E-Learning Courses. Food and Agriculture Organization of the United Nations - FAO, USA (2012)
55. Kumar Dubey, S., Rana, A., Sharma, A.: Usability evaluation of object oriented software system using fuzzy logic approach. Int. J. Comput. Appl. **43**, 1–6 (2012). https://doi.org/10.5120/6208-8778
56. Torrente, M.C.S., Prieto, A.B.M., Gutiérrez, D.A., de Sagastegui, M.E.A.: Sirius: a heuristic-based framework for measuring web usability adapted to the type of website. J. Syst. Softw. **86**, 649–663 (2013). https://doi.org/10.1016/j.jss.2012.10.049
57. Şenol, L., Gecili, H., Durdu, P.O.: Usability evaluation of a Moodle based learning management system. In: Proceedings of the World Conference on Educational Media and Technology (EdMedia 2014), Tampere, Finland, pp. 850–858 (2014). ISBN 978-1-939797-08-7
58. Thuseethan, S., Achchuthan, S., Kuhanesan, S.: Usability evaluation of learning management systems in Sri Lankan Universities. Adv. Hum. Comput. Interact. **15**, 1–13 (2015)
59. Gupta, D., Ahlawat, A., Sagar, K.: A critical analysis of a hierarchy based Usability Model. In: Proceedings of the 2014 International Conference on Contemporary Computing and Informatics (IC3I 2014), Mysore, India, pp. 255–260 (2014). https://doi.org/10.1109/IC3I.2014.7019810

60. Paz, F., Paz, F.A., Villanueva, D., Pow-Sang, J.A.: Heuristic evaluation as a complement to usability testing: a case study in web domain. In: Proceedings of the 12th International Conference on Information Technology - New Generations (ITNG 2015), Las Vegas, NV, USA, pp. 546–551 (2015). https://doi.org/10.1109/ITNG.2015.92
61. Issa, T., Isaias, P.: Sustainable Design: HCI, Usability and Environmental Concerns. Springer, Heidelberg (2015). https://doi.org/10.1007/978-1-4471-6753-2
62. Rogers, Y., Preece, J., Sharp, H.: Interaction Design: Beyond Human-Computer Interaction. Wiley, Hoboken (2015). ISBN 978-1-119-02075-2
63. Farmanesh, P., Samani, A.A.: Heuristic evaluation of the usability of Learning Management System (Moodle) at Eastern Mediterranean University, pp. 1–25 (2015). https://doi.org/10.5281/zenodo.59517

Identification of Patterns in Children with ADHD Based on Brain Waves

Alfredo Garcia[1]([🖂]) [iD], Juan Manuel Gonzalez[1] [iD],
and Amparo Palomino[2] [iD]

[1] Facultad de Ciencias de la Computación, BUAP, Puebla, Mexico
alfredo_amigo18@hotmail.com, jumagoca78@gmail.com
[2] Facultad de Ciencias de la Electrónica, BUAP, Puebla, Mexico
Ampalomino@gmail.com

Abstract. There are several disorders that affect the level of attention of people both in their childhood and adulthood. One of the most recognized disorders is attention deficit hyperactivity disorder (ADHD) and is usually diagnosed for the first time in childhood, and the symptoms persist in adolescence and adulthood. Some ways of knowing if a person presents ADHD are: through questionnaires, intellectual tests, types of behavior, medical diagnoses, among others. These tests require a long period of time where an observation and analysis process is performed in order to obtain a reliable diagnosis. This paper presents the development of an experiment for the identification of ADHD, using an electronic system where brain waves are involved as a physiological variable. The comparative analysis is described on a sample of children with diagnosed ADHD, and a sample of children without ADHD. This analysis is performed using statistical tools that graphically demonstrate some differences in the behavior of the level of attention of a child with ADHD with respect to the behavior of the level of attention of a child without ADHD. Finally, the obtained characteristics from a child with ADHD are described and a strategy is proposed for identify reliable patterns based on the user's level of attention.

Keywords: Attention level · Brain signals · Dispersion of attention · Diagnostic ADHD · Non invasive system

1 Introduction

ADHD is characterized by lack of attention, impulsivity and hyperactivity. Recently it has been estimated that it affects 3.5% of school-age children worldwide and is said to be one of the most common psychiatric disorders among young people. Children with these problems are often unpopular and lack reciprocal friendships, but are not always aware of their own unpopularity. Although these symptoms tend to decrease with age, at least 50% of children with ADHD still have symptoms that decrease in adulthood. Despite the vast literature that supports the efficacy of stimulant medication in the treatment of attention deficit/hyperactivity disorder (ADHD), several limitations of

P. H. Ruiz and V. Agredo-Delgado (Eds.): HCI-COLLAB 2019, CCIS 1114, pp. 255–268, 2019.
https://doi.org/10.1007/978-3-030-37386-3_19

pharmacological treatments highlight the clear need for effective alternative psychosocial treatments. There is also evidence of interventions that involve both the school and the training of parents that have resulted in classifying them as "empirically validated treatments" [1]. Attention deficit hyperactivity disorder (ADHD) is a common neurobiological condition that affects school-age children. One of the main symptoms is the lack of attention, which is a key factor of low academic performance, especially in tasks that require a lot of concentration time [2]. Children with Attention Deficit Hyperactivity Disorder (ADHD) experience a deficit in cognitive processes responsible for behaviors aimed at specific objectives, known as executive functioning (FE) [3]. The biggest challenge for adults with attention deficit hyperactivity disorder (ADHD) is the management of information and tasks [4].

2   Systems to Measure the Level of Attention

The study of physiological signals such as brain waves, heart rate, body temperature, among others, has revealed great advances in recent times obtaining significant results in applications from different fields of study such as medicine, robotics, psychology, among others. Currently there are low-cost commercial devices to obtain the reading of brain signals with which it is possible to know the level of attention of the user in an unreliable way. The performance of these devices is limited to the software and hardware established by the manufacturer for a specific task, added to the lack of accuracy in reading the signals, because the devices do not have a robust system for data acquisition and processing. The performance of these devices is limited, since their manufacture is oriented to simple tasks or didactic games. Another cause of the low performance of these devices is that they are invasive or intrusive; Tiaras, helmets, blood samples are used to obtain the signals of the user's physiological variables, any error in the calibration could generate an error in the final diagnosis [5].

To know the degree of affectation that ADHD produces in people, it is necessary to have tools that can provide a feedback of the percentage of attention when executing a specific task. Currently there is a variety of commercial devices that quantitatively provide the level of concentration, meditation, relaxation and user care, but in some cases are achieved in an invasive way, affecting the response of the user and consequently the final diagnosis. These devices usually use a physiological variable to infer the levels of attention in people, they are of the single-user type and of an accessible cost. The performance of these devices is limited since they have restrictions on the part of the manufacturer regarding the software and hardware implemented. Data acquisition and processing speeds of MINDWAVE, EMOTIV EPOC, MUSE devices, among others; they have delays and can not obtain a reading of the acquired variables in a time approximated to the real time. Another disadvantage presented by this type of device is its low usability and versatility in practice, since the user requires a long time for the devices to recognize the physiological signals that are desired to be acquired. Some devices have a graphic interface designed by the manufacturer, whose feedback is based solely on the indication of the level of attention graphically. Various applications in areas such as: psychology, education, business, health, among others require a system that accurately identifies the level of attention in people, and that in turn provides an instant response of what happens, as well as a reliable final diagnosis for decision making. It is also desirable to obtain a feedback that encourages the user to raise the level of attention at the same time as executing a specific task [6].

Biofeedback training systems foster a specific mental or physical state in a user through a closed cycle of bio-feedback. These systems gather the physiological state of a person through the detection of hardware, integrate this state into a computer-based interactive system and present the comments so that the user can work to adjust their status [7]. In this research work we propose to implement a system to measure the level of attention in children with ADHD, generating an analysis on the samples obtained, with the purpose of characterizing the behavior of their brain waves and obtaining statistical patterns that allow us to identify the presence of ADHD in students through the use of this device. The system is non-invasive and has an interface centered on the user, with the aim of obtaining a final diagnosis that reliably describes the level of attention.

2.1 Physiological Variables Related to the Level of Attention

The variety of techniques applied in the field of research to quantify the level of attention of people leads toward a descriptive analysis that is presented in this work [8].

Starting from the review in the literature of the variables used to relate the level of attention in people, has been found that the brain waves are the physiological variables with greater relevancy due to the cognitive relationship that exists between thinking and brain activity. Therefore its implication is direct [9–11].

The graph of the Fig. 1 shows the relevance that each one of the physiological variables has on the level of attention of the people. This analysis is obtained from the state of the art of the related works.

Depending on the physiological variable used, the device is chosen to perform the data acquisition. Within the most devices used in the literature are: the electroencephalogram, WEB cam, motion sensors, gyroscopes, electrodes, mouse, electrocardiogram, electrochemical sensors, keyboard, transducers, cameras and optical sensors [12–14].

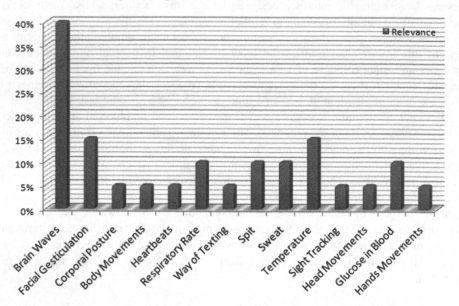

Fig. 1. Relevance of the physiological variables related to the level of attention in the literature.

In the Table 1 are compared the physiological variables, applied techniques and impact with the levels of attention obtained from various sources and scientific articles.

2.2 MindWave Headband

To realize the implementation of the electronic system in this work we use the MindWave device developed by the manufacturer Neurosky (www.neurosky.com), which allows obtaining EEG signals through a headband type interface that is placed on the head and it is powered by a 1.5 V type AAA battery. It uses a wireless interface to communicate with the computer and acquires the signals through passive bio-sensors connected to an electrode that makes contact with the forehead. In addition, it has a reference terminal is connected to the earlobe. This feature is used to determine the origin of a signal. In the brain-computer interfaces, the location of the electrodes allows obtaining different representations of the EEG. The MindWave device has only one terminal placed on the front of the subject, in what is formally known as a pre-frontal zone. Figure 2 shows the correct way in which the device is used [15].

Table 1. Comparison of physiological variables, techniques and relation with the levels of attention.

Reference number	Physiological variable used	Technique applied	Relationship and impact with the levels of attention
1	Facial Gesticulation	Digital image processing	The automated recognition of emotions can be directly correlated with the levels of attention of a teenager
2	Binaural waves (auditory waves)	Modification of the frequency range of the incident waves	Binaural waves cause a positive impact on mental states such as active concentration and creative visualization
3	Brain waves (Alfa, Beta, Delta, Theta y Gamma)	Wavelet Transform	Use of the Mindwave headband for reading brain signals, which are classified in levels of attention
4	Brain waves produced by facial gestures	Suites of EmotivEpoc: *Affective, *Expressiv, *Cognitiv	Use of the EmotivEpoc headband for the reading of brain signals, which are classified in levels of attention
5	Brain waves (Alfa, Beta, Delta, Theta y Gamma)	Classification of brain waves in emotions through their frequency variations	The automated recognition of emotions can be directly correlated with the levels of attention of a teenager
6	Brain waves (Alfa, Beta, Delta, Theta y Gamma)	Bayesian classification and Hill Climbing search algorithm	The automated recognition of emotions can be directly correlated with the levels of attention of a teenager
7	Brain waves (Alfa, Beta, Delta, Theta y Gamma)	Digital image processing Affective computing	Automatic feedback can improve levels of adolescent care
8	Facial gesturing Body movements	Digital image processing Mouse movement	Application of tasks that require cognitive processes such as attention, memory and reasoning
9	Brain waves Heart waves	Characterization of signal changes Classification of brain and heart waves in emotions through their frequency variations	The automated recognition of emotions can be directly correlated with the levels of attention of a teenager
10	Text	E-learning (Identification of emotions through the way of writing a text)	The automated recognition of emotions can be directly correlated with the levels of attention of a teenager

Fig. 2. Correct positioning of the Neurosky MindWave headband.

3 Affectation of ADHD in the Brain

The dispersed attention deficit (whose abbreviation is ADD and ADHD if it is with hyperactivity that is the most frequent) is a disorder of unclear cause, probably with the intervention of genetic and environmental factors, in which there is an alteration at the system level central nervous system, manifesting itself through an increase in activity, impulsivity and lack of attention, and frequently associating other alterations.

The genetic factor is demonstrated, since ADHD is 5 to 7 times more frequent in siblings and 11 to 18 times more frequent in twin siblings. Several genes possibly involved have been described.

ADHD is one of the most frequent causes of school failure and social problems in children.

3.1 Brain Regions and Their Functions

Several brain neuroimaging studies have shown that there are several brain regions affected in children with ADHD. Alterations have been described in [16]:

The prefrontal cortex: responsible for the executive function as planning actions, initiate them, realize the errors and correct them, avoid distractions by irrelevant stimuli, be flexible if there are changes in the circumstances.
The corpus callosum: serves as communication between the two cerebral hemispheres, to ensure a joint and complementary work.

The basal ganglia: involved in the control of impulses by coordinating or filtering the information that arrives from other regions of the brain and inhibiting automatic responses.

The anterior cingulate: is responsible for affective management and the management of emotions.

3.2 Neurotransmission

Neurotransmitters act as chemical messengers that serve so that neurons communicate with each other through receptors. In this way the neuronal impulses are transmitted from one neuron to another and from one brain region to another.

Studies indicate that ADHD causes problems in the regulatory circuits that communicate two brain areas: prefrontal cortex and basal ganglia. These areas communicate through dopamine and norepinephrine. By having a deficit release of these neurotransmitters and a high level of reuptake thereof, neurotransmission is altered, affecting attention, alertness, working memory and executive control.

The decrease in the synaptic metabolism of neurotransmitters produces the following consequences:

- Decrease attention
- Reduces the ability to initiate and continue activities
- Difficulty working memory (or short-term memory)
- It hinders the neutralization of irrelevant stimuli
- It hinders the ability to block inappropriate responses
- It hinders the planning of complex activities
- Difficulty organizing
- Increase physical activity
- Increase impulsivity

4   Development of the Attention Test

The experimental tests were conducted using the MindWave commercial device of the Neurosky company, to detect the level of attention in Mexican primary level students.

A sample of 22 students with diagnosed ADHD and 11 students without ADHD was evaluated whose ages are between 6 and 12 years.

The test consisted of a test to identify colors, which was obtained from the demos of the company Brain HQ (https://www.brainhq.com/why-brainhq/about-the-brainhq-exercises/attention).

To obtain the data of brain signals, a graphical interface was implemented, using the LABVIEW software. Figure 3 illustrates the graphic interface where you can observe the behavior of brain signals, body posture, temperature, a traffic light as feedback, a vector where the sampled data and the variation of the user's attention level are stored. In Fig. 4 the electronic system used to acquire the signals is shown.

Fig. 3. Graphical interface implemented in LABVIEW.

Fig. 4. System used for the acquisition of signals.

The test was done in the tablet modality for both cases (students with diagnosed ADHD and students without ADHD). The practical development is shown in the Figs. 5 and 6 respectively.

Fig. 5. Development of the test in students with ADHD.

Fig. 6. Development of the test in students without ADHD.

The experiment was developed in a classroom where the environment was controlled and adequate to avoid distracting agents and obtain a natural response and a better user performance.

5   Analysis and Results

The tabulation and graphing of the attention levels of each subject is performed individually with the data collected from the experiment. In the Fig. 7 are shown the graphs of the behavior of the level of attention along the time domain in students with ADHD and in the Fig. 8 are shown the graphs of the behavior of the level of attention throughout the time domain in students without ADHD.

In each graph the vertical axis "y" corresponds to the percentage of attention and the horizontal axis "x" denotes the time in seconds.

Each of the samples that are plotted were obtained through the Mindwave headband, using the interface developed for this system. The sampling time that was applied to the sampling was 500 ms.

Subsequently, various statistical tools are applied to find behavior patterns in the level of attention of both students with ADHD and in students without diagnosed ADHD.

The tools used in general were: standard deviation, average and dispersion.

In the Fig. 9 the standard deviation is plotted for both students with ADHD (Image on the left) and for students without ADHD (Image on the right).

In the Fig. 10 the average concentration is plotted on a scatter map where the average attention is shown on the left in students with ADHD and on the right the average attention in students without ADHD.

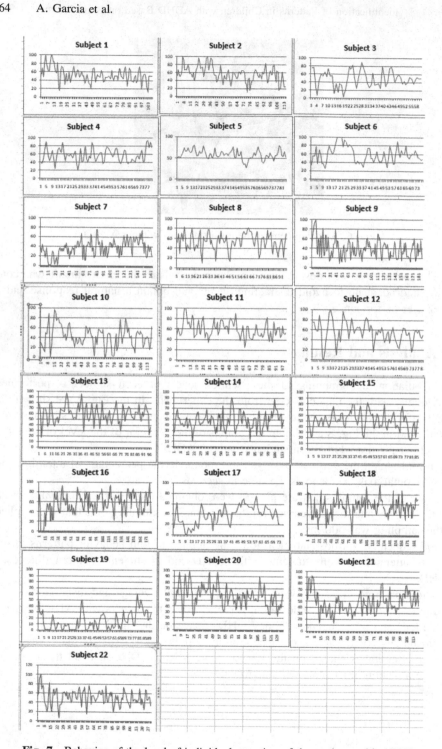

Fig. 7. Behavior of the level of individual attention of the students with ADHD.

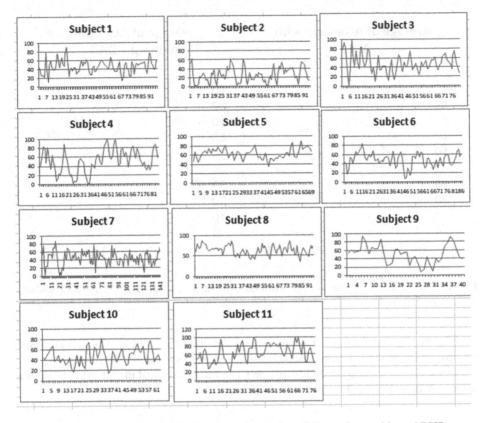

Fig. 8. Behavior of the level of individual attention of the students without ADHD.

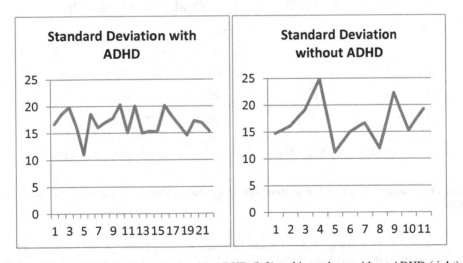

Fig. 9. Standard deviation in students with ADHD (left) and in students without ADHD (right).

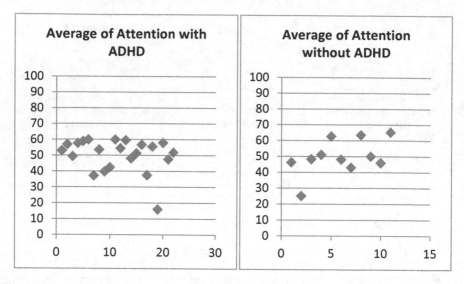

Fig. 10. Accumulation of the average attention in students with ADHD (left) and in students without ADHD (right).

The average level of general attention of the students without ADHD diagnosed was 52.35% and the calculated general dispersion of the samples gave 14.73.

In the Fig. 11 a comparison is made between the behavior of the attention level of a student with ADHD and a student without ADHD.

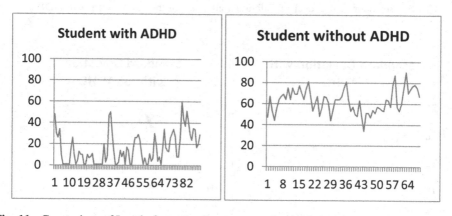

Fig. 11. Comparison of Level of attention between a student with ADHD and a student without ADHD.

In the Fig. 12 a comparison is made between the dispersion of the attention of a student with ADHD and a student without ADHD, obtained from a normal distribution and graphed in the form of a Gaussian bell.

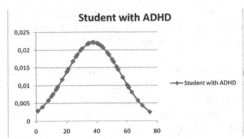
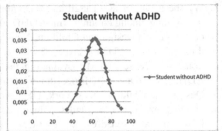

Fig. 12. Comparison of Dispersion between a student with ADHD and a student without ADHD.

With the results obtained from the attention level and the dispersion, a quantification can be performed to determine if a student presents characteristics of being a carrier of ADHD. This condition is satisfied if a student when performing the test obtains an average of attention less than **50.1531%** and its dispersion of attention is greater than **16.8647**.

6 Conclusions

The statistical analysis performed on the samples obtained showed that the level of attention in students with ADHD is lower compared to the level of attention of students without ADHD.

The attention of students with ADHD is more dispersed than the attention of students without ADHD, because it presents very abrupt changes over time. The behavior of attention in students with ADHD reaches high and low peaks which is a characteristic of scattered attention.

The statistical tools used show us differences in the behavior of the level of attention of students with ADHD with respect to students without ADHD, these results are the basis of future work to find predominant patterns for the identification of populations of students with ADHD using this system.

Acknowledgment. Special recognition to teacher "Claudia Gonzalez Calleros" for her valuable collaboration in taking samples with students with ADHD.

References

1. Pascual, M.F., Begoña, Z., Buldian, K.M.: Adaptive cognitive rehabilitation interventions based on serious games for children with ADHD using biofeedback techniques: assessment and evaluation. In: COMPUTE 2010 Proceedings of the Third Annual ACM Bangalore Conference, Article 29, Bilbao, España, pp. 1–4 (2010). http://dx.doi.org/10.4108/icst.pervasivehealth.2014.255249
2. Asiry, O., Shen, H., Calder, P.: Extending attention span of ADHD children through an eye tracker directed adaptive user interface. In: ASWEC 2015 Volume II: Proceedings of the ASWEC 2015 24th Australasian Software Engineering Conference, Australia, vol. 1, pp. 149–152 (2015). http://dx.doi.org/10.1145/2811681.2824997

3. Weisberg, O., et al.: TangiPlan: designing an assistive technology to enhance executive functioning among children with ADHD. In: IDC 2014 Proceedings of the 2014 Conference on Interaction Design and Children, New York, USA, vol. 1, pp. 293–296 (2014). http://dx. doi.org/10.1145/2593968.2610475

4. Sonne, T., Jensen, M.M.: Evaluating the ChillFish biofeedback game with children with ADHD. In: IDC 2016 Proceedings of the 15th International Conference on Interaction Design and Children, New York, USA, vol. 1, pp. 529–534 (2016)

5. Domínguez, C.: Las Ondas Binaurales y sus Efectos. In: Tesis de Investigación Experimental, Ciudad Cooperativa Cruz Azul, vol. 1, pp. 1–22 (2015)

6. Aballay, L., Aciar, S., Reategui, E.: Propuesta de un Método para Detección de Emociones en E-Learning. In: ASAI 2015, 16º Simposio Argentino de Inteligencia Artificial, Porto Alegre, Brasil, pp. 121–128 (2015). http://dx.doi.org/10.1145/2930674.2935981, ISSN 2451-7585

7. Sonne, T., Jensen, M.M.: ChillFish: a respiration game for children with ADHD. In: TEI 2016 Proceedings of the TEI '16: Tenth International Conference on Tangible, Embedded, and Embodied Interaction, New York, USA, vol. 1, pp. 271–278 (2016). http://dx.doi.org/ 10.1145/2839462.2839480

8. Marín, E.J.: Detección de emociones del usuario. In: Tesis Pontificia Universidad Católica de Valparaíso, Chile, vol. 1, pp. 1–67 (2014)

9. Hernández, A., Vásquez, R., Olivares, B.A., Cortes, G., López, I.: Sistema de detección de emociones para la recomendación de recursos educativos. In: Programación Matemática y Software, Orizaba, México, vol. 8, no. 1, pp. 58–66 (2016). ISSN 2007-3283

10. Saneiro, M.M.: Apoyo psico-educativo y afectivo en entornos virtuales de aprendizaje. Int. J. Dev. Educ. Psychol. 1(2), 233–241 (2015). http://dx.doi.org/10.17060/ijodaep.2015.n2. v1.338. De INFAD Base de datos, Badajoz, España

11. Campazzo, E., Martinez, M., Guzmán, A.E., Agüero, A.: Entornos Virtuales de Aprendizaje integrado a tecnología móvil y detección de emociones. In: Secretaría de Ciencia y Tecnología/Departamento de Ciencias Exactas Físicas y Naturales/Universidad Nacional de La Rioja, La Rioja, vol. 1, pp. 1–5 (2014)

12. Rojas, S., Garzón, J., Martínez, D., Escobar, M., Robayo, C.: Lector de ondas cerebrales para implementar un sistema alternativo y aumentativo de comunicación. In: 10th Latin American and Caribbean Conference for Engineering and Technology, vol. 10, pp. 1–9 (2012)

13. Campazzo, E., Martínez, M., Guzmán, A., Agüero, A.: Desarrollo de interface de detección de emociones para su utilización en redes sociales y entornos virtuales de aprendizaje. In: XV Workshop de Investigadores en Ciencias de la Computación, Paraná, vol. 1, pp. 1–5 (2013)

14. García, A.E.: Análisis de ondas cerebrales para determinar emociones a partir de estímulos visuales. In: Universidad Veracruzana Facultad de Estadística e Informática, Xalapa, Veracruz, México, vol. 1, pp. 1–137 (2015)

15. Torres, F., Sánchez, C., Palacio, B.: Adquisición y análisis de señales cerebrales utilizando el dispositivo MindWave. In: MASKANA, I+D+ingeniería 2014, vol. 1, pp. 1–11 (2014)

16. Centers for Disease Control and Prevention (CDC). Attention-Deficit/Hyperactivity Disorder (ADHD). https://www.cdc.gov/ncbddd/adhd/facts.html

Organizing Knowledge on Nonverbal Communication Mediated Through Haptic Technology

Hector M. Camarillo-Abad[1]([⊠]) [iD], J. Alfredo Sánchez[2] [iD],
and Oleg Starostenko[1] [iD]

[1] Universidad de las Américas Puebla, Ex-Hacienda Sta. Catarina Mártir S/N.
San Andrés, Cholula, Mexico
{hector.camarilload, oleg.starostenko}@udlap.mx
[2] National Laboratory of Advanced Informatics (LANIA), Rébsamen 80,
91090 Xalapa, Mexico
alfredo.sanchez@lania.edu.mx

Abstract. Nonverbal communication (NVC) can benefit from any human sense. The sense of touch, or haptic sense, is often used as a channel of NVC. This paper organizes existing knowledge on the use of technology to communicate nonverbally through the haptic sense (HNVC). The analysis of reported work and ongoing projects in the area during the last five years has resulted in an initial taxonomy that is based on three major dimensions, based upon the intent of the messages exchanged: interpretive, affective, and active communication. Thus, haptic devices are used to convey meaning in interpretive HNVC, to convey or to generate emotional reactions in affective HNVC, or to request specific actions or tasks in active HNVC. We characterize existing work using these major categories and various subcategories. This initial organization provides a general overview of all the areas that benefit from technology as a NVC channel. Analysis shows that using the haptic sense as a communication means still has many open research areas and potential new applications, and has proven to date to be an effective mechanism to communicate most of what humans would want to: messages, emotions, and actions.

Keywords: Nonverbal communication · Haptic technology · Technology mediated communication · Nonverbal interaction mediated through haptic technology

1 Introduction

Even though technology has been changing the ways in which people exchange information, the essence of human communication remains the same. Human communication is composed mainly of language and nonverbal communication (NVC). Any signal other than speech or writing is considered NVC, and is important because it can complement, repeat, accent, contradict, regulate, and even substitute language entirely. Arguably, just being human involves the constant use and interpretation of

© Springer Nature Switzerland AG 2019
P. H. Ruiz and V. Agredo-Delgado (Eds.): HCI-COLLAB 2019, CCIS 1114, pp. 269–283, 2019.
https://doi.org/10.1007/978-3-030-37386-3_20

nonverbal signals. NVC was not considered a formal research subject until the 1950's, when it was recognized as a new field [1].

NVC is thus a fundamental component of communication as humans, and it must be investigated further from the perspective of Human-Computer Interaction. The role of various technologies in supporting or enabling new forms of NVC deserves special attention, from machine vision or motion sensing to wearable and haptic technologies. We present an extensive literature review of existing work in the specific area of NVC mediated by haptic devices, as we consider there is great potential of this technology to support and enhance NVC.

Our work provides perspective of NVC mediated by haptic technologies by following specific criteria (Sect. 2), organizing knowledge in the field through a taxonomy (Sect. 3) that considers dimensions derived from the intent of the messages exchanged: affective, active and interpretive communication. We use our taxonomy to contextualize salient projects in each category and to facilitate comprehension of their approaches and interrelationships. We discuss challenges, open issues and research directions for the community interested in advancing the field (Sect. 4). Finally, we present our ongoing work on haptic NVC and its applications (Sect. 5).

2 Criteria for Inclusion

Given the vast amount of work that has been undertaken on NVC, we adopted a few criteria in order to narrow down the field of study. Firstly, published work relevant to our research must involve some kind of NVC, even though authors may not mention it explicitly. Some examples of NVC include [1]: body movements (the study subject of kinesics), facial movements, gestures, eye movement (the study subject of oculesics), haptics, sounds different from speech (known as paralanguage), use of space (studied by proxemics), and use of time (studied by chronemics).

Secondly, works considered must focus on the haptic sense, either for sending or receiving purposes in the NVC. Haptics includes all touch behavior, and it is considered an area in need of research [1]. Haptics is the term used for the investigation of human-machine communication using the sense of touch, both as input and output [2]. Touch can broadly be divided into discriminative and affective touch, the difference being feeling stimuli outside or inside the body respectively [3]. Functionally speaking, touch can also be divided into the cutaneous and kinesthetic senses. Kinesthesia is related to body movement, information about position of the body, muscular effort and force-feedback. Haptic interfaces are generally associated with the kinesthetic sense. The cutaneous sense is more skin-centered and is generally addressed by temperature and vibrotactile technology. Vibrotactile is the term used to refer to vibrations felt through the skin. The scope of our work also includes multisensory works, with the sole condition that the haptic sense must be present.

Thirdly, the communication means employed by the projects we have reviewed include some form of technology. Mediation through technology can happen in real time or asynchronously. This technology can either be a robot, wearable technology, or grounded technology. Wearable technology refers to small body-worn devices. This implies a new form of human-computer interaction also known as constant user interface [4], and thus it is of significant interest to this article.

Using haptic technology as a nonverbal medium to communicate has, theoretically, applications in every daily life scenario. However, exactly to what extent haptic technology is being used has not been systematically studied. We provide a general overview of all the different applications reported in the literature, organizing them according to their goals and applications. We propose a taxonomy that comprises every application found in our literature review, with the ultimate goal of fitting any new application into a category, or perhaps adding subcategories of the taxonomy.

Our literature search started by limiting the publications' years from 2015 to date. The search included all related terms: nonverbal, mediated, movements. Furthermore, results included at least one of the following terms: wearable, wearables, haptic, tactile. Using the variety of applications yielded by the search, we started constructing the taxonomy from the bottom up, adding or removing words in the search to find area-specific works relevant to NVC mediated by technology.

3 Proposed Taxonomy

We have developed a taxonomy for haptic-based NVC mediated by technology (HNVC) that considers mainly the purpose of communication, focusing on reported uses and applications of haptic technology in daily human activities. The taxonomy is intended to classify the wide range of HNVC applications and to inspire researchers to fill any gaps in the depth of the taxonomy. As a starting point to classify research works in the area of HNVC, works are divided into three major categories: interpretive, affective and active (Fig. 1).

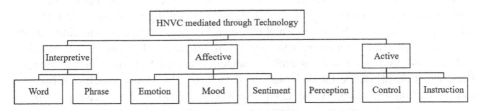

Fig. 1. General classification of HNVC.

This classification differs from the work of MacLean et al. [5], since they divided communication through touch into three main categories: signaling and monitoring, expression of affect, and sharing control with intelligent systems. Our classification is also inspired on the ultimate goal of communication, and is intended to further classify current works found in literature, thus making the initial classification more general. If the goal of the research is mainly to help users understand some meaning, it falls under the interpretive area. If it is related to emotion, it falls under the affective area. And if the communication is intended to convey actions, it falls under the active area. An alternative perspective for this classification considers the most common purposes of verbal communication: sharing a story (interpretive), an exchange of feelings towards something or someone (affective), or instructions to achieve something (active).

3.1   Interpretive HNVC

Interpretive HNVC refers to research work that focuses exclusively on using haptic devices for conveying meaning associated to nonverbal cues. Its main intention is that communication can be understood. Examples of interpretive HNVC includes representing words with different haptic sensations instead of words or phrases. Interpretive HNVC can be further subdivided into two subcategories, depending on the granularity of the signals: word-oriented and phrase-oriented, as discussed below.

Word-Oriented HNVC Works in the literature that focus on transmitting some meaning using haptic stimuli analogous to a word in verbal communication fall under this category. The work by Enriquez et al. [6] investigate how to convey words related to plants and fruits using haptic feedback to users. They even relate their research to phonemes and not words. They refer to a haptic phoneme as "the smallest unit of a constructed haptic signal to which a meaning can be assigned". Their aim is associating arbitrary meanings to haptic phonemes, testing how well users remember them. The technology they rely on is a grounded haptic knob. They used self-guided and enforced learning in sequence to train users. They pose that a smarter training method is needed to avoid some interpretation errors made by the users. The work by Chen et al. [7] compared guided learning, self-guided learning and mnemonics for the acquisition of haptic words. They highlight the importance of an effective learning method for users to fully adopt haptic communication. Their chosen technology is a wearable device for the forearm, consisting of 24 actuators. They mapped 13 letters into vibrotactile stimuli, including six vowels and seven consonants. Their experiment involved 100 English words using the coded vowels and consonants, with native and non-native speakers. Their findings support the use of guided learning, reporting an accuracy superior to 90% using different modes: incremental rehearsal, flashcards, explore, and video game. They discuss the need of training being more comprehensive, their device to be smaller, and planned to extend the research to sentence comprehension, not just words. Brewster et al. [8] define tactile icons called *tactons*. Their work is relevant because tactons are building blocks of tactile communication, adjusting vibrotactile parameters such as intensity, frequency, waveform and body location to assign a meaning to the vibration.

Phrase-Oriented HNVC. When research aims to convey haptic complex meanings analogous to phrases or sentences, it falls under this category. The work by Oliveira et al. [9] focuses on directional cueing and obstacle detection; hence their meanings are more complex than just one word. They research different tactile vocabularies with and without prefixation to communicate effective navigation. Their technology is a belt with eight actuators, arranged in a compass setting. They research first the perception of the vibrations, then interpretation, and finally the navigation task. They report that vibrotactile patterns in sequence present perception difficulties for the users. The work in Schelle et al. [10] involves inclusion of people with cognitive disabilities, and uses a textile pillow that allows for communication between patients with dementia and their families or caregivers. A single pillow is used, and all participants in the communication process must be at the same physical location touching the pillow. One of their main aims is the effect on personalization of the haptic stimuli on the patients. Their goal is to establish a dialogue in an alternative bodily manner, in what is known as tangible interaction. Their experiment consisted of three sessions, a mirroring and design of personalization, the personalized patterns, and mirroring and personalization. The work by Velázquez et al. [11] reports research on assisting visually impaired people in their situational awareness. They achieve this by testing the recognition of words coded with haptic stimuli, and then progress to even more complex sentences (involving two, three and four words). Their aim is to understand the learning processes and memory capabilities of the subjects, defining three main tactile concepts: leaning, language, and memory. The technology they use is a tactile display for the foot, including four vibrotactile actuators on the foot's plantar surface. They stress that their technology could be inserted into a shoe, concealing it completely, thus making it more wearable than other approaches. Their results include the feasibility of combining individual tactons to make sentences, achieving high recognition accuracy. They discuss long time memory, finding that after a month of their experiment, not a single user could recall meanings. Work they consider for the future includes means for users being able to concentrate on tactons, independently from noisy environments or crowded places.

3.2 Affective Communication Mediated Through Haptic Technology

The affective communication category involves work with the aim of understanding, emulating, or even creating an emotional reaction of the users. In turn, the affective area can be further subdivided into emotion, mood, and sentiment (Fig. 1). This classification is in line with the theory of Brave et al. [12]. According to them, emotion is object directed, intentional and short-lived (seconds). Mood is nonintentional and undirected at an object, therefore being diffuse and general. Mood influences appraisal of external events, and are processed over a longer time (hours or days) than emotions. Sentiments last longer (persist indefinitely) than both emotions and moods. Sentiments guide which situations and objects humans seek out or avoid [12]. Examples of the affective category include making people feel a certain emotion through vibration, exploring cultural differences in emotion representation, or using robots to elicit certain human emotions.

Emotion-Oriented HNVC. In this first subcategory, only instantaneous affective perception of humans is considered. The work by Morrison et al. [13] enables users to interact through a vest and a wall, both of which are endowed with vibrotactile technology. The vest is wearable, and has 32 vibrotactile actuators. Their goal was to make people feel a given emotion (relaxed, calm, and aware of danger). Their vibrotactile patterns were inspired by conversations with a therapist. Their experiment consisted on fitting the vest, training, interaction with the wall, and evaluation. They report that users lack the proper language to express vibrotactile sensations. Their future work suggests familiarizing users with the proper vocabulary. The research done by Haritaipan et al. [14] presents a conceptual design of communication using tactile and gestural interactions. Their main objective is to identify the difference between the Japanese and the French cultures. The interpersonal emotions they consider are love, gratitude and sympathy. Their technology includes hand-held and wrist-worn tactile devices. They conclude that cultural background does have an impact on the representation of emotions. The work by Hirano et al. [15] centers on the interaction between humans and robots, and how visual and haptic interaction affects the way the user feels. They used the robot Pepper for their research. They mention that human-robot interaction through touch can be divided into touching a robot, being touched by a robot, and mutual touch. Their findings encourage that human initiate touch, and not the robot. Mutual touch is the one area in need of more research. They point to future work researching gaze difference in different touch situations.

Mood-Oriented HNVC. The work by Ahmed et al. [16] shows that users associate moods to the system, and said moods have an influence on them. They researched different forms of touch interaction, vibrotactile and force-feedback, to gain insight of which is referred by users to convey affection. Their setting involves a user interacting with a 3D model of a virtual agent, which interacts through haptic signals sensed by the user's hand. Their findings also suggest that force-feedback interactions are preferred over vibrotactile for mood and affection purposes. The work by Mazzoni et al. [17] explores how a wearable vibrotactile globe can enhance moods watching a film. Their experiment consists of selecting a movie clip associated with a mood, then designing vibrotactile stimuli and evaluating the users' mood response, and finally pairing movie clips and vibrotactile stimuli. Their findings show that the intensity and frequency of the vibrotactile stimuli can produce anticipation, tension, and calmness.

Sentiment-Oriented HNVC. The work of Goedschalk et al. [18] is a good example of a negative sentiment towards a virtual agent. They use haptic feedback to enhance believability to a virtual "bad guy", trying to inspire negative sentiments on the user. Their haptic feedback was provided by a push sensation on a wearable vest, thus mimicking a common aggression nonverbal cue. Although their results are reported to have non-statistical significant effects, they highlight the importance to further research this interaction scenario. Their planned future work includes effect of speech loudness, alternative and repeated haptic feedback. Bosse et al. [19] also research virtual "bad guys": although no real threat was presented to users, only a threatening non-functioning device was used. Users were made to believe the device could send a small electrical shock in their finger area. Their findings highlight that only feeling a device that can potentially hurt rises the anxiety sentiments of the users. They point to future research in exploring these effects on different personalities, and reducing the predictability of the virtual agent.

3.3   Active Communication Mediated Through Haptic Technology

Active HNVC in our taxonomy refers to emotion-free messages intended not only to be understood, but to be performed as well. In this category users need to understand the message and then perform the required action. The active HNVC category is one we have elaborated with more detail, and hence involves more subcategories. It can be first divided, according to the messages' main purpose, into either perception-, control- or instruction-oriented HNVC (Fig. 2). Examples of the active category include navigation, control and interaction with virtual environments.

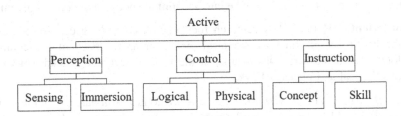

Fig. 2. Active HNVC sub-classifications.

Perception-Oriented HNVC. This category involves all applications focusing on sensing virtual objects, or people sensing their own motions and reactions. Research in this category explores HNVC without regard of emotional or affective implications. The category can be further divided into sensing- and immersion-based HNVC.

Sensing-Based HNVC. Sensing-based HNVC focuses on either enhancing or complementing any human sense. It is of special interest for inclusion of people with disabilities. Houde et al. [20] performed a review of what is known about deaf people experiencing their own bodies, body-related abilities and body-related processing. Typical users of research in this sub-area are both deaf and blind people. They advise future research relating deafness and its effects on body-related process, Bǎlan et al. [21] focus on how visually impaired people can benefit from auditory and haptic senses to construct a mental representation of their environment. Their findings include that visually impaired people successfully use other senses, including touch, to acquire and model spatial information.

Immersion-Based HNVC. Any work that relies on HNVC aiming to remove users from their actual environment, either in a presentation or in a virtual environment, falls under this subcategory. Of particular interest of this sub-section are virtual environments and games. Kruijff et al. [22] focus on navigation of particularly large virtual environments or games. They used three senses: haptic, visual, and auditory. The haptic sense is achieved through vibrotactile cues under the participant's feet, using bass-shakers. They compared their approach with other techniques to navigate virtual environments, namely regular seated joystick and standing learning locomotion. They conclude their multisensory method can enhance self-motion perception and involvement/presence. An interesting finding was that participants appreciated the benefits of walking-related haptic cues, independent of joystick or standing mode. Feng et al. [23] worked on enhancing a non-fatiguing walking in a virtual environment. They used tactile cues such as movement wind (the wind resistance felt by walking), directional wind (environmental wind), footstep vibration and footstep sound. They also conclude that tactile cues are of significant improvement for the activity. Bernardet et al. [24] developed an open source software framework to construct real-time interactive systems based on movement data. They highlight the importance of recording, sensing, storing, retrieving, analyzing, understanding and displaying movement data through various senses, while all these components communicate with each other. They provide further justification for this field by stating: "to better understand humans, and/or to build better technology, we need to take into account the body, and with it, movement".

Control-Oriented HNVC. Any research focusing on controlling certain technology using the haptic sense, either as a control means or as feedback of the controlled technology is included here. Distinctions in the type of technology lead to two subcategories: logical and physical HNVC.

Logically-Based HNVC. Any work that aims to control software is included here. Saunders et al. [25] focus on controlling desktop applications through the feet, using discrete taps and kicks. They used motion capture technology for their experiment. They propose ten design guidelines to be followed, the most general of which are: tapping for frequent actions, consider both feet as dominant ones, prefer toe taps, and sensing techniques should be robust. Their planned future work involves developing a fully working system in a real setting, researching other foot related gestures, or including other objects for interaction with the foot. The work by Costes et al. [26] use pseudo-haptics effects to virtually evoke some haptic properties: stiffness, roughness, reliefs, stickiness, and slipperiness. They refer to pseudo-haptics as additional visual effects that enhance the touch experience in touchscreens. Their results show that haptic properties can be successfully conveyed to a user interacting with a software. Their future work includes quantitative evaluation, thresholding methods, and models to improve quality, different effects, and the use of haptic databases.

Physically-Based HNVC. In contrast to logical HNVC, physical HNVC involves research of controlling robotic mechanisms or hardware in general. Bufalo et al. [27] focus on a disturbance rejection task of a controlled element. They considered three different modalities of haptic feedback: Variable Haptic Aid (VHA), Constant Haptic Aid (CHA), and No Haptic Aid (NoHA). Technology they used includes a display and a grounded electrical control-loaded sidestick, movable only laterally. Their results show that VHA is the best modality to help users learn the task. They point to further research on changing both the amount of help given on the CHA modality and the stiffness of the control, as to improve experimental results of this category. D'Intino et al. [28] focus on haptic feedback used to learn a compensatory tracking task. Their experiment uses two groups, one without any haptic feedback, and the other training with feedback and evaluating without feedback. They relied on a grounded sidestick with only lateral axis movement. Their conclusion is that users of haptic feedback learn more rapidly. Van Oosterhout et al. [29] explored the possible effects of inaccuracies in haptic shared control. They found out inaccuracies do have a negative effect in using haptic control tasks, and therefore any system should be accurate to work properly. Xu et al. [30] used wearable technology to develop a motion capture of arm movement. MYO armbands are located in the upper arm and forearm, so the motion of the operator's arm is obtained. They used this data to control a virtual robotic arm that mimics the movement of the operator.

Instruction-Oriented HNVC. This category involves all works and research that include HNVC for learning or training. It includes acquisition, improvement, and assistance of both skills and knowledge. Instruction-oriented HNVC is divided into two main types of applications: concept- and skill-oriented. Concept-oriented work focuses on abstract knowledge, while skill-oriented research involves any physical ability.

Concept-Based HNVC. This area does not deal with movement, but with teaching abstract ideas using tangible methods. Robotti works on helping students with difficulties in algebra, especially the ones with developmental dyscalculia [31]. Help is based on providing meaning to algebraic notations through visual, nonverbal, and kinaesthetic-tactile systems. They stress the importance of supporting abstract concepts with "visual non-verbal and kinaesthetic channels of access to information". The work by Magana et al. [32] is aimed to improve learning of electricity and magnetism concepts, using a visuohaptic simulation approach. *Visuohaptic* refers to the use of both visual and haptic sense. Their work compares visuohaptic to visual only and instructional multimedia. Their results show that visuohaptic did better, although not significantly. Their findings include that force feedback is a novelty for the majority of the users, and therefore might contribute to overloading work memory. They point to future work in the implementation of guided-inquiry approaches, designing materials for instruction and assessment more haptic-centered, learning strategies for touch interaction, and personalized calibration of force feedback.

Skill-Based NVC. The skill-oriented HNVC category involves human-human interaction mediated through technology, with the purpose of teaching a new skill to the user. According to Yokokohji et al. [33] training is a skill mapping from an expert to a learner, also called trainer and trainee, respectively. Their work highlights the importance of skill transfer, because it is time consuming and thus not easy to achieve. Furthermore, motor skills add the challenge of being difficult to describe with language. Schirmer et al. [34] use a tactile interface for eyes-free pedestrian navigation in cities. They used only two actuators and divided their experiments into compass and navigation modes. Prasad et al. [35] use a vibrotactile vest to provide navigation and obstacle detection to the wearer. Their findings include that vibration produces less cognitive load and greater environmental awareness than other navigational approaches.

Narazani et al. [36] work on feet-related skill transfer. They centered in dance and gymnastics, using both tactile and visual feedback. They refer to their users as instructor and recipient, respectively. Their goal is to achieve "real-time performance-oriented telexistence context". Their methodology consisted of three stages: First, the instructor performs a move that is interpreted and sent to recipient. Second, the movement is displayed visually or haptically to the recipient who will attempt the directed action. Third, feedback on accuracy is provided to the recipient. They also mention that, in general, the process involves feedforward (sending the move) and feedback (on the accuracy of the move), both of which can be either visual or haptic. The work by Ros et al. [37] use a robot as a dance tutor for children. Their focus is on how children accommodate to the tutor across interaction sessions.

Aggravi et al. [38] present a communication between an instructor and the student. Their aim is to assist the student, who is visually impaired, to learn to ski. They achieve it with the help of two vibrating bracelets in order to improve communication between instructor and student. Valsted et al. [39] use a haptic wristband and chest belt that assist runners achieve a technique called rhythmic breathing. Their results show that the runner context must be taken into account in designing the interaction mode, and that, overall, runners prefer to feel the feedback while exhaling.

Yang et al. [40] work on a handwriting tutor-tutee scenario mediated by a robot, using haptic feedback for corrections. Their setting involved the computer capturing an expert's motion skills, and then the robot can handle multiple tutees by itself. Pedemonte et al. [41] also work on transferring handwriting skills. They researched remote user communication with the goal of improving their handwriting skills. They focus on human-human interaction mediated by a haptic device between novice and expert. Their findings encourage the use of haptic guidance in the handwriting learning process.

Rajanna et al. [42] developed a system based on wearable technology for long periods of rehabilitation after surgery based on vibro-haptic feedback. Their system is able to set personal goals, track the progress, and easy to include in daily life. Their feedback works as follows: A vibro-haptic feedback is delivered when the body part being tracked is lifted to a required angle of elevation [42]. Ostadabbas et al. [43] propose a system that can be controlled with the tongue for people recovering from a stroke. They implemented a novel interaction system with the tongue to use an already existing rehabilitation system for the hand. Their goal is to improve the quality of life and the upper limbs' movements of people post-stroke.

Choi et al. [44] study a simulator for closing a wound with suturing procedures. Their aim is focused not only in medicine, but in nursing as well. They use both hands for the procedure and are aided by haptic feedback to learn the correct procedure. Uribe et al. [45] study the feasibility of using robots to assist brain surgery. Their robot is able to differentiate tissues, thus being of great help to the surgeon in high quality measurements. The work of Guo et al. [46] designed a robotic catheter system to protect surgeons and improve the overall surgery. Vascular interventional surgery is the specific application of the robot. They use force-feedback as the interaction with the surgeon. Their results include errors in the order of a few millimeters; errors reported to be acceptable in the surgery.

4   Research Directions

Based upon our review of the field, we have generated a taxonomy that provides perspective on existing work. In this section, we discuss directions for research in each of the three major categories of the taxonomy: affective, interpretive and active HNVC.

The affective category involves work that started with recognizing emotions, and then evolved to be able to communicate and simulate them. Given the popularity and feasibility of using the haptic sense to convey emotions, recent research directions are shifting towards emotions that linger through time: moods and feelings. It is expected that HNVC will be able to identify and change the affective states of humans even better than we as humans can. Because touch is strongly related to expressing emotions with human beings, it is important to continue to research the effects on artificial touch for interaction with robots, or with other humans mediated by technology.

The interpretive category has also evolved from users being able to differentiate single words, to understand multiple words that form full sentences. This area has also achieved to convey complex ideas and instructions with iconicity, much like every icon we use to save or open a document. This area is expected to achieve a high level of communication between humans using only the tactile sense. There is still need for research about differentiability of tactile patterns, the cognitive capacity to associate each pattern with a meaning, and if the association lingers in time. This research is fundamental to continue to progress in both the affective and active categories. The more we know about the foundations of tactile interpretations and meaning, the more HNVC can be explored in diverse real-life scenarios.

The active category has the most variants and subcategories in our proposed taxonomy. This is only natural, as humans perform a variety of activities in daily life, so we cannot turn off the haptic sense for any of them. In the control area the main goal is to achieve full controllability over the technology, being as natural and error-free as possible. Therefore, future research directions need to focus on the mutual understanding of human and technology. It is also important to explore different modalities of feedback depending on the current control capabilities of the users, without users heavily relying on the feedback. Perception strives to enhance our haptic sensory capabilities, possibly to compensate another sense or just to enhance an experience. Future research directions are to what extent our different senses correlate and can compensate each other, and which sensations help users to feel a more realistic virtual immersion in games and simulators, without causing dizziness or distractions. This research is central to be inclusive with people with sensorial disabilities, and to learn more about how humans use and perceive touch. The instruction area is very open, because it deals with acquiring new skills using technology. This area needs to benefit from the others, since it needs understanding of interpretive HNVC, and also of some degree of control between human and technology. The concept instruction subarea is still very open, as normal classroom settings do not use currently the haptic sense to help students understand abstract concepts. There are many abstract and even not abstract concepts that would definitely benefit with a better understanding of how human beings rely on the sense of touch to perceive and understand the world. The health applications have attracted attention because of the high level of training doctors need, and also because of the importance for everyone's well-being. Research must focus on providing realistic tactile and haptic sensations to the doctors in training, so that the training is as similar as possible to a real-life surgery or intervention.

HNVC has a wide range of application domains. Applications may range from analyzing cultural backgrounds for understanding emotions to using robots for assisting medical doctors in surgery. Understanding this diversity demands a rich taxonomy to encompass all existing research, and also to show the full potential of the human haptic sense to communicate and to perform different tasks. The use of the haptic sense also allows applications to be more inclusive, because visually impaired and deaf people can use their touch sense to compensate for deficiencies in their other senses. People with some sort of cognitive deterioration (such as dementia) may also benefit from HNVC, because the haptic medium offers them a novel way to express themselves and understand what others are trying to say. Everyone can benefit from advances in HNVC research, therefore there is a current need to continue research in this area. To formalize HNVC protocols and languages is of general importance, because all other subareas will benefit from having a solid basis in the general area.

5   Ongoing and Future Work

While our taxonomy provides a general overview of HNVC, specific details could potentially have been overlooked. Even though our proposed taxonomy focuses mainly on the purpose and applications of HNVC, we are aware of other transversal attributes that could further characterize the taxonomy, such as human senses or technology used. These attributes could further refine the proposed taxonomy, and potentially give insight of good practices depending on each area and sub-area of the taxonomy. They could also help identify under-researched technologies or senses in certain categories, further expanding the discussion on research directions. We are currently working on refining our taxonomy by considering those cross-category dimensions.

Since we have focused on finding diverse applications of HNVC, and this is a very active research area, there may be more recent works that can be reviewed and included in the proposed taxonomy. Therefore, we are also currently working on an extended literature review, fitting new works that fit under our criteria for HNVC categorization. These new works will expectedly further enrich each sub-area or the taxonomy, and provide more detailed research directions and good practices within each specific area. Overall, the more insight and information we have about how humans use the haptic sense and associated HNVC, the more we will understand ourselves, improve our daily activities, be more inclusive as a society, and develop technology that feels more natural and we can understand better.

References

1. Schroeder, M.L.: A research framework for second nonverbal code acquisition. Globe: J. Lang. Cult. Commun. **5**, 103–124 (2017). https://doi.org/10.5278/ojs.globe.v5i0.1943
2. Hayward, V., Astley, O.R., Cruz-Hernandez, M., Grant, D., Robles-De-La-Torre, G.: Haptic interfaces and devices. Sens. Rev. **24**(1), 16–29 (2004). https://doi.org/10.1108/02602280410515770
3. Huisman, G.: Social touch technology: a survey of haptic technology for social touch. IEEE Trans. Haptics **10**(3), 391–408 (2017). https://doi.org/10.1109/TOH.2017.2650221
4. Mann, S.: Humanistic computing: "WearComp" as a new framework and application for intelligent signal processing. Proc. IEEE **86**(11), 2123–2151 (1998). https://doi.org/10.1109/5.726784
5. MacLean, K.E., Pasquero, J., Smith, J.: Building a haptic language: communication through touch. Computer Science Department, University of British Columbia TR-2005-29, pp. 1–16 (2005). ftp://ftp.cs.ubc.ca/local/techreports/2005/TR-2005-29.pdf. Accessed 11 October 2019
6. Enriquez, M., MacLean, K., Chita, C.: Haptic phonemes: basic building blocks of haptic communication. In: 8th International Conference Proceedings on Multimodal Interfaces, pp. 302–309. ACM, Canada (2006). https://doi.org/10.1145/1180995.1181053

7. Chen, J., Turcott, R., Castillo, P., Wahyudinata, S., Lau, F., Israr, A.: Learning to feel words: a comparison of learning approaches to acquire haptic words. In: 15th ACM Symposium Proceedings on Applied Perception, pp. 1–7. ACM, Canada (2018). https://doi.org/10.1145/3225153.3225174

8. Brewster, S., Brown, L.M.: Tactons: structured tactile messages for non-visual information display. In: Cockburn, A. (eds.) 5th Conference on Australasian User Interface. AUIC 2004 Proceedings, vol. 28, pp. 15–23. Australian Computer Society Inc. (2004)

9. de J. Oliveira, V.A., Maciel, A.: Assessment of tactile languages as navigation aid in 3D environments. In: Auvray, M., Duriez, C. (eds.) EUROHAPTICS 2014. LNCS, vol. 8619, pp. 104–111. Springer, Heidelberg (2014). https://doi.org/10.1007/978-3-662-44196-1_14

10. Schelle, K.J., Gomez, N.C., Bhömer, M.T., Tomico, O., Wensveen, S.: Tactile dialogues: personalization of vibrotactile behavior to trigger interpersonal communication. In: 9th International Conference Proceedings on Tangible, Embedded, and Embodied Interaction, pp. 637–642. ACM, USA (2015). https://doi.org/10.1145/2677199.2687894

11. Velázquez, R., Pissaloux, E.: Constructing tactile languages for situational awareness assistance of visually impaired people. In: Pissaloux, E., Velázquez, R. (eds.) Mobility of Visually Impaired People, pp. 597–616. Springer, Cham (2018). https://doi.org/10.1007/978-3-319-54446-5_19

12. Brave, S., Nass, C.: Emotion in human-computer interaction. In: The Human-Computer Interaction Handbook: Fundamentals, Evolving Technologies and Emerging Applications, pp. 81–96. L. Erlbaum Associates Inc., Hillsdale (2003). https://doi.org/10.1201/b10368-6

13. Morrison, A., Knoche, H., Manresa-Yee, C.: Designing a vibrotactile language for a wearable vest. In: Marcus, A. (ed.) DUXU 2015. LNCS, vol. 9187, pp. 655–666. Springer, Cham (2015). https://doi.org/10.1007/978-3-319-20898-5_62

14. Haritaipan, L., Mougenot, C.: Cross-cultural study of tactile interactions in technologically mediated communication. In: Rau, P.-L.P. (ed.) CCD 2016. LNCS, vol. 9741, pp. 63–69. Springer, Cham (2016). https://doi.org/10.1007/978-3-319-40093-8_7

15. Hirano, T., et al.: Communication cues in a human-robot touch interaction. In: 4th International Conference Proceedings on Human Agent Interaction, pp. 201–206. ACM, USA (2016). https://doi.org/10.1145/2974804.2974809

16. Ahmed, I., Harjunen, V., Jacicci, G., Hoggan, E.: Reach out and touch me: effects of four distinct haptic technologies on affective touch in virtual reality. In: 18th International Conference Proceedings on Multimodal Interaction, pp. 341–348. ACM, USA (2016). https://doi.org/10.1145/2993148.2993171

17. Mazzoni, A., Bryan-Kinns, N.: Mood glove: a haptic wearable prototype system to enhance mood music in film. Entertain. Comput. **17**, 9–17 (2016). https://doi.org/10.1016/j.entcom.2016.06.002

18. Goedschalk, L., Bosse, T., Otte, M.: Get your virtual hands off me! – developing threatening IVAs using haptic feedback. In: Verheij, B., Wiering, M. (eds.) BNAIC 2017. CCIS, vol. 823, pp. 61–75. Springer, Cham (2018). https://doi.org/10.1007/978-3-319-76892-2_5

19. Bosse, T., Hartmann, T., Blankendaal, R.A.M., Dokter, N., Otte, M., Goedschalk, L.: Virtually bad: a study on virtual agents that physically threaten human beings. In: 17th International Conference Proceedings on Autonomous Agents and MultiAgent Systems, pp. 1258–1266. International Foundation for Autonomous Agents and Multiagent Systems, Richland (2018)

20. Houde, M.S., Landry, S.P., Pagé, S., Maheu, M., Champoux, F.: Body perception and action following deafness. Neural Plast. **2016**, 1–7 (2016). https://doi.org/10.1155/2016/5260671

21. Bălan, O., Moldoveanu, A., Moldoveanu, F., Butean, A.: Auditory and haptic spatial cognitive representation in the case of the visually impaired people. In: 22nd International Congress Proceedings on Sound and Vibration, Italy, pp. 1–5 (2015)

22. Kruijff, E., et al.: On your feet!: enhancing vection in leaning-based interfaces through multisensory stimuli. In: 2016 Symposium Proceedings on Spatial User Interaction, pp. 149–158. ACM, Japan (2016). https://doi.org/10.1145/2983310.2985759

23. Feng, M., Dey, A., Lindeman, R.W.: An initial exploration of a multi-sensory design space: tactile support for walking in immersive virtual environments. In: 2016 IEEE Symposium Proceedings on 3D User Interfaces, pp. 95–104. IEEE, USA (2016). https://doi.org/10.1109/3dui.2016.7460037

24. Bernardet, U., et al.: m+ m: a novel middleware for distributed, movement based interactive multimedia systems. In: 3rd International Symposium Proceedings on Movement and Computing, pp. 21–30. ACM, USA (2016)

25. Saunders, W., Vogel, D.: The performance of indirect foot pointing using discrete taps and kicks while standing. In: 41st Graphics Interface Conference Proceedings, pp. 265–272. Canadian Information Processing Society, Canada (2015)

26. Costes, A., Argelaguet, F., Danieau, F., Guillotel, P., Lécuyer, A.: Touchy: a visual approach for simulating haptic effects on touchscreens. Front. ICT **6**, 1–11 (2019). https://doi.org/10.3389/fict.2019.00001

27. Bufalo, F., Olivari, M., Geluardi, S., Gerboni, C.A., Pollini, L., Bülthoff, H.H.: Variable force-stiffness haptic feedback for learning a disturbance rejection task. In: 2017 IEEE International Conference Proceedings on Systems, Man, and Cybernetics, pp. 1517–1522. IEEE, Canada (2017). https://doi.org/10.1109/smc.2017.8122829

28. D'Intino, G., et al.: Evaluation of haptic support system for training purposes in a tracking task. In: 2016 IEEE International Conference on Systems, Man, and Cybernetics Proceedings, pp. 2169–2174. IEEE, Hungary (2016). https://doi.org/10.1109/smc.2016.7844560

29. Van Oosterhout, J., et al.: Haptic shared control in tele-manipulation: effects of inaccuracies in guidance on task execution. IEEE Trans. Haptics **8**(2), 164–175 (2015). https://doi.org/10.1109/TOH.2015.2406708

30. Xu, Y., Yang, C., Liang, P., Zhao, L., Li, Z.: Development of a hybrid motion capture method using MYO armband with application to teleoperation. In: 2016 IEEE International Conference Proceedings on Mechatronics and Automation, pp. 1179–1184. IEEE, China (2016). https://doi.org/10.1109/icma.2016.7558729

31. Robotti, E.: Designing innovative learning activities to face difficulties in algebra of dyscalculic students: exploiting the functionalities of *AlNuSet*. In: Leung, A., Baccaglini-Frank, A. (eds.) Digital Technologies in Designing Mathematics Education Tasks. MEDE, vol. 8, pp. 193–214. Springer, Cham (2017). https://doi.org/10.1007/978-3-319-43423-0_10

32. Magana, A.J., et al.: Exploring multimedia principles for supporting conceptual learning of electricity and magnetism with visuohaptic simulations. Comput. Educ. J. **8**(2), 8–23 (2017)

33. Yokokohji, Y., Hollis, R., Kanade, T., Henmi, K., Yoshikawa, T.: Toward machine mediated training of motor skills-skill transfer from human to human via virtual environment. In: 5th IEEE International Workshop Proceedings on Robot and Human Communication, pp. 32–37. IEEE, Japan (1996). https://doi.org/10.1109/roman.1996.568646

34. Schirmer, M., Hartmann, J., Bertel, S., Echtler, F.: Shoe me the way: a shoe-based tactile interface for eyes-free urban navigation. In: 17th International Conference Proceedings on Human-Computer Interaction with Mobile Devices and Services, pp. 327–336. ACM, USA (2015). https://doi.org/10.1145/2785830.2785832

35. Prasad, M., Taele, P., Olubeko, A., Hammond, T.: HaptiGo: a navigational 'tap on the shoulder'. In: 2014 IEEE Haptics Symposium Proceedings, pp. 1–7. IEEE (2014). https://doi.org/10.1109/haptics.2014.6775478

36. Narazani, M., Seaborn, K., Hiyama, A., Inami, M.: StepSync: wearable skill transfer system for real-time foot-based interaction. In: 23rd Annual Meeting Proceedings, pp. 1–4. Virtual Reality Society of Japan (2018)
37. Ros, R., Coninx, A., Demiris, Y., Patsis, G., Enescu, V., Sahli, H.: Behavioral accommodation towards a dance robot tutor. In: 9th ACM/IEEE International Conference Proceedings on Human-Robot Interaction, pp. 278–279. ACM, USA (2014). https://doi.org/10.1145/2559636.2559821
38. Aggravi, M., Salvietti, G., Prattichizzo, D.: Haptic assistive bracelets for blind skier guidance. In: 7th Augmented Human International Conference Proceedings, pp. 1–4. ACM, USA (2016). https://doi.org/10.1145/2875194.2875249
39. Valsted, F.M., Nielsen, C.V.H., Jensen, J.Q., Sonne, T., Jensen, M.M.: Strive: exploring assistive haptic feedback on the run. In: 29th Australian Conference Proceedings on Computer-Human Interaction, pp. 275–284. ACM, USA (2017). https://doi.org/10.1145/3152771.3152801
40. Yang, C., Liang, P., Ajoudani, A., Li, Z., Bicchi, A.: Development of a robotic teaching interface for human to human skill transfer. In: 2016 IEEE/RSJ International Conference Proceedings on Intelligent Robots and System, pp. 710–716. IEEE, USA (2016). https://doi.org/10.1109/iros.2016.7759130
41. Pedemonte, N., Laliberté, T., Gosselin, C.: Bidirectional haptic communication: application to the teaching and improvement of handwriting capabilities. Machines 4(1), 1–15 (2016). https://doi.org/10.3390/machines4010006
42. Rajanna, V., et al.: KinoHaptics: an automated, wearable, haptic assisted, physio-therapeutic system for post-surgery rehabilitation and self-care. J. Med. Syst. 40(3), 1–12 (2016). https://doi.org/10.1007/s10916-015-0391-3
43. Ostadabbas, S., et al.: Tongue-controlled robotic rehabilitation: a feasibility study in people with stroke. J. Rehabil. Res. Dev. 53(6), 989–1006 (2016). https://doi.org/10.1682/JRRD.2015.06.0122
44. Choi, K.-S., Chan, S.-H., Pang, W.-M.: Virtual suturing simulation based on commodity physics engine for medical learning. J. Med. Syst. 36(3), 1781–1793 (2012). https://doi.org/10.1007/s10916-010-9638-1
45. Uribe, D.O., Schoukens, J., Stroop, R.: Improved tactile resonance sensor for robotic assisted surgery. Mech. Syst. Signal Process. 99, 600–610 (2018). https://doi.org/10.1016/j.ymssp.2017.07.007
46. Guo, J., Yu, Y., Guo, S., Du, W.: Design and performance evaluation of a novel master manipulator for the robot-assist catheter system. In: 2016 IEEE International Conference Proceedings on Mechatronics and Automation, pp. 937–942. IEEE, USA (2016). https://doi.org/10.1109/icma.2016.7558688

Parallel Simulation of Digital Logic Circuits Using Message Passing via CSP as an Educational Tool

Mario Rossainz-López$^{(\boxtimes)}$ [iD], Carmen Cerón-Garnica$^{(\boxtimes)}$ [iD],
Etelvina Archundia-Sierra$^{(\boxtimes)}$ [iD], Patricia Cervantes-Márquez$^{(\boxtimes)}$ [iD],
David Carrasco-Limón$^{(\boxtimes)}$, and Bárbara Sánchez-Rinza$^{(\boxtimes)}$ [iD]

Benemérita Universidad Autónoma de Puebla, Avda. San Claudio y 14 Sur,
San Manuel, 72000 Puebla, Pue., Mexico
{rossainz, mceron, etelvina, patty, brinza}@cs.buap.mx,
odondavidcarrasco95@gmail.com

Abstract. The present work shows an educational application of practical utility for the learning of the Parallel and Concurrent Programming with passage of messages, through the simulation of the digital logical circuits, as an excellent example of the inherent parallelism in the behavior of this type of systems. The Java class library called JPMI is used, which provides the base classes to generate processes, channels and composition of processes: sequential, parallel and alternative; for the parallel implementation of the most useful gates in the area of digital systems such as, the AND, OR and NOT gates. It shows a basic case study of the use of the JPMI library for the parallel implementation of a simple digital logic circuit and with this implementation simulate its logical behavior. But the full implementation of a 4-bit digital logic counter as an educational application or simulator is also shown. The objective of this work is, on the one hand, to demonstrate that the proposed implementations help the student through the simulation to understand and learn both the construction and the functioning of the digital systems, and on the other hand to show the inherent relationship of the parallelism with the operation of these systems.

Keywords: Digital logic circuit · Digital systems · Logic gates · JPMI · CSP · Educational simulation · Parallel programming · Message passing

1 Introduction

A computer simulation is a computer program whose purpose is to create a scenario of an abstract model of a given system [1]. Computer simulations have become an important and useful part of the mathematical models of many natural science systems such as physics, electronics, astrophysics, chemistry and biology; as well as human systems of economics, psychology and social sciences [1]. In addition, it is used in the design of new technology to better understand its operation. With the help of parallel programming we propose a simulation through an educational application, of a 4-bit digital logic counter formed by AND, OR and NOT gates. The system shows the user a simple and friendly graphical interface with which it interacts to provide the initial

© Springer Nature Switzerland AG 2019
P. H. Ruiz and V. Agredo-Delgado (Eds.): HCI-COLLAB 2019, CCIS 1114, pp. 284–298, 2019.
https://doi.org/10.1007/978-3-030-37386-3_21

binary values of the circuit and see the results in the simulation of an electronic display. The objective of this application is to facilitate the understanding of the theory and practice of the analysis and design of programmable logic circuits with the support of the computational discipline, and to understand the inherent relationship between digital systems and parallelism. The proposal is original in the use of parallel programming with message passing under the object orientation paradigm [2], using a JPMI class library that implements the process algebra of the Hoare CSP [3]. The CSP is a mathematical model with which we can formally write parallel programs using message passing and demonstrate the behavior of these and their correctness [4, 5]. The JPMI library provides classes to generate processes, channels and composition of processes to be able to communicate and synchronize them: the sequential composition of processes, the parallel composition of processes and the alternative composition of processes [6, 7]. The document starts with the section where the concept of parallel simulation is explained and continues with the explanation of the simulation as a tool of learning. The next section talks about the digital logic circuits, we continue with the parallel simulation of the digital logic circuits. We incorporate the basic concepts of the CSP process algebra to understand how it is programmed, using the JPMI class library and we finish with a case study that shows how to simulate a simple digital logic circuit using parallelism. We explain the implementation of a 4-bit digital logic counter using JPMI for its simulation. The document ends with the results and conclusions.

2   Parallel Simulation

A computer simulation is a computation that models the behavior of some real or imagined systems over time. Simulations are widely used today to analyze the behavior of systems such as air traffic control and future generation telecommunication networks without constructing the systems and situations of interest. Constructing a prototype may be costly, infeasible and/or dangerous. Another important use of simulation today is to create computer-generated virtual worlds into which humans and/or physical devices will be embedded. An aircraft flight simulator used to train pilots is one such example [8]. Parallel Simulation and Distributed Simulation refer to technologies that enable a simulation program to execute on a computing system containing multiple processors, such as personal computers, interconnected by a communication network. Suffice it to say that parallel simulations execute on a set of computers confined to a single cabinet or machine room, while distributed simulations execute on machines that are geographically distributed across a building, university campus, or even the world [8]. There are primarily four principal benefits to executing a simulation program across multiple computers:

1. Reduced execution time: By subdividing a large simulation computation into many sub-computations, and executing the sub computations concurrently across, say, ten different processors, one can reduce the execution time up to a factor of ten.
2. Geographical Distribution: Executing the simulation program on a set of geographically distributed computers enables one to create virtual words with multiple participants that are physically located at different sites.

3. Integrating simulators that execute on machines from different manufacturers: The simulation computation to be distributed across multiple computers.
4. Fault Tolerance: Another potential benefit of utilizing multiple processors is increased tolerance to failures. If one processor goes down, it may be possible for other processors to pick up the work of the failed machine.

Parallel simulation then refers to the use of technologies that allow a simulation program to run in a computer system that contains several processors physically speaking, or several heavy or light processes at the programming language level. In this work we make use of the second, distinguishing Parallel Simulation with shared memory, where processes that share resources are used through the use of common memory for all of them and Parallel Simulation with Message Passing, where we use the distributed model thinking about processes that do not share memory and that communicate between them through the use of a passive object called a channel under the concept of rendezvous.

3 Simulation as a Learning Tool

Educational simulation is a powerful technique that teaches some aspects of the real world through its imitation or replication. It is based on a model of a system or phenomenon of the real world in which some elements have been simplified or omitted to facilitate learning. Simulation involves a process: the design of a model, which is a cut-out of a real system to carry out experiences with it, with the aim of recognizing, understanding, evaluating, self-evaluating and modifying strategies and acquiring new ones [9]. Suggests that the importance of simulations, from the educational point of view, lies in involving the user in an experience that is fundamental for the development of habits, skills, mental schemes, etc. that can influence their behavior. Currently, simulation as a learning tool has a very close relationship with the use of ICTs. The inclusion of ICT in education has allowed generating processes in learning environments; as for example: greater freedom to explore, observe, analyze and build knowledge; stimulate imagination and creativity; offer multiple sources of updated information; facilitate scientific understanding of natural phenomena and allow for multisensory learning experiences. Therefore, the educational use of computer simulations provides a more direct interaction between the student, the area of knowledge and the learning process. It allows the student to confirm predictions by simulating a specific situation created from certain initial conditions and by managing the variables that intervene in it. Software tools have been developed for some time, which allow to simulate real processes constituting a very useful educational resource for the teaching and learning of sciences. Software applications in general that show simulations, usually present the possibility of modifying the parameters of the simulation in order to observe and analyze the consequences of these changes on the phenomenon studied [10].

4 Digital Logic Circuits

A digital logic circuit is one that uses binary information (values of "1" and "0"). Digital design deals with the design of digital electronic circuits. Digital circuits are used in the design and construction of systems such as digital computers, data communication, digital recording and many other applications that require digital hardware [11]. A characteristic of digital logic circuits is their ability to manipulate discrete elements of information. In them, the discrete elements of information are represented by physical quantities called signals, but in almost all current electronic digital systems, signals employ only two discrete values, so we say they are binary. A binary digit, called a bit, has two values: 0 and 1. Discrete elements of information are represented by groups of bits called binary codes. A digital logic circuit is a system that manipulates discrete information elements represented internally in binary form. Like digital computers, almost all digital devices are programmable. If we modify the program of a programmable device, we can use the same hardware for many different applications [11].

4.1 Logic Gates

Logic gates are electronic circuits that operate with one or more input signals to produce an output signal. In digital systems, electrical signals, which could be voltages or currents, exist with one of two recognizable values. Voltage-operated circuits respond to two different voltage levels that represent a binary variable whose value is logical 1 or logical 0. In Fig. 1 (taken from [12]), the graphic symbols, their truth tables and their axioms with which the three most common types of gates are represented: AND, OR and NOT. The gates are hardware blocks that produce output signals equivalent to logic 1 or logic 0 when the logical input requirements are met.

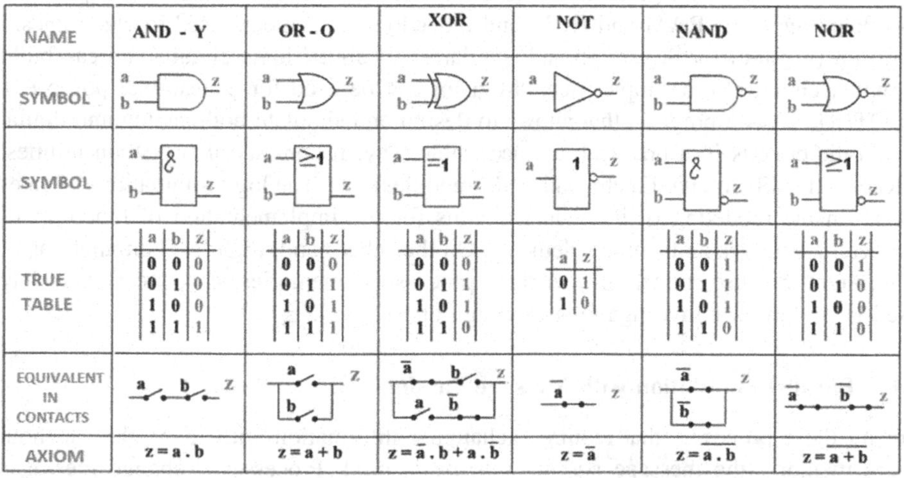

NAME	AND - Y	OR - O	XOR	NOT	NAND	NOR
SYMBOL						
SYMBOL						
TRUE TABLE	a b z 0 0 0 0 1 0 1 0 0 1 1 1	a b z 0 0 0 0 1 1 1 0 1 1 1 1	a b z 0 0 0 0 1 1 1 0 1 1 1 0	a z 0 1 1 0	a b z 0 0 1 0 1 1 1 0 1 1 1 0	a b z 0 0 1 0 1 0 1 0 0 1 1 0
EQUIVALENT IN CONTACTS						
AXIOM	$z = a \cdot b$	$z = a + b$	$z = \bar{a} \cdot b + a \cdot \bar{b}$	$z = \bar{a}$	$z = \overline{a \cdot b}$	$z = \overline{a + b}$

Fig. 1. Most used logic gates

The AND gate responds with an output signal of logic 1 when both input signals are logic 1. The OR gate responds with an output signal of logic 1 when any input signal is logic 1. The NOT gate is commonly referred to as an inverter, and in the timing diagram the output signal reverses the logical direction of the input signal. The NAND gate is the complement of the AND gate, as indicated by its graphic symbol consisting of an AND graphic symbol followed by a bubble. The NOR function is the complement of the OR function and its graphic symbol is that of OR followed by a bubble. The exclusive OR gate has a graphic symbol similar to the OR gate, only that it has an additional curved line on the input side. The equivalence gate, or exclusive NOR, is the complement of the exclusive OR, as indicated by the bubble on the output side of the graphic symbol of Fig. 1.

5   Parallel Simulation of Digital Logic Circuits

Like telecommunication networks, the simulation of digital electronic circuits and computer systems is the second area where parallel simulation plays an important role. For example, the computer-aided design community is interested in obtaining a rapid simulation of logic circuits because the simulation they perform in CAD systems regularly generates important bottlenecks in the design cycle. The final verification of a computer system may require weeks using conventional sequential simulation techniques. Much of the work in the application of parallel simulation techniques in logical circuits has focused on using the VHDL hardware description language. Several parallel simulation systems of prototypes have been developed with VHDL in scalar supercomputers, with different degrees of success reported in the literature; As examples we can mention Simulink (is a simulation tool of logical and digital models or systems, with a certain degree of abstraction of the physical phenomena involved in them.), CEDAR (It is a tool that allows you to design digital logic systems. It provides the user with basic logic gates, inverters and connectors, decoders, adders, comparators, flip-flops, registers, RAM and ROM and other logical elements used in electronics.), Logisim (is a tool for the design and simulation of digital logic circuits and can build complex circuits from simpler ones. Logisim can be used for educational purposes), PROTEUS (It is a program that allows to design and simulate both analog and digital electronic circuits in a practical and accessible way. It consists of two main utilities: ARES and ISIS, and the Electra and VSM modules), etc. The logic simulations of gates focus on the modeling of individual circuits for the implementation of functions of Boolean primitives and storage elements. On the other hand, high-level simulations of equipment that use models of switches, processors, memories, etc., are also widely used in preliminary investigations of design alternatives.

5.1   Parallel Simulation with Message Passing

For all those processes that require exchanging information with each other, without share memory, the message passing scheme is used. Processes exchange messages between them through explicit sending and receiving operations that are the basic primitives of any communication system of this type. The general communication model is represented in Fig. 2, where the fundamental elements that intervene in communication are identified in systems with message passing (a sending process, a receiving process, a communication channel, the message to send/receive and the sending and receiving operations).

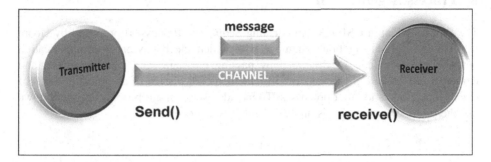

Fig. 2. Process Communication Model via message passing

5.2   Process Synchronization

- Asynchronous communication. The sending process can carry out the sending operation without it being necessary for it to coincide in time with the receiving operation by the receiving process [13]. This requires storing the messages in buffers until they are removed by the receiving process.
- Synchronous communication. There is a coincidence in time of the sending and receiving operations by the sending and receiving processes, that is, the sending process is blocked in the sending operation until the receiving process is ready to receive the message or vice versa [13]. This is called rendezvous.

5.3   Communication Channels and Messages

- Data flow. Once a communication channel has been established between a transmitting process and a receiving process, the latter, according to the flow of data passing through it, can be of two types: unidirectional or bidirectional.
- Channel capacity. It is the possibility that the channel has to store the messages sent by the sender process when they are not picked up by the receiving process.
- Message size: Messages traveling on the channel can be of fixed length or variable length.
- Channels with type or without type: Some communication schemes require defining the type of data that will flow through the channel, imposing the restriction of sending data only of the type for which the channel was declared.
- Step by copy or by reference: The communication by passing messages requires sending information between the processes involved in the communication. This can be done in two ways: make an exact copy of the data (message) that the sender process wants to send from its address space to the address space of the receiving

process (step by copy or value) or simply send it to the receiving process the address in the address space of the sender process where the message is located (step by reference).

6   Process Algebra CSP

The Process Algebra CSP (Communicating Sequential Processes) proposed by Hoare in 1978 is a formal algebraic language with which the behavior of communication between processes can be described by passing messages and can be verified and demonstrated. In CSP a process describes the behavior pattern of an object in terms of events, operators, and other processes. To include events in our process description, we use the prefix operator: if a is an event and P is a process, then

$$(a \rightarrow P) \tag{1}$$

is a process which may engage in a before behaving as P. An event can also be a communication event, which is represented by the pair c.v where c is the name of the channel on which the event takes place, and v is the value of the message that is passed. The input and output are respectively the read action c?v and write action c!v which are performed when both processes are ready and communication over channel c is performed. We define an input process

$$(c?(v : T) \rightarrow P(v)) \tag{2}$$

as a process that behaves as process P(v) after the value v is read by channel c. The value v is of type T denoted as $(c?(v : T) \rightarrow P(v))$. We define an output process:

$$(c!v \rightarrow P) \tag{3}$$

as a process that behaves as process P after the value v is sent by channel c. This tightly defined communication protocol is called rendezvous communication.

6.1   Process Compositions

- Sequential Process Composition: A thread is a sequential flow of control. The processes P and Q can be considered threads of control that invoke read and write actions on both channels each in a sequential order. If this order is not correctly chosen by the programmer or by the flow of control, then deadlock may be the result.
- Parallel Process Composition: The read and write actions of process P and the read and write actions of process Q are mutual independent. The read and write action can be executed in arbitrary order because the order is undefined. A more secure approach is using a parallel composition which eliminates deadlock.

- Alternative Process Composition: The actions of reading or writing by a process P and a process Q are carried out through an election which can be deterministic or non-deterministic. If P is chosen to be executed, then Q will not be executed and vice versa.

6.2   Communication Between Processes

The processes P and Q communicate through shared channels. The read and write actions on a channel are considered shared events that are performed when they are both ready. A channel provides one-way communication between two processes. For two-way communication two channels should be used. A channel that is used only for output by a process will be called an output channel of that process and one used only for input will be called an input channel (see Fig. 3).

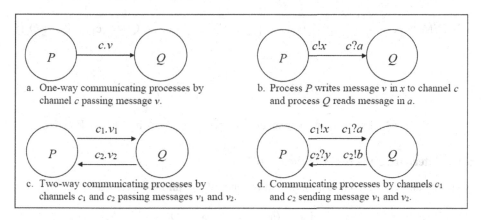

a. One-way communicating processes by channel c passing message v.

b. Process P writes message v in x to channel c and process Q reads message in a.

c. Two-way communicating processes by channels c_1 and c_2 passing messages v_1 and v_2.

d. Communicating processes by channels c_1 and c_2 sending message v_1 and v_2.

Fig. 3. Ways of communication between two processes P and Q (taken from [14])

6.3   Sequential Process Composition

A thread is a sequential flow of control. The processes P and Q can be considered threads of control that invoke read and write actions on both channels each in a sequential order. If this order is not correctly chosen by the programmer or by the flow of control, then deadlock may be the result. Both processes will then wait on communication infinitely. The processes P and Q are described as:

$$P = (c_1 \rightarrow c_2 \rightarrow P') \, y \, Q = (c_2 \rightarrow c_1 \rightarrow Q') \tag{4}$$

$$SYSTEM = ((c_1 \rightarrow c_2 \rightarrow P')|[\{c_1, c_2\} \mid \{c_1, c_2\}]|(c_2 \rightarrow c_1 \rightarrow Q')) = STOP \tag{5}$$

The processes P' and Q' are suffix processes of respectively P and Q after the composition. We simply see that $c_1 \rightarrow c_2$ and $c_2 \rightarrow c_1$ only can be performed when

$c_1 = c_2$. This is never true and therefore the processes P and Q are mutual exclusive or deadlocked. It is concluded that sequential communication in an erroneous order can cause an interlock.

6.4 Parallel Process Composition

The read and write actions of process P and the read and write actions of process Q are mutual independent. The read and write action can be executed in arbitrary order because the order is undefined. As mentioned before, in a sequential composition, such as in a sequential process, the order of the read and write actions should be carefully chosen. A more secure approach is using a parallel composition which eliminates deadlock. Let sequential-P in its composition and parallel-Q in its composition then we have:

$$P = (c_1 \to c_2 \to P') \, y \, Q = (c_2 \to c_1 \to Q') \, \Box \, (c_1 \to c_2 \to Q') \tag{6}$$

$$SYSTEM = \left(c_1 \to c_2 \to P' \right) \| \{c_1, c_2\} | \{c_1, c_2\} \| ((c_2 \to c_1 \to Q') \Box (c_1 \to c_2 \to Q')) \tag{7}$$

$$SYSTEM = c_1 \to c_2 \to \left(P' \| Q' \right) \tag{8}$$

The SYSTEM Process can be executed in both events c_1 and c_2, of P and Q.

6.5 Alternative Process Composition

A simple alternative composition based on one event can be described by the process:

$$ALT = (a \to P) \, \Box \, (\neg a \to Q) \tag{9}$$

The ALT will behave as P if it can engage in a else it will behave as Q. This behavior continues immediately and is analogous to a simple if-then-else statement. The process for the if-then statement – without the else – can be described as:

$$ALT = (a \to P) \, \Box \, (\neg a \to SKIP) \tag{10}$$

7 Parallel Programming Using JPMI

JPMI (Java Passing Message Interface) it's a library which implements the CSP model, i.e., processes, compositions and channels, in Java. An important advantage of CTJ is that the designer or programmer has a rich set of rules or guidelines available that help eliminate undesirable conditions during d sign and implementation phases. In JPMI a process represents an active object with execution capacity in itself [14]. The communication between processes is carried out using communication channels. The channels themselves are primitive data structures, that is, passive objects that the processes can use to send or receive information and that take into account the synchronization, planning and delivery of messages [14]. The channels are synchronized according to the rendezvous principle. A class that is a JPMI process, must implement the interface Jpmi. Proceso and must provide an implementation of the run() method which will contain the task that the process wants to perform when this method is invoked by another process. The process constructor specifies the input channels, the output channels and additional parameters to initialize the status of the process. The run() method is the only public method that a process can invoke directly in another process.

8 Case Study

The simulation of a digital logic circuit is shown, making use of the JPMI library in parallel programming with message passing. The objective is to show how simulation can be used in an educational way to teach real aspects of digital logic circuits, facilitating the learning of its components, as well as its inherently parallel functioning. The digital logic circuit that is simulated is formed of AND, OR and NOT gates connected in different ways that could be defined by the user. Each AND and OR gate has two inputs and one output. Each NOT gate has an entry and an exit. The gates are implemented as Processes using the JPMI library, and these receive Boolean values from other gates or from the user for simulated execution. The data for this program is stored in a matrix that defines the interconnections and functions of the gates (Table 1). With this, the logic circuit shown in Fig. 4 (taken from [15]), whose operation is simulated in its execution (see Fig. 5). Then the user or programmer, through simulation as a learning technique, could easily propose an implementation for the rest of the gates in Fig. 1; modifying the program to create any type of gate using the properties of object orientation such as inheritance and/or implementation of interfaces or use of abstract classes.

Table 1. Description of the logic circuit of Fig. 4

Gate	Function	Input 1	Input 2	Output
1	AND	Test 1	Test 2	Gate 1
2	OR	Gate 1		Output 1
3	NOT	Test 3	Gate 1	Output 2

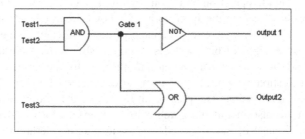

Fig. 4. Simple digital logic circuit (taken from [15])

9   Implementation of the Case Study Using JPMI

See Fig. 5.

```
import Jpmi.*;

public class And implements Proceso
{
  public CanalSimple in1,in2,out;
  public MsgBool num1,num2,num3;

  public And(CanalSimple in1,CanalSimple in2,CanalSimple out)
  {
    this.in1=in1;
    this.in2=in2;
    this.out=out;
  }

  public void run()
  {
    Lee lee1=new Lee(in1);
    Lee lee2=new Lee(in2);
    Proceso par=new Paralelo(new Proceso[]{lee1,lee2});
    par.run();
    num1=lee1.getMsg();
    num2=lee2.getMsg();
    if((num1.valorBool==1)&&(num2.valorBool==1))
        num3=new MsgBool(1);
    else num3=new MsgBool(0);
    System.out.println(num1.valorBool+" AND "+num2.valorBool+
                     "= "+num3.valorBool);
    out.send(num3);
  }
}
```

```
import Jpmi.*;

public class Or implements Proceso
{
  public CanalSimple in1,in2,out;
  public MsgBool num1,num2,num3;

  public Or(CanalSimple in1,CanalSimple in2,CanalSimple out)
  {
    this.in1=in1;
    this.in2=in2;
    this.out=out;
  }

  public void run()
  {
    Lee lee1=new Lee(in1);
    Lee lee2=new Lee(in2);
    Proceso par=new Paralelo(new Proceso[]{lee1,lee2});
    par.run();
    num1=lee1.getMsg();
    num2=lee2.getMsg();
    if((num1.valorBool==1)||(num2.valorBool==1))
        num3=new MsgBool(1);
    else num3=new MsgBool(0);
    System.out.println(num1.valorBool+" OR "+num2.valorBool+
                     "= "+num3.valorBool);
    out.send(num3);
  }
}
```

```
import Jpmi.*;

public class Not implements Proceso
{
  public CanalSimple in1,out;
  public MsgBool num1,num2;

  public Not(CanalSimple in1,CanalSimple out)
  {
    this.in1=in1;
    this.out=out;
  }

  public void run()
  {
    num1=(MsgBool)in1.receive();
    if(num1.valorBool==1)
        num2=new MsgBool(0);
    else num2=new MsgBool(1);
    System.out.println("NOT("+num1.valorBool+")="+
                          num2.valorBool);
    out.send(num2);
  }
}
```

```
import Jpmi.*;

public class Circuito
  {
   public static void main(String args[])
    {
      MsgBool valor1=new MsgBool(1);
      MsgBool valor2=new MsgBool(0);
      MsgBool valor3=new MsgBool(1);
      CanalSimple test1=new CanalSimple();
      CanalSimple test2=new CanalSimple();
      CanalSimple test3=new CanalSimple();
      CanalSimple gate1=new CanalSimple();
      CanalSimple gate1Out1=new CanalSimple();
      CanalSimple gate1Out2=new CanalSimple();
      CanalSimple output1=new CanalSimple();
      CanalSimple output2=new CanalSimple();

      Paralelo par=new Paralelo(new Proceso[]{
           new Entrada3(valor1,valor2,valor3,test1,test2,test3),
           new And(test1,test2,gate1),
           new Delta(gate1,gate1Out1,gate1Out2),
           new Or(gate1Out2,test3,output2),
           new Not(gate1Out1,output1),
           new Display(output1,output2)});
      par.run();
    }
  }
```

Fig. 5. JPMI code of the AND, OR and NOT gates and main program that implements the Digital Logic Circuit of Fig. 4.

10   Educational Application: Simulator of a 4-Bit Digital Logic Counter with JPMI

A simulator showing the operation of a 4-bit digital logic counter using the parallelism with message passing through the Jpmi library is shown as an educational application [16]. A counter is a digital logic circuit capable of counting electronic events, such as pulses, through a sequence of binary states. Figure 6 shows the logic diagram of the digital counter and shows also the application that is used for the simulation of the logic circuit. This application was developed using the Java JPMI library to program in parallel with message passing. The programming is like the one shown in Sect. 8 of this article but it has also included a graphical user interface for user-friendly use. To analyze the performance of the proposed application, an acceleration analysis of the execution of the 4-bit digital logic counter was carried out on a computer with an Intel

Core i5 processor at 2.30 GHz, with 8 Gb RAM and a graphics card NVIDIA Geforce GTX. The graph of Fig. 7 (left) shows the decrease in the execution time of the application by the CPU as the cores were used, going from a sequential execution time of 95 s to an execution time of 78 s, 65 s and 62 s using two, three and four cores respectively. Figure 7 (right) shows the analysis of the acceleration of the digital logic counter by applying the speedup formula and contrasting it with Amdahl's law as the upper limit of said acceleration. In it you can see that the acceleration with 2 cores was 1.54, with 3 cores was 1.87 and with four cores was 2.10, all of them below Amdahl's law with a non-parallel code fraction of 30% of the total of the programmed code.

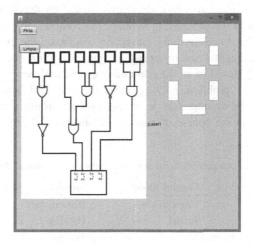

Fig. 6. Application programmed with JPMI that shows the simulation of a 4-bit digital logic counter

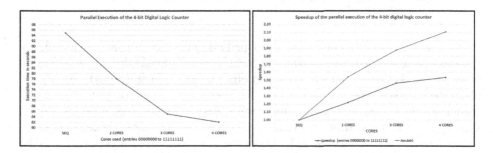

Fig. 7. Left: decrease in the execution time of the digital logic counter. Right: analysis of the speedup of the digital logic counter

11 Results

The sample of the population was 40 students, corresponding to 30% of the students enrolled in the course of concurrent and parallel programming, in the Faculty of Computer Science of the BUAP. The other groups worked with the traditional teaching-learning model. In this fieldwork, the students were divided into two groups of 20 students each. One group was identified as the "control" group, and worked under the traditional teaching modality, the other was called a "simulation" group and worked individually and in groups with the simulator. We worked individually and collaboratively to develop autonomous and collaborative learning in both groups. In the simulation group, impacts were obtained in the cognitive area, in practice and in attitudes that favored the learning process. They had a good performance using as a measure parameter the obtained grades, in comparison with those of the control group. The professional competency model establishes three levels: basic, generic and specific or technical (disciplinary) competences [17]. The competence can be defined as the ability of a professional to make decisions, based on the knowledge, skills and attitudes associated with the profession, to solve the complex problems that arise in the field of their professional activity [18]. Based on the above, the evaluation focused on measuring some instrumental and interpersonal generic (transversal) competences that were taken from [19]. Based on it, the competences and abilities were valued, from the criteria: technological, problem solving capacity and collaborative learning (see Table 2), which are the fundamental learnings that according to the curriculum, the student must acquire in the course of concurrent and parallel programming.

Table 2. Comparison of competences and abilities shown with/without the use of the simulator

Criteria	Control group	Simulation group
Work attitude	Unmotivated	Participatory
Attention	Partial	Continuous
Resolution time problems	Major	Minor
Learning scenarios	Scattered	Concrete
Resources	School notes	Laboratory, use of the simulator
Results of the practice	Miscellaneous results	Exact and similar results

On the other hand, the competences grouped under these criteria indicate a tendency towards action, directed more towards the "achievement" of tasks than to the impact on other people. Actions to influence or direct other people to improve productivity or to obtain better results are qualified in the "achievement" competition [20]. To achieve mastery of the competence, a performance test was used that served as an evaluation strategy to determine student achievement at a certain level of competence. To obtain a result in terms of learning with and without the simulator, the ratings obtained in the corresponding tests of the control group and the simulation group were used as a measurement parameter, and it was observed that the impact in the cognitive area of the students favored to the simulation group (see Fig. 8). The evaluation criteria considered were the tests or exams and the laboratory practices with the simulator. To measure the competences with the evaluation criteria above, checklists were used to measure: The installation and configuration of applications and development of techniques, Interconnection of mobile and wireless or wired devices to exchange information and data,

Test different cases and obtain simulator reports. The weighting of the competencies in the tests were: Instrumental 30%, Personal 30%, Disciplines 40%.

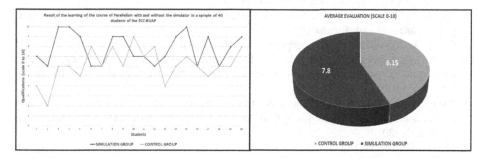

Fig. 8. (Left): Evaluation of learning with and without the simulator. (Right): Average evaluation on the scale of 0 to 10.

12 Conclusions

A 4-bit digital logic counter has been implemented as an educational application to learn Concurrent and Parallel Programming both in the construction of said counter and in the simulation of its behavior. The coding of the logic counter as a simulator was carried out with the use of parallel programming with message passing through the JPMI library, which implements the Process Algebra of Hoare or CSP. The logical gates AND, OR, NOT was implemented as processes (active objects) communicated through the compositions provided by JPMI: parallel composition of processes, sequential composition of processes and alternative composition of processes, using the concept of channel (passive objects) in their communications and synchronizations. The utility and relationship of the area of digital logic circuits with parallel programming was demonstrated by means of a case study (Sect. 8) and of educational application proposal that generates a simulation of an original digital 4-bit logic counter (Sect. 9). With this application the student in this area can better understand the reality of the operation of these circuits without need to have it physically and the importance that Concurrent and Parallel Programming has in the area of simulation of this type of systems. Finally, it was demonstrated that with the use of the simulator, the learning of the concurrent and parallel programming was easier and better, than without the simulator.

References

1. Fujimoto, R.M.: Parallel and Distributed Simulation Systems. Wiley, Hoboken (2000). https://doi.org/10.1109/wsc.1999.823061
2. Lea, D.: Concurrent Programming in Java. Addison-Wesley, Boston (1996)
3. Hiderink, J., Broenink, J., Bakkers, A.: Communicating Threads for Java. University of Twente: Draf-Rev 5, Netherlands (2000). https://doi.org/10.1109/isorc.2000.839557

4. Davies, J., Schneider, S.: Real-Time CSP, UK (1995)
5. Hoare, C.A.R.: Communicating Sequential Processes. Prentice Hall, London (2003)
6. Andrews, G.R.: Concurrent Programming. Principles and Practice. Benjamin Cummings Publishing Company Inc., San Francisco (1991)
7. Capel, I.M., Rodriguez, V.S: Sistemas Concurrentes y Distribuidos. Teorìa y Pràctica: Copycentro Editorial, España (2012)
8. Farley, J.: JAVA Distributed Computing, pp. 138–188. O'Really, Newton (1998)
9. Cataldi, Z., Lage, F.J., Dominighini, C.: Fundamentos para el uso de simulaciones en la enseñanza. Revista de Informática Educativa y Medios Audiovisuales 10(17), 8–16 (2013). ISSN 1667-8338
10. Alzugaray, M., Carreri, R., Marino, L.A.: El software de Simulación en Física. Herramienta para el aprendizaje de contenidos. V Congreso de Tecnología en Educación y Educación en Tecnología (2010)
11. Morris, M.: Diseño Digital. Pearson Ed – Prentice Hall, México (2003). https://doi.org/10.1109/pgec.1964.263740
12. Sánchez Santos, V., et al.: Electrónica Digital. Facultad de Ingeniería Mecánica Eléctrica (FIME). Universidad Veracruzana, México (2008). https://sites.google.com/site/electronicadigitaluvfime/home
13. Palma, J.T., Garrido, M.C., et al.: Programación Concurrente. Thomson, España (2003)
14. Arnold, K., Gosling, J.A.: The Java Programming Language. Addison-Wesley, Boston (1996)
15. Lewis, B., Berg, D.J.: A Guide to Multithreading Programming. Prentice Hall, Upper Saddle River (1996)
16. Wilkinson, B., Allen, M.: Parallel Programming. Techniques and Applications Using Networked Workstations and Parallel Computers, pp. 38–81, 227–264. Prentice Hall, Upper Saddle River (2000)
17. Parlamento Europeo: Comisión de las Comunidades Europeas sobre las competencias clave para el aprendizaje permanente, Bruselas (2005)
18. Valiente, A., Galdeano, C., Professional Competences. Educación Química, vol. 21, no. 1, México (2010)
19. COPA: Concepts and Methods of the Competency Outcomes and Performance Assessment, New York (1999)
20. Spencer, L.M., Spencer, S.M.: Competence at Work. Models for Superior Performance. Wiley, New York (1993)

Prevention of Diabetes Mellitus Through the Use of Mobile Technology (mHealth): Case Study

M. Hazael Guerrero-Flores[1]([⊠]) [iD], Huizilopoztli Luna-García[1] [iD],
Carlos E. Galván-Tejada[1] [iD], Hamurabi Gamboa-Rosales[1] [iD],
José M. Celaya-Padilla[2] [iD], Jorge I. Galván-Tejada[1] [iD],
Alfredo Mendoza-González[3] [iD], Vanessa Alcala-Rmz[1] [iD],
Adan Valladares-Salgado[4] [iD], and Miguel Cruz[4] [iD]

[1] Centro de Investigación e Innovación Biomédica e Informática (CIIBI),
Universidad Autónoma de Zacatecas, Francisco García Salinas,
Jardín Juárez #147, Centro Histórico, 98000 Zacatecas, Zac., Mexico
{hazaelgf, hlugar, ericgalvan, hamurabigr, gatejo,
vdrar.06}@uaz.edu.mx
[2] CONACYT, Universidad Autónoma de Zacatecas, Francisco García Salinas,
Jardín Juárez #147, Centro Histórico, 98000 Zacatecas, Zac., Mexico
jose.celaya@uaz.edu.mx
[3] PRODEP, Centro de Investigación e Innovación Biomédica e Informática
(CIIBI), Universidad Autónoma de Zacatecas, Francisco García Salinas,
Jardín Juárez #147, Centro Histórico, 98000 Zacatecas, Zac., Mexico
mendoza.uaa@gmail.com
[4] Unidad de Investigación Médica en Bioquímica, Hospital de Especialidades,
Centro Médico Nacional Siglo XXI, Instituto Mexicano del Seguro Social,
Av. Cuauhtémoc 330, Col. Doctores, Del. Cuauhtémoc,
06720 Mexico City, Mexico
adanval@gmail.com, mcruz@yahoo.com

Abstract. Currently advances in technology have allowed the development of tools focused on the field of medicine, such as mobile technology applied to health or mHealth, through which it seeks to improve the health and quality of life of people. In 2017 there were more than 200 million downloads in mHealth apps from online app stores, however, likewise, the dropout rate was high due to the problems faced by the users when using those apps. On the other hand, in the field of health, one of the main causes of death in Mexico is diabetes mellitus. Derived from the above, this article presents the design of a mobile application prototype as a support tool in the prevention of this disease, taking as reference the Risk Factors Questionnaire (RFQ). For the development of the prototype, the stages of the User Centered Design (UCD) process were implemented in accordance with the ISO 9241-210:2010. The purpose of the final application, is to provide an easy-to-use tool that provides the user with information about the possible risk of developing diabetes, based on user-provided data and analyzed with artificial intelligence algorithms, also to provide recommendations that impact on the people's lifestyles, as well as providing a list of doctors and

© Springer Nature Switzerland AG 2019
P. H. Ruiz and V. Agredo-Delgado (Eds.): HCI-COLLAB 2019, CCIS 1114, pp. 299–313, 2019.
https://doi.org/10.1007/978-3-030-37386-3_22

nutritionists located around locality. As a result of the UCD implementation, a low-fidelity prototype was designed and evaluated using user testing to determine usability and user satisfaction.

Keywords: Mobile technology · mHealth · Diabetes mellitus · User Centered Design (UCD) · Prototype · AI · Multiple linear regression

1 Introduction

In recent years, technology has been included in every area of our lives, changing the way we live, using knowledge to solve problems, or develop techniques and improve our quality of life, one of them is the mobile technology that has had a great growth, it is known that there are more mobile devices than people in the world and technology is heading towards a future in which most of it will be mobile [1].

Because of this, the market for mobile applications has increased, every day new applications are developed, from those aimed at entertainment, to those that directly or indirectly seek to improve the health or quality of life of people. This type of mobile technology intended for the area of health has been given the name "mhealth".

Mhealth can be defined as the use of wireless technologies that provide assistance and medical information through mobile devices. The mHealth applications are mainly developed for two large operating systems such as IOS and Android, some of which are aimed at allowing people to keep track of their own health and well-being, while others are aimed at providing care or medical tools to facilitate the care patients [2].

During 2017 more than 200 million mHealth applications were downloaded, but also the dropout rate was too high, this is because if a user encounters problems in usability, performance, security or compatibility, generates a bad experience with these technologies, which makes them less willing to use them in the future. So it is necessary, the creation of mhealth applications, carefully designed and tested before going on the market, to avoid problems that lead to the abandonment of the application [2].

There are currently mobile apps that are used to assist health care, whether they provide lifestyle recommendations, eating plans or fitness exercises that can be performed from home [3], as well as applications to schedule appointments and carry out procedures of the Instituto Mexicano del Seguro Social (IMSS) [4].

On the other hand, artificial intelligence (AI), a branch of computing, is able to analyze complex medical data, thereby finding meaningful relationships between the data, managing to diagnose or predict certain medical scenarios, so it is considered a critical tool for providing medical care efficiently [5].

Among the most common and frequent diseases in Mexico is diabetes mellitus, which is a degenerative chronic disease that is seen when the pancreas no longer produces enough insulin, the hormone responsible for regulating blood sugar and with over time causes damage to the body and even death [6]. Diabetes is a big problem in Mexico, due to its high prevalence, it causes between 15% and 20% of the expenditure of public health institutes [7]. From 2000 to 2008 the percentage of deaths increased from 10.7% to 14%, and by 2013 it caused a total of 89,420 deaths. In the state of Zacatecas, it caused 9.83% of deaths in 2016 [8, 9].

Currently there are many applications aimed at people with diabetes, for example, those that give recommendations on the necessary insulin dose, however, these applications have several drawbacks, one of them is that they do not provide information about the factors or formula with which they calculate the insulin dose, so the patient is not entirely sure if that dose is appropriate to their needs, in addition, that these applications may have been created by programmers without medical knowledge, so mHealth applications need to be designed considering already validated medical tools [10].

There are several techniques and methodologies that are used for the design and development of a mobile application, but one of them, is designed to meet the needs of the user, called User-Centered Design (UCD) that originates in 1955 based on methods used in industrial design, with the idea that designers should adapt their products to people's needs and not the other way around, when people no longer had to adapt to machines, man no longer had to memorize and to train too much to use them, now they had to adapt to people, they had to become more friendly, understandable and easy to use. It was Henry Dreyfuss in his 1955 book "Designing for people" who popularized this approach and until 30 years later the computer engineers applied these techniques, because previously they only focused on the proper functioning of their system and not in that it was easy to understand and use. The goal of User-Centered Design is to understand people, how they interact with each other, discover their needs and thereby develop efficient, useful, usable and attractive systems for people [11].

Derived from the above in this project is the design and development of a mobile application prototype, using the stages of User Centered Design (UCD) according to the ISO 9241-210:2010 standard [12], it is intended when the application is developed in its entirety, be a support tool for the diabetes prevention, by analyzing data provided by the user, taking as a reference the tool that helps to obtain the risk of developing diabetes, called the Risk Factors Questionnaire [13] and use artificial intelligence techniques, to provide the user with a quick and reliable risk to the disease, giving recommendations based to the percentage obtained, in addition to a list of doctors and nutritionists in their city.

2 Related Works

While there are already mobile applications that help their users with their health care, it is not the purpose of this article to evaluate or compare them, they are only taken as a reference, that there are in digital stores, such is the case of Samsung Health, developed by the company that bears the same name (Samsung), which helps to keep track of the user's lifestyle, such as their diet, physical activity, stress, heart rate, among others, to provide feedback on progress and help the user to eat a healthy diet [3].

IMSS Digital is an application of the government of México that serves to carry out various procedures at the Instituto Mexicano del Seguro Social (IMSS), such as scheduling appointments with doctors, assigning Social Security Number, change or discharge of clinic, as well as location of clinics according to the postal code, for this it is only necessary to have the Unique Population Registration Code (Clave Única de Registro de Población) (CURP), the Electronic Signature and an email [4].

There are applications developed in the topic of health especially for diabetes, such as Diabetes - Diario de glucosa, which helps people with diabetes to keep a daily record of their glucose levels, which the user enters on a daily basis, it allows you to create alarms and reminders so that the person does not forget to take their medications and/or their doctor's appointments [14].

The application prototype raised in this work differs from those mentioned above, because in addition to only giving recommendations to the user for the care of their health, it provides a list of doctors and nutritionists located in their city of residence so that these keep a check on your health. In addition, for the final application it is intended to apply Artificial Intelligence techniques.

There are currently research papers using artificial intelligence techniques, as well as data mining to be able to predict and diagnose various diseases, such as diabetes, where computer prediction models are implemented such as genetic algorithms, neural networks, decision trees, among others, to obtain models that are statistically and medically significant. This to diagnose and predict early-stage diabetes or predict the blood glucose level, managing to reduce the harmful effects of this disease, in addition to calculating the insulin needed for a patient daily [15, 16].

3   Materials and Methods

The design of the application was done using the UCD that relies on placing the end user at the center of development, so it influences the final result of the design. The ISO 9241-210:2010 standard was defined by the International Organization for Standardization, which provides recommendations for the entire design process, consisting of several stages shown in Fig. 1 [12].

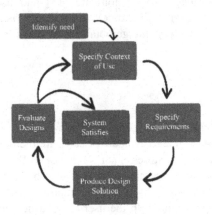

Fig. 1. User centered design stages [17].

UCD stages according to ISO 9241-210:2010 [12]:

1. Specify Context of Use: This is the stage at which end users of the application will be identified, the reason, under what conditions and where they will use it.

2. Specify Requirements: It is based on the identification of the user's needs and objectives, in addition to the requirements of the application and its use.
3. Produce Design Solutions: Based on the data obtained in the previous two phases, the design of the application is carried out.
4. Evaluate Designs: At this stage the application is evaluated to know if it meets the requirements above and manages to meet the needs for which it was developed, if so the process ends, otherwise it is necessary to repeat the process from its first stage.

3.1 Specify Context of Use

The first stage is to identify the user's needs and the goals they want to meet when using the app. Surveys were conducted to learn about people's opinions about mHealth apps, as well as their previous experiences with mHealth apps. The application of the surveys was conducted in person in the Plaza Bicentenario located in the capital city of Zacatecas, Mexico, in that place you can find a lot of people of all ages since this is the entrance to the center of the city [18]. It was also done electronically with the Google Forms tool, which allows to create and apply surveys for free, organizing the information obtained in graphs [19].

3.2 Specify Requirements

According to the results obtained with the surveys of the previous stage, graphs and tables are made for a better interpretation of the data, identifying the potential users of the tool, as well as the age at which there is a greater concern of people for their health, interest and acceptance to use an mHealth app.

To find out the questions to be included in the questionnaire, to be asked in the app and calculate the percentage of possible risk to develop diabetes, the Risk Factors Questionnaire was used, as it is approved by the Government of México and is used to find out if a person is at risk for diabetes, hypertension or obesity [13].

3.3 Produce Design Solutions

At this stage the design of a low fidelity prototype is proposed as it is a cheap and easy way to provide prototypes for evaluation, low fidelity means that the prototypes to be used do not contain the actual and final appearance of the interface even though these operate in a similar way, serve to obtain a lot of information about the interaction between the interface and the user [20].

The Balsamiq Mockups 3 software was used to create the application prototype, is a low-fidelity user interface design tool called wireframes or mockups without the need to write codes, this tool allows the creation of mockups as if you were working with paper and pencil, but adding the ease of modifying and rearranging the designs as digitally [21].

3.4   Evaluate Designs

For the prototypes evaluation created in the previous stage, the Justinmind software was used, it allows to create interactive prototypes without writing code, which allows to evaluate the functionality of the application on the computer or in the mobile application for Android that bears the same name [22]. In addition, it allows the creation of mockups from previously created images, which allowed the use of prototypes created in Balsamiq Mockups.

In order to obtain demographic data and the user's point of view towards the application prototype, focus groups and a small questionnaire were applied, as this technique allows to know the user's experience and preferences regarding the prototype, in addition, to be able to ask for your opinion [23].

The number of users required to carry out the evaluation, according to Jakob Nielsen, who is considered the father of usability, declares that the evaluation of a software by a small group of users, provides the same or better results as a large group, therefore, with its research, states that to evaluate large products it takes 5 to 8 users, while, for a small product, only 3 to 5 users are needed [24].

3.5   Database, Algorithm Training and Evaluation

The database corresponding to the experimentation of this research, is provided by the Medical Center XXI Century. This consists of 1019 Mexican patients of which 520 are cases of subjects with diabetes and 499 are subjects with absence of the disease. It should be mentioned that, of the 1019 patients, 517 are men and 502 women. Among the characteristics used to obtain the classification model are age, gender, height, weight, waist measurement, hip measurement, this data is related to the questions that are asked in the questionnaire included in the application prototype.

To perform the classification of the data, the decision trees model was used, so named because the knowledge obtained can be represented visually by a tree diagram, this model obtains its knowledge from inductive learning logical constructions. In order to carry out the classification process, questions are asked to the data, and with it to make a decision, in order to continue on a path until reaching the final decision corresponding to the classification [25].

The evaluation of the algorithm was performed using the area under the curve (AUC), as this allows us to determine the ability of the algorithm to distinguish between subjects with presence and absence of diabetes. This is because the curve plotted corresponds to the sensitivity values against specificity, measures that give us the probability of the algorithm to correctly classify patients with diabetes and patients who do not suffer from the disease. Because these measurements only take values from 0 to 1, the curve is limited to a maximum area of 1, if a value of 1 was obtained for the AUC, this would indicate that the algorithm perfectly classifies all patients. When the value of the AUC is 0.5 a straight line is formed from the point (0.0) to the point (1.1) indicates that the algorithm is unable to distinguish or discriminate between classes, so the closer the AUC value is to 1, the algorithm shows better performance [26].

4 Results

According to the implementation of each of the stages of User Centered Design (UCD) in the development of the prototype, the results that were obtained at each stage, using graphs and tables for a better understanding of the information, is shown. In addition, the results of the training and evaluation of the artificial intelligence algorithm are shown. To conduct the training and evaluation, the database divided into 2 subsets containing 70% and 30% from the data, for training and evaluation respectively.

4.1 Specify Requirements

From the surveys conducted in person and in the google forms, together the total opinion of 76 people was obtained, of whom their ages are in the range of 15 to 65 years. The results obtained from the surveys, show that the highest number of people interviewed, is in the age range between the ages of 18 to 28 with a total of 47 people, the data can be seen in Table 1, the elderly were noted to refuse answer to the survey, this was the cause of getting few surveys to people over the age of 39.

Table 1. Age of respondents.

Age range (years)	Total
−18	1
18–28	47
29–38	16
39–49	6
+50	6
Total	76

One of the main reasons for a person to make use of an mHealth app, it is necessary that it exists in it, a concern to know their health status and know how they can improve it. With the data obtained in the survey, it can be observed that more than 50% of the respondents are on the level of interest level 3 (medium) of concern for their own health, the data can be seen in Table 2.

Table 2. Percentage of concern for your health regarding age ranges.

Level of interest in your health (Five is the highest index)					
Age range (years)	1	2	3	4	5
−18	0.00%	0.00%	100.00%	0.00%	0.00%
18–28	6.38%	2.13%	31.91%	27.66%	31.91%
29–38	6.25%	0.00%	31.25%	25.00%	37.50%
39–49	16.67%	0.00%	50.00%	33.33%	0.00%
50	16.67%	0.00%	0.00%	16.67%	66.67%

Although there is a concern for their health, 44.7% of those surveyed have not been tested for diabetes, although 80.3% claim to have family members with the disease.

An interesting fact is that not many people are familiar with health care applications, and people who, if they have used them, have been mainly for fitness. The positive aspects of these experiences, was that it tracked the progress obtained, as well as providing reminders and warnings so that the user does not forget to perform the exercises, of the negative points mentioned, was were that for some applications it was always necessary to be connected to the internet for its proper functioning and had a large number of advertisements, in addition to the complexity of these, which made it difficult to use and because of their complexity they needed time to learn how to use it.

The acceptance of users for the use of an application, which through a short questionnaire shows them the percentage of their possible risk to developing diabetes, was high and more than half of users claimed that they would use it. Acceptance data for age ranges are shown in Table 3 and Fig. 2.

Table 3. Interest of people to use the application that provides their possible risk of contracting diabetes.

Level of interest for the use of the application (Five is the highest index)					
Age range (years)	1	2	3	4	5
−18	0.00%	0.00%	100.00%	0.00%	0.00%
18–28	2.13%	4.26%	12.77%	27.66%	53.19%
29–38	6.25%	0.00%	18.75%	25.00%	50.00%
39–49	16.67%	0.00%	16.67%	33.33%	33.33%
+50	16.67%	0.00%	50.00%	0.00%	33.33%

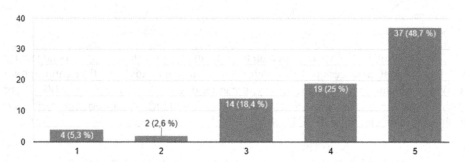

Fig. 2. Interest of people to use the application that provides their possible risk of contracting diabetes.

In addition, it is noted that there is a great interest of users to know the location of doctors and/or nutritionists in their city (see Fig. 3), they also showed acceptance that the percentage of their potential risk obtained in the application can be reviewed by a doctor and/or nutritionist, in order to keep track of the state of your health. So the idea of integrating a list of these, was accepted, the results obtained are shown in Figs. 4 and 5.

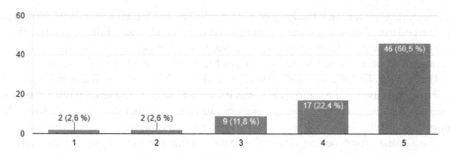

Fig. 3. Level of acceptance of people to meet doctors and/or nutritionists within their city

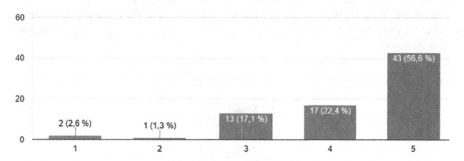

Fig. 4. Level of acceptance for doctors to monitor the result obtained in the app.

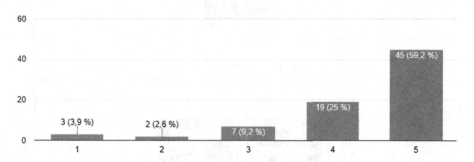

Fig. 5. Level of acceptance for nutritionists to monitor the result obtained in the app.

4.2 Produce Design Solutions and Evaluate Designs

With the data obtained in the previous stages of the User Centered Design (UCD) a low fidelity prototype was made as it is cheap and can be done in a short time which facilitates its evaluation and redesign. This type of prototype does not plan to show the final appearance of the application, however, you can use to evaluate the functionality [20].

A first prototype was made which consisted of 11 screens of which 5 presented the questionnaire questions, to navigate these questions it was necessary for the user to press a button, either back tracking or forward to answer the questions, this prototype did not consist of different colors, it contained only black and white. Similarly, these were designed with Balsamiq Mockups software, these obtained screens were passed to Justinmind to be evaluated by users and get feedback on design and ease of use.

The results obtained with the survey showed that the prototype was somewhat difficult to use, as users commented that it was difficult to be pressing several times a button to answer the questionnaire, another comment to note, was that they should change the colors used for the first prototype, as it was not pleasant for most evaluator users.

The second prototype consists of 5 screens, so that the user in just one manages to answer all the questions of the questionnaire and with a tap manage to get the percentage of their possible risk of getting diabetes, so the number of keystrokes was reduced, as well as the change in the colors used in the first prototype.

The colors used for the app can be seen on the screens in Figs. 6 and 7 showing the home screen and the start of the questionnaire that calculates your risk percentage of getting diabetes.

Fig. 6. App home screen.

Fig. 7. Questionnaire for calculating the percentage of your possible risk of getting diabetes.

On the screen presenting the percentage of your possible risk to getting diabetes was divided into 3 levels of risk, the low, medium and high level, which can be seen in Fig. 8.

Fig. 8. Screens showing all 3 risk levels.

After the percentage has been obtained, they are shown the corresponding recommendations, also from the Risk Factors Questionnaire, which can be seen in Fig. 9.

Fig. 9. Recommendations presented to users.

The final screen shows the list of both doctors and nutritionists separating them with an index to differentiate them (see Fig. 10). In addition to placing a button to return to the main screen of the application.

Fig. 10. List of doctors and nutritionists in the user's city.

With the second prototype, 5 users were tested, according to Jakob Nielsen [24], who were explained that the percentage they obtained in the app would not be true, since that was not the final app, only one of the first prototypes and only its functionality was simulated and it did not perform any calculations (see Fig. 11).

Fig. 11. Evaluation of the prototype by users.

The users participating in the focus group were of different ages, ranging from 18 to 35 years old (see Table 4), who in order to know their satisfaction with the prototype and obtain demographic data, were given a small questionnaire of 7 Questions. Which are listed below:

1. How old are you?
2. What is your sex?
3. On the scale of 1 to 5 (5 being the most difficult), how complicated is the use of the application?
4. On the scale of 1 to 5, 5 being the highest index. How much do you agree that the application meets the objective?
5. What did you like most about the application?
6. What did you not like about the application?
7. In general, what would improve the application?

The surveyed users are students of industrial electronic engineering from the Universidad Autónoma de Zacatecas.

Table 4. Ages of people who used the prototype app.

Age range (years)	Total
18	1
19	2
33	1
35	1
Total	5

The above questions resulted in the achievement of 2 types of results, which were obtained through the questions and those obtained through observation and additional comments made by users.

The following results were obtained with the questions: from question 3, mentioned above, it was obtained that the prototype was simple to use since its answer in the degree of difficulty was found on scale 1 and 2, being 1 easy and 5 difficult. With question 4 it was obtained, that the prototype meets the objective of giving the user his potential risk to get diabetes, which is based on answering a short questionnaire. What they liked most was the idea, that it is a support tool for the prevention of diabetes, as well as showing them a list of doctors and nutritionists who are in their city. Similar answers were obtained in Question 6 and 7, as some felt that the aesthetics of the app prototype needed to be improved.

Results obtained by observation and additional feedback: while users were conducting the assessment, it was observed that they showed no difficulty in answering the questionnaire, and responded quickly. Users commented that despite being only a prototype and not showing the actual risk percentage, it was alarming to get a high percentage to get the disease, which made them aware and encouraged them to look for ways to improve their health. They responded that the colors and aesthetics of the app still needed to be improved to make it more visually appealing.

4.3 Algorithm Evaluation

For the evaluation of the decision trees algorithm, 30% of the data was applied, with which an AUC of 0.758 was obtained, the curve of which can be observed in Fig. 12.

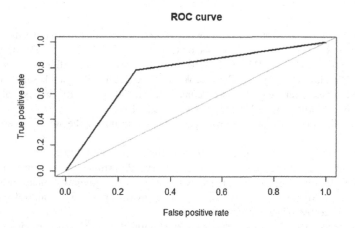

Fig. 12. Curve of sensitivity (True positive rate) against specificity (False positive rate)

5 Discussions and Conclusions

Because the questionnaire included in the application, it is based on the tool already validated by the government of Mexico to be able to know if a person is at risk of suffer diabetes, it is necessary to have a database of patients are presence and absence of diabetes, which answers all the questionnaire questions included in the application, it should be noted that the database used contains only the data that answers a few questions and not all of them.

However with the implementation of the User-Centered Design (UCD) process, an easy-to-use mHealth mobile application prototype that meets the needs of the end user was achieved. As a result of user testing in the prototype evaluation, positive feedback was obtained about the functionality and usability of the mobile app.

It is important to mention that this work is the result of the initial stage of a project that aims to develop a solution based on mobile technology for the health problem identified in México, diabetes mellitus, therefore, as a work and with the purpose of differentiating this solution from those available in the community, is intended to implement more artificial intelligence techniques such as (data mining, bigdata, deep learning, genetic algorithms) both for the analysis of information obtained by the application, as for the recommendations and feedback that will be given to the end user.

Acknowledgments. The authors be grateful for the support received to the academic and student community of the Maestría en Ciencias del Procesamiento de la Información and Ingeniería en Electrónica Industrial of the Universidad Autónoma de Zacatecas - México, as well, to the Consejo Zacatecano de Ciencia, Tecnología e Innovación (COZCyT).

References

1. Alonso, J., Mirón, J.: Aplicaciones móviles en salud: potencial, normativa de seguridad y regulación. Revista Cubana de Información en Ciencias de la Salud (2017). http://scielo.sld.cu/scielo.php?pid=S2307-21132017000300005&script=sci_arttext&tlng=pt
2. Ruiz, E., Proaño, Á., Ponce, O., Curioso, W.: Tecnologías móviles para la salud pública en el Perú: lecciones aprendidas. Revista Peruana de Medicina Experimental y Salud Pública (2015). http://dx.doi.org/10.17843/rpmesp.2015.322.1634
3. Samsung Health. https://www.samsung.com/mx/apps/samsung-health/. Accessed 07 Oct 2019
4. IMSS Digital. http://www.imss.gob.mx/imssdigital. Accessed 07 Oct 2019
5. Ramesh, A., Kambhampati, C., Monson, J., Drew, P.: Artificial intelligence in medicine. Ann. R. Coll. Surg. Engl. (2004). https://www.ncbi.nlm.nih.gov/pmc/articles/PMC1964229/
6. Organización Mundial de la Salud. https://www.who.int/es/news-room/fact-sheets/detail/diabetes. Accessed 07 Oct 2019
7. Soto, G., Moreno, L., Pahua, D.: Panorama epidemiológico de México, principales causas de morbilidad y mortalidad. Revista de la Facultad de Medicina de la UNAM (2016). http://www.scielo.org.mx/scielo.php?script=sci_arttext&pid=S0026-17422016000600008
8. Diabetes, tercera causa de muerte en Zacatecas. http://ntrzacatecas.com/2016/11/13/diabetes-tercera-causa-de-muerte-en-zacatecas-2/. Accessed 07 Oct 2019

9. Cuéntame   INEGI.   http://cuentame.inegi.org.mx/monografias/informacion/zac/poblacion/dinamica.aspx?tema=me&e=32. Accessed 07 Oct 2019
10. Klonoff, C.: The current status of mHealth for diabetes: will it be the next big thing?. J. Diab. Sci. Technol. (2013). https://doi.org/10.1177/193229681300700321
11. Galeano, R.: Diseño centrado en el usuario. Revista Q (2008). https://revistas.upb.edu.co/index.php/revista_Q/article/view/7831. ISSN 1909-2814
12. Ergonomics of human-systems interaction – Part 210: Humancentred design for interactive systems, traduced from (ISO 9241-210) (2010)
13. Cuestionario de Factores de Riesgo. https://www.gob.mx/salud/documentos/cuestionario-de-factores-de-riesgo. Accessed 07 Oct 2019
14. Diabetes - Diario de glucosa. https://play.google.com/store/apps/details?id=com.szyk.diabetes. Accessed 07 Oct 2019
15. Taherian, S., Khatibi, A., Zahedi, M.: Prediction and diagnosis of diabetes mellitus using a water wave optimization algorithm. J. AI Data Min. (2019). http://jad.shahroodut.ac.ir/article_1567.html
16. Gyuk, P., Vassányi, I., Kósa, I.: Blood glucose level prediction with improved parameter identification methods. IEEE Xplore Digit. Libr. (2017). https://doi.org/10.1109/NC.2017.8263257
17. User-Centered Design Basics. https://www.usability.gov/what-and-why/user-centered-design.html. Accessed 07 Oct 2019
18. Plaza Bicentenario recuerda el antiguo pueblo minero. http://ntrzacatecas.com/2015/06/16/plaza-bicentenario-recuerda-el-antiguo-pueblo-minero/. Accessed 07 Oct 2019
19. Crea formularios atractivos. https://www.google.com/intl/es_mx/forms/about/. Accessed 07 Oct 2019
20. Prototipado de Baja Fidelidad (Low-Fidelity prototyping). https://www.sidar.org/recur/desdi/traduc/es/visitable/tecnicas/Low.htm. Accessed 07 Oct 2019
21. Balsamiq Mockups 3 Application Overview. https://docs.balsamiq.com/desktop/overview/. Accessed 07 Oct 2019
22. Free wireframing tool. https://www.justinmind.com/free-wireframing-tool. Accessed 07 Oct 2019
23. Entrevistas y Grupos Orientados (Interviews and Focus Groups). https://www.sidar.org/recur/desdi/traduc/es/visitable/indagacion/Interv.htm. Accessed 07 Oct 2019
24. Vega, R., Rodríguez, Z., Justo, Y.: Procedimiento para realizar pruebas de usabilidad. Universidad de las Ciencias Informáticas. http://www.informatica-juridica.com/wp-content/uploads/2014/01/Procedimiento_para_realizar_pruebas_de_usabilidad.pdf
25. Quinlan, J.R.: Induction of decision trees. Mach. Learn. 1, 81–106 (1986). https://doi.org/10.1007/BF00116251
26. Fan, J., Upadhye, S., Worster, A.: Understanding receiver operating characteristic (ROC) curves. Can. J. Emerg. Med. (2015). https://doi.org/10.1017/S1481803500013336

Self-reported Methods for User Satisfaction Evaluation: A Bibliometric Analysis

Andrés F. Aguirre-Aguirre[1]([⊠]) , Ángela Villareal-Freire[1]([⊠]) ,
Jaime Díaz[2]([⊠]) , Carlos González-Amarillo[3]([⊠]) , Rosa Gil[4]([⊠]) ,
and César A. Collazos[1]([⊠])

[1] IDIS Research Group, University of Cauca, Popayán, Colombia
{afaguirre, avillarreal, ccollazo}@unicauca.edu.co
[2] Department of Computer and Information Sciences, University of La Frontera,
Temuco, Chile
jaimeignacio.diaz@ufrontera.cl
[3] GIT Research Group, University of Cauca, Popayán, Colombia
amarillo@unicauca.edu.co
[4] Research Group on Human Computer Interaction and Data Integration,
University of Lleida, Lleida, Spain
rgil@diei.udl.cat

Abstract. This research analyzes self-reported methods for user satisfaction evaluation through science mapping. The focal point of the domain fields of a user satisfaction evaluation must be fully established according to the current reality (challenges, issues and gaps) and future scientific perspectives (patterns and trends). The foregoing motivates the authors of the present article to use tools such as SciMAT to analyze the bibliographical production on user satisfaction and to identify the thematic patterns related to the user experience of particular interest in this study, such as self-reported methods, specifically SUS, SUMI and QUIS. Self-reported methods are the most frequently used evaluation tools due to their simplicity and low cost. Such methods offer information about users' subjective reactions and can become one of the most important inputs to collect and understand users' behavior, preferences and perceptions. Identifying these methods in science mapping provides understanding of their evolution throughout a certain period of time: 2001–2019 (based on a corpus of bibliographic references from 359 documents). Thanks to the analyzed information, some research opportunities were identified regarding the evaluation instruments that motivate the present study, such as the neglect of any connection between the emotional and the use of software, variety of contexts to evaluate; in addition to the promising future that is possible in the field of user satisfaction evaluation if methodologies and tools are generated or adapted for this purpose.

Keywords: User satisfaction · User experience · Self-reported methods · Subjective methods · SUS · SUMI · QUIS · SciMAT · Science mapping

© Springer Nature Switzerland AG 2019
P. H. Ruiz and V. Agredo-Delgado (Eds.): HCI-COLLAB 2019, CCIS 1114, pp. 314–331, 2019.
https://doi.org/10.1007/978-3-030-37386-3_23

1 Introduction

The world's bibliographical production has exponential numerical behaviors according to the area as well as to the historical, technological, social and political moment of societies. Therefore, it is important to include the greatest possible number of scientific studies with a diversity of approaches to have the broader picture of a field of study more precisely. Bibliometric studies not only provide information related to the areas and subareas related to the central topics in the desired field of research, but also make it possible to find research patterns and trends.

The evolution of a research field can be discovered through science mapping. In the case of user satisfaction, it is possible to learn how technological phenomena have impacted the generation of evaluation methods, in what contexts and the approach with which they are used. All these events pose the challenge of investigating the dynamics that have been constructed on the issue. Moreover, a bibliometric analysis offers the means to reach the current historical point of the area and show how the use of methods that seek to provide an understanding of the perceptions that users have of technology and quality of the user experience (UX) in general, has extended over time.

Some decades ago, digital technology was popular and used mainly by people with advanced technical knowledge [1]. Nowadays, with the appearance of emergent technologies and the evolution of the already existing ones, users have increased exponentially (and continue to grow), because technology covers almost every aspect and context of society [2]. This has meant a radical change in the way in how people interact with systems and even how they interact with one another through different digital tools.

This shows the importance of having tools that can evaluate digital technology in terms of the impact and relevance they have for the needs of current users. Although there are widely used methods to evaluate user satisfaction in the software industry and academic environments, it seems that they were not designed with the explicit approaches that support current technological development. The traditional methods have a pragmatic approach, *i.e.*, they mainly evaluate efficiency and effectiveness that users perceive regarding the system with which they are interacting [3]. However, there are aspects of the UX, like fun, entertainment and other subjective characteristics, that affect the users' overall satisfaction to the same degree or more than the pragmatic aspects do.

It is important to consider that user satisfaction is a multimodal construct that includes people's emotions, evaluations and perceptions about the different aspects inherent in their interaction with a system. Although it is certain that users could differ in what they consider more important or what gives them greatest satisfaction, there is a consensus about the multimodal nature inherent in user satisfaction [2].

This aspect highlights the importance of enriching the evaluation of user satisfaction, especially from an emotional approach, given its importance and the shortage of instruments that can measure it [4, 5]. To achieve this end, a deep understanding and attention to each detail of the interaction is required. Although the self- reported questionnaires that evaluate user satisfaction are only one type of instrument in the wide gamut of options to evaluate UX, they can (and should) be closer to covering a broader and more accuracy range of the needs that can be evaluated with this type of instruments. This poses a tremendous challenge for researchers, since their efforts should also converge on emphasizing the intangible (those aspects of an abstract nature like emotions), of course without neglecting those aspects on the pragmatic side of the UX, including usability, functionality, efficiency, etc.

In this sense, this paper presents a bibliometric study that compare different self-reported methods widely used in the academic area and software industry for the evaluation of user satisfaction. The purpose is to contribute to knowledge about the approaches, differences, limitations and level of relevance to the current technology, in particular, the way in which they assess interactions with this technology. Interaction with technology is not only what people do, but also what people feel [6]. Therefore, knowing what methods can appropriately measure and analyze user satisfaction (or at least approaching that purpose), is imperative in the current field of UX, because it becomes one of the main inputs in technology design that is consistent with the different needs of the users, their expectations and all those interaction-related aspects.

The article is organized as follows: the present introduction; Sect. 2 with the description of the research questions posed for the development of the study. Next, Sect. 3 enumerates and describes the self-reported methods considered in the study; while Sect. 4 describes the methodology followed to conduct the study. Section 5 presents the results obtained in each of the periods studied; in turn, the analysis of these periods and a general analysis of the study are provided. The conclusions of the study are presented in Sect. 6, while Sect. 7 describes some of the limitations identified. Finally, Sect. 8 offers some final observations on the results.

2   Research Questions

The evaluation of user satisfaction has been a constant challenge for the scientific community and professionals in the area of Human Computer-Interaction (HCI), since the conceptualization of user satisfaction has had different connotations and interpretations over time. Thus, it is important to gain an overview of its evolution, which can describe how the different self-reported instruments have been used to obtain and evaluate those characteristics that affect user satisfaction. In this context, the research questions addressed in this study and which guide its aims:

Can trends be identified with respect to the topics that have greatest relevance in the self-reported methods?

What are the approaches of the self-reported methods used to evaluate user satisfaction?

Is there a correspondence between the characteristics that evaluate the self-reported methods and those found in the study?

3   Design of the Study

3.1   Selection of the Instruments

As previously mentioned, there are different methods to evaluate user satisfaction. The methods highlighted by Tullis and Albert [7] serve as the starting point of this study. From these methods, an analysis was performed that could show relations among them or estimate their differences and similarities. Next, each of the user satisfaction evaluation instruments considered in this study are described:

System Usability Scale (SUS) is a variation of the traditional questionnaires. It presents a combination of statements written positively and negatively, so that the user really pays attention to each of their answers [8, 9]. SUS consists of a 10 item questionnaire, each with a Likert scale of 5 (or 7) points, which provides an overview of satisfaction with the software [8].

Software Usability Measuring Inventory (SUMI), is a method of evaluating the quality of software that allows measuring satisfaction and assessing user perception [10]. SUMI is a commercially-available questionnaire for assessing usability of software developed, validated and standardized on international databases [10, 11]. This method is referred to in standards ISO 9126 [12] and ISO 9241 [13] as a recognized tool for evaluating user satisfaction via five dimensions of usability. This tool is also available in several languages [10, 11].

Questionnaire for User Interaction Satisfaction (QUIS), is a tool developed by researchers at the University of Maryland Human-Computer Interaction Lab. Designed to assess the subjective satisfaction of users on specific aspects of the human-computer interface [14]. The current version, QUIS 7.0, assesses the user's overall satisfaction in 6 hierarchically organized facets in each of the nine interface-specific factors defined in this tool. Each facet, in turn, consists of a pair of semantic differentials arranged on a 10-point scale [14, 7]. The questionnaire is designed to be adjusted according to the analysis needs of each interface, in which only sections of interest can be considered.

Website Analysis and Measurement Inventory (WAMMI) is an online service that emerged from SUMI. Both were developed at the Human Factors Research Group (HFRG) at University College, Cork. Unlike SUMI, which is designed for the evaluation of desktop software applications, WAMMI focuses on evaluation of websites [7, 15]. This instrument consists of 20 questions that use 5-point Likert scales as answers [16, 7], and makes it possible to create a questionnaire and link it to WAMMI classification scales [7]. The result of a WAMMI analysis is a measure of "global satisfaction" [16], that is divided into 5 dimensions.

Measuring Usability of Multi-Media System (MUMMS), was developed by the same group that designed SUMI and WAMMI. MUMMS consists of a questionnaire that enables assessment of quality of use for multimedia software products [17]. Measurement aspects are the same as those SUMI takes account of and it incorporates a new one related to the user's emotional perception toward the use of the system. This tries to capture information about the fascination the multimedia application exerts on users [17].

The characteristics evaluated in each of the previously described instruments are described in Table 1:

Table 1. Characteristics of user satisfaction evaluated by different self-reported methods

Method	Characteristics evaluated
SUS	Ease of use, Usefulness, Helpfulness, Functionality, and Learnability [7]
SUMI	Efficiency, affection, utility, control, and learning [11]
QUIS	Screen factors, terminology and system feedback, learning factors, system capabilities, technical manuals, online tutorials, multimedia, teleconferencing and software installation [18, 19]
WAMMI	Attractiveness, control, efficiency, utility and learning, usability [7, 16]
MUMMS	Attractiveness, Controllability, Efficiency, Helpfulness, and Learnability [7]

4 Conduct the Study

In order to compare the methods of user satisfaction evaluation compiled, a science mapping of each of them was done using SciMAT. SciMAT is a powerful open source software tool for the analysis of the evolution and relevance of scientific production around a specific scientific area. The steps followed for this study are those generally carried out in a science mapping [20, 21]: data retrieval; data pre-processing and applying filters; design and normalize the network; science mapping; visualization and analysis. Finally, a visual interpretation of the science mapping is presented.

4.1 Data Retrieval

The first step is to construct the data set with which the study will be conducted. In this case, the Web of Science (WoS)[1] database is used, one of the most important and significant scientific databases that exists. Considering the aim of the study, the general criteria are established that define the search strings, the type of fields relevant to the search and the timeframe for the study. Consequently, the following criteria are defined:

- *Search string:* given the nature and purpose of this study, the search strings used correspond to the exact names of each instrument, *i.e.*, "*System Usability Scale*", "*Software Usability Measuring Inventory*", "*Questionnaire for User Interaction Satisfaction*", "*Website Analysis and Measurement Inventory*" and "*Measuring Usability of Multi-Media System*".
- *Search field:* the search criteria chosen is "Topic", since it has greater coverage than the rest of the criteria available in WoS, and allows the search in key fields for this study such as title, abstract, author's keywords and keywords plus.
- *Period:* the period for the longitudinal analysis is defined for studies published between 2001 and 2019.

Table 2 shows the results obtained in this phase:

---

[1] https://www.webofknowledge.com.

Table 2. Number of records obtained from WoS per method

Method	Number of records obtained from WoS
SUS	324 (*318 Articles; 6 Proceedings Paper; 4 Reviews, 2 Editorial Material*)
SUMI	16 (*16 Articles; 2 Proceedings Paper*)
QUIS	13 (*13 Articles; 3 Proceedings Paper*)
WAMMI	2 (*2 Articles*)
MUMMS	The search yielded no results

Given the results obtained in this phase, the comparison study focused mainly on SUS, SUMI and QUIS. It is worth noting that the shortage or absence of WAMMI and MUMMS records, respectively, does not mean that they have not been used in the scientific area, simply that they have not been the main object of research or that they have not had the sufficient relevance in a particular study, to prompt their appearance in the title, abstract or keywords.

4.2 Pre-processing

For the pre-processing of the compiled data set, SciMAT is used to detect and eliminate duplicate records. Since the corpora generated with each of the searches are relatively small[2], no citation thresholds for the inclusion or exclusion of documents were established.

4.3 Design and Normalize the Network

In this phase, a network is designed using descriptive terms or words as the unit of analysis; and the type of relation established for the network is co-occurrence[3]. As a similarity measure to normalize the network, an *equivalence index* is used, which makes it possible to adopt of statistical indices that represent the measure of connection between key words [22].

4.4 Science Mapping

The science mapping is the graphical representation of the scientific production around a field of research; this representation classifies the importance, the indexes associated with the production and the number of documents produced in the analyzed period.

To generate the science mapping, the algorithm of "simple centers" is used [23, 24]. This algorithm allows to locate networks of keywords that are strongly related to each other and that correspond to prominent centers of interest in the scientific community [25].

---

[2] The corpora analyzed in science mapping studies are generally thousands of records. For that reason, it is considered that those used in this study are relatively small.

[3] Co-occurrence, when two analysis units appear together in a set of documents.

4.5   Visualization and Analysis Schemes

This study focuses on the behavior of the publications, the authors and the references in different fields that center on each of the instruments for evaluating user satisfaction, seeking to detect patterns and trends in the related research topics, employing the following steps:

(1) Identification of research topics, with the normalization of the network, different research topics are identified. This process allows the grouping of keywords in the network that are strongly linked to research topics of great interest.

(2) Strategic diagram of clusters, this type of diagram shows the groups for every period and orders them in a two-dimensional space determined by *centrality* (x axis) and *density* (y axis). *Centrality* corresponds to the degree of cohesion of a network with other networks (external cohesion of the network). On the other hand, *density* represents the level of internal strength of the network (internal cohesion of the network).

The measures of centrality and density allow to categorize the clusters detected in a certain period [22]. These clusters represent the research topics of a given research field, and they are mapped in the two-dimensional space of the strategic diagram. According to the positioning that the cluster has in this space, it can be classified in one of the four groups: (1) *upper-right quadrant* holds the motor clusters; (2) *upper-left quadrant* shows highly developed and isolated clusters; (3) *lower-left quadrant* includes emerging topics or declining topics; (4) *lower-right quadrant* contains basic and transversal clusters. While the location of a cluster shows what a topic represents within a certain period (according to the classification of the quadrants of the strategic diagram), the volume of a sphere is proportional to the number of documents that belong to it.

In this sense, the strategic diagram of clusters offers essential information to reveal and understand the dynamics of a research field, and therefore, it is one of the main analysis inputs in this study.

5   Results Analysis

In order to perform the analysis of the compiled information, 19-year study period (2001–2019) was divided into two subperiods, organized according to the number of publications that mark a milestone in the increase or decrease in publications related to the methods of user satisfaction evaluation. Hence, an effort was made so that the years established to delimit the periods would make notable changes in the research initiatives recognizable, *i.e.*, it was designed in such a way that the trends and patterns of use of the instruments would be evident in the change of period.

5.1   First Sub-period

The first subperiod (2001–2010) is characterized by a similarity in the contexts and approaches in which SUS, SUMI and QUIS are used. In the following, the behavior of different areas (shown as spheres) for each of the instruments is explained in detail.

Presentation of First Period Results. In the strategic diagram of SUS (see Fig. 1), two spheres are highlighted that correspond to *usability* and *functionality*.

For the case of *usability*, its location and volume illustrate that it has neutral centrality, but with strong density. This behavior responds to the objective nature of usability, *i.e.*, its relation with other topics is neutral given that it is not an abstract concept like other areas that comprise user satisfaction. The high density that the diagram shows on *usability* is understood as a strong cohesion of the topics that comprise *usability*.

On the other hand, *functionality* is characterized as having strong centrality, but neutral density. Since *functionality* is related to multiple functions that make up the system, it is logical to see that it has strong centrality. The density of the *functionality* shown in the diagram, describes a dynamic behavior of the topics related to *functionality*, derived from the multiple contexts, applications, functions that are evaluated.

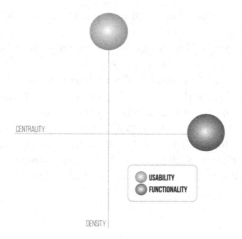

Fig. 1. Strategic diagram of SUS from period one (SciMAT adaptation)

In the strategic diagram of SUMI (see Fig. 2), two spheres corresponding to *usability* and *cognitive science* are highlighted.

As can be seen, *usability* maintains the location and volume of SUS, *i.e.*, its approaches and interpretation are equal.

The cluster *cognitive science* shows strong centrality and neutral density, as well as a small volume compared to usability. *Cognitive science* is an area related to the creation of mental models, design, analysis of experiments, etc.; therefore, it is possible to see that it has strong centrality. The density that shows this cluster describes the diversity of areas that comprise cognitive science.

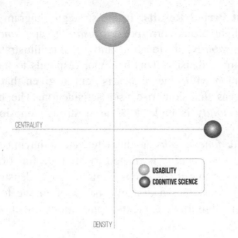

Fig. 2. Strategic diagram of SUMI from period one (SciMAT adaptation)

In the strategic diagram of QUIS (see Fig. 3), mainly two spheres can be observed that correspond to *functionality* and *interface design*.

In the case of the *interface design* cluster, there is neutral centrality with high density. Neutral centrality is due to it being an area that focuses on the style and appearance of the interfaces, that although it is related to other areas, its approach is concrete and limited. The high density that this cluster shows is understood as how strongly linked are the topics that underlie the interface design field.

The *functionality* cluster is characterized as having strong centrality, but neutral density. Given that this behavior is similar to that of SUS in the first period, its interpretation is similar.

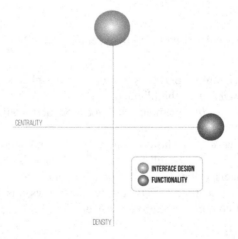

Fig. 3. Strategic diagram of QUIS from period one (SciMAT adaptation)

General Analysis of First-Period Results. In this period the predominant approaches of user satisfaction evaluation are the areas of *functionality* and *usability*, *i.e.*, these are motors topics and are characterized by their pragmatic approach to evaluation. As can be seen in Table 3, *functionality* and *usability* appear in more than one method, whereas the areas of *cognitive science* and *interface design* only stand out in one method (SUMI and QUIS, respectively).

Table 3. Predominant topics in each method during the first period (2001–2010)

	Functionality	Usability	Cognitive science	Interface design
SUS	X	X		
SUMI		X	X	
QUIS	X			X

In short, *functionality* and *usability* are indeed the topics of greatest relevance in this period. When analyzing the location of these topics in the strategic diagram, two main aspects are noted:

(1) Spatial location of the outstanding topics, both *functionality* and *usability* keep their positioning in the diagram, which suggests that the dynamics, treatment and relevance afforded to these topics is the same although they have been detected in different self-reported methods.

(2) Nature of the highlighted topics, although *functionality* and *usability* are motors topics, they are different in nature. As suggested in previous sections, high centrality and neutral density that shows *functionality* reveal that it is a significant topic and of great importance, but its development continues throughout this period. On the other hand, the topic of *usability* is characterized as having high density with neutral centrality, which shows that it is a highly developed area, characterized as being too specialized and peripheral.

5.2 Second Sub-period

In the second sub-period (2011–2019), the change in the volume of the spheres that represent the research topics is apparent. However, some disappear and new ones appear. The extant topics change their location according to the patterns and trends of the studies. Next, the interpretation of different areas drawn in each strategic diagram for each of the instruments is explained:

Presentation of Second-Period Results. In the SUS strategic diagram (see Fig. 4), three nodes related to *acceptance*, *design* and *health* stand out.

The cluster that represents *design* has a location with relatively weak centrality and density. This is due to the *design* being a broad and dynamic concept that can cover various fields, from interaction design, to interface design, which although they can be strongly related, are significantly different. It is also worth noting that despite not having a large volume (compared to health), it is considered one of the motor clusters of this period.

The cluster that represents *acceptance* shows low centrality and density. The location of this cluster on the two-dimensional space can be interpreted as an emergent yet poorly evolved area.

The cluster that represents *health* has remarkably strong centrality and density. For its volume and location, it is considered as a motor cluster in this period. Its appearance reveals that it is a context in which SUS is widely used.

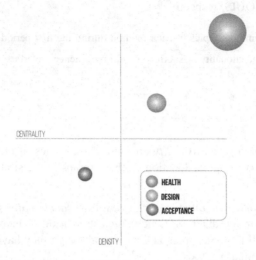

CENTRALITY

HEALTH
DESIGN
ACCEPTANCE

DENSITY

Fig. 4. Strategic diagram of SUS from period two (SciMAT adaptation)

The strategic diagram of SUMI (see Fig. 5) contains 2 clusters that belong to *functionality* and *usability*.

The cluster that represents *usability* shows high centrality and neutral density. The neutrality of the cluster density expresses the discrete approach that usability has with respect to other topics to which it can be related. As already mentioned, the strong centrality that characterizes *usability* in this period shows the internal strength that links the areas that comprise *usability*.

The functionality cluster is characterized as showing strong centrality and neutral density. Given that this behavior is similar to that of SUS in the first period, its interpretation is similar.

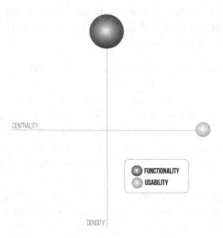

CENTRALITY

FUNCTIONALITY
USABILITY

DENSITY

Fig. 5. Strategic diagram of SUMI from period two (SciMAT adaptation)

In the strategic diagram of QUIS (see Fig. 6), mainly two clusters can be observed that correspond to *interface design* and *cognitive science*.

For the case of the *interface design* cluster, neutral centrality and density can be observed. This can be understood as interface design ceasing to be a motor cluster in the treatment of QUIS.

In the case of the *cognitive science* cluster, it is characterized as having very strong centrality and density, and it is constituted as a motor cluster in this period. Its appearance reveals it as one of the important areas that revolve around QUIS.

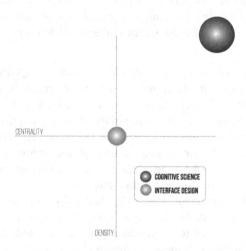

Fig. 6. Strategic diagram of QUIS from period two (SciMAT adaptation)

The diagrams shown previously demonstrate that the volume of the clusters and their location in the two-dimensional plane maintains strong similarities between them. Another evident aspect in the two periods is the conservation of the motor clusters, mainly those that comprise *usability* and *functionality*. Current publications related to SUS, SUMI and QUIS continue to turn on these two topics, neglecting other aspects equally or more important that make up user satisfaction in the new technological era.

General Analysis of Second-Period Results. Unlike the first period, this period is characterized because none of the topics detected in each of the self-report methods compiled in this study being repeated in another, *i.e.*, in SUS, SUMI and QUIS different topics are detected that are not common among them (Table 4 provides the predominant topics in each of the methods). However, not only are characteristics detected but also complex areas that include other areas (better known as umbrella terms), and that extend the range of topics and characteristics that commonly revolve around user satisfaction.

Table 4. Predominant topics in each method during the second period (2011–2019)

	Functionality	Usability	cognitive science	Interface design	Acceptance	Health	Design
SUS					X	X	X
SUMI	X	X					
QUIS			X	X			

The topics detected in this period were diverse and with similar positioning and volume. This makes it difficult to highlight the topics of greatest relevance. However, when analyzing the location of these topics in the strategic diagram, two main aspects are noted:

(1) Spatial location of the outstanding topics, SUS and QUIS are different from SUMI mainly because in them motors topics of considerable importance are detected: *health* (in SUS) and *cognitive science* (in QUIS) are cases that stand out from the others because their positioning in the strategic diagram indicates that they are highly developed and important topics for the construction of the scientific field around the evaluation of user satisfaction through self-reported methods. Similarly, this could be indicated for the topic of *design* but on a smaller scale than to the other two, given its size and positioning in the diagram.

On the other hand, *acceptance* is the only cluster that appears in another quadrant different from the others; its location supposes that it is still developing and thus still lacks importance compared to the remaining topics detected in the study.

(2) Nature of the highlighted topics, although almost all the topics detected in this period are motors (with the exception of *acceptance*), they are highly diverse in nature. The measures of centrality and density vary in most cases, *i.e.*, there is no pattern of similarity between the results obtained, each one offers different information, and for that reason its interpretation varies as has been indicated in the description of each strategic diagram.

5.3   General Analysis of the Results of the Science Mapping

Can trends be identified with respect to the topics that have greatest relevance in the self-reported methods?

The change in the volume and location of the spheres that represent the research topics is seen clearly in the transition from one period to another.

Usability is a topic that has transcended from period to period (detected in SUMI). The change in the volume of the cluster that represents usability shows that there is a decrease in the works related to the topic. As reported in recent studies, the usability of a product cannot be the only determinant factor, not even the main one, in user satisfaction [26, 27]. In terms of location, it can be seen that centrality increases from one period to another, which shows the strengthening that usability has with group structures from other topics, *i.e.*, how it affects and is affected by other aspects inherent in the UX. This has also entailed a reduction in its density, since its understanding has changed over time, something that is reflected in its conceptual redefinition, an example of this is the concept established in the standard ISO/IEC 9126-4 [12] and how it has been redefined in the standard ISO/IEC 25010:2011 [28].

Another topic that has remained in the two periods studied, is the *interface design* (detected in QUIS), its initial volume decreases compared to the second period, which indicates that there are fewer investigations on the *interface design* in the works published about QUIS. On the location of this cluster, a reduction in its density is noted, which may be related to the evolution of the technology and therefore that of its interfaces. This constant and accelerated change has involved a restructuring of the related areas, and that is a topic in permanent development.

What are the approaches of the self-reported methods used to evaluate user satisfaction?

With respect to the topics detected in both periods, the Fig. 7 illustrates which topics transcended from one period to another. The figure shows that *usability* and *interface design* are topics that have maintained in both periods, which suggests they are key topics in the evaluation of user satisfaction with SUMI and QUIS respectively.

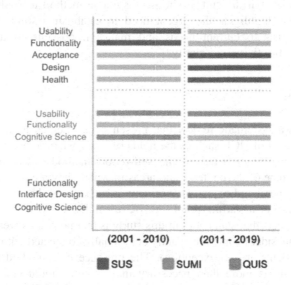

Fig. 7. Topics detected in each self-reported method during the two study periods

On the other hand, SUS presents the most noteworthy changes, since the topics that are characteristic in the first period disappear completely in the second, where not only characteristics (like *functionality* and *usability*), but also areas (like *design* and *acceptance*) and contexts (like *health*), are highlighted. This is consistent with the dynamism and coverage in the conceptualization of user satisfaction.

It is worth mentioning that topics disappearing from a period does not mean that they do not continue to be related to the research fields in which they were highlighted at the beginning; but that they did not have sufficient relevance to be detected and located in some quadrant of the two-dimensional space of the strategic diagram of the later period.

Is there a correspondence between the characteristics that evaluate the self-reported methods and those found in the study?

Another of the main findings in this study is that the topics detected in the scientific mapping performed on each of the self-reported methods compiled (SUS, SUMI and QUIS) do not correspond entirely to the characteristics that each of these methods evaluates (see Table 1). This is largely due to the lack of conceptual clarity regarding user satisfaction, a consequence of the various approaches in how user satisfaction is understood, which differ according to the context or aim of the study. Added to this is the constant technological progress and widespread growth inherent in the use of interactive systems generally. This has brought a constant change and evolution in the interactions between users and technology, and has posed a great challenge to find a consensus about the conceptual structure of user satisfaction. In fact, many of the methods used nowadays for their evaluation continue to be governed under the anachronistic parameters with which user satisfaction used to be understood. This aspect not only makes it difficult to choose a suitable method to evaluate user satisfaction, but it also highlights the urgent need to establish a solid theoretical construction that adjusts to current needs and makes it possible to understand user satisfaction with objectivity and clarity.

6   Conclusions

This study offers a systematic review that presents the research trends on user satisfaction in the context of HCI, such as the fields of study where most of the research is focused, the main characteristics of the self-report methods used to evaluate user satisfaction, and some of the contexts and areas to which they are most closely related. This provides a general and objective overview of each one of the methods, which can serve as a reference or a starting point for UX researchers.

One of the aspects that stands out in this study is that no results were found related to users' emotional side. People are usually emotionally connected with the things they use (software systems are no exception). The presence of a method that covers the emotional spectrum is more than necessary in this new digital era. This aspect is becoming increasingly relevant and invites the redesign of the different user satisfaction evaluation mechanisms, so as to encompass a holistic overview of user satisfaction.

The scientific overview generated from the perspective of user satisfaction evaluation from the bibliometric analysis determined a promising horizon in the possible adjustment of tools and methodologies to better approach the understanding of the factors that influence the quality of experience according to the context in which the user performs. For this reason, the self-reported methods need an adaptation to the today's historical and technological moment, in which the quality of the experience mapped out by emotions, perceptions, expectations, etc., plays a decisive role in individuals' daily activities.

Microelectronics, the Internet of Things (IoT) ecosystems, the ubiquity of sensors, record systems and data transparency (security), added to data analysis (Artificial

Intelligence, Big Data) for decision-making, demand useful data with more rigor for the generation of services based on experience in fields like Smart Cities, Learning, Automotive Autonomy, Health, Recreation, Agriculture and all those in which satisfaction is the main quality factor. Therefore, it is essential to devise alternatives of user satisfaction evaluation with application domain approaches. Factors that will influence and determine the future of technologies and the way they are designed.

7 Limitations

It is important to have a significantly larger corpus to perform a science mapping that allows obtaining more revealing and significant findings for a longitudinal and conceptual analysis of a scientific topic. Of course, this is subject to the research topic and to the publications that have been generated around it.

8 Discussion

WoS and Scopus are considered the main sources of data for bibliometric studies [29]. In fact, the comparison of these two main databases has been an active area of study and discussion, and has produced several scientific publications.

In this study, WoS was taken as the main source of data, but given the reduced size of the corpus obtained, Scopus was also considered. However, the results obtained with Scopus were quite similar to those of WoS. A report published in [29], highlights that in most cases the studies that compared WoS and Scopus from a bibliometric perspective obtained similar results between the two databases through a variety of indicators. In this report they also highlight that the quality of the data collected with Scopus has a poor performance compared to those in WoS. It should be underscored that the quality of the data also has a direct impact on the quality of the bibliometric indicators that can be compiled. This aspect and the similarity of the data collected with the two bibliographical databases, motivated the authors of this article to stay with WoS.

Acknowledgements. This work was (partially) financed by the Dirección de Investigación, Universidad de La Frontera.

References

1. Moggridge, B.: Designing Interactions. The MIT Press, Cambridge (2007)
2. Calvo, R.A., Vella-Brodrick, D., Desmet, P., Ryan, R.M.: Positive computing: a new partnership between psychology, social sciences and technologists. Psychol. Well Being **6**, 10 (2016)
3. Aguirre, A.F., Villareal-Freire, Á., Gil, R., Collazos, C.A.: Extending the concept of user satisfaction in e-learning systems from ISO/IEC 25010. In: Marcus, A., Wang, W. (eds.) DUXU 2017. LNCS, vol. 10290, pp. 167–179. Springer, Cham (2017). https://doi.org/10.1007/978-3-319-58640-3_13

4. Aguirre, A.F., Villareal, Á.P., Collazos, C.A., Gil, R.: Aspectos a considerar en la evaluación de la satisfacción de uso en Entornos Virtuales de Aprendizaje. Rev. Colomb. Comput. **16**, 75–96 (2015)
5. Capota, K., Van Hout, M., Van Der Geest, T.: Measuring the emotional impact of websites: a study on combining a dimensional and discrete emotion approach in measuring visual appeal of university websites. In: Proceedings of the 2007 Conference on Designing Pleasurable Products and Interfaces, 22–25 August 2007. ACM (2007). https://doi.org/10.1145/1314161.1314173
6. Shahriar, S.D.: A comparative study on evaluation of methods in capturing emotion (2011)
7. Tullis, T., Albert, W.: Measuring the User Experience: Collecting, Analyzing, and Presenting Usability Metrics. Morgan Kaufmann (2013). https://doi.org/10.1016/c2011-0-00016-9
8. Brooke, J.: SUS - A quick and dirty usability scale. In: Jordan, P.W., Thomas, B., Weerdmeester, B.A., McClleland, I.L. (eds.) Usability evaluation in industry, pp. 189–194. Taylor & Francis, Abingdon (1996)
9. Hartson, R., Pyla, P.: The UX Book: Process and Guidelines for Ensuring a Quality User Experience. Morgan Kaufmann, Burlington (2012)
10. Kirakowski, J., Corbett, M.: SUMI: the software usability measurement inventory. Br. J. Educ. Technol. **24**, 10–12 (1993)
11. Software Usability Measurement Inventory (SUMI). Human Factors Research Group, University College Cork (1993). http://sumi.ucc.ie/index.html. Accessed 22 Jan 2015
12. ISO/IEC TR 9126-4: Software engineering – Product quality – Part 4: Quality in use metrics (2004)
13. ISO 9241-11: Ergonomic requirements for office work with visual display terminals (VDTs) – Part 11: Guidance on usability (1998)
14. Chin, J.P., Diehl, V.A., Norman, K.L.: Development of an instrument measuring user satisfaction of the human-computer interface. In: Proceedings of the SIGCHI Conference on Human Factors in Computing Systems, pp. 213–218 (1988)
15. Kirakowski, J., Claridge, N., Whitehand, R.: Human centered measures of success in web site design. In: Proceedings of the Fourth Conference on Human Factors & the Web (1998)
16. Lindgaard, G., Dudek, C.: What is this evasive beast we call user satisfaction? Interact. Comput. **15**, 429–452 (2003)
17. Measuring the Usability of Multi-Media System (MUMMS). Human Factors Research Group, University College Cork (1996)
18. Chin, J.P., Diehl, V.A., Norman, K.L.: Questionnaire For User Interaction Satisfaction (QUIS). Human-Computer Interaction Lab, University of Maryland at College Park (1988). https://isr.umd.edu/news/news_story.php?id=4099. Accessed 19 Nov 2018
19. Johnson, T.R., Zhang, J., Tang, Z., Johnson, C., Turley, J.P.: Assessing informatics students' satisfaction with a web-based courseware system. Int. J. Med. Inform. **73**, 181–187 (2004)
20. Börner, K., Chen, C., Boyack, K.W.: Visualizing knowledge domains. Ann. Rev. Inf. Sci. Technol. **37**, 179–255 (2003)
21. Cobo, M.J., López-Herrera, A.G., Herrera-Viedma, E., Herrera, F.: Science mapping software tools: review, analysis, and cooperative study among tools. J. Am. Soc. Inf. Sci. Technol. **62**, 1382–1402 (2011)
22. Callon, M., Courtial, J.P., Laville, F.: Co-word analysis as a tool for describing the network of interactions between basic and technological research: the case of polymer chemsitry. Scientometrics **22**, 155–205 (1991)
23. Coulter, N., Monarch, I., Konda, S.: Software engineering as seen through its research literature: a study in co-word analysis. J. Am. Soc. Inf. Sci. **49**, 1206–1223 (1998)

24. Cobo, M.J., López-Herrera, A.G., Herrera-Viedma, E., Herrera, F.: An approach for detecting, quantifying, and visualizing the evolution of a research field: a practical application to the fuzzy sets theory field. J. Informetr. **5**, 146–166 (2011)
25. Cobo, M.J., Martínez, M.A., Gutiérrez-Salcedo, M., Fujita, H., Herrera-Viedma, E.: 25 years at knowledge-based systems: a bibliometric analysis. Knowl.-Based Syst. **80**, 3–13 (2015)
26. De Angeli, A., Sutcliffe, A., Hartmann, J.: Interaction, usability and aesthetics: what influences users' preferences? In: Proceedings of the 6th Conference on Designing Interactive Systems, pp. 271–280 (2006)
27. Sonderegger, A., Sauer, J.: The influence of design aesthetics in usability testing: effects on user performance and perceived usability. Appl. Ergon. **41**, 403–410 (2010)
28. ISO/IEC 25010:2011, Systems and software engineering – Systems and software Quality Requirements and Evaluation (SQuaRE) – System and software quality models. International Organization for Standardization (2011)
29. Grégoire, C., Roberge, G., Archambault, É.: Bibliometrics and Patent Indicators for the Science and Engineering Indicators 2016. SRI International (2016)

Software System for the Support
of Mouse Tracking Tests

David Alejandro Albornoz[1]([✉]) [iD], Sebastián Alejandro Moncayo[1] [iD],
Samir Ruano Hoyos[1] [iD], Gabriel Elías Chanchí Golondrino[2] [iD],
and Patricia Acosta-Vargas[3] [iD]

[1] Institución Universitaria Colegio Mayor del Cauca, Popayán, Colombia
{alejo.albornoz, sebastian.moncayo,
samir.ruano}@unimayor.edu.co
[2] Universidad de Cartagena, Cartagena, Colombia
gchanchig@unicartagena.edu.co
[3] Universidad de Las Américas, Quito, Ecuador
patricia.acosta@udla.edu.ec

Abstract. Among the tests that contribute to improve the usability of a software product are those based on mouse tracking. Currently, there are tools for the execution of mouse tracking tests, most of which do not allow to discriminate the analysis by areas of the screen or the analysis of the trace in a specific task of a user test. In this paper we present a software system for the execution of usability tests under the mouse tracking approach, which allows the capture of the mouse trace, the analysis of the areas of interest per task and the generation of the video of the session. Through the proposed software system, we hope to obtain specific recommendations regarding the adequate disposition of the elements on the screen. The proposal can serve as a starting point in future work and help in the development of more usable applications.

Keywords: Mouse tracking · Software system · Usability · Usability test

1 Introduction

The rise of new technologies such as the internet of things and the exponential development of the network of networks have enabled the growth in the number of applications deployed on the Internet, as well as the need for those applications to be more appropriate at the quality level to user needs [1]. Therefore, usability [2] has become a fundamental issue for the development of computer systems, since it defines the productivity of the user and companies with respect to a software application.

According to ISO 9241-11, usability is defined as the degree to which a product can be used by certain users to achieve its objectives with effectiveness, efficiency and satisfaction in a specific context of use [3]. This definition describes the three attributes (efficiency, effectiveness and satisfaction) that must be taken into account to estimate the degree of usability of a software product [4]. The efficiency attribute is referred to the fulfillment of the user's objectives, while the efficiency to the optimization of the

© Springer Nature Switzerland AG 2019
P. H. Ruiz and V. Agredo-Delgado (Eds.): HCI-COLLAB 2019, CCIS 1114, pp. 332–344, 2019.
https://doi.org/10.1007/978-3-030-37386-3_24

resources, being time the most important resource for the user. Finally, the satisfaction attribute is associated with the comfort of a user during the interaction [5].

In a test developed within a usability laboratory, efficacy can be obtained from the percentage of tasks performed by the test user. With regard to efficiency, this can be measured by the time spent by the user to perform the tasks defined by the test coordinator [6]. For its part, the attribute satisfaction, defined according to ISO 9241-11 as "absence of discomfort and existence of positive attitudes towards the use of a product" [3], is directly related to the emotionality of a user during the interaction with the evaluated software [7].

Similarly, one of the indicators that can be used to estimate the efficiency attribute is the number of clicks or mouse trace that a user performs during a given task in a usability test [6]. In this order of ideas, mouse tracking tests allow us to obtain relevant indicators in order to organize the different elements on screen in a more adequate way, with the purpose of making the interaction of the user with the evaluated software more efficient. In this way, from the mouse trace it is possible to detect the interface sectors of a certain software that can be redesigned in areas of higher hierarchy [8, 9].

According to Rayner [10] since the 1970s, monitoring systems have been used, among which the ocular systems stand out in the area of human computer interaction. These systems have a wide range of movement behaviors including the eyepiece that have been associated with mouse movements. On the other hand, there are multimodal data acquisition devices such as those presented in [11], where relevant data are provided for studies related to monitoring and ocular sampling. Although these eye tracking systems have a comparatively long history, the mouse tracking field has developed several interesting approaches to mouse movements. This is largely related to usability testing of web pages in order to improve the user experience.

Although there are commercial and academic tools for the execution of mouse tracking tests, most do not allow the analysis discriminated by areas of interest on the screen, or the analysis of the trace in a given task of a user test developed in a usability laboratory. In this way, in this article we present as a contribution a software system for the execution of mouse tracking tests, which in addition to capturing the mouse trace, allows the analysis of different areas of interest during the different tasks of a test of usability, as well as recording a video of the session. In this order of ideas, through the analysis by tasks and areas of interest of the screen, the software system intends to support the coordinators of the test in terms of detecting frequently used options that are located in areas of low hierarchy.

The proposed software system was developed in the Java language, making use of the EasyCapture, OpenCSV and JFreeChart libraries, which respectively allow the recording of the video session, the storage of the coordinates and the time in a CSV file, and finally the generation of statistical graphs from the data captured in the usability test. The rest of the article is organized as follows: in Sect. 2 the methodology considered in this research is presented. Section 3 describes the relevant concepts that were taken into account in this work. In Sect. 4, a set of tools that were considered for the design of the proposed software system are presented. Section 5 shows the functional diagram of the software system and its final interfaces. Section 6 describes a case study in which the software system was used. Finally, Sect. 7 presents the conclusions and future work derived from this research.

2 Methodology

This research applies the user-centered design (UCD) [12, 13], for the development of the usability testing tool under the mouse tracking approach. User-centered design is an iterative process in which designers focus on users and the needs of each phase of software development. Figure 1 contains the UCD including six phases (1) characterize usability tests, (2) inspect mouse tracking tools, (3) record tool requirements. (4) design the tool, (5) develop the tool, (6) expert user evaluation. For its part, the scrum methodology was used to develop the software system, which was proposed by Ken Schwaber and Jeff Sutherland [14]. Scrum allows rapid prototyping under an environment where requirements are incomplete at inception and change during the software development cycle [15].

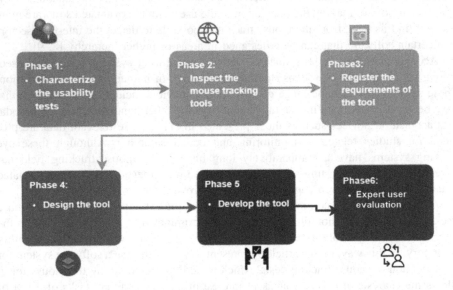

Fig. 1. Proposed methodology

Phase 1: Characterize the usability tests, in this phase the developers together with the evaluators carried out a study of the structure of the user tests developed in the usability laboratory, with the purpose of adapting the tool to the needs of the tests. Usability testing consists of procedures and techniques applied in the design and development of software, through which evaluators evaluate the degree of use, using empirical methods to optimize the user experience. The information obtained from the tests serve as support when applying changes in the tool, besides they are essential in the agile development of a software.

Phase 2: Inspect the mouse tracking tools, in this phase the developers selected a set of tools in order to evaluate and examine whether they meet the needs of a usability test. The developers explored and interacted with the Mouseflow, User-Track, and IoGraph tools.

Phase 3: Register the requirements of the tool, in this phase the developers registered the most important characteristics of the tool for the execution of usability tests under the mouse tracking approach. For example, it must be user-friendly and intuitive, multi-platform, offering visual reports of recordings made in individual sessions, with the registration of hot and cold clicks.

Phase 4: Design the tool, after characterizing the usability tests and inspecting the mouse tracking tools the developers obtained prerequisites to design the tool. Previously the developers designed Mockups to assist in the design of the tool's user interfaces.

Phase 5: Develop the tool, during this phase the developers built the tool with the requirements of the previous phases. The evaluators consider that the user tests are focused on the development of tasks.

Phase 6: Apply in a case study, in this phase, a group of experts in the area of human computer interaction, inspected the usability of the software system, taking into account Nielsen's heuristic principles.

3 Conceptual Framework

This section presents the main concepts that were taken into account for the development of this work. Among these are: usability laboratory, usability test and efficiency attribute.

3.1 Usability Laboratory

A usability laboratory is a physical space generally composed of two modules, one for the test user and the other for the test coordinators, in which usability evaluations are performed on products, systems and devices, by means of software and hardware specialized in monitoring and recording the user's actions with the product to be evaluated. A usability laboratory must be able to obtain indicators of the attributes of efficiency, effectiveness and satisfaction in accordance with ISO 9241-11 [7, 16].

3.2 Usability Test

It is a technique used in the software development process, by means of which the degree of use of these is evaluated, by inspecting the interaction of the test user with these applications. The main characteristics are the use of isolated physical spaces and constant monitoring with specialized software and hardware [17]. Among the usability tests, the mouse tracking approach stands out, through which it is possible to determine interface elements that are not properly distributed and whose location can contribute to improving the efficiency of the evaluated software [18]. According to ISO 9241-11 [3], efficiency is defined as the relationship between the resources employed and the precision and degree of achievement with which users achieve their objectives. Among the metrics used to determine the efficiency attribute are: time spent completing a task, number of keys pressed per task, time spent on each screen, relative efficiency compared to an expert user [6].

4 Mouse Tracking Tools

This section presents a set of tools that allow the support of usability tests under the mouse tracking approach. Within these tools are: Mouseflow, UserTrack, IoGraph.

4.1 Mouseflow

It is a tool for the analysis of the mouse trace in web applications, which runs in the background, allowing screen recordings, recordings of the movement of the mouse and generating statistics on the points where the user focuses attention when navigating in a web portal. The above in order to redistribute the different elements of a web portal such as: color, text, multimedia components, the location of different options, in order to improve the experience of a user on the site and make more efficient interaction. The tool includes five main components: session repetition (recordings), heat maps (click, movement, displacement, attention), funnels, shape analysis and user comments. Although Mouseflow allows monitoring of points of interest in which the user focuses attention during the interaction, the tool does not include the analysis of areas of interest on the screen, nor does the discrimination of the mouse trace by tasks [19].

4.2 UserTrack

It is an analytical tool that is currently under active development, which is designed to contribute to the improvement in the design of web portals, by defining from the mouse trace possible components of the interface to be relocated. This tool besides enabling the control of visitors to a website, allows the generation of heat maps and videos with the trace of a user's mouse during the interaction with a website. Heat maps are generated using three colors: green, yellow and red, depending on the trace and the time the mouse remains in a certain location on the screen. The green color is used when the time that the mouse remains in a position is short, the red color is used when the mouse stays longer in a position, while the yellow color corresponds to an intermediate time. Although UserTrack obtains data of interest about the mouse trace and where the user focuses its attention, it does not allow the analysis of the mouse trace by tasks or areas of interest by tasks of a usability test [20].

4.3 IoGraph

IoGraph is a free desktop tool developed in Java, which runs in the background and allows the capture and graphic representation of the mouse trace during a usability test. This tool also allows the capture of a background image and superimposes the captured mouse trace on it, to later enable the analysis of the test results. This tool also includes the feature of drawing points of interest in which the mouse remains still. Although this tool is intuitive and easy to use, it does not allow the analysis of the mouse trace by areas of interest, nor the analysis by tasks in a user test [21].

From the tools explored in this section, it is possible to conclude that none of these focuses on the analysis by time of each task, which is very useful in usability tests, in order to determine what is the behavior of a user in a given test task. In this sense, the tool proposed in this paper includes the analysis by areas of interest in each test task.

5 Proposed Software System

This section describes the flow and block diagram of the software system, as well as its final interfaces.

5.1 Software System Flow Diagram

Based on the different characteristics of a test developed in a usability laboratory, Fig. 2 shows the flow diagram of the software system for mouse tracking. In the first instance, once the software system has been executed, the test coordinator chooses whether to register a new session or to analyze the data previously stored in previous sessions. In case of choosing the option to register a new session, the test data such as the name of the session, the date, the name of the users among other basic data are entered. Then, parallel to the start of the usability test, the software system proceeds to obtain and store continuously and temporarily the x and y coordinates of the mouse

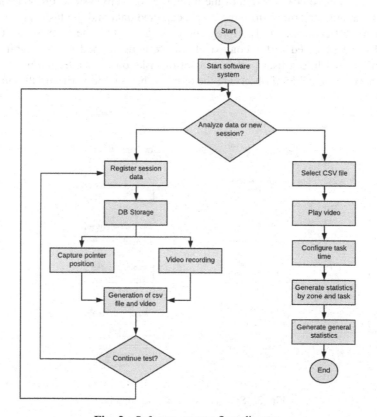

Fig. 2. Software system flow diagram

pointer, as well as the time elapsed since the test starts. While the pointer coordinates and time are recorded, the proposed software system is responsible for starting the recording of the video that captures the different user interactions with the software evaluated, using the EasyCapture library. Once the test is finished by the user, the software system generates a report with the data stored in a plain text file type CSV. This format was chosen in order to also allow the test coordinator to review the data in an excel spreadsheet.

Once the data is stored in the CSV file, it is possible to proceed with the recording of a new user session (repetition of the previous phase) or it is possible to continue with the analysis of the data captured and stored in the CSV. In the same way the test coordinator can proceed with the reproduction of the video generated in the session with each of the participating users. For the analysis of the areas of interest in the different tasks of a test, it is important that the test coordinator has recorded the duration in seconds of each of the tasks developed by users during the test, so that once provided the times of the tasks of each user, it is possible to make an analysis by area of interest of the tasks and the test in general.

5.2   Software System Block Diagram

Figure 3 shows the block diagram of the proposed software system, differentiating the functions that are performed from the user's captured data and the tasks performed by the usability test coordinator. The foregoing considering that the software system was designed to be executed in the context of user tests developed in the usability laboratory, in which while a user performs a set of tasks on a specific software, the test coordinator is responsible of observing the user's behavior and verifying the fulfillment of the tasks.

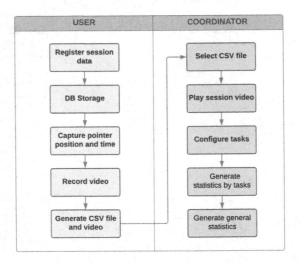

Fig. 3. Software system block diagram

In that order of ideas, in the first instance the software system allows to register the test data and store it in a database. Then, based on the tasks performed by the user within the usability laboratory, the tool is responsible for capturing in real time the pointer positions and the time associated with these captures. Also, while the user is performing the interaction, the software system is responsible for capturing a video of the session, which will allow the test coordinator to perform a detailed analysis of the user's behavior in a given task or at a general level. Once the different usability test tasks have been completed, the software system generates a.csv file that contains mouse trace information and the time in which each pair of coordinates has been captured.

When the usability test has finished, the coordinator is in charge of analyzing the results obtained, loading in the first instance the generated CSV file. Subsequently, the test coordinator can access the different videos generated, in order to verify the duration of each of the tasks performed by a specific user. From the completion of the times of the different tasks in the software system, it is possible to visualize the analysis by zones in each task and in a general way. By means of these results it is possible to make decisions related to the readjustment in the location of the components of the interface towards zones of more hierarchy in screen, looking for that the evaluated software offers a greater efficiency to the user.

5.3   Final System Software Interface

Based on the functionalities described in Sects. 5.1 and 5.2, Fig. 4 shows the main graphic interface of the proposed software system. To the left of the interface the different options of the tool are shown, which allow the configuration of the sessions, the capture of the mouse trace, the configuration of the tasks and the graphical analysis of the mouse trace by tasks and of general way. On the right side, by default, there is an interface that allows the loading of a CSV file from a previous session, as well as displaying the video associated to that session. In the same way it is possible to type the duration of the different test tasks associated with the loaded session, by means of which it is possible to analyze the mouse trace by areas of interest.

Fig. 4. Main interface of the software system

After loading the CSV file and specifying the duration of the different tasks of the test, the test coordinator can press the "Start Analysis" button, which allows to visualize in the option: "Partial Graphs", the mouse trace per task and in the option: "Total Graph", the complete trace of the test, as shown in Fig. 5. This allows the test coordinator to identify if the disposition of certain interface elements involved in each of the tasks is adequate.

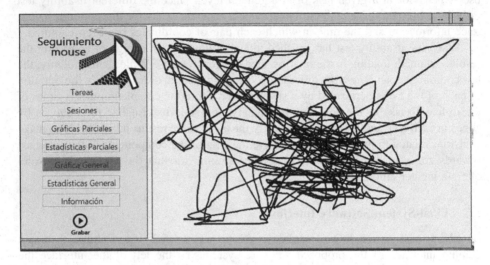

Fig. 5. Mouse trace generated by the software system

Finally, as shown in Fig. 6, it is possible to perform an analysis by areas of interest on the screen, according to the different tasks of a usability test. This allows you to visualize the areas of the screen most used in a test task, and then identify if certain elements of the screen are correctly located in a specific test task.

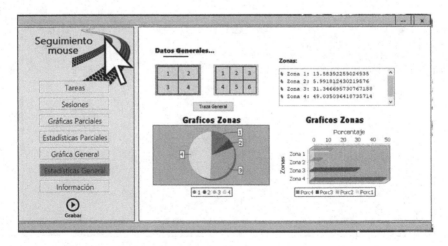

Fig. 6. Analysis by areas of interest

6 Expert User Evaluation

In order to evaluate the software system proposed in this article, a usability inspection was carried out with three experts in the area of human computer interaction. Usability testing is the generic name for a set of effective ways to evaluate user interfaces for usability problems, which are informal and easy to use. This method consists of forming a group of usability experts who analyze or inspect a particular application. The evaluators make a report commenting on different aspects of usability of the application, based on their experience in the area and taking into account a set of previously defined principles. This method consists of forming a group of usability experts who analyze or inspect a particular application. The evaluators make a report commenting on different aspects of usability of the application, based on their experience in the area and taking into account a set of principles previously defined. The generated report is used by the developers of the inspected software, in order to solve the usability problems identified by the evaluators. Two of the most used of such methods are: heuristic evaluation and cognitive walkthrough [6]. In this research work, an inspection method was used taking into account Nielsen's heuristic principles.

As a result of the inspection carried out on the proposed software system, the evaluators highlighted the advantages in terms of segmentation of the mouse trace by tasks and the analysis of the results by areas of interest on the screen. Similarly, Table 1 presents the main suggestions made by the evaluators according to Nielsen's heuristic principles.

Table 1. Evaluators suggestions

Heuristic	Suggestions
H1. Visibility of system status	It is suggested in each of the interfaces of the software system to include the title of the corresponding section, in order to locate the coordinator of the test on the task being performed
H2. Match between system and the real world	It is recommended to improve the functionality of discriminating tasks, since separating tasks by using ";" can be confusing for the test coordinator It is suggested to provide an additional option to the software system that allows the test coordinator to customize the number of zones to be analyzed on screen
H9. Aesthetic and minimalist design	It is suggested to separate the analysis by 4 zones and by 6 zones in different sections in order not to overload the information presented on the screen
H10. Help and documentation	Although the software system generated is mostly intuitive, it is suggested to include a help option and/or contextual help to guide the test coordinator in conducting a usability test under the mouse tracking approach

7 Conclusions and Future Work

The importance of usability tests under the mouse tracking approach, is that through the better distribution of the elements on screen, it is possible to improve the indicators of the efficiency attribute, so that a user can take less time to execute a certain task within the evaluated software.

The software system proposed in this investigation was built according to the characteristics of a conventional user test developed in a usability laboratory, so that it allows the analysis of mouse traces per test task, which is a input regarding similar tools, taking into account that usability tests are conducted by tasks. In the same way, the software system provides the use of different areas of interest, which can contribute to making decisions about possible areas of the screen that are not being used properly. Finally, the proposed software system also presents as a contribution the generation of a video with the interaction made by the user during the test, which allows the test coordinator to control the time of the tasks performed by the user.

The proposed software system stores the data of the user interaction with the software to be evaluated (mouse coordinates and time trace) in a CSV-type file and processes this data according to the duration of the usability test areas. This allows to present and filter in a graphic way the mouse trace in the different tasks, which is intended to help in the decision making of the test coordinator on the interface elements that can be relocated to make more efficient the software evaluated with respect to the different tasks.

The software system proposed in this article aims to be supportive in terms of the execution of usability tests, so that it allows obtaining complementary data that can generate recommendations about the appropriate location of the interface elements. This thanks to the advantages provided by the software system with respect to the analysis by areas of interest and by tasks of a usability test. In this sense the software system allows an analysis of the screen to 4 and 6 areas of interest divided equally.

Among the suggestions made to the software system by expert evaluators, the need to customize the number of areas of interest for analysis and improve the functionality of task discrimination is highlighted. Likewise, the evaluators highlighted the advantages of the software system in terms of the analysis of the mouse trace by areas of interest and by tasks of the test.

At the level of the technologies used for the construction of the proposed software system, it is important to emphasize that the Java language has the advantage of having a set of APIs that enable the capture of the mouse trace, the recording of videos of the interaction and the storage of the traces in CSV files. In this sense, unlike other programming languages, Java allows for easy integration of these libraries into the project, without requiring additional installations. Thus, the technologies used are intended to serve as a reference for the construction of projects for the study of the mouse trace in different contexts of application.

The importance of usability tests under the mouse tracking approach, is that through the better distribution of the elements on screen, it is possible to improve the indicators of the efficiency attribute, so that the user can take less time to execute a specific task within the evaluated software. In the same sense, it is intended to conduct affective computing studies from the mouse trace captured during a usability test, in order to contribute to the estimation of the satisfaction attribute.

References

1. Arroyo, E., Selker, T., Wei, W.: Usability tool for analysis of web designs using mouse tracks. In: CHI 2006 extended abstracts on Human factors in computing systems, April 2006, pp. 484–489. ACM (2006). https://doi.org/10.1145/1125451.1125557
2. Sánchez, W.: La usabilidad en Ingeniería de Software: definición y características. Revista de Ingeniería e Innovación de la Facultad de Ingeniería - Universidad Don Bosco 1(2), 7–21 (2011)
3. ISO 9241-11. https://www.iso.org/obp/ui/#iso:std:iso:9241:-11:ed-2:v1:en
4. Mascheroni, M., Greiner, C., Petris, R., Dapozo, G., Estayno M.: Calidad de software e Ingeniería de Usabilidad. In: XIV Workshop de Investigadores en Ciencias de la Computación. Universidad Nacional de Misiones (UNM), La Plata-Argentina (2012)
5. Cepeda, C., et al.: Mouse tracking measures and movement patterns with application for online surveys. In: Holzinger, A., Kieseberg, P., Tjoa, A.M., Weippl, E. (eds.) CD-MAKE 2018. LNCS, vol. 11015, pp. 28–42. Springer, Cham (2018). https://doi.org/10.1007/978-3-319-99740-7_3
6. Enriquez, J.G., Casas, S.I.: Usabilidad en aplicaciones Móviles. Revista Informe Científico Técnico UNPA 5(2), 25–47 (2013)
7. Delgado, D., Girón, D., Chanchí, G., Márceles, K.: Propuesta de una herramienta para la estimación de la satisfacción en pruebas de usuario, a partir del análisis de expresión facial. Revista Colombiana de Computación 19(2), 6–15 (2018). https://doi.org/10.29375/25392115.3438
8. Hehman, E., Stolier, R., Freeman, J.: Advanced mouse-tracking analytic techniques for enhancing psychological science. Group Processes Intergroup Relat. 18(3), 384–401 (2014). https://doi.org/10.1177/1368430214538325
9. Freeman, J., Ambady, N.: MouseTracker: software for studying real-time mental processing using a computer mouse-tracking method. Behav. Res. Methods 42(1), 226–241 (2010). https://doi.org/10.3758/brm.42.1.226
10. Rayner, K.: Eye movements in reading and information processing: 20 years of research. Psychol. Bull. 124, 372 (1998). https://doi.org/10.1037/0033-2909.124.3.372
11. Tobiipro: Eye tracking for research (2019). https://www.tobiipro.com/. Accessed 31 May 2019
12. Hassan, Y., Martín Fernández, F., Iazza, G.: Diseño web centrado en el usuario: usabilidad y arquitectura de la información. Hipertext net 2 (2004)
13. Salvador-Ullauri, L., et al.: Development of an accessible video game to improve the understanding of the test of Honey-Alonso. In: Nunes, I.L. (ed.) AHFE 2019. AISC, vol. 959, pp. 289–298. Springer, Cham (2020). https://doi.org/10.1007/978-3-030-20040-4_26
14. Schwaber, K., Beedle, M.: Agile Software Development with Scrum, vol. 1. Prentice Hall, Upper Saddle River (2002)
15. López-Martínez, J., Juárez-Ramírez, R., Huertas, C., Jiménez, S., Guerra-García, C.: Problems in the adoption of agile-scrum methodologies: a systematic literature review. In: Software Engineering Research and Innovation, pp 141–148. IEEE (2016). https://doi.org/10.1109/conisoft.2016.30

16. Perurena, L., Moráguez, M.: Usabilidad de los sitios Web, los métodos y las técnicas para la evaluación. Revista Cubana de Información en Ciencias de la Salud **24**(2), 176–194 (2013). https://doi.org/10.36512/rcics.v24i2.405.g306
17. Calvo-Fernandez, A., Ortega, S., Valls, A.: Métodos de evaluación con usuarios. Editorial Universidad de Cataluña, Cataluña-España (2004)
18. Unrau, R., Kray, C.: Usability evaluation for geographic information systems: a systematic literature review. Int. J. Geogr. Infor. Sci. **33**(4), 645–665 (2019). https://doi.org/10.1080/13658816.2018.1554813
19. Mouseflow. https://mouseflow.com
20. UserTrack. https://www.usertrack.net/
21. IoGraph. http://iographica.com/

Storytelling with Holograms
for the Development of Reading Competence

Julio Vera Sancho[1]([⊠]) [iD], Keyda De la Gala Quispe[1] [iD],
and Klinge Villalba Condori[2] [iD]

[1] Universidad Nacional de San Agustín de Arequipa, Arequipa, Peru
{jveras, kdelagala}@unsa.edu.pe
[2] Universidad Continental, Huancayo, Peru
Kvillalba@continental.edu.pe

Abstract. The use of emerging technologies such as interactive 3D virtual environments has improved the learning process in different areas in recent years, but their lack of interest and lack of interest in Educational Institutions for the use of these technologies and the use of traditional development strategies of reading competence, resulting in poor school performance in the area of communication and a decrease in PISA (Program for International Student Assessment). This paper proposes the creation and implementation of a low-cost, real-time holographic image generation model, using Blender, Kinect to detect the movements of a person and Ni-Mate that manages the data captured by the Kinect device. The research consists of five stages, the first one analyzes, designs and develops the assessment tools for reading competence, as the second stage the compilation of appropriate readings within the framework of the reading competence in PISA, so the third stage is an analysis and 3D model design, based on a satisfaction survey, as fourth the adequacy of space for better visualization and interaction of the teacher who tells the stories with the holograms generated and finally consider the research variables to make a comparison of the results obtained. In this project that proposes the use of hardware and software for the generation of low-cost interactive holograms, it will improve reading skills in students of Regular Basic Education (EBR) of primary level.

Keywords: Augmented reality · Holograms · Educational software · Reading comprehension

1 Introduction

In the last Sampling Evaluations of 2018 applied in Peru, in reading there was a percentage decrease of 8.6% compared to last year, in the satisfactory level 46.4% to 37.8%, in process 47.3% to 56.4% and beginning of 6.3% to 5.8% [1], this has led to low academic performance, consequently not being able to understand any type of texts causing frustration and rejection of complex readings that are carried out.

The rapid development of information and communication technology (ICT) is affecting several aspects of human life, including education. ICT in educational contexts is an electronic network to search, collect, store, process, transport and deliver

© Springer Nature Switzerland AG 2019
P. H. Ruiz and V. Agredo-Delgado (Eds.): HCI-COLLAB 2019, CCIS 1114, pp. 345–355, 2019.
https://doi.org/10.1007/978-3-030-37386-3_25

information effectively and quickly. Today, hologram technology is one of the rapidly evolving technologies. Although hologram technology in the educational environment is still new, it has the potential to help the student's learning process. The use of hologram technology in teaching and learning can train active students in the process of acquiring knowledge it can provide opportunities for students to observe, classify, develop and modify their personal knowledge, in addition to participating actively and collaboratively [2].

Therefore, emerging technologies such as holograms have the potential to be used in the classroom to complement other teaching and learning materials being a real challenge in the educational plan, since this technological tool is increasingly interactive and with greater applicability and communicative potential, so it would contribute to improve their student reading skills by allowing them to interact in a natural, active, participatory and practical way.

2 Related Jobs

In the present paper, 3D hologram technology in the learning environment presents the importance of this technology in our lives, and in the learning environment in particular, identifying the strengths and weaknesses of holograms as a teaching tool, with the end of a teacher survey in the United Kingdom and, therefore, the questionnaire has been used as a data collection technique. However, show that 45.5% of respondents confirm the importance of holograms as an effective teaching tool for the future. However, 47.3% of the teacher in all the mentioned stages that this technology cannot change the aspect of education, but can help in the way of teaching, the main barriers that can hinder the integration of holograms in the Researcher's environment have become a very interesting topic tool, as well as in the cost of teaching, and also in the cost of implementation today, the researcher believes that it is very interesting to use this technology in the teaching process, even if it is very expensive to currently implement [3].

In 2018 Magdalena Wójcik Holograms in libraries-the potential for education, promotion and services addresses the issue in the application of holograms in cultural institutions. The purpose of this project is to define the potential areas for the use of holograms in libraries, particularly in education, promotion and also in services. Three methods are used, the analysis method, the literature critique as well as the comparative method to determine the potential application areas of the holographic techniques in the libraries and finally, the situational analysis method known by the management sciences was used, determine the SWOT with the use of holograms in cultural institutions. The document can help initiate the debate on the opportunities and risks of the use of holograms in cultural institutions and their impact on the reader, the analysis carried out showed that holograms have a wider potential use in the library than initially assumed because it is not limited to education, promotion and services, but also includes documentation, research and exhibitions. Holograms could bring many benefits, but it is very important to ensure that both managers and employees of cultural institutions have the opportunity to expand their knowledge of new technologies to make responsible decisions about the introduction of these tools in their institutions and be prepared to counteract any negative aspect that arises from its use [4].

In the present paper Sharon Golder, Augmented 3D Holograms in Higher Education, Increasing Students' Learning Outcome Scores: A Mixed-Methods Study increased scores of student learning outcomes: a mixed methods study, the current study begins with first-year medical students, focusing on themselves the use of 3D holograms achieves a better score on student learning outcomes and experiences with holograms for educational purposes, designating two groups for the treatment and control group, showing that the survey and interview data of 82.9% stated that their experiences with the use of 3D holograms had a positive effect on their learning compared to 17.1% of the students who declared that their experiences with the use of 3D holograms had little or no effect on their learning. The results showed that 84.7% of the students had a significant positive experience with the use of 3D holograms compared to 15.3% of the students who did not have significant experiences, 87.5% of the students had a positive outlook on the use of 3D holograms as a tool, compared to 12.5% of students who had a negative perspective on the use of 3D holograms as a learning tool, the implications of the current study indicate that most students look for new ways to learn and they perceive the treatment as a new learning tool, also improving in the implementation of the treatment and the learning environment that play an important role since it significantly increases their results, in conclusion the students are not only welcome with new ways of learning but also seek New ways of learning [5].

In 2017 Rose Khairunnisa Roslan, 3D Spatial Visualization Skills Training Application for School Students Using Hologram Pyramid proposes a concept called 3D model of spatial visual skills training (3D SVST), this SVST 3D model is applied as the basis for developing a application to improve 3D visualization skills among elementary students using a floating imaging technology known as Hologram Pyramid, as a sample had a total of fifty fourth grade students from local schools in the state of Selangor, participants were students 10 years of different races like Malay, Chinese and Indian. The instruments before and after the test were developed based on the standardized test of visualization skills, these tests were divided into three sections, the first in mental rotation task (MRT), the second virtual construction component (VBC) and the third as a paper folding task (PFT), each section has two questions, the objective of the pretest is to obtain the performance level of the students' visualization ability through exercises using ordinary paper tests by rotating them before were exposed to the hologram pyramid. Once the pre-test was conducted, participants received exposure to visualization training using the hologram pyramid, in general, students need help to improve their visualization skills to perform better in STEM-related subjects, this study showed that the floating imaging technology used by the hologram pyramid can provide a potential solution to improve student visualization skills and can create the interest of students in the field of Science, Technology, Engineering and Mathematics [2].

3 Theoretical Fundament

3.1 Competence of the Communication Area

This competence is defined as a dynamic interaction between the reader, the text and the sociocultural contexts that frame reading. The reading competence is understanding, use, evaluation, reflection and commitment to texts in order to achieve their own goals, develop personal knowledge and potential, and participate in society [6].

This competence involves the combination of the following capabilities:

- Obtain information from the written text: This process consists in finding a specific data, information or text according to the purpose of the reader. In everyday life, readers often use texts to locate - for example - a particular data that interests them or browse the Internet to search for a text with particular characteristics.
- Infers and interprets text information: The student builds the meaning of the text, establishes relationships between the implicit and explicit information based on these, the student integrates the information to build the general meaning of the text and explain the purpose and intention of the author.
- Reflect and evaluate the form, content and context of the text: In this process of reflection and evaluation both relate as the student moves away from written texts. Now reflecting involves comparing and contrasting aspects of the content of the text. Evaluating involves analyzing, assessing and constructing an opinion and critical judgment about the different aspects of text content and the relationship with other texts, in their socio-cultural context of the reader and the text.

3.2 Reading Comprehension

Reading comprehension is the ability of an individual to capture as objectively as possible what an author wanted to convey through a written text. Therefore, reading comprehension is a concept encompassed by a broader one that is reading competence. Reading competence is the ability of a human being to use his reading comprehension in a productive way in the society that surrounds him [7]. The levels of reading comprehension are [8]:

a. Literal level: In this first level the reader has to assert two fundamental abilities such as recognizing and remembering; At this level, questions addressed to the [9]:

- Recognition, location and identification of elements.
- Recognition of details: Names, characters, time, etc.
- Recognition of the main ideas.
- Recognition of secondary ideas.

b. Inferential level: The second level implies that the reader makes conjectures and hypotheses of the reading, will be consigned in this level questions addressed to [10]:

- The inference of additional details that the reader might have added.
- The inference of the main ideas, for example, the induction of a meaning or moral teaching from the main idea.
- The inference of the secondary ideas that allows to determine the order in which they must be if in the text they do not appear ordered.

c. Criterial level: The third level corresponds to the critical reading or evaluative judgment of the reader, and with a [11]:

- Judgment on reality.
- Judgment on fantasy.
- Judgment of values, this level allows reflection on the content of the text.

3.3   Blended Learning

Blended learning is nowadays a frequently used term in media manuals and teaching technologies [12] It was defined as "the mixed use of face-to-face and non-face-to-face environments" [13] but it has evolved towards pedagogical designs in which the type of activities and the relationship between both environments are required, for example, the flipped classroom. As a result, today's blended learning environments present a wide variety of formats and pedagogical designs. [14] classifying it into four categories:

- Type of instruction: master, active, etc.
- Distribution medium
- Location: at home, in a public place or in a specific place.
- Synchrony: simultaneous, successive activities in the timeline.

3.4   Hologram

The word, hologram is composed of the Greek terms, "holo" for "full vision"; and the meaning of the "written" gram. A hologram is a three-dimensional record of the positive interference of laser light waves [3]. The form of execution of the holograms is creating the illusion of three-dimensional images. A light source is projected onto the surface of an object and dispersed. A second light illuminates the object to create an interference between the two sources. Essentially, the two light sources interact with each other and cause difficulties, which appears as a 3D image.

The word 'holography' is defined as a whole record, the holography can record all the information about an object in the form of an image [15]. It is the saving of the audiovisual resources, to then be projected on a surface, it allows a transformation of images, relocating the light that reflects it and placing it in such a way that in human view the object that is represented can be seen in different planes at the same time, that superimposed on reality, modify the vision we have of our environment.

4   Materials and Methods

4.1   Blender

Blender is a software open source for the creation of 3D models. It is compatible with all 3D pipe modeling, animation, simulation, rendering, composition and motion tracking, including video editing and game creation. Blender is cross-platform and works equally well on Linux, Windows and Macintosh computers. Its interface uses OpenGL to provide a consistent experience. To confirm specific compatibility, the list of supported platforms indicates that the development team tests regularly [16].

Blender was written in the Python programming language and, through the use of it, enables the implementation of add-ons, which provides the function of new functions without the need to change the source code, some resources are presented for the creation of animations in this tool.

Animation in Blender. In Blender the concept of keyframe is used to perform the animation manually. Thus, the animator positions the characters and objects of the scene in a certain time of the animation and then modifies its positioning, recording it in a new time position. With the keyframes recorded, Blender automatically generates the intermediate images, through the interpolation of the points that compose the image, being that this interpolation is called F-Curve [17].

4.2 Kinect

The Kinect is a sensor capable of detecting the movements of a person and determine the distance between the sensor and that person or other objects, created by Microsoft in association with PrimeSense, unlike ordinary cameras, the Kinect works as a depth camera [17]. The RGB camera (Red, Green, Blue) is used to capture the surroundings, colors and their shape. The IR matrix is responsible for locating objects in space. To do this, use two techniques [18]:

- The closer an object of the IR emitter is, the brightness of the reflection determines the proximity of that object.
- The location of the IR emitter and the IR camera is different, therefore, on one side of the object, a shadow is created which, depending on the proximity between objects, will be more or less large.

From the techniques of exposed operation, it is possible to obtain a good precision the position and shape of each object that is in front of the camera. In addition, with the image captured by the camera RGB, you can easily create a 3D simulation of the object with its colors and other elements. An additional advantage is that since it consists of several emitters and the IR camera, it does not need external lighting for proper operation.

4.3 Ni-Mate

It is a program that is responsible for receiving and managing the data captured by the Kinect V2 device. Thanks to a dedicated plug-in for Blender, you can make animations and applications with this 3D tool. The free version is the one used and can also be used for other types of sensors such as Leap Motion, PrimeSense Carmine, Intel RealSense, OpenNI and OpenNI2. With this, it is sufficient for the work that is going to be done with the application to be developed. With the paid version, up to 6 different users can be detected, in addition to adding more sensors to be managed at the same time and other functions [19].

5 Proposal

We propose the create a model of architecture at low cost for the creation of holograms, to improve reading competence, motivating students of Regular Basic Education the importance of understanding the texts, and demonstrate that in an immersive way you can learn and improve reading skills.

5.1 Preliminary Evaluation of Students

In this stage, the tools for the evaluation of reading competence are analyzed, designed and developed for 2nd and 4th grade students of the Regular Basic Education, this evaluation is through scenarios, which describe communicative situations that allow the reader to move from one text to another according to a reading purpose. Generally, the scenarios involve reading two or three texts that respond to the proposed communicative situation. Additionally, from the situations, questions are posed that evaluate different abilities and that have different levels of difficulty. An evaluation based on scenarios seeks to represent in an authentic and contextualized way the way in which a reader interacts with texts [20].

We will evaluate the reading competence, according to the abilities to locate information, comprehension, evaluation and reflection, through their abilities, then we will create a tool to evaluate the preferences of different readings, which can be modeled in 3D and later projected through holograms.

5.2 Compilation of Readings

In this stage a compilation of appropriate readings will be made within the framework of the reading competence in PISA, these readings will have a structure based on scenes that will make it possible to measure the reading competence, in Fig. 1, the structure of a stage and its elements: description of the communicative situation, texts, transitions and questions. It should be noted that the structure of the scenes is not fixed: the number of texts, transitions and questions is variable.

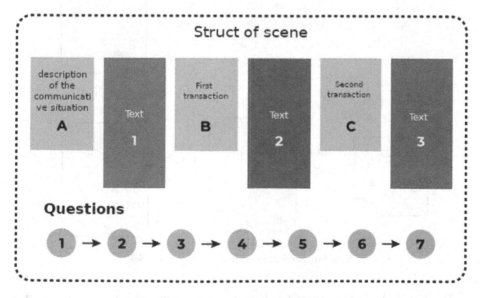

Fig. 1. Struct of a scene [20]

5.3   Analysis and Design of 3D Models

For a better user experience, an analysis and design of the 3D models will be carried out, based on a satisfaction survey carried out on a group of students, based on the selected readings. As part of the design is that we will use Blender for modeling and Kinect to make the animations so you have a better flow of movements. The connection of Kinect to Blender is that the Ni Mate complement is used, this complement will allow us to preview a Full Skeleton to see the movements captured by the Kinect.

5.4   Generation of Holograms

In this stage we will generate low cost holograms, for which we will prepare a space that will be adapted for a better visualization and interaction of the teacher who narrates the stories with the holograms, for this we will use the following structure. In Fig. 2, the structure for generation of holograms is shown, for this, we will have two people, the teacher narrator, who interacts with an assistant who is hidden, the assistant will make the movements according to the interaction with the teacher narrator; the Kinect team will read the movements of the assistant to process it, and generate the movements in real time of the 3D models, and the projector will be responsible for projecting the processed and animated movements of the 3D model to a structure that we will call holographic equipment, that will generate the holograms.

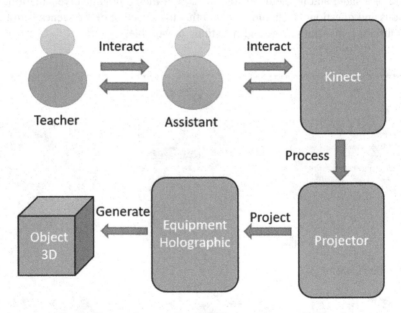

Fig. 2. Struct of generation of hologram. Source: Self made

The Fig. 3 shows the low-cost holographic equipment, which is a structure that receives the projection of images, on a transparent surface, that crosses diagonally on a cube-shaped structure, which will cause a 3D image is projected, and with the help of the kinect and the help of the assistant, interactive 3D images will be generated with the teacher narrator, which acts as a motivational factor for the development process of reading competence.

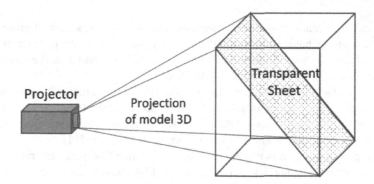

Fig. 3. Equipment holographic of low cost. Source: Self made

The Fig. 4 shows the holographic equipment and its projection of a 3D model, it should be noted that the transverse mesh that crosses the equipment, must be transparent to highlight the 3D model.

Fig. 4. Equipment Holographic. Source: Self made

5.5   Final Evaluation

To perform an evaluation, we must take into account our research variables, where our dependent variable is reading competence, and our independent variable is holograms, and we must see the relationship and effect that holograms have on reading competence.

For them an evaluation will be carried out, and two groups, a control group and an experimental group have to be formed, to which has been made in both groups of similar conditions, two evaluations, a preliminary evaluation and a final evaluation, for later make a comparison of the results obtained.

As part of the results obtained from both groups for reading competence, the following aspects were taken as indicators: Understand, evaluate and reflect, where an analysis with normal adjustment test of the Kolmogorov - Smirnov sample will be made, where we will determine if it has a normal distribution [11].

For the part of holograms is that the factors of Human Computer Interaction (HCI), of which we select, ergonomics and usability, will be taken as an indicator, for which an instrument based on questionnaire and observation is created.

6   Conclusions

In this research work has presented the architecture and implementation of a model of generation of holographic images of low cost in real time, which will help in the process of development of reading competence, has presented a set of technologies that are at scope and that can be used for the benefit of learning and encouragement for students to motivate them to read.

In this research work has presented the architecture and implementation of a model of generation of holographic images of low cost in real time, which will help in the process of development of reading competence, has presented a set of technologies that are at scope and that can be used for the benefit of learning and encouragement for students to motivate them to read, a process of development and evaluation has been presented for the use of emerging technologies focused on education and its importance in the future short term.

The development of holograms and their application in education, offers us great advantages for your learning process, such as: offering an attractive and interactive visualization of a representation of something real or fictitious, attractive and efficient communication between the teacher and the students, motivate students in their learning process and improve creativity in the presentation of educational content.

7   Further Work

As a continuation of this research work, it is still possible to follow research in holograms and other similar technologies, which help in a more interactive way the work of the teacher in the teaching and learning process, can use low-cost alternatives of technologies that are within the reach of teachers, and improving and creating more creative solutions and innovating in the field of education, there is also open blended learning research with the use of these technologies.

References

1. MINEDU: Resultados de la evaluación censal de estudiantes 2018 (2018)
2. Roslan, R.K., Ahmad, A.: 3D spatial visualization skills training application for school students using hologram pyramid. JOIV: Int. J. Inf. Vis. **1**(4), 170–174 (2017). https://doi.org/10.30630/joiv.1.4.61
3. Ghuloum, H.: 3D hologram technology in learning environment. In: Informing Science & IT Education Conference, pp. 693–704 (2010)
4. Wójcik, M.: Holograms in libraries–the potential for education, promotion and services. Library Hi Tech **36**(1), 18–28 (2018). https://doi.org/10.1108/LHT-11-2016-0142
5. Golden, S.A.: Augmented 3D holograms in higher education, increasing students learning outcome scores: a mixed methods study. Ph.D. thesis, Keiser University (2017)
6. MINEDU: Resultados de la evaluación censal de estudiantes 2018 (2019)
7. Pérez, E.J.: Comprensión lectora vs competencia lectora: qué son y qué relación existe entre ellas. Investigaciones sobre lectura (1), 65–74 (2014). https://doi.org/10.19052/ap.1048
8. Gordillo Alfonso, A., Flórez, M.d.P.: Los niveles de comprensión lectora: hacia una enunciación investigativa y reflexiva para mejorar la comprensión lectora en estudiantes universitarios (2017). https://doi.org/10.19052/ap.1048
9. Pinzás García, J.: Se aprende a leer, leyendo, ejercicios de comprensión de lectura para los docentes y sus estudiantes. Un Nuevo Maestro para el Milenio (2001)
10. Cassany, D.: Aproximaciones a la lectura crítica: teoría, ejemplos y reflexiones. Tarbiya, Revista de investigación e innovación educativa (32) (2017)
11. De la Gala Quispe, K., Vera, J.: Uso de la realidad aumentada mejora los niveles de comprensión lectora en estudiantes de quinto grado del nivel primario
12. Bartolomé Piña, A., García-Ruiz, R., Aguaded, I., et al.: Blended learning: panorama y perspectivas (2018). https://doi.org/10.5944/ried.21.1.18842
13. Bartolomé Piña, A.R.: Blended learning. conceptos básicos. Pixel-Bit: Revista de Medios y Educación **23**, 7–20 (2004)
14. González-Gómez, D., Jeong, J.S., Rodríguez, D.A., et al.: Performance and perception in the flipped learning model: an initial approach to evaluate the effectiveness of a new teaching methodology in a general science classroom. J. Sci. Educ. Technol. **25**(3), 450–459 (2016). https://doi.org/10.1007/s10956016-9605-9
15. Ramachandiran, C.R., Chong, M.M., Subramanian, P.: 3D hologram in futuristic classroom: a review. Periodicals Eng. Nat. Sci. **7**(2), 580–586 (2019). https://doi.org/10.21533/pen.v7i2.441
16. Blender: Free and open source 3D creation. Free to use for any purpose, forever (2019). https://www.blender.org/about/
17. Melo, F.C.: Kinected blender: uma solução para criação de animações 3D utilizando kinect e blender (2017)
18. Conjero Vila, R.: Diseño y desarrollo de una aplicación de control de ejercicios defisioterapia mediante el uso del dispositivo kinect v2. Ph.D. thesis (2017)
19. Ni-Mate: Motion capture made simple (2019). https://ni-mate.com/about/
20. MINEDU: Pisa la competencia lectora en el marco de pisa (2018). http://repositorio.minedu.gob.pe/bitstream/handle/MINEDU/5908/La%20competencia%20lectora%20en%20el%20marco%20de%20PISA%202018.pdf

Structure of a Guide for Usability Evaluation in Virtual Learning Environments

Vanessa Agredo-Delgado[1,2(✉)] [ID], Juan David Pinto-Corredor[2] [ID],
Cesar A. Collazos[2] [ID], Pablo H. Ruiz[1,2] [ID],
and Habib M. Fardoun[3,4] [ID]

[1] Corporación Universitaria Comfacauca – Unicomfacauca,
Street 4 Number 8–30, Popayán, Colombia
{vagredo, pruiz}@unicomfacauca.edu.co
[2] Universidad del Cauca, Street 5 Number 4–70, Popayán, Colombia
juandavidpinto4444@gmail.com,
ccollazo@unicauca.edu.co
[3] Information Systems, Faculty of Computing and Information Technology,
King Abdulaziz University, Jeddah, Saudi Arabia
hfardoun@kau.edu.sa
[4] Computer Science Department, College of Arts and Science,
Applied Science University, Al Eker, Bahrain

Abstract. Usability is an important factor in determining software quality, therefore, its evaluation is very important for the design process of usable software systems, as well as for the development of tests about its final performance to suggest improvements in different stages of the development life cycle. The usability evaluation of an interactive system is an important step in the User-Centered Design since it allows obtaining the usability characteristics of the system and the measurement in which usability principles are being applied, besides that it implies several activities that depend on the evaluation method to be implemented. To make this evaluation there are different methods, which present methodological defects and whose application depends on many variables, which makes it unreliable its use and it more complicated choosing methods to evaluate a Virtual Learning Environment (VLE). For this reason, this paper proposes a guide to be applied a usability evaluation in these contexts, in whose construction process a literature analysis was made to identify and select the usability evaluation methods that were subsequently applied in a VLE, to choose the ones that best adapted to the context and with them generate the guide. In addition, a case study was conducted to validate the usefulness, applicability, and complexity of the guide. According to the case study results, it can be considered that the guide is useful and applicable despite considering a lot of information that makes it complex and difficult to use.

Keywords: Education · Virtual learning environments · Usability · User experience · Usability evaluation methods

© Springer Nature Switzerland AG 2019
P. H. Ruiz and V. Agredo-Delgado (Eds.): HCI-COLLAB 2019, CCIS 1114, pp. 356–368, 2019.
https://doi.org/10.1007/978-3-030-37386-3_26

1 Introduction

Technological progress, with the great impact it has represented in various areas of human life, has also extended its influence in the education sector and fortunately, with this advancement it is easier to expand knowledge, where online learning has become a model that has revolutionized education as a great alternative to tradition-al education [1]. In the same way, educational institutions use available technologies and advances to provide more information to a growing audience. While the online educations systems proposals and modalities are growing, the number of people who use them too, so it is necessary to consider the diversity in the people's needs and characteristics to design Virtual Learning Environments (VLE) [2]. In this way, it is necessary to design and to build online education systems in order for the people to be able to use them in a simple, effective and efficient way, and the learning process provides a positive user experience [3]. Currently, the VLE has a large inexperienced public in its use, which is growing, for this reason, the User Experience (UX) is a fundamental part of the success of the VLE [4]. The UX refers to "how people feel about a product and its satisfaction when they use it, look at it, sustain it, open it or close it" [5]. The UX covers different facets related to software product quality such as accessibility, emotionality, usability, among others [6]. In this sense, this paper focuses exclusively on the UX "usability" facet and its characteristic "ease of learning" (which is defined as: "The time that a user, who has never seen an interface, can learn to use it well and perform basic operations, how much does it take to a typical community user to learn how to use relevant commands from a set of tasks?" [7]), specifically, in the usability evaluation of VLEs.

On the other hand, the usability evaluation of an interactive system is an important step in the User-Centered Design since it allows obtaining the usability characteristics of the system and the measurement in which usability principles are being applied, besides that it implies several activities that depend on the evaluation method to be implemented [8]. For this, it is necessary to perform the usability evaluation to validate if the final product meets the requirements and is easy to use, in addition to evaluating the system functionality scope and accessibility, the user experience in its interaction, and to identify specific problems [9]. To perform this evaluation, there are different Usability Assessment Methods (UAM), whose realization depends on variables such as costs, time availability, human resources in order to interpret the results, among others [10]. Some of these methods present methodological defects and whose application depends on many variables, which makes it unreliable its use and it more complicated choosing methods to evaluate a Virtual Learning Environment (VLE) [11]. A series of UAM can be applied on a VLE, but the question is how accurate the information is given for each one and/or a combination of them. Similarly, there is no standardization regarding what, how and when to perform the usability evaluation, but methods have been developed and used in isolation way and with specific criteria to evaluate a particular product [12]. However, usability assessment methods have strengths and weaknesses, focus on assessing certain aspects of usability requirements, so it is advisable to combine them in evaluation to complement each other in terms of their strengths and to cover a greater number of evaluation aspects [13]. The selection and evaluation methods combination will depend on financial and time constraints, the development cycle phases and the system nature [14].

Based on that, the problem arises when deciding which of the existing evaluation methods or combination is appropriate to evaluate the VLE usability. The objective of this paper is to validate the usability evaluation guide, validating its utility, applicability, and complexity in this context, guide that was built focusing on the study and methods set selection for evaluating usability in this context. These methods, after being selected, characterized and analyzed, generate a proposed guide that is formed by a new combination of methods to evaluate the VLE usability, which can provide usability information more completely and integral, regard to the realization of the evaluation methods indiscriminately and independently.

This paper is structured as follows: Sect. 2 shows a theoretical context of relevant research concepts. Section 3 contains some related work to usability evaluation in VLE. In Sect. 4, the process to build the guide and its validation. Finally, in Sect. 5 the conclusions and future work are described.

2 Theorical Context

Some important concepts are presented below for understanding the paper context:

2.1 Virtual Learning Environments (VLE)

A Virtual Learning Environment (VLE) is part of the computer applications set designed for educational purposes via the web, which contributes to reaching the educational objectives by providing a tools series that facilitate the user and course management, communication processes, evaluation, collaboration, and content distribution [15]. They present functionalities to facilitate the teaching and learning processes can unfold in a mediated way according to the needs of each specific context [16].

2.2 User Experience (UX)

The term User Experience (UX) refers to "how people feel about a product and their satisfaction when they use it, look at it, sustain it, open it or close it" [4]. Currently, there are different UX definitions used by professionals in the HCI area, one of the most outstanding is the ISO 9241-210 standard definition [17]: "Perceptions and person responses resulting from the use and/or anticipated product, system or service use". The UX covers different facets related to software product quality. The ISO/IEC 25010 standard [18] considers in a general way the following UX facets: accessibility, dependability, emotivity, playability, usability, among others.

2.3 Usability

Usability is part of the broader term "user experience" and refers to the "ease of access and/or use", whether it is a web page, a computer application or any other system that interacts with a user [19]. In addition, to be the extent to which a product can be used by specified users to achieve specified goals with effectiveness, efficiency, and satisfaction in a specified context of use, it is one of the most important features to define the quality of web applications as well as reliability and security [20].

2.4 Usability Evaluation

The usability evaluation has been determined as the activity comprising methods set that analyze the use quality of an interactive system, at different development life cycle stages, through user satisfaction with the process [21]. Usability evaluation is a fundamental part of the software development iterative approach because evaluation activities can produce design solutions to be applied in the next development cycle or, at least, greater knowledge about the interaction problem nature detected [22].

2.5 Usability Assessment Methods (UAM)

The methods have become an interesting study source by the usability researchers. Their application characteristics, the existing methods variety and the results generated [23] allow the usability characteristics evaluation such as the ease of learning, the ease, and efficiency of use, the ease to remember how it works, the frequency and error severity, its purpose is identifying usability problems and/or obtaining usability measures. There are four major categories of these methods: usability testing; usability inspections; surveys, interviews, and focus groups; and field methods [24].

3 Related Work

Gutierrez in [23], presents a work in which the UAMs have been studied in transactional web applications, contrasting their characteristics and generating a methodological evaluation proposal, in order to obtain the largest amount of relevant information regarding of the usability of this kind of applications. In the same way, Plantak et al. [25] examine e-learning usability evaluation methods, compare them and propose a criterion set that should be consulted when choosing the appropriate method to evaluate this context. The research shows that none of the methods examined has allowed integral e-learning platforms usability evaluation and none of them addresses all relevant specific topics for the learning systems and modules. On the other hand, Reyes in [26] presents methodological criteria to evaluate the Course Management Systems (CMS) usability. The evaluation was carried out by combining different methods and instruments with the potential platform users. Traditional usability evaluation methods were used, they were mixed and some new were originated to evaluate not only the elements that make up the usability but also the functionality and the pedagogical aspect of the CMS. Ferreira for this part in [27] proposes a model to evaluate the VLE quality, specifically the usability. The model is called MUsa, because it is a model based on usability, and is oriented to evaluate products in use. The general ideas are based on a four levels strategy, where the usability definitions, among attributes and heuristics, form the model core. Similarly, Martinez [22] focused on analyzing the virtual learning environment usability for undergraduate university students, emphasizing psycho-pedagogical aspects that allow evaluating both the contents quality and the system that contains them.

4 Building Activities for the Guide Definition

4.1 Research Methodology

In this work was developed the research methodology based on multi-cycle action with bifurcation [28]. The strategy starts dividing the work into three research cycles: conceptual cycle, methodological cycle, and evaluation cycle, which are detailed below.

Conceptual Cycle
In this cycle, a contextual analysis is carried out, to locate the problem to be studied. This cycle has three research phases: literature study about the important concepts, which are analyzed from an extensive literature review. The second phase is the identification of the appropriate UAMs for executing in VLE, where, from the literature, possible methods set are established to make up the combination proposed in this research, this phase was based on the work "Usability integration in the framework of the software development process [6]". Finally, after selecting those that are suitable for VLEs, activities, resources, and responsibilities are assigned to each selected method.

As a result of the conceptual cycle, according to the UAMs analyzed, it was determined that heuristic evaluation takes some advantages over the other methods, mainly because of the ease of carrying it out. For the methods of action analysis and standards inspection, highest level experts are required, and for the routes (cognitive and pluralistic) must be considered task definition methodologies and certain training, characteristics that increase the complexity of carrying them out. However, the inspection methods potential is not in doubt, because, if the time and conditions necessary to carry them out are available good results can be obtained. On the other hand, regarding the test methods, their advantages and disadvantages are quite varied. Thus, it is possible to establish certain comparisons between the test methods. The interrogation methods (questionnaires and interviews) are the simplest test methods to perform. Its characteristics allow, with few economic resources and with a preparation that does not consume too much time, to obtain satisfactory results regarding the system's usability evaluation. These characteristics find their counterpart when analyzing the information type provided by these test methods. The interrogation methods are aimed to obtain subjective information from the system under evaluation, getting, in many cases, information that cannot be obtained through other evaluation methods. Despite the advantages and disadvantages identification for each usability evaluation methods, in order to select the evaluation methods to be the study object in this investigation, summary information is required to facilitate decision making.

Finally, the usability assessment methods (test and inspection) object of study, that were selected after the execution of this cycle are:

Test methods

- Formal experiments
- Questionnaires and interviews
- Constructive interaction
- Driver's method

Inspection methods

- Heuristic evaluation
- Cognitive Tour

Methodological Cycle

Each one of the selected methods was applied individually on an object of study VLE. With these results, a metrics series were defined in order to make an objective comparison of the results that the application of the individual methods yielded, so, that from this new set you could choose the ones that could really be applied in VLEs. In this way, it was possible to select the most outstanding characteristics of the UAMs that were finally chosen, these were combined to build the guide for the evaluation of usability in VLEs. In the same way, was selected a new study object VLE.

After this steps, it was decided that a part of the guide should cover an evaluation carried out exclusively by expert evaluators, because the experience of this evaluators is a very important aspect to take into account since, through it, the evaluation is made with criteria that most likely are not taken into account by representative users of the system. On the other hand, it was decided to carry out an exclusive evaluation for representative users of the system, in order to consider, the interaction that they have with the VLE of the evaluation. In this way, we aim to have a guide that makes a thorough and thorough evaluation of the usability in VLE.

When was applied individually the VLEs on a study object, each one was applied under three stages of development (planning, execution, and analysis of results), it was decided to keep these stages within this guide in order to facilitate the monitoring and execution of the evaluation. Having that, five modules were defined that make up the guide, each of them with a different function and with a series of steps that give explicit indications to the participants of the evaluation.

The guide is composed of steps and each step has attached documents that allow the participants to generate deliverables of the activities they are doing, as well as facilitate the evaluation process. Each one of these documents and attached formats indicates to the participant of the evaluation how they must be completed in a clear and concrete manner so that the evaluation is carried out.

The guide consists of the following modules:

- Module 1 is about the previous activities executed exclusively by the representative of the organization (See Fig. 1). The document that must be completed in this module is: VLE Presentation letter.

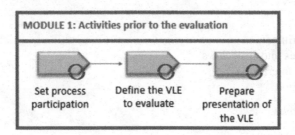

Fig. 1. Process diagram that follows Module 1

- Module 2 is about the activities that include the planning of evaluation and are executed exclusively by the evaluators (See Fig. 2). The documents that must be completed in this module are: the evaluation document in Excel, the user guide, the questionnaires pre-test and post-test, and the evaluators guide.

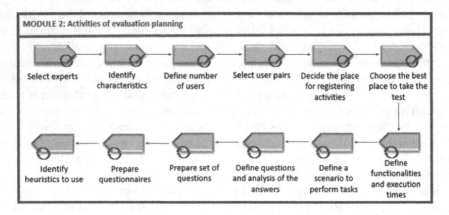

Fig. 2. Process diagram that follows Module 2

- Module 3 is about the activities that include the execution of the evaluation by the expert evaluators (See Fig. 3). The documents that must be completed in this module are: the evaluators guide, the individual evaluators and the evaluators documents in Excel.

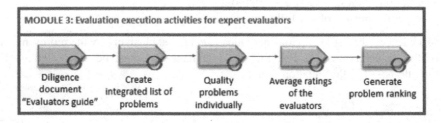

Fig. 3. Process diagram that follows Module 3

- Module 4 is about the activities that include the execution of the evaluation to the significant users of the VLE (See Fig. 4). The documents that must be completed in this module are: the user guide, the evaluators documents in Excel and the questionnaires post-test.

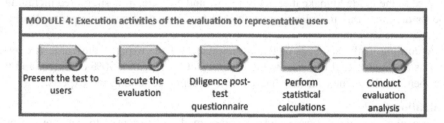

Fig. 4. Process diagram that follows Module 4

- Module 5 is about the activities that comprise the analysis of the result of the evaluations performs to experts and representative users of the VLE (See Fig. 5). The document that must be completed in this module is: the final result document.

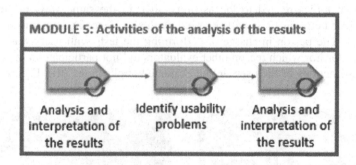

Fig. 5. Process diagram that follows Module 5

After building the guide for the usability evaluation in VLE, collaboration was requested from some experts on usability, to carry out an objective analysis of the guide. The analysis was carried out through a questionnaire using the google drive tool; the main objective of this analysis was to refine the guide, eliminating elements that according to the experience of the experts, those were not necessary to include in the guide and adding others that would make it more complete.

According to the experts, the VLE evaluation should not be done only through questions from a questionnaire, they suggested defining concrete metrics that allow the evaluator(s), to analyze if the VLE fulfills the objective for which it was created and if the students also achieve these tasks correctly. To complete this, some metrics that generate quantitative values of the evaluation were defined within module 3, in the activity "Perform statistical calculations" of the guide. The aim of these metrics was to enable experts to better analyze the results obtained. Likewise, they recommended deepening the aspects of the usability characteristic: "Ability to recognize its adequacy". For this reason, a checklist was included in the guide for expert evaluators, which would not only deepen that characteristic, but also the other characteristics that are part of usability. The experts suggested also, change the name to the documents annexed to the guide to make it easier to follow and execute, they suggested including a process diagram, this in order to give an idea to the evaluation participants about the process to be executed.

According to the statistics of the questionnaire of the experts, the guide is constituted as a valuable tool to evaluate the usability in VLE with a 50% obtained, and the documents and attached formats had an 80% acceptance among the experts.

Evaluation Cycle
In the evaluation cycle, a case study was designed and executed to validate the proposed guide would enable us to verify that meets the desired characteristics between them the utility, the applicability, and the complexity.

Case study context
The case study was developed in a virtual UNIVIDA learning environment of the virtual and remote academic unit of a higher education institution in the city of Popayan, Colombia. The group of evaluators was basically made up of researchers from different topics related to the usability area, in the same way, the users who participated are between 17 and 40 years old, with experience in the use of information technologies. The person in charge of performing the tests with users was the supervising evaluator, for which reason other evaluators did not participate in the process of observing the actions of the users in the evaluated applications (See Figs. 6 and 7).

Fig. 6. Case study context

Fig. 7. Supervising evaluator

Research question
To evaluate the guide, we defined the follows question: ¿Is the usability evaluation in VLEs carried out in a complete, clear, deep and systematic way by using the guide, consolidating itself as a useful tool and applicable?

Case study objective
The objective of the case study was to verify that the guide is useful and applicable in virtual learning environments and that the evaluation results improve the results obtained by applying the UAMs individually.

Indicators and metrics
For evaluate this study case objectively, it was necessary to define a set of metrics and indicators, which are described below:

Utility: is defined as the property by which the guide defined in this proposal acquires the status of useful value to evaluate usability in virtual learning environments. The metrics that have been established to calculate the utility are:

- The normalized value of the average finished tasks metric is greater than or equal to 0.8.
- The range of expert evaluators who consider that evaluation guidance is a useful tool in the VLE usability evaluation process is between 80% and 100%.
- The value that the supervising evaluator considers that the guide for the evaluation is a useful tool in the evaluation process of usability in VLE is between 80% and 100%.
- The value that the organization representative considers that the evaluation is a useful tool in the evaluation process of usability in VLE is between 80% and 100%.

Applicability: is defined as the property by which the guide can be easily used to obtain efficient results in the evaluation of usability in virtual learning environments. The metrics that have been established to determine the applicability are:

- The applicability degree of the guide obtained from the perception of the supervising evaluator that is between four and five (five being the highest degree of applicability) must be greater than or equal to 80%.
- The average of the applicability degree of the guide obtained from the perception of the expert evaluators that is between four and five (five being the highest degree of applicability) must be greater than or equal to 80%.
- The applicability degree of the documents annexed to the guide obtained from the perception of the supervising evaluator that is between four and five (five being the highest degree of applicability) must be greater than or equal to 80%.
- The average degree of applicability of the documents annexed to the guide obtained from the perception of the expert evaluators that is between four and five (five being the highest degree of applicability) must be greater than or equal to 80%.

Complexity: is defined as the diversity of elements that make up a situation, which is intertwined and/or interconnected that contains additional information and hides the supervising evaluator. The metrics that have been established to determine the complexity are:

- The average of complexity degree of the guide obtained from the perception of the expert evaluators that is between 1 and 5 (5 being the highest degree of complexity).
- The complexity degree of the guide obtained from the perception of the supervising evaluator that is between 1 and 5 (5 being the highest degree of complexity).

- The average of the complexity degree of the documents annexed to the guide obtained from the perception of the expert evaluators that is between 1 and 5 (5 being the highest degree of complexity).
- The complexity degree of the documents annexed to the guide obtained from the perception of the supervising evaluator that is between 1 and 5 (5 being the highest degree of complexity).

5   Case Study Execution and Results

For the case study execution, it was decided to execute the guide in the same environment that the UAMs were applied individually, this, in order to make a final comparison between the results obtained with the proposed guide and each UAM applied individually, and thus we achieve to see each of the advantages and disadvantages guide.

Utility: according to the proposed indicators and metrics, both the expert evaluators, the supervising evaluator and the representative of the organization indicated that the guide is consolidated as a useful tool in the usability evaluation process because the answers to the questionnaires yielded values above 80%, so because the 4 proposed indicators complied with the proposed metrics.

Applicability: regarding the indicators and metrics proposed, they were very close to not meeting the minimum range for approval, according to the data obtained from the expert evaluators and supervisory evaluator. They said that, when carrying out a complete usability evaluation process, the guide can become a bit extensive, and although the attached documents are very useful tools, these can be difficult to apply.

Complexity: regarding the complexity of the guide implementation, it was close to the minimum range for approval, the reasons for this situation are directly linked to the previous indicator, due since the guide and its documents provide a comprehensive usability assessment, these are considered somewhat complex in their execution, this is why the experts suggested including a general diagram of the usability evaluation process.

6   Conclusions and Future Work

Given the literature analysis carried out in this research, no guide clear was found for the usability evaluation that would pose to what, how and when the evaluation types should be carried out. The result presented in this research provides a clear guide for the usability evaluation in VLEs, structured in 5 modules, with their respective steps, roles, deliverables and documents to perform, with a sequence of well-defined activities, and the communication process specification. In this way, the guide is a first step in the objective of conducting usability evaluations in VLEs in a complete and effective manner following a guideline that facilitates the evaluations.

Although the guide was executed within a case study satisfactorily, the experts stated that the guide execution is expensive and difficult to perform, this is undoubtedly balanced by the results obtained at the end of the execution in which great improvement with respect to the individual execution of the methods, with which despite the extra effort that must be made to execute the guide, it carries out complete and effective evaluations.

It can be concluded that the guide is established as a useful tool in the usability evaluation process in VLEs, with regard to the applicability, it can be determined that it is moderately applicable, since a bit extensive, and the annexed documents can be difficult to apply, on the other hand, taking into account the complexity and its relationship with the applicability, it can be determined that the guide and its documents are complex, due to their extension and a large amount of time necessary to be executed.

As future work, it is necessary to improve the guide proposed in order to incorporate new elements and improve its description to make it easier to use and validate it in other usability contexts, this through new case studies, and with the use of technology or software to help the execution.

References

1. Swan, K.: Building learning communities in online courses: the importance of interaction. Educ. Commun. Inf. **2**(1), 23–49 (2002)
2. Mimirinis, M., Bhattacharya, M.: Design of virtual learning environments for deep learning. J. Interact. Learn. Res. **18**(1), 55–64 (2007)
3. Mor, E., Garreta, M., Galofré, M.: Diseño Centrado en el Usuario en Entornos Virtuales de Aprendizaje, de la Usabilidad a la Experiencia del Estudiante. In: SPDECE (2007)
4. Rogers, Y., Sharp, H., Preece, J.: Interaction Design Beyond Human - Computer Interaction (2012)
5. Hassenzahl, M., Tractinsky, N.: User experience-a research agenda. Behav. Inf. Technol. **25**(2), 91–97 (2006)
6. Ferré Grau, X.: Marco de integración de la usabilidad en el proceso de desarrollo software, (Doctoral dissertation) – Diss (2005)
7. Sanchez, W.: La usabilidad en Ingeniería de Software: Definición y características. Ingnovación. Revista de Ingeniería e Innovación de la Facultad de Ingeniería. Universidad Don Bosco, vol. 2, pp. 7–21 (2011)
8. Nielsen, J.: The usability engineering life cycle. Computer **25**(3), 12–22 (1992)
9. Petrie, H., Bevan, N.: The evaluation of accessibility, usability, and user experience. In: The Universal Access Handbook, vol. 1, pp. 1–16 (2009)
10. Granollers, T.: MPIu + a. Una metodología que integra la Ingeniería del Software, la Interacción Persona-Ordenador y la Accesibilidad en el contexto de equipos de desarrollo multidisciplinares, Universitat de Lleida (2007)
11. Solano Alegría, A.F.: Propuesta metodológica para la evaluación colaborativa de la usabilidad de aplicaciones de Televisión Digital Interactiva, Diss (2012)
12. Obeso, A., Elena, M.: Metodología de medición y evaluación de la usabilidad en sitios web educativos (2004)
13. Bevan, N., Macleod, M.: Usability measurement in context. Behav. Inf. Technol. **13**(1), 132–145 (1994)

14. Nielsen, J.: Paper versus computer implementations as mockup scenarios for heuristic evaluatio. In: de Proceedings of the IFIP Tc13 Third Interational Conference on Human-Computer Interaction (1990)

15. Thüer, S., Ferreira Szpiniak, A.: Entornos Virtuales de Aprendizaje: Diseño de experiencias de usuario para la web 2.0. In: de Conferencia Internacional ICDE–UNQ (2011)

16. Martinelli, S., Cicala, R., Perazzo, M., Bordignon, F., De Salvo, C.J.: nvestigación sobre entornos virtuales de aprendizaje utilizados para la enseñanza en profesorados y universidades nacionales. In: UNIPE-OEI Conectar Igualdad (2011)

17. International Organization for Standardization: ISO/TC 159/SC 4 Ergonomics of human-system interaction (Subcommittee). Ergonomic Requirements for Office Work with Visual Display Terminals (VDTs).: Guidance on Usability (1998)

18. Organización Internacional de Normalización: ISO-IEC 25010: 2011 Systems and Software Engineering-Systems and Software Quality Requirements and Evaluation (SQuaRE)-System and Software Quality Models (2011)

19. International Organization for Standardization: IEC 9126-1: Software engineering-product quality-part 1: Quality model (2001)

20. Offutt, J.: Quality attributes of web software applications. IEEE Softw. **19**(2), 25–32 (2002)

21. Reyes Vera, J.M., Berdugo Torres, M.I., Machuca Villegas, L.: Evaluación de usabilidad de un sistema de administración de cursos basado en la plataforma Lingweb. Ingeniare - Revista chilena de ingeniería. **24**(3), 435–444 (2006)

22. Ponce Martinez, M.P.: Usabildiad en un sistema de E-Learning. Pontificia Universidad Católica de Valparaíso (2007)

23. Gutiérrez Godoy, E.J.: Usabilidad y Comunicabilidad en Aplicaciones Web Transaccionales, Tesis de Grado - Magíster en Ingeniería Informática Pontificia Universidad Católica de Valparaíso (2011)

24. Jeng, J.: Usability assessment of academic digital libraries: effectiveness, efficiency, satisfaction, and learnability. Libri. **55**(1), 96–121 (2005)

25. Plantak Vukovac, D., Kirinic, V., Klicek, B.: A comparison of usability evaluation methods for e-learning systems. In: de DAAAM International Scientific Book, Vienna, Austria, DAAAM International, pp. 271–288 (2010)

26. Reyes Vera, J.M., Berdugo Torres, M.I., Machuca Villegas, L.: Evaluación de usabilidad de un sistema de administración de cursos basado en la plataforma Lingweb. Ingeniare. Revista chilena de ingeniería. **24**(3), 435–444 (2016)

27. Ferreira Szpiniak, A.: Diseño de un modelo de evaluación de entornos virtuales de enseñanza y aprendizaje basado en la usabilidad, Universidad Nacional de La Plata (2013)

28. Pino, F.J., Piattini, M., Horta Travassos, G.: Managing and developing distributed research projects in software engineering by means of action-research. Revista Facultad de Ingeniería Universidad de Antioquia **68**, 61–74 (2013)

The Human and the Context Components in the Design of Automatic Sign Language Recognition Systems

Soraia Silva Prietch[1]([⊠]) (iD), Polianna dos Santos Paim[1] (iD),
Ivan Olmos-Pineda[2] (iD), Josefina Guerrero García[2] (iD),
and Juan Manuel Gonzalez Calleros[2] (iD)

[1] Universidade Federal de Mato Grosso (UFMT),
Rondonópolis, MT 78.735-901, Brazil
soraia@ufmt.br, poliannapaim@gmail.com
[2] Benemérita Universidade Autónoma de Puebla (BUAP),
72592 Puebla, PUE, Mexico
ivanoprkl@gmail.com, josefina.guerrero@correo.buap.mx,
juan.gonzalez@cs.buap.mx

Abstract. To classify an Automatic Sign Language Recognition (ASLR) System as an Assistive Technology product is to affirm that it may contribute to a more inclusive and independent living for people who are Deaf or hard of hearing and who are sign language users. In this aspect, we consider important to take into account the Human Activity Assistive Technology Context (HAAT) model, in order to analyze all the aspects involving a proposed AT product. Since the goal of an ASLR system (AT component) is automatically convert sign language communication of one person into text or speech (Activity component), and since this type of system must have at least one human involved (Human component) in a specific context of use (Context component), in this paper, our goal is to present how related investigations are addressing the Human and the Context components of the HAAT model in the design of ASLR systems. As one of the findings from the exploratory literature review, we noticed a gap in the ASLR systems design, which did not include Deaf Community as co-designers and did not explore issues involving user experience.

Keywords: Assistive Technology · Deaf persons · User study · Human · Context

1 Introduction

According to Ibrahim, Selim and Zayed [1] "Sign language recognition system (SLRS) is one of the application areas of human computer interaction (HCI)". Also, if we are classifying an Automatic Sign Language Recognition (ASLR) System as an Assistive Technology product, in the sense that this type of solution mediated by technology contribute to a more inclusive and independent living for people who are Deaf or hard of hearing and who are sign language users, we must take into account the Human Activity Assistive Technology (HAAT) model, proposed by Cook and Polgar [2].

© Springer Nature Switzerland AG 2019
P. H. Ruiz and V. Agredo-Delgado (Eds.): HCI-COLLAB 2019, CCIS 1114, pp. 369–380, 2019.
https://doi.org/10.1007/978-3-030-37386-3_27

The HAAT model is composed by four components for assistive technology design: Human, Activities, Assistive Technology (AT) and Context. The Human component comes in the first place in order to design or to select an AT product/service/strategy for someone, in those cases, to know the person's physical, cognitive and emotional characteristics, skills and abilities are fundamental. The Activity component is defined depending on the context component the human is, whether someone is at home, at school, at work or at a leisure environment. However, when the same barrier is a constant in a life experience (context) of someone (human), then the assistive technology component (physical and extrinsic enablers) may be a useful product/service/strategy to provide individual autonomy and collective interaction in various contexts (physical, social, cultural, and institutional contexts) [2].

Since the goal of an ASLR system (AT component) is automatically convert sign language communication of one person into text or speech (Activity component) [3], and since this type of system must have at least one human involved (Human component) in a specific context of use (Context component), in this paper, our goal is to present how related works are addressing the Human and the Context components of the HAAT model in the design of ASLR systems.

The remainder of this paper is structured as follows. In Sect. 2, we present the human component by briefly showing an overview of sign language as the voice of the Deaf Community. In Sect. 3, we ideate scenarios of ASLR systems use as a mean to show what one may need to take into account on the context component. In Sect. 4, we present related works on ASLR systems design by conducting an exploratory literature review, observing whether the human and the context components are taken into account in such investigations. In Sect. 5, we analyze information found in exploratory literature review; and, in Sect. 6, we present final considerations.

2   The Human Component: Sign Language (SL) as the Voice of the Deaf Community

From García, Guimarães, Antunes e Fernandes [4], "Deaf culture is an expression applied to the social movement that holds deafness to be a difference in human experience – which includes the right to use their natural language: Sign Language (SL) – rather than a disability". According Hersh and Johnson [5], persons are part of the Deaf Community when they identify themselves with Deaf Culture, mostly related to the use of sign language as the main mode of communication, rather than written mode or oral speech. Huenerfauth and Hanson [3] inform that a subset of the people who are deaf and who are sign language users have difficulty in reading and writing; authors mention that "the reasons may be varied, but this phenomenon is replicated worldwide, regardless of sign language or written language of the country" (p. 38-2). This also educates us that each country has its own sign language, according to Quesada, López and Guerrero [6], there are "137 different sign languages around the world"; for instance, the Brazilian Sign Language (Libras) was recognized as the official language of the Brazilian Deaf Community in 2002 [7].

Other particularity is that many people believe that knowing the manual alphabet (dactylology), "a set of special handshapes to spell words" [3], someone may know how to communicate in sign language; however, this is a misunderstanding. For Huenerfauth and Hanson [3], "Signers typically reserve fingerspelling for titles, proper names, and other specific situations". Sign language dictionaries and glossaries have been created containing signs of general purpose (daily life signs) or signs of specific domain (e.g., Capovilla, Raphael, Temoteo and Martins [8]), proving that sign languages also have rich vocabularies.

As an official mode of communication, a specific sign language has distinct linguist structure from spoken language of the same country [3]. Sign languages, in general, are structured in five main parameters [8–10]: (a) Hand shape: hand configuration to communicate a sign; (b) Hand location (articulation point): place in the head or the body, where the sign is communicated, which can be touched (or not); (c) Hand movement: movement of the hand in space; (d) Hand orientation: change during communication; and, (e) Non-manual (facial and body) expression: it can define meanings of signs.

Furthermore, Rezende, Castro and Almeida [11] inform that "One sign is composed of various simultaneous elements [sign language parameters]" (p. 01). For instance, there are signs that does not need any movement to be understood; in other cases, some or all parameters must be used to produce an intelligible performance. In this sense, Nel, Ghaziasgar and Connan [12] affirm that "The use of a single parameter has meant that only a limited number of signs can be recognized [...]" (p. 179) by an ASLR system.

Also, phrase construction in sign language may have a different composition from phrase construction in written or spoken language [10, 13]. Syntactic structures of both languages are distinct, once sign order may be subject of variation (subject-verb-object (SVO), subject-object-verb (SOV), verb-subject-object (VSO), object-subject-verb (OSV)). According to authors [13], this variability is related to the grammatical dynamics and to the use of specific non-manual expressions. Moreover, according to Strobel and Fernandes [14] "[...] articles, prepositions, conjunctions are not used because these connectives are incorporated into sign communication" (p. 16); and, affirmative, interrogative, exclamatory and negative phrases are emphasized using facial and body expressions.

In terms of human component, people may have other disabilities in addition to a hearing loss [5]. Moreover, in a natural communication using sign language, people do not spell other people's name whenever they want to refer to someone who is not present, they use the person's sign. The person's sign can be defined as a "nickname" that only can be assigned by a Deaf person and it may represent the visual look or personality of someone. Using an ASLR system, a person's sign is a challenge for computing, since, in theory, each person has its own sign, being impossible to generate and store all possibilities. This is only one characteristic of sign language and still can affect user experience, especially, during a real-time communication. Finally, another aspect, mentioned by Rao and Kishore [15], as an intrinsic human factor is that two signers cannot perform the same sign similarly, if one may consider hand, arms, head and body combined with the five parameters of a given SL. People feel, think, do and perceive the world differently, it is a natural diversity of the human being; not natural for computing to identify all these nuances.

3 The Context Component: Ideation of Scenarios of ASLR Systems Use

According to Rojano-Cáceres *et al.* [16], in any domain, "we could identify different scenarios where the complexity of the communication varies" (pp. 01–02). In this sense, authors classified three levels of complexity in a conversation (or interaction) related to the degree of language' use: low, medium and high levels. ASLR systems may be classified as a high level, because they require "full use of grammar and syntax in complex interactions" [16]. Below we present nine potential scenarios (Figs. 1, 2 and 3), given the use of an ASLR system to generate written and/or oral communication (as output) from a sign language communication (as input).

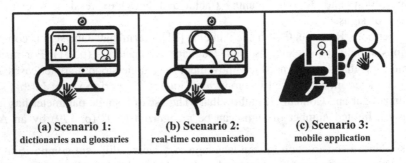

Fig. 1. ASLR system scenarios of use: (a) Scenario1: Dictionaries and glossaries; (b) Scenario2: Real-time communication; (c) Scenario3: Mobile application. [Authors' proposition]

Scenario 1 (Fig. 1a) refers to dictionaries and glossaries with ASLR system, were someone, asynchronously, could look up for an unknown sign just by gesturing it to a set of natural data capture. Considering this context, the system may have educational potential for people who want to learn sign language; and, it may support HCI field investigations, when interpreters are not available to intermediate communications between Deaf participants and researchers. Scenario 2 (Fig. 1b) presents ASLR system for Real-Time Communication (RTC), in which someone could communicate in sign language and obtain the translation in oral/written language, enabling one way of human-human interaction (HHI). This scenario also may provide educational potential, such as e-learning, where users (students, teachers or tutors) could maintain a synchronous communication; and, it could help in HCI remote investigations, such as conducting interviews, evaluating usability or communicability, among others. In Scenario 3 (Fig. 1c), the ASLR system is shown as a mobile application, where a hearing person who is not a sign language (SL) user, could use the camera to capture SL communication and use the system to translate it into written language, enabling one way of HHI. This scenario can happen in different environments of daily life, such as education, work, leisure, home, whenever individuals want or need to communicate. This type of technology would allow environment-independent communication due to the use of mobile technology; however, it could embarrass the signer being observed through the lens/screen of the smartphone.

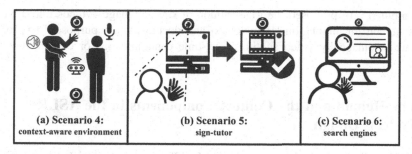

(a) Scenario 4:
context-aware environment

(b) Scenario 5:
sign-tutor

(c) Scenario 6:
search engines

Fig. 2. ASLR system scenarios of use: (a) Scenario4: Context-aware environment [Authors' proposition]; (b) Scenario5: eLearning evaluation [17, 18]; (c) Scenario6: Search engines [19].

Scenario 4 (Fig. 2a) illustrates a context-aware environment, in which a necessary set of devices to use an ASLR system should be available. The environment could be a classroom, a government service setting, a medical assistance room, a workplace, a controlled setting for HCI investigation, among others. This type of technology could provide a natural communication between people; however, it is environment-dependent, since a set of devices would be installed in a given environment. In Scenario 5 (Fig. 2b) an eLearning environment is presented, which includes an automatic sign language evaluation system [17, 18], in which learners perform sign language and verify whether their performance are correct. Scenario 6 (Fig. 2c) refers to ASLR system used for "indexing task, providing the required basis for sign language search engines" [19] (p. 2). The most commonly way to search for an information is with written language, what can be a barrier for deaf people who are illiterate.

(a) Scenario 7:
SignWriting generator

(b) Scenario 8:
selfie record

(c) Scenario 9:
transcription of sign language

Fig. 3. ASLR system scenarios of use: (a) Scenario7: SignWriting generator [4]; (b) Scenario8: Selfie record [15]; (c) Scenario9: Transcription of sign language [20].

In Scenario 7 (Fig. 3a), García, Guimarães, Antunes e Fernandes [4] proposed, as part of their framework, a SignWriting [21] generator by using an ASLR system, even though, in many countries, written sign languages are not recognized as official. In Scenario 8 (Fig. 3b), Rao and Kishore [15] proposed to record sign language videos with smartphone and translate it to written language. In this scenario someone can hold a selfie stick in one hand and sign with the other hand. In Scenario 9 (Fig. 3c), Borg and Camilleri [20] proposed the transcription of sign language "videos into a written representation for annotation [HamNoSys] and documentation purposes" (p. 163) to generate automatically video subtitles, real-time captioning [3] or class/lecture note taking.

4   The Human and the Context Components in the ASLR Systems Design

According to Melnyk, Shadrova and Karwatsky [22], "computer assisted recognition of sign language have been presented in the literature since nineteen eighties", mentioning that the first registered idea was made by Grimes, in 1983, as a patent of a glove interface device for manual sign recognition in American Sign Language (ASL) and the first experimental work, on fingerspelling recognition, was conducted by Hall, in 1985. Nowadays, in order to understand how one may contribute with human-computer interaction (HCI) research community interested on automatic sign language recognition (ASLR) systems, an exploratory literature review on related works is presented in this section. The reviewed papers were written in one of the three languages: Brazilian-Portuguese, Spanish and English, in order to find potential partners for continuity of this research.

Concerning with sensor-based data collection techniques, Quesada, López and Guerrero [6] proposed a handshape recognition system using the Leap Motion sensor and performed evaluations with 24 participants. Authors defined eleven signs (Number: 1 to 5, Letters: S, F and T, Thumb to the left, Thumb to the right, and the sign "I love you"), being the number 5 chosen as the control sign, since in pre-tests its recognition accuracy was 100%. Participants were organized in three groups, using one script with 20 signs each, also, each script had the eleven signs repeated twice in different orders. During the test, participants should perform each sign of the script, using the control sign between each one. As results, the Number 2 was the sign which obtained greater accuracy in recognition (100%); Letter S, Thumb to the left and the sign "I love you" were recognized in 90% of the cases; and, Letters F and T, and Thumb to the right were not recognized very well. Authors [6], also, verified some patterns in results that suggest the order of the signs, depending on the sign movement, influence in recognition accuracy.

Rivas et al. [18] proposed an educational system for learning Ecuadorian Sign Language for people who are Deaf or hard of hearing, using Leap Motion sensor for data capture. In this system, users can perform sign language and verify their learning outcomes, including their level of knowledge determined by the correct number of letters per time. Tests were conducted with 06 children who are Deaf or hard of hearing and 07 children who are hearing, in which interface and functionalities were shown before users started to accomplish tasks through the learning modes (sorted, random and time trial). Authors [18] noticed an improvement on learning outcomes after a certain period of use and task repetition, also, they mentioned the use of System Usability Scale (SUS), however, no results of this applied instrument were shown.

Paudyal, Lee, Banerjee and Gupta [23] used sensors and electromyogram signals associated with a mobile application for training, testing and user data collection of a fingerspelling recognition system. Authors [23] performed evaluation with 09 users, in which they tested three user interface elements to improve accuracy and execution time of an ASLR system. The first user interface element were GIF images of the 26 alphabet letters used for training; the second was an optional element for the user to correct the automatically recognized letters results; and, the third element was a feature able to show close matches in ranked order for the user to select the correct recognition result. Results showed increase in recognition rate, being especially useful for low processing speed devices/infrastructures.

With respect to works that uses computer vision-based techniques, Rao and Kishore [15] presented a mobile application for sign language video capture using selfie, which is sent and converted into text. An 18 words sentence, performed by 10 different signers, was used for training in the right order of written language and for testing in a different order for the same words. In spite of mentioning user participation for training and testing the system, nothing was mentioned about user experience design, usability or user study. Authors [15] reported two challenges of this scenario, the first was related to the fact that the user should use only one hand for signing, since the other would be holding a selfie stick and, the second was related to background variations, since the user would be moving around with the smartphone; for that authors decided to use an homogeneous background during investigation.

Nyaga and Wario [24] conducted a usability test to verify effectiveness, efficiency and satisfaction by 07 deaf participants, considering the use of an automatic South African Sign Language (SASL) recognition system. Participants were 10th grade students from a special school for Deaf and each participant should place one hand in front of a box (region of interest) and perform four tasks one at a time (Finger spelling for number 1, Finger spelling for number 2, Finger spelling for number 3 and Finger spelling for number 4). Techniques used were performance measurement technique (number of errors and task completion rate), observation and structured interviews, where the two former techniques conducted in a scale style. As number of errors, two were detected: "hand out of region of interest" and "head and hand within the region of interest", from these errors, task completion rate was affected, showing 100% for Task 1 and Task 3, 86% for Task 2 (one person/error), and 71% for Task 4 (two persons/one type of errors each). According to authors [24], in the observation scale, 100% of the participants gave the impression of being "interested", "involved" and "focused", 86% "motivated", 43% "calm", and 29% "impatient"; and, the structured interview showed that, in Question 1, 01 participant informed that he/she had "no idea what to improve" the evaluated system, 04 informed "no improvements" are needed, 01 asked to "include more tasks" and 01 mentioned "there should be improvements"; in Question 2, 03 participants reported "no challenges in use", 03 found "difficult to put hand in region of interest" and 01 mentioned the "system was slow"; in Question 3, 02 participants informed to like the system, 01 expressed that to interact with the system was exciting, 02 reported that they "find it useful (can detect hand)" and 02 had "no idea"; and, in Question 4, 02 reported to find the system "very helpful" and 05 "helpful".

Moreover, in spite of being a technical review of 1 patent, 18 papers and 22 language databases on ASLR systems, Melnyk, Shadrova and Karwatsky [22] compared outcomes by using vision-based and hardware-based techniques, for which they mention to provide good and inconvenient user experience, respectively, based on the understanding that holding or wearing a technological object would not provide a natural interaction. Also, González, Sánchez, Díaz and Pérez [25] informed they created their own dataset with Spanish alphabet letters for training and testing, where 25 Deaf participants only performed the signs to be recorded and stored.

Finally, there were found papers who reported design and/or development of ASLR systems that do not mention user studies: Ibrahim, Selim and Zayed [1]; Rezende, Castro and Almeida [11]; Nel, Ghaziasgar and Connan [12]; Borg and Camilleri [20]; Porfirio, Wiggers, Oliveira, and Weingaertner [26]; Barros, Pontes and Almeida [27]; Cervantes *et al.* [28]; Deaney *et al.* [29]; Gattupalli, Ghaderi and Athitsos [30]; Guerrero-Balaguera and Pérez-Holguín [31]; Rajaganapathy *et al.* [32]; Rodriguéz and Martínez [33]; Ronchetti [34]; Wang *et al.* [35]; Wiggers, Ré and Porfírio [36].

5   Analyzing Information Found in Exploratory Literature Review

From 24 papers included in the exploratory literature review, we categorized information found to analyze how investigations on ALSR systems have being concerned about the human and the context components. The categories include the human component, the context component, and, goals, HCI research techniques and built dataset reported in related works.

Regarding the human component, from Sect. 3, one may be aware of the complexity to recognize and to translate sign language into written/spoken language. This complexity reflects on the characteristics of many researches [6, 18, 23, 24, 26, 27, 31, 34, 36], which attack the big problem taking as a first step the recognition of hand configuration (numbers, letters of a written language alphabet, fingerspelling, and static signs of a specific sign language). Furthermore, despite of much interest of the computing community on the ASLR systems subject, a finding in literature review is that there still are researchers not familiarized with inclusive terms [3, 38]. In some papers, we may find terms, such as, "normal families", "deaf-mute", "deaf and dumb", "suffer from impairment", among others, that can be offensive to people who are involved and will potentially benefit from this type of research.

Concerning with the context component, if we critically observe the presented potential scenarios (Sect. 4), stakeholders usually expect a quick development by the research team and an ideal interaction through communication (fast in recognition time, complete and correct translation). However, due to an ASLR system complexity, a project may take many years to result in a slow, incomplete and partially correct translation. In this sense, expectation and real results can affect user experience and human-human interaction. Furthermore, in the case scenarios presented, systems should translate from sign language to text/speech and, the other way around, translate from text/speech to sign language, in order to guarantee full human-human interaction (HHI). To translate text/speech to sign language is necessary to generate a 3D avatar to communicate in real-time what is being written or spoken [3]. One example of investigation that considers full HHC is García, Guimarães, Antunes e Fernandes [4].

Taking into account the goals and the research techniques reported in 24 related works that mentioned to include users in some stage of an ASLR system design (total 05 works), we highlight the following findings:

- 03 (three) had technical outcome expectations, such as, recognition rate [6, 15, 23] and execution time [23] as goals;
- 03 (three) had HCI and/or educational outcome expectations, such as, learning outcomes [18], interface usability [18, 23, 24] as goals;
- 02 (two) reported specifically the participation of Deaf person in their investigations: 06 among 11 [18]; and, 07 in total [24];
- 05 (five) conducted some type of usability test [6, 15, 18, 23, 24] and, 01 conducted educational evaluation [18].

From these topics on goals and research techniques of the exploratory literature review, we found a gap in the ASLR systems design, which a small number of investigations include Deaf Community in the design process and none of the works report findings on user experience or participatory design.

On the matter of built dataset, Rezende, Castro and Almeida [11] inform that "There is currently no standardized database containing signs in a format that allows the validation of computational classification systems" (p. 01). Wang *et al.* [35] also affirm that "publicly available datasets are limited in this area", for which, Melnyk, Shadrova and Karwatsky [22] present examples of SL databases. Furthermore, researchers who created their own dataset to use for ASLR system design did not mention protocol or standards for dataset creation [1, 6, 11, 12, 25–28, 31, 32, 34–36].

6 Final Considerations

The problem complexity can be evidenced by observing different aspects of the same domain of application, taking into account the HAAT model components. The human components can be viewed through the eyes of the natural users of sign languages and their cultural experiences. The context can be previewed through those possible scenarios and many others. The activity can be stated as the full human-human communication between signers and non-signers. The assistive technology can include computing challenges, such as, datasets, algorithms, among others, to support the other three HAAT model components.

As we stated at the beginning of this paper, our goal was to present how related investigations are addressing the Human and the Context components of the HAAT model in the design of ASLR systems. With the exploratory literature review, we could observe that among 24 papers, only 05 included users in HCI evaluations. Except for one work [18], the contexts of research conduction were placed in controlled environments, mostly to test technical issues, such as, recognition rate, execution time, dataset acquisition.

To sum up, the exploratory literature review also was a motivator for the continuity of this work, for which we intend to analyze cultural aspects in the user experience design of an automatic sign language recognition system, taking into account the human and the context components of the Human Activity Assistive Technology (HAAT) model with stakeholders in different Latin American countries.

References

1. Ibrahim, N.B., Selim, M.M., Zayed, H.H.: An automatic arabic sign language recognition system (ArSLRS). J. King Saud Univ. Comput. Inf. Sci. **30**, 470–477 (2018). https://doi.org/ 10.1016/j.jksuci.2017.09.007. Accessed 2 Aug 2019
2. Cook, A.M., Polgar, J.M.: Cook & Hussey's Assistive Technologies: Principles and Practice. Mosby Elsevier, St. Louis (2008)
3. Huenerfauth, M.; Hanson, V.: Sign language in the interface: access for Deaf signers. In: Stephanidis, C. (eds.) The Universal Access Handbook. CRC Press (2009). https://doi.org/ 10.1201/9781420064995. Accessed 2 Aug 2019
4. García, L., Guimarães, C., Antunes, D., Fernandes, S.: HCI Architecture for deaf communities cultural inclusion and citizenship. In: ICEIS (2013). https://doi.org/10.5220/ 0004451201260133. Accessed 2 Aug 2019
5. Hersh, M., Johnson, M.: Assistive Technology for the Hearing-Impaired, Deaf and Deafblind. Springer, London (2003). https://doi.org/10.1007/b97528
6. Quesada, L., López, G., Guerrero, L.A.: Sign language recognition using leap motion. In: García-Chamizo, J.M., Fortino, G., Ochoa, S.F. (eds.) UCAmI 2015. LNCS, vol. 9454, pp. 277–288. Springer, Cham (2015). https://doi.org/10.1007/978-3-319-26401-1_26
7. Brazil. Brazilian Federal Law n. 10436: Provides on the Brazilian Sign Language - Libras and gives other measures (2002). https://goo.gl/X4BHZo. Accessed 04 Aug 2019
8. Capovilla, F., Raphael, W., Temoteo, J., Martins, A.: Dicionário da Língua de Sinais do Brasil: A Libras em suas Mãos, 1st edn. EdUSP, São Paulo (2017)
9. Brentari, D.: Phonology. In: Pfau, R., Steinback, M., Woll, B., (eds.) Sign Language: An International Handbook. Handbooks of Linguistics and Communication Science (HSK37), De Gruyter Mouton, Chap. I. (2012). http://bit.ly/2YBSOk7. Accessed 4 Aug 2019
10. Felipe, T.A.: Os processos de formação de palavra na Libras. ETD - Educação Temática Digital **7**(2), 200–217 (2006). https://doi.org/10.20396/etd.v7i2.803. Accessed 2 Aug 2019
11. Rezende, T., Castro, C., Almeida, S: An approach for Brazilian Sign Language (BSL) recognition based on facial expression and k-NN classifier. In: 29th SIBGRAPI, Workshop on Face Processing Applications, on Proceedings, pp. 1–2. SBC, São José dos Campos (2016). https://goo.gl/P9dtkg. Accessed 19 Sept 2018
12. Nel, W., Ghaziasgar, M., Connan, J.: An integrated sign language recognition system. In: SAICSIT 2013, East London, pp. 179–185. ACM (2013). https://dl.acm.org/citation.cfm? doid=2513456.2513491. Accessed 18 Feb 2019
13. Quadros, R., Pizzio, A., Rezende, P.: Língua Brasileira de Sinais II, 1st edn. UFSC, Florianópolis (2008). https://goo.gl/wRrKAX. Accessed 11 Oct 2018
14. Strobel, K., Fernandes, S.: Aspectos lingüísticos da LIBRAS. SEED/SUED/DEE, Curitiba (1998)
15. Rao, G.A., Kishore, P.V.V.: Selfie video based continuous Indian sign language recognition system. Ain Shams Eng. J. **9**, 1929–1939 (2018). https://doi.org/10.1016/j.asej.2016.10.013. Accessed 2 Aug 2019

16. Rojano-Cáceres, J., Sánchez-Barrera, H., Martínez-Gutiérrez, M., Guillermo, M., Ortega-Carrillo, J.: Designing an interaction architecture by scenarios for Deaf people. In: XVII International Conference on Human Computer Interaction (Interacción) on Proceedings, Salamanca, pp. 38:1–38:2. ACM (2016). https://dl.acm.org/citation.cfm?doid=2998626.2998642. Accessed 19 Sept 2018

17. Aran, O., et al.: SignTutor: an interactive system for sign language tutoring. IEEE Comput. Soc. 1(16), 81–93 (2009). https://doi.org/10.1109/MMUL.2009.17. Accessed 11 Oct 2018

18. Rivas, D., et al.: LeSigLa_EC: learning sign language of ecuador. In: Huang, T.-C., Lau, R., Huang, Y.-M., Spaniol, M., Yuen, C.-H. (eds.) SETE 2017. LNCS, vol. 10676, pp. 170–179. Springer, Cham (2017). https://doi.org/10.1007/978-3-319-71084-6_19. Accessed 3 Aug 2018

19. Agris, U., Zieren, J., Canzler, U., Bauer, B., Kraiss, K.: Recent developments in visual sign language recognition. Univers. Access Inf. Soc. 6(4), 323–362 (2008). https://doi.org/10.1007/s10209-007-0104-x. Accessed 04 Aug 2019

20. Borg, M., Camilleri, K.: Towards a transcription system of sign language video resources via motion trajectory factorisation. In: Proceedings of DocEng, Valletta on Proceedings, Valletta, Malta (2017). https://doi.org/10.1145/3103010.3103020. Accessed 19 Sept 2018

21. SignWriting® Site. http://www.signwriting.org/

22. Melnyk, M., Shadrova, V., Karwatsky, B.: Towards computer assisted international sign language recognition system: a systematic survey. Int. J. Comput. Appl. 89(17), 0975–8887 (2014). https://doi.org/10.5120/15727-4698. Accessed 2 Aug 2019

23. Paudyal, P., Lee, J., Banerjee, A., Gupta, S.: DyFAV: dynamic feature selection and voting for real-time recognition of fingerspelled alphabet using wearables. In: IUI 2017, Limassol, pp. 457–467. ACM (2017). https://doi.org/10.1145/3025171.3025216. Accessed 24 Sept 2018

24. Nyaga, C.N., Wario, R.D.: Sign language gesture recognition through computer vision. In: Cunningham, P., Cunningham, M. (eds.) IST-Africa 2018 Conference Proceedings, IIMC International Information Management Corporation (2018). Electronic ISSN: 2576-8581. http://bit.ly/2GJYcHO. Accessed 2 Aug 2019

25. González, G., Sánchez, J., Díaz, M., Pérez, A.: Recognition and classification of sign language for Spanish. Computación y Sistemas 22(1), 271–277 (2018). https://dx.doi.org/10.13053/cys-22-1-2780. Accessed 04 Aug 2019

26. Porfirio, A., Wiggers, K., Oliveira, S., Weingaertner, D.: Libras sign language hand configuration recognition based on 3D meshes. In: IEEE International Conference on Systems, Man, and Cybernetics (2013). https://doi.org/10.1109/smc.2013.274. Accessed 3 Aug 2019

27. Barros, R., Pontes, A., Almeida, J.: Reconhecimento de linguagem de sinais: aplicação em LIBRAS. In: V Jornada de Informática do Maranhão on Proceedings, São Luís, Maranhão (2014). https://goo.gl/uWG6y1. Accessed 24 Sept 2018

28. Cervantes, J., García-Lamont, F., Santiago, J.H., Cabrera, J.E., Trueba, A.: Clasificación del lenguaje de señas mexicano con SVM generando datos artificiales. Revista Vínculos, vol. 10, Número 1, Enero - Junio de (2013). https://doi.org/10.14483/2322939X.4684. Accessed 2 Aug 2019

29. Deaney, W., Venter, I., Ghaziasgar, M., Dodds, R.: A comparison of facial feature representation methods for automatic facial expression recognition. In: SAICSIT 2017 on Proceedings. Thaba Nchu, South Africa (2017). https://doi.org/10.1145/3129416.3129455. Accessed 19 Sept 2018

30. Gattupalli, S., Ghaderi, A., Athitsos, V.: Evaluation of deep learning based pose estimation for sign language recognition. In: PETRA 2016 on Proceedings, Greece, pp. 12:1–12:7. ACM (2016). https://doi.org/10.1145/2910674.2910716. Accessed 24 Sept 2018

31. Guerrero-Balaguera, J.D., Pérez-Holguín, W.J.: FPGA-based translation system from colombian sign language to text. Dyna **82**(189), 172–181 (2015). https://doi.org/10.15446/dyna.v82n189.43075. Accessed 2 Aug 2019

32. Rajaganapathy, S., Aravind, B., Keerthana, B., Sivagami, M.: Conversation of sign language to speech with human gestures. Procedia Comput. Sci. **50**, 10–15 (2015). https://doi.org/10.1016/j.procs.2015.04.004. Accessed 2 Aug 2019

33. Rodríguez, J., Martínez, F.: A kinematic gesture representation based on shape difference VLAD for sign language recognition. In: Chmielewski, L.J., Kozera, R., Orłowski, A., Wojciechowski, K., Bruckstein, A.M., Petkov, N. (eds.) ICCVG 2018. LNCS, vol. 11114, pp. 438–449. Springer, Cham (2018). https://doi.org/10.1007/978-3-030-00692-1_38

34. Ronchetti, F.: Reconocimiento de gestos dinámicos y su aplicación al lenguaje de señas. In: XX Workshop de Investigadores en Ciencias de la Computación, RedUNCI - UNNE, 26 y 27 de Abril de 2018. http://bit.ly/2LZUX2Z. ISBN 978-987-3619-27-4. Accessed 2 Aug 2019

35. Wang, H., Chai, X., Hong, X., Zhao, G., Chen, X.: Isolated sign language recognition with grassmann covariance matrices. ACM Trans. Access. Comput. **8**(4), 14:1–14:21 (2016). https://doi.org/10.1145/2897735. Accessed 19 Sept 2018

36. Wiggers, K., Ré, A., Porfírio, A.: Classificação das Configurações de Mão da Língua Brasileira de Sinais Mediante Rede Neural Artificial Kohonen. Recen **16**(2), 175–197 (2014). https://doi.org/10.5935/recen.2014.02.02. Accessed 18 Sept 2018

37. VLibras. http://www.vlibras.gov.br/. Accessed 11 Dec 2018

38. Hanson, V., Cavender, A., Trewin, S.: Writing about accessibility. interactions. In: XXII.6, page 62, November–December 2015. https://doi.org/10.1145/2828432. Accessed 4 Aug 2019

The RASE Model Applied to the Development of Communicative Competence Online

María de los Milagros Cruz-Ramos[1]([✉])(iD),
Juan Manuel González-Calleros[1](iD), and Luz Edith Herrera-Díaz[2](iD)

[1] Benemérita Universidad Autónoma de Puebla,
Av. San Claudio 14, 72592 Puebla, Mexico
tutor.milycruz@gmail.com, jumagoca78@gmail.com
[2] Universidad Veracruzana, Calzada Juan Pablo II s/n, 18071 Veracruz, Mexico
ehd63@hotmai.com

Abstract. This paper reports on an ongoing project aimed at determining if the integration of *language skills* and interaction, under the principles of the RASE model and the communicative approach, have an impact on the development students' *communicative competence* in an online English course for beginners. The modifications to the instructional design of the experimental group's online course are founded on the revised version of the Interaction Hypothesis, the study of *communicative competence*, the principles of the CLT approach, and those of the RASE model. Results are drawn from the application of communicative tests as part of a quantitative multiple time series quasi-experimental design. The tests are complemented with the use of a rubric specifically created to measure aspects related to the dimensions of the competence under study. The progress of those students working with the modified instructional design seems more evident that the progress of those in the control group, in particular when it comes to their oral *communicative competence*. The results in other areas of language and the other three *language skills* are not as clear since statistical analysis still needs to be carried out. Nevertheless, early results suggest that interaction and the use of integrated skills under a techno-pedagogical model do indeed aid the development of learners' *communicative competence*. Unlike previous studies, this project collects data related to all three dimensions of said competence.

Keywords: EFL · Techno-pedagogical model · Communicative competence

1 Introduction

Instructional design can be defined as a process aimed at the improvement and application of methods and models of instruction. The selection of instructional methods is necessary so as to achieve the desired changes in the knowledge and abilities of the students in a specific context and course [1]. In the case of courses that rely on the use of technology, such as those that involve blended or online learning, the principles of instructional design are translated into instructional design models [2]. These models work around a learning theory which orients the planning and execution of instruction.

© Springer Nature Switzerland AG 2019
P. H. Ruiz and V. Agredo-Delgado (Eds.): HCI-COLLAB 2019, CCIS 1114, pp. 381–395, 2019.
https://doi.org/10.1007/978-3-030-37386-3_28

Such models can also be called *techno-pedagogical* [3] due to the two dimensions they usually consider: (1) the technological, which deals with the tools and resources to be applied within the learning environment; (2) the pedagogical, concerned with the learners' characteristics and needs, as well as with the learning objectives, skills and competences to be achieved, the materials and activities to be designed and implemented, among other factors. However, it has been argued that disciplinary differences are rarely taken into account when designing or researching instruction in online courses [4].

This lack of disciplinary differences applied into instructional design seems evident when analyzing existent research around interaction and communication in a foreign language online. As matter of fact, EFL (English as a Foreign Language) online courses in general do not seem to take into account two essential disciplinary elements: EFL approaches to teaching and learning [5], and their implications for interaction and communication [6, 7]. This turns out to be problematic to say the least, due to the fact that regardless of the modality of instruction, EFL courses tend to have an objective in common: the development of skills that allow students to communicate in the target language. These skills, referred to as *communicative*, involve the integrated use of four different language skills (speaking, writing, listening, and reading).

A systematic literature review carried out last year [5] found that it was necessary to do further research on the development of *communication skills*, and the influence of techno-pedagogical strategies (product of instructional design) aimed at both the integration of language skills and learner interaction in the target language. Said literature review found that even those projects aimed at studying the effects that strategies, interaction and language skill integration have on students' actual *communicative competence* [8–13] either do not obtain conclusive results or focus exclusively on linguistic aspects which do not necessarily guarantee communication.

In consequence, this paper reports on the quantitative methods involved in an ongoing project that seeks to determine if an instructional design modified to incorporate interaction and communication in the target language under the principles of a communicative approach and the RASE model influences the development of a group of online students' *communicative competence*. This paper is organized as follows: Sect. 2 presents the literature review that serves as a theoretical framework to the modifications undergone by the instructional design; Sect. 3 presents the methodology followed, comprised by the implementation and data collection procedures; Sect. 4 synthesizes the preliminary results obtained in the first half of the project; Sect. 5 discusses the results and their implications; and Sect. 6 presents the conclusions and further research to be carried out in the second half of the project.

2 Literature Review

Language is considered a social process. Thus, we can assume that interaction with other people is relevant in learning how to communicate. This section revolves around four main concepts and theories that explain how communication in a target language can be achieved online under the principles of a teaching approach and a techno-pedagogical model.

2.1   Language and Interaction

Thanks to interaction, students are exposed to language models that constitute input. The role this input plays in the development of language is often analyzed from three points of view: the behaviorist, focused on the linguistic environment, that is, the stimuli and feedback obtained from the medium; the nativist, focused on the internal way in which each individual processes the language; and the interactionist, which considers the two previous ones [14]. A revised version of the Interaction Hypothesis [15] proposes that three things are necessary to acquire a new language through interaction: (1) noticing, the individual perceives and is aware of the linguistic characteristics of the input; (2) comparison, the individual compares the characteristics of the input with that of his own output, or his own speech; (3) integration, the individual constructs his own linguistic knowledge, thanks to the two previous elements, and internalizes it.

Regarding this revised version of the interaction hypothesis, [16] noted that there are additional aspects to be taken into account, such as student ability, and how prepared they are to negotiate meaning; yet, the author of said revised version concludes that his version of the hypothesis has generated sufficient research in the area and demonstrated explanatory power. The interaction hypothesis is still one of the most coherent and consistent ones, since it does not seem to contain internal contradictions and the terminology used is clearly and widely explained [17]. Although the role of instruction is not taken into account, the interaction hypothesis is capable of explaining the learning process [18]. Within this study learning is defined as the process through which an individual receives input in the target language via the interaction with other individuals. In turn, this input constitutes models of language whose patterns the student is able to understand, reproduce and adapt so as to express meaning.

2.2   Communicative Competence

The term *communicative competence* emphasizes the importance of learning what is grammatically correct while also understanding what is appropriate [19]. Although this concept was not originally created in relation to foreign languages, it gave rise to the work of other linguists [20, 21], who reevaluated the original definition; determined that this competence should be observable in communicative acts; and identified the need to look for ways to contribute to the development of *communicative competence* and its assessment.

This concept has been defined and studied by different authors over four decades [20–24]. In this particular study, *communicative competence* is understood as the use that individuals give to their grammatical knowledge of morphology, phonology, and syntax, as well as to their social knowledge in order to emit, interpret and adapt the messages received during their interaction with others in the target language, English.

2.3   Communicative Approaches in EFL

The TBLT (Task-Based Language Teaching) approach and the communicative approach (better known as CLT) stand out among other communicative approaches to language teaching due to the fact that they allow the integration of the four language skills while heightening the role of interaction among participants in the target language [25]. However, there are major differences between these two approaches. On the one hand, under the TBLT approach communication and interaction are likely to favor communication and interaction over linguistic forms; on the other hand, the CLT approach focuses on students learning and using forms, meanings and linguistic functions that enable them to communicate in the target language. Consequently, the CLT approach is aimed at the development of students' *communicative competence* [25, 26]. Instruction under the CLT approach follows a series of principles [25], which are considered applicable in online synchronous instruction and interaction [27]:

(a) Authentic language should be used and introduced into the classroom whenever possible.
(b) A part of being communicatively competent is being able to understand the intentions of the interlocutor.
(c) The use of language is not only the objective; it is also the means to achieve it.
(d) Errors are a natural result of the development of communication. They must be observed and addressed without diverting attention from communication.
(e) The teacher must establish situations that can promote communication.
(f) The communicative interaction among students gives them the opportunity to negotiate a meaning.
(g) The communicative context is essential to give meaning to expressions.
(h) It is important to learn to use language forms appropriately.

A balance among communication and linguistic form is attainable through this approach, as made evident in principles (b) and (h) above.

2.4   RASE as a Techno-Pedagogical Model

The theories, principles and approaches heretofore mentioned have important implications for instructional design in virtual environments at the system, course and lesson level [2]. The RASE model (acronym for Resources, Activities, Support, Evaluation), contemplates the design and implementation of resources, activities and evaluation. Additionally, it highlights the importance of the support provided to students. This model contemplates multiple concepts based on the Theory of Activity proposed by Vygotsky and articulated more specifically by Engeström [28]. Its focus is primarily constructivist, because it focuses learning on the activities carried out by the students in an environment that encourages the construction of knowledge, beyond its mere transmission. The RASE model can be approached from two perspectives: (1) instructional - it helps teachers to focus on the student while integrating educational technologies; and (2) learning - it helps students learn disciplinary content and develop new knowledge [29].

Each of the four RASE aspects has its own set of core characteristics [28, 29]: (a) Resources constitute easily accessible contents, materials and tools students can interact with; (b) Activities should be student-centered and authentic, clear instructions and models should be provided, and resources are to be used as tools; (c) Support should be both anticipatory and ongoing, available in multiple modes; (d) Evaluation can have multiple outcomes, and it must be aligned to the learning activities while offering feedback and opportunities for improvement.

2.5 Theoretical Articulation

The works cited in this section suggest that interaction in the target language is key in the development of students' *communicative competence*. Moreover, if disciplinary principles are followed when planning instruction, then students can acquire linguistic and functional tools that enable them to communicate in the target language. However, within an online environment, this can only be achieved with the support of a techno-pedagogical model. The RASE model seems particularly useful due to the simplicity of its own tenets, which have major points in common with the CLT approach.

3 Methodology

This ongoing study attempts to analyze the development of students' communicative skills in an online EFL course in order to determine if the integration of language skills and student interaction in the target language are correlated to students' *communicative competence* at the end of the course. The study followed two groups of undergraduate students in a public university in southeast Mexico. These groups were enrolled in a compulsory online English II course during the 2019 spring semester. Students' *communicative competence* was measured three times throughout the course as part of a quantitative quasi-experimental multiple time series design using an experimental and a control group. The multiple measurements help the design gain strength since certainty is gained in the interpretation of the results [30, 31].

However, threats to the internal validity of this type of study must be acknowledged. Such is the case of sample size, the loss of data, and subjects possibly withdrawing from the implementation [32]. Some solutions to control these threats include keeping a balance between the size of experimental and control groups, matching (pairing) subjects based on a specific characteristic or variable in order to emulate random assignment, as well as calculating the size of the effect in relation to the size of the sample [32].

3.1 Context and Subjects

Under the university's current system students need to take either two or four compulsory English courses, depending on their undergraduate program. Online courses are available for beginner levels I and II on the institutional platform Eminus. The target population was constituted by the 221 students enrolled in the online English II course offered by the university during the 2019 spring semester across five different regions and cities where the university has a campus.

The accessible population was constituted by the 46 students enrolled in the Veracruz-Boca del Rio area. These 46 students belonged to 21 different undergraduate programs and were distributed in two groups: 24 of them belonged to the experimental group (EG) and 22 to the control group (CG). In turn, the sample consisted of those students who were active throughout the course and was thus selected nonrandomly.

The following Table 1 details the distribution the sample by gender, in relation to the accessible population.

Table 1. Accessible population and sample.

	EG		CG	
	Accessible population	Sample	Accessible population	Sample
Male	14	9	13	6
Female	10	8	9	7

The course covered 10 thematic units. The original course design included the use of asynchronous tools for individual and group tasks, showing some similarities to the Dick and Carey techno-pedagogical model due to the fact that the platform works as the medium where instruction is carried in all its stages [33]. Said techno-pedagogical model defines instruction, as a set of examples, materials, and activities to be carried out by students, all of which are aimed at prompting a desired behavior or learning [34]. In contrast, and as we have previously established, this study understands learning as the process through which an individual receives information that constitutes input.

From this input, individuals must discern, reproduce and adapt language models so as to express meaning in the target language. Nevertheless, the original course design limits students' opportunities to receive input in English either from the resources or from interaction with others. Group forum tasks are frequently carried out completely in Spanish. In addition, study materials available on the platform contain explanations in Spanish and examples in English. Moreover, the lack of oral and written interaction in the target language among individuals, whether synchronously or asynchronously, goes against the tenets of the CLT approach. Consequently, there is an evident disparity between the instruction provided and the objective online English courses within the institution pursue and assess in students: communication.

3.2 Changes to the Instructional Design

In the case of the experimental group (EG), the original course design was altered based on the principles of both the RASE techno-pedagogical model and the principles of the CLT approach so as to ensure that technological tools were used to support the development of students' communication in the target language. Resources, activities, support and evaluation were all modified or enriched. New resources included: (a) multimedia presentations and videos, which focused on presenting language as it would be used in real contexts and giving instructions for activities to be carried out synchronously under the guidance of the instructor, or asynchronously for reinforcement; (b) audios, recorded by speakers with a C2 level according to the Common European Framework of Reference (CEFR) in order to provide listening practice, a language skill which was not considered in the previous design; (c) interactive vocabulary flashcards that students could access online contained visual and written representations of the vocabulary from each unit, as well as the words' pronunciation.

Resources were later retrieved as part of two main kind of activities: asynchronous forums on the institutional platform and synchronous practice sessions on the web conferencing tool Zoom. Audios were sometimes introduced in the forums and used to set a model for student interaction. Different language skills were integrated in the forums, thus providing greater opportunities for contextualized practice of the language. An additional change to the forums consisted in the exchange of audio messages recorded using a free online tool named VoiceSpice. Synchronous web conferencing sessions provided students with contextualized practice of the language based on the principles of the CLT approach, found to be applicable online by [27]. Multimedia presentations were used to explain/review the language presented in the unit, followed by activities that helped students practice grammar and ultimately demanded them to use the language in a contextualized manner. The interaction during the sessions involved the use of all four language skills.

Support was provided both asynchronously (via personal and institutional email) and synchronously (at the end of the practice sessions). The support provided was ongoing as students could have access to it at any point throughout all ten units. Similarly, anticipatory support was made available in the form of manuals that expanded on technical aspects anticipating student needs, as well as in the form of weekly assignment reminders and monthly progress reports. A messaging service was also used so as to provide additional support options to students. Evaluation, the last element of the RASE model, was also modified with the help of the web conferencing tool Zoom. Partial oral exams and final project presentations took place online constituting in themselves opportunities for students to get additional feedback on their progress.

3.3 Data Collection

Standardized tests provided by the institutional English department were used to asses students' progress in three moments. A pre-test was administered a week prior to the start of the course, a control test was administered on the eighth week, and final test took place towards the end of the course on week sixteen. All tests had a written and an oral component. The former assessed students' grammar and vocabulary, as well as three language skills (listening, reading and writing). The latter assessed the fourth language skill (speaking, also considered oral production). However, in order to measure students' *communicative competence*, an additional quantitative instrument was designed to complement the oral component of the standardized tests.

This instrument consisted in a rubric that assessed elements corresponding to each of the three dimensions of the variable *communicative competence*. The design process took into account the guidelines and examples offered in the CEFR [35], as well as the operationalization of said variable into dimensions and indicators. In order for the rubric to be as manageable as possible, only six aspects directly related to the indicators established in the operationalization were included.

These aspects were selected based on two conditions- how representative they were of each dimension, and how applicable they would be to the expected production of an EFL leaner at a beginner's level:

1. Lexical and grammatical accuracy and precision
2. Lexical and grammatical range
3. Pronunciation
4. Style and Register
5. Fluency and coherency
6. Contextual appropriateness.

Along with the rubric, a detailed set of scoring criteria was developed so as to let potential examiners know how to score each aspect. The rubric uses a scale between 1 and 5, with 5 being the highest possible score for each of the six aspects. This results in a total of 30 possible points overall. The rubric was validated both qualitative and quantitatively by two different groups of TEFL (Teaching English as a Foreign Language) experts. The first group of experts validated the design by emulating the operationalization process originally followed, whereas the second group of experts validated the relevance and coherence of each indicator to measure its corresponding dimension. The rubric was then tested to determine if two different scorers would reach an acceptable agreement.

4   Preliminary Results

This section reports on the results obtained by both groups in the Pre-Test, Test Control and Post-Test in terms of score means, before in-depth statistical analysis. It also reports on the performance of five pairs of learners matched mechanically taking one student from the EG and one from the CG. These ten students were paired based on the *communicative competence* they demonstrated in the oral component of the pre-test as advised by [32]. These five pairs were selected as a means of purposive sampling [31] so as to obtain varied data on typical, high and low performances for maximum variation, but discarding those cases considered extreme.

4.1   Group Scores

The following Table 2 summarizes the mean scores obtained by each group in each of the five sections comprised in the written component in the three moments of the time multiple time series: The Pre-Test, the Control Test and the Post-Test.

Table 2. Mean scores obtained in the written component of the standardized tests.

	Experimental group			Control group		
Area	Pre-test	Control test	Post-test	Pre-test	Control test	Post-test
Vocabulary	4.48	7.39	8.57	6.33	8.24	8.13
Grammar	5.97	5.64	6.36	7.45	5.45	6.41
Listening	6.29	6.92	7.65	8.16	7.87	7.09
Reading	8.86	8.32	9.49	8.37	7.47	9.12
Writing	5.78	5.10	5.83	7.62	5.38	5.26

The global mean scores obtained by the groups in the written component are shown next (see Fig. 1).

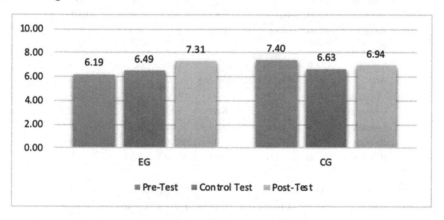

Fig. 1. The chart shows the mean scores obtained by each group in the written component of the pre-test, control test and post-test.

The mean scores obtained by each group in the oral test in relation to their *communicative competence* are shown below (see Fig. 2).

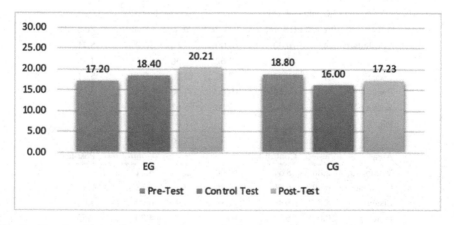

Fig. 2. The chart shows the mean oral score obtained by each group in the pre-test, control test and post-test.

4.2   Pair Scores

The following Table 3 shows the results each pair of students obtained in the three moments of the time series.

Table 3. Pair scores in the written component.

Pair 1

Area	EG (student 9)			CG (student 4)		
	Pre-test	Control test	Post-test	Pre-test	Control test	Post-test
Vocabulary	10.00	8.57	10.00	5.71	7.14	10.00
Grammar	8.26	7.27	8.57	5.65	5.45	8.57
Listening	10.00	9.23	9.29	8.57	10.00	8.57
Reading	10.00	10.00	8.57	8.57	10.00	10.00
Writing	10.00	5.00	8.33	8.33	5.00	3.33

Pair 2

Area	EG (student 8)			CG (student 17)		
	Pre-test	Control test	Post-test	Pre-test	Control test	Post-test
Vocabulary	4.29	8.57	10.00	10.00	8.57	10.00
Grammar	8.26	6.82	6.67	9.13	9.09	7.62
Listening	10.00	8.46	9.29	10.00	8.46	9.29
Reading	10.00	10.00	10.00	10.00	10.00	10.00
Writing	10.00	5.00	5.00	10.00	8.33	8.33

Pair 3

Area	EG (student 4)			CG (student 2)		
	Pre-test	Control test	Post-test	Pre-test	Control test	Post-test
Vocabulary	2.86	7.14	10.00	7.14	7.14	8.57
Grammar	6.96	5.45	6.67	7.83	4.55	10.00
Listening	8.57	7.59	8.57	7.14	5.38	7.14
Reading	10.00	7.14	10.00	5.71	4.29	10.00
Writing	8.33	5.00	8.33	6.67	5.00	6.67

Pair 4

Area	EG (student 11)			CG (student 12)		
	Pre-test	Control test	Post-test	Pre-test	Control test	Post-test
Vocabulary	1.43	10.00	10.00	7.14	10.00	5.71
Grammar	4.78	5.45	7.62	6.96	3.18	4.76
Listening	5.71	5.38	7.86	10.00	5.38	5.71
Reading	7.14	7.14	10.00	10.00	5.71	7.14
Writing	3.33	5.00	5.00	6.67	5.00	5.00

Pair 5

Area	EG (student 12)			CG (student 18)		
	Pre-test	Control test	Post-test	Pre-test	Control test	Post-test
Vocabulary	2.86	8.57	10.00	2.86	5.71	7.14
Grammar	6.09	6.36	8.10	5.65	2.73	6.19
Listening	8.57	8.46	7.86	4.29	6.92	5.00
Reading	10.00	10.00	10.00	7.14	4.29	8.57
Writing	8.33	6.67	5.00	3.33	3.33	3.33

The global written and oral scores for each pair throughout the time series are presented below (see Fig. 3). Also shown, are the oral scores for each pair in the three moments of the time series (see Fig. 4).

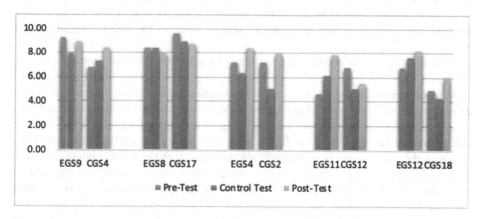

Fig. 3. The chart shows the global scores each pair of students obtained in the written tests.

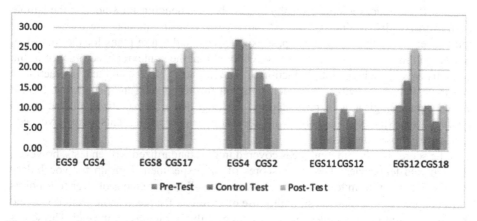

Fig. 4. The chart shows the scores each pair of students obtained in the oral tests when measuring *communicative competence*.

5 Discussion

Both individual and group scores show that, in average, the control group started ahead of the experimental group. This is made evident in the average scores obtained in the standardized written Pre-Test. Given that all students enrolled into English II courses credited the previous course, albeit in different modalities and temporalities, they share a similar starting point at least as far as their linguistic knowledge concerns. Still, the mean scores for the two areas related to linguistic knowledge, vocabulary and grammar, were over a point lower for the experimental group. Something similar occurred with the *language skills* listening and writing. For reading, however, the experimental group scored almost half a point higher. This difference in scores per section, is congruent with the global score for the same written tests. The experimental group's overall score of 6.19, was almost a point and a half below the 7.40 score averaged by the students in the control group. The disparity in scores when measuring students' oral *communicative competence*, was as steep as the one shown in written tests.

Nevertheless, and in line with the findings of a previous quantitative study [7], oral communication was expected to be the aspect to improve the most, from the pre-test to subsequent measurements, thanks to an intervention that fostered interaction in the target language among peers. This research implemented such a change through the modification of some course elements according to the principles of the RASE techno-pedagogical model [28, 29]. Accordingly, when comparing the results obtained by both groups in the three moments of the multiple time series, the experimental group's oral *communicative competence* rose steadily, whereas the average scores for the control group decreased from pre-test to control test. Even though the control group managed to recover to some degree from control test to post-test, the group's *communicative competence score* for the post-test was almost three points lower than the one obtained by the experimental group.

An apparent cause for the control group's oral score decrease could be the fact that English II introduces a topic typically considered challenging for students: the simple past. Additionally, during the second half of the course, students are asked to start mixing tenses to discuss routines, past experiences, and future plans for the first time. Keeping in mind that other authors have claimed that the contextualized practice of the contents aids the subsequent production of the language [25, 26] and that interaction is key in providing students with models they can further modify and personalize [15], it would seem illogical to expect students lacking that contextualized interaction to produce contextualized language with the same results as students who have been exposed to those conditions.

The scores for the different areas covered in the standardized written tests, however, show mixed tendencies. The mean scores of the experimental group for vocabulary increased steadily from test to test to show an overall improvement of over four points from the pre-test to the post-test; in the case of grammar the mean score went down and then up, amounting to a modest improvement of only four tenths by the end. The scores for the *language skills* showed three different behaviors: listening increased steadily by seven tenths from test to test; the score for reading decreased only to increase again at the end, reaching an overall improvement of over six tenths; writing was the least benefited area, with a score than went down seven tenths from pre-test to control test and barely recovered them from control test to post-test. Then again, the written tasks for the second and third tests also involved the use of new topics.

The mean scores of the control group showed mixed tendencies as well, with scores going up or down from test to test. Consequently, the group scores for the different sections as well as the global written score ended up being lower than those of the experimental group by the time of the post-test. The most affected skill in their case was also writing, which decreased by over two points between the start and the end of the course.

Even before an in-depth statistical analysis, the results of the individuals paired with a member of the other group, do not seem to show a clear tendency. There have been individuals in each pair whose scores have increased and decreased in the different areas of the written test, while their counterpart's either show a similar behavior or do the opposite. The only exception is the linguistic skill vocabulary, where four out of the five students from the experimental group saw their scores soar in the post-test. It must be noted that even when their counterparts' original scores for vocabulary had been higher, within all five pairs the members of the experimental group managed to match or even surpass them in that area. The scores individuals obtained when measuring their oral *communicative competence* show that, within four of the five pairs, the members of the experimental group performed better in both the control test and the post-test than the members of the other group did.

The comparison between the group's global written scores seems to make things clearer. The global mean scores of the experimental group increased by three tenths, from the pre-test to the control test, while the global means of the control group decreased by over almost eight tenths. Still, the average written score of the experimental group was below that of the control group in that second test, turning what originally was a difference 1.21 points to a difference of only 0.14 points. The tendency continued from the control test to the post-test, which lead the experimental group eventually surpass the control group.

6 Future Work

SPSS, a statistical analysis program, will be used to explore the causal relations among the different variables involved in this project. Due to the fact that ANOVA tests are usually run to verify if certain characteristics of two groups differ significantly at the end of an intervention [26], such a test will be considered to verify if the experimental and control group's *communicative competence* differed significantly after the intervention finished.

7 Conclusions

The body of work behind the idea that integrated skills and interaction are key in the development of communication is wide to say the least [7, 10, 14–16, 19–26]. As previous literature reviews have demonstrated [5], researchers around the world are interested in the use of synchronous and asynchronous communication technology in EFL courses. However, the correlation between instructional designs, strategies implemented, and actual communicative results are not typically studied.

The preliminary results shown in this paper seem promising, even if the time frame for the implementation and data collection was quite limited. It is too soon to determine whether the improvement in students' *communicative competence* was indeed significant between groups. That is to say: until a statistical analysis has been carried out, it will not be possible to assert whether the intervention has actually been beneficial or not. The extent of the benefits, given they exist, remains unknown. The outlook, however, is optimistic.

References

1. Reigeluth, C.: Instructional Design Theories and Models. An Overview of their Current Status, 1st edn. Lawrence Erlbaum Associates, Hillside, New Jersey (1983). https://doi.org/10.4324/9780203824283
2. Universidad Veracruzana. http://www.uv.es/~bellochc/pedagogia/EVA4.pdf. Accessed 15 Sept 2016
3. Coll, C., Mauri, T., Onrunbia, J.: Los entornos virtuales de aprendizaje basados en el análisis de casos y la resolución de problemas. Psicología de la educación virtual, 1st end. Morata, Spain (2008)
4. Smith, G., Torres-Ayala, A., Heindel, A.: Disciplinary differences in e-learning instructional design: the case of mathematics. J. Distance Educ. 23(3), 63–88 (2019). https://files.eric.ed.gov/fulltext/EJ812564.pdf. Accessed 10 July 2019
5. Cruz-Ramos, M., González-Calleros, J., Herrera-Díaz, L.: Desarrollo de Habilidades Comunicativas en Cursos de Inglés en Línea: Una Aproximación desde el Estado del Conocimiento, 1st edn. CIATA.org-UCLM, Ciudad Real (2018). https://www.researchgate.net/publication/326357243_Tecnologias_y_Aprendizaje_Investigacion_y_Practica. Accessed 18 June 2019
6. Fincham, X.: Metacognitive knowledge development and language learning in the context of web-based distance language learning: a multiple-case study of adult EFL learners in China. Order No. 3718760, Michigan State University, Ann Arbor (2015)
7. Flesvig, N.: Examining the relationship between interaction and linguistic outcomes: is the online learning environment a viable alternative to traditional classroom instruction for beginning language learners? Order No. 3612411. The Florida State University, Ann Arbor (2013)
8. Arias, L.: Impacto de un curso mediado por la Web 2.0 en el desarrollo profesional de un grupo de futuros docentes de inglés. Folios 36, 51–76 (2012). https://doi.org/10.17227/01234870.36folios51.76
9. Chang, H., Windeatt, S.: Developing collaborative learning practices in an online language course. Comput. Assist. Lang. Learn. 29(8), 1–16 (2016). https://doi.org/10.1080/09588221.2016.1274331
10. Cruz, M., Sandoval, M.: Retroalimentación entre iguales en sesiones virtuales síncronas. Recopilación de Ponencias del Congreso Internacional de Investigación Acad. J. Celaya 7 (4),1169–1174 (2015)
11. Herrera Díaz, L., González Miy, D.: Developing the oral skill in online English courses framed by the community of inquiry. Profile 16(1), 73–88 (2017). http://dx.doi.org/10.15446/profile.v19n1.55957
12. Rosales, B., Zárate, J., Lozano, A.: Desarrollo de la competencia comunicativa en el idioma inglés en una plataforma interactiva. Sinéctica. Revista Electrónica De Educación 41, 1–11 (2013). https://doi.org/10.31391/s2007-7033
13. Vine, A., Ferreira, A.: Mejoramiento de la Competencia Comunicativa en Español como Lengua Extranjera a Través de la Videocomunicación. Revista De Lingüística Teórica Y Aplicada 50(1), 139–160 (2012)
14. Ellis, R.: Understanding Second Language Acquisition, 1st edn. Oxford University Press, Oxford (1985)

15. Ellis, R.: The Interaction Hypothesis: A Critical Evaluation. Regional Language Centre Seminar, Singapore pp. 3–46 (1991)
16. Ellis, R.: The Study of Second Language Acquisition, 2nd edn. Oxford University Press, Oxford (2008)
17. Ghaemi, F., Salehi, N.: Interaction hypothesis: a comprehensive theory of SLA? Int. J. Teach. Engl. 4(4), 23–33 (2014)
18. Gass, S., Mackey, A.: Input, Interaction, and Output in Second Language Acquisition. Theories in Second Language Acquisition, 2nd edn. Routledge, New York (2015). https://doi.org/10.4324/9780203628942
19. Hymes, D.: On communicative competence. In: Sociolinguistics. Selected Readings, 1st edn. Penguin, London (1972)
20. Canale, M., Swain, M.: Theoretical bases of communicative approaches to second language teaching and testing. Appl. Linguist. 1, 1–47 (1980). https://doi.org/10.1093/applin/I.1.1
21. Savignon, S.: Communicative Competence: Theory and Classroom Practice. Texts and Contexts in Second Language Learning, 1st edn. Addison-Wesley Publishing Company, Reading Massachusetts (1983)
22. Widdowson, H.: Learning Purpose and Language Use, 1st edn. Oxford University Press, Oxford (1983)
23. Bachman, L.: Fundamental Considerations in Language Testing, 1st edn. Oxford University Press, Oxford (2011)
24. Pilleux, M.: Competencia comunicativa y análisis del discurso. Estudios Filológicos (36), 143–152 (2001). https://doi.org/10.4067/s0071-17132001003600010
25. Larsen-Freeman, D., Anderson, M.: Techniques and Principles in Language Teaching, 3rd edn. Oxford University Press, New York (2011)
26. Richards, J.C.: http://www.professorjackrichards.com. Accessed 20 July 2018
27. Sandoval, M., Cruz, M.: The CLT approach in online synchronous sessions. In: Memorias del Congreso Internacional de Investigación Academia Journals Celaya 2018, vol. 10, pp. 5096–5101. Academia Journal, Celaya (2018)
28. Churchill, D., King, M., Fox, R.: Learning design for science education in the 21st century. Zbornik Instituta Za Pedagoska Istrazivanja 45(2), 404–421 (2013). https://doi.org/10.2298/ZIPI1302404C
29. Fox, R.: The Rise of Open and Blended Learning. Studies and Practices for Advancement in Open and Distance Education, 1st edn. Open University of Hong Kong Press, Hong Kong (2015)
30. Campbell, D., Stanley, J.: Experimental And Quasi-Experimental Designs for Research, 1st edn. R. McNally, Chicago (1966)
31. Fraenkel, J., Wallen, N., Hyun, H.: How to Design and Evaluate Research in Education, 8th edn. McGraw-Hill, New York (2012)
32. Fernández-García, P., Vallejo-Seco, G., Livacic-Rojas, P., Tuero-Herrero, E.: Validez Estructurada para una investigación cuasi-experimental de calidad: se cumplen 50 años de la presentación en sociedad de los diseños cuasi-experimentales. Anales de Psicología 30(2), 756–771 (2014). https://doi.org/10.6018/analesps.30.2.166911
33. Chávez-Espinoza, J., Balderrama-Trápaga, J., Figueroa-Rodríguez, S.: The Dick and Carey Systems Approach Model: Acercamiento y fundamentación. Creative Commons, Ciudad de México (2014)
34. Dick, W., Carey, L., Carey, J.: Introduction to Instructional Design. The Systematic Design of Instruction, 8th edn. Pearson, New Jersey (2015)
35. Council of Europe: Common European Framework of Reference for Languages: Learning, Teaching, Assessment, 1st edn. Cambridge University Press, Strasbourg (2018)

Towards a Technological Strategy for Using Sources of Reliable Information on the Internet

Mayra Nayeli Márquez-Specia$^{(\boxtimes)}$ ⓘ, Josefina Guerrero-García ⓘ,
and Yadira Navarro-Rangel ⓘ

Doctorado en Sistemas y Ambientes Educativos,
Facultad de Ciencias de la Electrónica, Benemérita Universidad Autónoma
de Puebla, Ciudad Universitaria, Av. San Claudio y 14 sur, Puebla, PUE, Mexico
{mayra.specia,yadira.navarro}@correo.buap.mx,
joseguga01@gmail.com

Abstract. This is a study with pre-test and post-test design whose main objective is to know the effectiveness of a sequence of activities designed to develop the skills in the search of reliable information on the Internet, this, in university students of the first semester in a degree in the Chemical Biological area. Throughout this study, ICTs are used as a tool for the search of specialized information, through the use of databases as well as for the co-evaluations of information sources carried out by the students, using the C.A.R.S. checklist for the evaluation of information sources on the internet. To obtain results in this research, a comparison is made of the data obtained in the co-evaluations, so the methodological design is divided into two stages, one before and one after the application of the sequence of activities, to verify the effectiveness of the sequence the comparison of means is made by the t-Student statistic.

Keywords: Information search · Higher education · Co-evaluation of sources · C.A.R.S. Checklist

1 Introduction

In the educational field there is a great diversity of competences, in the case of this study, it refers to one of the primary stages in the teaching of the research process and the development of research competencies, that is, the search and evaluation of reliable information, particularly in students of the Chemical Biological Sciences area.

To put on context, we understand by investigative competence the set of skills and attitudes required for the development of a research project [1], on the other hand, the search for reliable scientific information is undoubtedly one of the most important elements in the teaching and development of skills for research.

So, for the development of these skills and abilities, students go through a process where they acquire epistemological, methodological and instrumental foundations, in order to build scientific knowledge [2].

In such a way that the teaching of the research process should be adapted in the way of producing and using scientific knowledge, through the application of didactic

© Springer Nature Switzerland AG 2019
P. H. Ruiz and V. Agredo-Delgado (Eds.): HCI-COLLAB 2019, CCIS 1114, pp. 396–407, 2019.
https://doi.org/10.1007/978-3-030-37386-3_29

research strategies, presenting significant moments in the process of teaching scientific research [3].

The curriculum of university students should evolve along with current professional needs, where the context is the knowledge society, since professionals must not only master their area of knowledge but must know the utility and potential of Information and Communication Technologies (ICT).

According to Fernández and Villavicencio [4] the support to research nurseries is of importance for students to develop the necessary skills for research among which the skills in information search and bibliometric analysis are considered, which is a requirement to achieve a training based on research.

From this point of view, higher education institutions require the definition and application of ICT integration strategies and innovation in didactic - pedagogical mediation, to help students develop a profile of scientific competencies that guide the search for pertinent information and construction of significant knowledge [5].

A task of great importance when doing a documentary search is, without a doubt, to evaluate the quality of the information sources that are consulted, since in the case of the Internet, it is a powerful resource of free access, so that the user is obliged to recognize the sources of reliable and high-quality information [6].

Meanwhile, studies show that students overestimated their search skills and their ability to evaluate sources, while students expressed comfort by developing searches, researchers found that they were not familiar with the basic search concepts, in addition to selecting web sources more frequently than peer-reviewed articles [7].

The initial phase of any research process is the search and review of information, so obtaining reliable sources with scientific support becomes a primary task of any researcher, therefore developing the necessary skills for students to perform this task in an effective way should be a priority in educational programs.

For the development of this research, a study with a pre-test post-test design is contemplated, taking as sample students of the Pharmacobiologist Chemistry Degree from a public university in México, with whom a sequence of activities was applied, focused on developing in students the necessary skills for the search and evaluation of information sources with the support of ICT.

In such a way, that the main objective of this research is based on knowing the effectiveness of the sequence of activities through the comparison of the co-evaluations of information sources obtained from the internet in the pre and post test.

1.1 C.A.R.S. of Harris Checklist for the Co-evaluation of Information Sources

Some of the tasks of university students in all disciplines is that they write essays and research reports, being an important requirement of these tasks the use of evidence to support the assertions that appear in the work, so teachers consider the evaluation of the sources with their students with greater relevance, however, students have problems to understand what these concepts mean [8].

As the critical attitude in the search for information has already been raised, the use and knowledge of pertinent search tools and the use of reliable scientific information are important requirements for the development of research competences in university students of any area.

Since students follow a sequential process to evaluate the content of a website; opening and reviewing the pages, prioritizing websites that contain information that covers more elements required in the assigned task, seeking to find the complete answer on a site [9]; it is important that they consider the quality of the information and in order to obtain such quality it is necessary to do specialized searches.

In order to develop these competencies and skills in information management, students must have access to various search tools, whether search engines or specialized databases, however, the evaluation of the information obtained is still of great importance, since that not only reliability is important, but also its accuracy.

Regarding the evaluation of information sources, there are several models or checklists that allow the evaluation of information sources in an effective way, being the C.A.R.S. of Harris Checklist one of the most used, which has been previously implemented in the University.

The C.A.R.S. (Credibility, Accuracy, Reasonableness and Support) Checklist is designed to help researchers evaluate the sources of information, probably few sources will comply with each of the criteria in this list, but if you learn to use and apply these criteria, it will be possible to separate the quality information from the bad quality information [10].

To clearly understand the C.A.R.S. Checklist, a summary of the four elements that comprise it is presented (see Table 1).

Table 1. Summary of the elements of the CARS Checklist for the evaluation of information sources [11].

Element	Description
Credibility	Trustworthy source, author's credentials, evidence of quality control, known or respected authority, organizational support. Goal: an authoritative source, a source that supplies some good evidence that allows you to trust it
Accuracy	Up to date, factual, detailed, exact, comprehensive, audience and purpose reflect intentions of completeness and accuracy. Goal: a source that is correct today (not yesterday)
Reasonableness	Fair, balanced, objective, reasoned, no conflict of interest, absence of fallacies or slanted tone. Goal: a source that engages the subject thoughtfully and reasonably, concerned with the truth
Support	Listed sources, contact information, available corroboration, claims supported, documentation supplied. Goal: a source that provides convincing evidence for the claims made

2 Methodology

As part of the design of a didactic strategy, a series of activities focused on developing specific research skills in university students who are studying the first semester of an educational program in the Chemical Biological area are being implemented.

The application of the sequence of activities has been carried out with two groups of new students to the degree of Chemist Pharmacobiologist, the 2 groups are made up of 20 and 23 students respectively, the tests that are currently performed correspond to a general piloting of the methodology proposed for a doctoral study in order to detect areas of opportunity and necessary adjustments to it.

Among the main characteristics of the participants in this study, we found that 66% are female and 34% male, where 82% come from public higher secondary education, while 18% from private education (see Fig. 1), within the sample of the 43 students, the predominant ages are 18 and 19 years. It is worth mentioning that the selection of the sample was made for convenience since the two groups available for the spring 2019 period were used.

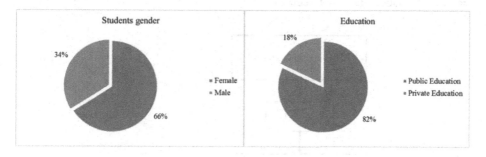

Fig. 1. Student's gender and type of education previous to university.

Considering what has been established in the syllabus proposed for the subject and approved by the Faculty of Chemical Sciences, topics from 1.1 to 1.4 corresponding to Unit 1 have been selected (see Table 2).

Table 2. Subjects corresponding to Unit 1 of the syllabus of the subject Computational Tools.

Unit	Topics
1. Search for reliable information	1.1 How to define the need for information
	1.2 Reliability of information: selection of sources
	1.3 Tools for searching information on the internet
	1.3.1 Google Scholar
	1.3.2 Electronic resources provided by the general management of BUAP libraries
	1.4 Databases: SciELO, SpringerLink, SCOPUS, etc.
	1.5 Information search strategies

The subject of Computational Tools is taught in one of the computer labs of the Faculty of Chemical Sciences at the university, this laboratory has a total of 36 computers with Internet access, and since the total number of students is divided into two groups, each student has access to a computer in each session, as well as an own account in the Blackboard institutional platform, which is being used to store the virtual portfolios of the students divided into teams of 3 to 4 members.

To test these activities a total of 5 sessions of two hours each per group were used, the indications and links necessary for the development of each activity are published by group in the announcement section of Blackboard.

The work and the topics were divided into two stages, the first stage where the students, select a scientific topic by team, use their own strategy and the tools they already know to search for information and obtain 2 sources of information per person, later they are divided into pairs, selecting a person from a team different from their own, to perform the co evaluation applying the C.A.R.S. Checklist for the evaluation of information sources on the internet (see Fig. 2), which was adjusted for its application in Google forms, which raises a scale from 1 to 5, being 1 = Very poor, 2 = Poor, 3 = Fair, 4 = Good and 5 = Excellent.

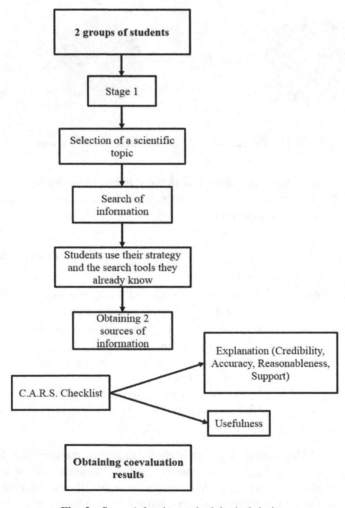

Fig. 2. Stage 1 for the methodological design.

Stage 2 (see Fig. 3), began with the activities proposed for each topic, making readings and visiting university pages to collect the most important points to define the need for information, reliability of the sources and types of information.

Subsequently, the students entered Google Scholar and databases available in the electronic resources of the web page of university libraries, as well as databases of free access.

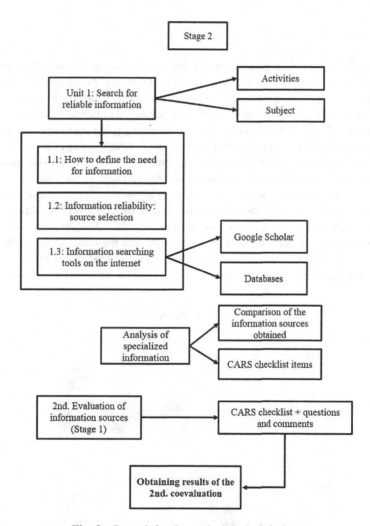

Fig. 3. Stage 2 for the methodological design.

Having covered the topics from 1.1 to 1.4 of Unit 1, the students again seek sources of information regarding the previously selected scientific topic and make a comparison between the first sources obtained and those obtained from the databases.

Finally, they carry out a second co evaluation of the sources obtained in stage 1 through the C.A.R.S. Checklist, for the post-test, a different form was used than the pre-test, the same elements of the C.A.R.S. Checklist however, questions such as: Are there changes in your way of evaluating the web reference? This question is applied to the two sources obtained, the next item asks for the explanation of the previous answer, the last question: Which of the items of the C.A.R.S. evaluation checklist seems more important to determine the quality of the information we find on the internet? This seeks to know which element is most important for students.

3   Results

For the results obtained, a comparison of the co-evaluation of sources is presented through the CARS Checklist in the first and second stages for each item (see Figs. 4, 5 and 6), where the students' approach to the items proposed in the checklist for evaluation of information sources obtained from the Internet changed noticeably. This is reaffirmed when observing that the results obtained in the questions referring to the students shows they changed their way of evaluating sources 1 and 2 with respect to the co-evaluation carried out in stage 1, to which 100% of the students answered affirmatively, that means, all the students modified their evaluation in the second stage of the study.

Regarding the comments made by the students about the explanation of this change, they agree that in the first stage they did not understand the concept of reliability, they did not consider determining factors such as the date of publication, author's data, source support and type of source among others; generally that they did not know the importance of the reliability criteria and already knowing and understanding their importance, the vision they have on the reliability and type of sources obtained has changed.

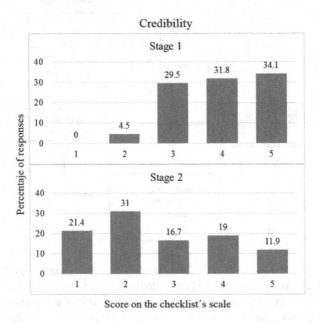

Fig. 4. Comparison of Stages 1 and 2 of the credibility items.

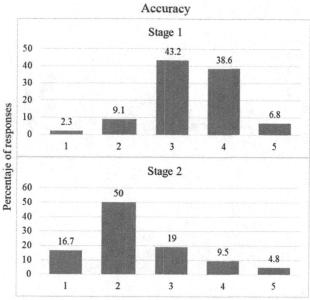

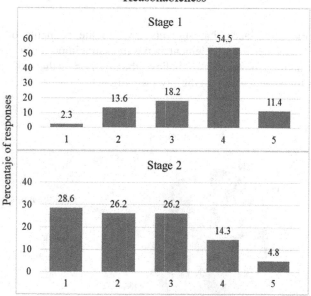

Fig. 5. Comparison of Stages 1 and 2 of the accuracy and reasonableness items.

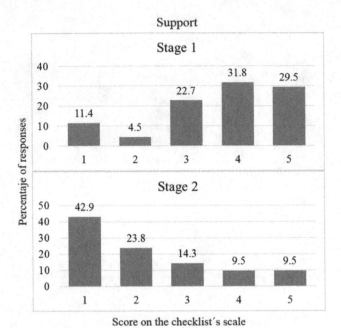

Fig. 6. Comparison of Stages 1 and 2 of the support items.

Regarding the importance that students give to the elements of the C.A.R.S. Checklist 78.6% consider that all elements have the same importance to determine the quality of information sources, 11.9% believe that support is the most important element, followed by accuracy and credibility (see Fig. 7).

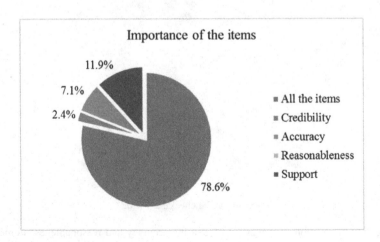

Fig. 7. Importance of items according to students.

Subsequently, to verify if there is a significant difference between the results obtained from the co-evaluation performed in the first stage and those obtained in the second stage, a t-Student test was performed for paired samples, for which the IBM SPSS Statistics statistical software [12] was used, considering the means obtained for each of the four elements of the information source evaluation model, prior to the t-test, a normality test was performed where it is verified that due to the P-value obtained, the data of the two stages of the study come from a normal distribution (see Table 3), in contrast to the value of $\alpha = 0.05$.

Table 3. Shapiro-Wilk test for normality distribution in data.

	Kolmogorov-Smirnov[a]			Shapiro-Wilk		
	Statistical	gl	Sig.	Statistical	gl	Sig.
Stage 1	.232	4	.	.915	4	.511
Stage 2	.266	4	.	.952	4	.727

Regarding the results obtained in the t-Student test for paired samples (see Table 4), in the comparison of the means obtained in the co-evaluations of the pre-test and the post-test, it was found that there is a significant difference in the results before and after the sequence of activities carried out with the students, so it is concluded that the sequence does have significant effects on the students' understanding regarding the reliability of the sources of information, this in contrast with the P-value obtained and the value of $\alpha = 0.05$.

Table 4. t test of paired samples, for comparison of means

	Paired differences					t	gl	Sig. (bilateral)
	Man	Standard Dev.	Standard error	95% confidence interval of the difference				
				Inferior	Superior			
Stage 1 – Stage 2	1.29770	.08129	.04064	1.16835	1.42705	31.928	3	.000

4 Conclusions

In accordance with the main objective of this research which focuses on knowing the effectiveness of the sequence of activities through the comparison of the co-evaluations of information sources obtained from the internet in the pre and post test, it is concluded that the activities proposed for the sequence have had sufficient effect to generate a change in the understanding and application of the students on the 4 elements addressed in the Harris' C.A.R.S. Checklist.

In addition to obtaining a significant difference according to the statistics made, the total of the students participating in the study claim to have modified their criteria to perform the co-evaluation, since within the activities it includes the verification of the central points to determine the reliability of the sources, visit specialized databases, search and obtain information about these resources and compare the type of information obtained in stages 1 and 2 of the study, which allows the students themselves to determine the differences in the information obtained and reflect on the type of information required for their university education.

It is clear the change that the students had when co-evaluating the sources obtained through the search tools that they use on a regular basis, being predominant the use of Google, since by understanding the importance of the origin of the sources of information reflect on the use of tools for the search of specialized information, and the use of available resources including search time, so that from the activities carried out they prefer to spend the greatest amount of time in determining the descriptors for the search.

Finally, it should be mentioned that for each of the elements of the model: Credibility, Accuracy, Reasonableness and Support, there was a difference between the means obtained in the pre and post test, which indicates that the decrease in the points achieved for each element is because the students were more rigorous and careful in the application of each criterion, adhering to the quality standards of the specialized information that is requested for their professional training, the results obtained in this study are part of the preliminary analysis of data for the doctoral research of which it is a part.

References

1. Jaik Dipp, A.: Competencias investigativas: una mirada a la educación superior, 1st edn., pp. 3–16, 50–60. Red Durango de investigadores educativos a. C. REDIE, México (2013). http://redie.mx/librosyrevistas/libros/competenciasinvestigativas.pdf. Accessed 23 Oct 2018
2. Rojas Soriano, R.: Formación de investigadores educativos Una propuesta de investigación, 12th edn. Plaza y Valdes, México, D.F. (1992). http://raulrojassoriano.com/cuallitlanezi/wp-content/themes/raulrojassoriano/assets/libros/formacion-investigadores-educativos-rojas-soriano.pdf. Accessed 03 Feb 2019
3. Rojas-Betancur, H., Méndez-Villamizar, R.: Cómo enseñar a investigar. Un reto para la pedagogía universitaria. Educ. Educ 16(1), 95–108 (2013). http://dx.doi.org/10.5294/edu.2013.16.1.6. Accessed 05 Feb 2019
4. Fernández-Espinosa, C.E., Villavicencio-Aguilar, C.E.: Habilidades investigativas para trabajos de graduación. ACADEMO Revista De Investigación En Ciencias Sociales Y Humanidades 4(1) (2017). https://revistacientifica.uamericana.edu.py/index.php/academo/article/view/61/58. Accessed 20 Mar 2019
5. Marín, F.V., Inciarte, A. de J., Hernández, H.G., Pitre, R.C.: Estrategias de las Instituciones de Educación Superior para la Integración de las Tecnología de la Información y la Comunicación y de la Innovación en los Procesos de Enseñanza. Un Estudio en el Distrito de Barranquilla, Colombia. Formación universitaria, 10(6), 29–38 (2017). https://dx.doi.org/10.4067/S0718-50062017000600004. Accessed 23 Mar 2019
6. Landgrave-Ibáñez, S., Rosas, E.P., Esquivel, L.B., Coria, A.I., Jiménez Galván, I., Sámano Sámano, A.: Uso de la Web e internet como herramientas para la búsqueda de información médica científica. Archivos en Medicina Familiar 18(4), 95–106 (2017). https://www.medigraphic.com/cgi-bin/new/resumen.cgi?IDARTICULO=72102. Accessed Mar 19 2019

7. Perry, H.B.: Information literacy in the sciences: faculty perception of undergraduate student skill. Coll. Res. Libr. **78**(7), 964 (2017). https://doi.org/10.5860/crl.78.964. Accessed 12 July 2019
8. Auberry, K.: Increasing students' ability to identify fake news through information literacy education and content management systems. Ref. Libr. **59**(4), 179–187 (2018). https://doi.org/10.1080/02763877.2018.1489935. Accessed 28 Mar 2019
9. Hinostroza, J.E., Ibieta, A., Labbé, C., Soto, M.T.: Browsing the internet to solve information problems: a study of students' search actions and behaviours using a 'think aloud' protocol. Educ. Inf. Technol. **23**(5), 1933–1953 (2018). https://doi.org/10.1007/s10639-018-9698-2. Accessed 28 June 2019
10. North Hennepin Community College: CARS Checklist. https://nhcc.edu/student-resources/library/doinglibraryresearch/cars-checklist. Accessed 23 Mar 2019
11. Harris, R.: Evaluating Internet Research Sources. VirtualSalt (2015). https://www.virtualsalt.com/evalu8it.htm. Accessed 23 Mar 2019
12. IBM SPSS Statistics for Windows. IBM Corp, Armonk (2013)

Towards Reinforcing Generic Competences in Higher Education Students Using Gamification

Sara Muñoz$^{(\boxtimes)}$, Edwin Gamboa , Oscar Bedoya ,
and María Trujillo

Universidad del Valle, Cali, Colombia
{sara.munoz, edwin.gamboa, oscar.bedoya,
maria.trujillo}@correounivalle.edu.co

Abstract. Deficiencies in generic competences (e.g. critical reading and quantitative reasoning) have been identified in Colombian undergraduate students. Tackling this problem, a gamified system for motivating students to reinforce generic competences has been developed by Universidad del Valle using a player centred design methodology. The gamification strategy is composed by four mechanics: First, a training zone where students can improve generic competences (e.g., quantitative reasoning and reading comprehension). Second, an improvement shop where students exchange earned points for power-ups. Third, a badge system, which presents different tasks that students must perform to win a set of medals. Lastly, an abilities diagram that measures students' performance. A web prototype was built to support the gamification strategy. The prototype was iteratively tested using functional and non-functional testing, to guide the development process. Also, the gamification strategy was validated using a heuristic evaluation, confirming that the content to be used in the gamification strategy should be designed according to student's preferences, otherwise, the strategy may fail. The main limitation of this research is that the sample of users is not representative of *Universidad del Valle* student population and some evaluated features and graphical resources of the application are still being developed.

Keywords: Education · Gamification · Generic competences · Undergraduate students

1 Introduction

According to [7], students desertion is defined as a phenomenon of abandonment of an institution that can be explained by socioeconomic, individual, institutional and academic variables. This is one of the main problems faced by the Colombian higher education system. Despite the increment in coverage and admission rates to higher education, in recent years, the number of students who complete undergraduate program is low, showing a large number of students drop out, mainly in the first semesters [7].

In that context, *Universidad del Valle* is committed to reduce the students drop out rate by involving ICT (information and communication technology) in the university's

© Springer Nature Switzerland AG 2019
P. H. Ruiz and V. Agredo-Delgado (Eds.): HCI-COLLAB 2019, CCIS 1114, pp. 408–422, 2019.
https://doi.org/10.1007/978-3-030-37386-3_30

educational processes and proposed the development of a pedagogical intervention to strengthen generic competences: critical reading and quantitative reasoning.

According to [21], generic competences are defined as: Learning levels which are common to all students in higher education and are focused on critical reasoning, interpersonal understanding, creative thinking, analytic reasoning, and problem solving. Quantitative reasoning evaluates the understanding, design and correct application of methods, procedures and arguments based on mathematical contents called generics. This will allow professionals to raise critical positions, make decisions and generate strategies [21]. And critical reading evaluates people's ability to interpret and evaluate texts found in everyday academic life. The main objective is to determine the level of reading comprehension of a student in operations of interpretation, learning and critical posture in writings, which should happen without the need of extra textual information [21]. The intervention is framed in the development of a Virtual Skills Gymnasium (VSG), this platform includes gamification techniques since gamification has potential to enhance learning experiences [23]. The VSG aims to support three levels of student knowledge. The first level focuses on students who have knowledge deficiencies that had to be acquired at the secondary school. The second level focuses on students who require a deeper understanding of specific knowledge. The last level focuses on students with advanced knowledge who are conducting the final career project.

In this paper, we present a gamification strategy included in the VSG. The remaining of the paper is organised as follows: in Sect. 2, the related works are outlined. In Sect. 3, we present a gamification strategy based on the self-determination theory. In Sect. 4, technical details of the prototype are presented. In Sects. 5 and 6, we present and discuss the preliminary results of an evaluation of the gamification strategy and the prototype. Finally, we summarise the results of this work and draw conclusions in Sect. 7.

2   Related Work

In the context of higher education, gamification has been mainly employed with educational platforms to motivate users and provide them with a better experience. For instance, in [10], a gymnasium-laboratory in higher education was developed to allow the collection, classification, evaluation and transmission of materials created by teachers. In the gymnasium-laboratory, students can find tutorials on the topics that cause them most difficulties. Each tutorial contains interactive exercises, videos, examples of past exams (some of them with solution and interactive explanations), course materials, simulators and various activities to develop mathematical thinking or specific objectives of the course topics. However, the authors do not include evidence of the effect of using the application with students.

In [1], a tool called *CodeTraining* is proposed to motivate students to improve programming skills. The platform allows instructors to create and edit programming exercises and students to take available courses and solve the available exercises. They are allowed to compile and run code on the web interface receiving instant feedback.

After solving problems, students receive points based on the difficulty level of the problem (normal, hard, and advanced). In order to evaluate the efficiency of the system, some tests were carried out involving 40 students from the *Culiacan Technological Institute*. However, the obtained results are not presented in this research.

In [2], a zombie-themed evidence-based medicine game was developed to allow medical students to test their EBM (evidence-based medicine) skills. The game is a "choose your own adventure" style that takes students through a scenario where a disease outbreak is taking place and a resident is asked to use EBM skills to select a screening and diagnostic tool to use on potentially infected patients. Within the story, the resident uses her evidence-based medicine skills to choose a screening and diagnostic tool. This game is an example of a self-assess tool for students. However, as the game was designed as a proof-of-concept only, the story is left at a cliffhanger, leaving room for future expansion. The game has been viewed over 443 times with 343 unique users between April 2016 and May 2017. Nevertheless, this research does not include any evaluation of the effect of the game on students' learning process.

In [19] Duolingo, a popular language learning application, is described. The platform uses a playfully illustrated, gamified design that combines point-reward incentives with implicit instruction, mastery learning, explanations and other best practices. Also, the application uses a half-life regression-based algorithm that allows students to remember what they had learned and identify the vocabulary that is most difficult for them to master. In this research, two experiments were carried out and both concluded with successful results, about the impact of half-life regression in student's engagement.

3   Virtual Skills Gymnasium Prototype

The Virtual Skills Gymnasium (VSG) is focused on reinforcing generic competences of quantitative reasoning and critical reading of higher education students. A team of experts in pedagogy designed a bank of questions to feed the VSG. These questions are intended to strengthen one or more of the generic competences. A gamification strategy is integrated in the VSG in order to motivate students to use the VSG. The gamification strategy consists of four mechanics, which are: a training zone, an improvement shop, a badge system and an abilities diagram that measures the generic competences of a student according to his/her performance throughout the application. The details of the methodology used to design the gamification strategy are explained in [3], the design process, concerning to the audience, will be presented below.

3.1   Gamification Strategy Design Process

We followed the Player Centred Design, approach presented in [3], to design the proposed gamification strategy, which is based on a player centred design process. This approach aims to accomplish players' and organisations' goals. Accordingly, the following steps were carried out to define the audience of the gamification strategy:

Define the Target Audience. In agreement with [3], defining the target audience for any gamified solution is critically important. Therefore, four provisional *personas* [5] were modelled to represent the possible profiles of the student population of *Universidad del Valle*. Due to the huge diversity of the student's population at the university and the difficult access to student information, it was decided to use provisional *personas* [5], which are used when there is not enough time, resources, or corporate buy-in to perform the necessary fieldwork [5]. Figure 1 shows the four provisional *personas* created for this purpose.

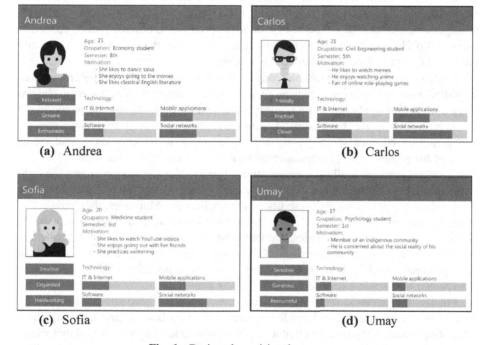

Fig. 1. Designed provisional *personas*.

Define Player Goals. Nine interviews were conducted involving 14 students of the Engineering Faculty to know their motivations and opinions regarding Internet, mobile applications, video games, social networks, student drop-out, generic competences and expectations regarding this project. They belong to first, second and sixth semester of Systems, Electrical and Food engineering academic programs. Their ages range from 16 to 25 years. A thematic analysis of user interviews was performed, according to the methodology proposed in [13].

After the thematic analysis, a profile of the interviewed students was developed. Most of them have a close relationship with technology, meaning they are recurrent users of the Internet, mobile applications, video games and social networks. They described themselves as people who like to be in touch with their parents and friends.

However, student population of *Universidad del Valle* is highly diverse, some of the students stated that they do not have permanent Internet or television service. Regarding their daily activities, students consider the Internet and technology to be very useful, especially for searching and sharing information. Their main devices of use are the computer, mobile phone and tablets.

The students expressed their opinions about the desertion rates in the university. They consider that many causes influence this problem. External factors such as low quality of education in some of the city's public schools, which causes students to face the subjects of the first semesters with insufficient bases and gaps in previous knowledge. Selection of students' careers that is affected by the *SABER 11*[1] test score required for career entry or family influences, students' poor discipline and time management, the lack of methodology of some professors, besides social, economic and emotional issues that students must deal throughout their university years and prevent their optimal performance in the academic environment.

Students mentioned the possible context in which they would use the application, identified tentative moments such as their free time and moments between classes. They consider the application as a reinforcement tool for their classes and would like it to be promoted by the professors. Accordingly, students would appreciate that the application would have short step-by-step explanations, in which audio visual media are used for greater clarity, complemented with didactic exercises, that fit their learning curve and progress gradually. Likewise, students expect the application to provide them with initiative to reinforce what they have learned, where frustration is avoided through the freedom of navigation and usability of the application. Moreover, they would like social interaction to be promoted, users to be supported and distractors to be avoided using a visually pleasing application that provides them with useful information. Additionally, they mentioned some mechanics with which they would like to interact in the application such as on boarding, trivia, levels, competition, scoring, badges, unexpected things and extrinsic rewards such as grades.

Finally, the intrinsic motivations were discussed, here students expressed their interest in strengthening their knowledge, share things on Internet and knowing about interesting topics. They consider that a gamified application might be a tool that would increase their motivation to learn. Also, they would like that specific learning levels of their academic programs are included. Figure 2 shows the thematic analysis representation of target potential users.

3.2   Gamification Strategy Mechanics

We used the structure proposed in [6] to design the mechanics of the gamification strategy. Figure 3 illustrates the designed mechanics and their relations with the main gamification strategy.

---

[1] SABER 11 test: The SABER 11 test evaluates the level of Secondary Education from 2014 onwards, is aligned with the evaluations of Basic Education to provide information to the educational community on the development of the basic competencies that a student must develop during the passage through school life [4].

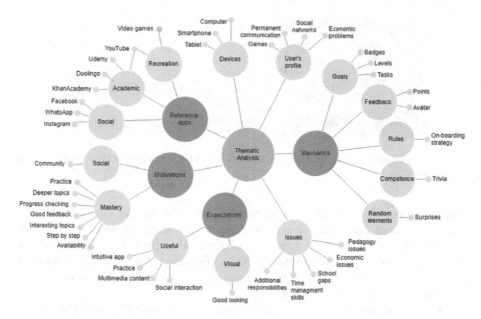

Fig. 2. Thematic analysis representation of target potential users

This strategy was designed based on the self-determination theory [16]. According to [22], this theory considers humans as inherently proactive, with a strong internal desire for growth. With this idea, external environments should support human internal motivators to avoid frustration. Our gamification strategy intends to address two of the three motivators:

- Competence or mastery: People attempt to be effective in dealing with the external environment. This motivator is satisfied with the training zone and abilities diagram, which help to improve students' competences; and the badge system, which gives recognition to students when they improve their competences.
- Autonomy: The innate need to feel in charge of life, while doing what is considered meaningful and in harmony with the values of each person. This motivator is satisfied with the training module, badge module and shop module since these modules are open tools that students can use when they need it.
- Relatedness: Involves social connection with family, friends and others. Also, it can also be expressed as a desire to "make a difference" in a group. This motivator will be supported by a future version of the application.

In the following sections, we describe these mechanics in detail.

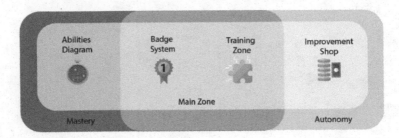

Fig. 3. The relation between the designed mechanics and the main gamification strategy. Icons designed by: [18]

Training Zone. This mechanic is intended to identify the sub-competences (e.g. connectors, macro proposals) of generic competences in which students have performed poorly. For this purpose, a selection of questions is made according to students' deficiencies based on their performance in the main zone. Priority is given to those questions that correspond to the weakest competences of students. Figure 4a presents the UI of this mechanic in the application.

A training algorithm was specially designed for the question selection in this module, explained in [14].

Badge System. In this module, we include a series of medals and awards that students can obtain according to their performance in the application. These badges are distributed throughout the world, relate students' performance to narrative and recognise their effort in the application. The badges are also proposed as an alternative path made up of more complex challenges, which students are free to accomplish. Two types of badges were defined, the first type is *Record Badges*, oriented to promote behaviours such as persistence and correct performance in students. The second type is *Mastery Badges*, aimed at improving the student's learning levels, these are granted when the student has correctly answered the most difficult questions of each learning level. Table 1 shows the designed record badges and Table 2 shows a few of the designed mastery badges. Meanwhile, Fig. 4b presents the UI of this mechanic in the application.

Improvement Shop. In this module, students can exchange points earned previously for power-ups that serve as support tools to overcome some challenges that are presented by the application, such as the Time Trial Challenge where a student has a certain amount of time to answer the question. This mechanic is oriented to give value to the points obtained by the player. Figure 4c illustrates the UI of this mechanic in the application. Table 3 shows the designed power ups.

Table 1. Designed record badges. Source: Universidad del Valle

Icon	Badge title and description
	Reconstructed area (100%) You've successfully rebuilt your first area. Continue to help your character, practice your skills and get more badges to improve your performance
	Defeat *Did* You're very agile. You have surpassed Did and his time challenge in 3 guided zones in the same environment
	Perfect game You exceed expectations. You answered correctly to 3 questions in sequence

Table 2. Designed mastery badges. Source: Universidad del Valle

Icon	Badge title and description
	Technician of the letters Identifies the formal categories that Spanish offers to establish linear cohesion in written texts
	Gold tongue Identifies speech acts in written texts
	Number collector Recognize and obtain pieces of information from different representations
	Making the right choices Selecting relevant information and establishing relationships between viable solutions to a problem

Abilities Diagram. This mechanic is composed of a diamond-shaped graph where the performance of student's skills is measured. Also, this module is part of the feedback system of the application, particularly, reinforcement feedback is provided [9] since it highlights both positive and negative performed areas on which students should improve. Figure 4d shows the UI of this mechanic in the application.

This graph measures 5 parameters: persistence, adaptability, progress, effectiveness, engagement.

Table 3. Designed power ups. Source: Universidad del Valle

Icon	Power up title and description
	Okoku Gem You can use this improvement when you have a question that is too complex and you don't know how to solve it. With this gem of the inhabitants of *Okoku* you will be able to fly from there, run away and not answer, immediately
	Infinity This improvement will be useful to you when *Did* appears and puts the time limit challenge on you. With infinity, you can extend the time you need to answer *Did*'s question and challenge
	Arkkit flower The arkkit flower helps you focus and choose the best option, so when you feel overwhelmed by the number of options to answer a question, you can use this enhancement, and its powers.

(a) Training zone

(b) Badge system

(c) Improvement shop

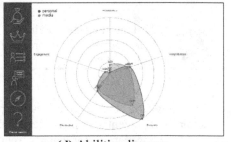

(d) Abilities diagram

Fig. 4. Gamification strategy designed mechanics. Source: *Universidad del Valle*

4 Technical Details

This section explains the technical details of the prototype. In Sect. 4.1, the layered architecture is shown, along with a deployment diagram. Also, in Sect. 4.2, the technologies selected for the implementation are presented.

4.1 Architecture

According to [11], a system's architecture is the set of principal design decisions made during its development and any subsequent evolution. Moreover, an architecture manifests itself in all major facets of a software system, including its structural elements: components, connectors and configurations.

The architecture of VSG is based on a layer model architecture. It is described by four standard layers: presentation, business, persistence, and database; each layer has a specific role and responsibility in the prototype. The presentation layer is responsible for handling all user interface and browser communication logic. The business layer is responsible for executing specific business rules associated with the request. And the persistence layer makes SQL queries to the database layer to retrieve the customer data [17]. Figure 5 shows the layered architecture of the prototype.

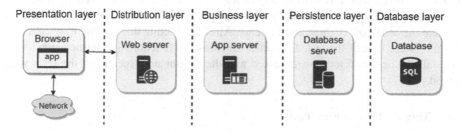

Fig. 5. Layered architecture of VSG prototype

Also, Fig. 6 presents the deployment diagram of the prototype used in development and testing environment. The execution architecture of the prototype shows nodes such as hardware or software execution environments, and the middleware connecting them.

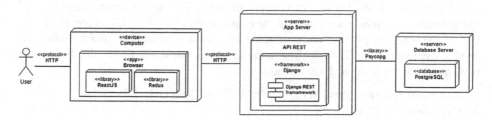

Fig. 6. Deployment diagram of VSG prototype

4.2   Technologies

The technologies selected by *Universidad del Valle* to implement the application are:

- *Front-end*: HTML5, CSS3, JavaScript: ReactJS
- *Back-end*: Python 3.6.5, Django 1.11, Django REST Framework 3.7.1 (DRF)
- *DBMS*: PostgreSQL.

In addition, the Bitbucket platform was selected as hosting service.

5   Evaluation

We employed a multi-method approach to assess the quality of the gamification strategy. The following section presents functional and non-functional testing applied to the prototype. Also, a heuristic evaluation and its results are outlined.

5.1   Automated Smoke Tests

The application captures information from the events generated by a student in the UI. For this reason, smoke tests of 6 repetitive functionalities (e.g. navigation through the modules, pop-up dialog on badges module, select an answer option on questions and training module, answer a question in questions and training module, navigation through questions, and buy power-ups) of the UI were performed with Selenium web driver to validate the behaviour of these components. After conducting this test, we may conclude that the interaction of the tested modules satisfies the functionality defined previously since all the designed tests were passed and the originated issues from the tests were solved.

5.2   Manual End-to-End Tests

Manual end-to-end tests were performed for 23 functionalities. An end-to-end test evaluates functionality in the backend and front-end of the application. These tests were represented in test cases and were supported by the acceptance criteria of user stories. These tests were executed iteratively until they were approved successfully.

5.3   Performance Tests

For the development of performance tests, the response times to resolve requests were tested according to the number of concurrent users. Those tests were executed with JMeter tool. Performance tests include the response time of the back-end and the front-end of the VSG. The tests were conducted in a local environment, and the obtained results are reported in Table 4. The computer equipment on which the tests were performed has the following specifications:

- Processor: Intel(R) Core(TM) i5-7200U CPU @ 2.50 GHz 2.71 GHz
- Ram memory: 12 GB
- System type: 64 bits
- Cache memory: 3 MB.

Table 4. Obtained results in performance test

Concurrent users	Max time response (s)	Average response time (s)	Standard deviation (s)
100	0.150	0.107	0.015
300	1.575	0.315	0.274
500	3.798	0.398	0.432
1200	7.434	0.406	0.568

We took the Training zone module since we consider it as the most expensive computing module. According to [15], 1.0 s is about the limit for the user's flow of thought to stay uninterrupted. Then, as Table 4 shows, the application satisfies the acceptable average response time proposed by the author.

5.4 Heuristic Evaluation

A heuristic evaluation was performed by 4 evaluators, using the heuristics to evaluate gameful designs presented in [20]. The assessors consider that:

- The reconstruction of zones is incomplete, which may be confusing for students.
- They emphasised that the level of questions should grow accordingly with the level of users as it happens in the training zone, but it should be complemented in the main zone.
- The application only presents two zones: the main zone and the training zone, thereby the displayed navigation route is always the same, which may be boring for students.
- The social interactivity is a key factor to enable user engagement since students could collaborate and compete.

6 Discussion

The obtained results show that some mechanics in the application are confusing for students, which may be due to the incomplete description of the available modules and the incomplete zone module, which shows the available zones that a student has and their reconstruction progress.

In this strategy, structural gamification was applied [3] since the content to be delivered was designed by a group pedagogy experts from *Universidad del Valle*. The obtained results show that the content may be not adequate for students since it was designed for accomplishing the goals of *Universidad del Valle* rather than students' goals, which is one of the primary reasons of failing of gamified solutions [3]. Consequently, the content of a strategy should always be user oriented even if structural gamification is applied. Otherwise, users may feel overwhelmed and leave the application. Which confirms that successful gamification is a process, that involves time-consuming work of gaining a real understanding of the target audience and their motivations and goals, this knowledge is acquired taking time to understand users [3].

Moreover, the lack of meaningfulness between the mechanics, the story and the content may be demotivating for students since the acquired knowledge is not reflected in the gamification strategy. For example, if a student had to apply his/her knowledge in quantitative reasoning to calculate the amount of resources to rebuild a zone or repair a building, the mechanics would be meaningful for students. Meaningful mechanics gives more weight to student's choices, making them feel more autonomous. Hence, the correct association between content and mechanics would guide us to avoid "Pointsification" [22], which is defined by the author as focusing on the rewards and not enough on the appeal of the experience.

The evaluation shows that using player centred design and self-determination theory for the mechanics design was appropriate, the positive results obtained in the heuristic evaluation correspond with the motivators stated by this theory. Also, using technologies like ReactJS, Django, DRF allowed us to have reusable code and have a modular application. Finally, this gamification strategy may have potential to be used by all Colombian universities.

6.1 Limitations and Future Work

The development of this research had a few limitations. First, the results obtained in the evaluation process are preliminary; in order to assess the long-term impact, more rigorous tests must be conducted during a meaningful period of time (e.g. one semester, one year). For instance, long-term motivation can be evaluated with a test in which students using the application are compared against students that do not use it, during a significant period of time. Also, these evaluations can be corroborated with results obtained in the SABER PRO test[2].

Relatedness, the third need of the self-determination theory, should be addressed including new mechanics (e.g. social forum, social networks integration, etc.) to the gamification strategy. Moreover, future work may include the design of new mechanics specially targeted at the players type. For instance, in [12], the authors propose a set of mechanics appropriate for each type and conclude that personalised gameful systems will be more engaging if they adapt to personality traits or player types.

Also, we highlight that some features of the application should be extended, the questions bank should be larger and the topics and dynamics should be built with students, according to their interest topics. Finally, some negatively evaluated features are still under development, thus, the evaluation results were affected by those gaps.

7 Conclusions

A complementary gamification strategy was designed, implemented and tested using a multi-method approach for the VSG. This gamification strategy is composed of four mechanics based on self-determination theory: a badges system, a shop, an abilities diagram module and a training zone. These mechanics are related to the

---

[2] Test conducted by *Instituto Colombiano para el Fomento de la Educación Superior* ICFES, it is aim to evaluate and provide a report on the degree of development of skills and general knowledge of students who have passed 75% of the credits of their respective academic programs in higher education [8].

self-determination theory since the training zone, abilities diagram and badges system are intended to promote the mastery of a student. Also, the autonomy in the application can be supported by the training zone, badges system and shop since students may use those mechanics when they want it. The designed mechanics are intended to motivate students in the reinforcement of generic competences.

Evaluation results show that the content of the gamification strategy should be redirected to student's interests and the mechanics should have a deeper relation with the content. In order to achieve this, students should be constantly included in the development process, to ensure that the gamification strategy is oriented towards the motivations and expectations of the students. Finally, this research may be a precedent in gamification and higher education field, it may have the potential to be used by Colombian universities.

References

1. Barrón-Estrada, M.L., Zatarain-Cabada, R., Lindor-Valdez, M.: CodeTraining: an authoring tool for a gamified programming learning environment. In: Pichardo-Lagunas, O., Miranda-Jiménez, S. (eds.) MICAI 2016. LNCS (LNAI), vol. 10062, pp. 501–512. Springer, Cham (2017). https://doi.org/10.1007/978-3-319-62428-0_41
2. Blevins, A., et al.: Courting apocalypse: creating a zombie-themed evidence-based medicine game. Med. Ref. Serv. Q. **36**, 313–322 (2017). https://doi.org/10.1080/02763869.2017.1369239
3. Burke, B.: Gamify: How Gamification Motivates People to Do Extraordinary Things. Bibliomotion, Brookline (2014)
4. Colombia Ministerio de Educación: Estándares Básicos de Competencia. https://www.mineducacion.gov.co/1759/w3-article-244735.html
5. Cooper, A., et al.: About Face 3: The Essentials of Interaction Design. Wiley, Hoboken (2007)
6. Francisco-Aparicio, A., et al.: Gamification: analysis and application. In: Penichet, V.M.R., et al. (eds.) New Trends in Interaction, Virtual Reality and Modeling, pp. 113–126. Springer, London (2013). https://doi.org/10.1007/978-1-4471-5445-7_9
7. Guzmán, C., et al.: Deserción estudiantil en la educación superior colombiana. metodología de seguimiento, diagnóstico y elementos para su prevención. Ministerio de Educación Nacional. Colombia. https://www.mineducacion.gov.co/sistemasdeinformacion/1735/articles-254702_libro_desercion.pdf
8. ICFES Instituto Colombiano para la Evaluación de la Educación: Información general del examen de estado de la calidad de la educación superior, Saber Pro - Icfes Instituto Colombiano para la Evaluación de la Educación (2015). http://www2.icfes.gov.co/instituciones-educativas-y-secretarias/saber-pro/informacion-de-la-prueba-saber-pro
9. Kapp, K.M., et al.: The Gamification of Learning and Instruction Fieldbook: Ideas into Practice. Wiley, San Francisco (2012)
10. Medina Herrera, A., et al.: Newton Gymlab: gimnasio-laboratorio virtual de física y matemáticas (2013). http://hdl.handle.net/11285/621356
11. Medvidovic, N., Taylor, R.N.: Software architecture: foundations, theory, and practice. In: Proceedings of the 32nd ACM/IEEE International Conference on Software Engineering, vol. 2, pp. 471–472 (2010). https://doi.org/10.1145/1810295.1810435

12. Mora, A., et al.: Effect of personalized gameful design on student engagement. In: 2018 IEEE Global Engineering Education Conference (EDUCON), pp. 1925–1933 (2018). https://doi.org/10.1109/educon.2018.8363471

13. Mortensen, D.: How to Do a Thematic Analysis of User Interviews | Interaction Design Foundation. https://www.interaction-design.org/literature/article/how-to-do-a-thematic-analysis-of-user-interviews

14. Muñoz, S., Bedoya, O., Gamboa, E., Trujillo, M.: A training algorithm to reinforce generic competences in higher education students. In: Serrano C., J.E., Martínez-Santos, J.C. (eds.) CCC 2018. CCIS, vol. 885, pp. 201–212. Springer, Cham (2018). https://doi.org/10.1007/978-3-319-98998-3_16

15. Nah, F.F.-H.: A study on tolerable waiting time: how long are web users willing to wait? Behav. Inf. Technol. **23**(3), 153–163 (2004). https://doi.org/10.1080/01449290410001669914

16. Pink, D.H.: Drive: The Surprising Truth About What Motivates us. Penguin, London (2011)

17. Richards, M.: Software architecture patterns (2015). https://www.oreilly.com/ideas/software-architecture-patterns/page/2/layered-architecture

18. Roundicons: Games. https://www.flaticon.com/packs/games-3

19. Settles, B., Meeder, B.: A Trainable Spaced Repetition Model for Language Learning. Presented at the (2016). https://doi.org/10.18653/v1/p16-1174

20. Tondello, G.F., et al.: Heuristic evaluation for gameful design. In: Proceedings of the 2016 Annual Symposium on Computer-Human Interaction in Play Companion Extended Abstracts - CHI PLAY Companion 2016, pp. 315–323. ACM Press, New York (2016). https://doi.org/10.1145/2968120.2987729

21. Unigarro, M., Maldonado, D.: Sistema Institucional de Evaluación de Competencias. Marco teórico sobre competencias genéricas: Razonamiento cuantitativo y lectura crítica 4, (2018). https://doi.org/10.16925/greylit.2304

22. Werbach, K., Hunter, D.: For the Win: How Game Thinking Can Revolutionize Your Business. Wharton, Philadelphia (2012)

23. Zaric, N., Scepanovic, S.: Gamification of e-learning based on learning styles –design model and implementation. In: E-Learn: World Conference on E-Learning in Corporate, Government, Healthcare, and Higher Education, pp. 723–729 (2018). https://www.learntechlib.org/p/185026/

Usability in ICTs for Industry 4.0

Horacio René Del Giorgio$^{(\boxtimes)}$ (iD) and Alicia Mon (iD)

Departamento de Ingeniería e Investigaciones Tecnológicas, Universidad
Nacional de La Matanza, San Justo, Buenos Aires, Argentina
horacio.delgiorgio@gmail.com, alicialmon@gmail.com

Abstract. Information and Communication Technologies (ICTs) are a key piece in industrial development on the way to digital transformation that requires the development of Industry 4.0. The impact generated by the new technologies in the industry enables the detection of failures, the improvement of processes, and the acceleration of production times. These are factors that may significantly modify the levels of productivity in the different industrial sectors. Although industries currently use various Software Products in their management, marketing and logistics processes, among others, the insertion of technologies in the automation and control of production processes is generating a new industrial revolution that modifies the process control paradigm, directly impacting in productivity and competitiveness. The software industry faces the challenge of developing accessible and usable products for specific users, analyzing their behaviors, knowledge and characteristics, in order to apply techniques that may be adapted to the production processes and knowledge that work within an industry. This article raises the application of usability techniques to the development of products that can be implemented in the manufacturing industry, regardless of the branch of activity, and for this purpose, a model of Design/ Development Process of Specific Software Products for the industry is suggested. This model applies and customizes the different usability techniques to the particularities of this type of user in its real context of use.

Keywords: Industry 4.0 · ICTs · Usability

1 Introduction

The development of the ICTs that described the third industrial revolution is in a process of transformation by a set of scientific and technological advances that take the way of innovation and express themselves both in people's daily lives and in processes that are developed in the economic activity of the industrial production of goods, as well as in the provision of services. In this context of transformation, digitalization adopts a leading role and it has become essential in some productive and service sectors.

This is how the term *Industry 4.0*, which refers specifically to the fourth industrial revolution, generates a significant qualitative leap in the organization and management of value chains [1].

The development of ICTs allows linking the physical world and the digital world through devices, materials, products, equipment, facilities and communications,

© Springer Nature Switzerland AG 2019
P. H. Ruiz and V. Agredo-Delgado (Eds.): HCI-COLLAB 2019, CCIS 1114, pp. 423–436, 2019.
https://doi.org/10.1007/978-3-030-37386-3_31

expressed through collaborative systems and Software Products interconnected with a wide variety of devices to enhance the development of Industry 4.0.

The impact generated by the Software shows up mainly in production systems, especially with the help of artificial intelligence, robotics and wireless communications. The different parts of the production process not only adopt intelligent functions, but also interconnect automatically and autonomously between them through the Internet of Things [2], where knowledge management is part of production systems [3, 4].

Faced with this great transformation, today's industry needs urgent technological changes, given that the competitiveness of companies goes through globalization, productivity and innovation. However, no previous works have been found to define exactly what degree of technological development is currently implemented in the industries to determine what the specific update requirements and usability attributes are, such as defined in usability standards [5–7].

The addition of new technologies in the industrial sectors requires a deep knowledge of the existing capacity. That is to say, without information related to the Software Products implemented and used in the different processes, it is not possible to define technological incorporation needs to generate a reconversion in the value chains.

That is why this article describes the specific features of the Software Products that are currently implemented in the manufacturing industries, regardless of the branch in which they are cataloged internationally, in order to establish what types of software they take part in the current technologies of the industry that are heading towards Industry 4.0. From the definition of the specific Software Products, a Design/ Development Process that contains the particularities of the users is suggested. In this sense, Software Engineering has as a challenge to adapt its knowledge to the application of particular techniques as an indispensable support for the development of industrial production.

2 Software Product Differentiation

The typology developed in the present article allows analyzing the Software Products in the different areas within the industries grouped in 3 categories of products with the same level of hierarchy, interaction and dependence among them that match with different types of technological development, but which are needed and complement each other. In this sense, the typology organizes and differentiates between Software Products, Equipment or Hardware, and Communications or Infrastructure [8, 9].

In the different categories, the products are grouped according to their evolution and contribution to the level of innovation within the Industry. The defined categories, as well as the specific products, have been validated in a study carried out with experts from the ICT area, through interviews and surveys, in order to establish different levels of development [8].

The following figure (Fig. 1) shows the taxonomy with the typology of older Software Products according to their incorporation in the market, which is called "Basic", grouped by type of function that they fulfill regardless of the functional area of the industry in which they are implemented [10].

	WEB Technologies - WEB Page (External Site)
	WEB Technologies - Intranet (Internal Site)
	Collaborative Systems - Instant Messaging
	Collaborative Systems - Email
Software Products Basic Level	Collaborative Systems - Social Networks
	Office Tools - Word Processor
	Office Tools - Spreadsheet Tool
	Office Tools - Presentations Tool
	Office Tools - Scheduling and E.Mail Tool
	Office Tools - PDF Reader

Fig. 1. Software products - basic level. Source: Author's own editing [10]

Figure 2 shows the typology of products of an intermediate level, with Software Products that can be found in the industries and integrate more recent technologies available in the market (which is called "Intermediate") but not necessarily constitute innovation products.

	WEB Technologies - Extranet
	WEB Technologies - On Line Advertising
	Collaborative Systems - IP Telephony
	Collaborative Systems - File Synchronization
	Collaborative Systems - Mobile Applications
	Office Tools - Database Manager
	Office Tools - PDF Files Manager
	Management Systems - Enterprise Resource Planning (ERP)
	Management Systems - Customer Relationship Manager (CRM)
Software Products Intermediate Level	Management Systems - Support/Claim Management
	Management Systems - Logistics/Supply
	Management Systems - Quality Management
	Management Systems - Human Resources Management
	Production Management Systems - Product Quality
	Production Management Systems - Plant/Maintenance Engineering
	Product and Process Design Systems - Computer Aided Design (CAD)
	Geolocation Systems - Distribution and Logistics
	Security Systems - Infrastructure Security
	Security Systems - Information Security

Fig. 2. Software products - intermediate level. Source: Author's own editing [10]

Finally, Fig. 3 shows the typology of the most advanced Software Products that must be integrated and complemented to generate a substantively more advanced level of innovation. This is how, at this level of technological development (called "Advanced"), the following are the detected products that are necessary for the transformation of a manufacturing industry into an Industry 4.0.

Software Products Advanced Level	Collaborative Systems - Videoconference
	Management Systems - Balanced Score Card (BSC)
	Management Systems - Business Intelligence
	Management Systems - Big Data
	Management Systems - Machine Learning
	Management Systems - Energy Control Software
	Production Management Systems - Material Requirements Planning (MRP)
	Production Management Systems - Product Data Management (PDM)
	Production Management Systems - Automation Control Systems
	Production Management Systems - SCADA Systems
	Production Management Systems - Embedded Systems
	Product and Process Design Systems - Computer Aided Manufacturing (CAM)
	Product and Process Design Systems - Computer Aided Engineering (CAE)
	Product and Process Design Systems - Virtual Reality
	Product and Process Design Systems - Augmented Reality
	Geolocation Systems - Advertising

Fig. 3. Software products - advanced level. Source: Author's own editing [10]

The types of Software Products that are at the most advanced level perform the following functions, in interaction with the appropriate Hardware and Infrastructure/ Communications equipment.

2.1 Collaborative Systems

Collaborative Systems are a set of tools and applications that help people, in general dispersed geographically, to work as a team through means to carry out projects and tasks together, allowing communication, conducting conferences and coordination of activities. These collaboration tools allow the exchange of information in real time with remote employees, and with customers and suppliers from other geographical areas.

Among some of the advantages, these tools allow performing virtual meetings, giving the organization a better response to unforeseen situations. The bandwidth of the communications infrastructure must be appropriate to allow the transmission of multimedia content to multiple recipients. The areas involved are very variable. Essentially these systems can reach all functional areas that require interaction of people geographically dispersed. Many organizations deploy these tools as extensions of other applications, such as E.Mail [11].

In the communications and business of an organization, **videoconferences** are a simple communication tool that substantially reduces the costs of face-to-face meetings.

There are a huge number of platforms with features for different classes of users. All platforms give users the opportunity to use them for free, but with limited features.

The following options can be mentioned among the most outstanding features of videoconferencing applications: connection to social networks, drawing tools, surveys, chat, telephone line to participate in the conference, and options for smartphones, among others.

2.2   Management Systems

Management Systems are those where the information that is produced by the different activities that the organization carries out is collected, stored, modified and retrieved; like the receipt of a purchase order, the issuance of an invoice, the clearance of merchandise, a claim, the high of a new collaborator, among others. Some of them are essential for any organization regardless of the size and type of activity, as in the case of an ERP (Enterprise Resource Planning), since accounting records rest mainly on them. The rest of the systems have a more specific application and their justification is associated with the industry/type of organization segment, its size and the competitive strategy.

The **BSC (Balanced Score Card)** systems link the achievement of long-term strategic goals with the daily operations of an organization. BSC systems combine traditional financial measures with non-financial factors. In fact, the term *Balanced* indicates that it seeks the balance between financial and non-financial indicators, the short term and the long term, the results and process indicators and a balance between the environment and the inside of the organization. BSC systems allow to quickly and easily identifying the achievement of objectives defined by the strategic plan, as well as allowing the control of deviations. BSC systems are an appropriate tool for communication to the entire organization, about its vision, milestones and objectives [11].

Business Intelligence systems contain tools that enable the mining and the use of data from the organization, by grouping them statistically for the creation of a knowledge base for itself. Among the main benefits of BI systems is the fact that they provide foundation and support for decision making. BI systems, in addition, allow data mining; that is, analyze patterns, correlations, trends, among other parameters. They include greater control through a control panel (BSC), faster reporting, and integrity and consistency of information.

Generally, BI systems involve management positions, as users and management control analysts, which require aggregate data for decision making. Normally the implementation of a BI system requires a standard product, on which adaptations are made including the construction of a Data Warehouse, and data extraction processes.

The quantification of the benefits of the BI systems comes mainly from the potential better decisions.

Big Data is a set of techniques that help in making real-time decisions that involve a large volume of data, typically from various sources. ECommerce projects find, in Big Data techniques, a tool to maximize the conversion rate. Big Data is usually characterized by three attributes: volume, variety and speed. The processing of Big Data typically requires non-SQL databases, capable of managing unstructured and structured data, such as mongoDB, Cassandra or Apache Jackrabbit [11].

In the case of **Machine Learning** it is pointed out that the machine (the computer) can learn. In this context, *Learning* does not imply memorizing and collecting data. Here it aims to develop the ability to *generalize and associate*. When this concept is adapted to a machine or computer, it means that these teams should try to replicate these cognitive faculties of the human being, developing models that generalize the information introduced to them in order to make their predictions.

That is why the concept refers to a method of data analysis that automates the construction of analytical models. It constitutes a branch of Artificial Intelligence based on the idea that systems can learn from previous data, and thereby identify patterns and make decisions with minimal human intervention from the programming of an algorithm.

The iterative aspect of Machine Learning is that, as models are exposed to new data, they can adjust their parameters independently. They learn from previous calculations to produce reliable and repeatable decisions and results. That is to say, with Machine Learning it is possible to change the philosophy from *reactive* Software Products into *predictive* Software Products.

In the Industry, the mediation of IoT for obtaining data or managing massive data can help Machine Learning reach even higher levels of efficiency, making it easier for the Machine Learning system to gradually learn to recognize any factor related to internal and external production, optimize use and consumables, and improve the efficiency of the entire production process or predict equipment failures.

The **Energy Control Software** requires electronic devices or sensors that, centrally and automatically, from any personal desktop computer, may collect the energy power data. This type of platform allows companies to have an integral control of luminaires and electrical equipment, allowing the adoption of energy saving strategies based on schedules, occupation of areas and lighting levels.

Even though lighting generally represents the highest power load for an organization, efforts to implement savings and control strategies are not only limited to controlling the lighting of lights based on motion sensors. By means of incorporating measurement sensors, the system can increase the number of strategies that can be implemented; for example, considering the amount of available sunlight, types of tasks that are being performed, and employee preferences, among others.

2.3 Production Management Systems

With the help of the Management Systems mentioned above, the Production Management Systems allow the control of the resources used in the manufacturing process, as well as the different processes that are carried out to obtain the final product. In the definition of the different production processes, the costs, the resources used and the final result obtained can be controlled. These systems connect each step of the supply chain to be able to carry out traceability and real-time monitoring, ensuring efficient delivery and quality of the product, as well as compliance with safety standards. They also help maintain a connected production chain, which means the permanent collection of data for decision making. With the help of these systems, industries can now see exactly where a problem came from and prevent it from continuing further in the supply chain. With the ability to access and analyze data collected from a connected supply chain, companies can react to unforeseen and unplanned events as soon as they happen. This means that, if an inappropriate part or product is identified during a stage in the supply chain, the material can be identified and tracked.

The **MRP (Material Requirements Planning)** is a software application for the planning of production and the acquisition of materials. The main functions that this application performs are to indicate which materials are necessary to buy/produce to comply with the master production plan. On the other hand, it also makes recommendations to eventually modify the scheduling of material orders and, as time goes by, it also makes recommendations to reschedule open orders when they do not match the dates of delivery and requirements, and also include programming techniques or methods to establish and the dates of the orders valid, ranked by priorities [12].

Organizations that handle batch production, or manufacture products on demand, can separate the cost of direct material and manpower in each production order, as is the case of companies that make furniture, tools, and assemblers, among others. Through the production orders, these applications, allow the separation of the cost elements for each work order, or determine the quantity of products that have been requested, or the availability of existing merchandise.

Finally, in the production order there is a count of the raw materials, manpower and indirect expenses that were used in that order to obtain the unit cost of the product of that specific order, so as to have concise and total data [3].

PDM (Product Data Management) tools provide the means to manage all information related to both the product itself and the processes used throughout its entire life cycle.

The type of information that can be managed by PDM tools includes information on the configuration of the product (the structure of parts and components, versions, revisions, among other parameters), as well as data or documents used to describe the product (drawings, CAD files, specification documents) and their manufacturing processes (process sheets, numeric control programs).

In terms of process management, PDM tools support the various work flows and current procedures in force during the life cycle of a product, while contemplating the definition of the people profiles that perform these tasks, their functions and responsibilities in the processes mentioned above [12].

In the control instrumentation, the three basic elements capable of carrying out sequential control or continuous regulation within the control of industrial processes are the PLC (Programmable Logic Controller), the industrial computer and the industrial regulators (both analog and digital version). Automation control systems replace PLCs and allow interaction with the rest of the company's systems (ERP, MRP, among others).

Usually, these are custom systems, capable of giving orders and interacting with a network of automatons and measurement devices, with a graphic environment of the systems being monitored. Its objective is to provide fast and updated information on the status of a machine or plant, recorded breakdowns, numbers of carried out work cycles, among other parameters, as well as to be able to activate the different elements that are appropriate in each time and situation. All information can be processed by these software products to provide additional details; for example, if a certain element has exceeded its average number of movement cycles or starts and if it is therefore recommended to change it, or a fault register that alerts an element with an excessive level of breakdowns and allows to analyze possible solutions.

Complementing the **Automation Control Systems**, a **SCADA (Supervisory Control And Data Acquisition)** system is a set of software and hardware used to interconnect, control and manage various field devices, as well as remotely control the entire production process. On the other hand, and like the software products mentioned above, an HCI (Human Computer Interface) is usually integrated to allow a much more intuitive and faster process control. All this is intended to help operators and supervisors, giving them better control and the possibility of making changes almost immediately.

An **Embedded System** is a system generally based on a microprocessor, sensors and actuators, and designed to perform dedicated functions. These are electronic equipment that perform data and information processing. Unlike a personal computer, they are designed to satisfy a specific function, such as a watch, a cell phone, the control system of a car, among other functions. It is an electronic system that is contained (embedded) in complete equipment that includes, for example, mechanical and electromechanical parts. This type of systems has gained great importance from the point of view of information systems with the use of Arduino-type platforms for rapid prototype development.

2.4   Product and Process Design Systems

These systems allow the design of serial and/or industrial products, looking for the improvement of the qualities of them, emphasizing the form factor, function and use with a priority focus on the user. In addition to seeking the satisfaction of the needs of users as the main goal, the life cycle of the product, the rational use of materials and resources in its manufacture is also taken into account. Through its use, interpretation errors can be eliminated, time and control tasks can be reduced, and tasks duplication can be eliminated, among other advantages. They also allow simulations, which are used to represent a process through another one that makes it much simpler and more understandable. These simulations include very large, numerous and diverse areas, such as the analysis of the environmental impact caused by various sources, stress analysis of materials, among other areas, in order to avoid destructive tests and to be able to carry out eventual re-planning prior to the launch of the manufacturing process.

The introduction in the industry of the machine-tool of numerical control, robots and automatic warehouses, among others, is causing significant advantages over traditional production methods.

CAM (Computed Aided Manufacturing) tools are computer systems that allow to manufacture the pieces in numerical control machines, calculating the trajectories of the tool to achieve correct machining, based on the geometry information of the piece (obtained from of the drawing of the piece, made in 2D or 3D by means of a CAD system), the type of operation desired, the chosen tool and the defined cutting conditions.

Among others, a series of advantages offered by Computer Aided Manufacturing, compared to other traditional methods, it eliminates human errors when performing operations with the machine tool, reduces manufacturing costs by reducing wear and tear of the elements of the machine and also reduces the time when programming the numerical control of the machine tool.

As a direct result, it is possible to manufacture intermediate series of parts with costs comparable to those of the large series, in addition to introducing the possibility of using new approaches in the manufacturing organization [13].

Although the reference to product design is covered by CAD tools, the simulation of the design as well as the optimization and monitoring of the production process can be carried out with the help of CAE tools.

CAE (Computer Aided Engineering) is another step in traditional CAD systems, because not only helps in the design of the model, but also allows the integration of its properties, conditions to which it is submitted, materials, among others.

In this way, existing CAE tools allow to calculate how the piece or structure will behave in reality, in diverse aspects as deformations, resistance, thermal features and vibrations.

For that purpose, it is necessary to move from the geometry created into a CAD environment to the CAE system [13].

Virtual Reality is a three-dimensional environment generated by computers that creates in the user the feeling of being immersed in it. This environment is visualized through virtual reality lenses, and sometimes accompanied by other devices, such as gloves or special suits, which allow greater interaction with the environment, as well as the perception of different stimulus that intensify the sensation of reality. Virtual Reality is mostly applied in the field of entertainment and video games, but it has been extended to other fields such as medicine, artistic creation, and military training or flight simulations [4].

This technique allows a much more efficient mental and locomotive learning than in a conventional course with videos and manuals. With this technology, work accidents can be simulated, simulations of risky operations, virtual visits to facilities in the industries, action tests in case of emergency and escape routes.

Augmented Reality is the real-time visualization of visual and/or audible elements overlapped on a real-world environment. Thus, while Virtual Reality allows users to experience a completely virtual world, Augmented Reality adds virtual elements to an existing reality, instead of creating that reality from scratch.

One of the main achievements of this technology is a highly motivating user experience. Beyond the known uses (like in the *Pokemon Go* application), in disciplines such as education, Augmented Reality will allow training in real environments by adding extra information, or even simulate those real environments that perhaps, due to availability or location, they are not always accessible [4].

In the production line, it helps to have a global vision of the manufacture of a product, details of the layers, among others. As regards to logistics, it allows visual indications of work orders, hands-free on the operators to manipulate the merchandise while interacting with their surroundings. For maintenance and support, it allows to help in the detection of problems in the workplace, indicating the physical points to review, make visual indications from a remote support, being able to have the most centralized expertise and optimize tasks through virtual visits, among other advantages.

2.5 Geolocation Systems

Usually, these types of systems allow the association of a digital resource with a physical address. Site information is obtained through a calculation based on altitude and length coordinates to indicate a specific place anywhere in the world. The use of these systems allows the integration of these technologies for online services through collaborative use.

The **Geolocation Systems for Advertising**, also called *Geomarketing*, point to a discipline of great potential that provides information for making business decisions supported by the spatial variable. Born from the confluence of marketing and geography, they allow an interdisciplinary analysis of the situation of a business through the exact location of customers, points of sale, branches, competitors, among other variables, locating them on a digital or printed map through symbols and custom colors. The inferences and predictions within this discipline go beyond the traditional use of qualitative and quantitative analysis, and belong to a growing strand of analysis called *geospatial analysis*.

Geomarketing is the marketing area oriented towards the global knowledge of the customers, their needs and behaviors within a given geographical environment, which helps to have a more complete vision of them and to identify their needs. These tools allow information on what happens in a given geographical area, going down to detail [14].

A Geomarketing system consists of statistical and cartographic information, market studies and an adequate processing of the information, called ESDA (Exploratory Spatial Data Analysis) that, when applied to large volumes of microdata is also usually called *Spatial Datamining*.

The geographical analysis of the economic-social reality, through cartographic instruments and tools of spatial statistics, allows the addressing of critical and usual questions of commercial distribution, which could be outlined by the following question: *who buys where?* [15].

3   Hardware and Infrastructure/Communications Products

The sophistication of the Software Products described before requires the joint incorporation of specific Hardware equipment and appropriate Communications and Infrastructure equipment for their correct operation and integration.

Just as an example, the types of Hardware or Equipment and Infrastructure and Communications products that are at the most advanced level of technology development are: 3D Printers, Plotters, Shared Disks, Internet of Things Networks and Sensors, among others.

The increasing speed of the computing power of Hardware equipment makes possible the local, remote or cloud processing of significantly higher data volumes and capabilities such as the associated use of complex mathematical methods.

The computing power allows having even smarter sensors, although this intelligence is not enough until it is combined with the appropriate Software and application knowledge through an appropriate HCI (Human Computer Interface). The intelligent match of application knowledge and the flexibility of more advanced software architectures allow this stage to be reached in the development of sensors.

4 Industrial Software Design/Development Process

The task of the Software Products designers lives in solving problems creatively from the point of view of the users' workspace. Software Engineering, when designing, should focus on the observation of specific users and not on possible solutions. Assuming that the raw material of the Software is the knowledge, it must be contained at the time of designing/developing the Software Products.

For this purpose, there are 3 possible types of knowledge to which the software design and development team must focus and integrate with the user in their context when obtaining knowledge:

- **Knowledge of the problem to be solved**: it requires that the Software Product Design/Development team know the main aspects of the problem. That is to say, the routine, the methodology and the technical features of the manufacturing or the production line must be done under a deep analysis. This knowledge matches to the realm of the problem domain and the software to be implemented will work as a support for the existing production.
- **Knowledge of the techniques to be used**: it requires that the Design/Development team must know the technology and methodologies that it will use to understand the problem, design and build the solution. This knowledge is typical in the field of Software Engineering for the development of an application, which must include the knowledge about the ICTs necessary for the software to work properly for the user.
- **User Knowledge**: means knowing the user, understanding how the user understands the problem, knowing how the user operates in everyday resolution; that is to say, that the Design/Development team must understand how the user works in the routine and systematic tasks. This knowledge matches to the user's field and it requires a set of specific observation and analysis techniques that must be performed in the user's workspace.

The design of this type of Software Products requires a process in the analysis of the interaction between the user and the equipment that contains the Software. Initially, it requires starting from the *observation* of how the user performs routine tasks, in order to *understand* the movements and knowledge. Once this routine is understood, the problem must be *analyzed*, in order to create some possible *solution plans* that improve the task performed. Such ideas should not only include the software, but also and especially the equipment and infrastructure necessary for the software to function properly in the times of the operation. Once the viable ideas have been defined as a solution, the process requires the construction of a *prototype* that will be *tested* in the real context of use, *evaluated* and measured in terms of the improvement in the performance of the task, then *refine* the solution and start again the observation cycle if required by the Design/Development of the Software Product.

The following figure (Fig. 4) shows the Process of Design/Development of Software Products for the industry in which all the ICT products essential for user interaction must be analyzed. The dotted arrow between the *Refine and Observe* processes refers to the fact that it is a process of continuous improvement that begins with observation, as already mentioned, ends with refinement and begins again with a more refined observation.

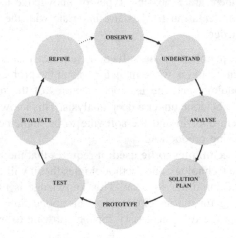

Fig. 4. Design/Development process. Source: Author's own editing

The techniques to be used in the process of Design/Development of software for the industry require the combination of various resources, such as: ethnography of a user, simulation of experiences, map of user experience, concept map, person profile, technological routes and focus group.

The proposed process defines that, in the instances of testing and evaluation with the user, theoretical surveys with a large number of questions should be avoided, given that users are not accustomed to these activities in their routine tasks. It is necessary to use all available techniques that are closest to the user's task for validation instances.

Since the innovation process constitutes an interdisciplinary and collaborative field that must contemplate the needs of users, the development of Software Products must include the incorporation of knowledge from other disciplines for the development of usability techniques, such as anthropology or sociology. The appropriate techniques should be applied with the controlled knowledge of these disciplines. The new technological possibilities that allow the development of products, processes or services that improve the quality of life, add value to the expertise of a user as they are directly absorbed from their knowledge. If this process focuses on human factors, it makes innovation as a result from the needs of users and not from the perception of technologists.

In this sense, the design, development and implementation of technologies in the industry constitutes a focal point as support for productive development, and it is from this perspective that software engineering should focus on the usability of its products.

5   Conclusions

This article introduces the progress of an ongoing investigation that allows the detection of Software Products that directly impact in the productivity levels in the various industrial sectors where they are implemented.

The detection of specific ICT products at different levels of development and their integration with the total information generated in a company according to the different functions they fulfill directly impacts in productivity levels and allows the turning of a company into an Industry 4.0.

The design of the interfaces of these complex products requires strategies focused on specific users, so that they acquire a high level of usability by integrating the necessary infrastructure and equipment for the type of Software Products to be developed.

From this perspective, a model that represents the process of Design/Development of Software Products for the industry has been introduced, focusing it on the user profile as well as the specific techniques to be applied as part of a process for this productive sector.

It is also suggested that the development team must be integrated into the context of the user to acquire their knowledge. Once the types of ICTs that define a company as Industry 4.0 are validated, the next activities will be carried out in the future towards the interaction criteria, specific to all the ICT products that are integrated into the Software Products, given that the levels of usability of the software developed.

References

1. Ministerio de Ciencia, Tecnología e innovación Productiva: Industria 4.0: Escenarios e impactos para la formulación de políticas tecnológicas en los umbrales de la Cuarta Revolución Industrial (2015). http://www.mincyt.gob.ar
2. Hewlett Packard: The Internet of Things. Today and Tomorrow (2016). http://chiefit.me/wp-content/uploads/2017/03/HPE-Aruba_IoT_Research_Report.pdf
3. ANETCOM: La TIC en la estrategia empresarial. Valencia. España (2017). https://datos.portaldelcomerciante.com/userfiles/167/Biblioteca/93d0cb62098a0ea3055eLaTICenlaestrategiaempresarial.pdf
4. Barraco Mármol, G., Bender, A., Mazza, N.H.: nTIC 2018. Buenos Aires: Universidad del Salvador (2018). http://www.sustentum.com/nTIC/nTIC2018.pdf
5. ISO/IEC 25000: System and Software Quality Requirements and Evaluation – SquaR. International Standards Organization (2014). https://iso25000.com/index.php/normas-iso-25000/iso-25010/23-usabilidad
6. ISO 13407: Human Centred Design Processes for Interactive Systems. International Standards Organization (1999). https://www.iso.org/standard/21197.html

7. Bevan, N.: UsabilityNet Methods for User Centred Design. Human Computer Interaction: Theory and Practice (Volume 1). Lawrence Erlbaum Associates (2003). https://www.researchgate.net/publication/228703678_UsabilityNet_Methods_for_user_centred_design

8. Mon, A., Del Giorgio, H.: Análisis de las tecnologías de la información y la comunicación y su innovación en la industria. In: XXIV Congreso Argentino de Ciencias de la Computación (CACIC 2018) (2018). http://sedici.unlp.edu.ar/handle/10915/73560

9. Del Giorgio, H.R., Mon, A.: Niveles de productos software en la industria 4.0. Int. J. Inf. Syst. Softw. Eng. Big Co. (IJISEBC) 5(2), 53–62 (2019). http://uajournals.com/ojs/index.php/ijisebc/article/view/398

10. Mon, A., Del Giorgio, H., De María, E., Figuerola, C., Querel, M.: Observatorio de inserción de TICs en los procesos industriales. Proyecto de Investigación C.187. Universidad Nacional de La Matanza, Buenos Aires, Argentina (2017)

11. Mazza, N.H.: Gestión Estratégica de Recursos Informáticos. Buenos Aires: Sustentum (2014). http://www.sustentum.com/sustentum/pubs/geri.pdf

12. Bonilla, A.: Aplicación de las Tecnologías de la Información y Comunicación en la industria (2001). http://www.bizkaia.eus/Home2/Archivos/DPTO8/Temas/Pdf/ca_GT_INDUSTRIA.pdf

13. Bonilla, A.: Herramientas de Diseño e Ingeniería (2003). http://www.bizkaia.eus/Home2/Archivos/DPTO8/Temas/Pdf/ca_GTcapitulo1.pdf

14. Alcaide Casado, J.C., Calero de la Paz, M., Hernández Luque, R.: Geomarketing: Marketing territorial para vender y fidelizar más. ESIC, Madrid (2012). ISBN 13 9788473568357

15. Chasco Yrigoyen, C.: El Geomarketing y la Distribución Comercial (2003). https://dialnet.unirioja.es/servlet/articulo?codigo=663345

Author Index